Thinking Film

ALSO AVAILABLE FROM BLOOMSBURY

*New Philosophies of Film: An Introduction to Cinema as a Way of
Thinking*, Robert Sinnerbrink
The Continental Philosophy of Film Reader, ed. Joseph Westfall
Movies with Meaning: Existentialism through Film, Dan Shaw
*European Cinema and Continental Philosophy: Film as Thought
Experiment*, Thomas Elsaesser

Thinking Film

Philosophy at the Movies

Edited by
Richard Kearney and
M. E. Littlejohn

BLOOMSBURY ACADEMIC
LONDON • NEW YORK • OXFORD • NEW DELHI • SYDNEY

BLOOMSBURY ACADEMIC
Bloomsbury Publishing Plc
50 Bedford Square, London, WC1B 3DP, UK
1385 Broadway, New York, NY 10018, USA

BLOOMSBURY, BLOOMSBURY ACADEMIC and the Diana logo are trademarks of
Bloomsbury Publishing Plc

First published in Great Britain 2023

Cover design: Ben Anslow
Cover image: The audience at a film screening in an English village, 1940.
Original publication: Picture Post - 339 - Life In A Village - unpub.
(© Bert Hardy / Picture Post / Hulton Archive / Getty Images)

A catalogue record for this book is available from the British Library.

A catalog record for this book is available from the Library of Congress.

ISBN: HB: 978-1-3501-1345-9
PB: 978-1-3501-1346-6
ePDF: 978-1-3501-1344-2
eBook: 978-1-3501-1347-3

Typeset by Deanta Global Publishing Services, Chennai, India
Printed and bound in Great Britain

To find out more about our authors and books visit www.bloomsbury.com and
sign up for our newsletters.

In memory of Stanley Cavell (1926–2018)

CONTENTS

ACKNOWLEDGMENTS

The genesis of this book originated in the classroom, both at the University of New Brunswick over the many classes on Stanley Cavell's philosophy and the movies he treasured, and at Boston College where Gilles Deleuze and the Continental Tradition were added to the mix. The editors would like to thank all those students who participated and shared their thoughts and reflections on Cavell, Deleuze, and the films they loved. We would be remiss if we did not thank Joe and Linda, Fanny, Bill, Simone, Sarah, Anne and others who shared their inspiration and enthusiasm over many "dinner, movie and discussion" nights at the Kearney home in West Newton. We are grateful for the kind encouragement and ongoing support of our editors, Liza Thompson and Lucy Harper, and the whole production team at Bloomsbury Press.

M. E. Littlejohn would like to thank the Harrison McCain Foundation Grant in Aid of Scholarly Book Publishing at UNB which generously supported the publication of this book.

He would like to thank Heidi MacDonald, Dean of Arts, for her ongoing support and encouragement. And finally, he would like to express his indebtedness to Stephanie Rumpza, for her discerning counsel and her generosity which knows no bounds.

EDITORIAL ACKNOWLEDGMENTS

The editors and publisher gratefully acknowledge the permission granted to reproduce the copyright material in this book.

Stanley Cavell, "The Thought of Movies," was originally published in *The Yale Review* 72.2 (Winter 1983): 181–200. Published with permission.

Selections of Gilles Deleuze, "On Cinema," were originally published in *Cinéma 1. L'Image-Mouvement*, Copyright 1983 by Les Editions de Minuit, English translation by H. Tomlinson and B. Habberjam, Copyright 1986 by Athlone Press, US edition published by the University of Minnesota Press; *Cinéma 2, L'Image-temps*, Copyright 1985 by Les Editions de Minuit, English translation H. Tomlinson and R. Galeta, copyright 1989 by Athlone Press, US edition published by the University of Minnesota Press; and *Two Regimes of Madness: Texts and Interview 1975 – 1995*, ed. David Lapoujade, translated by Ames Hodges and Mike Taormina (New York/Los Angeles: Semiotext(e), 2006). The selection was curated by David Deamer. Reprinted with permission of Les Éditions de Minuit, University of Minnesota Press and Semiotext(e).

A version of "On Sidney Lumet's *Serpico*" was originally published by Sam B. Girgus in *Generations of Jewish Directors and the Struggle for America's Soul. Wyler, Lumet, and Spielberg* (Cham, Switzerland: Palgrave Macmillan, 2021), reproduced with permission of Palgrave Macmillan.

Selections of Richard Kearney, "Rethinking Monster Movies," were originally published in *Strangers, Gods, and Monsters: Interpreting Otherness* (London and New York: Routledge, 2003), pp. 47–62 and *On Stories* (London and New York: Routledge, 2001), pp. 110–14. Reproduced with permission.

Richard Kearney, "On Wim Wenders's *Paris, Texas*" was originally posted in *Wake of the Imagination: Toward a Postmodern Culture* (Routledge, 1988), pp. 322–9. Reproduced with permission of Routledge.

Naomi Scheman, "Missing Mothers/Desiring Daughters: Framing the Sight of Women" is a shortened, edited version of the original piece printed *Critical Inquiry*, Vol. 15, No. 1 (Autumn, 1988), pp. 62–89, and reprinted in her volume of collected papers, *Engenderings: Constructions of Knowledge, Authority, and Privilege* (Routledge, 1993). Published with permission of Copyright Clearance Center.

Vivian Sobchack, "'The Active Eye' (Revisited)" originally appeared in the special issue of Film and Phenomenology for *Studia Phaenomenologica* vol. 16 (2016), pp. 63–90. Reprinted with permission.

An earlier version of Anthony J. Steinbock, "*I Wake Up Screaming*" appeared in *Film International* (filmint.nu), November 22, 2016; available at http://filmint.nu/i-wake-up-screaming-anthony-j-steinbock/ (accessed May 25, 2021). Reprinted courtesy of Daniel Lindvall and Matthew Sorrento.

Cheek to Cheek
from the RKO Radio Motion Picture TOP HAT
Words and Music by Irving Berlin
Copyright © 1935 BERLIN IRVING MUSIC CORP.
Copyright Renewed
All Rights Administered by UNIVERSAL MUSIC CORP.
All Rights Reserved Used by Permission
Reprinted by Permission of Hal Leonard LLC.

Every effort has been made to trace copyright holders and to obtain their permission for the use of copyright material. The publisher apologizes for any errors or omissions in the foregoing list and would be grateful if notified of any corrections that should be incorporated in future reprints or editions of this book.

Introduction

Richard Kearney and M. E. Littlejohn

From images on the cave walls to the moving images that brought nations to cinemas, human beings have made art to understand the world. Even as the technology and delivery of the art form has changed, the medium of film has been an integral part of our lives. How is it that shadow and light projected on a screen brought collective audiences to laughter and tears, consoled and healed, challenged and interrogated by means of images, words, gestures, and sounds? How is that people can walk into a theater and leave the experience reflective and transformed: the same, but different? For having viewed the world in film, they now view themselves and their world differently.

Half a century ago, American philosopher Stanley Cavell pointed out that to cross between high art and low art is a quintessential mark of American culture and its two great original art forms: jazz and film. This realization arose early in Cavell's career after he took a break one evening from serious philosophy dissertation writing to watch Ingmar Bergman's *Smiles of a Summer Night*. He returned home to write on the film all night. He recognized that the film he had viewed truly mattered, and that, like any other serious art form, everything within the film mattered. Each frame, the particular lighting, posture, dialogue, and tone of voice conspired together to present the whole work in its perfection. Like all serious art, film was just as worthy of serious reflection. Cavell thus goes even beyond recognizing film as a powerful aesthetic medium. He had realized that film demanded "serious" reflection, just like his "serious" dissertation. Thus began his intense thinking and writing about film. Cavell later wrote, "to my way of thinking the creation of film was as if meant for philosophy—meant to reorient everything philosophy has said about reality and its representation, about art and imitation, about greatness and conventionality, about judgment and pleasure, about skepticism and transcendence, about language and expression."[1]

Cavell pointed out that in the first half of the twentieth century, it was through film that America did its *thinking*. Directors from around the world, schooled by these popular early American classics, would go on to craft their own film masterpieces. So why have these films, with their critical role in shaping an international cultural discourse, never become a staple of philosophical conversation? When they stray from the strict confines of the philosophical canon, why are philosophers more comfortable referencing a novel than a film? While Cavell's work contributed to the founding of film studies departments in universities, as an important achievement as this is, he joked that such a development was not unlike "creating a Department of Books." He wanted films to become an integral part of philosophical discussion, not separated off as a specialization. Can films contribute to philosophical reflection, or even more radically, can film themselves do the work of philosophy? But this immediately leads us to a third question, for we must ask: What *kind* of philosophy is a film meant to challenge or perform?

While trained in Analytic philosophy, Cavell chose to do his thinking along the tear of the Analytic and Continental philosophical divide. But the division between the Analytic and Continental European traditions remains all too often a chasm, and the two philosophies often continue to live in different worlds, so alien are their questions and starting points at times. Indeed, if we started from certain branches within these traditions, no conversation would be possible. Yet, at the same time, other strains within both of these traditions have brought rich resources to the task of reflecting on film; already early in the last century Bergson and Merleau-Ponty had begun to reflect on the philosophical significance of the moving image. As multiple traditions and movements of cinema began to develop, journals of film criticism inaugurated and deepened the discourse. In 1971 Cavell's *The World Viewed: Reflections on the Ontology of Film* became the first serious work of philosophy dedicated to film, while Gilles Deleuze became the first major philosopher to devote extended attention to film on the continent. In the decades that followed, philosophers in both traditions began to read and reflect on film, increasingly less mindful of the borders that divide, and more focused on the developing art medium that was calling them to engagement and reflection. Some use film to explore philosophical theories, like asking whether or not an imaginary story of a horror movie can provoke real fear. Others use films to illustrate common philosophical problems and questions, like using *The Matrix* or *Inception* to illustrate forms of metaphysical skepticism. What interests us in this volume is something else: an approach that treats film as a discussion partner with its own perspective, its own questions and reflections to offer, speaking in its own language that is very different from the one that philosophy speaks but not necessarily inferior. This is an approach that both Cavell and Deleuze have in common: instead of coming with predetermined philosophical theories for film to illustrate or fill in, they each made space to let film speak for itself. If we take this approach, perhaps film can be a productive meeting place of traditions. For instead of first deciding which philosophy to follow, we can instead allow the conversation to be led by film, by whatever philosophy will allow film to take its place as an equal in the dialogue. Admittedly, it is more work for a philosopher to enter dialogue as an equal instead of presiding over it, but this is what the contributors to this volume attempt to do.

Film thus stands at an intersecting point of three crossings: high and low art, aesthetics and philosophy, and the Anglo-American and Continental traditions. If film forms a frontier of philosophy, it can also serve as common ground on which the philosophical traditions can meet. By affirming the lasting and universal value of one of America's original art forms now well beloved all over the world, this book aims to provide new resources for belonging to, critiquing, and developing an international contemporary culture of thinking along this trifold intersectionality.

Part I orients the reader by presenting classic texts from the two pioneers of serious philosophical engagement with film from both philosophical traditions. It opens with Stanley Cavell's "The Thought of Movies," originally delivered as the Patricia Wise Lecture in 1982, one year after his *Pursuits of Happiness: The Hollywood Comedy of Remarriage,* and a decade after *The World Viewed.* He took this occasion to respond to criticisms of his work on remarriage comedies in particular, as well as wholesale dismissal of his project crossing philosophy and film. In the process he reflects on his own path to thinking seriously in and through film and its significance for understanding the American cultural inheritance. This is followed by a chapter by Gilles Deleuze, who, from the other side of the ocean and from another philosophical tradition, wrote a massive two-volume study *On Cinema* published in 1983 and 1985. This chapter features a guide to the key themes of this major work through accessible selections, interspersed with Deleuze's own commentary in later interviews. Cavell and Deleuze, giants in their respective traditions, serve here as examples and models of a philosophy that aims to take film seriously as a conversational partner.

While Part I lays out the historical foundation for our approach to film, Part II opens the discourse up to the present, featuring contemporary thinkers from both traditions taking up the same themes. Robert Sinnerbrink's overview of the contemporary discussion on philosophy and film introduces a synthesis of key ideas from Cavell and Deleuze, and his introduction on how this conversation has developed will serve as a valuable pedagogical guide for readers new to this area of study. We then include four chapters that enter dialogue with film following the example of Cavell. By way of introduction to this great American philosopher, M. E. Littlejohn provides an introduction to how American films from the 1930s to 1940s anticipate and prepare the ground for a number of central ideas Cavell would later develop in his dialogue with Wittgenstein, Emerson, Thoreau, and others. Naomi Scheman provides a thoughtful feminist critique to Cavell's analysis of *Philadelphia Story.* Stephen Mulhall discusses the reasons a recent box office rom-com fails to meet the standards of a Cavellian Remarriage Comedy it tries to emulate. Sandra Laugier reflects on Cavell's insights into the transformation of self through film and explores how these ideas can be transposed to contemporary television series, particularly given their increasing cultural relevance. In the second half of Part II, six contributors take up the more multifaceted Continental approach to cinema, beginning from Deleuze and broadening into other significant approaches of phenomenology and hermeneutics. If the technical language of Deleuze feels intimidating to new readers, David Deamer's chapter will come as a welcome entry point, for he patiently and lucidly unfolds Deleuze's key ideas while illustrating their use in a single film. Guided by the phenomenology of Maurice Merleau-Ponty, Vivian Sobchack here re-presents her groundbreaking work on the phenomenology of cinema which first appeared in the 1990s, paving an influential avenue beyond structuralist and post-structuralist film theory so prevalent in the prior decade. Richard Kearney, meanwhile, takes up films from a hermeneutic perspective, exploring how cinematic concerns with aliens and monsters can shed light on the central philosophical relations between self and other, discerning strangers as guests or monsters, responding in hospitality or hostility. Anna Westin, Anthony J. Steinbock, and Stephanie Rumpza extend and apply these insights of phenomenology and hermeneutics to particular films and under the scope of more specific philosophical challenges of mediation, belonging, and transcendence. Approaching from different philosophical traditions, the chapters of Part II thus reflect on what philosophy can learn from film and what critical and creative tensions exist within this relationship.

Part III brings this dialogue of philosophy and film into lived practice. Each author has been tasked with exploring how one particular film incites their thinking, and the variety of responses that result is telling. This is first due to the contributors themselves—in addition to emerging and seasoned philosophers, authors of this part also hail from theology, film studies, and popular film media and even include renowned poet and novelist Fanny Howe. The films discussed, meanwhile, range from contemporary to classic, from art films to blockbusters, following Cavell's insistence that all of these genres can give rise to thinking. Far from offering a representative overview of the dialogue of philosophy and film, these chapters only scratch the surface of where this conversation can take us. And so we issue an invitation to our readers to make your own contribution to Part III, taking up a conversation with your own favorite film: How and why has it inspired your serious thinking?

Philosophy and film met, at first uncertain of what to make of each other, but after some time, and through a long engagement, representatives of the 2,500-year tradition of philosophy wed with film, for better, and not for worse. Film indeed brings us to thought and sets us talking. This volume aims to celebrate the daring liaison.

Note

1 Stanley Cavell, *Contesting Tears: The Hollywood Melodrama of the Unknown Woman* (Chicago, IL: University of Chicago Press, 1996), Epigraph.

PART I

Classic Philosophers on Film

1

The Thought of Movies

Stanley Cavell

It must be the nature of American academic philosophy (or of its reputation), together with the nature of American movies (or of their notoriety), that makes someone who writes about both, in the same breath, subject to questions, not to say suspicions. The invitation to deliver this year's Patricia Wise Lecture is the first time I have been questioned about this combination of concerns, or obsessions, by a group of people committed to sitting quietly for the better part of an hour while I search for an answer.

The question has, I think without fail, come my way with philosophy put first: How is it that a professor of philosophy gets to thinking about Hollywood films?—as though becoming a professor of philosophy were easier to accept than thinking and writing about movies. So defensive have I grown that it took me a while to recognize that for most of my life the opposite direction of the question would have been more natural: How is it that someone whose education was as formed by going to the movies as by reading books, gets to thinking about philosophy professionally?

For a long time I believed the connection to be a private crossroads of my own. It became explicit for me during that period in my life I learned later, in a calmer time, to call my identity crisis. After college, in the late 1940s, I was accepted by the extension program of the Juilliard Conservatory as a composition major, following some two years of increasing doubts that music was my life. Almost as soon as I arrived in New York and established myself in school, I began avoiding my composition lessons. I spent my days reading and my nights in a theater, typically standing for the opera or a play, and then afterwards going to a film revival on 42nd Street, which in the late forties was a rich arena within which to learn the range and randomness of the American talkie. What I was reading all day I privately called philosophy, though I knew no more about what other people meant by the word than

I knew why it was in philosophy that I was looking for the answer to the question my life had become.

Since I had spent my undergraduate years torn between the wish to be a writer and the fact of composing music for the student theater—for anything ranging from numbers for our annual musical revues to incidental music for nothing less than *King Lear*—what I learned in college would scarcely, I mean by European standards, have added up to an education at all. But I was encouraged to go on learning from the odd places, and the odd people, that it pleased my immigrant, unlettered father and my accomplished mother to take me to—he who was in love with the learning he never would have, and she who while I was growing up made a living playing the piano for silent movies and for vaudeville. The commonest place we went together was to movies. So while before I entered college I would not have heard a performance of, say, the Beethoven Ninth, and lacked any obvious preparation for it in the history of music and of German culture, I had known enough to attend carefully, for example, to the moves of Fred Astaire and Ginger Rogers and Jerome Kern, so that when the chorus in the last movement of the Ninth sings the two principal themes in counterpoint, the ecstasy this caused me had been prepared by my response to the closing of *Swingtime*, in which one of the pair is singing again "A Fine Romance" while the other is singing again "The Way You Look Tonight." This would not have constituted the preparation I claim for high art unless it had gone beyond cleverness. It is essential that each of the Kern songs is as good individually as it is, so that when the pair modify and cast them together in the reprise, each can be seen capable, so to speak, of meaning the separate song he and she have on their minds.

In the same way the lyrics of such songs were preparation for the high poetry I had yet to discover. In my early adolescence lines such as

Heaven, I'm in heaven
And the cares that hung around me through the week
Seem to vanish like a gambler's lucky streak,
When we're out together dancing cheek to cheek

A stanza such as this *was* what I thought of as poetry—nothing else will be poetry for me that cannot compete with the experience of concentration and lift in such words. It seems to me that I knew this then to be an experience not alone of the behavior and the intelligence of the words with one another, nor only, in addition, of the wit and beauty of invoking the gambler's run of luck, but that it was an experience of these (though I would have lacked as yet words of my own in which to say so) together with the drama of using the vanishing of the streak, which is a bad thing, as a simile for the vanishing of cares and the access to heaven, which is a good thing— as if beyond bad and good there were a region of chance and risk within which alone the intimacy emblematized or mythologized in the dancing of

Astaire and Rogers is realizable. Eventually I would be able to note that happiness and happenstance spring from the same root, that the pursuit of happiness—whether this is an occasion for a step into selfhood or into nationhood—requires the bravery to recognize and seize the occasion, or as Emerson had put it, "the courage to be what you are." I am not claiming that I, then, on 42nd Street, had already planned my book on the Hollywood comedy of remarriage; but rather that that book is in part written in loyalty to younger versions of myself, some of whom were, or are, there. Certainly I can sympathize with Steve Martin's half-crazed hero in the recent *Pennies from Heaven* when he says, crying from the heart about the songs he peddles and believes, "Listen to the words!" And I am, I guess, claiming that that younger version of myself, playing hooky from Juilliard and in the poverty of his formal education reading all day and spending half the night in theaters, was already taking to heart Henry James's most memorable advice to aspiring writers. In "The Art of Fiction" James says:

> The power to guess the unseen from the seen, to trace the implications of things, to judge the whole piece by the pattern, the condition of feeling life in general so completely that you are well on your way to knowing any particular corner of it—this cluster of gifts may almost be said to constitute experience. . . . Therefore, if I should certainly say to a novice "Write from experience and experience only," I should feel that this was rather a tantalizing monition if I were not careful immediately to add, "Try to be one of the people on whom nothing is lost."

By the time, the time came for me to write my book about a set of Hollywood romances (*Pursuits of Happiness*), I had come to count on myself as one of the people willing not to be lost to his or to her experience, hence to count on being able to survive the indignities of sometimes guessing unconvincingly and of sometimes tracing things in thin air. So, for instance, in my book I build a sense of the shared structure of the comedies of remarriage out of an understanding of Shakespearean romance; and I discuss the blanket in *It Happened One Night* in terms of the censoring of human knowledge and aspiration in the philosophy of Kant; and I see the speculation of Heidegger exemplified or explained in the countenance of Buster Keaton; and I find in *The Awful Truth* that when the camera moves away from an imminent embrace between Cary Grant and Irene Dunne to discover a pair of human figurines marking the passage of time by skipping together into a clock that has the form of a house, that in that image something metaphysical is being said about what marriage is, that it is a new way of inhabiting time, and moreover that that is a way of summarizing the philosophy, among others, of Thoreau and of Nietzsche.

So I suppose I should not be surprised that this book of mine has met with some resistance from its reviewers. More than once it has been called pretentious. Put aside for the present the possibility that its ideas are poorly executed or voiced in the writing—there is nothing I can do about that now. If that is not the whole story, then the charge of pretension must have to do with the connections I make between film and philosophy; at any rate, the charge leveled against either separately would hardly be worth responding to. But what in the connections may strike one as pretentious? It is important to me to bring out what I find to be a harmless way of issuing the charge, and a harmful way.

The harmless way takes the connections as a matter of preference, and on this basis I can see that one who is not familiar with the texts I mention may prefer that I not drop their names. I have two excuses for doing so. First, since I find in movies food for thought, I go for help in thinking about what I understand them to be thinking about where I go for help in thinking about anything, to the thinkers I know best and trust most. Second, as is typical of a certain kind of American, I find what I do to be pertinent to any and all of my fellow citizens, and I secretly believe that if they saw it as I do, they would all immediately devote themselves to doing it too.

This accounts in part for an American's readiness to lecture his fellows, a practice that made an impression on de Tocqueville during his visit to us in the 1830s, the decade before Thoreau moved out to Walden to prepare his kind of lecturing, or dressing down. It is a practice some will find insufferable and others generous. The practice raises for me the issue whether Americans have anything to their name to call a common cultural inheritance, whether you can name three works of high culture that you can be sure all the people you care about have read or seen or heard. This lack of assured commonality would be another part of the cause for our tendency to lecture rather than to converse with one another.

The harmful way of charging my book with pretension takes it for granted that philosophy and Hollywood movies occupy separate cultural intentions, with nothing to say across their border, indeed with not so much as a border between them. The immediate harm in this view lies in its closing off an exploration of what those Americans to whom it matters may be said to have instead of a common inheritance of high culture, namely an ability to move between high and low, caring about each also from the vantage of the other. This has its liabilities, naturally; for example, of indiscriminateness and of moments of incomprehensibility to the outside learned world. But it also, to my mind, accounts for what is best, or special, in our work; for example, for the reach in Thoreau's prose from the highest sublimity to the lowest pun. I am reminded that de Tocqueville also remarked a liveliness among the populace of our democracy that he missed in his populace at home and which he attributed to the fact that in America there is genuinely public business which requires learning and intelligence to take part in. This seems to me the condition for the kind of mutual respect called upon in putting together the high and the low.

For someone, or most people, to take for granted that there is no border between philosophy and movies, for this to carry its apparent conviction, there must be available fairly definite, if unconscious, interpretations both of what philosophy is and of what the Hollywood movie is. Philosophy would have to be thought of as a more or less technical discipline reserved for specialists. But this would just interpret what it is that makes philosophy professional; and however internal that state is to philosophy and indeed to the growing professionalization of the world, it does not say what makes philosophy philosophy.

I understand it as a willingness to think not about something other than what ordinary human beings think about, but rather to learn to think undistractedly about things that ordinary human beings cannot help thinking about, or anyway cannot help having occur to them, sometimes in fantasy, sometimes as a flash across a landscape; such things, for example, as whether we can know the world as it is in itself, or whether others really know the nature of one's own experiences, or whether good and bad are relative, or whether we might not now be dreaming that we are awake, or whether modern tyrannies and weapons and spaces and speeds and art are continuous with the past of the human race or discontinuous, and hence whether the learning of the human race is not irrelevant to the problems it has brought before itself. Such thoughts are instances of that characteristic human willingness to allow questions for itself which it cannot answer with satisfaction. Cynics about philosophy, and perhaps about humanity, will find that questions without answers are empty; dogmatists will claim to have arrived at answers; philosophers after my heart will rather wish to convey the thought that while there may be no satisfying answers to such questions *in certain forms*, there are, so to speak, directions to answers, *ways to think*, that are worth the time of your life to discover. (It is a further question for me whether directions of this kind are teachable, in ways suited to what we think of as schools.)

It would not become me to proceed, in speaking on this occasion of my interest in movies, other than by way of faithfulness to the impulse to philosophy as I conceive it. Apart from the best I can do in this attempt, I would not have approached the question whether the same sensibility that is drawn to and perplexed about philosophy is drawn to and perplexed about movies.

There is, I suggested, an interpretation of Hollywood movies that is the companion of the interpretation of philosophy as a specialized profession. This interpretation takes movies as specialized commodities manufactured by an industry designed to satisfy the tastes of a mass audience. Conventional capitalists as well as conventional Marxists can equally take such a view. It is no more false than is the interpretation of philosophy as a profession, but it is no less partial, or prejudicial. Just as it would be possible to select films carefully with an idea of proving that film can attain to art (people interested in such selections will on the whole not include Hollywood talkies in this selection), so one could heap together abysses of bad and meretricious movies with an idea of proving one's bleakest view of Hollywood. These are not my interests, and have nothing special to do with assessing the life of movies.

What interests me much more in these terms about Hollywood is that for around fifteen years, say from the middle thirties to the early fifties, it provided an environment in which a group of people, as a matter of its routine practice, turned out work as good, say, as that represented by the seven movies forming the basis of my book on remarriage comedies—work, that is to say, as good, or something like as good, as *It Happened One Night* (1934*), The Awful Truth* (1937), *Bringing Up Baby* (1938), *His Girl Friday* (1940), *The Philadelphia Story* (1940), *The Lady Eve* (1941), and *Adam's Rib* (1949)—work that must participate in any history of film as an art that I would find credible. I am not, perhaps I should say, claiming that this work is the best work in the history of world cinema, nor that these films are better than the experimental or nonfiction films contemporary with them. I am, I guess, claiming that they are good, worthy companions of the best; and also that we have as yet no way of knowing, no sufficient terms in which to say, how good they are.

So it is no part of my argument to insist that major work can only come from such an environment or to deny that significant movies continue to be made in Hollywood. But I expect that no one still finds that they come almost exclusively from there, and routinely, say every other week, something like twenty or twenty-five times a year. Over a period of fifteen golden years, that comes to between three hundred and four hundred works, which is a larger body of first-rate or nearly first-rate work than the entire corpus of Elizabethan and Jacobean drama can show.

How could we show that it is equally, or anyway, sufficiently, worth studying? Now we are at the heart of the aesthetic matter. Nothing can show this value to you unless it is discovered in your own experience, in the persistent exercise of your own taste, and hence the willingness to challenge your taste as it stands, to form your own artistic conscience, hence nowhere but in the details of your encounter with specific works.

It is time for some more extended examples. I choose two principally, one beginning from a question I have about a moment in *The Philadelphia Story*, the second from a question I have about the mood of *Pennies from Heaven*.

The Philadelphia Story is in some ways the central member of the remarriage comedies brought together in *Pursuits of Happiness*, but beyond allowing me the pleasure of saying something consecutive about my commitment to these comedies, the example here is meant to isolate for attention one of those apparently insignificant moments in whose power a part of the power of film rests. If it is part of the grain of film to magnify the feeling and meaning of a moment, it is equally part of it to counter this tendency, and instead to acknowledge the fateful fact of a human life that the significance of its moments is ordinarily not given with the moments as they are lived, so that to determine the significant crossroads of a life may be the work of a lifetime. It is as if an inherent *concealment* of significance, as much as its revelation, were part of the governing force of what we mean by film acting and film directing and film viewing.

We need always to be returning to the fact of how mysterious these objects called movies are, unlike anything else on earth. They have the evanescence of performances and the permanence of recordings, but they are not recordings (because there is nothing independent of them to which they owe fidelity); and they are not performances (because they are perfectly repeatable).

If what I might call the *historical* evanescence of film will be overcome when the new technologies of video cassettes and discs complete the work of late-night television and revival theaters, and the history of movies becomes part of the experience of viewing new movies—a relation to history that we take for granted in the rest of the arts—this should serve to steady our awareness of the *natural* evanescence of film, the fact that its events exist only in motion, in passing.[1] This natural fact makes all the more extraordinary the historical fact that films are still on the whole viewed just once and reviewed on the basis of just one viewing, hence that the bulk of the prose even dedicated moviegoers read about movies is the prose of reviewing, not the demanding criticism and the readings and appreciations one takes for granted as being devoted to other arts. It will compensate my having to choose examples that I cannot be assured we have in common if doing so serves to bring this contingency of film viewing and reading into question.

The moment in *The Philadelphia Story* occurs late, when Katharine Hepburn, hearing from Jimmy Stewart that he did not take advantage of her drunken state the previous night, turns from the assembled audience and says, in a sudden, quiet access of admiration, "I think men are wonderful." Nothing further comes of the line; its moment passes with its saying, like a shadow passing. Struck with the strangeness of this moment, I found in composing *Pursuits of Happiness*—and it is something that one of my reviewers, and on the whole a sympathetic and learned one, found more hysterically inappropriate than any other of my perceptions—that to my ear this line alludes to the moment in *The Tempest* at which Miranda exclaims, "How beauteous mankind is!" Evidently I had not, for that reader, made sufficiently clear my general need for the Shakespearean connection in relation to remarriage comedy; nor had I gained sufficient credit with him to get him to put his sense of appropriateness in abeyance for the moment and specifically to try out what I called an allusion amounting almost to an echo. This is something I am going to ask you to consider doing. Let me go over what I am basing myself on in such cases.

The point of the title "remarriage" is to register the grouping of a set of comedies which differ from classical comedy in various respects, but most notably in this, that in classical comedy the narrative shows a young pair overcoming obstacles to their love and at the end achieving marriage, whereas comedies of remarriage begin or climax with a pair less young, getting or threatening their divorce, so that the drive of the narrative is to get them *back* together, together *again*. The central idea I follow out along various paths, but *roughly* the idea is that the validity or bond of marriage is assured, even legitimized, not by church or state or sexual compatibility (these bonds, it is implied, are no deeper than those of marriage), but by something I call the willingness for remarriage, a way of continuing to affirm the happiness of one's initial leap. As if the chance of happiness exists only when it seconds itself. In classical comedy people made for one another find one another; in remarriage comedy people who *have* found one another find that they *are* made for each other. The greatest of the structures of remarriage is *The Winter's Tale*, which is, together with *The Tempest*, the greatest of the Shakespearean romances.

But I want the Shakespearean connection with remarriage comedy also for less stupendous structural reasons. Shakespearean romantic comedy lost out, so a way of telling the history goes to the newer Jonsonian comedy of manners as setting the standard for the future of the English stage. Now I claim that the emergence of film, especially of the talkie, discovered another theater, several centuries later, for that older, Shakespearean structure. Some features of the older comedy that found new life on film are, for example, that it is the woman rather than the man who holds the key to the plot and who undergoes something like death and transformation; that there is some special understanding she has with her father, who does not oppose (as in conventional comedy) but endorses the object of her desire; that the central pair are not young, so that the issue of chastity or innocence, while present, cannot be settled by determinations of literal virginity; that the plot begins and complicates itself in a city but gets resolved in a move to a world of nature—in Shakespeare this is called the green world or the golden world; in four of the seven major Hollywood comedies of remarriage this world is called Connecticut.

But such structural connections are in service of a further reason for the Shakespearean connection, namely to locate the mode of perception called upon in movies, anyway in movies of this kind. The connection in effect implies that what allows film to rediscover, for its own purposes, Shakespearean romance is that unlike the prose of comic theatrical dialogue after Shakespeare, film has a natural equivalent for the medium of Shakespeare's dramatic poetry. I think of it as the poetry of film itself, what it is that happens to figures and objects and places as they are variously molded and displaced by a motion-picture camera and then projected and screened. Every art, every worthwhile human enterprise, has its poetry, ways of doing things that perfect the possibilities of the enterprise itself, make it the one it is; each of the arts has its own poetry, of course, so has each sport, and so I am sure have banking and baking and surgery and government. You may think of it as the unteachable point in any worthwhile enterprise.

I understand it to be, let me say, a natural vision of film that every motion and station, in particular every human posture and gesture, however glancing, has its poetry, or you may say its lucidity. Charlie Chaplin and Buster Keaton live on this knowledge, and perhaps bring it to its purest expression; it is my claim in *Pursuits of Happiness* that the Hollywood talkie finds an equivalent for this expressiveness, this expression of lucidity, in the way certain pairs of human beings are in conversation. (An implied threat to their happiness is that they are, somehow because of this fortune, incomprehensible to everyone else in the world they inhabit.) Any of the arts will be drawn to this knowledge, this perception of the poetry of the ordinary, but film, I would like to say, democratizes the knowledge, hence at once blesses and curses us with it. It says that the perception of poetry is as open to all, regardless as it were of birth or talent, as the ability is to hold a camera on a subject, so that a failure so to perceive, to persist in missing the subject, which may amount to missing the evanescence of the subject, is ascribable only to ourselves, to failures of our character; as if to fail to guess the unseen from the seen, to fail to trace the implications of things—that is, to fail the perception that there is something to be guessed and traced, right or wrong—requires that we persistently coarsen and stupefy ourselves.

Business people would not run a business this way; this was something Emerson admired about American business; it is why Thoreau asks for what he calls "a little more Yankee shrewdness" in our lives. And Emerson and Thoreau are the writers I know best who most incessantly express this sense of life as missed possibility, of its passing as in a dream, hence the sense of our leading lives of what they call quiet desperation. The movies I name comedies of remarriage find happiness in proposing that there is relief from just that Emersonian loss, that there are conditions under which opportunities may be discovered again and retaken, that somewhere there is a locale in which a second chance is something one may give oneself. (It is my argument about *The Philadelphia Story* in *Pursuits of Happiness*—which I won't try to go into here—that the Philadelphia in its title is the site of the signing of the Declaration of Independence and of the Constitution of the United States, so that America is the name of the locale of the second chance, or it was meant to be. Remarriage is the central of the second chances.)

Now I'm taking that apparently insignificant moment of *The Philadelphia Story*, the evanescence of the seven syllables "I think men are wonderful," as one in which a character is taking such an opportunity, and the movie proposing one to us. It may help to note that the companion line from *The Tempest*—"How beauteous mankind is!"—is also seven syllables long and that both lines occur at the late moment in their dramas at which the principal female is about to undergo a metaphysical transformation. The Hepburn character is to move from the state of chaste goddess (a state each of the four men in her life either accuses her of or praises her for) into what she calls feeling like a human being; and in *The Tempest*, in response to Miranda's exclamation, Ferdinand's father asks whether she is a goddess, to which Ferdinand replies

Sir she is mortal,
But by immortal providence she's mine.

By the way, while the line of Miranda's I am measuring Hepburn's with does not contain the word "wonderful," its more familiar, wider context runs this way:

> O wonder!
> How many goodly creatures are there here!
> How beauteous mankind is! O brave new world
> That has such people in it!

Remember that we are what has become of the new world, the idea and the fact of which so fascinated Shakespeare and his age. If one is interested enough to go this far with the conjunction of Hollywood comedy and Shakespearean romance, one will be bound to ask what the point of such a moment is, I mean why this crossroads of wonder is marked so carefully in these dramatic structures. My answer for the comedies of remarriage would run in something like the following way. I think of them, as a group, to be dedicated to the pursuit of what you might call equality between men and women (and of this as emblematic of the search for human community as such—but I am letting this pass for the present), the pursuit of their correct independence of, and dependence upon, one another. What the comedies of remarriage show is that, as the world goes, there is an unfairness or asymmetry in this pursuit, because women require an education for their assumption of equality, and this must be managed with the help of men. The first task for her, accordingly, is to choose the best man for this work. Because of the history between them—both their private history and the history of their culture—they are struggling with one another, they have justified grievances against one another; hence I sometimes characterize these movies as revenge comedies. If their relationship is to go forward the pair must get around to forgiving one another, and, continuing the asymmetry, it must primarily be the woman who forgives the man, not just because she has more to forgive but because she has more power to forgive. And yet in these movies it may be hard to see what the particular man in question needs such radical forgiveness for. He has done nothing obvious to harm the woman, and the specific charges the women bring against the men—Clark Gable's disdainfulness in *It Happened One Night*; Cary Grant's craziness in *The Awful Truth*, and his deviousness in *His Girl Friday*, and his gorgeous thirst in *The Philadelphia Story*; Henry Fonda's sappiness in *The Lady Eve*; Spencer Tracy's forcefulness, even brutishness, in *Adam's Rib*—these are features the woman honors as well as hates the man for, which is doubtless why she can forgive him. It is not fully explicit until the last of the definitive remarriage comedies, *Adam's Rib* in 1949, that what the woman has against the man is fundamentally the simple villainy of his *being* a man; hence that is what her happiness with him depends on her getting around to forgiving him for. The form this takes in the line from *The Philadelphia Story* about men being wonderful, I take, accordingly, as an expression of admiration at the sheer fact of their separateness, wonder as it were that there should be two sexes, and that the opposite one is *as such* admirable. This is hardly the end of anger between them; there are always their differences. But it is a kind of promise to spend as long as it takes—say till death them do part—to work out what those differences are, what they come to.

At some point—always supposing that one can believe that a conjunction of Shakespeare and Hollywood comedies is not hysterically inappropriate—a more sympathetic doubt about the conjunction may seem called for, prompting one to want to know how *serious* I am about it, whether when I say, for example, that film has a natural power of poetry equivalent to the power of Shakespeare's dramatic poetry, I really mean poetry in the same sense. Here I might just respond by saying that that is not a question to which I have an answer apart from the thinking and the writing I do and have done, about movies among other matters. But I want to pause, before turning to my concluding example, to sketch an answer more openly philosophical, in particular one that accounts more openly for the periodic appearance of Emerson and Thoreau in my thoughts, those here tonight and those in *Pursuits of Happiness*. Because while my insistence on writing about philosophy and movies in the same breath, insisting on both of them, but especially on their conjunction, as part of my American intellectual and cultural inheritance—while this has caused me a certain amount of professional tension, it has caused no more than my insistence on inheriting Emerson and Thoreau as philosophers.

Do I really mean philosophers? In the same sense that Plato and Descartes and Kant are philosophers? While this is not a moment to argue the point, I take the moment to ask you to conceive the following possibility: that Emerson and Thoreau are the central founding thinkers of American culture but that this knowledge, though possessed by shifting bands of individuals, is not culturally possessed. It would be an expression of this possibility that no profession is responsible for them as thinkers. Mostly they do not exist for the American profession of philosophy; and the literary professions are mostly not in a position to preserve them in these terms. They are unknown to the culture they express in a way it would not be thinkable for Kant and Schiller and Goethe to be unknown to the culture of Germany, or Descartes and Rousseau to France, or Locke and Hume and John Stuart Mill to England. I do not think it is clear how we are to understand and assess this fact about our cultural lives, but you can see that someone with my interests might wish not to miss the occasion for noting the fact out loud in the nation's capital.

(Here I am seeing our reception of our best writers, like our reception of the best Hollywood movies, as part of America's tendency to overpraise and undervalue its best work, as though the circus ballyhoo advertising of Hollywood movies were covering doubts we have that they are really any good at all. I guess this is a preachy thing to say; and maybe that is what's meant sometimes when I'm called pretentious. But preachiness is equally part of the American grain in me, a risk you run in hanging around Emerson and Thoreau as much as I have lately. It is a tone associated in remarriage comedies especially with Katharine Hepburn's high-mindedness. She gets lectured about it by the men in her life, repeatedly dressed down. And once, in *Adam's Rib*, Spencer Tracy allows himself to say to her, "You get cute when you get causey." Of course this makes her sore. And I think I know just how she feels.)

But now if our central thinkers are unpossessed, unshared by us, it will not be expected that we can readily come to intellectual terms on the issues that matter most to us, as say the fundamental issues of art and of philosophy can matter to us. Emerson and Thoreau fully knew this difficulty in getting themselves understood. I have taken as a parable of Emerson's dedication of himself as a writer the following sentences from one of his early, most famous essays, "Self-Reliance":

> I shun father and mother and wife and brother when my genius calls me. I would write on the lintels of the door-post, Whim. I hope it is somewhat better than whim at last, but we cannot spend the day in explanation.

Two remarks about this. First, shunning father and mother and wife and brother is, according to the New Testament, required of you when the Lord calls you and you seek the kingdom of heaven. And according to the Old Testament, writing on the lintels of the door is something you do on Passover, to avoid the angel of death, and it is also where writings from Deuteronomy are placed, in mezuzahs, to signify that Jews live within and that they are obedient to the injunction of the Lord to bear his words and at all times to acknowledge them. So Emerson is putting the *calling* and the *act* of his writing in the public place reserved in both of the founding testaments of our culture for the word of God. Is he being serious?

My second remark about Emerson's passage is that it acknowledges his writing to be posing exactly the question of its own seriousness. In the parable I just cited, he both declares his writing to be a matter of life and death, the path of his faith and redemption, and also declares that *everything* he writes is Whim. I understand this to mean that it is his mission to create the language in which to explain himself, and accordingly to imply both that there is no such standing discourse between him and his culture, and that he is to that extent without justification before himself. The course open to him is to stake the seriousness of his life, his conviction, on what, before his life's work, we will have no words for: call it whim. So if I answer that my insistence on, for example, aligning movies and Shakespeare and philosophy is based on whim, you will know how to take me.

Now I'm ready to offer as my concluding example, to challenge our convictions in the worth of movies as subjects of thought, *Pennies from Heaven*, a much less lucky movie than, say, the seven thirties comedies I listed in the original genre of remarriage. Those movies are likeable and comprehensible enough to be worth taking and treasuring as light comedies, without working to consciousness any more of the material in *Pursuits of Happiness* than occurs to you casually. Whereas if the brilliance of *Pennies from Heaven* doesn't strike you right off, if you don't become convinced at any rate fairly swiftly that the shocking juxtaposition of attitudes it presents is part of a study, among other things, of the unsettling power of movies, it is likely to seem too unpleasant and confused to think about at all. It is bound to be somewhat hard to think about since it is a Hollywood musical that apparently seeks to undermine the conventions that made possible the Hollywood musical. The subsequent paradox is that its success depends on its undermining itself. If it absorbs the power of conviction of the Hollywood musical then it has not undermined that power. If on the other hand it does not absorb the power of the Hollywood musical, then it lacks the power of conviction altogether. It would answer this paradox to say: This movie has the conviction of a work that undermines the conventional sources of conviction in its medium, precisely by reconceiving the sources of that conviction. This sounds like something that might be said of the course of modernism in the other major arts; it is a reason I have sometimes said that art now exists in the condition of philosophy, since it has always been the condition of philosophy to attempt to escape itself, which for several centuries has taken the form of each new major philosopher wishing to repudiate the past of the subject—I mean repudiate it philosophically. As famous, and successful, as any such effort in the arts is Bertolt Brecht's repudiation of theatricality by means of theater itself; theater, hence, reconceived. But in thinking about movies this is so far merely words; it is an idea that has no commonly appreciated and acknowledged realization in film itself. It tells us nothing about whether, for example, *Pennies from Heaven* succeeds or fails in the new terms we allow for it. The moral remains that nothing but the details of the individual work can tell.

Take the two most obvious details in which this film calls into question the conventions of classical Hollywood musicals, the fact that they employ the dubbing of voices, and the fact that they go to any fictional lengths in order to motivate realistically their fantastic songs and dances. When the small-time hero, refused financing by the banker, breaks into a happy duet with him, his voice dubbed by a woman's; or when the crippled, mumbling beggar takes on an athletic, dazzlingly mounted performance of the title song; the violence of emotion I felt as I stared at the conventions of the Hollywood musical brought to trial was only increased by the fact that I found the numbers expert and gripping. So if *Pennies from Heaven* is parody, it is at the same time tribute, homage: it acknowledges that the reputedly naive musicals on which it lives were as artful and as mysterious as anything it can claim for itself. It shows that conventions of the Hollywood musical are deeper than we may have thought, that their discovery of human desires and satisfactions cannot be undone or outpaced merely by exaggerating them, and indeed in no obvious way at all. And if this is true of the Hollywood musical, where in successful film, or in art generally, is it not true?

Yet this film fails its own knowledge at the end and strikes, to my ear, so false a note as to help ensure its lack of consideration. What happens is this. The hero is arrested for a terrible crime we know has been committed by the crippled beggar, and the film's examination of the human voice and the sentiments of popular song climaxes with the hero's finding his own voice not in song but in plain speech as, on the gallows, he speaks the words of what may be recognized as the verse to the song "Pennies from Heaven." To ask a writer's words to be so sound that they can be said on the gallows is an ambitious test of writing; I find that these words, said by Steve Martin, passed well enough. If so, then nothing should stand in the way of the fiction's happy ending. The governor might have driven up in a limousine, his way cleared by screaming motorcycles, and sung a song of pardon to our hero. Instead the movie slinks to a conclusion by having the hero reappear to his sweetheart for no reason within the fiction, mouthing something like, "We've worked too hard not to get a happy ending." This is roughly to suppose that the conventions that lend the movie its power are disposable at will.

How wrong this is, is reinforced if we notice that the climax of the movie alludes to a more famous dramatic work with pennies in its title, the Brecht-Weill *Threepenny Opera*, which concludes with its bourgeois criminal hero singing on the gallows and being brought a reprieve by a messenger on horseback. So in failing to find out how to say that its hero deserves a pardon, perhaps in the form of an ironic consolation, *Pennies from Heaven* is faithless at once to its Hollywood medium and to its source in the Brechtian theater of estrangement.[2]

Let us end on this movie's other and most dangerous moment of imitation and homage, the reenactment by Steve Martin and Bernadette Peters of the Astaire-Rogers routine on Irving Berlin's "Let's Face the Music and Dance." What the movie is studying here most extravagantly is the nature of what is called our identification with the figures of drama. This reenactment, along with the voices that take over the characters as they go into song, reveals the identification with figures on film not as a process of imitating them but as a product of being possessed by them. Now of all the impersonations one might have tried of the distinctive stars in the history of Hollywood, from Chaplin to Gable and Hepburn, the one no normal person in his right mind would have tried to translate from the realm of fantasy into the public realm is the sense of himself in an Astaire routine: no one else could perfectly enough lend his body to the demands of that spirit. So one must ask how good the Martin-Peters enactment is of this impossible possession. And I find the answer to be that it is convincing enough to make me ask how convincing the original is, whether *it* fulfills its own dramatic invitation to face the music and dance.

I note that it is perhaps the most weirdly motivated of all the memorable Astaire productions. He prefaces the dance with a little drama in which he loses his money at a casino and then, wandering outside with a pistol to use on himself, sees a woman in an evening gown mount a parapet; he grabs her before she can leap, throws away the pistol, and begins the song and dance. Described in this way, apart from its experience, it may be wondered how they get through all this without laughing.[3] But within the experience, or in remembering such experiences, we know that Astaire has thought about what motivates dancing, about what provides its occasions, as well as anyone who ever lived; so we had perhaps better think further about it in the present case.

The little opening drama, in which the actions set in music are neither spoken nor sung nor danced, invokes the condition of mime, of what the Elizabethans called a dumb show, of the sort used in *Hamlet* by the players of the play-within-the-play who act out their drama silently before they speak their parts. If you take this undanced prelude or invitation to dance in this way, as a kind of prophecy or parable of Astaire's understanding of his dancing, then he can be taken to be declaring that it is meant as a removal not from life but from death. Though the idea of escaping life is a more common view of dance and of comedy, and I guess of art in general, than Astaire's idea of redeeming death, it is no less metaphysical. Astaire's view of dancing as facing the music, as a *response* to the life of inexorable consequences, which turn out to be the consequences of desperate pleasures, would then be a concrete translation of what such a thinker as Nietzsche meant by dancing (as when Zarathustra speaks, urging: "Raise up your hearts, my brothers, high, higher! And don't forget your legs! Raise up your legs, too, good dancers!")—something I guess he would have learned, among other things, from Emerson, from such a passage in another of Emerson's early essays as this: "All that we reckoned settled shakes and rattles; and literatures, cities, climates, religions, leave their foundations and dance before our eyes." Can an Astaire-Rogers dance, projected on a screen, be this good? How good would this good have to be?—This is serious business.

Postscript

It was pointed out to me by a student at Yale, on my return for other matters some months after I had given a version of this lecture there, that the ending of *Pennies from Heaven*, which I criticize as faithless to its sources in the Hollywood musical and in Brechtian theater in its avoidance of a stance toward the hero's threatened execution, is readable as a further reflection of the hero's fantasy life, hence as his last moments on the gallows. We hadn't more than a few minutes in which to pursue the idea, so I may have misunderstood what he said. My response is this.

Dennis Potter's novelized version of the material to *Pennies from Heaven* fairly obviously does not know what its own end should be, whether part of the hero's fantasy life, or a further appeal on its behalf, or some final regret that there is no use in such an appeal, or a complaint against society for not listening more carefully, or a complaint against the songs for being dismissable. Regarded as the prospectus for a movie, these alternatives may well have seemed undecidable, for the movie must work its own way into such matters. The possibility that the movie takes the option of adopting the hero's fantasy is one that crossed my mind, but it makes matters worse, I think, than I said, worse than making some cheap fun of itself.

The hero's prior bursts into song and dance have the effect of authenticating his inner life, convincing us not only of its existence but of the justice, however mad in imagery (in, some might say, the Utopianism), of its demands. An accomplishment worthy of any art. After these outbursts, it followed (as a kind of price of their elations) that the film's return to grim reality was a return to something no less indebted to the Hollywood past than its treatment of the musical is. A way to tell the structure of *Pennies from Heaven* is as one that alternates musical absorptions of Hollywood (of the thirties and early forties) with counterabsorptions of that same Hollywood; the counterabsorptions work as a kind of negative Utopianism to match the mad positive Utopianism of its music and its music's words. An obvious source for the returns, the counterabsorptions, is such a "woman's film" or "tearjerker" (as if we knew what these are) as George Stevens's *Penny Serenade* of 1941, with Irene Dunne and Cary Grant. I suppose this is deliberate, not only because of the connection in name, but because one of the married pair in the earlier film (in this case the woman) is a hawker of popular music (of records, not sheet music), and a spinning record recurrently punctuates the narration as the film works its way through the death of an innocent and the death of innocence. A less specific source of the counterattitude to reality, to reality as consisting of a planet without music, seems to me something like a Fritz Lang *film noir* early in his American career, for example, *You Only Live Once* of 1937, also about a loser condemned to die for a crime of which he is innocent, which also ends (almost) in a prison yard, with a succeeding ironic fantasy of freedom.

The sources of negative or dashed Utopianism will be harder to recognize than those of the musical numbers, but the alternation of genres provides at once an interpretation of the hero's sensibility, of the commonness of his craziness, and an insight of significance into the Hollywood of its golden age, namely that it depicted a unified world, a universe. The "fugitive couple" of certain of its melodramas are negations of just those pairs in certain Hollywood comedies who are hardly less isolated from society, hardly less incomprehensible to it, but whose isolation and incomprehensibility work themselves out with fortune more willing to smile. (The happier pairs have easier access to money. It remains to be determined how far this is the difference that matters, and how far it is the symbol of the difference.)

It is up to each of us to find our participation in these high-hat highs and low-down lows. Now if the conclusion of *Pennies from Heaven* is to be identified as the hero's fantasy, and it is to be taken on the model of his earlier bursts into song, then, since it has no follow-up, it forces us to read his fantasy as merely some apparently well-understood, ironic escape from some well-understood reality.

And this seems to me faithless at once to the hero's inner life, refusing the just appeal in its tawdriness; and to the freedom it seemed to assign us in determining our relation to these events; and to the power of film itself, whose dangers and values of seduction it had honored, if feared, in its own production, but now seems, in an act of self-disrespect, to claim to transcend-to claim some privileged position from which to assess the value of movies, of fantasy, of art, of such freedom as we can find the means to express and hence to claim. Far be it from me to deny the connection between high and low tawdriness, or escape; but to discount them is not something we need art for, high or low.

I take this moment to avert a related ambiguity in what I was saying in my lecture. When I note the extraordinary persistence of the conventions in viewing movies just once (interspersed with the odd cult-object viewed countless times), and reviewing them on the basis of one viewing, I am objecting not to the practices in themselves but to their dominance, and lack of assessment, in general movie culture. Certainly I am not recommending repetitive viewing to no particular point, as the better alternative. On the contrary, the casual, or surprised, appeal to memorable passages has a value that studiedness may sacrifice, a value not merely of spontaneity (whatever that is), but of a depth that only a certain immediacy will capture, as by surprise. The sacrifice of literary immediacy to studiedness is more familiar ground, and I can imagine that the practical difficulties in the way of checking one's reactions to the events of film (for all the technology of cassettes, etc.), or one's recall of them, may at some time have a leavening effect on our literary culture, remembering the value there was (however practically necessitated by its own economy) in citing common literary works from memory, a time when a smaller literary world had works in common, a time (except for such things) not to be envied. It resulted in some misquotation (of a particular kind), but its outcome was of contexts in which one recognized the point of having a memory, a public memory. This is something I want from an eventual film culture as much as I want film's rigorous, orderly study. Such is my justification for continuing to explore *Pennies from Heaven* on the basis of one viewing. My excuse is not having had it available since needing to see it again. (How hard did I look for it? A new question for one's intellectual conscience.)

Notes

1 Norton Batkin took me back to this idea. His work, represented by
Photography and Philosophy, the doctoral dissertation he submitted to the

Department of Philosophy at Harvard in May 1981, goes far with it, into the nature of photography's stillness.

2 I have added a postscript that amplifies this claim.

3 Arlene Croce testifies to such a feeling in her elegant and useful *The Fred Astaire and Ginger Rogers Book* (New York, 1972), 88.

2

On Cinema

Gilles Deleuze

On the *Cinema* books

From **Cinema 2,** *Conclusion*

The usefulness of theoretical books on cinema has been called into question (especially today, because the times are not right) [. . .]. For many people, philosophy is something which is not "made," but is pre-existent, ready-made in a prefabricated sky. However, philosophical theory is itself a practice, just as much as its object. It is no more abstract than its object. It is a practice of concepts, and it must be judged in the light of the other practices with which it interferes. A theory of cinema is not "about" cinema, but about the concepts that cinema gives rise to and which are themselves related to other concepts corresponding to other practices, the practice of concepts in general having no privilege over others, any more than one object has over others. It is at the level of the interference of many practices that things happen, beings, images, concepts, all kinds of events. The theory of cinema does not bear on the cinema, but on the concepts of the cinema, which are no less practical, effective or existent than cinema itself [. . .]. Cinema's concepts are not given in cinema. And yet they are cinema's concepts, not theories about cinema. So that there is always a time, midday-midnight, when we must no longer ask ourselves, "What is cinema?" but "What is philosophy?" Cinema itself is a new practice of images and signs, whose theory philosophy must produce as conceptual practice.[1]

From "Cinema-1, Premiere"

You are wondering why so many people write about cinema. I ask myself the same question. It seems to me to be because cinema contains a lot of ideas. What I call Ideas are images that make one think. From one art to another, the nature of images varies and is inseparable from the techniques used: colors and lines for painting, sound for music, verbal descriptions for novels, movement-images for cinema, etc. And in each case, the thoughts are inseparable from the images; they are completely immanent to the images. There are no abstract thoughts realized indifferently in one image or another, but concrete images that only exist through these images and their means. Drawing out cinematic ideas means extracting thoughts without abstracting them, grasping them in their internal relationship with the movement-images. That is why people write "about" cinema. The great cinematic authors are thinkers just as much as painters, musicians, novelists and philosophers (philosophy has no special privilege).[2]

From "On The Movement-Image"

Bergson's position, in *Matter and Memory*, is unique. Or *Matter and Memory*, rather, is a unique, extraordinary book among Bergson's work. He no longer puts motion in the realm of duration, but on the one hand posits the absolute identity of motion-matter-image, and on the other hand discovers a Time that's the coexistence of all levels of duration (matter being only the lowest level). Fellini recently said we're in infancy, old age, and middle age all at once: that's thoroughly Bergsonian. So there's a marriage in *Matter and Memory* of pure spiritualism and radical materialism. At once Vertov and Dreyer, if you like, both directions. But Bergson didn't continue along this path. He relinquished these two basic advances touching the movement-image and the time-image. Why? I think it's because Bergson was here working out new philosophical concepts relating to the theory of relativity: he thought relativity involved a conception of time which it didn't itself bring out, but which it was up to philosophy to construct. Only what happened was that people thought Bergson was attacking relativity, that he was criticizing the physical theory itself. Bergson considered the misunderstanding too basic to dispel. So he went back to a simpler conception. Still, in *Matter and Memory* (1896) he'd traced out a movement-image and a time-image that he could, subsequently, have applied to cinema.[3]

From "Portrait of the Philosopher as a Moviegoer"

[W]hen I was about ten years old, I started going to the movies all the time, more so than my peers. I still have fond memories of the actors and the films of that era. I loved Danielle Darrieux, and I got a kick out of Saturnin

Fabre because he scared me and made me laugh. He had a diction all his own. But after the war, I rediscovered movies long after everyone else. It wasn't until very late that the obviousness of film as art or creation in its own right struck me. By then I thought of myself only as a philosopher. What led me to start writing about film was that I had been wrestling with a problem of signs for some time [. . .]. And yet film was no pretext or field of application. Philosophy is not in a state of exterior reflection on other fields or disciplines, but in a state of active and interior alliance with them. It is no more abstract than they are, nor any more difficult.

I didn't imagine I was doing philosophy on cinema. I considered cinema for itself through a classification of signs. This classification is flexible and can be altered. Its only value resides in what it allows you to see. The book may have a complicated organisation, but this is because the material itself is difficult. What I had hoped to do was to invent sentences that function like images, that "show" the great works of film. My argument is simple: the great auteurs of film are thinking, thought exists in their work, and making a film is creative, living thought.[4]

[. . .] It does happen that I feel like I "absolutely need" to see some film or the other, and that if I don't, I won't be able to continue the work. And then I give up—I'm forced to do without it; or it reappears, having been re-released. It also happens that when I do see a film, if it seems really beautiful, I know I will want to write about it. This changes the writing conditions.[5]

[. . .] Crying, or causing tears to flow, and provoking laughter are the functions of certain images. You can cry because it's too beautiful or too intense. The only thing that bugs me is the knowing laughter of the cinephiles. This kind of laughter is supposedly on some higher level, a second level. I'd rather see the whole house in tears.[6]

[. . .] The first volume, *The Movement-Image*, should have the feel of a complete work, but it should also leave the reader asking for more. The sequel is the time-image, but not as an opposition to the movement-image. Rather, the movement-image implies in itself only an indirect image of time, one that is produced by editing. The second volume must therefore examine the kinds of images that have a direct impact on time.[7]

From Cinema 1, *"Preface"*

This study is not a history of the cinema. It is a taxonomy, an attempt at the classification of images and signs. But this first volume has to content itself with determining the elements, and the elements of only one part of the classification.

We will frequently be referring to the American logician Peirce (1839-1914), because he established a general classification of images and signs, which is undoubtedly the most complete and the most varied. It can be compared with Linnaeus's classifications in natural history, or even more with Mendeleev's table in chemistry.

Another comparison is no less necessary. Bergson was writing *Matter and Memory* in 1896: it was the diagnosis of a crisis in psychology. Movement, as physical reality in the external world, and the image, as psychic reality in consciousness, could no longer be opposed. The Bergsonian discovery of a movement-image and, more profoundly, of a time-image, still retains such richness today that it is not certain that all its consequences have been drawn.[8]

From Cinema 1, *"Preface to the English Edition"*

It is not a matter of saying that the modern cinema of the time-image is "more valuable" than the classical cinema of the movement-image. We are talking only of masterpieces to which no hierarchy of value applies. The cinema is always as perfect as it can be, taking into account the images and signs which it invents and which it has at its disposal at a given moment. This is why this study must interweave concrete analyses of images and signs with the "monographs" of the great directors who have created or renewed them.[9]

From Cinema 2, *"Preface to the English Edition"*

Over several centuries, from the Greeks to Kant, a revolution took place in philosophy: the subordination of time to movement was reversed, time ceases to be the measurement of normal movement, it increasingly appears for itself and creates paradoxical movements. Time is out of joint: Hamlet's words signify that time is no longer subordinated to movement, but rather movement to time. It could be said that, in its own sphere, cinema has repeated the same experience, the same reversal, in more fast-moving circumstances. The movement-image of the so-called classical cinema gave way, in the post-war period, to a direct time-image. Such a general idea must of course be qualified, corrected, adapted to concrete examples.

Why is the Second World War taken as a break? The fact is that, in Europe, the post-war period has greatly increased the situations which we no longer know how to react to, in spaces which we no longer know how to describe. These were "any spaces whatever," deserted but inhabited, disused warehouses, waste ground, cities in the course of demolition or reconstruction. And in these any-spaces-whatever a new race of characters was stirring, kind of mutant: they saw rather than acted, they were seers. Hence Rossellini's great trilogy, *Europe 51, Stromboli, Germany Year 0*: a child in the destroyed city, a foreign woman on the island, a bourgeois woman who starts to "see" what is around her. Situations could be extremes, or, on the contrary, those of everyday banality, or both at once: what tends to collapse, or at least to lose its position, is the sensory-motor schema which constituted the action-image of the old cinema. And thanks to this loosening of the sensory-motor linkage, it is time, "a little time in the pure state," which rises up to the surface of the screen. Time ceases to be derived from the movement, it appears in itself and itself gives rise to false movements [. . .].

In any case, what we call temporal structure, or direct time-image, clearly goes beyond the purely empirical succession of time—past-present-future. It is, for example, a coexistence of distinct durations, or of levels of duration; a single event can belong to several levels: the sheets of past coexist in a non-chronological order. We see this in Welles with his powerful intuition of the earth, then in Resnais with his characters who return from the land of the dead.

There are yet more temporal structures: the whole aim of this book is to release those that the cinematographic image has been able to grasp and reveal, and which can echo the teachings of science, what the other arts uncover for us, or what philosophy makes understandable for us, each in their respective ways. It is foolish to talk about the death of the cinema because cinema is still at the beginning of its investigations: making visible these relationships of time which can only appear in a creation of the image.[10]

On Bergson—Movement and Time

From Cinema 1, *Chapter 1*

Bergson does not just put forward one thesis on movement, but three. The first is the most famous [. . .] you cannot reconstitute movement with positions in space or instants in time: that is, with immobile sections. You can only achieve this reconstitution by adding to the positions, or to the instants, the abstract idea of a succession, of a time which is mechanical, homogeneous, universal and copied from space, identical for all movements. And thus you miss the movement in two ways. On the one hand, you can bring two instants or two positions together to infinity; but movement will always occur in the interval between the two, in other words behind your back. On the other hand, however much you divide and subdivide time, movement will always occur in a concrete duration; thus each movement will have its own qualitative duration. Hence we oppose two irreducible formulas: "real movement → concrete duration," and "immobile sections + abstract time."

In 1907, in *Creative Evolution*, Bergson gives the incorrect formula a name: the cinematographic illusion. Cinema, in fact, works with two complementary givens: instantaneous sections which are called images; and a movement or a time which is impersonal, uniform, abstract, invisible, or imperceptible, which is "in" the apparatus, and "with" which the images are made to pass consecutively. Cinema thus gives us a false movement—it is the typical example of false movement. But it is strange that Bergson should give the oldest illusion such a modern and recent name ("cinematographic"). In fact, says Bergson, when the cinema reconstitutes movement with mobile sections, it is merely doing what was already being done by the most ancient thought (Zeno's paradoxes), or what natural perception does. In this respect, Bergson's position differs from that of phenomenology, which instead saw the cinema as breaking with the conditions of natural perception. "We take snapshots, as it were, of the passing reality, and, as these are characteristics of the reality, we have only to string them on a becoming abstract, uniform and invisible, situated at the back of the apparatus of knowledge . . . Perception, intellection, language so proceed in general. Whether we would think becoming, or express it, or even perceive it, we hardly do anything else than set going a kind of cinematograph inside us." Does this mean that for Bergson the cinema is only the projection, the reproduction of a constant, universal illusion? As though we had always had cinema without realising it? But then a whole range of problems arises.

Firstly, is not the reproduction of the illusion in a certain sense also its correction? Can we conclude that the result is artificial because the means are artificial? Cinema proceeds with photogrammes—that is, with immobile sections—twenty-four images per second (or eighteen at the outset). But it has often been noted that what it gives us is not the photogramme: it is an intermediate image, to which movement is not appended or added; the movement on the contrary belongs to the intermediate image as immediate given. It might be said that the position of natural perception is the same. But there the illusion is corrected "above" perception by the conditions which make perception possible in the subject. In the cinema, however, it is corrected at the same time as the image appears for a spectator without conditions (in this respect, as we will see, phenomenology is right in assuming that natural perception and cinematographic perception are qualitatively different). In short, cinema does not give us an image to which movement is added, it immediately gives us a movement-image. It does give us a section, but a section which is mobile, not an immobile section + abstract movement. Now what is again very odd is that Bergson was perfectly aware of the existence of mobile sections or movement-images. This happened before *Creative Evolution*, before the official birth of the cinema: it was set out in *Matter and Memory* in 1896. The discovery of the movement-image, beyond the conditions of natural perception, was the extraordinary invention of the first chapter of *Matter and Memory*.[11]

[. . .] Now *Creative Evolution* advances a second thesis, which, instead of reducing everything to the same illusion about movement, distinguishes at least two very different illusions. The error remains the same—that of reconstituting movement from instants or positions—but there are two ways of doing this: the ancient and the modern [. . .]. The modern scientific revolution has consisted in relating movement not to privileged instants, but to any-instant-whatever. Although movement was still recomposed, *it was no longer recomposed from formal transcendental elements (poses), but from immanent material elements (sections)* [. . .]. Bergson forcefully demonstrates that the cinema fully belongs to this modern conception of movement. But, from this point, he seems to hesitate between two paths, one of which leads him back to his first thesis, the other instead opening up a new question. According to the first path, although the two conceptions may be different from the scientific point of view, they nevertheless have a more or less identical result. In fact, to recompose movement with *eternal poses* or with *immobile sections* comes to the same thing: in both cases, one misses the movement because one constructs a Whole, one assumes that "all is given," whilst movement only occurs if the whole is neither given nor giveable. As soon as a whole is given to one in the eternal order of forms or poses, or in the set of any-instant-whatevers, then either time is no more than the image of eternity or it is the consequence of the set; there is no longer room for real movement. Another path, however, seemed open to Bergson. For, if the ancient conception corresponds closely to ancient philosophy, which aims to think the eternal, then the modern conception, modern science, calls upon another philosophy. When one relates movement to any-moment-whatever, one must be capable of thinking the production of the new, that is, of the remarkable and the singular, at any one of these moments: this is a complete conversion of philosophy. It is what Bergson ultimately aims to do: to give modern science the metaphysic which corresponds to it, which it lacks as one half lacks the other. But can we stop once we have set out on this path? Can we deny that the arts must also go through this conversion or that the cinema is an essential factor in this, and that it has a role to play in the birth and formation of this new thought, this new way of thinking? This is why Bergson is no longer content merely to corroborate his first thesis on movement. Bergson's second thesis—although it stops half way—makes possible another way of looking at the cinema, a way in which it would no longer be just the perfected apparatus of the oldest illusion, but, on the contrary, the organ for perfecting the new reality (2002a:3-4;7-8).[12]

[. . .] And this is Bergson's third thesis, which is also contained in *Creative Evolution*. If we tried to reduce it to a bare formula, it would be this: not only is the instant an immobile section of movement, but movement is a mobile section of duration, that is, of the Whole, or of a whole. Which implies that movement expresses something more profound, which is the change in duration or in the whole. To say that duration is change is part of its definition: it changes and does not stop changing [. . .]. The upshot of this third thesis is that we find ourselves on three levels: (1) the sets or closed systems which are defined by discernible objects or distinct parts; (2) the movement of translation which is established between these objects and modifies their respective positions; (3) the duration or the whole, a spiritual reality which constantly changes according to its own relations.

Thus in a sense movement has two aspects. On the one hand, that which happens between objects or parts; on the other hand, that which expresses the duration or the whole. The result is that duration, by changing qualitatively, is divided up in objects, and objects, by gaining depth, by losing their contours, are united in duration. We can therefore say that movement relates the objects of a closed system to open duration, and duration to the objects of the system which it forces to open up. Movement relates the objects between which it is established to the changing whole which it expresses, and vice versa. Through movement the whole is divided up into objects, and objects are re-united in the whole, and indeed between the two "the whole" changes. We can consider the objects or parts of a set as *immobile sections*; but movement is established between these sections, and relates the objects or parts to the duration of a whole which changes, and thus expresses the changing of the whole in relation to the objects and is itself a *mobile section* of duration. Now we are equipped to understand the profound thesis of the first chapter of *Matter and Memory*. (1) There are not only instantaneous images, that is, immobile sections of movement; (2) there are movement-images which are mobile sections of duration; (3) there are, finally, time-images, that is, duration-images, change-images, relation-images, volume-images which are beyond movement itself.[13]

The Movement-Image and Its Varieties

From Cinema 1, *Chapter 4:* Bergson constantly says that we cannot understand anything unless we are first given the set of images [. . .].

If the cinema does *not* have natural subjective perception as its model, it is because the mobility of its centres and the variability of its framings always lead it to restore vast acentred and deframed zones. It then tends to return to the first régime of the movement-image; universal variation, total, objective and diffuse perception. In fact, it travels the route in both directions. From the point of view which occupies us for the moment, we go from total, objective perception which is indistinguishable from the thing, to a subjective perception which is distinguished from it by simple elimination or subtraction. It is this unicentred subjective perception that is called perception strictly speaking. And it is the first avatar of the movement-image: when it is related to a centre of indetermination, it becomes *perception-image*.

However, we should not think that the whole operation consists only of a subtraction. There is something else as well. When the universe of movement-images is related to one of these special images which forms a centre in it, the universe is incurved and organised to surround it. We continue to go from the world to the centre, but the world has taken on a curvature, it has become a periphery, it forms a horizon. We are still in the perception-image, but we are already entering the action-image as well. In fact, perception is only one side of the gap, and action is the other side. What is called action, strictly speaking, is the delayed reaction of the centre of indetermination. Now, this centre is only capable of acting—in the sense of organising an unexpected response—because it perceives and has received the excitation on a privileged facet, eliminating the remainder. All this amounts to recalling that all perception is primarily sensory-motor: perception "is no more in the sensory centres than in the motor centres; it measures the complexity of their relations." If the world is incurved around the perceptive centre, this is already from the point of view of action, from which perception is inseparable. By incurving, perceived things tender their unstable facet toward me, at the same time as my delayed reaction, which has become action, leams to use them [. . .].

This is therefore the second avatar of the movement-image: it becomes *action-image*. One passes imperceptibly from perception to action. The operation under consideration is no longer elimination, selection or framing, but the incurving of the universe, which simultaneously causes the virtual action of things on us and our possible action on things. This is the second material aspect of subjectivity. And, just as perception relates movement to "bodies" (nouns), that is to rigid objects which will serve as moving bodies or as things moved, action relates movement to "acts" (verbs) which will be the design for an assumed end or result.

But the interval is not merely defined by the specialisation of the two limit-facets, perceptive and active. There is an in-between. Affection is what occupies the interval, what occupies it without filling it in or filling it up. It surges in the centre of indetermination, that is to say in the subject, between a perception which is troubling in certain respects and a hesitant action. It is a coincidence of subject and object, or the way in which the subject perceives itself, or rather experiences itself or feels itself "from the inside" (third material aspect of subjectivity). It relates movement to a "quality" as lived state (adjective). Indeed, it is not sufficient to think that perception— thanks to distance—retains or reflects what interests us by letting pass what is indifferent to us. There is inevitably a part of external movements that we "absorb," that we refract, and which does not transform itself into either objects of perception or acts of the subject; rather they mark the coincidence of the subject and the object in a pure quality. This is the final avatar of the movement-image: the *affection-image* [. . .]. All things considered, *movement-images divide into three sorts of images when they are related to a centre of indetermination as to a special image*: perception-images, action-images and affection-images. And each one of us, the special image or the contingent centre, is nothing but an assemblage of three images, a consolidate of perception-images, action-images and affection-images [. . .].

It is easy, in the cinema, to recognise on a practical level these three kinds of images which pass across the screen, without even making use of explicit criteria. The scene from Lubitsch's *The Man I Killed* which was mentioned previously is an exemplary perception-image: the crowd seen from behind, at waist height, leaves a gap which corresponds to a cripple's missing leg; through this gap another cripple, who is legless, sees the parade which passes. Fritz Lang provides a famous example of the action-image in *Dr Mabuse the Gambler*: an organised action, segmented in space and in time, with the synchronised watches whose ticking punctuates the murder in the train, the car which carries off the stolen document, the telephone which warns Mabuse. The action-image will remain marked by this model, to the point of finding a privileged milieu in the *film noir* and the ideal of a detailed segmentarised action in the hold-up. In comparison, the Western presents not only action-images, but also an almost pure perception-image: it is a drama of the visible and of the invisible as much as an epic of action; the hero only acts because he is the first to see, and only triumphs because he imposes on action the interval or the second's delay which allows him to see everything (Anthony Mann's *Winchester '73*). As for the affection-image, we will find striking cases in the face of Dreyer's *Joan of Arc*, and in most of the close-ups of the face in general.

A film is never made up of a single kind of image: thus we call the combination of the three varieties, montage. Montage (in one of its aspects) is the assemblage of movement-images, hence the inter-assemblage of perception-images, affection-images and action-images. Nevertheless a film, at least in its most simple characteristics, always has one type of image which is dominant: one can speak of an active, perceptive or affective montage, depending on the predominant type. It has often been said that Griffith invented montage precisely by creating the montage of action. But Dreyer invents a montage and even a framing of affection, with other laws, in so far as *The Passion of Joan of Arc* is the case of an almost exclusively affective film. Vertov is perhaps the inventor of properly perceptive montage, which was to be developed by the whole of the experimental cinema. These three kinds of spatially determined shots can be made to correspond to these three kinds of varieties: the long-shot would be primarily a perception-image; the medium-shot an action-image; the close-up an affection-image. But, at the same time, according to one of Eisenstein's instructions, each of these movement-images is a point of view on the whole of the film, a way of grasping this whole, which becomes affective in the close-up, active in the medium-shot, perceptive in the long-shot—each of these shots ceasing to be spatial in order to become itself a "reading" of the whole film.[14]

[. . .] We already have, therefore, four kinds of images: firstly *movement-images*. Then, when they are related to a centre of indetermination, they divide into three varieties—*perception-images*, *action-images*, *affection-images*. There is every reason to believe that many other kinds of images can exist [. . .] in so far as they result from a comparison of movement-images between themselves, or from a combination of the three varieties [. . .]. C. S. Peirce is the philosopher who went the furthest into a systematic classification of images.[15]

From Cinema 1, *Chapter 12*

After having distinguished between affection and action, which he calls Firstness and Secondness, Peirce added a third kind of image: the "mental'" or Thirdness. The point of thirdness was a term that referred to a second term through the intermediary of another term or terms. This third instance appeared in signification, law or relation [. . .]. Therefore thirdness gives birth not to actions but to "acts" which necessarily contain the symbolic element of a law (giving, exchanging); not to perceptions, but to interpretations which refer to the element of sense; not to affections, but to intellectual feelings of relations, such as the feelings which accompany the use of the logical conjunctions "because," "although," "so that," "therefore," "now," etc.

Thirdness perhaps finds its most adequate representation in relation [. . .]. It is an image which takes as its object, relations, symbolic acts, intellectual feelings. It can be, but is not necessarily, more difficult than the other images. It will necessarily have a new, direct, relationship with thought, a relationship which is completely distinct from that of the other images [. . .]. Take the example of burlesque [. . .]. The Marx brothers [. . .] are distributed in such a way that Harpo and Chico are most often grouped together, Groucho for his part looming up in order to enter into a kind of alliance with the two others. Caught in the indissoluble group of 3, Harpo is the 1, the representative of celestial affects, but also already of infernal impulses, voraciousness, sexuality, destruction. Chico is 2: it is he who takes on action, the initiative, the duel with the milieu, the strategy of effort and resistance. Harpo hides, in his immense raincoat, all kinds of objects, bits and pieces which can be used for any kind of action; but he himself only uses them in an affective or fetishistic way, and it is Chico who uses them for organised action. Finally, Groucho is the three, the man of interpretations, of symbolic acts and abstract relations. Nevertheless each of the three equally belongs to the thirdness that they make up together. Harpo and Chico already have a relationship such that Chico throws a *word* to Harpo, who has to provide the corresponding object, in a series which is constantly denatured (for example the series *flash-fish-flesh-flask-flush* . . . in *Animal Crackers*); conversely Harpo proposes to Chico the enigma of a language of gestures, in a series of mimes that Chico must constantly guess in order to extract a *proposition* from them. But Groucho pushes the art of interpretation to its final degree, because he is the master of *reasoning*, of arguments and syllogisms which find a pure expression in nonsense: "Either this man is dead, or my watch has stopped" (he says, feeling Harpo's pulse in *A Day at the Races*). In all these senses, the greatness of the Marx Brothers is to have introduced the mental-image into burlesque.[16]

From Cinema 2, *Chapter 2*

Peirce's strength, when he invented semiotics, was to conceive of signs on the basis of images and their combinations, not as a function of determinants which were already linguistic. This led him to the most extraordinary classification of images and signs, of which we offer only a brief summary. Peirce begins with the image, from the phenomenon or from what appears. The image seems to him to be of three kinds, no more: firstness (something that only refers to itself, quality or power, pure possibility; for instance, the red that we find identical to itself in the proposition "You have not put on your red dress" or "You are in red"); secondness (something that refers to itself only through something else, existence, action-reaction, effort-resistance); thirdness (something that refers to itself only by comparing one thing to another, relation, the law, the necessary). It will be noted that the three kinds of images are not simply ordinal—first, second, third—but cardinal: there are two in the second, to the point where there is a firstness in the secondness, and there are three in the third. If the third marks the culmination, it is because it cannot be made up with dyads, but also because combinations of triads on their own or with the other modes can produce any multiplicity. This said, the sign in Peirce apparently combines the three kinds of image, but not in any kind of way: the sign is an image which stands for another image (its object), through the relation of a third image which constitutes "its interpretant," this in turn being a sign, and so on to infinity. Hence Peirce, by combining the three modes of the image and the three aspects of the sign, produces nine sign elements, and ten corresponding signs (because all the combinations of elements are not logically possible) [. . .].

We saw in Volume 1 that firstness, secondness and thirdness corresponded to the affection-image, the action-image and the relation-image. But all three are deduced from the movement-image as material, as soon as it is related to the interval of movement. Now this deduction is possible only if we first assume a perception-image. Of course, perception is strictly identical to every image, in so far as every image acts and reacts on all the others, on all their sides and in all their parts [. . .]. And perception will not constitute a first type of image in the movement-image without being extended into the other types, if there are any: perception of action, of affection, of relation, etc. The perception-image will therefore be like a degree zero in the deduction which is carried out as a function of the movement-image: there will be a "zeroness" before Peirce's firstness. As for the question: are there types of image in the movement-image other than the perception-image?, it is resolved by the various aspects of the interval: the perception-image received movement on one side, but the affection-image is what occupies the interval (firstness), the action-image what executes the movement on the other side (secondness), and the relation-image what reconstitutes the whole of the movement with all the aspects of the interval (thirdness functioning as closure of the deduction). Thus the movement-image gives rise to a sensory-motor whole which grounds narration in the image.

Between the perception-image and the others, there is no intermediary, because perception extends by itself into the other images. But, in the other cases, there is necessarily an intermediary which indicates the extension as passage. This is why, in the end, we find ourselves faced with six types of perceptible visible images that we see, not three: *perception-image, affection-image, impulse-image* (intermediates between affection and action), *action-image, reflection-image* (intermediate between action and relation), *relation-image*. And since, on the one hand, deduction constitutes a genesis of types, and, on the other, its degree zero, the perception-image, gives the others a bipolar composition appropriate to each case, we shall find ourselves with at least two signs of composition, and at least one sign of genesis for each type of image [. . .].

Thus the signs of composition for the perception-image are the *dicisign* and the *reume*. The dicisign refers to a perception of perception, and usually appears in cinema when the camera "sees" a character who is seeing; it implies a firm frame, and so constitutes a kind of solid state of perception. But the reume refers to a fluid or liquid perception which passes continuously through the frame. The *engramme*, finally, is the genetic sign or the gaseous state of perception, molecular perception, which the two others presuppose. The affection-image has the *icon* as sign of composition, which can be of quality or of power; it is a quality or a power which are only expressed (for example, a face) without being actualized. But it is the *qualisign* or the *potisign* which constitutes the genetic element because they construct quality or power in an any-space-whatever, that is, in a space that does not yet appear as a real setting. The impulse-image, intermediate between affection and action, is composed of *fetishes*, fetishes of Good or Evil: these are fragments torn from a derived setting, but which refer genetically to the *symptom* of an originary world operating below the setting. The action-image implies a real actualized setting which has become sufficient, so that a global situation will provoke an action, or on the contrary an action will disclose a part of the situation: the two signs of composition, therefore, are the *synsign* and the *index*. The internal link between situation and action, in any case, constitutes the genetic element or the imprint. The reflection-image, which goes from action to relation, is composed when action and situation enter into indirect relations: the signs are then *figures*, of attraction or inversion. And the genetic sign is *discursive*, that is, a situation or an action of discourse, independent of the question: is the discourse itself realized in a language? Finally, the relation-image relates movement to the whole that it expresses, and makes the whole vary according to the distribution of movement: the two signs of composition will be the *mark*, or the circumstance, through which two images are united, according to a habit ("natural" relation), and the *demark*, the circumstance through which an image finds itself torn from its natural relation or series; the sign of genesis the *symbol*, the circumstance through which we are made to compare two images, even arbitrarily united ("abstract" relation).

The movement-image is matter itself, as Bergson showed. It is a matter that is not linguistically formed, although it is semiotically, and constitutes the first dimension of semiotics. In fact, the different kinds of image which are necessarily deduced from the movement-image, the six kinds, are the elements that make this matter into a signaletic material. And the signs themselves are the features of expression that compose and combine these images, and constantly re-create them, borne or carted along by matter in movement.[17]

The Time-Image and Its Varieties

From Cinema 2, *Chapter 10*

We can now summarize the constitution of this time-image in modern cinema, and the new signs that it implies or initiates. There are many possible transformations, almost imperceptible passages, and also combinations between the movement-image and the time-image. It cannot be said that one is more important than the other, whether more beautiful or more profound. All that can be said is that the movement-image does not give us a time-image [. . .].

[W]hat brings this cinema of action into question after the war is the very break-up of the sensory-motor schema: the rise of situations to which one can no longer react, of environments with which there are now only chance relations, of empty or disconnected any-space-whatevers replacing qualified extended space. It is here that situations no longer extend into action or reaction in accordance with the requirements of the movement-image. These are pure optical and sound situations, in which the character does not know how to respond, abandoned spaces in which he ceases to experience and to act so that he enters into flight, goes on a trip, comes and goes, vaguely indifferent to what happens to him, undecided as to what must be done. But he has gained in an ability to see what he has lost in action or reaction: he SEES so that the viewer's problem becomes "What is there to see in the image?" (and not now "What are we going to see in the next image?"). The situation no longer extends into action through the intermediary of affections. It is cut off from all its extensions, it is now important only for itself, having absorbed all its affective intensities, all its active extensions. This is no longer a sensory-motor situation, but a purely optical and sound situation, where the seer has replaced the agent: a "description." We call this type of image opsigns and sonsigns, they appear after the war, through all the external reasons we can point to (the calling into question of action, the necessity of seeing and hearing, the proliferation of empty, disconnected, abandoned spaces) but also through the internal push of a cinema being reborn, re-creating its conditions, neorealism, new wave, new American cinema. Now, if it is true that the sensory-motor situation governed the indirect representation of time as consequence of the movement-image, the purely optical and sound situation opens onto a direct time-image. The time-image is the correlate of the opsign and the sonsign. It never appeared more clearly than in the author who anticipated modern cinema, from before the war and in the conditions of the silent film, Ozu: opsigns, empty or disconnected spaces, open on to still lifes as the pure form of time. Instead of "motor situation—indirect representation of time," we have "opsign or sonsign—direct presentation of time."

But what can purely optical and sound images link up with, since they no longer extend into action? We would like to reply: with recollection-images or dream-images. Yet, the former still come within the framework of the sensory-motor situation, whose interval they are content to fill, even though lengthening and distending it; they seize a former present in the past and thus respect the empirical progression of time, even though they introduce local regressions into it (the flashback as psychological memory). The latter, dream-images, rather affect the whole: they project the sensory-motor situation to infinity, sometimes by ensuring the constant metamorphosis of the situation, sometimes by replacing the action of characters with a movement of world. But we do not, in this way, leave behind an indirect representation, even though we come close, in certain exceptional cases, to doors of time that already belong to modern cinema (for instance, the flashback as revelation of a time which forks and frees itself in Mankiewicz, or the movement of world as the coupling of a pure description and dance in the American musical comedy). However, in these very cases, the recollection-image or the dream-image, the mnemosign or the onirosign, are gone beyond: for these images in themselves are virtual images, which are linked with the actual optical or sound image (description) but which are constantly being actualized on their own account, or the former in the latter to infinity. For the time-image to be born, on the contrary, the actual image must enter into relation with its *own* virtual image as such; from the outset pure description must divide in two, "repeat itself, take itself up again, fork, contradict itself." An image which is double-sided, mutual, both actual and virtual, must be constituted. We are no longer in the situation of a relationship between the actual image and other virtual images, recollections, or dreams, which thus become actual in turn: this is still a mode of linkage. We are in the situation of an actual image and its own virtual image, to the extent that there is no longer any linkage of the real with the imaginary, but *indiscernibility of the two*, a perpetual exchange. This is a progress in relation to the opsign: we saw how the crystal (the hyalosign) ensures the dividing in two of description, and brings about the exchange in the image which has become mutual, the exchange of the actual and the virtual, of the limpid and the opaque, of the seed and the surrounding. By raising themselves to the indiscernibility of the real and the imaginary, the signs of the crystal go beyond all psychology of the recollection or dream, and all physics of action. What we see in the crystal is no longer the empirical progression of time as succession of presents, nor its indirect representation as interval or as whole; it is its direct presentation, its constitutive dividing in two into a present which is passing and a past which is preserved, the strict contemporaneity of the present with the past that it will be, of the past with the present that it has been. It is time itself which arises in the crystal, and which is constantly recommending its dividing in two without completing it, since the indiscernible exchange is always renewed and reproduced. The direct time-image or the transcendental form of time is what we see in the crystal; and hyalosigns, and crystalline signs, should therefore be called mirrors or seeds of time.

Thus we have the chronosigns which mark the various presentations of the direct time-image. The first concerns the *order of time*: this order is not made up of succession, nor is it the same thing as the interval or the whole of indirect representation. It is a matter of the internal relations of time, in a topological or quantic form. Thus the first chronosign has two figures: sometimes it is the coexistence of all the sheets of past, with the topological transformation of these sheets, and the overtaking of psychological memory toward a world-memory (this sign can be called sheet, aspect, or *facies*). Sometimes it is the simultaneity of points of present, these points breaking with all external succession, and carrying out quantic jumps between the presents which are doubled by the past, the future and the present itself (this sign can be called point or accent). We are no longer in an indiscernible distinction between the real and the imaginary, which would characterize the crystal-image, but in undecidable alternatives between sheets of past, or "inexplicable" differences between points of present, which now concern the direct time-image. What is in play is no longer the real and the imaginary, but the true and the false. And just as the real and the imaginary become indiscernible in certain very specific conditions of the image, the true and the false now become undecidable or inextricable: the impossible proceeds from the possible, and the past is not necessarily true. A new logic has to be invented, just as earlier a new psychology had to be. It seemed to us that Resnais went furthest in the direction of coexisting sheets of past, and Robbe-Grillet in that of simultaneous peaks of present: hence the paradox of *Last Year in Marienbad*, which participates in the double system. But, in any event, the time-image has arisen through direct or transcendental presentation, as a new element in post-war cinema, and Welles was master of the time-image . . .

There is still another type of chronosign which on this occasion constitutes *time as series*: the before and after are no longer themselves a matter of external empirical succession, but of the intrinsic quality of that which becomes in time. Becoming can in fact be defined as that which transforms an empirical sequence into a series: a burst of series. A series is a sequence of images, which tend in themselves in the direction of a limit, which orients and inspires the first sequence (the before), and gives way to another sequence organized as series which tends in turn toward another limit (the after). The before and the after are then no longer successive determinations of the course of time, but the two sides of the power, or the passage of the power to a higher power. The direct time-image here does not appear in an order of coexistences or simultaneities, but in a becoming as potentialization, as series of powers. This second type of chronosign, the genesign, has therefore also the property of bringing into question the notion of truth; for the false ceases to be a simple appearance or even a lie, in order to achieve that power of becoming which constitutes series or degrees, which crosses limits, carries out metamorphoses, and develops along its whole path an act of legend, of storytelling. Beyond the true or the false, becoming as power of the false [. . .].

Sometimes again, in the third place, characters dissolve of their own accord, and the author is effaced: there are now only attitudes of bodies, corporeal postures forming series, and a gest which connects them together as limit. It is a cinema of bodies which has broken all the more with the sensory-motor schema through action being replaced by attitude, and supposedly true linkage by the gest which produces legend or storytelling. Sometimes, finally, the series, their limits and transformations, the degrees of power, may be a matter of any kind of relation of the image: characters, states of one character, positions of the author, attitudes of bodies, as well as colours, aesthetic genres, psychological faculties, political powers, logical or metaphysical categories [. . .] this thought outside itself and this un-thought within thought. This is the unsummonable in Welles, the undecidable in Resnais, the inexplicable in the Straubs, the impossible in Marguerite Duras, the irrational in Syberberg. The brain has lost its Euclidean coordinates and now emits other signs. The direct time-image effectively has as noosigns the irrational cut between non-linked (but always relinked) images, and the absolute contact between non-totalizable, asymmetrical outside and inside [. . .].

These new signs are lectosigns, which show the final aspect of the direct time-image, the common limit: the visual image becoming stratigraphic is for its part all the more readable in that the speech-act becomes an autonomous creator. Classical cinema was not short of lectosigns, but only to the extent that the speech-act was itself read in the silent film, or in the first stage of the talkie, making it possible to read the visual image, of which it was only one component. From classical to modern cinema, from the movement-image to the time-image, what changes are not only the chronosigns, but the noosigns and lectosigns, having said that it is always possible to multiply the passages from one regime to the other, just as to accentuate their irreducible differences.[18]

This selection of work by Gilles Deleuze
on cinema has been curated by David Deamer.

Notes

1 Extract from the final page and conclusion of the *Cinema* books. Gilles Deleuze, *Cinema 2: The Time Image*, trans. H. Tomlinson and R. Galeta (Minneapolis, MN: University of Minnesota Press, 2001), 280. Hereafter C2.

2 Extract from Deleuze's first interview on the *Cinema* books, conducted by Serge Daney for *Libération*. Gilles Deleuze, "Cinema-I, Premiere," in *Two Regimes of Madness: Texts and Interview 1975–1995*, ed. David Lapoujade; trans. Ames Hodges and Mike Taormina (New York/Los Angeles: Semiotext(e), 2006), 210.

3 Extract from a conversation with Pascal Bonitzer and Jean Narboni for *Cahiers du Cinema* #352. Gilles Deleuze, "On *The Movement-Image*," in *Negotiations: 1972–1990*, trans. Martin Joughin (New York: Columbia University Press, 1995), 46–56, 47–8.

4 Extract from an interview conducted by Hervé Guibert for *Le Monde*. Gilles Deleuze, "Portrait of the Philosopher as a Moviegoer," in *Two Regimes of Madness: Texts and Interview 1975–1995*, ed. David Lapoujade; trans. Ames Hodges and Mike Taormina (New York/Los Angeles: Semiotext(e), 2006), 213–21, 219–20.

5 Extract from Deleuze, "Portrait of the Philosopher as a Moviegoer," 220–1.

6 Extract from Deleuze, "Portrait of the Philosopher as a Moviegoer," 216.

7 Extract from Deleuze, "Portrait of the Philosopher as a Moviegoer," 220.

8 Extract from "Preface," Gilles Deleuze, *Cinema 1: The Movement-Image*, trans. H. Tomlinson and B. Habberjam (London: Athlone Press, 2002), xiv. Hereafter *C1*.

9 Extract from "Preface to the English Edition" (1985), *C1*, x.

10 Extract from "Preface to the English Edition" (1989), *C2*, xi–xii.

11 *C1*, 1–2.

12 *C1*, 3–4; 7–8.

13 *C1*, 8; 11.

14 *C1*, 62–70.

15 *C1*, 68–9.

16 *C1*, 197–200.

17 *C2*, 30–3.

18 *C2*, 270–9.

PART II

Thinking on Films

3

Film as Philosophy and Cinematic Thinking

Robert Sinnerbrink

The recent "philosophical turn" in film theory is described as commencing during the 1990s, thanks to the intervention of analytic-cognitivist approaches to film theory and to the growing reception of works by Stanley Cavell and Gilles Deleuze.[1] Thomas Elsaesser, for example, cites Deleuze's *Cinema* books as having inaugurated the current wave of interest in film and philosophy, while he credits Cavell as the first major Anglophone philosopher to make cinema central to his philosophical work.[2] Both Cavell and Deleuze go beyond merely including cinema within the purview of aesthetics, opening up a new way of thinking by claiming a profound affinity between film and philosophy. Indeed, Cavell describes his conception of the film-philosophy relationship as challenging received definitions of what philosophy might be:

> A way to put the difference in what I might like to see become the field of Film and Philosophy, anyway in how I have conceived my writing on film to be motivated philosophically, is that it takes the fact of film itself to become a challenge for philosophy.[3]

"Film and Philosophy," according to Cavell, is distinguished by how the "fact of film"—its artistic potentials and philosophical possibilities—poses a challenge to philosophy's exclusive claims to knowledge and to being the privileged path to self-knowledge. Cavell contrasts this with the more conventional "Philosophy and Film," which uses films as examples of established problems and arguments, whether from the history of philosophy or from "recent analytical philosophy arranged by topic."[4] Cavell's imagined field of "Film and Philosophy," which his work has helped inspire and realize, takes film to pose questions to philosophy: to challenge philosophy's claims to best articulate what art—especially the art of moving images—endeavors to show. Cinema enacts a more vivid disclosure of aspects of experience than philosophy can do by means of argumentative discourse alone. It can disclose the everyday in ways that bring to our attention many things: the unfamiliarity of the familiar, the difficulty of acknowledging others, the meaning of being human, the problem of skepticism, the difficulties of love, or the pursuit of happiness. These are all things that philosophy has traditionally asked about and that film has now rediscovered and reanimated in its own ways. Film and philosophy respond to shared questions and problems that open up a cultural space of engagement that brings together aesthetic experience and conceptual reflection. Cavell can thereby claim a common ground for cinema and philosophy as different yet complementary ways of confronting skepticism, retrieving the ordinary, re-enchanting the world, and transforming the self. As he writes in the Preface to *Contesting Tears*:

> to my way of thinking the creation of film was as if meant for philosophy—meant to reorient everything philosophy has said about reality and its representation, about art and imitation, about greatness and conventionality, about judgment and pleasure, about scepticism and transcendence, about language and expression.[5]

Many take this passage as a statement of Cavell's theoretical "position" on the film-philosophy relationship. Cavell's suggestion, however, is that some of the received problems of philosophy—above all the problem of skepticism—are transfigured thanks to philosophy's encounter with cinema. The invention of film is an event of thought, an audiovisual technology and artistic medium capable of exploring some of the problems and questions that have traditionally preoccupied philosophy. It can also explore questions pertaining to cinema itself not only as a medium, an art form, and as genre but also as a medium enabling moral reflection and self-questioning in profoundly engaging ways. This reorientation not only concerns how we think but the means by which thinking can happen; it implies a reorientation in our preconceptions regarding how we can communicate philosophical and ethical thought.

Deleuze, for his part, argues that film explores problems in its own domain that are of direct relevance to philosophy. Indeed, it is no surprise that a philosopher concerned with "making thought move" would discover the philosophical attraction of cinema, as Deleuze remarks: "How could I not discover cinema, which introduces 'real' movement into the image? I wasn't trying to *apply* philosophy to cinema, but I went straight from philosophy to cinema. The reverse was also true, one went right from cinema to philosophy."[6] The point, for Deleuze, is neither to merely apply a readymade philosophical theory to film nor to simply reflect upon film as a theoretical object. The encounter between film and philosophy happens, rather, "when one discipline realizes that it has to resolve, for itself and by its own means, a problem similar to one confronted by the other."[7] Both philosophy and cinema respond to problems posed by experience, problems to which they respond in different, yet related ways, using concepts or images as diverse ways of expressing thought.

Both philosophy and art, for Deleuze, are ways of thinking that use different means to respond to experience (philosophy thinks with concepts, art with "percepts" or blocs of sensation communicated through artistic works).[8] Philosophy can respond to cinema by constructing its concepts, which concepts refer to ways of thinking and experiencing the world that the cinema explores in its own manner (e.g., dealing with movement, time, memory, expression, the body, the brain, politics, history, and film itself). Philosophy and film become related practices of thought, the one creating concepts that pertain to the other, but which do not reduce the other to thereby illustrate the former. The encounter between them, rather, offers both new ways of thinking philosophically and new ways of experiencing and engaging with film.

Both thinkers articulate in complex ways the possibility of a mutually productive encounter between film and philosophy. How are we to understand this film-philosophy relationship? Are film and philosophy contraries or complementaries, friends or foes? This question motivates one of the more original contributions to contemporary aesthetics: the idea of film *as* philosophy. Defenders of the "film as philosophy" thesis have argued that certain kinds of film are capable of screening philosophical thought experiments.[9] They argue that film can philosophize on a variety of topics, including reflection on its own status, in ways comparable to philosophy,[10] or that film has its own affective ways of thinking that alter the manner in which philosophy can be experienced.[11] Critics of the "film as philosophy" thesis, by contrast, have argued that such claims are merely metaphorical: for these critics, film, as a visual narrative art, does not give reasons, make arguments, or draw conclusions; hence it cannot be understood as "philosophical" in the proper sense.[12] Alternatively, given the ambiguity of film narrative, if there are philosophical aspects to a film, these are usually subordinate to its artistic and rhetorical ends.[13] Critics also argue that any philosophy gleaned from a film is either due to the philosophical acumen of the interpreter, or else is due to the expression of an explicit aesthetic intention on the part of its maker(s).[14] The difficulty with such contentions, however, is that they often assume a too narrow or reductive conception of what counts as philosophy, or else fail to reflect on the variety of ways in which film and philosophy—or indeed philosophy and art—can be related. The most productive way of exploring the idea of film as philosophy, I suggest, is as an invitation to rethink the hierarchical relationship between philosophy and art. The encounter between film and philosophy invites us to explore novel ways in which our conventional understanding of philosophy, and aesthetic receptivity to new kinds of experience, might be renewed and transformed. It also requires that we reflect upon and rethink our conceptions of philosophy and what counts as a philosophical contribution or philosophical understanding. The debate over "film as philosophy," in short, is as much a meta-philosophical dispute over the meaning and practice of philosophy as it is a debate within aesthetics or philosophy of film.

Film-Philosophy/Film as Philosophy

As remarked earlier, the idea of film-philosophy (or "film as philosophy") has gained recognition in recent years as a dynamic strand of contemporary film theory. As the hyphen suggests, it expresses a way of thinking at the intersection between film and philosophy, linking the two in a shared enterprise that seeks to illuminate the one by means of the other. Inspired by Cavell and Deleuze, film-philosophers claim that film and philosophy are related intimately and productively, sharing problems to which they respond in distinctive ways, thereby opening up new possibilities of thought.[15] More generally, we can define film-philosophy as a style or "genre" of philosophical film theory with close links to film aesthetics as well as earlier traditions of film theory. It seeks to explore the relationship between philosophy and film in a non-reductive, mutually transformative manner, and thus overlaps with, but is not reducible to, traditional philosophy of film. As remarked, film-philosophers have claimed that films can make innovative contributions to our philosophical understanding by cinematic means.[16] From this point of view, one might call Cavell a film-philosopher and Noël Carroll a philosopher of film; they are both concerned with similar problems but philosophize on (and with) film in distinctive yet complementary ways.

We can gain a better understanding of the specificity of film-philosophy by examining two of the more influential recent texts that played a key role in the ongoing "film as philosophy" debate: Mulhall's *On Film* and Wartenberg's *Thinking on Screen*.[17] Both of these works argue that film can make creative contributions to our philosophical understanding via cinematic means. These and other works defending the "film as philosophy" thesis generated a vigorous debate with other theorists who questioned whether film can make genuine contributions to philosophy.[18] This debate opens up important questions concerning our assumptions about the practice of philosophy, about the power of film to transform our horizons of meaning, and about the language we should use in philosophizing on film.[19]

"Bold" Film-Philosophy (Mulhall)

Inspired by the work of Stanley Cavell, Stephen Mulhall's *On Film* is one of the more influential versions of contemporary film-philosophy. In his "Introduction," Mulhall outlines his reasons for selecting the *Alien* quadrilogy—*Alien* (Ridley Scott, 1979), *Aliens* (James Cameron, 1986), *Alien³* (David Fincher, 1992), and *Alien Resurrection* (Jean-Pierre Jeunet, 1997)—as a case study demonstrating the idea of "film as philosophy."[20] These fascinating genre films are distinguished, for Mulhall, by their sustained interest in questions of human identity and embodiment, concerns that have been central to the modern philosophical tradition since Descartes. Far from being trivial, Mulhall argues that these films treat identity and embodiment with a "sophistication and self-awareness" that suggests they are "making real contributions" to our philosophical understanding.[21] In an oft-quoted passage, Mulhall restates this claim as describing his own approach to film-philosophy:

> I do not look to these films as handy or popular illustrations of views and arguments properly developed by philosophers; I see them rather as themselves reflecting on and evaluating such views and arguments, as thinking seriously and systematically about them in just the ways that philosophers do. Such films are not philosophy's raw material, nor a source for its ornamentation; they are philosophical exercises, philosophy in action—film as philosophizing.[22]

This passage has provoked a storm of debate, with both critics and defenders of film-philosophy arguing over its meaning and implications. Many have taken it as defining Mulhall's settled "position" as a film-philosopher, treating his remarks as representative of a general thesis or methodology for the study of cinema, one that remains in need of theoretical justification and conceptual elaboration.[23] Mulhall has since defended his approach, rejecting "theory"-based approaches from a Wittgensteinian perspective and maintaining that the real argument is to be found in his sustained philosophical interpretations of the *Alien* films, a point mostly ignored by his critics.[24]

Mulhall presents this passage at the conclusion of a paragraph highlighting the *Alien* films' philosophical interest in the problem of "the relation of human identity and embodiment."[25] These films' thematic exploration of "the bodily basis of human identity," in turn, raises the question concerning the conditions of cinema. For this is a medium dependent upon "the projection of moving images of embodied human individuals presented to a camera."[26] These two issues, for Mulhall, suggest that a film like *Alien* explores questions about "the nature of the cinematic medium" that one might otherwise expect to find in the philosophy of film.[27]

This Cavellian insight leads Mulhall to specify three senses in which film can "philosophize." We can describe films as akin to the *philosophy of film*, exploring issues that philosopher-theorists might consider (like "the nature of the medium"). We can also talk of *film as philosophizing*, where films explore recognized philosophical ideas, themes, or problems (like human identity and embodiment). Finally, we can talk of *film in the condition of philosophy*, where films reflect upon their own conditions of possibility or the presuppositions of their own practice (the dialectic of "originality and inheritance," for example, inherent to the creation of cinematic sequels). These are overlapping concerns and the distinctions between them are not always sharp; but they help us articulate the different ways in which we might speak of "film as philosophy."

There are some ambiguities, however, in Mulhall's account. He cites *Alien*'s concern with human embodiment and identity as suggesting that it engages in "film as philosophizing"[28] but also as what relates it to the "philosophy of film."[29] Reflection upon the nature of the cinematic medium, by contrast, is a sign that the *Alien* films emulate the "philosophy of film"[30] but also that they are instances of "cinematic modernism,"[31] which he identifies with "film in the condition of philosophy."[32] Is "art in the condition of modernism" to be identified with art that exists "in the condition of philosophy"?[33] If so, this would seem to exclude non-modernist cinematic works from enjoying philosophical status, or at the very least raise questions about the philosophical status of modernist versus non-modernist works. Conversely, any work that exhibits elements of self-reflection—say, episodes of *The Simpsons* or recent horror movie franchises—could count as modernist and hence as philosophical, which would weaken the category considerably as to its discriminating power. We need not tether film-philosophy, however, to modernist self-reflection; nor should we assume that self-reflection is the only hallmark of a philosophical work. Film can be philosophical in many ways. Nonetheless, Mulhall's Cavellian emphasis on the power of cinema to explore philosophical questions even contribute to philosophical understanding, by cinematic means, continues to provoke debate. So too does his insistence on the "primacy of the particular" in aesthetics, along with his Wittgensteinian and Cavellian-inspired mode of film-philosophy, which avoids offering any philosophical theory of cinema in favor of questioning our assumptions about the film-philosophy relationship.[34]

"Moderate" Film-Philosophy (Wartenberg)

Thomas Wartenberg has also addressed these criticisms and defended what he calls a "moderate" version of film-philosophy (or cinematic philosophy, to use his term). In *Thinking on Screen*, Wartenberg questions whether there are good reasons to accept the Platonic "philosophical disenfranchisement of film" that underpins the most common criticisms of film-philosophy; "a priori criticisms" that "do not refer to actual films, but make general claims about what films cannot do."[35] Consequently, Wartenberg remarks, critics have tended to posit "a fundamental theoretical problem" at the heart of film-philosophy, rather than questioning their own assumptions about the relationship between philosophy and film.[36]

Wartenberg summarizes these criticisms as the *explicitness, generality*, and *imposition* objections.[37] The first objection turns on the claim that film, as a visual rather than linguistic medium, "lacks the explicitness to formulate and defend the precise claims that are characteristic of philosophical writing."[38] Films are taken to be ambiguous, rhetorically driven, and hence epistemically inferior to philosophy; or they are taken as making implicit philosophical claims that critics must then make explicit.[39] The idea that only interpreters make arguments in relation to film, however, is misguided. Although viewers or critics may make such arguments explicit, this does not mean that they, rather than the film, are the source or bearers of the arguments as such. Even if arguments are implicit in films, they do not necessarily have to be imprecise (in historical genre films, science fiction, or documentaries, for example). For that matter, many philosophical arguments are ambiguous, so "ambiguity" is not a sound criterion for distinguishing between the claims of film and those of philosophy.[40] What such criticisms end up showing, rather, is that film-philosophy is *difficult* rather than impossible; it requires not only a capacity for theoretical argument but also an ability to engage in philosophically oriented film interpretation.

The generality objection, however, challenges this idea: philosophy deals with issues characterized by their "abstractness and generality," whereas narrative film deals with the particularity of characters, situations, and events.[41] Wartenberg responds, however, by pointing to nonfiction or documentary films, which can make important contributions to our understanding of historical events or social issues.[42] What of fictional film? Wartenberg underlines in response the significance of narrative film as a way of screening complex "thought experiments" involving hypothetical narrative situations that prompt us to reflect upon the plausibility and coherence of our beliefs, moral assumptions, or philosophical commitments.[43]

The third and most common complaint about film-philosophy is the "imposition objection": that film theorists are often guilty of "imposing" inappropriate or unintended theoretical meanings upon their chosen films. According to Wartenberg, we can reformulate this as a maxim, rather, that ought to guide philosophical interpretation: namely, to avoid imposing inappropriate interpretations on a cinematic work, and to ensure that its creator could have intended any interpretation attributed to it.[44] Here Wartenberg usefully distinguishes between *creator*-oriented and *audience*-oriented interpretations: reconstructing the meaning that an author of a work could have intended versus that which audiences might find relevant to understanding or appreciating a work. Only the former, Wartenberg claims, "can justify the claim that the film itself is philosophical"; a point he takes up in his Aristotelian interpretation of Carol Reed's *The Third Man* (1948) as an exploration of the philosophical concept of friendship.[45]

So how can films "do philosophy"? Philosophers have sought to show how this is possible in two ways. The first is a global or "universalist" approach, which posits an intrinsic connection between film and philosophy (Cavell on film and skepticism for example, or Deleuze on thought and cinema); the second is a local, particularist, or empirical approach, which "investigates the question of film's relationship to philosophy by paying attention both to individual films and specific philosophical techniques."[46] Along with other film-philosophers like Mulhall, Wartenberg champions the latter approach, examining what philosophical questions a film raises and how, in specific terms, films screen these philosophical issues.[47]

As remarked, such an approach implicitly raises a meta-philosophical question, namely what conception of philosophy as such participants in the film-philosophy debate hold or assume. Wartenberg identifies three distinct conceptions that are pertinent here: philosophy as a discipline addressing basic human concerns or "eternal questions"; philosophy as a discipline that asks questions of other disciplines; and philosophy as a distinctive mode of discourse involving "the argument, the counterexample, and the thought experiment."[48] As we saw with Mulhall, there are many ways in which films can "screen" philosophy: they can illustrate philosophical ideas in innovative ways; they can make arguments concerning philosophical and moral issues; they can reflect upon the medium of cinema; and they can stage cinematic thought experiments that serve as philosophical counterexamples or provoke reflection on our assumptions and beliefs. From this perspective, we can defend a "moderate" film-philosophy against the standard objections, and can show, in particular cases, how films make creative contributions to our philosophical understanding using cinematic means.

Wartenberg thus rejects "bold" versions of film-philosophy (like Mulhall's), which risk assuming a conception of philosophy that is either too encompassing (that almost anything related to abstract ideas, social themes, or morality can count as philosophy) or too esoteric (assuming a "controversial" definition of philosophy, like that of Heidegger or the later Wittgenstein). Mulhall's strong claim that films can philosophize in "just the ways philosophers do," for example, is criticized for failing to explain "how a cultural form other than philosophy itself"—namely film—"can make a substantial contribution to the specifically philosophical discussion of an issue such as that of human embodiment."[49] In a similar vein, radical exponents of film-philosophy are criticized for claiming that film's expressive capacities sometimes outstrip what we can readily articulate in standard philosophical discourse, which means we require a new kind of idiom— perhaps a new kind of thinking—in order to describe and conceptualize what film enables us to experience.[50]

Defending "Bold" Film-Philosophy

Can we defend a bold or radical version of the idea of film-philosophy? Do some films make innovative contributions to our philosophical understanding and ethical experience via cinematic means? Can they also pose a challenge to philosophy, suggesting new ways of thinking, even a "cinematic thinking"? As Mulhall remarks, addressing such questions requires close engagement with particular films, or put differently, the presentation of persuasive cases of philosophical film criticism and ethical analysis.[51] There is, however, an important meta-philosophical point we can make here. Arguments over the relationship between film and philosophy always assume a given conception of what counts as philosophy, and hence how cinema may (or may not) contribute to philosophical understanding. If film can contribute to philosophy by *showing* what philosophy finds difficult to state, then the demand that we need to "paraphrase" the relevant content of a film into a recognized philosophical discourse might overlook precisely how film can question our conception of philosophy and how it ought to be communicated.[52] Some philosophical and ethical problems, for example, may be articulated and elaborated in a more subtle, complex, or comprehensive manner in the form of a narrative film than in a philosophical debate. There may also be films that challenge the idea that there are philosophical "solutions" to moral problems or that one can produce an ethical argument to decide whether a given course of action is right or wrong.[53] In short, this is both an aesthetic and a meta-philosophical debate: one that challenges us not only to think through the philosophical significance of cinema but to entertain the possibility that cinema may also enlarge our conception of philosophy, demonstrating different ways in which thought can happen.

Indeed, the idea of film-philosophy or film as philosophy invites us to explore how our encounter with film can transform philosophical thinking. If the aesthetic form of a film is intrinsic to the expression of its philosophical meaning, then we require a language that is at once aesthetically receptive and philosophically reflective if we are to do it justice as a philosophically significant work of art. What counts as a philosophical contribution and the manner in which we best communicate such thinking are therefore questions that film can force us to consider. This experience, both aesthetic and philosophical, is what brings film and philosophy together in a mutually productive encounter. This is especially so in cases where films enact a "resistance to theory," which makes them challenging test cases to explore the idea of cinematic thinking—a non-conceptual or aesthetic thinking in images that resists cognitive closure or theoretical subsumption.[54]

It is still important, however, to clarify the ways in which films *do not* always philosophize "in just the ways philosophers do": how they express thought in non-philosophical ways (by aesthetic means, through affect, sensation, or emotion; via cinematic style, using visual ideas or aesthetic abstractions; and through narrative form, deploying all the devices of the narrative arts).

Indeed, it might be better to speak of films "thinking" or expressing thought in ways that embrace *both* philosophical and non-philosophical means of expression. This openness to the "non-philosophical" manner of cinematic thinking might make us more attuned to transforming our horizons of meaning, questioning what was hitherto familiar and opening up new paths for thinking—all of which contribute to the practice of film-philosophy, or of what it might become.

To end with a speculative remark, the recent surge of interest in cinephilia, I suggest, might be understood as a cultural-cinematic renovation of the ancient (but also romantic, existentialist, and perfectionist) idea of "philosophy as a way of life."[55] This is not to subsume film into a "traditional" conception of philosophy but to learn from the encounter with cinema that we can experience and explore philosophy in new ways. From this perspective, film-philosophy has the potential to become a richly experiential mode of shaping our existence ethically and aesthetically through the thoughtful engagement with film. It can become a form of cultural practice defined by a love of cinema (and of philosophy), and a commitment to the idea that cinema can reveal the world anew, disclosing the everyday in new ways, or wiping away, as Bazin once wrote, "that spiritual dust and grime with which my eyes have covered it."[56] Cinema opens up an aesthetically intensified experience of reality, expressing a care for existence—for nature and spirit—that includes whatever exceeds our habitual ways of knowing or opens new paths for thinking. It brings film and philosophy together as complementary ways of understanding and transforming ourselves thanks to the virtual worlds that cinema reveals and the kinds of experiences—both philosophical and ethical—that cinema makes possible. The film-philosophy relationship, in short, is a "thinking encounter," at once creative and conceptual, in which the relations between thought and image are explored in a manner that has the potential to transform our ways of being.

Notes

1   See Robert Sinnerbrink, *New Philosophies of Film* (London and New York: Continuum/Bloomsbury, 2011), 3–5.

2   Thomas Elsaesser and Malte Hagener, *Film Theory: An Introduction Through the Senses* (New York: Routledge, 2010), 8–12, 187.

3   Stanley Cavell, "Foreword: On Eyal Peretz's *Becoming Visionary*," in *Becoming Visionary: Brian de Palma's Cinematic Education of the Senses*, ed. Eyal Peretz (Palo Alto, CA: Stanford University Press, 2007), xiv.

4   Ibid.

5   Stanley Cavell, *Contesting Tears: The Melodrama of the Unknown Woman* (Chicago, IL: University of Chicago Press, 1996), xii.

6   Gilles Deleuze, "The Brain Is the Screen: An Interview with Gilles Deleuze," trans. Marie Therese Guirgis, in *The Brain Is the Screen: Deleuze and the*

Philosophy of Cinema, ed. Gregory Flaxman (Minneapolis, MN: University of Minnesota Press, 2000), 366.

7   Ibid., 367.

8   Gilles Deleuze and Félix Guattari, *What is Philosophy?* trans. Hugh Tomlinson and Graham Burchell (New York: Columbia University Press, 1996), 164.

9   See Thomas E. Wartenberg, *Thinking on Screen: Film as Philosophy* (London/New York: Routledge, 2007).

10 Stephen Mulhall, *On Film* (London and New York: Routledge, 2002); Mulhall, *On Film*, 2nd ed. (London and New York: Routledge, 2008); Mulhall, *On Film*, 3rd ed. (London and New York: Routledge, 2016).

11 Daniel Frampton, *Filmosophy* (London: Wallflower Press, 2006).

12 Julian Baggini, "Alien Ways of Thinking: Mulhall's *On Film*," *Film-Philosophy* 7, no. 3 (2003): http://www.film-philosophy.com/index.php/f-p/article/view /745/657; Bruce Russell, "The Philosophical Limits of Film," in *Philosophy of Film and Motion Pictures: An Anthology*, ed. Noël Carroll and Jinhee Choi (Malden, MA/Oxford: Blackwell Publishing, 2006), 387–90.

13 Murray Smith, "Film, Art, and Ambiguity," in *Thinking Through Cinema: Film as Philosophy*, ed. Murray Smith and Thomas E. Wartenberg (Malden, MA/Oxford: Blackwell Publishing, 2006), 33–42.

14 Paisley Livingston, "Theses on Cinema as Philosophy," in *Thinking Through Cinema: Film as Philosophy*, ed. Murray Smith and Thomas E. Wartenberg (Malden, MA/Oxford: Blackwell Publishing, 2006), 11–18; P. Livingston, *Cinema, Philosophy, Bergman: On Film as Philosophy* (Oxford: Oxford University Press, 2009).

15 See Cavell, *The World Viewed: Reflections on the Ontology of Cinema*, Enlarged ed. (Cambridge, MA and London: Harvard University Press, 1979); Gilles Deleuze, *Cinema 1: The Movement-Image*, trans. High Tomlinson and Barbara Habberjam (Minneapolis, MN: University of Minnesota Press, 1986); Gilles Deleuze, *Cinema 2 The Time-Image*, trans. Hugh Tomlinson and Robert Galatea (Minneapolis, MN: University of Minnesota Press, 1989).

16 Mulhall, *On Film*; Robert Sinnerbrink, "Re-enfranchising Film: Towards a Romantic Film-Philosophy," in *New Takes in Film-Philosophy*, ed. Havi Carel and Greg Tuck (Basingstoke/New York: Palgrave Macmillan, 2011), 25–47; Sinnerbrink, *New Philosophies of Film*; Aaron Smuts, "Film as Philosophy: In Defence of a Bold Thesis," *The Journal of Aesthetics and Art Criticism* 67, no. 4 (2009): 409–20; Wartenberg, *Thinking on Screen*.

17 Mulhall, *On Film*, 2nd ed., 3–11; and Wartenberg, *Thinking on Screen*, 15–31.

18 See Livingston, "Theses on Cinema as Philosophy," 11–18; Livingston, *Cinema, Philosophy, Bergman*; Russell, "The Philosophical Limits of Film," 387–90; Smith, "Film, Art, and Ambiguity."

19 See Sinnerbrink, *New Philosophies of Film*, 120–35.

20 Mulhall, *On Film*, 1–11.

21 Ibid., 2.

22 Ibid.

23 See Baggini, "Alien Ways of Thinking"; Smith, "Film, Art, and Ambiguity."

24 Mulhall, *On Film*, 2nd ed., 130–4.

25 Ibid., 2.

26 Ibid., 3.

27 Ibid., 3–4.

28 Ibid., 2.

29 Ibid., 4.

30 Ibid., 3–4.

31 Ibid., 6.

32 Ibid.

33 Ibid.

34 In response to critics of his book *On Film* (2002), Mulhall remarks that
    his aim, in the Second Edition of *On Film* (2008), is "to identify and put in
    question a range of assumptions about what film and philosophy must be
    whose apparent prevalence has helped to occlude the kinds of possibilities my
    book always aspired to realize." Mulhall, *On Film*, 2nd ed., 155.

35 Wartenberg, *Thinking on Screen*, 16.

36 Ibid.

37 Ibid., 16–31.

38 Ibid., 16.

39 Russell, "The Philosophical Limits of Film," quoted in Wartenberg, *Thinking
    on Screen*, 19.

40 Wartenberg, *Thinking on Screen*, 19–20.

41 Ibid., 21.

42 Ibid., 22–4.

43 Ibid., 24–5; Chapter Four.

44 Ibid., 26. See also Sinnerbrink, *New Philosophies of Film* and Sinnerbrink,
    Cinematic Ethics: Exploring Ethical Experience Through Film (London and
    New York: Routledge, 2016).

45 Wartenberg, *Thinking on Screen*, 26. See also Livingston, *Cinema, Philosophy,
    Bergman*.

46 Wartenberg, *Thinking on Screen*, 26. Cavell's readings of particular remarriage
    comedies and melodramas of the unknown woman would fit into this second
    approach.

47 Wartenberg, *Thinking on Screen*, 28.

48 Ibid., 30. There are, of course, other conceptions of philosophy that one could
    mention here, but Wartenberg keeps to generic senses of philosophy rather
    than assuming "controversial" definitions.

49 Ibid., 37.

50 See Frampton, *Filmosophy*; Sinnerbrink, "Re-enfranchising Film" and *New
    Philosophies of Film*, 137–9.

51 See Mulhall, *On Film*; Sinnerbrink, *New Philosophies of Film: An Introduction to Cinema as a Way of Thinking*, 2nd ed. (London and New York: Bloomsbury Academic, 2022), 249 ff. and Sinnerbrink, *Cinematic Ethics*, 109 ff.

52 See Livingston, "Theses on Cinema as Philosophy," and Sinnerbrink, *New Philosophies of Film*.

53 See Sinnerbrink, *Cinematic Ethics*.

54 Sinnerbrink, *New Philosophies of Film*, 139.

55 Pierre Hadot, "There Are Nowadays Professors of Philosophy but No Philosophers," trans. J. Aaron Simmons, *Journal of Speculative Realism* 19, no. 3 (2005): 229–37.

56 André Bazin, *What is Cinema? Volume I*, trans. Hugh Gray (Berkeley/Los Angeles/London: University of California Press, 1967), 15.

4

Philosophical Therapy at the Movies

M. E. Littlejohn

How does one bring philosophy and film together? How did a philosopher like Stanley Cavell become so interested in film that he dedicated years of classes, four major books, and numerous articles to the subject? He writes:

> When a few years ago I was asked to say how as a philosopher I had become interested in film, I replied by saying, roughly, that the inflection more pertinent to my experience was how a lost young musician had come to recognise his interests as philosophical, one whose education (in narrative, in poetry, in song, in dance) had been more formed by going to the movies than by reading books.[1]

This response challenges a number of assumptions that might be lurking behind the initial question, and others like it. For when we pair philosophy and film, the "and" leads us to believe we are juxtaposing two separate and disparate things. Following this comes the assumption that it is the former's job to interrogate the latter, that the philosopher must extract content from film deemed philosophical or elevate cinematic elements to the level of philosophical reflection: in short, the philosopher must bring philosophy to the movies. But might it be the case that philosophy is already at the movies, awaiting the viewer? Cavell's words thus provide a reversal of assumptions: film entered his life prior to the formal study of philosophy and was perhaps even a condition for coming to recognize himself as a philosopher. So, his question is not: How can films capture the interest of a philosopher? but: How did film prepare the path for this young person to find his calling as a philosopher?

A child of Jewish immigrants growing up during the Depression, the young Cavell and his family joined the rest of the nation at the movies twice a week, and his mother had played piano at the silent movie houses. He shared her love of music and dreamed of entering a music conservatory, though his unlettered father insisted he attain a university degree first. A love of learning in his undergraduate years would prove fateful, for when he at last enrolled in the composition program at Julliard in the late 1940s, he found himself in spirit and interest a late arrival at the doorstep of his earlier dream. This precipitated a personal crisis: if he was not a musician and composer, then who was he? Cavell found himself ditching classes to frequent repertory theaters playing classic films he enjoyed from his earlier years. After returning to Berkley, this "lost musician" eventually found his way to philosophy.

As Harvard colleague Hilary Putnam recounts, a great "process of narrowing" was taking place in standard graduate programs of this era, training students out of their natural instincts and instructing "what not to like and what not to consider philosophy"—Kierkegaard was thus merely a poet, Marx merely a social theorist, Freud merely a psychologist, and so on, while philosophy increasingly emphasized its continuity with science.[2] It was not the first time that philosophy had become remarkably forgetful of life, abstracted from flesh and blood, disengaged from the communal creatures who are themselves doing the thinking. If Cavell turned to philosophy to find a way out of his personal crisis, he would soon return the favor by pointing a new way for this academic discipline which, though it did yet not realize it, was also in crisis.

It was under the influence of J. L. Austin, then visiting professor at Harvard, and subsequently through a reading of Wittgenstein's *Philosophical Investigations* that the full power of Cavell's own original voice would develop and the scope, depth, and originality of his thought would begin to emerge. From his earliest writing on the *Investigations*, Cavell had an uncanny grasp of how to understand this philosophical masterpiece. He recognized self-knowledge as one of its great themes, along with Wittgenstein's claim that philosophy does not put forward a thesis. He also recognized how philosophers underestimate the pull toward skepticism, and the difficulty of refuting it. Wittgenstein employed several key metaphors to describe the critical philosophy of his *Investigations,* notably "therapy," which did not work through a method, but rather various methods that would help relieve a philosopher from a habitual way of misconstruing a problem in order to attain a clear view of the phenomenon in question. Wittgenstein knew this danger of error firsthand. In his earlier *Tractatus-Logico Philosophicus*, he had, among other things, offered a powerful account of language. The problem was that he had come to recognize that his account was ultimately erroneous. How had he been so mistaken? The answer is complex, but at least in part it involves a tendency for thinkers to be predisposed to tacitly accepting primitive conceptual pictures that inform their most complex thinking. In the case of Wittgenstein, the "logicist thesis" predisposed him to view language in terms of a simple conceptual frame where every word stands for an object. From the opening of the *Investigations*, a consideration of a seemingly innocuous passage from St. Augustine's *Confessions*, Wittgenstein presents a series of critical-therapeutic exchanges between philosophical voices as he loosens the grip of the word-for-object picture, and guides his readers, step by step, from the disembodied, crystalline palace of the logic of language back to the rough ground of incarnate, fully embodied human exchange, the communal activities of language speakers engaged in the many activities of life. Instead of reading the opening passage of Augustine as presenting only the picture of the essence of languages: "Every word has a meaning. This meaning is correlated with the word. It is the object for which the word stands,"[3] we are able to recognize language in terms of "bodily movements, as it were the natural language of all peoples; the expression of the face, the play of the eyes, the movement of other parts of the body, and the tone of the voice which expresses our state of mind in seeking, having, rejecting, or avoiding something."[4] More than this, it matters who says what to whom, and why, and in what context and in what tone and with what accompanying gestures and facial expressions.

From this perspective, we can better understand what Cavell would mean when he wrote, "to my way of thinking the creation of film was as if meant for philosophy."[5] The American films of the 1930s and 1940s that he would write on depicted people in movement, engaging with each other in the flow of life: a stolen glance on a bus (*It Happened One Night*) or an icy judgmental glare (*The Philadelphia Story*), a walk of a transformed woman down the gangplank (*Now, Voyager*), and a woman riding a jail cell door as it swings open (*Bringing Up Baby*), a dance both awkward and amusing at the same time (*The Awful Truth*), a slap (*Adam's Rib*), a tickle behind the door (*The Awful Truth*), a childish push to end a childish fight (*The Philadelphia Story*), and a pull to bring the pristine George to the dirt (*The Philadelphia Story*), the art of reading the drama of a room through a handheld mirror (*The Lady Eve*), a shared language that creates a private space while open to public view (*His Girl Friday*), and the transformation of tears to triumph in a face that stares us down (*Stella Dallas*). And what unique voices, faces, eyes, and bodily stature: Cary Grant, Jean Arthur, Katherine Hepburn, James Stewart, Barbara Stanwyck, Bette Davis, to name just a few.

Cavell's turn to film remained a challenge for some philosophers for years afterward: Was he not projecting profundity onto the films, or extrapolating too far? Others were suspicious of his ongoing delight in the movies: Did he not enjoy them more than philosophy "proper"—philosophy on the written page? He recounts how *Cities of Words*, which alternates discussion of philosophy texts and film, was criticized because he seemed "more interested in the movies than in the books, the evidence for which is that [he] sometimes praise[d] the films as masterpieces but approach[ed] the philosophical texts spiritlessly."[6] That is, a "real philosopher" should always prefer the written word first.

This is to fail to see Cavell's breakthrough. It is not that he was retrospectively reading philosophy into the films, but that the films themselves were communicating themes central to Cavell's thinking: the tension of theory and therapy played out in philosophy and life, the to-and-fro of a conversation with traction; skepticism and self-knowledge; Emersonian perfectionism and the ongoing attainment of self; the particularity of voice and transcendentalism—in short, these films he had loved as a child and returned to again as an adult had ripened Cavell for his reception and original engagement with Austin, Wittgenstein, Emerson, Thoreau, Shakespeare, and psychoanalysis.

Yet it is not enough to make this argument by diagnosis from a distance. We must be attentive to these movies that Cavell has so brilliantly written about. Setting aside the texts, let us turn directly to the films, and show how Cavell saw them unfolding their own thinking. Only then can we begin to see the full force of Cavell's autobiographical inflection.[7] I will focus here on three themes in particular: the power of conceptual pictures to cloud self-knowledge, the non-theoretical work of the philosophical therapist, and the significance of conversations with or without traction in the ongoing path of attaining oneself.

A Picture Held Us Captive

If philosophy can be a "working on oneself," it can be an antidote to the human tendency to become caught in the grip of conceptual frames. Both of the major genres Cavell has discussed, the Comedies of Remarriage and the Melodramas of the Unknown Woman, dramatize the human propensity to become caught in the grip of conceptual frames; that is, to shun the particular for the universal, to smooth the rough ground of human interaction, and to elevate us beyond the limitations of human knowing by theoretical constructions we perceive as more robust. However, the attempt to get outside of human limitations leads to only a false sense of progress, thinking we are becoming more and more while becoming less and less. Just as Wittgenstein observes of the metaphysical tradition, the characters in these films "[come] to grief not in denying what we all know to be true, but in [their] effort to escape those human forms of life which alone provide the coherence of our expression." The solution is not to circumvent this limitation but to accept it, lest we be "chafed by our own skin, by a sense of powerlessness to penetrate beyond the human conditions of knowledge" which are no barriers to be escaped but the only path of self-knowledge, self-betterment, and transcendence.[8]

For example, some of the romantic pairs in these films are seduced by a false imagination that frames expectations of love and marriage, whether the romantic fixations of Ellie's "love at first encounter" (IHON) and Deeds's "damsel in distress" (MD), the jaded cynicism of both Jean (LE) and Babe (MD)—both in their own sphere cons and vendors of words—while Charlotte sees her path as the choice between a conventional marriage to Elliot and a conventional affair with Jerry (NV).[9] David is irritated by his madcap encounters with Susan, and doesn't even realize he needs rescuing from his imminent sexless marriage, because he is so accustomed to having his entire identity squeezed into the box of a disembodied brain (the film opens with his fiancée scolding, "Shh! Dr. Huxley is thinking!") (BB). In addition to false pictures of love, there are false pictures of money and class. Lower-class characters like Peter (IHON), Mike (PS), and Jean (LE) scorn those born to the purple. Old-money Stephen cannot help but judge through this prism, however much he tells Stella she does not have to change for him (SD), while George in his new-money insecurity is even more desperate to hold to the same externalities of proper dress and behavior (PS).

Frequently characters get caught up in "perfectionistic" ethics that leave no room for human frailty and therefore no room for flesh and blood human beings, no room to work through their issues on the rough ground of life. Clearly Tracy is the worst offender here (PS), but we also see a similar unyielding moral judgment in George when she slips (PS); in Stephen, whose confusion of etiquette and morality has him constantly projecting deficiencies upon Stella's moral character (SD); and in Charles/ Hopsy, who prefers the Edenic wild world of the jungle, where snakes can be named and categorized, to the confusing world of civilization, where (to paraphrase Jean) "the good girls are not quite as good as you think, and the bad not quite so bad" (LE). Whether love or class or ethics, as long as these characters remain captive to these projections, they remain in some way fixed and frozen, unable to progress in the story or in their own betterment.

In all of the above examples, we might say that the characters have somehow become caught by their own conceptual pictures. Yet there is a far more subversive possibility, when someone else's conceptual picture imposes, imprisons, and undermines the possibilities of a character who can do little to change this. We see this first of all in the crude folk theory of the "late child" held by the careless selfishness of Mrs. Vale, which subjects Charlotte's life to the role of companion and caregiver of her older mother. The totality of physical and psychic effacement robs Charlotte of her voice, brings her to collapse, and brings the family, steeped in social-psychological justification, to an inexplicable crisis—breakdowns are foreign to the Vale family.

Gaslight is an even more extreme example of the silencing and stealing of voice, this time through a conscious and malicious construction of a made-to-order skeptical frame which ensures the deepening of Paula's self-doubt at every turn. Gregory, for his part, is captive to his own conceptual picture, irrationally fixated on stealing, possessing, and contemplating timeless beauty. He is not interested in wealth—the jewels are too famous to be sold—but he is captive to a crazed desire, a "fire in his brain" he himself does not understand. In this pursuit, he is unable to appreciate—indeed has pathological disregard for—the particular human beauty in front of him. For he had first silenced the virtuoso musical voice of Alice Ahlquist by murder, and now he will systemically cut down Paula, her heir. Paula begins as a person of voice, with musical promise like her aunt, and yet we only see her failing to sing to her capacity, because she is distracted, "not *herself*." Her explanation: she is in love. This "love" from the beginning obliterates all else and only continues on the same course until she herself is nearly destroyed by it. When Gregory begins his lies, manipulation, and insinuated violence thinly veiled under patronizing tones, Paula is trapped, for in her love she places unquestioned trust in his word. She grasps desperately for any explanation, any concepts that can integrate these nonsensical accusations into an account of reality, even when it means negating and abandoning her own experience as a possible source of truth. She is led deeper and deeper to a radical skepticism, doubting her memory, her senses, the dimming lamps and the noises she hears in the attic, and by the end can hardly utter the word "I," as if she is wholly alien to herself. Under schemes born of Gregory's obsessive metaphysical craving for the timeless jewels, and the mental gymnastics Paula endures out of unquestioned trust in his word, she collapses into a doubt more radical than any Cartesian skepticism, from which no "Cogito ergo sum" is powerful enough to rescue her.

If Charlotte's voice is victimized by folk theories, and Paula by a violent madman, *Mr. Deeds* features this negation of voice through non-stop misinterpretation. Deeds elects to remain silent after discovering that his small-town sweetheart "Mary Dawson" is really only the invented alter ego of the reporter Babe Bennett, who manipulated his heart to gain firsthand access to his story, and then wrote a series of articles framing his every word and action as simple, foolish, or absurd. Building on these reports, eminent Austrian psychiatrist Dr. Von Hallor, introduced as "probably the greatest authority on the subject," appears as an expert witness, and is neatly able to adapt Deeds's various actions into an overarching theory of manic-depressive disorder. Whether in the high theory of legal or psychiatric "super-expressions," or in the nicknames and simplifications of a slick reporter, both pre-fashioned accounts about Deeds tailor the facts, ignore context, and fit the uniqueness of the person into a previously determined system of expectation that judges him as lacking. Submitted to misinterpretation and manipulation at every turn, Deeds's voice has been utterly robbed of its power, and so silence is his only recourse (Figure 4.1).

In all these cases, whether it is matter of self-seduction or becoming a seducer or victim of others, the misuse of theory which seeks a solid claim over reality in fact denies and supplants it by failing to see the particular case and particular context. Instead of denying human weakness and escaping human vulnerability, it only enslaves the voice and diminishes self-betterment by fixing it in place.

FIGURE 4.1 *Mr. Deeds through the lens of a theory. Everett Collection Inc/Alamy Stock Photo. Everett Collection Inc/Alamy Stock Photo.*

Signposts: "Not That Way, This Way"

The counter pull against such failed attempts at mastery can be found in the characters who serve as "therapists" or "philosophical sages," who help liberate those who have been caught in conceptual pictures, leading them back to the ordinary ground of life. Rather than trying to find a one-size-fits-all rule in advance, they see the unique, multifaceted dimensions of a problem and are unafraid of interpersonal engagement. They innovate from within changing circumstances and in response to the "patients" own initiatives, experience, and self-understanding.

In these films psychiatrists and medical authorities play a dual role, sometimes positive but often negative. Those who are theory-driven are threatening to the vulnerable. Again, Deeds's life and actions are at the mercy of the authoritative, reductive interpretation of Dr. Von Hallor (MD). Dr. Lehman seems high-minded as he corrects Susan's reference to "crazy" people, but his toleration for aberration proves quite thin as he later has Susan locked up as a lunatic when she talks about the leopard on his roof and dismisses her aunt as "hysterical" for being upset about it (BB). Paula fears the arrival of medical authorities, for she believes they will not help her but lock her up based on Gregory's diagnosis of her madness (GL). And at first Charlotte is suspicious of the psychiatrist called in by her mother to "fix" her and scrutinize her life, and fears she will become the victim of yet another, more sophisticated theory than that of the "late child" (NV).

Dr. Jacquith, however, is a contrast to all of these examples (NV). He is the therapist figure par excellence, who refuses to cooperate with any textbook diagnosis or clinicalization from a distance. He comes to see Charlotte in her lived context, her home, her room. He overturns Mrs. Vale's hope that he will side with her and rationalize away her daughter's ill health by authoritative proclamation. Contrary to Mrs. Vale's view, there is nothing shameful about psychiatry, nor not knowing one's way about.[10] Jacquith explains, "It's very simply, really, what I try to do. People walk along the road, they come to a fork in the road, they're confused, they don't know which way to take. I just put up a signpost, 'Not that way, this way.'"[11] He disarms Charlotte's defensive anticipations that she will be the object of projected, psychologized interpretations by responding from the ground of ordinary life, trust, and honest conversation. When Charlotte agrees to show him the elaborate boxes she carves as a hobby, an objective correlative of her captivity, Jacquith admires the artistry, and he transforms her secret vice of smoking into a shared practice by confessing he left his tobacco downstairs. Charlotte breaks down begging for his help, and Jacquith responds, "You don't need my help." That is, he will not provide a cure *for* her in the way she assumes, as an answer imposed from outside her life, a counterforce to the imposition of the "late child" role. Rather, he removes her from the madness of her poisoned environment to free her to continue the liberating conversation they have begun. This ongoing recovery of her own voice will slowly build in her a trust in her own judgments. The fruits of this approach bear out over the film, as Jacquith's conversation guides Charlotte even in his absence until she learns how to discern her own unique path through the subtler snares of alienating convention that await her after her cruise. As she works her way out of the romantic conversations she thought she needed, it is her conversation with Jacquith that has traction—and for them both, as they become partners in the shared project of healing others with Charlotte's care for Tina and her contribution to the expansion of Jacquith's sanitarium, Cascade (Figure 4.2).

The detective Brian (GL) is also an informal therapist figure, as he plays a critical role in the initial steps toward restoration of a silenced voice. Like Jacquith, he comes to Paula's lived context, addresses her by name, and refuses to listen to any account of her condition but her own. By presenting Paula the tangible evidence of a missing glove of her aunt's, he counters the many "missing" objects Gregory accused her of misplacing. After affirming her memory, he affirms her sense experience as well as her sound reason, for he encourages her to speak in her own voice the truth she has hidden from herself: that logically speaking, only Gregory could be the source of the strange sounds, that Gregory must be lying to her. Such affirming conversation had been denied to Paula at every turn, not only by Gregory but by the other

FIGURE 4.2 *Making plans together on the ground of life. PictureLux/The Hollywood Archive/Alamy Stock Photo. PictureLux/The Hollywood Archive/ Alamy Stock Photo.*

disaffirming characters he surrounded her with, the hearing-impaired cook and the insubordinate maid. Brian's affirmation initiates Paula's restoration of voice, which builds toward the climactic mock re-enactment of her madness before her captured husband, defiantly reclaiming her "I." Brian asks if he could visit the following day, "Let me come here and see you and talk to you," recognizing the conversation will be of help. Touched by his words, she touches his arm, recognizing that as she required a musical voice coach, she will require a therapeutic voice coach to continue to liberate her voice in the conversation of the ordinary after the long night of captivity.

Another model of the therapist is found in the examples of Charlotte (NV) and Dexter (PS), who are, each in their own ways, wounded healers. Both know how to show someone the way forward, because each of them has been in that place of weakness—Dexter in his weakness of alcoholism can be forgiving of Tracy, and Charlotte through her difficult relation with her mother can help bring healing to Jerry's wounded daughter Tina. Both are, in a way, implicated in their circumstances—Dexter loves Tracy and Charlotte loves Jerry—and yet both are committed to the other's flourishing above their personal desires. Dexter comes to the wedding not to win Tracy's hand, but to open her eyes, to prevent her from making the mistake of marrying beneath her. As he engages with the cast of characters involved, he rarely resorts to lectures and commands, but repeats questions and assertions, rephrases them, allows them to be rethought and reconsidered. Charlotte does not take in Tina to please Jerry, but out of compassion for

Tina. In this, Charlotte finds a greater purpose for her own life, however unconventional, for she has come to see that her own healing is not to be restored to the new constraints of a conventional life, which would turn her past experience into a meaningless obstacle to be overcome and forgotten— as young Paula is commanded at the beginning of the film to forget her trauma (GL). Rather, Charlotte recognizes in Tina that her painful youth under her tyrannical mother can become a meaningful source of healing for others, and that this is where Charlotte will most flourish.

Deeds, meanwhile, becomes a philosophical therapist of the people in his rejection of a society that identifies a happy life with the monetized life, that judges giving money away to help others gain their footing as an act of social subversion and personal madness (MD). In the courtroom, Deeds also proves himself to be an astute reader of the particular situation and the particular person, serving as the counterexample to Dr. Von Hallor's high psychological theory. He begins by pointing out the embodied idiosyncrasies that accompany thinking: one is an "'o'-filler," another is a nose-twitcher, another a knuckle-cracker, and the psychiatrist himself is a doodler. At each observation the characters recoil physically in surprise and embarrassment, revealing their dissociation and inattentiveness to their own embodiment, before they attempt to force their bodies into more "rational" (i.e., stiff and unnatural) behavior. It is then short work for Deeds to resolve the absurdity of the newspaper anecdotes and witnesses against him by recontextualizing them. Deeds's therapy is to restore the vitality of ordinary language, embodied experience, and nuanced common sense, after all these things had become hopelessly alien under the distortions of the theoretical, clinicalized, or caricaturized perspective. Yet this virtuoso display of returning to the ground of life is not possible for the silenced Deeds until after Babe takes the stand a second time, confessing her manipulation of an innocent man ("I crucified him!"), a moment followed by the plea of the farmers Deeds had promised to support. The credibility of Babe's testimony is called into question by the lawyers once she is forced to admit on the stand her love for Deeds, but it is this testimony of love and the cry of the people that give Deeds the ground to rise up to his own defense.

Thus, beyond the master therapist Jacquith, characters step into the role of signpost in a number of ways, pointing each other back to the ground of life when someone is caught or confused. Perhaps one of the most powerful and effective occasions for the therapeutic conversation in these films is the ongoing mutually educative discourse that takes place in marriage.

Conversations with Traction

Leonard Cohen once said that marriage is the hottest furnace of sanctity, and the remarriage comedies bear this out. It is in the furnace of conversation where the couples find themselves married, and remarried, unable to divorce themselves from the words they continue to have for each other. The binding force of marriage does not take the form of a rule imposed from without, but finding and being found from within. It yet offers the possibility of rejection. These remarriage comedies all begin with the real possibility of the marriage's breakdown. And yet, as these characters distance themselves from their marital bond and seek other partners, they discover that romance is not one-sized fits all: none of the other possible suitors "fit" them at all. Lucy discovers she can neither sing nor dance with Daniel, and though he guffaws at the most trivial things, they cannot share a laugh together, and he cannot match her wit (AT), not unlike the bad paring of Hildy and Bruce (GF) (both of these handsome yet dull, homespun domestics are played by Ralph Bellamy). Tracy brags of her taste in men ("Can I pick 'em, or can I pick 'em?"), but then immediately drags her too-clean fiancé to the ground to "dirty him up," to give him the character that she instinctively knows (but will not acknowledge) that he does not possess (PS). Even beautiful words prove unconvincing, as when George declares his lofty adoration for Tracy while denying her the grounded love she most desperately needs. Stephen encourages Stella to be who she is only to judge her at every turn, and even when she sacrifices the child she has raised and loved, Stephen is unable to read more than the surface of Stella's actions (SD). Jerry's love encourages Charlotte's growth as she sheds her "late child" persona, but he is unable to move past these romantic conventions to recognize her unique path (NV). A conversation with such partners will only lead to withering and not flourishing; their best selves will be stunted.

In the Melodramas, the characters only face conversations like these that prevent their betterment, since they either do not challenge or they challenge the wrong things, and so it is necessary to reject these relationships in order to come into their own. Some end up finding a conversational equal outside romance, as Charlotte finds hers in the shared project with Jacquith (NV), while Stella is thrown back on her own counsel as she navigates beyond the voices that repeatedly fail to understand her (SD). None of these films rejects the future possibility of a mutually educative marriage, but it is clear that this possibility has not yet been encountered.

By contrast, in the remarriage comedies, recognizing the unsuitability of new partners allows characters to rediscover the traction of their "abandoned" conversation. For despite their attempt to transcend or nullify their marriage, they find that divorce is "just a piece of paper" (AT), an arbitrary legal severing. The conversation of their marriage, however, endures and continues to have a formative hold on their lives. It is not just Tracy and Dexter who "grew up together" (PS), but all of these couples, for it was in this primary conversation that they have come to be who they are, and no other partner proves capable of stepping into this role. Whether she goes by Jean or Eve, and whether she calls him Charles or Hopsy, the two of them "were holding hands way back" (LE). Passing to the brink of separation has liberated these couples from the misconceptions that pulled them apart, and now they rediscover each other on newly won ground; they learn to see anew the value of their ordinary life together and the importance of this ongoing conversation. This step back is thus not a return to the beginning, but a step forward, as they are "the same, but different" (AT), resuming the ongoing attainment of self in the mutually educative conversation which is flexible, always in play, and never reaching a last word.

This dynamic ongoing conversation has a variety of languages in its service, as diverse and unique as the couples involved, from shared laughs and shared jokes, shared practices and gestures, shared worlds and shared stories. On the one hand, it can be zany and madcap, as Susan employs a radical "interruption" therapy of a spontaneous series of miscommunications, slapstick mayhem, double entendre, and play-acting, all with unforeseeable outcomes, to reach the abstracted David (BB). This destabilization is exactly what David needs to free him from the joyless, predictable world of work under the loveless tutelage of Miss Swallow, to awaken him to the festival of life that he is missing. In the process they, like Jerry and Lucy, share "some grand laughs" (AT), which, as Cavell tells us, is an important way of celebrating "marriage as festive existence."[12]

On the other end of the spectrum, we find the language of tough talk, another effective tool of authenticity, as it loosens the grip of the false picture of one's reality to help one to become one's truest self. But not just anyone gets to talk tough. It is a matter of who speaks, and not just what. They must have "moral standing" in each other's lives. Tracy is strong and unyielding and has condemned Dexter for his weakness, yet when he says difficult things, she endures it, fights back, but ultimately listens (PS). No one else could take this role for Tracy. Mike is embarrassed to have to witness such an intimate exchange, while George is bewildered that this "bickering" remains so unbroken between his fiancée and her former husband. Dexter pushes hard to help Tracy recognize the flaw of her high moral standards, that she judges others by a false measure of perfection which factors out her own weaknesses, just as he pushes her to recognize that George is not her equal conversation partner, only a high priest who will devote himself to her worship. Their exchange leaves Tracy shaken and thoughtful as she tries to explain to George why a model yacht is significant through the concept of "yar," and one recognizes there can and will be no marriage if, like George, one's partner cannot provide conversational traction. It is a long way from Dexter with his keen words and Socratic questions.

The tough talk in *The Philadelphia Story* is suited for the serious occasion, but knowing how to bicker at an everyday level is another important skill of this mutually educative conversation, as coupling must absorb and endure the irritations of everyday life as well as its joys. It is Peter and Ellie's pantomime of a bickering couple that convinces the detectives of their cover story (IHOM), the bickering between Adam and Amanda in the courtroom is in this place an unwanted betrayal of their intimacy (AR), and despite their protests Jerry and Lucy clearly love the friction of their virtuoso ribbing

(AT). It is in and through tough talk, constructive bickering, and the many other languages that both wound and heal, liberate and bind, that these characters gain and regain moral standing in each other's lives and help each other to see, "Not that way, this way."

Thus, far from a rigid rule or a strict legal contract, these mutual conversations flourish in the continuous play of sameness and difference, ongoing attainment and re-attainment of identity, and a keen recognition of the uniqueness of each person's path to becoming their best selves. Following the deeply American tradition of "moral perfectionism" articulated by authors Emerson and Thoreau, these films recognize the superficiality of seeing human perfection as a moral code or set of exterior rules, and show how the moral life is rooted in the ongoing reach toward one's best self. This contrast is clearly visible in the line that flows from the rule-bound scolding of George, scandalized by Tracy's apparent fall with Mike, to the liberating emphasis of Dexter (PS):

> George: A man expects his wife to—
> Tracy: —behave herself, naturally.
> Dexter: —behave herself *naturally*.

Dexter recognizes that for Tracy to be her best self, she must learn to behave herself naturally, as a flesh and blood human being in her uniqueness. In this experience of her frailty, Tracy's eyes are opened, and she now sees how George is caught in expectations and judgments, that this is how she has judged others, and that her unforgiving moral standard was an obstacle to her growth. Becoming a decent human being, the decent human being that each person alone can become, is the goal of life, and the mutually educative therapeutic conversation is able to discern how to help the other with their individual needs find their unique path to betterment.

If these characters' feet are on the ground, they are also at times aware of a transcendental longing. Charlotte tries to move Jerry to see a calling to something higher than conventional romance, telling him "don't let's ask for the moon. We have the stars" (NV). Peter meanwhile longs to share that higher sense of being with someone, "If I could ever meet the right sort of girl" to enjoy the

> nights when you and the moon and the water all become one. You feel you're part of something big and marvellous. That's the only place to live . . . where the stars are so close over your head you feel you could reach up and stir them around. . . . Boy, if I could ever find a girl who was hungry for those things (HOM).

Peter doesn't see it quite yet, but Ellie has already become that woman, just as he has again become that man. And that possibility is now open to them, now that they are no longer the same people who met on the bus, seeking the false freedom of rebellion and bravado. Whether alone or together, once they shed their doubt and confusion there is no limit to who they can be, what they can think, what larger world of community can be opened when they have found their footing.

The subtle theme of transcendental longing leads us to a final observation. The leading characters in Cavell's two genres of films do not often appeal to the word "love." Most are like Dexter, silent when the question is put to them point blank (PS), like Babe, who only admits it when on the stand (MD), or like Susan, who only blurts it out to her aunt as she rushes to prevent David from leaving (BB). Love, or its absence, is most often made manifest as these characters live out its history in their particular lives. It is too important a word to be thrown around, except by those who are unable to make it manifest, like George (PS), Kip (AR), Daniel (AT), or Jerry (NV). But there is a sense that love haunts these movies, just as love, or its absence, haunts life. Love travels free, and remains elusive in these films, sometimes incognito, for those who would fix it too easily into the conceptual frame of convention without being attentive to its particular manifestations unfolding on the screen. We will not find any false permanence of "happily ever after" here, only the ongoing movement manifest in life: "*this* is the way they lived."[13]

Conclusion

Thus, by attending to Cavell's careful readings of these classic Hollywood films, we see unfolded the major themes of his philosophy, rooted as they are in the rough ground of life. They manifest to us how our worlds are built upon words, and how our voices depend on the voices of others. While theorizing conversations insensitive to the particular case and individual person lead to deformation, dissolution, and even the loss of self and voice, in these mutually educative conversations, characters challenge, taunt, cajole, question, and ultimately wait for each other to break through to their true human identities, to put aside the masks, stereotypes, and faulty moral judgments they hide behind which prevent them from seeing themselves and others.

Film thus prepared the path of this "lost young musician," helping Cavell to "recognize his interests as philosophical."[14] They also continued to be an intimate companion to his life and thinking as it unfolded, which is evident in the penultimate entry of his brilliant, rigorously self-interrogating memoir, *Little Did I Know*. Now a mature scholar, after decades of achievements in teaching, writing, and discussing, he describes a night of insomnia where he finds himself watching the classic movie channel and reflecting on Howard Hawks's film adaptation of Hemingway's novel *To Have and Have Not* (1944). Where Cavell had first assumed the title referred to "society's haves and have-nots," he now realizes that Hemingway's early titles echoed "moments of imperishable writing" and so it must be a reference to 1 Cor. 13:2: "And though I have the gift of prophecy, and understand all mysteries, and all knowledge; and though I have all faith, so that I could remove mountains, and have not charity, I am nothing."[15] Relating this to Hemingway's novel, Cavell observes that we can never really know in advance what we "have" or "have not."[16] For charity, like compassion, perception, or luck, is something that only can be played out in the way we stake our lives, or, we might add, in the conversations that we set our stakes in. As he takes up this reflection that places Hawks and Hemingway's work in dialogue with Nietzsche, Wittgenstein, and Blanchot, Cavell issues a critique, in form and content, to any philosophy which sees itself as an activity of fabricating abstract arguments and shoring up knowledge as a secure possession. To cite the prior verse of Corinthians, we might call such philosophers "clanging gongs or noisy symbols" (1 Cor. 13:1) or, perhaps, "chatterboxes."[17] They only shield themselves from life "in attempting to explain something, clear themselves of it, when they have no explanation and cannot bear their own silence."[18] Cavell concludes, "We can say that what they then assert is nothing." The temptation "to speak in emptiness rather than to suffer being empty of speech" is a continual temptation for us.[19] But some things simply cannot be said. They are nevertheless manifest, shown in life.

Instead of the false clarity that seeks to clear us of thinking, Cavell wants us to embrace the ongoing balancing act of "have" and "have not" as we return thinking to the rough ground of life—and, eventually, of death. The question of mortality is one Cavell is deeply occupied with in the last pages of his memoir, and following Blanchot, he freely acknowledges that films will not do away with the "awkwardness in dying." Reflecting on Howard Hawks's film *Only Angels Have Wings* (1939), he states, "I am not exactly proposing that adolescent male Americans can learn from quite good movies what philosophically inclined grown-ups may learn from their peers, how to achieve the loss of companionability, to take farewell"—as if anything could. Yet film *does* address the question of how to speak "in the face of the dying." This "effort, however awkward," is, as Cavell says, "a failure I keep expecting of philosophy to correct."[20] Even in this all-too-brief gloss of Cavell's rich reflections, it is clear that, far from a disposable ornamentation to this great thinker's philosophical achievement, film is central to his thinking and in this case grounds a strong critique of philosophy's forgetfulness of life. It is no accident that it is a reflection on film, and not philosophy as an abstract science, which sets up the final entry and culmination of the book, where Cavell "the philosopher" is lost and without words as he lives out the impending death of his father.

Philosophers, as academics, at times indulge in making borders and reinforcing them. Those who make a hard separation between "philosophy *and* film" are often those who make a hard separation of "philosophy *and* life." But Cavell had the brilliant audacity to allow his questions to cross borders that can become a chasm. He transgressed the "borders" of high and low art, analytic and continental philosophy, and old-world colonialist pretensions and new-world frontiers of thought, joining the pioneering voices who have found their way out of the crystalline palace of logicism and scientism. In doing so, he sought to provide a way for us to regain our footing on the rough ground of everyday life, after our language had become alienated from everyday usage in the service of false conceptual prisons. It is there on this ground that philosophical questions arise, and it is there where philosophy and film meet—on the ground of a life lived deeply and fully and reflected upon. For these questions of life and death confront not just philosophers or specialists of other disciplines. The problems that give rise to philosophy present themselves to everyone. As America went to the movies, leaving in laughter or tears, it is certain that it was their lives that were being explored on the screen. Without moralizing, these films themselves serve as signposts for the unique crossroads of those who watch them: "Not that way, this way." And as these films did the work of philosophy, audiences left these movies theaters the same, but different.

Notes

1 Stanley Cavell, *A Pitch of Philosophy: Autobiographical Exercises* (Cambridge, MA: Harvard University Press, 1994), 131.

2 Hilary Putnam in *The American Philosopher: Conversations with Quine, Davidson, Putnam, Nozick, Danto, Rorty, Cavell, MacIntyre, Kuhn* ed. Giovanna Borradori (Chicago, IL: University of Chicago Press, 2014), 54–5.

3 Ludwig Wittgenstein, *Philosophical Investigations,* 4th ed., trans. Elizabeth Anscombe, P. M. S. Hacker, Joachim Schulte (Oxford: Wiley-Blackwell, 2009), §1.

4 Ibid., citing Augustine, *Confessions*, I. 8.

5 Stanley Cavell, *Contesting Tears: The Hollywood Melodrama of the Unknown Woman* (Chicago, IL: University of Chicago Press, 1996), Epigraph.

6 Stanley Cavell, *Little Did I Know: Excerpts from Memory* (Stanford, CA: Stanford University Press, 2010), 519.

7 In this discussion, my aim is to closely follow Cavell's insights, bringing them together in a way that will make their philosophical character apparent to readers new to his thought. I will thus draw freely from across his primary works on film: *Pursuits of Happiness: The Hollywood Comedy of Remarriage* (Cambridge, MA: Harvard University Press, 1981); Cavell, *Contesting Tears: The Hollywood Melodrama of the Unknown Woman* (1996); and *Cities of Words: Pedagogical Letters on a Register of the Moral Life* (Cambridge, MA: Harvard University Press, 2004). The films I will discuss later include *It Happened One Night*, 1934 (henceforth IHON); *Mr. Deeds Goes to Town*, 1936 (henceforth MD); *The Awful Truth*, 1937 (AT); *Stella Dallas*, 1937 (SD); *Bringing Up Baby*, 1938 (BB); *The Philadelphia Story*, 1940 (PS); *His Girl Friday*, 1940 (GF); *The Lady Eve*, 1941 (LE); *Now, Voyager*, 1942 (NV); *Gaslight*, 1944 (GL); *Adam's Rib*, 1949 (AR).

8 Stanley Cavell, *Must We Mean What We Say? A Book of Essays* (New York: Charles Scriber's Sons, 1969; Cambridge: Cambridge University Press, 1977), 61.

9 For film title abbreviations, see footnote 7.

10 Cf. Wittgenstein, *Philosophical Investigations*, 123.

11 As Wittgenstein writes, "Language sets everyone the same traps; it is an immense network of easily accessible wrong turnings. And so hence we see one person after another walking down the same paths & we know in advance the point at which they will branch off, at which they will walk straight on without noticing the turning, etc. etc. So what I should do is erect signposts at all the junctions where there are wrong turnings, to help people past the danger points." *Culture and Value*, 2nd ed., trans. Peter Winch (Oxford: Wiley-Blackwell, 1991), 25e. As with language, so with life.

12 Cavell, *Pursuits of Happiness*, 239.

13 Ibid.

14 Cavell, *A Pitch of Philosophy*, 131.

15 Cavell, *Little Did I Know*, entry from August 30, 2004, 542.

16 Ibid., 542–3.

17 Which is not, of course, the only form of speech: this latter term I take from Wittgenstein's translation of a line from Augustine's *Confessions*: "And woe to those who say nothing concerning thee just because the chatterboxes talk a lot of nonsense." *The Selected Writings of Maurice O'Connor Drury: On Wittgenstein, Philosophy, Religion and Psychiatry*, ed. John Hayes (London: Bloomsbury, 2017), 158.

18 Cavell, *Little Did I Know*, 544.

19 Ibid., 545.

20 Ibid., 545–6.

5

Missing Mothers/Desiring Daughters

Framing the Sight of Women

Naomi Scheman

Recent work in feminist film theory has focused on the nature of gaze, both of the characters within a film and of the spectator addressed by the film. Questions have been raised about the relations of the gaze to subjectivity, to gender, and to sexuality, and about the relations among those three.[1] In particular, it has been argued, most notably by Laura Mulvey in her essay "Visual Pleasure and Narrative Cinema,"[2] that the cinematic gaze is gendered male and characterized by the taking of the female body as the quintessential and deeply problematic object of sight. In such accounts, the female gaze— and along with it female subjectivity—comes to seem impossible.

Yet women do, of course, see movies. Furthermore, many classic Hollywood films were made with a specifically female audience in mind, clearly not addressing that audience as though it were in masculine drag. And there are movies, in particular many of the same movies, that include women characters who see in ways that are coded as distinctively female.[3] Olive Higgins poignantly suggests that neither the presence of active women on the screen nor the acknowledged presence of viewing women in the audience by itself challenges the patriarchal logic of the gaze as she writes of the classic maternal melodrama *Stella Dallas*, "How could she–oh how could she have become a part of the picture on the screen, while her mother was still in the audience, out there, in the dark, looking on?".[4] There are, however, also specifically feminist films, made from and for an oppositional spectatorial position, and there are feminist film viewers, critics, and theorists looking at all sorts of films.[5] How shall we account for all these gazes and for the subjectivities behind them?

One possible place to start looking for oppositional consciousness is in the films Stanley Cavell discusses in *Pursuits of Happiness*, extremely popular films that are little discussed by feminist film theorists.[6] These comedies from the 1930s and 1940s, particularly as Cavell discusses them, seem to offer counterexamples to the gaze-as-male theories. For example, though it has been argued that both the spectatorial gaze at a movie and the gazes of characters *within* a movie are normatively male—and conversely, that the female gaze is absent, stigmatized, or punished—in these films women are allowed, even encouraged, to look to (and for) their heart's content. Katharine Hepburn is told explicitly and repeatedly in *The Philadelphia Story* that to be a "real woman" she has to learn not to be a beautiful statue; she has to become a seer, not the seen. Rosalind Russell in *His Girl Friday* is a reporter, Ruth Hussey in *The Philadelphia Story* a photographer, and Hepburn in *Adam's Rib* a lawyer, who, although punished for making a spectacle of Spencer Tracy, transgresses—if at all—only in the nature of her orchestration of the gazes in the courtroom, not in her command of the gaze per se. Similarly, when Barbara Stanwyck as the Lady Eve undermines the authority of Henry Fonda's senses, we are allowed to sympathize with Fonda without concluding that epistemic authority in general is more rightfully his than hers.

On the narrative level, too, these films seem counterexemplary, and they address many of the same issues raised by discussions of the gaze, particularly by those twentieth-century theories of narrative that see the gaze as gendered male by its placement in a male Oedipal frame.[7] In these theories, the Oedipus story is seen as the quintessential narrative, and exclusive focus on the male version stems from the widespread acceptance of an essentially Freudian account of the genesis of female sexuality as the learned foregoing of active desire. The female story cannot stand as its own narrative; rather, we have the story of how a girl comes to embody the desired goal and the reward of the male developmental quest. But the fates of the heroines of the *Pursuits of Happiness* films are as interesting and as connected to their own desires as are the fates of the heroes, and the paths to those fates are as complex and as much, if not more, the subject of the films: these women are hardly milestones along a male Oedipal journey.

Connecting the issues of the female gaze and of the female narrative is the issue of desire. As Cavell repeatedly stresses, a central theme of these films is the heroine's acknowledgment of her desire and of its true object—frequently the man from whom she mistakenly thought she needed to be divorced. The heroine's acknowledgment of her desire, and of herself as a subject of desire, is for Cavell what principally makes a marriage of equality achievable. It is in this achievement (or the creation of the grounds for the hope of it) that Cavell wants to locate the feminism of the genre: it is the "comedy of equality" (*PH*, p. 82). There is, therefore, an obvious explanation in Cavell's terms for the anomalous nature of these films: if their vision is explicitly feminist in embracing an ideal of equality, in approvingly foregrounding female desire, and in characterizing that desire as active and as actively gazing, then they would not be expected to fit an analysis based on films whose view of female desire and the female gaze is passive, absent, or treacherous. If we accept Cavell's readings, these films provide genuine counterexamples to feminist claims of the normative masculinity of film (in general or in Hollywood).

My affection for these films, and the ways in which Cavell accounts for that affection, leads me to want to believe that his account, or something like it, is true: that there did briefly emerge a distinctively feminist sensibility in some popular Hollywood movies, one which unsurprisingly succumbed to the repressive redomestication of women in the post-war years. But, for a number of reasons, I can't quite believe it. Some version of the feminist critical theory of popular cinema does, in an odd way, apply to these movies: they are, to use a frequent phrase of Cavell's, the exceptions that prove the rule. Though they do have some claim to being considered feminist, their feminism is seriously qualified by the terms in which it is presented, by the ways in which female desire and the female gaze are framed.

The clue to my unease with Cavell's readings, with the films themselves, and with the feminism they embody is found in the double state of motherlessness (neither having nor being one) that is requisite for the heroines. By exploring the absence of mothers and maternity in these comedies, I want to illuminate some features of the distinctively female, though only stuntedly feminist, gaze they depict. I will argue that such a gaze is one a masculinist world has little trouble conscripting, and that its incompatibility with maternity functions to keep it within bounds.

Missing Mothers/Desiring Daughters: Take One

Cavell explicitly acknowledges that the motherlessness of the heroines in the films he discusses poses a problem. In his most extended discussion of the missing mothers, he admits that "no account of these comedies will be satisfactory that does not explain this absence, or avoidance," since it raises "a question about the limitations of these comedies, about what it is their laughter is seeking to cover" (*PH*, p. 57). The problem is not unique to these films: the mothers of comedic heroines are quite commonly absent—not dead or gone, but simply unremarkedly nonexistent, as they are notably in *The Lady Eve* and *It Happened One Night*. Although he recognizes the importance and the depth of this odd and troubling feature of the apparent paternal parthenogenesis of comedic heroines, Cavell goes on not to explain it, but to "offer three guesses about regions from which an explanation will have to be formed" (*PH*, p. 57)—the social, the psychological or dramatic, and the mythical. My sense is that to the extent that such explanations will be adequate, those very explanations undercut the laughter. The "limitations of these comedies" are, from a feminist perspective, fatal, if not to our pleasure in them,[8] then to our taking that pleasure seriously in the ways Cavell would urge us to do. The motherlessness of the heroines is the clue to the male framing of the desiring female gazes that provide so much of that pleasure.

In his guess about the region of the social, Cavell notes the generation to which the absent mothers would have belonged. He refers to this generation as the one that "won the right to vote without at the same time winning the issues in terms of which voting mattered enough" (PH, p. 58). As a result, the following generation—that of the heroines of these films—was the first in which American women grew up with the expectation of formal political equality, one of the effects of which is to raise the hopes of substantive equality and to make the traditional compromises of female selfhood no longer seem inevitable. Cavell suggests that the challenges thereby offered might appear sufficiently terrifying to account for the daughters' repression of the memory of those responsible for creating them. As an explanation, this is puzzling. The maternal erasure would seem to be in the service of the repression of the terror of those challenges, but it is integral to Cavell's account that the daughters confront the challenges: Why should they repress the mothers?

More adequate explanations can be found by exploring Cavell's other two regions, the psychological or dramatic and the mythical. The two are closely connected, not surprisingly, given Cavell's reliance on Freud and Freud's reliance on mythology.[9] Initially, however, Cavell's guess about the psychological or dramatic reasons for motherlessness is also puzzling, since it focuses not on the absence of women's mothers but on the presence of their fathers, as though one could have only one true parent. His argument is that "there is a closeness children may bear to the parent of the opposite sex which is enabling for a daughter but crippling for a son" (PH, p. 57). (The "crippled sons" in a number of these films are men who are permanently attached to their mothers; they are the men the heroines mistakenly turn to in flight from their own desires.) Beyond the puzzling shift of attention from absent mothers to present fathers, there is a further puzzle about why this should be so: Why should the love of a daughter for her father stand less in the way of her coming to love someone else than a son's love for his mother?

From a psychoanalytic perspective, the answer is that a girl's connection to her father is inherently more fungible—more replaceable by a substitute—than is a boy's connection to his mother.[10] The maternal connection for both males and females is the original one, the one wherein attachment is initially learned. The attachment of a girl to her father is always already a substitute; she enters into it through learning what it is to transfer love and desire from one object to another: it is the model of fungibility.

Males are supposed to learn to shift their desire from their mothers under the threat of castration attendant on Oedipal desires. For boys the Oedipus complex "is not simply repressed, it is literally smashed to pieces by the shock of threatened castration. . . . In normal, or, it is better to say, ideal cases, the Oedipus complex exists no longer, even in the unconscious; the super-ego has become its heir."[11] In the case of a girl's attachment to her father, no such destruction is either possible or necessary: it is impossible, since in Freud's view she is already castrated, and it is unnecessary, since, being both passive and secondary, her desire for her father poses no threat to her future development. What is necessary in her case is precisely that such an attachment occur, that is, that she shift her desire away from her mother.

Freud's account of the shift in a girl's desire, which takes her recognition of "the fact of being castrated" as its primary cause, is notoriously problematic.[12] But even if one rejects completely the idea that a girl's turning away from her mother pivots on her discovery of the supposedly obvious and natural inferiority of her genitals, one still needs to explain how the socially mandated shift of love object from mother to father could occur. Presumably such a shift requires some powerfully motivating forces, however different from the ones Freud postulates. It also must leave some considerable residue of loss, a grief at the heart of socially acceptable femininity, which Freud barely glimpses. Cavell more than glimpses it, but he leaves it largely buried: unearthed, it would dishearteningly reveal the costs, in the world Freud describes, of comedy and challenge its definition of ending in happiness defined as marriage. By the rules of such a world, not only is a girl's attachment to her father not inhibiting of later attachments, but it is positively necessary in establishing her heterosexuality by breaking her attachment to her mother beyond recollection.

Cavell notes that marriage in classical romance requires the discovery of one's origins, the identity of one's parents; in contrast, the comedies of remarriage (as he refers to the films in *Pursuits of Happiness*) require that one learn and acknowledge one's sexual identity. But typically for the heroine in both sorts of narrative, the acknowledgment of parents is the acknowledgment of fathers and the mandated repression of mothers, a move that is of a piece with the acknowledgment of (hetero)sexual identity. The girl is supposed to claim heterosexuality as her genuine sexual identity, the deepest expression of self, not just as a "haven of refuge" from the ambivalences of her attachment to her mother, as Freud describes its initial attraction.[13] Repressing the attachment to her mother amounts to identifying her father as her true parent, forgetting the love and desire that preceded her love and desire for him. Doing that also requires learning how to do it, that is, learning how to dispose of desire according to demands that are external to it, through cooperating in the fiction that the desires she newly acquires were the ones that were there all along.

Through such cooperation girls are learning that there is a connection between the particular fungibility of female desire and the normative passivity of that desire. By defining female desire as responsive to male—in the first instance, paternal—desire, the culture inscribes "father-daughter incest [as] a culturally constructed paradigm of female desire."[14] The paradigm shapes that desire as normatively passive, as responsive to another's active desire, even if only fantasized:

> Along with the abandonment of clitoridal masturbation a certain amount of activity is renounced. Passivity now has the upper hand, and the girl's turning to her father is accomplished principally with the help of passive instinctual impulses. You can see that a wave of development like this, which clears the phallic activity out of the way, smooths the ground for femininity. If too much is not lost in the course of it through repression, this femininity may turn out to be normal.

Freud takes it that a girl's initial turning to her father is motivated by the wish of acquiring a penis from him, but the "feminine situation is only established ... if the wish for a penis is replaced by one for a baby,"[15] ("F," 22:128), that is, if the desire for libidinal activity is renounced. The wish for a baby and other, ensuing, passive sexual aims require for their (fantasized) fulfillment another's (fantasized) activity. To fantasize the satisfaction of passive desires is to fantasize being the object of another's active desire. (The situation is, of course, not symmetric: one can, unfortunately, in fantasy or reality play out one's active desires on another whether the corresponding passive desire is present or not.) Thus, a father's desire—at least as represented in a daughter's mind—is a central feature of the acquisition of femininity: she learns to desire someone who (she fantasizes or believes) desires her. And, under the conditions of patriarchal control and compulsory heterosexuality,[16] her desire, if it enters into consideration at all, is meant to become fungible more or less on demand. Like Sleeping Beauty, she awakens to the man who lays claim to her.

This peculiar fungibility of female desire is very different from the fungibility of male desire. Men may be expected to shift their desires from one woman to another with ease and frequency, but they are not expected to desire automatically those who desire them. This difference is linked to the different fates of the attachment boys and girls have to their mothers. The "smashing to pieces" of the male Oedipus complex leaves the boy in possession of a large amount of power in the service of his becoming a civilized adult, largely in the form of the super-ego. Although he can experience this power as punitive and constraining, it is fundamentally empowering of him as an active member of society. Not so for the girl: her love for her mother is not transformed but repressed, and it succumbs to narcissistic humiliation, bitter disappointment, and a sense of betrayal. Finally, it is replaced by a love structured by her passive desires and a learned responsiveness to the desires and demands of others.

In Freud's account, not only girls' sexual identity but their gender identity is acquired with the Oedipus complex: "With their entry into the [developmentally earlier] phallic phase the differences between the sexes are completely eclipsed by their agreements. We are ... obliged to recognize that the little girl is a little man."[17] The attainment of gender identity, therefore, is portrayed as a peculiarly female problem, since girls need to turn away from the libidinal activity that is both common to all pre-Oedipal children and distinctively male.[18] In this story female gender identity gets linked both to the question of *origins*, as the gendered self comes into existence in relation to the father, and to *sexual identity*, as that relation is learned through a reorientation of desire. That is, the two forms of self-knowledge, about one's parentage and about one's sexual identity, which Cavell argues are demanded for a (true or happy) marriage, are in Freudian terms conflated in the case of women. On such an account, a woman needs to acknowledge that she came into existence as a female only in relation to the thought of her father's desire for her; that is, she needs to acknowledge him as her one true parent.

The claim of the primacy of paternity has a long history, and Freud is *descriptively* right in associating it with advances in civilization. Aristotle thought that mothers supplied only the matter that semen formed into a human being, and, as Susan Bordo has argued, the seventeenth-century *homunculus* theory of reproduction is of a piece with what she calls the Cartesian masculinization of thought.[19] Although it is usually *men* that men are required to be the parents of (since they are the ones who will thereby acquire the authority that comes of being "not of woman born"), there is at least one important example of the paternal parthenogenesis of a daughter: Athena's emergence from the forehead of Zeus, who became her sole parent by, literally, swallowing her mother. The conditions of Athena's birth are essential to her role as the goddess of wisdom, as, for example, when in the *Oresteia* she sides with Orestes against the matriarchal Furies, thereby helping to inaugurate patriarchal rule: she declares herself "unreservedly for male in everything / save marrying one."[20]

The requisite virginity of Athena and of other women—mortal and divine—who play her role of mediating between the worlds of maternal and paternal power (e.g., the modern stereotype of the spinster schoolteacher) is, I am beginning to suspect, less a matter of avoiding sex than of avoiding maternity, which, as Cavell points out in a related discussion, used to require (hetero)sexual abstinence (*PH*, p. 59). The difficulties women encounter today when they attempt to combine motherhood and career are rooted in part in their violating a long-standing taboo against combining the symbolically loaded power of maternity with power as constituted in the extradomestic world.[21] To be allowed to exercise that second sort of power, to act like a man, has generally meant thinking of oneself as a genetic fluke— parthenogenetically fathered and sterile.

Cavell's guess from the region of myth about the absence of heroines' mothers makes reference to this tradition: "Mythically, the absence of the mother continues the idea that the creation of the woman is the business of men; even, paradoxically, when the creation is that of the so-called new woman, the woman of equality" (*PH*, p. 57). Beyond obvious paradox, a deeper one appears in the claim that only as a father can a woman claim *either* public empowerment or feminine sexual identity. The paradox lies in the double cultural privileging of paternity grounding the authorities of civilization and as creating female desire. The message to a woman is clear: within the systems of male privilege neither her appropriately feminine sexual identity nor her ability to assume public power is compatible with her being her mother's daughter. (What is, of course, compatible with her having been mothered is her mothering—one reason why the heroines of these films cannot be mothers. As Nancy Chodorow argues in *The Reproduction of Mothering*, mothers are mothers' daughters.) It appeared to Freud in his work with adult women that

> Insight into [the] early, pre-Oedipus, phase in girls comes . . . as a surprise, like the discovery . . . of the Minoan-Mycenean civilization behind the civilization of Greece.
>
> Everything in the sphere of this first attachment to the mother seemed . . . so difficult to grasp in analysis—so grey with age and shadowy and almost impossible to revivify—that it was as if it had succumbed to an especially inexorable repression.

Freud goes on to speculate that his female patients' repression of pre-Oedipal material was reinforced during analysis with him, since the transference would have continued "the very attachment to the father in which they had taken refuge."[22] Women analysts, he suggests, have with more success evoked, *through* the transference, women's attachments to their mothers. One way of thinking about this observation is that heterosexuality both depends on and reinforces the loss of a daughter's attachment to her mother: that attachment is most likely to be rediscovered through an erotically experienced bond with another woman, or through the daughter herself becoming a mother. But in the terrain of these comedies—exclusively heterosexual and childless—the absence of even the memory of a mother is a necessary part of the identity these women embrace.

Consider the one film Cavell discusses in which the heroine does have a mother: *The Philadelphia Story*. When we first see mother and daughter together, a couple of days before Tracy's (second) wedding and just before the arrival of Dexter and the dragooned *Spy* reporters, their relationship is extremely close. We get an intimation, however, that they live that relationship in very different ways. Tracy is affectionately bossy toward her mother (and the others she approves of) and dismissively judgmental toward her father (and the others, notably Dexter, she disapproves of). Her mother is much less severe; even when she strongly disapproves of something, she tends to hold her peace (as when she admits to Dinah that it is "stinking" of Tracy not to allow her father to come to her wedding). Mother Lord's unconditional love, not only of Tracy, but notably of her philandering husband, can be taken, I think, as a model of how Tracy is supposed to learn to feel.

But if Tracy is meant to come to resemble her mother more closely, neither she nor the viewers of the film are meant to attend to that fate in those terms; in particular, neither she nor we are meant to pay much attention to Mother Lord. Rather, Tracy's education, as we are shown it, is entirely in the hands of men, who lecture her on how to be a real woman. (Cavell notes that "Katharine Hepburn seems to inspire her men with the most ungovernable wishes to lecture her. Four of them take turns at it in *The Philadelphia Story*" [*PH*, p. 56].) Tracy's mother's role in her daughter's education is precisely to allow herself to be replaced, to be silent in the face of the paternal claim.

Feminist critics of the Shakespearean romances that Cavell finds echoed in these films—notably *A Midsummer Night's Dream* in *The Philadelphia Story*—have argued that the marriages that constitute their happy endings are an assertion of patriarchal order that requires the rupture of bonds between women.[23] Since comedic heroines seem in general never to have had mothers, the mother/daughter bond is not usually among those whose rupture is enacted, but I think we can see its fate in *The Philadelphia Story* as emblematic of the long-buried prehistory to which Freud consigns a girl's pre-Oedipal attachment to her mother.

The scene in which Tracy's father asserts his claim to her affectionate attention contains, as Cavell notes, "words difficult to tolerate" (*PH*, p. 137), especially as we know them to be overheard by Mrs. Lord: they are simply and unredeemably cruel. Mr. Lord makes it clear that he considers his behavior none of his daughter's business, that far from occupying the high moral ground she takes herself to be on, she's "been speaking like a jealous woman," and, finally, that if he's been involved with another woman, it's *her* fault. The reason he gives for this accusation (one that I fear the film does not expect us to find outrageous) is that a man has a natural need—and, apparently, consequently a right—to be looked up to uncritically by a beautiful young woman, so if his daughter refuses to meet this need once her mother is no longer young and beautiful, she is guilty of his seeking to have it met elsewhere. It is, in Cavell's words, "essential to his aria that it occurs *in the presence of the mother*, as a kind of reclaiming of her from Tracy" (*PH*, p. 137). But it is equally and, for the narrative, more importantly a claiming of Tracy from her mother, an assertion of his claim to her love and attention. And Tracy goes on, oblivious to the effect of her father's words on her mother (it is not clear that she knows her to have been listening), to test what he has said against how the other men around her see her and how she wants to see herself and to be seen.

Cavell's discussion of the rupture between Tracy and her mother that follows this speech ("there is next to no further exchange between them in the film" [*PH*, p. 138]) connects it to Freud's discussion of women's unhappy first marriages in "Female Sexuality," but the connection is an odd one. Freud suggests that a woman's difficult marriage may be replicating a difficult relationship with her mother, but the film gives us no reason to attribute any particular difficulty to Tracy's relationship with her mother. Her bossiness seems to *manifest* itself in relation to her mother rather than to be a peculiar feature of that relationship or particularly grounded in it.

What the film *does* seem to be telling us, particularly in conjunction with the others in its genre and with the tradition of romantic comedy in general, is that a woman's happiness in marriage requires her abandonment both of her love for her mother and of the active aspects of her own sexuality. She needs to acknowledge her identity as a sexually desiring woman, and even to act in pursuit of those desires, but the structure of desire she needs to acknowledge is Oedipal. The right man is the one who, because of the nature of *his* desire for *her*, has a claim on her. In their unsuccessful attempts to escape the claims of the right man, the heroines of *The Awful Truth* and *His Girl Friday* turn, like Tracy Lord, to unsuitable substitutes, men who lack the power to make such a claim to a woman's desire, because they have not learned to turn their desire away from their mothers.

Thus, it seems to me that by exploring the regions of Cavell's guesses about the absence of the heroines' mothers in these films, I can adequately account for the absence, but the cost of the account is a serious compromising of the pleasure I can take in those films and of my ability to regard their endings as happy ones. Cavell is right to note that in these films "the creation of the woman is the business of men" (*PH*, p. 57): that this creation requires for its fictional enactment the erasure of the woman's mother confirms feminist suspicions that, like Athena from Zeus's forehead, women born of men will identify with them and will at best leave a dubious legacy of female self-realization.

Notes

1   See, for example, E. Ann Kaplan, *Women and Film: Both Sides of the Camera* (New York: Meuthen & Co., 1983). See also Teresa de Lauretis, *Alice Doesn't: Feminism, Semiotics, Cinema* (Bloomington, IN: Indiana University Press, 1984).

2   Laura Mulvey, "Visual Pleasure and Narrative Cinema," *Screen* 16 (Autumn 1976): 6–18; reprinted in *Movies and Methods: An Anthology*, ed. Bill Nichols, 2 vols. (Berkeley and Los Angeles, 1976–85), 2:303–15.

3   For an account of the issues raised by the centrality of women both in the narrative and in the address of a film genre, see Mary Ann Doane, *The Desire to Desire: The Woman's Film of the 1940's* (Bloomington, IN, 1987).

4   Quoted in Kaplan, "The Case of the Missing Mother: Maternal Issues in Vidor's Stella Dallas," *Heresies: A Feminist Publication on Art and Politics* 16 (Fall 1983): 81.

5   In addition to the works already cited, see the essays in the "Feminist Criticism" section of *Movies and Methods;* Michelle Citron et al., "Women and Film: A Discussion of Feminist Aesthetics," *New German Critique* 13

(Winter 1978): 83–107; Judith Mayne, "Feminist Film Theory and Criticism," *Signs: Journal of Women in Culture and Society* 11 (Autumn 1985): 81–100; and Mary C. Gentile, *Film Feminisms: Theory and Practice* (Westport, CT, 1985).

6   Stanley Cavell, *Pursuits of Happiness: The Hollywood Comedy of Remarriage* (Cambridge, MA, 1981); hereafter abbreviated *PH*. The films Cavell discusses are *The Lady Eve, It Happened One Night, Bringing Up Baby, The Philadelphia Story, His Girl Friday, Adam's Rib, and The Awful Truth.*

7   See de Lauretis, *Alice Doesn't*, 103–57.

8   On the loss of pleasure attendant on feminist film criticism, see Mulvey, "Visual Pleasure and Narrative Cinema," 2:306.

9   Cavell makes his reliance on Freud explicit in "Freud and Philosophy: A Fragment," *Critical Inquiry* 13 (Winter 1987): 386–93. This "fragment" has been integrated into Cavell's longer essay, "Psychoanalysis and Cinema."

10   I am indebted to Ronald de Sousa for the application of the concept of fungibility to emotions and their objects. See de Sousa, "Self-Deceptive Emotions," in *Explaining Emotions*, ed. Amelie Oksenberg Rorty (Berkeley and Los Angeles, 1980), esp. 292–4.

11   Sigmund Freud, "Some Psychical Consequences of the Anatomical Distinction between the Sexes," in *The Standard Edition of the Complete Psychological Works of Sigmund Freud*, ed. and trans. James Strachey, 24 vols. (London, 1953–74), 19:2.

12   See Freud, *Complete Psychological Works*, 19:253. See also Freud, "Femininity," *New Introductory Lectures on Psycho-Analysis*, *Standard Edition*, 22:126.

13   Freud, "Femininity," 22:129.

14   Sandra M. Gilbert, "Life's Empty Pack: Notes Toward a Literary Daughteronomy," *Critical Inquiry* 11 (March 1985): 372.

15   Freud, "Femininity," 22:128.

16   "Compulsory heterosexuality" is a term introduced by Adrienne Rich to refer to the complex of social, cultural, economic, political, and psychological forces that affect women's eroticism in heterosexist and male-dominant cultures. See Rich, "Compulsory Heterosexuality and Lesbian Existence," *Signs* 5 (Summer 1980): 631–60.

17   Freud, "Femininity," 22:118.

18   Nancy Chodorow discusses the "primacy of maleness" in Freud's developmental theories, along with a number of challenges to it, in "Freud: Ideology and Evidence," in *The Reproduction of Mothering: Psychoanalysis and the Sociology of Gender* (Berkeley and Los Angeles, 1978), 141–58. Chodorow argues that because all children experience an early undifferentiated attachment to a female caretaker, the attainment of gender identity is peculiarly a *male* problem.

19   See Susan Bordo, "The Cartesian Masculinization of Thought," *Signs* 11 (Spring 1986): 439–56. An expanded version of this chapter, "The Cartesian Masculinization Thought and the Seventeenth-Century Flight from the

Feminine," appears in her book *The Flight to Objectivity: Essays on Cartesianism and Culture* (Albany, NY, 1987), 118.

20   Aeschylus, *The Orestes Plays: The Agamemnon, The Libation Bearers, The Eumenides*, trans. Paul Roche (New York, 1962), 190.

21   For a discussion of the effects that women's bearing the sole symbolic power of infant caretakers have on a culture, see Dorothy Dinnerstein, *The Mermaid and the Minotaur: Sexual Arrangements and Human Malaise* (New York, 1976).

22   Freud, "Female Sexuality," *Standard Edition*, 21:226.

23   For a discussion of that rupture in *A Midsummer Night's Dream*, see Shirley Nelson Garner, "A Midsummer Night's Dream: 'Jack Shall Have Jill / Nought Shall Go Ill,'" *Women's Studies* 9 (1981): 47–63.

6

Why Is *Leap Year* Not a Comedy of Remarriage?

Stephen Mulhall

Some might think that a better question would be: "Why on earth would anyone think that it *was* a remarriage comedy?" So let me first acknowledge the apparent force of the case against my way of embarking on this chapter before trying to contest it.

Leap Year (2010: Anand Tucker) concerns a successful New York businesswoman (Anna: Amy Adams) who—frustrated by the failure of her surgeon boyfriend (Jeremy: Adam Scott) to propose on their fourth anniversary—follows him to Dublin in order to make use of a supposed, specifically Irish tradition that on February 29 women are allowed to propose to men. Travel problems leave her stranded in rural Ireland, where she has to enlist the help of a surly pub-owner and chef (Declan: Matthew Goode); and as the two make slow and bickering progress to her destination, they gradually fall in love, leaving Anna with a dilemma when Declan disappears after seeing Jeremy propose to her on their arrival in Dublin. When she discovers (back in the United States) that the proposal was primarily prompted by his desire to secure their joint lease on a swanky apartment in a very conservative condominium, she abandons Jeremy, returns to Ireland and proposes to Declan. The film ends as they depart on their honeymoon.

So, the film looks very much like a romcom, a genre with apparently indefeasible popular appeal, but this one met with a remarkably uniform hostile reception upon its release. Critics mocked its premise, viewing the idea of a leap day proposal not as an emancipatory romantic gesture (Anna's repeatedly declared view) but as a reactionary piece of gender politics; and they poured scorn on its vision of twenty-first-century Ireland, replete with genial drunks, awash with superstition and social conservatism, entirely lacking in public transport, mobile phones, or internet access, a land in which Dingle is closer to Wales than Dublin, and which generally exemplifies an unregenerate form of canonical Hollywood Oirishness. Even the established charms and talents of Adams and Goode were unable to overcome these obstacles and reach audience hearts: the overall US gross takings by 2020 barely doubled those of its opening weekend, and the worldwide gross takings were significantly less than double its small budget. In short, it was a popular and critical flop.

On the other hand, it didn't go entirely unnoticed that its makers might have intended—however ineptly—to acknowledge some kind of relation to the history of its own enterprise. In *Time*, under the headline "*Leap Year*— The Worst Movie of 2010*" (a declaration he was confident enough to make early in January of that year), Richard Corliss declared:

> You don't have to have seen the 1945 Brit film *I Know Where I'm Going!*, with Wendy Hiller as the prissy traveler [sic] who finds improbable love, to know that *Leap Year* is a simple ransacking of older, better movie romances. And of bad ones too: the scene in which Anna and Declan, barely on speaking terms, are forced to have a big smooch in public, got an airing in *The Proposal*; and the local dance where the warring parties start to fall in love was in . . . *The Morgans*? Doesn't matter; they're all the same deficient movie.[1]

Set aside the two latter reference points, where the critic's venom succeeds only in subverting the potential insight of his own comparative method (by implying that bad films, like Tolstoy's happy families, are essentially indistinguishable from each other): one can see why the Powell and Pressburger film might have come to mind. Hiller's Joan Webster is trying to reach a remote Scottish island named Killoran, on which she plans to marry a wealthy industrialist who has rented it from the laird, but as she waits out in the inclement weather that prevents her from making the final short boat journey from the mainland, she meets and quickly becomes attracted to that laird (Roger Livesey). As well as the shared Celtic culture and landscape (just how clear *is* Hollywood on the difference between Ireland and Scotland?), this film and *Leap Year* both make pivotal use of a ruined castle as the embodiment of a mythic vision of the power and the threat posed by genuine romantic passion. In the 1945 film, we are told that the laird has shunned the ruin ever since he heard his nanny reciting its history to him as a child, but his reason for doing so is shrouded in mystery until the very end, when Joan's apparent departure prompts him to overcome his reluctance. As he cautiously explores the building, we hear the voice of his nanny recounting an atrocity committed by one of his ancestors (who drowned his faithless young wife and her lover by chaining them together and throwing them in a well); with her dying breath the woman curses any future laird who enters the castle, prophesying that "never shall he leave it a free man; he shall be chained to a woman to the end of his days, and shall die in his chains." It is at this point that the laird sees Joan marching resolutely back to the ruin, and rushes to meet her—at which moment the film concludes.

Does this glimpse of their conjoined future show that they have fulfilled the curse, or that they have broken the spell? The weight of the question, and of the consequent realization that they have done both (and so can equally well be thought of as transforming a malediction into a blessing or as revealing enchantment to be a kind of imprisonment), has been amply prepared for by the film's carefully developed but ultimately uncanny ability to capture the enigmatic depth and power of this remote Scottish culture's synthesis of hard-nosed pragmatism, myth, and magic—something exemplified in particular by the way non-human animal lives are seamlessly interwoven with those of their human fellows, and both with the land's extremes of beauty and violence. This is why David Thomson calls *I Know Where I'm Going!* "a genuinely superstitious film";[2] it is one in which we effortlessly accept that Joan's increasingly passionate bouts of prayer for good weather, and the laird's sense that crossing the castle's threshold might be death-dealing, take the true measure of the transformative fate with which they are struggling. The only thing *Leap Year* has to offer by way of such cultural invocation is a series of supposedly comic exchanges about such burning questions as whether a black cat spells good or bad luck for an impending journey—a wholly superstitious idea of what superstition might be. So when Declan and Anna climb to a ruined castle, and Declan recites a similar tale, according to which two young lovers forced to travel incessantly to avoid the vengeful wrath of the woman's older husband find themselves incapable of leaving this very castle once they take in its glorious view, it's not difficult to see why his vision seems threadbare in comparison and its application to the film's couple essentially unearned.

We could stay a little longer than Corliss himself does with his openness to the relevance of accomplished historical exemplars, and note *Leap Year*'s equally clear reference to Peter Weir's 1990 film *Green Card*, in which a woman's desire to inhabit an apartment in a conservative condominium also leads to the mere pretense of a marriage transforming itself into the real thing; but the potential relevance of *I Know Where I'm Going!* is enough on its own to emphasize that a target missed is no less a target aimed at, and so to invite the following question. If Anand Tucker and his writers could plausibly be read as invoking other films from 1990 and 1945, however ineptly, might there not be other—even less recent, and potentially more pervasively formative—cinematic reference points to be identified? I want to suggest that *Leap Year* is in fact primarily under the influence of *It Happened One Night*—Frank Capra's Oscar-winning 1934 film starring Clark Gable (as Peter Warne) and Claudette Colbert (as Ellie Andrews). The correspondences are so extensive that it can be hard to achieve a perspicuous survey of them, so the following sequence of descriptive clauses—each equally applicable to both—should be regarded as open to extension.

Prompted by her father, a well-to-do and self-possessed young woman sets off in pursuit of the man she regards as the love of her life. Hindered by bad weather and a lack of money, she acquires an initially unwilling companion on her long and challenging journey who quickly sees that she might provide him with a way of solving problems he has created in his career, and who regards her as so naïve about the ways of the world that ordinary people such as himself inhabit that she needs to be both protected from them and educated in them. The education primarily takes the form of a series of more or less hectoring lectures; the protection involves a series of rescues—when her luggage is stolen, he recovers it by the use of violence; he provides a car when needed, as well as steering her through the vagaries of bus and train travel; and he provides a roof over their heads for a night by initiating the pretense that they are a married couple. That shared night involves the use of a blanket/shower curtain to divide their room, at once preserving their modesty and enhancing their erotic power over one another. It further involves the man's attempts to provide food for her in the form of carrots, as well as time spent beside a river from which he carries the woman, and in which the reflections of the stars are so bright that they can be stirred around. The same locale prompts him to articulate his private fantasy of having someone so captivated by the natural beauty of an unspoiled landscape that she would be willing to share it with him. Both narratives end with the same three scenes, although differently ordered: a large and elaborate wedding which is interrupted just when vows are to be exchanged; the man's insistence on a small, precisely calculated financial recompense for his travel expenses, while refusing outright to accept a large sum of money from which he could truly benefit; and the man's apparent inability to respond immediately and directly when the woman proposes to him by proposing to share his fantasy—first remaining mute, then absenting himself for reasons that barely make sense to him, let alone to the audience.

An even closer look at *Leap Year* strongly suggests that it's as if its makers had set themselves the task of ensuring that any given element of Capra's movie would have its analogue—however displaced or transposed—in their own. This applies as much to the smallest of details (as when Anna inflicts farcically excessive damage to her bedroom in Declan's pub, simply because that allows it to echo the brief early scene in which Ellie violently destroys crockery and furnishings on her father's ship) as it does to the most well-known set-piece (when, lacking any explicit analogue to the famous sequence in which Ellie flags down a ride by revealing her stockinged legs, *Leap Year* shoehorns in an allusion to it by having Anna say, for no particular reason, "I've been told that my legs are my best feature").

Few readers of this collection will be unaware that *It Happened One Night* is the earliest of the six films that Cavell offered as members of his genre of remarriage comedy. So once we see just how fanatically faithful *Leap Year* is to that earlier film, we may now want to reformulate my initial question once more, and ask "How could such a meticulous transcription of a remarriage comedy *not* be a remarriage comedy?" To ask this question is, in effect, to ask whether *Leap Year*'s mode of relating itself to a remarriage comedy actually instantiates the way in which two authentic members of that genre relate to one another. But before I attempt to answer *that* question, I must first briefly address the fact that Cavell himself sometimes appears to think that the very idea of there being contemporary members of his genre of remarriage comedy is problematic.

Cavell is perfectly happy to talk of, and to identify, more recent films as having "the feel" of remarriage comedy, or "keeping something like a remarriage surface," or "invoking the genre rather than continuing it" (all formulations to be found in his 2000 essay "The Good of Film"[3]); what he appears to object to is the idea that such films might constitute full-fledged members of that genre. And his primary objections relate to intervening shifts in historical context: "the fear of divorce has changed, the threat of pregnancy has changed, the male and female stars and the directors and writers who put them in action are gone" (CF, 342). But I can't say that I find any of these points decisive: I see no obvious reason for thinking that our contemporary context couldn't invite the projection of the symbolic significance of divorce, childlessness, and the possibility of offspring, as Cavell's genre established it; and I see no reason to think that there are no current stars, directors, and writers capable of bearing up under the standards set by their predecessors.

What seems to me a more decisive basis for skepticism here is the sheer depth and complexity that Cavell has incorporated from the outset into his characterization of remarriage comedy as a genre; and much of that flows from the unifying role he assigns to myth in his articulation of that genre's identity. On his account,[4] the members of a genre in his specific sense of that term (what he christens "genre-as-medium") "share the inheritance of certain conditions, procedures and subjects and goals of composition, and . . . each member represents a study of these conditions, something I think of as bearing the responsibility of the inheritance" (*PH*, 28); and what they inherit above or before all is a myth, which Cavell begins to recount as follows:

> A running quarrel is forcing apart a pair who recognize themselves as having known one another forever, that is from the beginning, not just in the past but in a period before there was a past, before history. This naturally presents itself as their having shared childhood together, suggesting that they are brother and sister. They have discovered their sexuality together and find themselves required to enter this realm at roughly the same time that they are required to enter the social realm, as if the sexual and the social are to legitimize one another. . . . The joining of the sexual and the social is called marriage. Something evidently internal to the task of marriage causes trouble in paradise—as if marriage, which was to be a ratification, is itself in need of ratification. So marriage has its

disappointment—call this its impotence to domesticate sexuality without discouraging it. . . . And the disappointment seeks revenge, as it were, for having made one discover one's incompleteness, one's transience, one's homelessness. Upon separation, the woman tries a regressive tack, usually that of accepting as a husband a simpler, or a mere, father-substitute. . . . This is psychologically an effort to put her desire, awakened by the original man, back to sleep. (*PH*, 31–2)

The unifying role of this myth should not, however, be envisaged as requiring that each member of the genre must exhibit one and the same narrative content (either the same narrative or one which amounts to a re-ordering of the same narrative elements). For on Cavell's understanding of myth, each telling of any myth is a retelling of it. The remarriage myth as Cavell just told it, for example, offers a psychoanalytically informed retelling of the Christian myth of the Garden of Eden, just as *The Lady Eve* offers its own retelling of that myth and just as Freud elsewhere retells what we might think of as the original Greek myth of Oedipus; but of course, Sophocles presents his own account of Oedipus as a recounting of an ancient tale, one always already familiar to his audience and their predecessors, hence as an inherited account of the otherwise-unaccountable origins of their community. If, as Cavell says elsewhere, "Myths will generally deal with origins that no-one can have been present at" (CR,[5] 365); and if no-one was or could have been present at the true beginning of the cosmos, the polis or distinctively human life; then second-hand accounts—that is, accounts which present themselves as recountings, as new versions of an absent earlier one—are the best we could possibly have, and so aren't really second-hand at all (since it makes no sense to talk of the original or firsthand version).

Cavell applies this general point to remarriage comedy in two ways: his recounting of the myth of remarriage not only implies that the pair who are its concern have an essentially mythological understanding of the unaccountable origin of their own relationship (and are contesting its best interpretation), but also entails that each member of the genre that inherits this myth constitutes a retelling of it. In other words, each member of the remarriage genre embodies a way of making sense of its identifying myth's way of making sense of things (of marriage, but also—in the terms of Cavell's construction of it—of sexuality, society, desire, separateness, finitude, and so on). Each such critical evaluation therefore amounts to a critical evaluation of the interpretations of all its fellow-members, a view of the myth that is also a view of all the other views of that myth. So we should expect each member's version of that myth to be distinctive; and if a given member of the genre (appears to) omit an apparently significant clause or provision in the myth, it can nevertheless maintain its claim to membership of the genre by compensating for that lack—for example, by introducing a new clause or provision to its retelling of the myth which proves to contribute to a description of the genre as a whole.

Take the fact that Cavell's fuller (re)construction of the myth includes the clause that, in order to achieve the perspective needed to recover from the threat of divorce, the central pair typically retreat from the city to what Cavell calls "the green world," akin to a Shakespearean forest, which is most often represented by Connecticut. Cavell himself points out that there is no such green world in *It Happened One Night*, but he claims that the film compensates for this absence by its emphasis upon their journeying together, thereby inviting us to view the necessary achievement of perspective as not so much a state or condition as a matter of directedness or orientation, a willingness for adventure, which invites a reinterpretation of marriage as itself a process of quest and adventure. And prompted by this perception, he finds that adventurousness in turn plays a significant role in each of the other films of remarriage; and so it continues (*PH*, 29).

Any defender of *Leap Year*'s claim to be a remarriage comedy might well take heart from these ideas of shared inheritance and compensatory recounting and regard the film's systematic fidelity to its source as doubly justified: first, because it establishes a connection to cinematic history that has to be massively emphasized, precisely because so few of its viewers can be expected to credit it; and second, because it establishes a background against which its specific differences from its source gain particular salience and force. They might, for example, argue that its transposition of *It Happened One Night*'s life on the road to Ireland amounts to an emphatic equation of improvisatory journeying with the inhabitation of the greenest of green worlds; and if that world is somewhat caricatured in order to facilitate the necessary achievement of perspective, then surely the same was true of the original remarriage comedies' ways of representing life in Connecticut. Likewise, they might see Anna's investment in proposing to her chosen man as a way of underlining and interpreting the fact that Ellie takes the lead when the possibility arises of collaborating in the realization of her man's imagination of what married life might be. Just as Ellie begins her journey by seeking to affirm her initial public choice of mate and ends by privately revising it, so Anna learns to distinguish submission to a baleful public tradition from personal enactments of autonomy.

I have two (or two kinds of) reasons for resisting any such defense. The first has to do with whether these transpositions are genuinely compensatory, in the sense Cavell specifies: Do they amount to revisions of the inherited myth that enrich our understanding of its capacity to make sense of things? Anna's experiences may educate her in some ways, but her second proposal seems just as much in thrall to the idea of a public declaration as was her first: it may not occur on leap day, but it certainly occurs in front of others, as if Anna cannot rid herself of the idea that being the proposer necessitates public exposure and the risk of humiliation. Is this an advance on Ellie's realization that she and Peter could inhabit a shared world of intimacy, but only by avoiding any truck with the social world's understandings of marriage—only by realizing that world privately? As for the green world of Ireland: if that world had contributed the kind of complex texture that it displays in *I Know Where I'm Going!*, then we might have learned something new about the way an authentic willingness to remarry must confront the internal relationship between erotic enchantment and spiritual enchainment. But *Leap Year*'s vision of the Celtic world is so lacking in imagination that its invocation does no more than repeat what *It Happened One Night* has already taught us. In other words, these differences don't make enough of a difference, or a difference of the right kind: since they either deaden or positively foreclose the myth's vision of human transformation or transfiguration, they don't constitute a study of the genre's defining conditions so much as a lifeless reiteration of another's member's enabling recounting of them.

And this takes me to my second (set of) reasons for resistance, which are rooted in the way Cavell uses the idea of conversation to characterize a feature of each film's narrative, a feature of their relation to each other, and a feature of their audience's relation to both. His readings of each film are intended first of all to show that their central pairs engage in a conversation about how best to account for the unaccountable origins of their relationship, and thereby more generally disclose marriage as aspiring to a condition of meet-and-happy conversation. And it is in coming to appreciate this that Cavell is enabled to appreciate how each comedy engages with the other comedies in a critical conversation about the best available account of their own founding and unifying mythological inheritance. Likewise, as the pairs in the comedies struggle to manage transfiguration, and in particular to reconceive marriage as itself a transfigurative condition—as unending remarriage—so the comedies effect compensatory transformations on one another which serve to disclose deeper reaches of shared significance in their relationship, and so disclose their individual mode of cinematic significance as itself always subject to reinterpretation in view of its present and future fellow-members of the genre. Just as the mode of being of the pairs in the comedies aspires to be one of continuous becoming, so the mode of being of the members of this and all genres-as-medium stands revealed as one of continuous becoming (as its meaning unendingly unfolds in view of future developments of the genre and of its critical reception).

Against this background, my second reason for denying genre membership to *Leap Year* can now be articulated as follows: the central pair of this film engage in something like the opposite of the meet-and-happy conversation we encounter in genuine members of the genre. Declan's surliness toward Anna is the negation of Peter's way of talking to Ellie: it reveals no general capacity to educate, and no specific desire to help Anna to cultivate her innate capacity for self-overcoming; and whereas Peter's nurturing impulses gradually modify and ultimately come to inform his exchanges with Ellie, Declan's merely occasionally interrupt his persistent mood of black cheerlessness. It's as if Declan and Anna spend most of their time together in the kind of cursed marriage that Peter and Ellie briefly pretend to share when private detectives invade their autohome cabin.

To be sure, *Leap Year* attempts to account for this, by giving Declan a romantic prehistory in which another woman betrayed him with a mutual friend. But then the film assigns to Anna the task of diagnosing this, and of devoting herself to the task of rescuing Declan from it, and so from himself; and that precisely inverts the relationship between the man and the woman of genuine remarriage comedies—in which the woman seeks education from the man, who must demonstrate his suitability for the role by demonstrating a willingness to be taught how best to occupy it, even if that requires sacrificing his pride. Declan exhibits no such willingness, and so Anna receives nothing resembling an education from him. And the inevitable result of depicting such a negation of meet and happy, mutually educative conversation is that *Leap Year* disqualifies itself from the meet and happy, mutually educative conversation between genuine members of the genre of remarriage comedy. Instead (rather like its male protagonist), it oscillates between neurotically elaborate reiterations of the contribution made to that conversation by one existing member, and unmotivated, essential meaningless modifications to it; and that is no way to illuminate the subject matter under discussion.

Another way of making this point would be to say that, unlike genuine members of this genre, *Leap Year* systematically fails to reward our engagement with it. It fails to provoke or invite genuinely illuminating critical conversation; it fails either to nurture or to educate our aesthetic (and ethical and philosophical) responsiveness to the topics and themes of which members of this genre are trying to make sense. In other words, *Leap Year* cannot be a remarriage comedy because it's a bad film[6].

Notes

1 *Time* magazine online: Saturday, January 9, 2010, http://content.time.com/time/arts/article/0,8599,1952703,00.html.

2 *The New Biographical Dictionary of Film*, 4th ed. (London: Little, Brown, 2002), "Michael Powell," entry, 695.

3 In Rothman (ed), *Cavell on Film* (Albany, NY: SUNY Press, 2005), hereafter CF.

4 In *Pursuits of Happiness* (Cambridge, MA: Harvard University Press, 1981), hereafter "PH."

5 *The Claim of Reason* (Oxford: Oxford University Press, 1979).

6 I'd like to thank my daughter, Ellie, for directing me to *Leap Year* as we endured a pandemic lockdown together.

7

Film and Television as Forms of Shared Experience

Sandra Laugier

Let us recall the controversy sparked by the proposal, in August of 2018, to create a new movie category for the Oscars—"best popular film"—which would have recognized blockbuster movies, including, for example, Ryan Coogler's *Black Panther* (2018), a superb film that is now being honored again due to the untimely death of its lead actor, Chadwick Boseman. Opponents argued that, in principle, the Oscars already recognize films that are both "great" and popular: from *New York-Miami* (1935) to *Titanic* (1998), *Gladiator* (2001), and *The Lord of the Rings* (2003). But for at least the last decade, it has been rare that a "popular" film (one with a very large audience such as *Black Panther*, which was a formative *experience* for many viewers) has been acknowledged by the institutions of cinema, and there is a certain virtuous hypocrisy in rejecting, even on the basis of excellent arguments, the creation of a specific category for movies that are in fact excluded from artistic recognition by the Academy.

The debate made clear the difficulty movie critics and the institutions of cinema have in accounting for the reality of "popular" culture. The audiences for art have changed since the end of the last century, and, due to a lack of study, adequate theoretical tools, and clear awareness of culture's shift toward "the common," philosophy has not yet sufficiently observed or analyzed this democratization of art in the age of digital media, or the constitution of a new set of values through the mass distribution of television series. And yet what we are witnessing today is simply the realization of what Ralph Waldo Emerson and later John Dewey called for: an art anchored in the spectator's experience and in everyday life;[1] an art that is not cut off from ordinary life or placed upon a pedestal.

In 1939, Walter Benjamin reflected on the effects of new technical possibilities for reproducing musical and plastic works of art; today, the expansion of the audience for art and the creation of new forms, agents, and models of artistic action and practice thanks to the digital turn have transformed the very definition of art and are contesting elitist understandings of "great art." As Marc Cerisuelo reminds us, citing Erwin Panofsky's 1936 essay "Style and Medium in the Motion Pictures," Panofsky was the first to insist on the fact that "film was first and foremost created as popular entertainment without aesthetic pretension, and 're-established that dynamic contact between art production and art consumption, which . . . is sorely attenuated—if not entirely interrupted—in many other fields of artistic endeavor.'"[2] Today, this understanding and defense of an art that has not lost contact with its audience extends beyond cinema and into television series and other widespread cultural practices (internet videos, etc.). A profound transformation of the cultural field and its hierarchies is underway, as evidenced by the academic world's change in attitude toward television series. TV series, previously seen as either mind-numbing or ideologically driven mass-market products—or as guilty pleasures for intellectuals in need of entertainment—have now become objects of study. Above all, and in line with the thinking of Stanley Cavell and with the pragmatist aesthetics that came before him, they have come to be seen as sites where artistic and hermeneutic authority is re-appropriated, and where spectators are re-empowered through the constitution of unique experiences. The question of their status as *art* remains. My goal here will be to use the Dewey's analysis in *Art as Experience* to affirm not only the importance of TV series in our lives but also their status as art.

Reflection on popular culture and its "ordinary" objects—such as "mainstream" movies—leads to a transformation of theory and of criticism, as Cavell was one of the first to realize. Cavell is less concerned with inverting artistic hierarchies or the relationship between theory and practice than with the transformation of self necessitated by our encounter with new experiences. The framework that he proposed for cinema—that of cultural democracy—is also valid for TV series. To use it, we must also prove the need for TV criticism and define its form—a challenge raised by the great critic and analyst of popular culture, Robert Warshow, who, in *The Immediate Experience* (a title that has the ring of a pragmatist proclamation), maintained that:

> We are all "self-made men" culturally, establishing ourselves in terms of the particular choices we make from among the confusing multitude of stimuli that present themselves to us. Something more than the pleasures of personal cultivation is at stake when one chooses to respond to

Proust rather than to Mickey Spillane, to Laurence Olivier in Oedipus Rex rather than Sterling Hayden in The Asphalt Jungle. And when one has made the "right" choice, Mickey Spillane and Sterling Hayden do not disappear; perhaps no one gets quite out of sight of them. There is great need, I think, for a criticism of "popular culture" which can acknowledge its pervasive and disturbing power without ceasing to be aware of the superior claims of the higher arts, and yet without a bad conscience.[3]

Beyond the question of popular and "mass" culture, it is a question of our capacity for unique aesthetic actions and choices in the midst of everything that is offered to us. This is a point Dewey also made when he insisted on the agency of the art lover, who contributes as much to the making of a work as its author does. In claiming this, he went against a museum-based understanding of the fine arts, and saw art as an essential practice and driver of social action, and thus a practice and driver of real democracy, if democracy is understood not only as an institutional construct but as the requirement that one participate in public life. This explains why thinking about popular culture is equally important in both Dewey's *Art as Experience* and in *The Public and Its Problems*.

Cavell only rarely referred to Dewey explicitly and may even seem to have neglected him. But we know from Cavell's autobiography, *Little Did I Know*, that he read and began to teach *Art and Experience* and *Human Nature and Conduct* quite early on, starting in 1948 at UCLA—even before becoming interested in Wittgenstein, who, on Cavell's first reading, appeared to contribute nothing more than what Dewey had. He even wrote a seventy-page paper on Dewey for one of his professors at UCLA, Donald Piatt.[4] It is thus high time to bring these two thinkers together on the question of popular culture in the broad sense, of which TV series are the clearest example—even if, for different reasons, neither Cavell nor Dewey discussed them directly.

Cavell noted with regard to Robert Warshow that when criticism turns to such objects, a specific form of attention is required, and a kind of "personal writing," since it is only by trusting oneself that one can write about an entirely unique kind of experience, one that is both particular and shared:

> While the likes of T.S. Eliot and Henry James . . . are great artists, unlike those who create the comic strip Krazy Kat and write Broadway plays and make Hollywood movies, the latter say things he (also) wants to hear, or rather things he (also) can and must understand his relation to; this relation manifests the way he lives, his actual life of culture. He concludes that to say what he finds in these more everyday concerns he needs to write personally, but it seems clear that the reverse is equally true, that he wants to attend to them because that attention demands of him writing that is personal, and inspires him to it.[5]

Like Dewey, Cavell and Warshow are deeply involved in the democratization of culture, the only way toward democratizing democracy itself and the only form of citizen education based on self-trust and self-confidence.[6] The arrival of popular culture onto the artistic scene displaces our conceptual categories, which have been challenged by the waning of autotelism and of an aestheticizing understanding of art. It definitively validates pragmatist aesthetics, which refuse to make art a sphere of activity separate from ordinary life or to see an individual creator as the sole "maker" of a work. It leads to reconsidering the relations between art and democracy, to doing away with fixed or institutionalized (whether politically or culturally) definitions of each of them, and instead to organizing them pragmatically around actual and shared values, practices, and forms of life. In this context, we may redefine popular culture: no longer as "entertainment" (even if that is part of its social mission) but also as a collective labor of moral education, as the production of values and ultimately of reality. This culture (comprised of blockbuster movies, TV series, music, videos shared on the internet, etc.) plays a crucial role in re-evaluating ethics and in constituting real democracy on the basis of images, scenes, and characters—on the basis of values that are expressed and shareable.

The question for Cavell remains that of the criticism that one can produce (and share) of this experience, and his philosophical ambition in *Must We Mean What We Say?* was to situate "modernism" during a period when criticism itself was struggling with skepticism and had to re-create self-trust out of the ashes of experience. Cavell explains what led him to write about cinema at a moment when no other philosopher was interested in it:

> Film had for me become essential in my relation to the arts generally, as the experience of my extended bouts of moviegoing in New York and Los Angeles and Berkeley proved to me . . . Philosophers, it seemed, had almost without exception left the field alone. Should this be taken for granted? Or oughtn't the fact of this neglect itself inspire suspicion? Given my restiveness with philosophy's treatment, or avoidance, or stylization, of human experience—a restiveness that is a treasured inheritance from my early reading of John Dewey and of William James—what better way to challenge the avoidance than through the worldwide phenomenon of cinema?[7]

Later, Cavell again evokes Dewey and James when he describes what he owes to their critique of empiricism: "to take a fundamental, I hope imperishable, insight of Dewey's and of William James's—the way the classical empiricists distort or stylize experience."[8]

This dissatisfaction or agitation in the face of philosophy's avoidance (a key concept in early Cavell) of experience—and in particular by philosophy that claims to be rooted in experience—is indeed what Cavell owes to his reading of Dewey, even if for him this reading was not sufficient to describe the unique experience of cinema—or, I would add, of television series.

Popular Culture and Ordinary Aesthetics

In spite of the progress that has been made in the philosophy of film, we are lacking analyses of the ethical stakes, modes of expressivity, and moral education at work in TV series and in the experiences of their viewers. We may begin with Cavell's *reading* of films, with how it is anchored in the works themselves, and with his way of showing that a film (taken as a whole, including its actors and production) brings its own intelligence into its making, and that this intelligence itself educates us, leading us to recognize and appreciate our own tastes as movie fans, and thus to come to know ourselves. This reading is even more valuable for TV series, and it opens the way for a pragmatist approach to our relations to the filmographic and televisual fields.

An ordinary aesthetics must defend not the specificity of the individuals who create works, nor works as such, but a common and shareable aesthetic experience. One of Cavell's aims and greatest achievements is to have shown the "intelligence that a film has *already* brought to bear in its making," which amounts to letting a work of art *have its own voice* in what philosophy will say about it.[9] Understanding the relation of cinema to philosophy thus implies learning what it means to "check one's experience," to use the expression from *Pursuits of Happiness*[10]—that is, what it means to examine one's own experience and "let the object or the work of your interest teach you how to consider it."[11] This means that one must educate one's experience so that one can be educated by it. There is an inevitable circularity at work here: *having* an experience requires trusting one's experience. This role of trust in education makes popular culture an essential resource for moral education.

For Cavell, there is a parallel between the relationship of cinema to high art and the relationship of ordinary language philosophy to "high" philosophy. In both cases it is a matter of a change in orientation and a shift of importance toward life, following one of Dewey's insights in *Art as Experience*. Philosophy, then, is connected to the self-education that cinema provides, and which can be defined as each person's *cinematographic autobiography*, to use Cavell's concept: the way in which our lives include fragments of movies and the way in which we orient ourselves in relation to these key moments, which are just as much a part of our experience as the dreams or real moments that haunt us are. Cinema, like TV series, presents us with important moments, moments of transformation—moments that in real life are fleeting and indeterminate, or which require years or an entire lifetime to understand. Such understanding requires a form of autonomy, of "self-reliance," to use Emerson's concept: learning to trust one's experience and to render one's judgment self-sufficient.

In *The Claim of Reason*, Cavell defined philosophy as "the education of grownups."[12] This definition parallels his goal in his works on cinema (where he focused primarily on Hollywood movies), which is to assign popular culture the role of changing us. For Cavell, as for Dewey, the value of culture lies in its capacity to transform us, and philosophy consists in "bring[ing] my own language and life into imagination" and in "a convening of my culture's criteria, in order to confront them with my life and words": "In this light, philosophy becomes the education of grownups. . . . The anxiety in teaching, in serious communication, is that I myself require education. And for grownups this is not natural growth, but *change*."[13]

Cavell also calls this philosophical undertaking "moral education," or "pedagogy," as in the subtitle to *Cities of Words*: "*Pedagogical Letters on a Register of the Moral Life*." This pedagogical claim regarding the task of philosophy recalls Dewey's involvement in the science of education. For both authors, the educational value of popular culture is more than anecdotal; it defines how both "popular" and "culture" (in the sense of *Bildung*) ought to be understood in the expression "popular culture." The vocation of popular culture is the philosophical education of a *public* (in Dewey's sense) rather than the institution and valorization of a socially targeted corpus. Popular culture does not refer to a primitive or inferior version of culture, but rather to a shared democratic culture that creates common *values* and serves as a resource for a form of self-education—or more specifically, a form of culture of the self, a subjective perfecting or subjectivation that occurs through sharing and commenting on ordinary and public material that is integrated into ordinary life.

It is in this sense that, to cite Warshow again, "we are all self-made men." Cinema is at the heart of popular culture: "movies . . . are the most highly developed and most engrossing of the popular arts, and . . . seem to have an almost unlimited power to absorb and transform the discordant elements of our fragmented culture."[14] In reading this passage, one cannot help but transfer the remark to TV series, which are certainly—even more than movies—a repository of all of culture and absorb and recycle elements from music, video games, classical television—and, of course, movies. That which Cavell claimed for Hollywood popular movies—their capacity to create a culture shared by millions—has been transferred onto other corpora and practices, in particular, onto TV series, which have taken up, if not taken over, the task of educating the public. Cavell's argument in *Cities of Words* was both ethical and perfectionist, if we redefine morality in new terms: no longer in terms of "the good" or judgment, but rather the *exploration* of our forms of life. For Cavell, there is an affinity between cinema—*good* movies—and a particular understanding of the good, an understanding that is foreign to so-called dominant moral theories. The importance and benefit of extending this aesthetic and ethical method to include TV series is equally ethical, for these works are as shared and public as movies were in the twentieth century; they reach a significant audience and play an educational role, and perhaps even more clearly than cinema, they make it possible to anchor the value of a work in the experience one has of it.

We need to rethink what we mean today by popular culture (which is no longer exactly popular in the social or political sense in which certain arts—songs, folklore—once were, even if popular culture sometimes draws on the resources of these arts) by connecting it more clearly to the notion of the *public*. TV series are the sites of the education of individuals, an education that amounts to a form of subjective perfecting through sharing and discussing public and ordinary material, which is integrated into individuals' lives and is a source of conversation.

Cavell's ordinary aesthetics deliberately goes against the traditional critical approach, where there is an obsession with art as a *separate domain*—a view admirably criticized by Dewey—and with the mystique of the individual creator, as well as with "representation" and image, to the detriment of the ordinary experience of seeing a movie, which is the subjective—but always shared—experience of *public* material. For Cavell, cinema is a form of shared experience, and in movies it is a matter less of aesthetics than of *practice*—an ordinary practice that connects and reconciles the private and the public, subjective expectation and the sharing of the common.

The forms of popular culture that interest me here are those that are capable of transforming our existences by educating and cultivating our ordinary experience, not only in the classical sense of training our aesthetic taste, but in the sense of a moral training that is constitutive of our singularity. Cavell, radically combining Emerson's analyses (in his essay "Experience") and Dewey's (in his chapter "Having an Experience" in *Art as Experience*) emphasizes that it is important to be able to *educate one's experience* in such a way that one can have confidence in it and in this way to live it. Cinephilia is a form of education of the self, and series-philia is even more so. This education does not occur through exposure to a set of universal masterpieces (even if such TV classics do now exist), but through the constitution of one's personal list of favorite movies or series and of scenes that are appropriate to various circumstances or occasions of one's life, when they are re-mobilized.

The question is what the ordinary does to philosophy. Cinematographic art, whether in the form of movies or TV series, is "popular" art because the experience of it underlies ordinary experience, just as Dewey maintained that aesthetic experience is emblematic of experience in general. This experience is *moral*—both mysterious and ordinary, personal and public. It is ordinary because nothing is more shareable and self-evident than going to see movies or watching shows and talking about them, and these are often moments in which we re-enact our agreement in language. It is a mysterious form of knowledge, this coming to know what counts for oneself, and there is nothing easy or immediate about it. The only source for verifying one's description of what counts is *oneself*—whence the role of confidence, of trust in one's own experience,[15] which is the source of moral perfectionism and the only basis for public education and public moral expression.

Cavell discusses "the importance of importance" in chapter 3 of *Pursuits of Happiness*. Television series continue the realist quest for the ordinary and the pedagogical task undertaken by cinema of providing an inseparably subjective and public education. Let us recall here that Cavell's point of departure for his study was Tolstoy's move to replace the question of art's essence with that of its *importance*. Importance is not something extra, an afterthought. To master a concept, in Wittgensteinian terms, requires knowing what role a word plays in our usages, which amounts to knowing its role, its importance in our lives, its place within our form of life. To master a concept is thus to know its importance: our criteria of usage spell out what counts for us, in the sense both of what is identified as falling under a concept (what "counts as"), and in the sense of what arouses our interest and represents a value for us. This priority of importance and mattering over the beautiful and the true (or the redefinition of the latter in terms of the former) as concepts governing ordinary experience is the heart of Cavell's definition of a culture of the ordinary. This does not imply some falsely revolutionary inversion of values, but rather a new assessment of importance.

Wittgenstein called for just such a new assessment of importance and of what counts in an essential passage in the *Philosophical Investigations*, where he calls for ordinary language philosophy and attention to real life:

> Where does our investigation get its importance from, since it seems only to destroy everything interesting, that is, all that is great and important? (As it were all the buildings, leaving behind only bits of stone and rubble.) What we are destroying is nothing but houses of cards and we are clearing up the ground of language on which they stand.[16]

This shifting of *the important* to the heart of thought can be said to define the ontology of popular culture, which constitutes a family (in the Wittgensteinian sense of family resemblances) rather than a distinct domain. There are clear connections here to pragmatism and its radical pluralism, since it is reality itself that is defined by the arts and their implication in our experience.

Elementary Forms of Shared Experience

Public and popular forms of cultural production are democratic in the sense that, today, as demonstrated by the proliferation of blogs, amateur criticism, or even just any conversation about a popular series demonstrates, they ascribe to each individual the capacity to *trust his or her judgment*. TV series and the place that they and their worlds have come to occupy in spectators' lives demonstrate series' relationship to individual experience and the fact that they pursue the pedagogical task undertaken by popular cinema—that of an inseparably subjective and public education. This intertwining of the private and the public is also an intertwining of modes of constitution of the public, and is equally expressed in new modes of subjectivation by the public.

Television series are typically collective works, and in a sense they are detached from the individuality of their creators. The best series (with a few exceptions, such as those by David Lynch) definitively do away with the mythology of the great author. They are also determined by the materiality of the work and by those who make it, as Dewey emphasizes.[17] Cavell includes in "the intention" of a work its authors, actors, and technicians, its production constraints, the expectations of the public in scriptwriting, and so on. This ordinary aesthetics of series opens the possibility of shifting the hierarchies of aesthetic interest by making clear the moral and intellectual value of ordinary practices and the expressivity of overlooked figures, as for example in classic HBO series such as Sex and the City and The Wire, which gave voice to women and to Black youth, respectively, and depicted their forms of life.

TV series connect the private to the public in a new way.[18] In The Public and Its Problems, Dewey defined the public on the basis of an encounter with a problematic situation, in which people experience a specific difficulty that they initially perceive as being part of private life. According to him, the concept of the public is the response to this difficulty, a response that is never predetermined and which emerges through the interactions of those who decide to give the problem public expression. Understood in light of this theory of the public, television inherits the task that Cavell saw as belonging to popular cinema: the moral education and constitution of a public.

Cavell explicitly took the popularity of cinema as his starting point. This realist quality comes not from any aesthetics or theory of "representation" but rather of "minding"; the interest is actually mobilized by the popular, and the care and commitment the popular in fact commands. What distinguishes cinema from other arts is this collective interest: everyone (at least at the time when Cavell was writing his first works) cares about movies.

> Rich and poor, those who care about no (other) art and those who live on the promise of art, those whose pride is education and those whose pride is power or practicality—all care about movies, await them, respond to them, remember them, talk about them, hate some of them, are grateful for some of them.[19]

And, of course, this is even more obvious in the case of TV series.

Thus, cinema belongs to the shared experience of minding, and from this emerges a new, pragmatist definition of culture. Cavell does not speak of seeing a movie, but rather of "moviegoing": it is not so much a matter of aesthetics as of a democratic practice that connects and reconciles the private and the public. This means that, as Dewey insisted, it is the experience of a work and its continuity with everyday life that is primary. The very invention of cinema challenged what Dewey called "a chasm between ordinary and esthetic experience."[20]

The educational value of popular culture is essential to its democratic quality. Today, this allows us to define what must be understood by "popular" in the expression "popular culture" and to revisit the concept of "pop culture"—a colloquial abbreviation that does not make it any easier to take these arts seriously. For Cavell and Dewey, the stakes of our relation to popular culture are political. Cavell dismisses the line of thought that claims that all art passes through a "popular" stage in its infancy, as if there were a natural hierarchy or evolution from popular art to great art, and as if it were possible to measure an art's life span and to see it as a living being with a period of youth and of maturity. Panofsky's view was that cinema took up the popular genres of tragedy, romance, crime, adventure, and comedy when moviemakers understood that these genres "could be transfigured . . . by the exploitation of the unique and specific possibilities of the new medium."[21] But for Panofsky, it is a matter of exploring new *aesthetic* possibilities; he does not consider in detail the practical possibilities of a widespread sharing of experience, the inclusion of this experience in the viewer's private life, or the education of one's viewing.

"Moviegoing" transforms our existences by educating our ordinary experience, shaping not only our aesthetic tastes but our morality as well. This is never as obvious as in our choice of the films or series that mark moments of our lives. The ordinariness of popular culture emerges in our capacity to define our uniqueness through our allegiances and values in relation to it; I am thinking here of things like the "Top 5" lists in the film *High Fidelity* (Nick Hornby and S. Frears, 2000), and more recently in the series *High Fidelity* (starring Zoë Kravitz), through which the characters not only enumerate but literally *are* their tastes. Thus, the way in which each individual creates his or her own experience out of cinema makes it a democratic art: the democracy of the singular.

A Democratic Ontology

By recalling the democratic stakes of cinema, we are better able to perceive what is at stake for pragmatist aesthetics in TV series, whether through the validation of individual experience, the social nature of pragmatism, or the democratic dimension of art. It remains to be seen how we can go even further, and understand TV series as pragmatist art par excellence within the present context, in which cinema has acquired the status of art, and is defined as "high-end" popular culture—frequently in contrast to TV series.

No reflection on ordinary aesthetics can ignore the issue Cavell confronted in refusing both the critic's contempt for forms seen as degraded and the contempt of intellectuals who might comfortably claim an interest in popular culture while maintaining the conviction that they occupy a position of superiority with respect to it. And it is even more difficult to convince people of the intelligence of popular TV series than it was for Cavell to convince readers of the intelligence of remarriage comedies, and today it is widely understood that there is a hierarchy between "quality" series (which are usually somber, cynical, and male-dominated) and the rest, a distinction that mirrors the hierarchy between "important" films and commercial movies.

The stakes have not changed since the birth of "modernism," which had to affirm itself in terms of self-trust. When Cavell's book *The World Viewed* was published, Rosalind Krauss considered it an "extreme curiosity"[22] from the point of view of those theoreticians of cinema who were readers and admirers of Eisenstein, Vertov, Brakhage, Snow, and Warhol. According to Krauss, Cavell combined historical ignorance with an inability to distinguish between *important*—that is, experimental— cinema and a form of entertainment that barely merits being called "cinematic." The similarity to arguments made against television series by cinema purists is obvious. But this redefinition of the important is the hallmark of Cavell's approach to popular culture. In "More of the World Viewed," which Cavell wrote several years after *The World Viewed*, he contests the possibility of determining the importance of a film from a solely theoretical or historical point of view.[23] In art as in politics, *I* alone can say what counts and can determine the importance and significance of the movies or series I see. This is the deeply *democratic* aspect of the experience of cinema, which stands in contrast to the condescension that marks conventional approaches to the aesthetics and criticism of popular culture, and especially of TV series.

Characters as Vehicles and Sources of Values

The material of television series allows for contextualization, historicity (thanks to regular rhythms of viewing and their duration over the long term), and the familiarization and education of perception through our attention to the expressions and gestures of characters whom we come to know. Here we may think, for example, of the series *Buffy the Vampire Slayer* (Joss Whedon, 1997–2003), a feminist work intended to morally transform a co- ed adolescent audience, which depicts an apparently ordinary teenage girl who is capable of fighting evil. In both mainstream movies and TV series, rather than the mystique of the author, we see the emergence of the force and impact of an actor's embodiment of a character.

The characters of television fiction are so well anchored, morally guided, and clear in their moral expressions—without being archetypal—that they can be "released" and opened to the imagination and usage of all viewers, "entrusted" to us—as if it were up to each of us to take care of them. Whence the great importance of the conclusions to series, which must teach their viewers to go on without them. *Lost*, *Mad Men*, and *The Americans* are recent illustrations of the work that series do to guide us in separating from their characters. The movie or television actor or actress has the mysterious capacity for what Cavell defined as "photogenesis": the ability to make him- or herself perceptible to spectators and thereby to constitute the spectator's experience. Thus, the modes of expression of TV series actors (their moral texture, style of speech, and gesture) are a veritable moral resource offered by popular culture. The question of morality is shifted toward the development of a common sensibility which is both pre-supposed and educated/transformed by the sharing of values.

Series create care and awaken affectivity through the representation of moving figures or situations. Their very form gives them their moral value and expressivity: the regularity with which viewers frequent them, the integration of characters into viewers' ordinary and familial lives, viewers' initiation into new and initially opaque forms of life and lexicons, viewers' attachment to characters, and finally, the methodology and modes of narration of series. This leads to revising the status of morality, and locating it not in rules, transcendental norms, or principles of decision-making, but rather in attention to ordinary behaviors, to everyday micro-choices, to individuals' styles of expressing themselves and making claims. These are transformations of morality that many philosophers, weary of overly abstract meta-ethics and overly normative deontological ethics, have called for. Some, like Martha Nussbaum, have tested this form of ethics on literary material. But the material of television series allows for an even more developed contextualization and a historicity of the public-private relation. One of the tasks of series philosophy would be to demonstrate, through a reading of the moral expressivity constituted by a series, the individual and collective moral choices, negotiations, conflicts, and agreements at the basis of moral representation: the choices and trajectories of fictional characters, the twists and turns of the plot.

In US series such as *Lost*, *Six Feet Under*, *Game of Thrones*, and *The Walking Dead*, there is a perfectionist moral quest that has democratic aims, since it seeks to be widely shared. Beyond their differences, these shows are all based on the desire to give public expression to despair, and on the hope that new conversations will be born—what Cavell called "cities of words." They testify to a hope in the educability of the viewer, who is obliged to pay attention, to mind. For both Warshow and Cavell, such perfectionism in the aesthetic and pragmatic imperative to invent a public defines popular culture and its "genres."

TV Series, a Twenty-First-Century Art

In an essay dedicated to Cavell's ontology of cinema, Emmanuel Bourdieu defined the realism of cinema in terms of its entanglement with everyday life.[24] Indeed, it is as *experience* rather than as *object* that cinema interests me, and this is the basis for an ordinary theory of cinema that can be applied to series, making it possible to solidify the concrete (although perhaps overly romantic) idea of a *shared experience*. I propose the following principles for such a theory of shared experience:

1) **Educating** one's experience so one may be educated by it. Both Emerson and Dewey point to the circularity that, as I have noted, is inevitable: *having* an experience requires trusting one's experience.

2) **Finding the words to speak** an experience: this is the central theme Cavell develops in *The Claim of Reason*: the possibility and necessity of finding one's voice within one's story.[25] Having an experience is inseparable from the question of expression, and of the possibilities, which cinema explores, of the natural expressivity of human beings. This discovery, rooted in Cavell's reading of Wittgenstein, is Cavell's favored mode of approach to images. "These film words thus declare their mimesis of ordinary words, words in daily conversation. A mastery of film writing and film making accordingly requires, for such films, a mastery of this mode of mimesis."[26]

3) **Technological inventions or developments** determine the transformation of experience: Cavell discovers that the development of talking movies constituted a stage in the expressivity of humans and of women in particular, who found sites of existence in the genres of remarriage comedy and melodrama. The inscription of words in experience occurs through an actor or actress's complex embodiment of a character—complex because our experience of a character's words is marked by our earlier experiences of the actor or actress in other roles. This is even more true in the case of TV series, where we regularly visit with characters over the long term: we saw Alyson Hannigan in the role of Willow for seven years on *Buffy* (1997–2003), and this affects our view of *How I Met Your Mother* (2005–14) and our attachment to the character of Lily and to her expressivity. Or, take the example of Kiefer Sutherland, known for his role as Agent Jack Bauer in *24* (2001–14), who also starred in in *Melancholia* (Lars von Trier, 2011), where he does not (really) save the world, and in *Designated Survivor* (2016–19), where he plays the president of the United States; our perception of the latter two is enriched by our familiarity with the actor's earlier exploits. What gives series their educative force is our ordinary and repeated contact with characters who become our friends—not on

the over-used model of identification, but rather that of contact, familiarization, and attachment.

4) **Regularity** and long-term repeated contact with characters allows us to *let ourselves* be educated by the experience of the series, by our *reception* of it. "Reception" here does not refer to some kind of pure passivity; cumulative experience and our openness to repeating it make the reception of series a combination of perception, cognition, and emotion, which can be analyzed in pragmatist terms. Cavell never focused on this point, but it is clear that the daily or weekly rhythm of series gives them a particular force, as does the way they fit into natural cycles (i.e., their "seasons"). Here we may think of Dewey's analysis of how aesthetic experience is rooted in "nature."

5) **The "small" screen of series** and the aesthetics specific to television are often used by cinephiles to devalorize them. But the format allows for additional expressivity; our nearness to the screen and its small size enhances close-up shots of characters' faces as they express emotions and increases our awareness of how they change physically over the years. Attachment to characters is also reinforced by the domestic context in which series are viewed. Although the domesticity of viewing has not disappeared, people now increasingly view series when they are away from home: while commuting on mass transit or on vacation. This in fact reinforces their integration into daily life, confirming Dewey's point that art is inscribed in the everyday.

6) **The genres of popular culture** certainly constitute the strongest conceptual link between cinema and TV series. Emmanuel Bourdieu, in the essay cited earlier, explains that one of cinema's particular characteristics is its internal reference to genres, the specific modality of its investigation into its own expressive potentialities. Other art forms appeal to the notion of genre, but they do so retrospectively, in order to classify earlier works or to differentiate one work within a genre. In contrast, cinema and series only exist within genres, which defines the popular: there is no essence of cinema just as for Wittgenstein there is no essence of language and just as for Dewey there is no essence of art. The development of popular culture puts forth the model of the "self-made" viewer, who forms his or her taste through his or her choice of favorite genres (for cinema, action movies, romantic comedies, Westerns, science fiction, vampire movies, vulgar comedies for teens; for TV series, procedurals, medical shows, family shows, fantasy, etc.), in contrast to the aristocratic distinction of art. Movies and series mutually influence one another along a continuum, an influence reinforced by the passing of actors and directors from one format to the other:

Michael Mann, David Fincher, Jane Campion, and, of course, David
Lynch.

Let us recall that for Cavell, the constitution of genres and their
importance is based on a property specific to the making of films:
the production of a movie is an enterprise that mobilizes not only
the team behind one work, led by its director, but also, indirectly,
the entire community of other filmmakers and all their works, since
members of one team are highly likely to participate or to have
participated in making other movies produced by the community in
question.

Popular culture is defined precisely by the *creativity* specific to
genre, which drives the creation of works. For example, given how
seductive the character played by James Stewart is to the heroine
of *The Philadelphia Story* (Cukor, 1942), the movie could easily
have ended with their marriage, a possibility the movie briefly
alludes to. But, as Cavell notes, it is the genre that decides—just as
we know, without even needing any confirmation, that *War of the
Worlds* (Spielberg, 2005) will also end with a remarriage (as most
catastrophe movies do) and just as genre allows us to understand
the somewhat strange ending of *The Affair* (Treem and Levi,
2014–19), which depicts the reconciliation of the original couple
in an apocalyptic future. Thus, cinema is full of explicit references
to archetypal works and to the genres that these works contribute
to constituting during a given period. TV series are themselves a
compendium of these references: references to films or classical
series through the "citation" of scenes or actors.

It is the openness of genre and its creativity that make possible
its later productivity, including in the derivation of new genres.
TV series have clearly inherited the conversational capacities of
couples from the remarriage comedy genre, which has given them
the grammar for their expressions, interactions, and emotions. Early
twenty-first-century series have supplied forms of morality to an
entire range of current genres: Mafia/cartel shows such as *Narcos*
and *Mafiosa* draw from *The Sopranos*; political shows such as
Baron Noir draw from *The West Wing*, metaphysical shows such as
The Leftovers draw from *Lost*, and feminist ones such as *Girls* or *I
May Destroy You* draw from *Sex and the City*. Thus, genre contains
an element of empowerment for the generations of characters that
follow, and it provides an expressive grammar, including for the
viewer, who finds within it resources for his or her own feelings and
situations. This creative aspect of genre, which was already present
in cinema, has become more radical with TV series, which are
explicitly terrains of ordinary expression and are themselves filled
with moments of conversation about recent or classical comedies,

which constitute their referential and moral universe, and with constant allusions to TV and movie characters. Thus, the viewer's ordinary competence is a capacity for expression furnished by his or her knowledge, or mastery, of a genre. Genre is not essence: its value comes from the expressive possibilities it opens for both actor and viewer, and Netflix productions, for example, are typical of this kind of recycling of genre. Genre provides proof of concept of popular culture, of the fact that an experience is literally shared between creators and viewers.

7) **The end of the author and of privileged experience**: by eliding the problematic of the author, a theory of aesthetic genre specific to popular culture de-dramatizes the process of making. For creators, it is no longer a question of measuring oneself against a lineage of isolated geniuses—that is, making a unique place for oneself in a universe of absolutely unique, already constituted positions—but rather of becoming part of a collective enterprise by collaborating in it through one's own contribution. This consists in exploring inherited and shared genres or in inventing new ones in concert with other creators, genres that will in turn serve as frameworks and engines for new collective explorations, and ultimately for the derivation of different genres, and so on. Netflix is part of this liberation and regularly opens the way toward creative explorations, in particular outside of the United States.

And it is no longer indispensable for the viewer or critic to create, in isolation, an entirely singular opinion of a work, without being influenced by anybody else. The pleasure and attachment that films and series create are above all collective experiences and evaluations, rather than individual judgments. We are now well aware of the sexist nature of the cult of the author, which has contributed to keeping women and other minorities at the margins of "visible" cinematographic production. The collective nature of production has been particularly successful in the work of female showrunners, of whom there are now many.

Thus, perhaps the definition of experience proposed by pragmatism, as rich and as suited to popular culture as it is, does not provide the means to analyze and be transformed by the experience of the new arts of the twentieth and twenty-first centuries. Cavell, citing Warshow, writes that:

[Warshow] expresses his sense of the necessarily personal in various ways . . . namely, a sense of the writer's having to invent his own audience, of the writer's having to invent all the meanings of experience (p. 16), of the modern intellectual's "facing the necessity of describing and clarifying an experience which has itself deprived him of the vocabulary he requires to deal with it." (p. 9)[27]

What is at stake is no longer simply *having* an experience or the recognition or enlargement of the concept of aesthetic experience, which Dewey put at the center of experience itself. The true legacy of pragmatist aesthetics lies not only in the radical changes proposed by Dewey—the refusal of an existence that would be separate from art, the affirmation of aesthetic experience as ordinary and shared, the recognition of the agency that exists within "reception." It is also the aesthetic and ethical exigency to take into account the productions of popular culture, what Warshow called its "pervasive and disturbing force."[28] It is the search for words to describe an experience that has precisely deprived you of the words you need to face it.

Translated by Daniela Ginsburg

Notes

1 John Dewey, *Art as Experience* (New York, NY: Perigree, 1980), chapter 1.

2 Marc Cerisuelo, "L'importance du cinéma," in *Stanley Cavell: Cinéma et philosophie*, ed. Marc Cerisuelo and Sandra Laugier (Paris: Presses de la Sorbonne Nouvelle, 2001), 19.

3 Robert Warshow, *The Immediate Experience: Movies, Comics, Theatre & Other Aspects of Popular Culture*, Expanded ed. (Cambridge, MA: Harvard University Press, 2001), xxxvii.

4 Stanley Cavell, *Little Did I Know: Excerpts from Memory* (Stanford, CA: Stanford University Press, 2010), 245.

5 Stanley Cavell, "After Half a Century," in Warshow, *The Immediate Experience*, 292.

6 Albert Ogien and Sandra Laugier, *Le principe démocratie: enquête sur les nouvelles formes du politique* (Paris: Découverte, 2014).

7 Cavell, *Little Did I Know*, 423.

8 Ibid., 497.

9 Stanly Cavell, *Pursuits of Happiness: The Hollywood Comedy of Remarriage* (Cambridge, MA: Harvard University Press, 1981), 10.

10 Ibid., 12.

11 Ibid., 10.

12 Stanley Cavell, *The Claim of Reason: Wittgenstein, Skepticism, Morality, and Tragedy* (Oxford: Oxford University Press, 1979), 125.

13 Ibid.

14 Warshow, *The Immediate Experience*, xxxviii.

15 Cavell, *Pursuits of Happiness*, 12; Dewey, *Art as Experience*, chapter 3.

16 Ludwig Wittgenstein, *Philosophical Investigations*, trans. G. E. M. Anscombe (Englewood Cliffs, NJ: Prentice Hall, 1958), §118.

17 Dewey, *Art as Experience*, chapters 1 and 3.

18 Sandra Laugier, *Nos vies en séries* (Paris: Climats Flammarion, 2019).

19 Stanley Cavell, *The World Viewed: Reflections on the Ontology of Film*, Enlarged ed. (Cambridge, MA: 1971), 4–5.

20 Dewey, *Art as Experience*, 10.

21 Erwin Panofsky, cited in Cavell, *The World Viewed*, 30.

22 Rosalind E. Krauss, "Rosalind Krauss on Dark Glasses and Bifocals," *Artforum* 12, no. 9 (May 1974): 59–62, https://www.artforum.com/print /197405/dark-glasses-and-bifocals-37376.

23 Cavell, "More of the World Viewed," in *The World Viewed*, 162–230.

24 Emmanuel Bourdieu, "Stanley Cavell—Pour une esthétique d'un art impur," in *Stanley Cavell: Cinéma et philosophie*, ed. Marc Cerisuelo and Sandra Laugier (Paris: Presses de la Sorbonne Nouvelle, 2001), 57.

25 Sandra Laugier, *Wittgenstein: le mythe de l'inexpressivité* (Paris: Vrin, 2010).

26 Cavell, *Pursuits of Happiness*, 11.

27 Cavell, in Warshow, *The Immediate Experience*, 292.

28 Warshow, *The Immediate Experience*, xxxvii.

8

What Does It Mean to Have a Cinematic Idea?

Deleuze and Kurosawa's *Stray Dog*

David Deamer

Drawing Legs on a Picture of a Snake

"What does it mean," asks Gilles Deleuze, "to have an idea in cinema?" Deleuze is talking at La Fémis film school in early 1987, a couple of years after the publication of the second of his two *Cinema* books (1983; 1985) and the conclusion of four years of his University of Paris *Cinema Seminars* (1981–5). "Ideas," continues the philosopher, "have to be treated like potentials already *engaged* in one mode of expression or another and inseparable from the mode of expression." (emphasis in original). There are no pure ideas, for Deleuze. That's to say, ideas are expressed "in a certain domain, an idea in cinema or an idea in philosophy."[1] Philosophy expresses ideas through the creation of concepts. "You do not invent concepts," Deleuze proposes to the audience of cineastes, "that is not your concern." Rather, filmmakers create "blocks" of movement and duration.[2] Philosophy and cinema are of course different disciplines. And each discipline expresses an idea (a problem, a question, a thought) in its own way. During his first interview on the *Cinema* books in 1983, Deleuze tells film critic Serge Daney that "philosophy has no special privilege," the "great cinematic authors are thinkers just as much as painters, musicians, novelists and philosophers."[3] Painters think through "lines and colours," musicians through "modes and rhythms," writers "words and syntax."[4] Filmmakers think by creating "images," blocks of movement, and duration.[5]

Filmmaker Kurosawa Akira puts it this way: "Everything I want to say is in the film itself; for me to say anything more is, as the proverb goes, like 'drawing legs on a picture of a snake.'" Taken from Kurosawa's book *Something Like an Autobiography* (1982), these words appear in relation to *Stray Dog* (1949). This film, writes Kurosawa, was made to express an "idea" (or "problem," or "vision").[6] Ideas are expressed as image-blocks for Kurosawa just as with Deleuze. One of the most astonishing images of *Stray Dog* comes toward the very end of the film. The detective and the fugitive lie side by side in long grass and wild flowers—both exhausted, fighting for breath. It is early morning, the height of summer, the verdure that surrounds them still damp from the rainstorm of the night before. Kurosawa captures the two young men with a ground-level mid-shot, the world silent but for their tortured breathing. Detective Murakami has been hunting Yusa Shinjiro for days. The once small-time crook began terrorizing the streets of post-war Tokyo after getting hold of a Colt semi-automatic pistol, the gun stolen from the rookie investigator at the opening of the film. Murakami has felt humiliation and shame, anger and responsibility for the other man's actions. Now, Yusa is in handcuffs after a vicious brawl and desperate chase through some woods outside the city. We become aware of the sound of children's voices. In the distance school kids are passing along a country lane on their way to lessons, singing a joyful song. Kurosawa gives us a close-up of Yusa's face, interposed with a series of loose point-of-view shots: a clear sky, framed by wild flowers, a bug flits across the screen. Cut to an overhead full-shot of both men. Yusa sobs. Wails, screams. His body squirms, writhes, convulses. Murakami slowly pushes himself up, sits watching the killer in horror.

What idea does this cinematic image express? We seemingly meet an impasse: If cinema expresses ideas through images of movement and duration, how can anyone, let alone a filmmaker, talk or write about cinematic ideas? It seems the formulations of both Kurosawa and Deleuze serve only to raise a far more difficult question. Yet we know people do talk and write about films. Cinemagoers, critics, scholars, theorists, even filmmakers! And there is something called (variously) film studies, film theory, film-philosophy. What then is the relation between cinematic ideas and philosophic concepts, between images and writing? What—for Deleuze—is film-philosophy?

That one discipline needs or requires another to think about itself—Deleuze tells his audience—is "comical."[7] Cinema does not deploy philosophic ideas, nor is a film explained by philosophy.[8] Even when philosophy believes this is its gift or purpose. Nonetheless, it is "perfectly natural to go from philosophy to cinema, and from cinema to philosophy."[9] Ideas in different domains "resonate," have "powerful encounters," and it is in this way an "affinity is revealed."[10] Cinematic blocks of movement and duration intersect with philosophical concepts. As Deleuze writes on the final page of the *Cinema* books, it is through the "interference of many practices that things happen."[11] Film-philosophy is thus—for Deleuze—film and philosophy together in alliance. Film-philosophy, just like film and just like philosophy, is a creative practice. What Deleuze says of his writing on the work of other philosophers would also be true of his adventures with cinema: "the author actually had to say everything I made him say. But it also had to be a monster because it was necessary to go through all kinds of decenterings, slips, break ins, secret emissions, which I really enjoyed."[12] Film-philosophy—in this way—is the love of drawing legs on pictures of snakes. Snakes become monstrous, strange beasts, *kaiju*. Snakes become dragons. Film-philosophy—for Deleuze—is philosophy, and filmmakers "become philosophers or theoreticians" when they talk about what they do.[13] If they wish to talk about what they do. Philosophers, theorists, writers, in the same way, go to the movies, think and write about cinema, and create film-philosophy.

Cinematic Images of Movement and Duration

Cinema is the art of composing audiovisual blocks of movement and duration. Every frame, shot, sequence, film, cycle, and oeuvre is such a block: an image itself and an assemblage of images within an assemblage of images. It is through cinematic movement that cinema creates images of space, and it is through cinematic duration that cinema creates images of time.[14] Movement and duration are, of course, simultaneous and inseparable aspects of spacetime. Nonetheless, there are fundamental differences of expression. Movement is a direct expression of space (giving us an indirect image of duration). Whereas duration is a direct expression of time (giving us an indirect image of movement). Cinematic images, accordingly, tend toward being expressed as either "blocks of movement / duration" or "blocks of duration / movement."[15] The former are what Deleuze calls movement-images, the latter time-images. Each "implies the reversal of the subordination" of the other.[16] Thus Deleuze's twofold formula of the essence of cinema:

$$\text{movement-images} = \frac{\text{movement}}{\text{duration}} \quad and \quad \text{time-images} = \frac{\text{duration}}{\text{movement}}$$

This formula is deduced from the two co-constitutive processes original to cinema: camera movement and filmic montage.

However, filmmaking began with a static camera and continuous images. The earliest films were fifty-second *actualités*, such as those first screened at the Cinématographe Lumière in December 1895. Such films, for Deleuze, are "primitive." A filmic image always captures movement and always captures time, yet during the early period films are neither movement-images nor time-images "properly speaking."[17] This is because both real cinematographic movement and true cinematographic duration are "concealed," remain "potential."[18] For example, some of the earliest movies were "stage views," where a static camera filmed a fictional scene in wide-shot. Here the camera functions as a device for capturing another pre-established art form; cinema is a recording of theatrical scenes projected as spectacle, an attraction. Cinema has yet to become cinema. Echoing philosopher Henri Bergson, Deleuze writes that the "essence of a thing never appears at the outset, but in the middle, in the course of its development, when its strength is assured."[19] Georges Méliès says something similar in his 1907 essay "Cinematographic Views": it was when film "was put in the service of theatrical art" that "its success was transformed into a triumph"; but it was only with "transformation views" that cinema began to create its own aesthetic domain.[20] As Ricciotto Canudo argues in "The Birth of the Sixth Art" in 1911, cinema discovers itself through the "conciliation of the Rhythms of Space" and "the Rhythms of Time" and thus becomes a "new Aesthetics."[21]

This transformation occurs when the cinema discovers its two fundamental, co-constitutive processes. "[T]he conquest of its own essence or novelty," writes Deleuze, "was to take place through montage" and "the mobile camera."[22] The camera is put into motion (pan, tilt, dolly, zoom, etc.) and films are composed through the editing together of different shots (spatiotemporal milieus; and types, wide-shots, medium-shots, close-ups, etc.). In this way, cinematic movement and cinematic duration were released as movement-images. Movement-images are images in movement over time, and images linking different spaces over time. The camera moves to follow people and objects, various shots of the same and different events are captured, and montage assembles these images into a film. Such discoveries are perfected and refined through dissolves, superimpositions, contrast of light and dark, intertitles, voice, music, and color. All this—and more—describes the "splendour of the classical image" of cinema.[23]

Yet, there must necessarily be another transformation. If the movement-image appears with the capture and release of movement and duration as movement/duration, the reverse must be possible: duration/movement, or the time-image. Echoing philosopher Friedrich Nietzsche, Deleuze writes: "it is never at the beginning that something new, a new art, is able to reveal its essence; what it was from the outset it can reveal only after a detour in its evolution."[24] The movement-image, the "so-called classical image," now appears as a detour between the "so-called primitive image" and the "so-called modern image," the time-image.[25] This is because the concealment of movement and duration is more far-reaching than first considered: "not only had the connections of montage to be imperceptible [. . .] but also the camera movements."[26] Camera movement follows people and things in motion, keeping them within the frame. It tends to invisibility, the movement within the frame capturing the eye of the spectator. And movements motivate and mask cuts. A movement is matched to another movement within another frame. The invisible camera and the invisible edit become the highest principles of cinema for the movement-image. In distinction, the time-image was revealed when the camera moved for itself independent of characters and objects, and when montage abandoned the seamless flow of images to embrace discontinuity. Such time-images, as we shall see, invite an encounter with duration. How does the time-image arise? In many ways, "some of which were social, economic, political, moral and others more internal to art."[27] "Over several centuries," writes Deleuze, "from the Greeks to Kant, a revolution took place in philosophy: the subordination of time to movement was reversed, time ceases to be the measurement of normal movement, it increasingly appears for itself and creates paradoxical movements." So too science and the arts, including—"in more fast-moving circumstances"—the cinema.[28] The "timing is something like: around 1948, Italy; about 1958, France; about 1968, Germany": neorealism, the new wave, new German cinema.[29] For Deleuze, "[t]he post-war period has greatly increased the situations which we no longer know how to react to, in spaces which we no longer know how to describe," "deserted but inhabited, disused warehouses, waste ground, cities in the course of demolition or reconstruction" where "a new race of characters was stirring," "they saw rather than acted, they were seers."[30] This period also revealed "the unsteadiness of the 'American Dream'" and the rise of the "new American cinema," as well as "the new consciousness of minorities" with "black American cinema's black-powerism."[31] There were many other just as important "historical and political" movements, "female authors, female directors," the cinemas of South America, Africa, and Asia, including the "mutation of an Americanised Japan."[32] Without doubt, there were precursors to the time-image (Ozu, Welles, Renoir, etc.), and the movement-image will continue to go from strength to strength. Nonetheless, after the Second World War, time-images attained critical cinematic mass; everywhere, in every way, duration began to surge forth from cinema.

Stray Dog seems to express the event of this transformation as it is happening, filmed as it is during the censorship of the American-led Allied occupation (1945–52), in the aftermath of the cataclysmic fire-bombings of Tokyo and atomic attacks on Hiroshima and Nagasaki, in the wake of the fascist Japanese war machine.[33] *Stray Dog* is a film in which the time-image is gnawing away at the movement-image from within, disrupting the flow of images, and creating temporal disjunctions. Where movement-images and time-images "coexist in the same film."[34] Such exchanges occur throughout the movie, but it is during the apogee of the finale sequence this reversal is felt most viscerally. Yusa's paroxysm is a time-image exploding onscreen.

Let's track back a bit . . . Again, Yusa fires the pistol at the detective, but the gun is now empty and the mechanism clicks uselessly upon itself. A brawl begins, the two men grappling in the dirt, rendered through a series of close-ups, then medium-shots where each movement within the frame motivates a cut to a new image. Yusa escapes Murakami, jumps up and sprints away, throwing the pistol at the detective: a close-up of it being thrown, a wide-shot as it travels through the air, then another close-up as Murakami retrieves it from the ground. The chase continues: a wide-shot of the detective wading through a marsh after Yusa, and as both men approach the camera appearing in medium-shot, the camera pans left and right keeping them within the frame. Here we see the logical trajectory of the movement-image: the linkage of images giving us a seamless flow. However, when we encounter the paroxysm, things change: no camera movement, no cutting, but a static long-take of the killer's scream as Murakami watches in horror. It may be objected that this shot is merely the outcome of the movement-images that precede it, with one of the antagonists "reduced to helplessness, bound and gagged, as a result of the ups and downs of the action." But Yusa is not attempting to escape. He is "animated in vain, the situation he is in outstrips his motor capacities on all sides, and makes him see and hear what is no longer subject to the rules of a response or an action," he becomes "prey to a vision."[35] Yusa is not attempting to escape; something is escaping Yusa. This is the reversal. A paroxysm of rage, fear, revulsion, misery. Something has broken through, torn open the skin of the film exposing a terrible wound. Kurosawa gives us a cinematic idea that resonates in painting with Edvard Munch's infinite scream of the universe. Or Kurt Cobain's wails of pain in Nirvana's final recording before the singer's suicide.[36] Or, as Nietzsche writes, "when you stare for a long time into an abyss, the abyss stares back at you."[37]

Not every image of duration is so explosive. Some are ever so subtle, almost imperceptible, though nonetheless very powerful. Take the three shots which Kurosawa seemingly attributes to Yusa gazing at the sky. These images—which divide a close-up of the killer's face—are from three slightly different perspectives, each a different spatiotemporal framing. Yet at the same time, the children's voices give us a diegetic audio continuity, accentuating the disjunctions of the visual image. Whose visions are these? The moment is delicate, beautiful. Nonetheless, the infinite sky—which gives us the whole of the past—is an abyss. Here we pass from undifferentiated shot to undifferentiated shot not through any logic of movement, but by the resonances of the vast infinity within each image and the little infinities between each image. Once again, we encounter time as duration. The universe stares at Yusa.

The Movement-image and the Time-image

In the finale of *Stray Dog* we witness (again and again) the movement-image trajectory dissolving into time-images, time-images solidifying into movement-images. Yet something else is immediately evident. The sky-abyss and the paroxysm-scream are very different images of duration. Similarly, there are different types of movement: facial close-ups, medium-shots of bodies, and establishing wide-shots. The movement-image and the time-image are composites. Thus the project of Deleuze's *Cinema* books, to create "a taxonomy," a "classification of images and signs" of films.[38] *Cinema 1: The Movement-Image* (1983) and *Cinema 2: The Time-Image* (1985) each explore how ideas are expressed through different cinematic images, how these images are encountered as signs, perspectives that philosophy can explore. To develop this cineosis Deleuze first turns to Bergson.[39]

Bergson was the first philosopher to write on film. "I saw it at its origins," he says of the movies, and "I realised it could offer something new to philosophy."[40] In *Creative Evolution* (1907), Bergson describes the cinema as giving us what has become known as the cinematographic illusion, the perfection of a worldview named, with daring anachronism, as the "cinematographical mechanism of thought."[41] The universe, the world, life, our bodies, and consciousness have a fundamental reality as movement and duration. However, throughout the history of human thought—be thought expressed through common language, art, science, or indeed philosophy—movement and duration prove elusive. The camera captures real movement and true duration as a series of static images. Thus "moving reality" and "change" are "immobilized" as "successive states."[42] The projector then returns mobility to the filmstrip of snapshots which appear continuous onscreen; nonetheless, "real time, regarded as a flux, or, in other words, as the very mobility of being, escapes."[43] Cinema gives us the illusion of movement and duration, but in so doing reveals the prevalence of the cinematographic status of all human production. Language cuts up reality into words, sculpture and painting create frozen idols, science reduces the universe to formulas, and philosophy proposes eternal forms. The invention of the cinema, however, is a flashpoint. For Bergson, film is not only a synecdoche but simultaneously the apotheosis of the cinematographic mechanism of thought. The cinema becomes an ally in Bergson's search for a new philosophy.

What *Creative Evolution* "ultimately aims to do," comments Deleuze, is "give modern science the metaphysic which corresponds to it." However, for Bergson, cinema itself cannot give us such movement or duration. It just reveals the illusion for philosophy. "But," asks Deleuze, "can we stop once we have set out on this path? Can we deny that the arts must go through this conversion or that the cinema is an essential factor in this, and that it has a role to play in the birth and formation of this new thought, this new way of thinking?."[44] Bergson privileges philosophy. Only the new philosophy can express the reality of movement and duration. The conditions for Bergson's folly, however, are historical. The cinematographic illusion necessarily corresponds to the concealments of the so-called primitive image of film. In 1895 and even 1907 Bergson could not have known what the cinema would become: movement-images, then time-images. Or could he? Deleuze does something utterly astounding, quickly passing through *Creative Evolution* for Bergson's previous book, *Matter and Memory* (1896). Published at the same time as the birth of film, Deleuze argues that this revolutionary but lesser-known text is all the more awesome as it "prefigure[s] the future or the essence of the cinema," the theory therein what the "cinema would rediscover" before Bergson encountered the Cinématographe Lumière. For Deleuze, the idea of real movement and true duration gives rise to both cinema and *Matter and Memory* at the same historical moment.[45] This is "the thesis of *Matter and Memory*, mobile sections" and "temporal planes."[46] As Deleuze summarizes: "(1) there are not only instantaneous images, that is, immobile sections": the cinematographic illusion of *Creative Evolution*. But, with *Matter and Memory*, "(2) there are movement-images which are mobile sections of duration," and "(3) there are, finally, time-images, that is, duration-images."[47]

The universe is composed of matter and appears as images. The matter of the universe is an image, the worlds within, and entities of all kinds from macrocosm to mesocosm to microcosm. Images are composed of images and compose images—and all images "act and react upon one another in all their elementary parts according to constant laws," the "laws of nature."[48] Images are determinate, the continuity of real movement. Among these matter-images, however, special images evolve: living bodies. A body not only perceives the images of the world in order to act upon the images of the world. Crucially, between the body as perception-image and the body as action-image there is an interval: the body as affection-image. The body is affected by perceptions, and affects inspire actions. And the more complex the body the more multiplicitous the affects and the more multiplicitous the possible actions. The living body thus evolves as a "*centre of indetermination*," of choice, of freedom.[49] But the body (and its brain) simultaneously evolves as master of affects, master of actions, master of perceptions: perceptions become selective, affects become controlled, actions become directed—perfected, pathologized, habitualized. In this way, the body-brain is also an image of memory, a mental-image. Bergson gives this reciprocal process a name, the sensory-motor system. However, there is another kind of memory: pure memory. This memory is not of the body and its brain, is not actual, but virtual, the genesis of bodies and their brains. The virtual has had many names, including the soul and the spirit, although Bergson prefers such concepts as consciousness, duration, and becoming. We are not only a sensory-motor system: a coherent body-brain in comprehensive space and chronological time. Our consciousness flows with the vital temporality of the present, we exist as a long duration with our whole past and the past, and we are always becoming new, reborn, other with the future. Duration, the virtual, consciousness, becoming, (pure) memory, (real) time—can, for Bergson, be used interchangeably, are essentially synonymous.

Deleuze sees that the two possible configurations of the two co-constitutive processes of cinema resonate with Bergson's sensory-motor system and duration as movement-images and time-images. So, in the first place, movement-images can be said to be composed: perception-images, affection-images, and action-images, with the reciprocity of mental-images. Thus Deleuze's basic taxonomy of the movement-image:

$$\underline{\text{perception-images} \leftrightarrow \text{affection-images} \leftrightarrow \text{action-images}}$$
$$\text{mental-images}$$

The final sequence of *Stray Dog* is beautifully woven from the weft and warp of such movement-images. Let's rewind to the beginning of the finale . . .

Murakami approaches Ohara train station searching for the fleeing criminal. We begin with *perception-images*. There is a wide-shot of the station and its environs through which Murakami moves, before he enters the waiting room slouching into a vacant seat. The room is filled with people, and the detective surreptitiously casts his gaze around, over the bodies and faces of the travelers, Kurosawa shooting this with point-of-view shots both static and flowing. Eventually, Murakami sees Yusa. And Yusa sees Murakami. Such are perception-images: the perception of a world which extracts characters as central images from all the images of the world, to the images of the perception of the characters, what they select from all the images of their world.

With the two men caught in each other's gaze we pass immediately into *affection-images*. Kurosawa cuts between close-ups of their faces. Yusa's face traverses a series of images: curiosity, uncertainty, fear. Murakami's face the series of relief, triumph, and (a pretense of) nonchalance. The affection-image expresses emotions: makes visible the invisible forces that course through and between bodies. And the most expressive images of such are close-ups of faces which react to perception and prefigure action. What will Yusa do next? What will Murakami do next?

Yusa turns and runs, Murakami jumps from his seat, giving chase. We encounter *action-images*. Kurosawa films the two men in wide-shot with a lateral camera movement as they run along the train track and with a series of medium-shots as they enter the woods. Action-images describe acts and reactions within the world. Murakami trips and falls; and as the detective rights himself he sees Yusa has also slipped, but the criminal has an advantage. Murakami is now facing his own pistol, defenseless. The action-image stalls, there is silence . . .

From perception-images through affection-images to action-images, we are carried full circle, back to perception with Murakami and Yusa staring at one another, to the affects of a face-off, the movement toward another action-image again in suspension. Yet in the silence of the grove do we not encounter something simmering beneath? As well as perception-images and affection-images are there not *mental-images*? Ricocheting back and forth between the killer and the cop, it is as if we can hear the thoughts of the two men in the tension of this moment: Murakami believes there are three bullets left in the gun, is he right? can he survive?—Yusa knows he can kill, he's even shot a cop before, but can he kill this cop, here, now? Mental-images are always simmering beneath. But such simmering is "different from making the mental the proper object of an image," an "explicit image."[50] As Murakami sat in the waiting room scanning the travelers, we hear the thoughts of the detective as voice-over. Murakami has never seen Yusa, so rather than awaiting recognition we are following a series of relations, a process of reasoning, the movement of thought: "Which is Yusa? Don't act on impulse, stay calm. Stay calm. Think things over. About twenty-seven or eight. A white linen suit. He may have changed his suit. What then?"[51] It is not that the visual image is a perception-image and the sound image a mental-image. Mental-images have risen to the surface. The detective remembers the downpour of the night before, Kurosawa pans around the room until the camera happens upon muddy shoes, the movement of the camera tilting to reveal dirty white linen trousers. The man takes out a cigarette and matches: "Left-handed!"[52] And thus the mental-image returns us to the perception-image, then affection-images, and action-images.

However, as Yusa and Murakami face each other in the woods, Kurosawa does something curious. The tension of movement toward another action-image begins to dissipate. Silence gives way to a sound image of a piano. At first this music has an uncertain status: Is it non-diegetic or off-screen? Through intercutting Kurosawa reveals a woodland cottage among the trees. This is the origin of the fragile, tentative tune carried on the morning breeze. Yusa—of course—must pull the trigger, despite Kurosawa switching focus from the face-off with Murakami. So, the killer fires. The cop is hit in the arm. The music stops. Blood drips to the forest floor. However, Kurosawa stymies the action to come, and takes us into the cottage. Filming first from the outside and through an open window (frame-within-frame) we see a woman sitting at her piano gazing back at us. Slowly, she pushes herself up and approaches the window. Cutting to a reverse angle shot within the room, Kurosawa films over-the-shoulder as she looks out into the woods (again frame-within-frame). A lovely little garden with picket fence, and beyond, obscured among the trees, two men in white linen suits facing one another, frozen. Kurosawa cuts back to outside the cottage (third frame-within-frame) as the woman rubs her eyes, blocks her vision, turns away. An image which gives "no response or reaction," an image "all the more profound because she cannot react in a way that softens or compensates for the violence of what she sees."[53] These three frame-within-frame images fracture cinematic space and create a temporal recursion: duration. The woman has seen too much: the Emperor's militaristic war machine, the killing and suicide of soldiers, the rape of women, slavery, the murder of civilians and prisoners, the atomic bombs, occupation. The two men—indistinguishable through distance (similar ages, dress, state)—are framed in the central image of the block as though we are looking through a portal into the past, history, and memory in the present which promises to extend brutal patriarchy into the future. A screen in a movie theater, the woman in her cottage lured toward but turning away in protest "against represented violence."[54]

A Multiplicity of Time-images

The time-image "no longer asks how images are linked, but 'What does the image *show*?.'" The relation "*sensory-motor situation → indirect image of time*" is replaced by "*pure optical and sound situation → direct image of time.*"[55] However, that the cinema undoes the linearity and layering of movement-images "was not enough."[56] For Deleuze, the time-image "asks the question: what are the new forces at work in the image, and the new signs invading the screen?."[57] This gives us a second moment of taxonomic creation, there are various time-images.

To explicate cinematic duration as a time-image Deleuze returns to an earlier work, *Difference and Repetition* (1968). "[T]he first book," writes Deleuze, "in which I tried to 'do philosophy.' All that I have done since is connected."[58] This treatise seeks to explore the givenness of the concept of identity through a theorizing of its genesis: the differences and repetitions— or syntheses—of time, space, and consciousness. Deleuze's three syntheses conceptualize the *grounding* of everyday existence: the trajectory of a coherent body-brain in comprehensive space and chronological time. Such spatiotemporal existence, for Deleuze, arises from a flux of disjunctions which occur both between the three syntheses and through their constitution. All three synthesis have their own *foundation, ground*, and *ungrounding*— are a tension of centripetal forces which cohere and centripetal forces which disperse. Accordingly, the project of *Difference and Repetition* is threefold: to map the myriad disjunctions of each of the three syntheses, to account for how cohesion arises from flux, and to explore how flux can free itself to produce new images of thought, of life, of the world.

The constitutive elements of the syntheses of time are presentness, pastness, and futureness: succession, memory, and becoming. Each of these three elements is a disjunctive syntheses as each are their own encounter with time; each a repetition of the dimensions of time as difference. Succession is the vital foundation, where presentness subsumes present, past, and future. Memory is the ground where pastness subsumes past, present, and future. Becoming is an ungrounding, where futureness subsumes the future, present, and past. Accordingly, each of the three syntheses of time has three temporalities which circulate within in their own way, and which in turn resonate with the three syntheses of space and the three syntheses of consciousness.[59] Succession resonates with surface in the syntheses of space, and the I in the syntheses of consciousness. Memory resonates with depth and the self. Becoming resonates with intensity and otherness. And just as succession, memory, and becoming are disjunctive conceptions of temporality—so are surface, depth, and intensity disjunctive conceptions of space as mesocosm, macrocosm, and microcosm; and so are I, self, and other disjunctive conceptions of consciousness causing the I to fracture and selves to dissolve as I and self are already other. "[P]erhaps," writes Deleuze, "the highest object of art is to bring into play simultaneously all these repetitions," to "embed them in one another," these repetitions "with their differences in kind and rhythm, their respective displacements and disguises, their divergences and decentrings."[60]

To explore this "perhaps," Deleuze creates the images and signs of the time-image in *Cinema 2*. The three time-images are called *hyalosigns*, *chronosigns*, and *noosigns*. The hyalosign resonates with succession, surface, and the fractured I: the image itself as foundation appearing as "the coalescence of an actual image and its virtual image." The chronosign resonates with memory, depth, and dissolved selves: "narration" as ground.[61] The noosign resonates with becoming, intensity, and otherness: an ungrounding narrative, the "force" which invites "us to think."[62] Thus—like a Chinese box, a Matryoshka doll, or a fractal (rather than the linearity and layering of movement-images)—Deleuze's fundamental formula of the time-image:

hyalosign

↕

chronosign

↕

noosign

Of course, these three time-images are each a perspective of time, so the hyalosign resonates with presentness expressed in the present, past, and future; the chronosign resonates with pastness expressed in the past, present, and future; while the noosign resonates with futureness expressed in the future, present, and past. Each of the time-images will thus unfold through three signs—and together they nest as a complex cinematic block of disjunctive images, dispersive narration, and discordant narrative. Perhaps this is why, as Mitsuhiro Yoshimoto comments, "[c]ritics have reacted strongly to the black market sequence" of *Stray Dog* (2005:160). The movement-image is in "crisis."[63] Differentiated perception-, affection-, action-, and mental-images collapse, become undifferentiated optical and sound images, *opsigns and sonsigns*, "aberrant movements and false continuity shots."[64] Donald Richie writes "*Stray Dog* is full of temporal miscalculations. One of them is the endless montage sequence," a "full ten minutes of double-exposure, dissolves, fades, multiple images."[65] However, believes Yoshimoto, "this sequence is what makes *Stray Dog* artistically so successful."[66] Such a reinterpretation is to affirm the sequence as a time-image: opsigns and sonsigns becoming time-images.

Some children have their backs to the camera. Yet we also see their faces staring at us; and as we watch, they turn toward and away from the camera running off simultaneously in two different directions. The kids had their heads pressed against a shop window, gazing at the unobtainable goodies within, the exterior daylight transforming the glass (for us) into a black mirror. This is a *mirror-image*, composing opsigns and sonsigns as the first hyalosign: the presentness of the present generating a multiplicity of perspectives. The reflection of a man appears. Dressed in old fatigues and a battered cap, he checks his appearance before moving on. This—we realize—is the detective. No longer in his crisp white linen suit and stylish fedora, Murakami has split in two, becoming a dark reflection. No longer does an actual image flow into the next image; but rather the actual image correlates to its virtual: becomes pictorial. The black market sequence is a series of such fragments, opsigns and sonsigns exchanged as the *limpid-opaque*, opaque becomes limpid and the limpid opaque, "the virtual image becomes actual" and "the actual image becomes virtual in its turn."[67] Cop becomes vagabond—walking the streets in battered boots; bedding down in cramped, flea-ridden doss houses—before vagabond becomes cop once more. Cop and vagabond, each the virtual past of the other as each are actualized in turn. The sequence is thus also a series of images describing the atmosphere of post-war Japan. These *seed-environment* images—multiple fragments composing wholes which retain their fragmentation—describe post-war Tokyo: shattered buildings, broken streets, populated by the flotsam and jetsam of a devastated Japanese society.[68] Accordingly, such images are simultaneously a narration, chronosigns: *sheets of the past, peaks of the present, powers of the false.* Yoshimoto sees that the sequence serves to create "metonymic references to key incidents from Murakami's past," where he "relives his past"; but also "experiences a kind of life that he might have chosen to live."[69] These two aspects of the narration are sheets of the past and peaks of the present—both a disruption to the linear order of time. The "coexistence of all the sheets of the past" plunges the character into the "circles of the past" as an "infinity of levels."[70] Kurosawa films such circles in a number of ways: Murakami's ragged clothes and ruined boots, images where nothing happens, blocks of seemingly endless repetition, faces that stare with suspicion and violence, the sound of a train that haunts the audio landscape. Kurosawa's brilliance here is to allow these sheets through which Murakami passes to be indeterminate as they appear, only to be drawn upon later in the film through movement-images. Murakami will go on to tell of how he was demobilized from the army, brought back to Tokyo as a prisoner by train, had his knapsack with all his possessions stolen, becoming destitute and without purpose. And while these images function as sheets of the past, they are simultaneously peaks of the present, capturing multiple parallel presents, all conceivable yet together impossible, where Murakami is an undercover cop, never became a cop, is a former cop fired for losing his gun. Or in another configuration, where Murakami is an actual of the virtual Yusa, a sense of the killer before the trajectory of the movement-image will reveal his name, that he too was in the army, had his knapsack stolen with all he owned. Yoshimoto may describe Murakami as choosing another path, but Kurosawa sees such an outcome in terms of serendipity, chance, accident: the dice throw. And it is this question—as we shall see—that will haunt Murakami. The third chronosign is the "power of the false," the final aspect of time-image narration.[71] Narration is ungrounded by the future, "truth is not to be achieved, formed, or reproduced," writes Deleuze, "it has to be created."[72] The whole of the black market sequence is a power of the false: it is through Murakami's masquerade that Kurosawa expresses the truth of post-war Tokyo. Poverty, starvation, resignation, desperation, subjugation, exploitation. Powers of the false are—in this way—the conditions for a new image of cinematic thought: the noosign. The story will "replace filmstock in a virtual film," writes Deleuze, "which now only goes on in the head."[73] The noosign is the narrative arising from chronosigns and hyalosigns. And this new image of thought appears through a reconfigured relation of bodies and world. In the movement-image, the sensory-motor system linked universe and character through plot. In the absence of actual links, hyalosigns and chronosigns require a virtual relinkage. In other words, time-images invite us to think. The first sign is the *body of attitude*, "the everyday body," no longer "a presence of bodies, in perception and action" but "a primordial genesis of bodies."[74] The black market sequence overflows with the difference and repetition of bodies: exhausted bodies, lost bodies, violent bodies, slave bodies, master bodies—cops, vagabonds, whores, pickpockets, yakuza, gamblers, drunks, and so on. These bodies are simultaneously a collective enunciation: the *body of gest*, a multiplicity-mass synthesizing the socius. The final image of the noosign concerns the mise-en-scène, the *cinema of the brain*. Here "landscapes are mental states, just as mental states are cartographies."[75] The screen becomes an image of the mind, "thought no longer appears on the screen as function of the body," but rather the whole sequence becomes a "cerebral space."[76] The black market scene expresses the idea of Kurosawa's Tokyo.

The time-image is the simultaneity of hyalosigns, chronosigns, and noosigns. Opsigns and sonsigns allow the ascension of new forces of the image, narration, and narrative. But as a block the time-image is a *lectosign*, "the common limit."[77] This limit is that which invites us "to treat the optical and sound image like something that is also readable."[78] The black market sequence is a new image of thought: a world populated by a people immersed in the event of the long duration of war, defeat and surrender, and occupation. And with such an event: the end of state Shinto, imperialism, and empire; the possibility of mass suicide; and the actualization of the death of god.

New Year's Day, 1946, Hirohito proclaims that Japan was "not predicated on the false conception that the Emperor is divine, and that the Japanese people are superior to other races and fated to rule the world."[79] Like a vortex in the trajectory of *Stray Dog*, the black market sequence is a time-image into which movement-images plunge: all coordinates are lost, causal trajectories disrupted, actors becoming seers. Kurosawa sees these

signs among "ruins of post-war Tokyo."[80] "The enemy has recently used a
most cruel explosive," announced the Emperor after the atomic bombs.[81]
Kurosawa remembers everyone "looked fully prepared for the Honourable
Death of the Hundred Million," the streets full of "shopowners who had
taken their Japanese swords from their sheaths and sat staring at the bare
blades."[82] "Should we continue to fight," Hirohito's voice crackled over the
radio, "not only would it result in the ultimate collapse and obliteration
of the Japanese nation, but also it would lead to the total extinction of
human civilization."[83] "I captured the atmosphere of post-war Japan very
well in *Stray Dog*," says Kurosawa.[84] For Deleuze, the "great post-war
philosophers and writers demonstrated that thought has something to do
with Auschwitz, with Hiroshima, but this was also demonstrated by the
great cinema authors."[85]

A Multiplicity of Movement-images

Little by little, opsigns and sonsigns are recaptured as movement-images.
With the amusement alley, the old fountain, the Conga Teashop, perception-
images, affection-images, action-images, and mental-images take shape.
Murakami encounters a young thug, leading to Tokyo's illegal gun trade,
and the detective is back in his white linen suit and dapper fedora. The
investigation—which was stymied, dissolving into the time-image of the
black market sequence—begins again, all the more assured. Murakami
is now on a trajectory that will team him up with veteran cop Sato, in
turn leading them to Yusa. This coalescence of movement-images describes
a coherent body-brain in comprehensive space and chronological time,
the cohesion of the three disjunctive syntheses into "[a]ctive synthetic
identity."[86] The "sensory-motor" system, "a rich domain of signs which
envelope heterogeneous elements and animate behaviour."[87] As Deleuze
puts it *Cinema 1*, "there is every reason to believe that many other kinds
of images can exist."[88] The expansion of the movement-image taxonomy is
thus a third moment of cineotic creation.

Deleuze invokes the semiotics of Charles Sanders Peirce from *Pragmatism
and Pragmaticism* (1903) not only because it aligns with Bergson's sensory-
motor system, but also as it offers a way of developing the movement-
image. "[W]hen he invented semiotics," writes Deleuze, the "strength" of
Peirce's process was "to conceive signs on the basis of images and their
combinations."[89] Peirce sees three levels of encounter with the world:
firstness, secondness, and thirdness. Firstness is "the Idea of that which is
such as it is regardless of anything else," a "Quality of Feeling." Secondness
is "the Idea of Reaction as an element of the Phenomenon." While thirdness
is the "Idea" of "Representation as an element of the Phenomenon."[90]
Deleuze aligns these levels with Bergson's affect (firstness-feeling), action
(secondness-reaction), and mental processes (thirdness-representation);

while perception is a given for Peirce (and so has zeroness).[91] Such is only the first of three moves, for what is essential in Peirce's system is that levels are inclusive of each other, offering logical combinations as an incremental trajectory: thirdness (three relations) is inclusive of secondness (two relations) in turn inclusive of firstness. Thus while firstness is composed only of itself, secondness is composed of firstness and secondness (three levels), and thirdness is composed of thirdness, secondness, and firstness (six levels). For Peirce, then, there are ten incremental levels of an encounter with the world. And for Deleuze, this means there can be ten types of movement-image beyond the zeroness of the perception-image: one affection-image, three action-images, and six mental-images. Finally, these images will each be expressed through three signs.[92] With respect to Peirce, this is the aspect of the sign itself, its relation to its object, and this relation to a subject. These perspectives—for Deleuze—are where undifferentiated opsigns and sonsigns are differentiated through capture in the orbit of one of the eleven movement-images and appear as degrees of emergence. Integrating Bergsonian terminology, gaseous genesis passes through a liquid transition toward solid composition.[93] Accordingly, there will be thirty-three signs, three for each image, giving us eleven images, which organize as narration and produce narrative.[94]

Stray Dog begins with *perception-images*: the degree zero of the film. From an infinity of images a central image, Murakami, is emergent. "Your pistol has been stolen?" asks a man sat at a desk, the camera panning right while tracking back in a fluid movement from this medium-shot to a static wide-shot.[95] Now revealed in the background, desks arc the room all with detectives looking on; in the foreground, dominating the frame, stands Murakami. "How many rounds were in it?" asks Chief Abe, a cutaway determining this is a police station; "All seven, sir," replies the forlorn detective.[96] From the vastness of images of a *gaseous perception* we pass through *liquid perception* as the formation of an ensemble to *solid perception*. Murakami is established at the center, becoming the image around which all other images will circulate, and from which all other images emerge.

We thus pass immediately into *affection-images*. The devastated cityscape is not only a background but an *any-space-whatever*, a genesis from which characters arise embodying the affects of post-war Tokyo. Kurosawa immediately gives us bus traveling through these streets, overcrowded and bursting with bodies, a *dividual* mass framing the central character as an *icon*. We get a close-up of Murakami's face covered in sweat, exhausted after his shift, distracted by the intensity of the heat, cramped among his fellow passengers, all drenched in perspiration. Murakami will have his gun stolen and will give chase through an any-space-whatever before his prey escapes. It is thus because of this tortuous journey that the action is initiated.

With *Stray Dog*, the domain of action will come to overwhelm the sensory-motor narration of the movement-image. In the first place, the *impulse-*

image describes how the forces of the universe are grounded in spontaneous acts. This is the world of Yusa, his cramped hovel "no place for people," an expression of "bad environments," a kennel for a "stray dog," this "mad dog."[97] Deleuze aligns such a universe with naturalism, an *originary world* producing animalistic drives stored up in *fetishes* and let loose as *symptoms*. Fetishes are objects that retain the forces of the primal universe, such as Yusa's scrawled confession of his torturing of a cat, the act itself a symptom. The fetish par excellence, however, is the gun. In Yusa's hands the pistol becomes a fetish that grounds all the desperation, misery, and horror of post-war Japan with each bullet fired. The impulse-image, accordingly, is how action-images designate Yusa's world and diagnose his symptoms as symptoms of the world.

In the second place, the investigation unfolds through the *small form action-image*. Murakami follows clues, each an action unveiling more of the social reality of contemporary Tokyo. The detective begins by attempting to identify the man he chased from the crowded bus, only to discover the actual pickpocket was a woman. Women—in this way—are revealed as the face of Tokyo criminality, a screen behind which men hide: after the pickpocket we meet the female gun dealer then the young dancer. Each of these women, in turn, reveals a way forward: the pickpocket to the black market; the gun dealer to the yakuza boss; and the dancer to her lover, Yusa. The small form creates ellipses, a series images of *lack* which disclose answers. However, such ellipses can remain *equivocal*, or map a *vector*. Kurosawa beautifully layers all three of these possibilities in the final reel of the film. Murakami and Sato split up following different lines of the investigation, creating a vectoral space, a complex, ambiguous world. Within this world, Murakami's path is one of equivocity by way of an encounter with the traumas of Yusa's girlfriend; while Sato's path is a series of resolutions leading to the killer's hideout.

"This is Realism" proclaims Deleuze of the *large form action-image*, the final avatar of pure action.[98] Here the forces of the *milieu* determine the behavior of characters, and are extracted as two oppositional lines which will clash and modify the situation. These lines of force are embodied through the *binomial*, or duel: in *Stray Dog* the ultimate conflict between Murakami and Yusa. But there are duels everywhere, such forces being expositional. So, the ongoing conflicts of the rookie Murakami and the more experienced Sato; or the collaboration between the two in opposition to the series of criminals. Furthermore, these forces can also *imprint* upon a single character, giving a "much more complex behaviourism" which takes into account "internal factors."[99] Here—once again—we encounter the gun, now from the perspective of Murakami. The theft of the pistol is internalized, the forces constituting the personal struggles the character must negotiate: setbacks, mistakes, unforeseen consequences, such as the effect on Murakami of Sato being shot by Yusa.

Mental-images arise with figures of reflection, the first of which is the *attraction-image*: cinematic tropes. Such tropes coalesce as *theatrical figures* (allegories, allusions) and *plastic figures* (metaphors, synecdoches). Kurosawa creates a wonderful plastic figure with the long scene at the baseball stadium—a metaphor for the investigation. The game expresses all the tension and impatience which Murakami feels, while for Sato it expresses strategy and even enjoyment. The lost child episode within this sequence, on the other hand, gives us as a theatrical figure. Sato stages a ruse to capture the gang boss, an allusion to one of Kurosawa's touchstones no doubt, Shakespeare, where Hamlet uses players to catch the king. In this way, the stadium sees these figures circulate as a mise-en-abyme: figure within figure, figure encompassed by and encompassing figure, a trope reflecting upon the genre of the film.

Such reflection is captured by the second figure, *inversion-images*, which critique the two forms of the action-image each through the other. The genetic sign is the *quotidian*. *Stray Dog* can be seen as a typical noir: a hollow man, two buddy cops, an irascible chief, a moll or two, a femme fatale, a series of henchmen, and a final nemesis. All the excesses of a narration of investigation and duels are the familiar givens of the genre—as if large and small forms produce a wave cancellation. However, such conventions can be accentuated for far more compelling critiques. The figure of the *sublime* explores the large form from the perspective of the small, heightening the necessities of action revealing "a crazy enterprise."[100] We have here a third aspect of the stolen gun, the viewpoint reflected upon by the senior officers of the police department. Murakami is obsessed, possessed; they just want him to do his job. For Kurosawa, this figure allows him to critique the pathology of Japanese obligation and duty harnessed during the Pacific War. Correspondingly, action can be *enfeebled* through "weaklings and idiots."[101] Take Sei, a comedic preening "Prince Charming," a "ladies" man who cons wealthy older women.[102] Sei reflects the pathetic image to which Yusa aspires, undermining the conventional grand motivations of a noir nemesis, and critiquing the violence as meaningless.

The third and final figure of reflection is the *discourse-image*, which has its genesis at the *limit of action-images* where nothing is ultimately resolved (through the large form) or revealed (through the small form). *Stray Dog* ends with a coda. Murakami arm in sling is visiting Sato, who has been hospitalized and is bedbound. Sato knows the rookie has been humiliated and still feels guilty about everything that has happened. But more than that, he feels something far deeper is troubling Murakami. "You'll forget as time passes," Sato keeps telling Murakami, "sympathy fades"—there is no triumph at the end of *Stray Dog*, in the criminal being brought to justice—"Look out of the window," Sato tries again, "Many bad things will happen beneath those roofs. Many good people will be hurt by men like Yusa."[103] Kurosawa takes us to the very limit of the action-image in the coda, developing a trajectory that began with the *limit of the small form* before passing through the *limit of the large form*. The limit of the small form is where actions no longer reveal a determined situation, but allow "a reality" to surge forth which is "disorientated, disconnected."[104] This limit structures the early third of the film, the various stymyings of Murakami's investigation concluding with the black market sequence. And it is this time-image that haunts the rest of the movie, actualized through the limit of the large form, when the character finds it "necessary to absorb a question in order to produce an action which would truly be a considered response."[105] When the two detectives talk with the sister, they discover everything began when Yusa had his knapsack stolen after the war. For Murakami this moment is ungrounding and pivotal, and mirrors his own experience. "In a way," he soon admits to Sato, "I'm sorry for Yusa."[106] The limit of the large form explores the "*a question* which is hidden in the situation."[107] Murakami's fate is bound up in Kurosawa's question: the dice throw of the difference and repetition—the synthesis—of Murakami and Yusa.

Attraction-images, inversion-images, and discourse-images are nascent mental-images, reflecting upon action-image narration. Mental-images proper ascend when images of thought appear for themselves. We begin with *dream-images*, conjured as *rich dreams* where the real is differentiated from the dream through "dissolves, super-impositions, deframings, complex camera movements, special effects."[108] The black market sequence uses many of these manipulations, yet would we want to call it a dream-image rather than a time-image? "It took the modern cinema to re-read the whole of cinema as already made up of aberrant movements and false continuity shots," writes Deleuze. The time-image "is the phantom which has always haunted the cinema, but it took modern cinema to give a body to this phantom."[109] In other words, while the black market sequence is a block of duration/movement, it is but a sequence in a wider block of movement/duration. Movement-images will corral, surround, and subsume this time-image within the sensory-motor trajectory. Accordingly, the black market sequence within the movement-image trajectory is a nightmare that begins as a rich dream, dissipates as a *restrained dream* where dream-world coalesces with real-world, and then haunts the rest of the film as a *movement of world* where the real and the nightmare are indistinguishable once Murakami discovers the origin of Yusa's criminality.

The second mental-image proper is the *recollection-image*, the flashback, memory actualized onscreen. Kurosawa utilizes the flashback at the very beginning of the film to frame Murakami's experience on the crowded bus. The flashback—according to Deleuze—gives us destiny, an event from the past brought into the present to propel the narration forward. Its varieties—or signs—are those of *strong destiny* which concerns action, *weak destiny* which captures more amorphous affects, and *forking paths* where memory complexifies thought. The flashback sequence in *Stray Dog* seems to layer all these signs: the stolen gun is not only the spur-to-action narration, but its loss is the genesis of the detective's shame and humiliation. Kurosawa goes further still, however, overlaying the visual images with a non-diegetic voice-over, transforming the film in to a kind of fable, a cultural, collective memory, a situation from which Kurosawa will go on to extract the question. This appears in visual form at the end of the sequence as Murakami stands alone at a crossroads.

Finally, we reach the *relation-image*, where the mental-image "finds its most adequate representation."[110] Relation-images render logical and symbolic thought onscreen. Logical progression proceeds through *marks*, a habitual or "a customary series."[111] Kurosawa gives us a magnificent series in relation to the gun—its fourth and final function—the seven rounds. The bullets identify the weapon as Murakami's Colt, ratchet up the tension of Yusa's crimes—"Once isn't a habit, twice is"—but most of all provide the beats of the film, a countdown toward the finale.[112] The three shots Yusa fires at the detective in the forest are thus the completion of these marks, or rather, the conclusion comes when the mechanism clicks uselessly upon itself, a *demark*, the derailing of the sequence which rises to significance for itself rendering the weapon and Yusa impotent. The relation-image, however, can also give us a *symbol*, the "abstract relation."[113] Kurosawa begins the film with this genetic sign. The opening credits run over a long-take of a dog panting in the summer heat. This image has a primacy effect: Yusa as stray dog becoming mad dog; Murakami as stray dog that has found a home; and together, at the apogee of the finale, the detective and the fugitive lying side by side among wild flowers, exhausted, fighting for breath in the summer heat.

Kurosawa is a virtuoso of movement-images in *Stray Dog*. Their constitution, transitions, and compositions, their logic and flow, their reciprocity, encircling, and layering.

Coda: The Domination of a Sign

"A film is never made up of a single kind of image," writes Deleuze.[114] Every film is composed of many movement-images and time-images, and may even be composed of all movement-images and all time-images—as with *Stray Dog*. Accordingly, it "is not a matter of saying that the modern cinema of the time-image is 'more valuable' than the classical cinema of the movement-image."[115] Such a saying is merely an echo of "the knowing laughter of the cinephiles."[116] Neither the time-image nor the movement-image is "more important than the other," neither "more beautiful," neither "more profound."[117] Rather, the cineosis explicates how movement-images disperse as time-images and time-images cohere as movement-images. Every film is the dance of movement and time. Hence, the cineosis "is essentially a symptomology, and signs are what you class in order to extract a concept, not as abstract essence, but as event," "it's like a vocabulary or dictionary. It's not what is most essential, but it is a necessary first step."[118] In this way, for Deleuze, a film "always has one type of image which is dominant," "a point of view on the whole film," "a 'reading' of the whole film."[119] A film is always dominated by one sign, a sign around which all other signs swarm, the encircling forces allowing that sign to ascend, but more importantly, permeating that sign and so expressing the idea. And as all films of a filmmaker are one image as an assemblage of images within an assemblage of images, so we can say that one sign comes to dominate the work of that filmmaker. Such is Deleuze's film-philosophy: "Everything has a story. Philosophy also tells stories. Stories with concepts. Cinema tells stories with blocks of movement / duration."[120]

Kurosawa—for Deleuze—is a filmmaker of the limit of the large form action-image. Kurosawa tells stories that explore questions.[121] In *Stray Dog* this is the question of the dice throw of the repetitions and differences of Murakami and Yusa. This question is given "intensity" through the variance of forces which organize the slow ascension of the sign. Kurosawa's "profound originality," writes Deleuze, means he must "tear from the situation the question it contains, discover the givens of the secret question."[122] This is why many of Kurosawa's films have a long exposition before a brutal concluding action, why the central character must discover and explore all the coordinates of the question before being allowed to act, and why there is an analysis of the opposition of lower depths and utopian heights.[123] And perhaps this is why Kurosawa prefers not to talk about the idea expressed in each of his films—the secret question must be a discovery in the story. Anyway, in the *Cinema* books, it is with the limit of the large form action-image and with *Stray Dog* where Deleuze's exploration of the films of Kurosawa will begin . . .

Notes

1   For Matthew J. Barnard. Too late? Thanks go to Robert Lapsley for posing the question all those years ago provoking an off-the-cuff response that has haunted me since, and to Murray Littlejohn and Richard Kearney for the opportunity to see if it had legs.

    Gilles Deleuze, "What is the Creative Act?" in *Two Regimes of Madness: Texts and Interview 1975–1995*, ed. David Lapoujade; trans. Ames Hodges and Mike Taormina (New York/Los Angeles: Semiotext(e), 2006), 312–24, 312.

2   Deleuze, "What is the Creative Act?," 314–5.

3   Gilles Deleuze, "Cinema-I, Premiere," in *Two Regimes of Madness: Texts and Interview 1975–1995*, ed. David Lapoujade; trans. Ames Hodges and Mike Taormina (New York/Los Angeles: Semiotext(e), 2006), 210–12, 210.

4   Gilles Deleuze and Félix Guattari, *What Is Philosophy?* trans. G. Burchell and H. Tomlinson (London/Brooklyn: Verso, 2009), 170, 166.

5   Deleuze, "Cinema-I, Premiere," 210.

6   Kurosawa Akira, *Something Like an Autobiography*, trans. Audie E. Bock (Vintage: New York 1983), 172–3.

7 Deleuze, "What is the Creative Act?," 316.

8 Gilles Deleuze, "Portrait of the Philosopher as a Moviegoer," in *Two Regimes of Madness: Texts and Interview 1975–1995*, ed. David Lapoujade; trans. Ames Hodges and Mike Taormina (New York/Los Angeles: Semiotext(e), 2006), 213–21, 213.

9 Gilles Deleuze, "The Brain is the Screen," in *Two Regimes of Madness: Texts and Interview 1975–1995*, ed. David Lapoujade, trans. Ames Hodges and Mike Taormina (New York/Los Angeles: Semiotext(e), 2006), 282–91, 283.

10 Deleuze, "What is the Creative Act?," 316.

11 Gilles Deleuze, *Cinema 2: The Time Image*, trans. H. Tomlinson and R. Galeta (Minneapolis, MN: University of Minnesota Press, 2001), 280. Hereafter *C2*.

12 Gilles Deleuze, *Bergsonism*, trans. H. Tomlinson and B. Habberjam (New York: Zone Books, 2002), 8.

13 *C2*, 280.

14 Gilles Deleuze, *Cinema 1: The Movement-Image*, trans. H. Tomlinson and B. Habberjam (London: Athlone Press, 2002), 61. Hereafter *C1*.

15 Deleuze, "What is the Creative Act?," 314–15.

16 *C2*, 271.

17 *C1*, 24.

18 *C1*, 25.

19 *C1*, 3.

20 Georges Méliès, "Cinematographic Views," in *French Film Theory and Criticism—A History / Anthology: 1907–1939*, ed. Richard Abel (Princeton, NJ: Princeton University Press, 1988), 35–47, 36;38.

21 Ricciotto Canudo, "The Birth of the Sixth Art," in *French Film Theory and Criticism—A History / Anthology: 1907-1939*, ed. Richard Abel (Princeton, NJ: Princeton University Press, 1988), 58–65, 58, 64.

22 *C1*, 3.

23 *C2*, 277.

24 *C2*, 43.

25 *C2*, 241; *C1*, 25.

26 *C1*, 25.

27 *C1*, 206.

28 *C2*, xi.

29 *C1*, 211.

30 *C2*, xi.

31 *C1*:206; *C2*:272;215.

32 *C2*, 220;19.

33 See David Deamer, *Deleuze, Japanese Cinema, and the Atom Bomb: The Spectre of Impossibility* (New York: Bloomsbury, 2014), 7–13.

34 *C2*, 4.

35 *C2*, 3.

36 Nirvana, "You Know You're Right," (*You Know You're Right* single: song written by Kurt Cobain; first released October 2, 2002: DGC Records).

37 Friedrich Nietzsche, *Beyond Good and Evil: Prelude to a Philosophy of the Future*, ed. Rolf-Peter Horstmann and Judith Norman; trans. Judith Norman (Cambridge: Cambridge University Press, 2010), §146.

38 *C1*, xiv.

39 Cineosis = cinematic semiosis: this term was created to foreground the taxonomic aspect of Deleuze's film-philosophy. See David Deamer, "A Deleuzian Cineosis: Cinematic Semiosis and Syntheses of Time," in *Deleuze Studies*, vol. 5.3 (Edinburgh: Edinburgh University Press, 2011), 358–82.

40 Louis-Georges Schwartz, "'Henri Bergson Talks to Us About Cinema' by Michel Georges-Michel from *Le Journal*, February 20, 1914," trans. Louis-Georges Schwartz, *Cinema Journal* 50, no. 3 (2011): 79–82, 81. Paul Douglass, "Bergson and Cinema: Friends or Foes?" in *The New Bergson*, ed. John Mullarkey (Manchester/New York: Manchester University Press, 1999), 218.

41 Henri Bergson, *Creative Evolution*, trans. A. Mitchell (London: Macmillan, 1911), 323, 287. Hereafter Bergson, *CE*.

42 Bergson, *CE*, 324.

43 Bergson, *CE*, 355.

44 *C1*, 7.

45 For a more detailed exploration of Bergson and the beginnings of film-philosophy, see David Deamer, "'Living Pictures': Bergson, Cinema, and Film-Philosophy," in *The Bergsonian Mind*, ed. Mark Sinclair and Yaron Wolf (Abingdon and New York: Routledge, 2022), 461–79.

46 *C1*, 3.

47 *C1*, 11.

48 Henri Bergson, *Matter and Memory*, trans. N. M. Paul and W. S. Palmer (London: George Allen and Unwin, 1911), 1. Hereafter Bergson, *MM*.

49 Bergson, *MM*, 28.

50 *C1*, 198.

51 *Stray Dog* (directed by Kurosawa Akira; from a story by Kurosawa; screenplay Kikushima Ryûzô and Kurosawa: Film Art Association, Shintoho Film Distribution Committee, Toho Company: Japan, 1949).

52 *Stray Dog*, Kurosawa.

53 *C2*, 2.

54 *C2*, 264.

55 *C2*, 41.

56 *C2*, 23.

57 *C2*, 271.

58 Gilles Deleuze, *Difference and Repetition*, trans. P. Patton (London and New York: Continuum, 2004), xiii. Hereafter *DR*. For a more detailed exegesis of the correlations between *DR* and time-images, as well as an overview of other expositions, see David Deamer, *Deleuze's Cinema Books: Three Introductions to the Taxonomy of Images* (Edinburgh: Edinburgh University Press, 2016), 41–69.

59 *DR*, 273; 289.

60 *DR*, 365.

61 *C2*, 127.

62 *C2*, 276; 189.

63 *C1*, 205–15.

64 *C2*, 41.

65 Donald Richie, *The Films of Akira Kurosawa* (Third Edition Expanded and Updated with the new epilogue), additional material by Joan Mellen (Berkeley, Los Angeles, London: University of California Press, 1998), 63.

66 Mitsuhiro Yoshimoto, *Kurosawa: Film Studies and Japanese Cinema* (Duke University Press, 2000), 160.

67 *C2*, 70.

68 *C2*, 71.

69 Yoshimoto, *Kurosawa*, 161–2.

70 *C2*, 99; 105.

71 *C2*, 126.

72 *C2*, 147.

73 *C2*, 215.

74 *C2*, 191; 201.

75 *C2*, 205.

76 *C2*, 211.

77 *C2*, 279.

78 *C2*, 24.

79 Marius B. Jansen, *The Making of Modern Japan* (Cambridge, MA: The Belknap Press of Harvard University Press, 2002), 669.

80 Kurosawa, *Something Like an Autobiography*, 175.

81 Jansen, *The Making of Modern Japan*, 660.

82 Kurosawa, *Something Like an Autobiography*, 145.

83 Jansen, *The Making of Modern Japan*, 660.

84 Kurosawa, *Something Like an Autobiography*, 176.

85 *C2*, 209.

86 *DR*, 109.

87 *DR*, 94.

88 *C1*, 68.

89 *C2*, 30.

90 Charles Sanders Peirce, *Collected Papers of Charles Sanders Peirce: Volume V & VI*, ed. C. Hartshorne and P. Weiss (Cambridge, MA: The Belknap Press of Harvard University Press, 1974), §66.

91 *C2*, 31–2.

92 *C2*, 32.

93 Bergson, *MM*, 263.

94 Deleuze gives two summaries, both partial, of the movement-image taxonomy (*C1*:217–18; *C2*:30–3). The full set here comes from across both the *Cinema* books. For a more detailed exegesis, see Deamer, *Three Introductions*, 16–40.

95 *Stray Dog*, Kurosawa.

96 *Stray Dog*, Kurosawa.

97 *Stray Dog*, Kurosawa.

98 *C1*, 141.

99 *C1*, 158.

100 *C1*, 184.

101 *C1*, 185.

102 *Stray Dog*, Kurosawa.

103 *Stray Dog*, Kurosawa.

104 *C1*, 195.

105 *C1*, 190.

106 *Stray Dog*, Kurosawa.

107 *C1*, 189.

108 *C2*, 58.

109 *C2*, 41.

110 *C1*, 197.

111 *C1*, 203.

112 *Stray Dog*, Kurosawa.

113 *C1*, 204.

114 *C1*, 70.

115 *C1*, xiv.

116 Deleuze, "Portrait of the Philosopher as a Moviegoer," 216.

117 *C2*, 270.

118 Deleuze, "The Brain is the Screen," 286, 285.

119 *C1*, 70.

120 Deleuze, "What is the Creative Act?" 314.

121 *C1*, 188–6; but also *C2*, 75; 128; 176; 201; see also Deamer, *Deleuze, Japanese Cinema, and the Atom Bomb*, 171–216.

122 *C1*, 189.

123 *C1*, 188.

9

"The Active Eye" (Revisited)

Toward a Phenomenology of Cinematic Movement

Vivian Sobchack

Introduction

In "The Film and the New Psychology," Merleau-Ponty asserts the strong affinity between phenomenology and the cinema.[1] Indeed, for him, cinema is perhaps the phenomenological art *par excellence*, given that its "technical methods" correspond to an "existential" and phenomenological "mode of thought."[2] Moreover, while phenomenological philosophy must use language "to make us see the bond between subject and world, between subject and others," the cinema uses the camera and projector to make this bond sensually visible.[3] Thus Merleau-Ponty writes: "The movies are peculiarly suited to make manifest the union of mind and body, mind and world, and the expression of one in the other."[4] Indeed, using technical methods of perception and expression that, to some degree, correspond to our own in structure and function, the movies not only enabled us to sensually perceive this union of mind, body, world, and others but they also dramatized this union's inherent and reversible dynamism.

Along with the *visible* dramas of this dynamic commingling of body, world, and others in motion on screen, what was radically new about the cinema were its *visual* dramas. Unlike works of theater, painting, or photography, the movies made visible for the very first time *visual perception in expressive action*—that is, prospectively moving in, and responding to, an objectively visible world it shared with things and others. Moreover, the unprecedented visibility of visual perception in meaningful motion implicated an intentional, situated, and material *seeing subject* of some sensually intelligible kind that, however anonymous and invisible onscreen, was not reducible to either its human filmmakers or the camera as mechanical apparatus. In sum, once only available to us as the "introceptive" or private visual activity that each of us experiences directly only through our own eyes, with the advent of cinema, this introceptive movement of vision became intersubjectively extroverted for all to see. Thus, as Merleau-Ponty writes (quoting Goethe), "What is inside is also outside."[5]

In what follows, my project is to elaborate Merleau-Ponty's discussion of cinema in his 1945 essay by expanding, yet also narrowing, his focus to the cinematic moving image *experienced as such*. As Arthur Danto writes: "With the movies, we do not just see *that* they move, we see them *moving*: and this is because the pictures themselves move."[6] Thus, I explore the dynamic union of mind, body, and world in the cinema through the fundamental relationship between the off-screen "technical methods" of *camera movement* and their phenomenological effects and as the *moving image* projected and perceived onscreen. In this regard, I draw not only upon Merleau-Ponty's phenomenological descriptions of perception and its expression in our embodied experience of vision and in the cinema, but also from my own phenomenological exploration of cinematic movement. Indeed, as my title suggests, what follows is a "revisiting" of an earlier essay, one which has been written over itself—and time—in three differently-inflected versions before this present one.

The first version, "Toward Inhabited Space: The Semiotic Structure of Camera Movement in the Cinema," was published in 1982, at the height of American film studies' embrace of structuralism, semiotics, and Lacanian psychoanalysis—to me, a theoretically oppressive triumvirate.[7] "The Active Eye: A Phenomenology of Cinematic Vision," the essay referred to in my title, was the second version.[8] Published in 1990, when many film scholars had become disenchanted with the negativity of theoretical paradigms that insisted cinephilia of any kind was both intellectually and politically disingenuous, it introduced two phenomenological formulations central to my then-forthcoming *The Address of the Eye: A Phenomenology of Film Experience*.[9] Further elaborated here, one was my description of the cinematic moving image as a "viewing view/viewed view," its shifting horizons and perspectival grasp of what was to see moving onscreen in a materially-grounded and finite way that was neither "transcendental" nor conflated with the spectator's vision (as some contemporary film theorists had influentially claimed).[10] The other formulation was what I called the "film's body." This was the material, yet transcendent, "other side" of the viewing view/viewed view that, off-screen and unseen, existentially enabled and configured the logical, psychological, and literal "coherence" of the unfolding perceptual field visible onscreen. Although dependent upon them, in the film experience, both the viewing view/viewed view and the film's body were not phenomenologically experienced as reducible to either the filmmaker or the camera and other components of the cinematic apparatus (unless specifically, and secondarily, so marked). Many years later, in 2014, the third version of my essay emerged as the first keynote on cinema ever presented to the Merleau-Ponty Circle.[11] Given the context, "The Film and the New Psychology" became my entry point into a discussion of cinematic movement that provoked the further thought about its *gestalt* structure addressed below.

Whatever their inflections, all versions of this essay owe much to Merleau-Ponty, and take up his grounding "existential" premise that "intentional consciousness" (whether pre-reflectively operative or reflectively deliberative) is manifest only as it is *embodied* and *in movement*—that is, actively perceiving, expressively responding to, and inhabiting a "given" lifeworld into which it has been existentially "thrown."[12] As a sensing and sentient but also material "lived body," our consciousness is not "transcendental," static, or ever in full possession of either itself or its world. Indeed, its intentional and physical movement is self-displacing and transformative—a "becoming," whose permutations cannot be completely disclosed to reflection or reduced to a phenomenological "essence." They can be provisionally "thematized" however—as, in relation to the moving film image, they shall be here.

Why Camera Movement?

The lengthy first part of "The Film and the New Psychology" is focused on the *gestalt* structure of existential perception. From the first, perception (whether human or cinematic) configures worldly stimuli into coherent "forms" that make sense both physically and cognitively. As Merleau-Ponty suggests, we "perceive in a total way with [our] whole being."[13] The given world thus "organizes itself in front of [us] as a unified perceptual field" of which we are an integral and perceptually transformative part, this is particularly evident in the philosopher's discussion of the perception of movement.[14] The essay's next, and much shorter, section is an explicit application of perception's *gestalt* structure to the correspondent *gestalt* perception of film editing. Indeed, "montage," the editorial connection *between* discrete moving images dramatizes perception's constitution of a "temporal *gestalt*"—a unified and meaningful form constituted from its separate parts but perceived and experienced as transcendent of them.[15]

But what of moving images as such? Although, in his conclusion, Merleau-Ponty refers to the "bond" that exists between consciousness, embodied movement, and space, he does not explicitly recognize that the moving image is that bond's most fundamental expression—and it, too, has a *gestalt* structure both off-screen and on.[16] Constituted off-screen by the "technical methods" of the active camera and passive projector, static photographic images are constituted onscreen as the "spatial *gestalt*" of visibly moving images. In its turn, the onscreen movement of these moving images reconfigures two-dimensional space into a "place" or "world" given depth and volume by the movement perceived in them. Without this fundamental bonding of movement and space both off-screen and on, there would be no cinema—and, secondarily, no montage. Indeed, the earliest films were perceived as such before editing became the cinema's dominant "technical method," and more recent films have also demonstrated the cinema's existence independent of editorial fragmentation in extremity— and by choice. With the development of digital cameras as well as mounts such as the Steadicam, the remote-controlled Louma crane, and now flying "drones" affixed with very small GoPro cameras, we have seen an increase not only in films with long continuous passages of movement but also in films that are one single "take," most acclaimed among them *Russian Ark/Russkij Kovcheg* (2002, Alexandr Sokurov) and the more recent *Fish & Cat/Mahi va gorbeh* (2013, Shahram Mokri).[17]

Historically, however, Merleau-Ponty's focus on editing and his lack of attention to the *gestalt* implications of the movement of the moving image as such is hardly singular.[18] In this regard, film scholar Tom Gunning has suggested that film studies has long paid more attention to editing than to camera movement for two basic reasons: first, its significance to the development—and primacy—of cinematic narrative; and second, its logical affinity with the discipline's primarily analytic orientation and modes of description.[19] Thus, as Gunning suggests, analysis of camera movement has been generally limited to aspects of narrative such as "point of view, revelation or emphasis of narratively salient elements, or following mobile characters."[20] Certainly, there are exceptions, perhaps the most notable Christian Metz's "On the Impression of Reality in the Cinema," which attributes the cinema's basic phenomenological "realism" (whatever a film's subject matter) to movement's presentational (rather than representational) presence to perception. He writes: "Because movement is never material but is always *visual*, to reproduce its appearance is to duplicate its reality. [. . .] In the cinema, the impression of reality is also the reality of the impression, the real presence of movement."[21] For the most part, however, work that correlates specific off-screen "technical methods" of camera movement with their phenomenological effects as onscreen "modes of being" that have a perceptual and expressive integrity of their own are few and far between.

Although the "technical methods" of editing and camera movement both achieve synthetic effects onscreen, these syntheses differ. Insofar as the temporal *gestalt* of editorially-mediated moving images configures and marks them through perceptible cuts, dissolves, and the like as having specific logical or psychological meaning only in perceived "spatial relation" to each other, its movement emerges as *reflective*. In contrast, albeit also often in cooperation, the perceived immediacy and continuity of camera movement is synthesized in—and as—the spatial *gestalt* of the onscreen image itself moving in time. Whether imminent or realized, this movement emerges as *pre-reflective*: a present and continuous configuration and reconfiguration of movement, space, and time perceived not in "relation" to each other but *as a unity* with depth, shape, and meaning that, however nascent, is, as Merleau-Ponty puts it, "scattered in the sensible world."[22] In sum, cinema's radical originality emerged in both history and perception from movement—not only the *visible* movement *in* its images but also the *visual* movement *of* its images. Thus, from the first, its pictures of movement were always also configured as an inherently open (and soon visibly shifting) perceptual field that made of them moving pictures.

The sections that follow elaborate this *gestalt* structure through the correspondence between moving images as perceived and expressed onscreen and four fundamental forms of camera movement that bring them into visible and visual being. Produced by the motion picture camera (or, these days, a mimetic digital equivalent, whether physical or virtual),[23] from the first, all four are inherent to the medium and "happen" in space and time not only *in* the image but also, and more significantly, *as* the image. All are also perceived in an "immediacy" expressed "in the moment," and, indeed, constitute the grounding premises of every film we see. Let me briefly introduce these movements as well as the four correspondent phenomenological "themes" that emerge from their respective onscreen effects. For clarity, my overall direction will be from movement *as* the image to movement *in* the image to movement *of* the image. However this might suggest a "progression," all four modes of movement are systemically relational rather than systematically hierarchical, and so are usually co-present and co-operative, each with the others. Thus, as shall become apparent in the "separate" sections to follow, it is impossible to focus on one without relating it to the others.

The *first* movement of the camera is so fundamental that it is often not regarded as movement at all, particularly when neither the moving image itself nor the things in it visibly displace themselves in screen space. Functioning as the "zero-degree" of cinematic perception and expression, this is the movement that commutes static photographic images into onscreen moving images through camera and projector. In the film experience, however, this technical method of achieving movement is phenomenologically transformed onscreen into the dynamic simultaneity and "intertwined" *gestalt* of the visual perception and visible expression that I've earlier referred to as the "viewing view/viewed view." This description of the moving image as such is meant to emphasize the *gestalt*'s two co-present and conjoined elements, neither of which precedes or antecedes the other onscreen, even as, in perception, each can reversibly become a figure or ground for the other. Moreover, in its ongoing, directed, and perspectival visual activity of seeing "something" that takes on meaning by being chosen to be seen that particular way, the viewing view/viewed view also appears, however latently, as *intentional*, and, in its visual activity, implicates an unseen but "embodied subject" of some kind. Thus, my elaboration of the grounding functions of the "film's body." As Merleau-Ponty writes, "The simplest perception of movement presupposes a subject who is situated spatially and initiated into the world."[24] The phenomenological theme that emerges from this foundational form of cinematic movement is that, from the first and without a thought, it allows us "to understand motility as basic intentionality," and, reversibly, intentionality as basic motility.[25]

The *second* form of cinematic movement is the optical movement of the camera. It is more reflexive than the first, insofar as its visual activity is more markedly visible and, to varying degree, directs us to the perceiving, expressive, and unseen subject of some kind that is always presently constituting the viewing view/viewed view onscreen. The camera, for example, may optically register an image at different speeds or may soften or blur it. It may, in onscreen effect, "hyperbolize" or "drain" the colors of the world at which it gazes through a variety of film stocks and filters. Or, enabled by a special lens, it and the onscreen viewing view may "zoom in" on a distant object, its visual attention visibly transcending physical space to locate itself in the object without having to physically move. Onscreen, optical *effects* phenomenologically *qualify* the viewing view's visual attention with subjective *affects* and *attitudes* that, visible in the viewed view, transform and transcend the normative spatiotemporality of the physical world it engages. The phenomenological theme suggested by the camera's optical movement is that embodied and intentional vision is not merely physically "grounded" in immanence. That is, whether qualified by affect, imagination, or mindful intelligence, the objective lived body (here the "film's body") is subjective and, however always grounded in a present "here" and "now," is also capable of *transcendence in immanence*.

Both the first and second cinematic movements emerge *as* the moving image, and, in their less dramatic forms, are often perceived either latently or transparently. The *third* emerges *in* the image as the objective movement of animate beings and animated things seen "there" in onscreen space. This is the movement first noticed in both film experience and cinema history. As is normatively the case with our own vision, both camera and spectator are intentionally directed toward the world's objective visibility rather than reflexively toward their own subjective visual activity. Thus, even in film studies, motion *in* the image is commonly, if problematically, called "subject movement"—a transparent "oversight" of its actual status as the "intentional object" of the unseen "seeing subject" presently seeing and making it visibly present to the spectator. The phenomenological theme revealed by this privileged attention to visible movement perceived as objectively "there" rather than visual movement perceived as subjectively "here" is that, from the first, vision (whether on or off-screen) is primarily *world- and other-directed*—even as, on occasion, it may itself become its own object of consciously reflexive awareness.

Such world- and other-directedness gives rise to the *fourth* fundamental form of camera movement. Off-screen, this is the *physical mobility* and displacement of the camera in relation to objects and others. Onscreen, the inherent motility and intentionality of the viewing view become visibly explicit and expressive as the visually mobile "framing" of a viewed view. The camera *qua* embodied subject's vision actively asserts itself in the world it inhabits, moving to change its viewing situation in relation to its contingent interests. Simultaneously, and in excess of the visual field presently visible, the vitality of the given world solicits and provokes the viewing view to visibly responsive and self-displacing movement. Thus, Merleau-Ponty's dynamic "union of mind and body, mind and world, and the expression of one in the other" becomes charged with *intersubjectivity*[26]—and, to be later elaborated, what I have elsewhere termed *interobjectivity*.[27]

This responsive physical motility in a world of others and objects attests not only to the existence of an unseen seeing subject but also—and explicitly—to its own *objective materiality*. Revealed in the changing viewing view, its visual movement appears finitely located, perspectival, and thus *driven* to physical movement by its material limits and existential finitude. Nonetheless, and again like our own vision, both the visual movement (the viewing view) generated by these constraints and the visual field itself (the viewed view) are transcendently opened by—and to—physical movement. Not reducible to the camera as mechanism, this other material and existential side of the viewing view/viewed view is what I've called the "film's body." The phenomenological theme of this fourth cinematic movement is that vision's material *premises* provide the *existential grounds* not only for its "union" with the objective world and others but also for the *maturation* of its *visually perceptive motility* into *visibly expressive mobility*. As mentioned earlier, all four movements fundamental to the moving image as such coexist, cooperate, and can be co-present in the image—and to the spectator. However, dependent upon both the specific film and the habituation and interests of the spectator, all also exist in varying degrees and ratios of latent or manifest appearance and perceptual transparence or opacity.

Motility as Intentionality: The Viewing View/Viewed View

In the 1970s, film scholars associated with what was called "apparatus theory" mounted a major—and politically-driven—critique of the cinema. Their focus was on the negative ideological and illusionary effects of the medium's constitutive "technical methods" as well as the correspondent "modes of thought" that informed its projected narratives.[28] Indeed, in an argument recalling Henri Bergson's on cinema as well as Zeno of Elea's spatiotemporal paradoxes, the movement that constituted "moving pictures" was deemed a *perceptual illusion*.[29] Given that each frame of a film was first recorded and then projected in *arrest*—held fixed for a fraction of a second before lens and light source and separated from other frames by a shutter—cinematic movement was not "real" movement at all. However, from the perspective of both phenomenology and the "new psychology," cinematic movement is not a *perceptual illusion* but a *perceptual reality*. Thus, writing in 1916, psychologist Hugo Münsterberg tells us in *The Photoplay: A Psychological Study*: "The perception of movement is an *independent* experience which cannot be reduced to a simple seeing of a series of different positions" as if it were an unprojected film strip.[30] Merleau-Ponty also critiques this analytic view of motion. Focusing on the perception of movement in his 1953 course, "The Sensible World and the World of Expression," he emphasizes that "once motion is cut off from its perceptual origins, it defies representation and is self-destructive"; indeed, the description of motion as relative to fixed points and coordinates (or separate frames of film) puts it in arrest, and, as he suggests, is "a *retrospective* schema [. . .] of our bodily experience of movement" that cannot account for the lived transitions that constitute being-in-motion.[31]

This is not to deny that the "technical methods" of synchronizing the rates of recording and projection with the physiological conditions of human vision provide the *necessary* conditions for commuting still photographs into the onscreen spatiotemporal *gestalt* perceived as *visible* movement. Nonetheless, these hardly provide the *sufficient* conditions for the cinema's radically original and, indeed, "independent" constitution of this *gestalt* as always also *visual* movement. When we actually view a film, this *gestalt* is perceived not solely, or even primarily, as a *post hoc representation* or simulacrum of movement (an already accomplished viewed view); rather, it is always also, and primarily, perceived as an *ad hoc presentation* of movement (a viewing view that acts in space and time in concert with its world's visibility). Thus neither the seeing nor the seen—the viewing view or the viewed view—is phenomenologically experienced as if one preceded the other. Unless otherwise (and secondarily) marked, much like the structure of our own vision, in the film experience, the viewed view is not perceived as a re-presentation. It is neither a "second" or "substitute" thing existing prior to its presently being seen—nor is it abstracted and separated from its present presence and movement in a world that we also access through our senses. As Merleau-Ponty writes in "Eye and Mind," "This precession of what is upon what one sees and makes seen, of what one sees and makes seen upon what is—this is vision itself."[32] Thus, for mechanism, film, and spectator, the *sufficient* condition for the commutation of a series of photographic stills into the perceptual reality of cinematic movement is this grounding *gestalt*—or synthetic composite—of cinematic vision that, onscreen, is always already the moving image.

From the first, this moving image is inherently charged not only with *motility* but also with *intentionality*, the latter brought to explicit visibility in two complimentary and non-hierarchical manifestations. One is the *coherence* and relative *constancy* of the *spatiotemporal boundaries* that *frame* the viewing view/viewed view, and the other is the *chiasmatic structure* of the visual/visible *gestalt* itself. In concert with a screen, the film's frame does much more than contain and display the viewing view/viewed view. Like our own bodies, because it is inherently mobile, the frame's articulated and finite boundaries *orient* and *organize* the viewing view's perceptual and motor access to—and in—the film's world. Thus, whether pre-reflectively operative or explicitly deliberative, where and how the viewing view settles itself or moves in that world appears intentional, and its vision sensed as a diacritically meaningful *choice*. Moreover, and again like our own bodies, the frame's *spatiotemporal coherence* and relative *constancy* (even when the viewing view/viewed view within its bounds is moving) significantly *synthesizes* the viewing view's sense perception and movement into a particular and unified "place." Indeed, by constituting a unity that accommodates and "goes along with" not only with the viewing view/ viewed view's own displacement in time and space but also with its internal ruptures and the occasional inconstancy of its contraction or expansion, the frame of a given film is always the *same* frame. Both the frame and the viewed view/viewed view within it thus emerge as unique to the film itself, and are not reducible to either the camera as apparatus or the filmmaker who directs it as s/he imaginatively "sees" it.

In its coherence, relative constancy, and syntheses of sense perception, in its providing a concrete and finite "place" for the viewing view, the frame bears a strong relation to some of the phenomenological functions of our own phenomenal—but also existentially lived—bodies. Hence the emergence of what I call the "film's body" to designate the film as materially and functionally embodied—as mentioned earlier, the "other" phenomenal side of the coherent and intentional viewing view onscreen. Constituted by the cooperative functions of the material camera, projector, screen, and their ancillary "appendages," and signaled by the frame, the film's body is certainly not anthropomorphic even as, given the cinematic primacy of narrative, it is most often (but not always) anthropocentric. Nonetheless, and despite its phenomenal dispersal in space and time, its cooperative functions parallel those of our own lived bodies, the latter described by phenomenologist Richard Zaner as the four fundamental ways in which the "perceptive body" engages us in the world. First, it functions as the "zero degree" orientational point from which spatiotemporal coordinates are organized and our world is structured. Second, it is our "organ of perception," encompassing several sensory fields that provide us our various means of access to the world. Third, as a systemic unity, it synthesizes these sensory fields in a coherent "place" on, and in which, our sensations are experienced. Fourth, enabling diacritical motion and expressive gesture, the "perceptive body" functions not only to actualize the projects of intentional consciousness (whether spontaneous or deliberative) but also to signify them.[33]

In this regard, even before it visibly moves, the frame externalizes at least three of these functions: its "zero degree" orientational status, its synthesis of several sensory fields, and its system unity as a coherent and sensate "place." Thus, like our own phenomenal lived bodies, the frame's objective geometry (its "aspect ratio") sets the film and spectator's (and sometimes a character's) non-geometric perceptual boundaries and instantiates their different existential horizons and subjective possibilities—and positioning— in the film's world. For example, about a troubled young man's fraught relationship with his mother, the frame in *Mommy* (2015, Xavier Dolan) is non-normatively narrow and experienced by both spectators and its main character as perceptually constricted. However, at the few times the character is happy, he deliberately pushes against the frame's sides to expand both the viewing view and, as a consequence, his own perceptual horizons. At whatever size, however, the framed viewing view situates itself in the film's world as a unity, synthesizing even its internal differences. *The Grand Budapest Hotel* (2014, Wes Anderson), for example, uses various aspect ratios consonant with those of the narrative's historical periods, but all are coherent as the same frame, whose perceptual field also reveals a character of its own. What the viewing view attends to is often kept at a distance and symmetrically composed in its vision. Not itself moving at these moments, its gaze contains, orders, and aestheticizes its world, thus creating tragicomedy from the human and historical chaos it sees before it. In sum, coordinated with, and as, the unity and coherence of the frame, the viewing view's particular stance in its world is perceived as intentional not merely because it sees "something" but because its vision and position have a certain behavioral integrity particular to it.

The perception of intentionality also emerges from the *chiasmatic structure* of the visual/visible *gestalt* that fills the film's frame and is dynamized by imminent or actual movement. The viewing view refers us to its objective world through its viewed view and the viewed view reverses this world-directedness to refer us to the presence of a presently seeing, if unseen, subject of some kind. Moreover, as discussed earlier, despite their difference—one the seeing and the other the seen—each mutually anticipates and refers to the other in a non-hierarchical temporal relation of "precession" in which neither is cause or effect of the other. As Merleau-Ponty writes of our own vision in "Eye and Mind," this structural *chiasmus* lights "the spark [. . .] between [the] sensing and [the] sensible" so that "a bonding of some sort takes place."[34] In the cinema, this "bonding" is a *composite* rather than *conflation* of the viewing view and viewed view and, as the seeing and the seen do in our own vision, both emerge as separate and yet inseparable.

Moreover, even when the viewing view/viewed view appears visibly motionless, it emerges as active and intentional because it *can* move. However quiescent, it is perceived as visibly marking a *visual choice* to maintain its intentional grasp on what it holds in its sight. Engaged in continuing to *arrest* its gaze, its gaze is thus never at rest. The world at which it gazes is also never still; given the continuous flux of light, shadow, and atmosphere, it never concedes its own motility, even when it, too, is relatively quiescent. The slightest change of light or flutter of a leaf on a tree in the viewed view reciprocates the viewing view's attention by charging it with the potentiality of its own visible movement. Thus, even when relatively motionless, the cinematic moving image is phenomenologically perceived as dynamized and different from a photograph or projected slide, both of which do not provoke anticipation of either visible movement *in* the image and/or visual movement *of* the image. Indeed, the cinema's viewing view/viewed view is also perceived differently from that of a surveillance camera. The cinema's viewing view appears consistently distanced from, and continuously disinterested in, the world at which it gazes, and thus its unchanging stance toward that world seems more mechanical than intentional and tends to refer us back not to a perceiving subject but to the camera as "apparatus." Even if the surveillant viewing view moves, its movement is unvarying in scope and rhythm. Although it is situated and visually intending something, that "something" is its entire visual field in which "no thing" provokes any particular interest. Consistently unselective even in motion, its intentionality seems nearly absent.

This difference between the cinematic and surveillant viewing view/viewed view is one of degree rather than of kind (as with the photograph and slide). Nonetheless, it is a difference that makes a difference—one, indeed, that structures the form, narrative, and disturbing viewing experience of *Caché* (2005, Michael Haneke). The film begins with an extremely lengthy and static "establishing shot" of a Paris side street held far beyond necessary to locate us in time and space. However, what appears as the *film's* first moving image is, in fact, revealed also to be footage from a *surveillance video*. Both shot with high-definition digital cameras, even after film and video are narratively separated, this conflation and confusion of intentional and mechanical vision occurs again at various moments, including the film/video's extremely ambiguous closing surveillant image. As one critic noted in a review aptly titled "Camera Obscure," the overall effect is "creepy." From *Caché's* beginning, he writes, "you are rarely confident about what you're watching, and never sure that watching will be enough"; unlike the cinematic viewing view/viewed view, surveillant seeing "doesn't necessarily entail perception or understanding."[35]

In sum, like our own vision, the spatiotemporal *gestalt* that is the cinematic moving image is not only perceptible, it is also perceptive. As such, it is inherently active and selective and, from the first, charged with movement and intentionality, each, as Merleau-Ponty has pointed out, the expression of the other. Thus, the viewing view's diacritical activity of choosing where to look, of arresting its gaze or moving it, visually and visibly circumscribes in the viewed view not only the perceptual horizons of significance but also an expressive field for intersubjective movement and signification. This is precisely what constitutes the cinema's viewing view/viewed view as the meaningful vision of an intentional "other"—and also why, counter to the argument advanced by the apparatus theorists, we do not ever experience the cinema's moving images as our own, but rather see "according to it, or with it."[36]

Optical Movement: Transcendence in Existence

The second fundamental form of cinematic movement in—and as—the moving image emerges technically through "visual" or "optical" effects. Although there are many kinds of such "effects" accomplished in the camera during filming or added later in a laboratory or now on a computer, here I am particularly interested in those in which the implicit "subject" of the film's viewing view/viewed view becomes explicit through the ways in which its *states of consciousness* and *affective moods* transform its onscreen perception and expression and transcend its existential imminence. That is, the humanly-lived body and the film's body do not only perceive what is objectively "there" in front of its eyes. As lived, both also subjectively feel, imagine, fantasize, dream, remember, think, and express their existence as not only "elsewhere" and "elsewhen" but also as "other" than it presently is in their respective "here" and "now."

Indeed, in "Film and the New Psychology," Merleau-Ponty emphasizes states of consciousness and affect as a "modification" of our relations with the world and others, and writes: "For the movies as for modern psychology[,] dizziness, pleasure, grief, love, and hate are ways of behaving."[37] Nonetheless, these ways of behaving are only related to the *visible behavior* of onscreen characters and not to the *visible visual behavior* of the embodied viewing view/viewed view. Thus, uncharacteristically proscriptive, Merleau-Ponty tells us: "If a movie wants to show us someone who is dizzy, it should not attempt to portray the interior landscape of dizziness [. . .].We will get a much better sense of dizziness if we see it from the outside."[38] Focused on onscreen "someones," the philosopher overlooks their phenomenological mediation through another seeing subject, whose visual grasp of the scene and seen is in *behavioral excess* of these "someones" and, indeed, has an independent, if also invested, relation to them. For example, during a scene in *Easy Rider* (1969, Dennis Hopper), four characters take LSD in a deserted New Orleans cemetery as we watch them from both "outside" and "inside" get high. However, at a certain point, the viewing view/viewed view moves away from its close (and transparent) identification with the characters. Ignoring them, it discloses through its own erratic movements and altered state of consciousness—its seeing and hearing marked by the non-normative graininess of 16mm film stock, hallucinatory lens flares and artifacts, overexposure, anamorphic distortion, and overbearingly rhythmic and collaged sound—that it and the film are also, and independently, "tripping out." As Kevin Fisher notes of the sequence: "What emerges are alternative cinematic ways of being and perceiving in the world not merely for the characters but also (and more globally) for the film's body—this irrespective of and sometimes even against the grain of the characters' [identification] with the drug experience."[39]

Whether attributed to characters or to the viewing view, onscreen optical movement brings to visible expression subjective consciousness as it audio-visually and texturally *qualifies* and *modulates* its world. Accomplished in the camera or added later, its effects co-emerge with the image itself, and visibly mark subjective moods, feelings, attention, and attitudes that simultaneously alter not only the viewing view's normative (or unmarked) mode of vision but also the visible world in its viewed view. Off-screen, the "technical methods" of optical movement entail constitutive choices and changes in such things as film stock, camera lenses and focal length, aperture settings, filters, frame recording rates, and so on. Many of these qualitative choices may be quite subtle in effect and are not explicitly noticed. Nonetheless, their variations and nuances are implicitly sensed and perceived, and when brought to consciousness in their extremity (ever more present in digital cinema), they are seen to dramatically alter what stands in any individual film as normative vision. Most of these active qualifications of the viewing view/viewed view accomplished in the camera have familiar, if impoverished, names such as the "zoom," "slow" or "fast" motion, "reverse motion," and "time lapse," all of which challenge normative anthropomorphic vision but are nonetheless kinetically, psychologically, imaginatively, and even intellectually, comprehensible to it. Each of these informs and/or modifies the viewing view/viewed, their various transformations of perception and the world owing more to subjective consciousness than to the laws of physics. Thus, optical movement makes visible not only vision's subjectivity (and the existence of a subject) but also consciousness's capacity for various forms of *transcendence in immanence*.

Perhaps the most obvious example of how optical movement reveals subjective vision's capacity for transcendence in immanence is the zoom, particularly when the camera itself remains in a fixed spatial position. A movement only of the camera's lens, in effect, the zoom optically advances toward or retreats from the object of its vision. What is visibly inscribed onscreen in this movement is not the *physical* displacement in space of either the viewing subject or viewed object. Rather, what is displaced is the viewing subject's *attention*. Its vision thus *transcends* its own fixed spatial position to bring the intentional object forward or thrust it backward in consciousness rather than in space. Indeed, words like "nearer," "closer," and "farther" seem inappropriate descriptors for the zoom, for its movement of attention does not change the physical spatial relationship between the viewing view and the intentional object in its viewed view. Rather, the viewing view traverses worldly space without materially inhabiting the distance between itself and, as in a forward zoom, the object that compels its attention. That object looms "larger" rather than "nearer" in the viewed view but, since it has not changed position, its worldly situation and relation to its background remain both perspectivally and proportionally static. Moreover, as the viewing view's attention collapses space and transcends distance, the world loses much of the depth that physical movement in space confers on it, and so, in the viewed view, the physical space between the intentional object and its background is not only fixed but also seems flattened. Here we see clearly the "union of mind and world" and the "expression of one in the other." As Merleau-Ponty writes: "Movement and rest distribute themselves in our surroundings [. . .] according to the way we settle ourselves in the world and the position our bodies assume in it [. . .]; the looked-at object in which I anchor myself will always seem fixed"—and, in the zoom, I would add, so will its background.[40]

In this regard, there is a radical difference between the optical movement of a zoom and a tracking shot toward or away from an object. In the zoom, the only movement is of the off-screen camera's lens and the onscreen viewing view's *subjective attention*. In the tracking shot, however, both the entire camera and the viewing view's embodied attention move *physically* through worldly space, neither collapsing nor transcending the substantial distance between intending subject and intentional object. The tracking shot thus implicates the seeing subject as having a *material existence* that inhabits the world objectively, and is subject to its physical laws. This difference between a movement of attention that can transcend physical distance with a look and an embodied movement through physical space is nowhere so marked as in *Vertigo* (1958, Alfred Hitchcock). In a key scene, both a forward zoom and backward tracking shot (a "dolly zoom") are used simultaneously to dramatize the main character's paralyzing fear of heights.[41] The camera lens zooms in as the terrified character looks down into a deep vertical stairwell, and, "borrowing" the viewing view as his own, his literally "transfixed" attention transcends the intervening space to locate itself at the stairwell's bottom. Simultaneously, the entire camera tracks backward in physical space, as the character's immanent body, aware of the fatal fall through space his transfixed attention threatens, rebels and intends itself in the opposite direction. The dizzying conflict between the transcendent and immanent aspects of conscious and material existence seen in the viewing view/viewed view is thus both affectively and physically enacted as "psychosomatic." There are complex confusions of perspective: through the forward zoom—the bottom of the stairwell expands and seems to rise upward—while simultaneously—through the tracking movement backward—the foreground remains constant in size. Thus the viewing view/viewed view reveals mind and body at odds with each other, and its disorientation is dizzying for both character and spectator. However, although both narrative and editing posit this vertiginous perception as isomorphic with the human character's, because its "technical methods" differ materially, if not functionally, from those of the human character, the viewing view/viewed view also retains a certain subjective (and, in this case, disturbing) integrity of its own that not only further dissociates the character in his extremity, but also reflexively directs us to the differently embodied existence of a subjective "other." This reflexivity may well have been why Merleau-Ponty did not appreciate the zoom, pointing, in a 1948 radio broadcast, to its "sensationalism" as among other "tics, mannerisms and devices" that were not "properly cinematic."[42]

In this regard, Merleau-Ponty tends to favor the cinema's *perceptual realism*, and the zoom is the mode of optical movement that most dramatically *transcends* perceptual realism (albeit not *perceptual reality*, in which our attention and focus, if through a different "technical method," similarly "zooms in" on our intentional objects all the time).[43] Indeed, the zoom and other optical qualifications of the moving image are the visible and sensible expression of the film's subjective and embodied "mind's eye." Thus, optical movement entails not only attention, but also affect, imagination and a carnal form of intellection that, in *The Visible and the Invisible*, Merleau-Ponty calls "sensible ideas."[44] As Mauro Carbone writes, these are "ideas" that are "inseparable from their sensible presentation" in images (here, moving images) and "instituted by these very images *as their own depth*."[45] In *Zero for Conduct/Zéro de conduite* (1933, Jean Vigo), the slow motion sequence of young boys having a pillow fight conveys the sensible idea—a space out of time—of a joyous but only temporary rebellion against the boys' repressive boarding school.[46] The "scarlet suffusions over the screen" in *Marnie* (1964, Alfred Hitchcock) emerge not only from the main character as sensible affect but also from the viewing view/viewed view as the sensible idea of trauma.[47] Generated by—and in—their specific situations, both slow motion and flood of color express and deepen their respective sequences with an "ideality" that is "constituted by those images *as their excess*," and makes both carnal and cognitive sense "precisely through [its manifest] appearance."[48]

Over all, optical movement is reflexive, its "technical methods" visibly different enough from our own in effect, if similar in visual function, to attract explicit notice. Hence it directs us, if not to the methods themselves, then to an unseen, anonymous, and intentionally directed subject that is different from ourselves but, nonetheless, engages its world, as we do, both affectively and cognitively. In this regard, the zoom is "sensational," its movement toward or away from its object one of the cinema's most dramatically reflexive modes of making the intentional movement of attention visible onscreen. Indeed, Merleau-Ponty considers paying attention a creative act that transforms "the mental field" and provides "a new way for consciousness to be present to its objects."[49] It does not just "elucidate pre-existing data," but subjectively "bring[s] about a new articulation of them as figures."[50] It also accomplishes a "synthesis of transition"—this most apparent onscreen through the movement of both the optical zoom and physical tracking shot.[51] Unlike the tracking shot, however, the zoom's onscreen synthesis of transition is more transitive than transformative. That is, its mode of attention moves to elucidate (or becomes disinterested in) pre-existing data but it does not newly articulate them since its transformation is only in size, not in perspective (this, perhaps, a better reason than its "sensationalism" for Merleau-Ponty to disparage it). It is thus another mode of optical movement—"rack focus"—that transforms the "mental field" and its relation to "pre-existing data." Entailing a change of lens and focal length, its onscreen effect visibly shifts the viewing view's literally focused attention to certain objects or events in the visual field to relocate its focus elsewhere in the field. In the process, we see intentional consciousness as being "present to its objects" in a "new way," the movement of its attention creating new figure/ground relations and ratios of significance (and signification) that rearticulate the world afresh.

The attention, affect, and ideation figured onscreen by optical movement are thus specific to each film. Indeed, as Merleau-Ponty tells us: "Attention, [. . .], as a general and formal activity, does not exist. There is in each case a certain liberty to be acquired, and a certain mental space to make the most of. There is literally a question of creation."[52] This liberty and mental space have existential limits however, even as these may be expanded in digital and virtual cinema. No matter how attention, affect, imagination, and intelligence transform and renew the world or transcend its physics and logic, they are, if to varying degree, still tethered to it—as well as dependent upon the entwined existential structure and functions of movement and vision. Nonetheless, the immanence and limitations of the lived-body subject (whether film or spectator) are precisely what enable its transcendence and freedom. That is, each of the two unseen viewing subjects in the film experience have a certain liberty and mental space in which to visually inscribe not only a visible narrative but also a moving autobiography.

Movement in the Visible World

Whether inside or outside the cinema, it is the visible world to which vision and movement are primarily, indeed primordially, directed. It is the world's motion that provides the *motive* for our and the cinema's own. Thus movement of animate beings and animated objects *in* the viewed view is the third fundamental form of cinematic movement. Sensed as immediately "given" to vision (even at the cinema), this objective movement and the viewed view in which it appears tend to dominate the viewing view—even as the latter subjectively co-constitutes not only their visibility but also their motion. As Merleau-Ponty writes, "What makes part of the field count as an object in motion, and another as the background is the way in which we establish our relations with them by the act of looking"; in sum, "the relation between the moving object and its background passes through our body."[53] However, since our eyes are "never *in* the perception of an object," this relation is latent.[54] Thus, he adds: "If we can ever speak of movement without an object in motion, it is pre-eminently in the case of our own body."[55] This is also the case of the "film's body," the camera its perceiving "eye." Invisible to itself as the "zero-degree" of the perception of movement, it looks outward at the world's movement, which appears in the viewed view "as an absolute."[56]

However, for the subject of vision, who co-constitutes the motion in the visual field as always relative to its own embodied situation and subjectivity, there are gradations in the perception of this seemingly "absolute" and world-generated movement. Certainly we perceive a difference between the movement of people—subjects like ourselves who run to fulfill their own intentions and contingent projects as we do—and the objective movement of trains that run on predetermined tracks and schedules but have no agenda of their own. Nonetheless, the movements of both resonate as they pass through our bodies, and, as both subjective objects (to ourselves) and objective subjects (to others), we cannot grasp (even as we can think) "absolute" objectivity. Thus, we often confer intentionality on (as well as give names to) the cars whose objective motility is perceived as an extension of our own bodies, and children, playing with outstretched arms at "being" an airplane, take up the plane's movement and perceived intentionality as their own. Indeed, throughout the history of cinema, moving objects have been perceived and viewed as intentional—whether, for example, the jealous and malevolent used car in *Christine* (1983, John Carpenter) or the "endearing" robot trash collector/compactor in *WALL-E* (2008, Andrew Stanton), who early on in the film behaves and moves with an intentionality and subjectivity clearly in excess of its programming.

Like sound, movement resonates in and through our bodies whether it is generated by us or by other subjects and objects. Seen objectively from the "outside," in its relation to others and the world, it is kinetically experienced and mimetically responded to "inside"—this long before the discovery of "mirror neurons." Particularly when we see other people's movements, whether off- or onscreen, we "recognize a certain common structure [. . .] or way of being in the world."[57] They are not simply moving; they are *behaving*: actively "having" their "being" in the world and with it. Hence Merleau-Ponty's primary focus on the cinema's unique capacity to show us the manifest "bond between subject and world, between subject and others."[58] For him, the "inside" of other subjects is given to us in their "outside" in visibly autonomous and contingent behavior. Indeed, the movies are "so gripping," he writes, precisely because "they directly present to us that special way of being in the world, of dealing with things and other people, which we can see in the sign language of gesture and gaze."[59]

In this regard, the movements of lived-body subjects (animals and humans) are perceived as in *intentional excess* of our—and the viewing view's—own co-constitution of them in our own intentional act of looking. That is, even as our vision comprehends the movements of others, their movements are contingent in a way that escapes predetermination and visual control, and what emerges between the seeing subject and the subject seen is an *intersubjective* relation of recognition that calls forth varying degrees of visual and motor coordination and negotiation that create dialogic tension. The cinema makes this coordination, negotiation, and tension visible in the relations between the movement *in* the viewed view and the movement *of* the viewing view. For example, in *Blood Wedding/Bodas de Sangre* (1981, Carlos Saura), a docudrama of a studio rehearsal of Antonio Gades's flamenco ballet, the tension between the moving dancers in the viewed view and the movement of the viewing view is almost palpable, the camera *qua* subject situating itself in close to their bodies and passion, its vision circling and moving not only with but also against them in its own curious and complementary choreography.

Indeed, the intentional and motor excess of lived-body subjects seen in the viewed view can "surprise" the camera *qua* subject, motivating a readjustment of its situation and thus its viewing view. This is particularly apparent in "nature films" focused on animals and the documentary mode called "direct cinema." Except to set up basic conditions for filming, direct cinema neither preplans its motor relations to the people who are the objects of its vision, nor do the filmmakers interact overtly with them other than through the camera's responsive movement which follows their lead. Thus we often see "errors" in visual judgment onscreen in relation to their intentions and movements. The viewing view "mis-takes" where to anchor its vision and may have to move abruptly so as to "catch up" with individuals "doing their own thing" by visibly shifting its focus or changing its physical situation. It is this *ad hoc* response to, and expression of, such intentional excess and contingent behavior that gives direct cinema much of its particular vitality. Vision becomes charged with a certain uncertainty that intensifies both the drama of intersubjectivity between lived-body subjects and the discrete intentionality and existential status of the viewing view/viewed view.

What direct cinema makes obvious is also found, if to a lesser degree, in narrative films. Although the movements of both camera and human actors are spatially as well as narratively plotted, the viewing view meets its match in the lived-body subjects that provoke its gaze, and are capable of surprising it—thus the difficulty of filming children or animals who cannot contain themselves under direction. There are also those "extras" in the background who, told to "act like people" doing "x" or "y," behave in particular ways that direction has merely generalized. Indeed, the many "takes" shot in narrative filmmaking attest to the impossibility of completely suppressing the always contingent movement and relations between intentional subjects. Some "takes" are regarded as "mis-takes," while others reveal something unexpected that surpasses what was planned. No "take" is exactly the same as another, and although the one selected for use in a film is determinate, its *now-fixed* viewing view/viewed view makes presently visible its *then-contingent* moment and motion. Thus what we see onscreen is not its fixity but its active "becoming" before us.

We—and the camera *qua* subject—are also fascinated by the passive and active movement of worldly objects. Transcending their expected and thus transparent "use value," objects onscreen are ambiguous. Their materiality is at once familiar and yet, focused upon by the viewing view, also mysterious, their apparent lack of intentionality and subjectivity irreconcilable with the fact of our own. Particularly in the cinema, close-up, their lack of motility seems sometimes expectant rather than static and, in long shot, their motion seems often purposive. This is, in part, a function of narrative, but also, in part, a function of the subjective human gaze. That is, we are objects as well as subjects, and we engage the material world and the things and people in it "interobjectively" as well as "intersubjectively." The other side of intersubjectivity is what I term "interobjectivity."[60] This a mode of corporeal engagement with the world's materiality in which we subjectively recognize the common "matter" that affords a certain reversibility between subjects and objects, each differentiated yet both related to the other through the grounding "element" or "condition" of existence that Merleau-Ponty eventually called "flesh."[61] Interobjectivity thus subjectively opens us up not only to fascination but also to identification with objects—fascination with their alterity and identification with their materiality. Although reducible to a simple attribution of our own egological subjectivity to non-sentient existents as in Disney's *Cars* (2006, John Lasseter & Joe Ranft), interobjectivity is a much more complex structure of reversible subject-object relations that vary in both ratio (how proportionately "in-itself," "for itself," or "for us" an object seems) and degree (how transparent or explicit and passive or active is the particular subject-object relation). Thus, as is the case off-screen, objects onscreen are never only—or—"absolutely"—objective to human eyes. Across a range of "live-action" and "animated" films, their modalities and movements entail subjectivity in different ratios and degrees of personification, anthropomorphism, animism, and fetishism—as well as what is not only perceived but also carnally sensed as an alterity that is both willful and obdurate.

Indeed, as Mikel Dufrenne suggests, subjectively engaged, at its limit, "the affectively qualified object is itself a subject and no longer a pure object or the simple correlate of an impersonal consciousness."[62] Also "affectively qualified" (in this instance, by me, if not all of us) the camera as object is subjectively engaged at its onscreen limit and becomes itself a subject, its viewing view further affectively qualifying all the objects seen in its viewed view. Thus, even if its movement is initially predetermined, the camera is not, as is the train, fixed by necessity but creatively open and responsive to the passive and active movement of both subjects and objects in the world toward which it is intentionally and subjectively directed. Indeed, the overarching theme of this third form of cinematic movement is that it is primarily preoccupied by a contingent world filled with others and things in intersubjective and interobjective relations that generate both latent and manifest motion.

Perceptive Motility Becomes Expressive Mobility

Refusing to wait passively until I was ready, the fourth fundamental form of cinematic movement has made its presence felt in all the previous sections as it has in almost all cinema. This is the physical movement in and through space of the off-screen camera *qua* subject that is perceived onscreen as the explicitly active movement of the film's viewing view. Displacing its finite and perspectival vision in visible movement, making diacritical choices about where and when to be and see, even as its eye is not in the picture, this unseen but situated seeing subject is perceived not only as intentional but also as materially *present* to its world—*inhabiting* space and time as an expressive entity intelligibly engaged in making sense and meaning of what it sees. Thus, the seeming "absoluteness" of movement *in* the viewed view is visibly subsumed and "subjectified" by the movement *of* the viewing view, its outward directedness toward the world and others reflexively reversing itself as its own movement becomes visible *in* the viewed view.

When the viewing view moves in space and time, as spectators, we sense the seeing before us as belonging to an "other," and our vision as not solely our own. Indeed, there are always two seeing subjects in the film experience, both physically invisible onscreen and yet both existentially present to and making meaning of the same seen (and scene). However, as Merleau-Ponty writes in *The Visible and the Invisible*, "There is here no problem of the *alter ego* because it is not *I* who sees, not [the *other*] who sees, because an anonymous visibility inhabits both of us, a vision in general."[63] This general vision only requires that the "other's" seeing before us be intelligible as a chiasmatic composite of the visual and visible that functions intentionally in a manner similar to—but not necessarily the same as—our own vision. Once met, this requirement also allows for existential specificity, and for differences of visual intention, interest, and movement between the film's vision and our own. Thus, the intentions, interests, and movements of that "other" seeing subject expressed in the viewing view/viewed view need not be (and often aren't) anthropomorphic or anthropocentric. We have seen according to the intentional and pixelated viewing view of an animatronic robot run amok in *Westworld* (1973, Michael Crichton), a dog rolling joyfully in leaves in *My Talks with Dean Spanley* (2008, Toa Fraser), and even a fly upon the wall in *The Fly* (1958, Kurt Neumann). We have also seen according to a viewing view that often loses interest in the human drama before it, as in *The Passenger/Professione: Reporter* (1975, Michelangelo Antonioni), in which, bored with the human characters, the viewing view follows the path of a wire up a wall, or moves out a hotel room window and into the street just as something—now unseen—happens inside critical to the anthropocentric narrative.

Indeed, in *Koyaanisqatsi* (1982, Godfrey Reggio), the viewing view almost completely ignores both human beings and human time as it soars or dives down to visually absorb the natural beauty and human decimation of our planet. For most of its length, it keeps significant distance from humans and, when they appear, "speeds them up" in fast motion as if to get them quickly out of its sight. Thus, although many scholars believe that "the film image becomes articulated [and] organized into a perceptual world" through "reference to and identification with [human] bodily motion," *Koyaanisqatsi* reveals that human motion is not necessary to the articulation and organization of onscreen space, or, for that matter, our ability to orient our vision in it.[64] We have no problem at all identifying perceptually with the dynamism of the viewing view and orienting ourselves in the perceived world "according to" its non-anthropocentric vision and non-anthropomorphic internal rhythms.[65] Cinematic vision need not be just like our own for its general structure, function, and movement to be intelligible and sensible to us. Sharing vision "in general" with the viewing view, we can see "according to, or with it," although, if its interests or movements are at significant odds with our own, we may also refuse its vision and cover our eyes or become disoriented and nauseous rather than thrilled by our differences.

In its movement through space, its visible alteration of its frame of reference, the viewing view expresses in the viewed view not only vision "in general" but also vision in particular. The moving image as such is explicitly selective—and vision "in general" becomes particularly meaningful in every film's specific context. Thus, the transcendence in immanence that Merleau-Ponty sees in the open-ended mobility and expressivity of our own embodied vision finds its visible correlate in the visual activity of the viewing view. In *The Prose of the World*, what he writes of our transcendent vision also describes the viewing view's transcendent movement onscreen. Part of a "system of systems" (here, the cinema of which the moving camera is a part), it is not only "devoted to the inspection of a world," but also "capable of leaping over distances, piercing into the perceptual future, and outlining, in the inconceivable platitude of being, hollows and reliefs, distances and gaps—in short, a meaning."[66]

As discussed, the viewing view's transcendence through movement need not be bound to a surrogate character such as the superhero in *Spider-Man* (2002, Sam Raimi), who swoops across and through the "hollows and reliefs, distances, and gaps," of New York City fighting crime. Indeed, the camera *qua* subject comes fully "into its own" when the implicit movement of its onscreen perception matures into the explicit mobility of subjectively expressive *gesture*. As Yvette Biró tells us: "Gesture [. . .] transforms feelings, intentions, and [. . .] thoughts into images of motion. It lends them sensory form while it remains the mysterious intermediary, providing us only points of reference."[67] Expressive movement or gesture thus emerges as what Merleau-Ponty has called "wild meaning."[68] Not yet specific, it broadly "outlines an intentional object," and "presents itself as a question, bringing certain perceptible bits of the world to [our] notice, and inviting our concurrence in them."[69] Given its dependence upon some degree of recognition and reciprocity that admits the question and allows us to "inhabit" the gestures of an "other," this concurrence is never secure. Nonetheless, affirming the visual/visible *gestalt* as perceiving the world and what it sees as significant, the expressive onscreen movement of the viewing view in relation to the content (and context) of its viewed view is inherently understood as meaningful—even when we are not sure of what it means. In sum, the phenomenological theme of this fourth cinematic movement is that the gestural movement of the viewing view is the communicative basis upon which film and spectator are mutually intelligible to each other as seeing subjects, their respective acts of embodied and situated seeing, both off-screen and on, constituting cinematic vision, like our own, as a "system of systems."

Conclusion

Although neglected in "The Film and the New Psychology," by 1953, in *The Sensible World and the World of Expression*, Merleau-Ponty had come to recognize the visual expressivity of the cinematic moving image as such. Explicitly emphatic in his course notes, he writes: "The cinema was invented as a means of photographing objects in movement or as a *representation of movement*, has discovered in the process [. . .] *the movement of representation*."[70] Moreover, he now identifies this latter movement—not itself a representation but its presentation—not only with editing but also with "changes of perspective."[71] Both are "a solicitation and, so to speak, a celebration of our openness to the world [. . .], an openness upon which the film can make continuous variations."[72]

Constituting the moving image as such, all four forms of cinematic movement I've elaborated here are essential to these "continuous variations." Indeed, in each and every film, they generate "sensible ideas" and comprehensible meaning through unique interrelations with each other as well as with sound and editing. As Merleau-Ponty tells us in "The Film and the New Psychology," each "film does not mean anything but itself."[73] Played out in—as—existential experience, each film thus moves and becomes what it will be before us in our mutual yet individual activity of constructing both a visibly moving narrative and a visually moving autobiography. In the particular rhythms of its intentional and perspectival behavior, its stillness, pauses, hesitations, fluidity and grace, the movements of, and as, each film's moving images visibly inscribe onscreen a postural schema and style of being that transcends its off-screen technical methods and makers to always become—and belong to—itself as well as to those of us who watch it.

In *The Visible and the Invisible*, unfinished at the time of his death in 1961, Merleau-Ponty writes eloquently of the transitivity and reversibility of vision: "As soon as we see other seers [. . .] henceforth, through other eyes we are for ourselves fully visible [. . .]. For the first time, the seeing that I am is for me really visible; for the first time I appear to myself completely turned inside out under my own eyes."[74] Certainly, the cinematic moving image uniquely expresses and magnifies this transitive and reversible structure in which we see and understand *in* the visible eyes and gestures of others the intentionality motility of our own vision. More radically, however, the cinema also lets us see the intentionality motility of our own vision *through* the visibly visual motility of an other's "eyes." Thus if, as Merleau-Ponty suggests, the cinema is the phenomenological art *par excellence,* it is because it realizes and reveals the "inside" of vision as it dramatizes its "outside." But there is more. The cinema is also the phenomenological art *par excellence* because it expands our perception through the expressive and experiential equivalent of phenomenology's "variational method." Indeed, the cinema's "continuous variations" of actively seeing "the" world or "a" world through the eyes of an "other" can open our own—offering us not only new sights but also new perspectives on "our" world outside the frame. In sum, and regardless of whether produced by physical or virtual camera, the viewing view/viewed view that constitutes cinema's "moving images" enables us not only to see different others and things onscreen but also, if we allow it (and sometimes even when we don't), to see, off-screen, differently than we had before.

Notes

1 Maurice Merleau-Ponty, *Sense and Nonsense,* trans. Hubert L. Dreyfus and Patricia Dreyfus (Evanston, IL: Northwestern University Press, 1964). The essay was initially a 1945 lecture presented at the Institut des Haute Études Cinématographiques.

2 Ibid., 59.

3 Ibid., 58.

4 Ibid.

5 Ibid., 59.

6 Arthur C. Danto, "Moving Pictures," *Quarterly Review of Film Studies* 4, no. 1 (Winter 1979): 1–21, at 17.

7 Vivian Sobchack, "Toward Inhabited Space: The Semiotic Structure of Camera Movement in the Cinema," *Semiotica* 41 (1982): 317–35.

8 Vivian Sobchack, "The Active Eye: A Phenomenology of Cinematic Vision," *Quarterly Review of Film and Video* 12, no. 3 (1992): 21–36.

9 Vivian Sobchack, *The Address of the Eye: A Phenomenology of Film Experience* (Princeton, NJ: Princeton University Press, 1992).

10 *Cf.* Jean-Louis Baudry, "Ideological Effects of the Cinematographic Apparatus," trans. Alan Williams, *Film Quarterly* 28 (1974): 39–47.

11 Vivian Sobchack, "'The Active Eye' Revisited: Toward a Phenomenology of Cinematic Movement," 39th Colloque Annuele du Merleau-Ponty Circle. Geneva, Switzerland: August 28, 2014.

12 On operative and deliberative intentionality, *cf.* Maurice Merleau-Ponty, *Phenomenology of Perception*, trans. Colin Smith (London: Routledge & Kegan Paul, 1962), xvii–xviii.

13 Merleau-Ponty, *Sense and Nonsense*, 50. *Cf.* Vivian Sobchack, *Carnal Thoughts: Embodiment and Moving Image Culture* (Berkeley, CA: University of California Press, 2004), 53–84.

14 Ibid., 51.

15 Ibid., 54–6.

16 Ibid., 59. By 1952–3, in his first course at the Collège de France, "Le Monde Sensible and Le Monde de l'Expression," the philosopher's focus had changed to the perceptive and expressive dimensions of movement, its last lecture on the cinema as "universal expression through movement." Maurice Merleau-Ponty, *Le Monde Sensible et le Monde de l'Expression: Cours au Collège de France Notes, 1953*, ed. Emmanuel de Saint Aubert and Stefan Kristensen (Geneva: MétisPresses, 2011 43).

17 Using the Steadicam and digital camera, *Russian Ark* is an unbroken 96-minute tracking shot; *Fish & Cat*'s, 140 minutes. Given the historical association of the "long take" with "realist aesthetics," it is important to note that both films were spatiotemporally "fantastic" narratives. Also significant is that their continuous images were often digitally modified in postproduction, albeit neither fragmented nor reordered. Such "editing" (not so-called) *within* the moving image dates to early cinema, in which lens "mattes" were used to block portions of the negative from exposure so as to allow two or more image elements to combine "in camera" and result in a single image. Today, these elements are "composited" digitally.

18 Rhetorically, editing is a more obvious example of *gestalt* reconfiguration and synthesis than is camera movement. For related discussion of why Merleau-Ponty neglects the moving image as such, *cf.* Pierre Rodrigo, "L'écart du sens: Cadrage et montage cinématographiques selon Eisenstein et Merleau-Ponty," *Chiasmi International* 12 (2010): 71–82, and Mauro Carbone, *The Flesh of Images: Merleau-Ponty between Painting and Cinema*, trans. Marta Nijhuis (Albany, NY: SUNY Press, 2015), 43–6.

19 Gunning, "Rounding out the Moving Image: Camera Movement and Volumetric Space," Unpublished manuscript circulated at the Lysebu workshop, "Precarious Mediation," 1–9. Oslo, Norway, August 8–11: 1–2.

20 Ibid., 2.

21 Christian Metz, *Film Language: A Semiotics of the Cinema*, trans. Michael Taylor (Chicago, IL: Chicago University Press, 1991), 9. On this issue, *cf.* Gunning, "Moving Away from the Index: Cinema and the Impression of Reality," *Differences: A Journal of Feminist Cultural Studies* 18, no. 1 (2007): 29–52.

22 Maurice Merleau-Ponty, *In Praise of Philosophy and Other Essays*, trans. John O'Neill (Evanston, IL: Northwestern University Press, 1970), 73.

23 Not all digitally achieved cinematic movement mimics that of a physical camera in actual space. However, even as virtual camera movement may differ, insofar as its movements are seen to change its perspective and perceptual

field and as intentional in directedness, it is mimetic of the spatial *gestalt* that grounds not only cinema but also vision itself. A radical example of both the differences and similarities between physical and virtual camera movement can be seen in *Enter the Void* (2009, Gaspar Noé).

24 Merleau-Ponty, *In Praise of Philosophy,* 72–3.

25 Merleau-Ponty, *Phenomenology of Perception,* 137.

26 Merleau-Ponty, *Sense and Nonsense,* 58.

27 Sobchack, *Carnal Thoughts,* 311–18.

28 *Cf.* Philip Rosen, ed., *Narrative, Apparatus, Ideology: A Film Theory Reader* (New York: Columbia University Press, 1986).

29 *Cf.* Henri Bergson, *Creative Evolution,* trans. Arthur Mitchell (New York: Dover, 1998), 321–31.

30 Hugo Münsterberg, *The Film: A Psychological Study: The Silent Photoplay in 1916* (New York: Dover, 1970), 26. Although Münsterberg sounds a good deal like Merleau-Ponty here, and was sympathetic to many aspects of *gestalt* psychology, his "new psychology" was primarily experimental and tended to privilege mental processes. Thus, in *Phenomenology of Perception,* Merleau-Ponty also critiques the "new psychology" for its "intellectualism," "empiricism," and "psychologism." *Cf.* Merleau-Ponty 1962, particularly the first chapters.

31 Merleau-Ponty, *In Praise of Philosophy,* 73.

32 Maurice Merleau-Ponty, *The Primacy of Perception,* ed. James E. Edie, trans. Carleton Dallery (Evanston, IL: Northwestern University Press, 1964), 188. For an in-depth discussion of Merleau-Ponty's use of "precession," *cf.* Carbone, *The Flesh of Images,* 56–61.

33 Richard M. Zaner, *The Problem of Embodiment: Some Contributions to a Phenomenology of the Body,* 2nd ed (The Hague: Martinus Nijoff, 1971), 249–53.

34 Merleau-Ponty, *The Primacy of Perception,* 163.

35 Michael Atkinson, "Camera Obscure," *Village Voice,* December 13, 2005. www.villagevoice.com (Accessed July 12, 2014).

36 Merleau-Ponty, *The Primacy of Perception,* 164. (I thank Mauro Carbone for emphasizing this particular formulation in "Eye and Mind" describing our relation not only to painting but also to cinema.)

37 Merleau-Ponty, *Sense and Nonsense,* 58.

38 Ibid.

39 Kevin B. Fisher, "Intimate Elsewheres: Altered States of Consciousness in Post-WWII American Film," Diss. University of California, Los Angeles. UMI, 2009: 204. For elaborated analysis *cf.* 200–25.

40 Merleau-Ponty, *Sense and Nonsense,* 52.

41 François Truffaut and Alfred Hitchcock, *Hitchcock/Truffaut* (New York: Simon & Schuster, 1967), 187.

42 Maurice Merleau-Ponty, *The World of Perception,* trans. Oliver Davis (New York: Routledge, 2004), 73.

43   *Cf.* Stephen Prince, "True Lies: Perceptual Realism, Digital Images, and Film
     Theory," *Film Quarterly* 49, no. 3 (Spring 1996): 27–37, at 32. "Perceptual
     realism" is "a nested hierarchy of cues which organize the display of light,
     color, texture, movement, and sound in ways that correspond with the viewer's
     own understanding of these phenomena in daily life."

44   Maurice Merleau-Ponty, *The Visible and the Invisible*, ed. Claude Lefort, trans.
     Alphonso Lingis (Evanston, IL: Northwestern University Press, 1968), 149–51.

45   Carbone *The Flesh of Images*, 60. Emphasis added.

46   Merleau-Ponty discusses the film's slow motion (and accompanying music); *cf.*
     Le Monde Sensible et le Monde de l'Expression, 119, and Carbone, *The Flesh
     of Images*, 32–54.

47   *Cf.* Robin Wood, in *The Trouble with Marnie*, *Marnie* DVD documentary
     (2000, Laurent Bouzereau).

48   Carbone *The Flesh of Images*, 9. Emphasis added.

49   Merleau-Ponty, *Phenomenology of Perception*, 29.

50   Ibid., 30.

51   Ibid.

52   Ibid., 29.

53   Ibid., 278.

54   Ibid., 279.

55   Ibid.

56   Ibid., 280.

57   Merleau-Ponty, *Sense and Nonsense,* 53.

58   Ibid., 58.

59   Ibid.

60   For development and elaboration of this concept, *cf.* Vivian Sobchack, *Carnal
     Thoughts*, 286–318.

61   *Cf.* Merleau-Ponty, *The Visible and the Invisible*. For a summary of the
     complex meaning of "flesh," *cf.* Gary Brent Madison, *The Phenomenology of
     Merleau-Ponty: A Search for the Limits of Consciousness* (Athens, OH: Ohio
     University Press, 1981), 168–83; and Carbone, *The Flesh of Images*.

62   Mikel Dufrenne, *The Phenomenology of Aesthetic Experience*, trans. Edward
     S. Casey, et. al. (Evanston, IL: Northwestern University Press, 1973), 442.

63   Merleau-Ponty, *The Visible and the Invisible*, 142.

64   Bruce Jenkins, "Structures of Perceptual Engagement in Film: Toward a
     Technology of Embodiment," *Film Reader* 2 (1977): 141–6, at 142.

65   Merleau-Ponty, *The Primacy of Perception*, 164. *Cf.* Carbone, *The Flesh of
     Images*, 3–4, on seeing "according to, or with."

66   Maurice Merleau-Ponty, *The Prose of the World*, ed. Claude Lefort, trans.
     John O'Neill (Evanston, IL: Northwestern University Press, 1973), 78.

67   Yvette Biró, *Profane Mythology: The Savage Mind of the Cinema*, trans. Imre
     Goldstein (Bloomington and Indianapolis, IN: Indiana University Press, 1982), 37.

68 Merleau-Ponty, *The Visible and the Invisible*, 155.

69 Merleau-Ponty, *Phenomenology of Perception*, 185.

70 Merleau-Ponty, *In Praise of Philosophy*, 78.

71 Ibid.

72 Ibid., 78–9. Later Merleau-Ponty will reject the word "representation" in relation to what I call the "viewed view" for its suggestion of a secondarily produced—rather than mutually emergent—phenomenon. *Cf.* Carbone, *The Flesh of Images*, 56.

73 Merleau-Ponty, *Sense and Nonsense*, 57.

74 Merleau-Ponty, *The Visible and the Invisible*, 143.

10

Rethinking Monster Movies

Men in Black, Alien Resurrection, and *Apocalypse Now*

Richard Kearney

There is, in our contemporary popular unconscious, a pervasive obsession with the monstrous which is symptomatic of the perduring role of sacrificial scapegoats in our culture, an ongoing syndrome of US (nationals) versus THEM (aliens) repeatedly played out in our cultural imaginary.[1] I review here three classic screenings of the sacrificial drama of aliens and monsters—*Men in Black*, *Alien Resurrection*, and *Apocalypse Now*.

The In-Human Alien

"Alien" films have long riveted popular attention, from TV serials like the *X-Files* and *Star Trek* to Hollywood blockbusters like *Mars Attacks, Independence Day, Star Wars*, and *Men in Black*. The "aliens" who feature in these movies and proliferate on the growing number of websites devoted to extraterrestrials go by such exotic names as "Greys," "Nordics," "Reptoids," "Chupas," and "Reptilians."

In Barry Sonnenfeld's cult movie *Men in Black*, we are treated to an intriguing opening sequence. Illegal aliens—that is, Hispanic workers or "wetbacks"—are being smuggled across the Mexican border into the United States. A group of Secret Service agents dressed in black suits are monitoring the unlawful immigration trail. At one point they hit upon a suspicious-looking transit vehicle transporting a cargo of legal "non-resident aliens." But on proceeding to arrest them, they discover they are actually extraterrestrial aliens in disguise!

That the film opens with a border-crossing is symptomatic of the alien syndrome. Borders have always been favorite places for alien invasion—of the immigrant, adversarial, or extraterrestrial kind. The Rio Grande in particular has been a borderland of much contention between Hispanic immigrants and the US government, a conflict zone made even more conflictual in recent years by a growing number of legal disputes concerning the Pueblo Indians, who have started to reclaim ancient territorial rights. A crisis exacerbated by Trump's Wall. It is also along this same southern frontier that most sightings of extraterrestrials and UFOs have occurred. Roswell, Area 51, and other controversial sites of "alien" landings are located in this no man's land between America and its "other."

Crises of national identity seek provisional resolution by displacing the internal conflict of US/THEM onto an external screen. Hence the recurring need to identify outside enemies—in the interests of national security—which usually goes by the name of *war*. In the past century, communists, fascists, Cubans, North Koreans, Vietcong, and Iraqis have played leading roles in the screening of the "enemy" without. But these roles have been largely played out. And when there are not enough spies, subversives or criminals to put on national trial, one tends to note a resurgence of traumas *internal* to the body politic. Examples of this may be witnessed in the brutal repression of African American and Native American communities; but in order to distract the "People" from such inner alien-nations and divisions, pretending that there is just one single nation after all, it becomes necessary to exteriorize the enemy again. And if there are no obvious candidates, one has to construct them. Hence the need to de-territorialize aliens, to see them as extraterrestrial, as coming to us from outer space, invading our homes, abducting our loved ones, penetrating both our bodies and minds.

The film proceeds on a roller-coaster ride of twists and turns with the law-and-order Men in Black (MIB Agents K and J) seeking out their non-human counterparts. The MIB "saints" and extraterrestrial "strangers" play the same role (as secret agents, albeit on opposite sides). And the viewer is hard put at times to know which exactly is which. The farmer-turned-alien epitomizes the alien-nation phenomenon of paranoid fear, namely, that it may well be those most familiar to us who are secretly most foreign—in this instance, those who harbor the "villainous bug" from outer space which is sent to destroy the all-American apple-pie home, and by extension New York City itself.

It is curious how similar monster movies like *Alien Resurrection, Predator, Bladerunner, Alien Nation,* and *Virus* operate on similar border-lines between human and inhuman—a fuzzy frontier-zone typical of the unconscious phenomenon of the "uncanny" so central to paranoia and phobia. It is interesting, moreover, that in the making of the *Alien* series the special-effect engineers were requested to make the alien creatures more "human-like" lest they proved unrecognizable and unbelievable to the viewer—hence the device of the mouth within the mouth: at once monstrous and anthropoid.

Nowhere is this more clearly illustrated than in the famous *Alien* series, shot during the two decades leading up to the third millennium. The four films—directed by directed by Ridley Scott, James Cameron, David Fincher, and Jean-Pierre Jeunet—offer a serial *monstration* of sacrificial monsters, exposing the ways in which our deepest fantasy fears can serve as uncanny doubles for our all-too-human selves. The series has already been critically analyzed in my earlier volume, *Strangers Gods and Monsters* and, more extensively, in Stephen's Mulhall's *On Film*,[2] so I confine myself here to a few remarks which I consider relevant to my present argument.

I think it telling that throughout the quadrilogy allusions are made to the interchangeability of human and extraterrestrial aliens. Human space travelers actually find themselves playing "host" to the hostile monster from outer space, thus discovering (to their horror) that the monster is not just "out there" but "in here." The dragon-shaped alien, recalling portraits of the satanic beast of the apocalypse, is capable of invading our most intimate being. So that the thing these human astronauts consider most foreign is in fact the most familiar.[3] What really terrifies them is the alien *within*, already inscribed in the homely but so secretly that it cannot be acknowledged or named. The extraterrestrials in the series thus serve, I am suggesting, as imaginary personifications of our inner alienation, reminding us that we are not at home with ourselves, even at home. They are, we might say, postmodern replicas of the old religious demons: figures of chaos and disorientation within order and orientation.[4]

Stephen Mulhall argues convincingly that the monsters in the *Alien* series symbolize our fear of our own carnality—for example, sexual difference, phallic penetration, genital violation, pregnancy, generativity, reproduction, labor, and birth-death. The alien, he writes, "represents the return of the repressed human body, of our ineluctable participation in the realm of nature—of life."[5] More specifically, for the androgenous Lieutenant Ripley, maternal fecundity represents her "monstrous other." But the monstrosity of the alien represents more than just life. It stems also from a deeper fear that nature may itself be reduced to the out-of-control and invasive culture of biotechnology. The alien's body, as Mulhall notes, *is* its technology; an unnerving phenomenon which suggests that science is amoral and inhuman, and terrifyingly "sublime." Indeed, in the last film in the series, *Alien Resurrection*, Ripley herself is replicated as a cloned, posthumous hybrid who behaves like an android but possesses the racial memory and flair of the alien who invaded her.

The sentiment that the monstrous nature of the alien is not in fact that alien to humanity at all is vividly captured in the scene in Ridley Scott's *Alien* (the opening film in the series) where the android Ash describes the monster-fetus that has exploded through Kane's chest as "Kane's son"—an allusion to the evil inherited from the original Cain of Genesis. Even Agent Ripley comes to resemble the alien in terms of physiognomic features by *Alien 3*, and at one point finds herself impregnated by the extraterrestrial beast whose offspring bursts through her torso in the final sequence. What most deeply defines Ripley is that she is so irrevocably obsessed by the Alien that she becomes incapable of recalling almost anything else.[6] In this sense, Ripley is not just one of the alien family, "she *is* the alien; it incarnates the nightmare that makes her who she is, and that she has been incubating." On this reading, Ripley's encounter with the impregnating alien is paralleled by her sexual intercourse with Clemens, marking the decisive point where she overcomes her deep antipathy toward human embodiment. For Ripley, "the sexual body is ultimately the long repressed and sublimated *das Ding* from which she has sought to flee."[7] Mulhall offers this reading of the final graphic scene (Figure 10.1):

> As she descends into the flames, the alien queen bursts out; Ripley holds it gently in her cupped hands, and lays its crowned head on her breast, as if to suckle it. The logic of the Alien universe, and of Ripley's own nature, is here finally consummated. Since the alien itself originates from within her, since it is an incarnate projection of her deepest fears, she can succeed in eliminating it only by eliminating herself.[8]

This uneasy sense that we humans are in fact the *real* aliens—or at least just as alien as the "others somewhere out there"—is a theme that is replicated in a number of other alien films. In *Men in Black* a farmer returns to his wife looking just like himself but somehow changed: within minutes of his return to the house his whole face and body begin to disintegrate as an alien creature convulses his skin. In *The Astronaut's Wife,* an alien virus enters the astronauts body during a mysterious space mission and then migrates from

FIGURE 10.1 *Agent Ripley's last sacrifice.* Alien 3, *directed by David Fincher* © *Twentieth Century Fox Film Corporation 1992. All Rights Reserved.*

him into his wife's womb ("Spencer is inside me," the violated Juliane says of her alienated spouse). In all three films—*Men in Black*, *The Astronaut's Wife*, and *Alien*—it is telling that the extraterrestrials reproduce themselves by invading a human womb. In the first film, an invaded woman (whose husband is exposed as a "resident alien" with two identifies) gives birth to a tentacled monster in the back of a car; in the second, the astronaut's wife gives birth to alien twins; and in the third, Agent Ripley gives birth to both human and monster offspring. This "undecidable" or "doppelgänger" character of the alien-human progeny is itself a perfect illustration of the "return of the repressed" as a disorienting mix of the biological and the mechanical, the real and the robotic.

This confusion is reinforced by a number of revealing puns and allusions throughout the *Alien* films themselves. The heinous criminals exiled in the outer space prison, Fiorina 161, in *Alien 3* are themselves so alienated from all humanity that some try to rape Ripley (just as the monster does). And they can only be saved by following their Christian-apocalyptic leader, Dillon, into the ultimate sacrificial encounter with their own "in-human" double, the face-hugging, chest-bursting monster itself. Moreover, the suggestion of collusion between robotic clones and galactic aliens in the first film of the series—where the android Ash is conspiring with *Nostromo's* central computer, Mother, to divert the ship to the alien-infested planet—is cleverly transposed in the second and third movies into a realization that the worst monsters are not: (a) the extraterrestrials who are simply following their nature (like their Alien Queen protecting her nursery); nor (b) the robotic clones and androids (Bishop actually saves Agent Ripley and her adopted daughter, Newt, from the exploding planet). The ultimate monsters turn out, in the final analysis, to be the all-too-*terrestrial* humans of The Company who have employed Ripley to hunt the outer-space monster with a view to bringing it back to earth as a deadly addition to their bio-weapons program. The crisis of the Anthropocene is deeply anthropological.

This reversibility between human and inhuman orders of monstrosity is underlined by James Cameron's own avowal that his depiction of the Marine mission to LV 426 is a replay of the Vietnam War. It is an anti-war protest. Indeed, while the *Alien* quadrilogy may be said to dramatize the rite of scapegoating, there is a radical religious inversion of this mechanism when Ripley finally chooses to transcend the mimetic order of sacrificial violence and offer herself up for the sake of the human race. In the final scene of *Alien 3*, Ripley defies the Company's plans to extract the monster-fetus from her womb, falling in cruciform position into a pit of molten lead.[9] Only, of course, to be miraculously reborn in the next sequel, *Alien Resurrection*.

This climactic reversal is, I think, key to the message of the series regarding the sacrificial phenomenon. For while ostensibly scapegoating monsters from other planets, the series actually suggests that the primary source of death and destruction is to be found in humanity's own will-to-power. The real culprits of the piece are the *human* manipulators of war technology and biogenetic engineering back on Earth. In sum, the most alienating and alien-making forces of all are shown to reside not out there in intergalactic space but within the human species itself. Left alone, the aliens would have just done their own survival thing: reproduce their biological species in their "natural" way. It is humanity's tampering with this different order of being that causes havoc and carnage. It is *we* who have turned these strangers into scapegoats, these aliens into monsters.

There is, one might say, nothing particularly new about this. Human interference with monsters goes back to Greek myths of the Minotaur, Kabbalistic stories of Golems, and Gothic tales of vampires, ghouls, and Frankensteins. Indeed, Dr. Pretorius sounds the typically apocalyptic note on this score when he makes his famous toast in *The Bride of Frankenstein*: "To a new world of gods and monsters!" But what sets the *Alien* series off from such prototypical versions of the human-inhuman monster is the fact that today we possess the technology that can travel into outer space and bring the *imaginary* world of aliens into contact with the *real* Earth. The boundary separating science from science fiction is blurred. Hence the inflation of our horror before the undecidability of the monstrous. As Stanley Cavell astutely observes:

> Isn't it the case that not the human horrifies me, but the inhuman, the monstrous? Very well. But only what is human can be inhuman. Can only the human be monstrous? If something is monstrous, and we do not believe that there are monsters, then only the human is a candidate for the monstrous.

Horror, Cavell deduces, is the name we give to the experience of the

> precariousness of human identity, to the perception that it may be lost or invaded, that we may be, or may become, something other than we are, or take ourselves for; that our origins as human beings need accounting for, and are unaccountable.[10]

Though he is not speaking of the *Alien* series as such, Cavell's deduction bears directly on the question at hand. The cinematic horror of the monsters betrays the secret horror of the human.

Horror and Monsters

"The Horror, the Horror." These last words of Conrad's *Heart of Darkness* are given contemporary celebrity by Coppola's film *Apocalypse Now Redux*. Coppola offers an alternative look at the theme of the sacrificial scapegoat and the US over THEM syndrome. The film transposes the characters of *Heart of Darkness* to Vietnam, recounting the story of a US Special Forces officer,

Lieutenant Willard, sent upriver in North Vietnam in search of a renegade Colonel, Walter Kurtz. Kurtz has left his high-ranking job in the Joint Chiefs of Staff in Washington to counter a threat by double agents endangering the lives of hundreds of American soldiers. Operating deep within Cambodian territory—then legally off-limits to US troops—Kurtz disobeys orders and eliminates the threat. Faced with disciplinary action, he escapes deeper into the jungle and starts carrying out indiscriminate raids against military stations and villages. His methods are ruthless and utterly effective, but the US Command judges that he has gone too far. Willard is called in to terminate Kurtz's command, and to do so "with extreme prejudice."

This last summary expression betrays how US war policy mirrors the "illegal" activities of Kurtz. The mirroring becomes more and more alarming as the film unfolds, charting Willard's journey toward the heart of darkness that is Kurtz's hideout. The parallel between righteous executioner and evil criminal is signposted from the opening scene of the film: Willard admits that his narrative and Kurtz's are inextricably bound up with each other. "There is really no way of telling his story without telling mine," he says, "if his is a confession, then so is mine." As he leafs through his dossier, Willard discovers that Kurtz was once just like him. He reads one of Kurtz's letters to his son, claiming that the charges leveled against him by the High Command are "quite simply insane" (the very term used by the High Command to describe Kurtz's behavior). In the same letter, Kurtz explains to his son that he is beyond the Army's "lying timid morality"—a morality which Willard has plenty of opportunity to realize is only skin deep. The photograph in the dossier is a shadowy silhouette marked "Believed to be Col. Walter Kurtz": a signal that as we approach the heart of darkness the Minotaur lurking in wait grows undecidable. The question of whether we are dealing with a neo-Nietzschean hero or a psychopathic monster becomes problematic. Who is the real demon? we find ourselves asking. This out-of-bounds unknown reprobate or his sanctimonious accusers back in Washington and Saigon? Should Willard embrace this estranged being or execute him? How, in short, is he to make the right call? How, in this night of fear and trembling, is he to *judge*?

The narrator's odyssey to the heart of the jungle serves to retrace Kurtz's own itinerary. From the sententious briefing with top brass at home base to the various detours through one horrifying US Army outpost after the next, Willard begins to realize that Kurtz's horrific acts are no more than efficient enactments of so-called "legitimate" military conduct. Kurtz, he finally acknowledges, is playing out the role of a sacrificial scapegoat as the High Command keeps its hands clean. The final scene where the execution of Kurtz is juxtaposed with graphic shots of animal sacrifice (a caribou cleft in two by a sword) aptly captures this.

Several premonitory scenes anticipate this sacrificial denouement. At the opening military briefing, Willard is told by his Senior Officer that Kurtz has crossed the line between "us" and "them." The General in question describes Kurtz as being "out there . . . with the natives . . . operating beyond the pale of any human decency." He tells how Kurtz, once a prized first-ranking Colonel, has supped with the devil to the point of no return, traversing the border between civilians and barbarians. Kurtz has broken with the norms of civilized, reasonable behavior. He has gone "insane," ultimately yielding to the temptation "to be a god." He has become the Other, the Monster, the pure passed over to the Hades of the impure. A friend turned enemy. He is damned.

The irony of these demonizing sentiments is breathtaking, of course, in light of what we soon discover the "civilized, reasonable behavior" of the officially approved US troops to be.

The discovery is brutal as Willard steers his gunboat up the river leading from North Vietnam to Cambodia. His nightmare encounter with two military commands says it all. The first of these is led by Colonel Kilgore, a Cavalry officer who shares the same rank as Kurtz but seems more zealous in bloodlust. He distributes "death cards" to his victims, orders his troops to surf on the river during military maneuvers and plays Wagner—the chosen music of Nazi machismo and *Birth of the Nation* suprematism—to accompany his helicopter gun missions. In contradistinction to Kurtz's crystalline logic of terminating war by any means, Kilgore keeps it going for the heck of it. The banality of evil could hardly be more lucidly illustrated than in these surreal scenes of gratuitous violence. If we are talking "insanity," this is it; though Kilgore is considered "legitimate" while Kurtz is not. Compared to this hellish mayhem, Kurtz's description of his incisive actions as "moments of clarity" begins to sound more convincing than the Army's dismissal of them as "unsound methods." (As if the actual *aim* of "exterminating the brutes" is quite acceptable!) The Army objects to the means, not the end.

The confusion of friend and foe, ally and alien, is compounded as Willard visits two US frontier outposts. At first we see GIs debauching themselves at an officially sponsored show of Playboy bunnies, while the second displays an inferno of military inefficiency, cowardice, and drug abuse. The US myth of the noble frontiersman takes a last dive here as one of Kilgore's super surfers collapses in a hail of shrapnel. Could Kurtz possibly be worse?

As Willard arrives at his destination—Kurtz's hideout—the enigma deepens. Willard is met by an American photographer who proclaims Kurtz to be a "poet warrior." He hails him as the prophet of a new "dialectic" which, far from making him mad, brings him beyond conventional categories of good and evil. "No maybes, no supposes, no fractions." Willard, full of maybes, vacillates one more time. He eventually meets Kurtz himself and is invited into his den.

So the pursuer confronts the monster. They talk for days without guard. Kurtz expounds his reasoning. He recounts how he learned from the Vietcong "enemy" the uncompromising logic of war. He tells the story of how he and his troops had vaccinated children in a certain village only to discover that, after they had left, the Vietcong had returned and cut off each inoculated arm. This enemy act struck Kurtz "like a diamond bullet through his forehead," revealing to him the inner truth of military action:

pure will to power without judgment. These were "not monsters but men," he learnt. These were "geniuses . . . perfect, genuine, complete, crystalline, pure of act." These were men who could both love and kill: love their own families with total passion and kill their enemies "without passion . . . without judgement." Why? "Because it is judgement that defeats us." And Kurtz ultimately confesses to Willard that if he had ten divisions of men like that he could have dispensed with hypocrisy and terminated the war. Even the corpses strewn on Kurtz's compound serve a specific purpose—to instill enough horror to bring the war to an end. What looks like madness is in fact a (perverse) obsession with peace, the desire to win the war as effectively and rapidly as possible. Here we have a morality of immorality. Kurtz's speech culminates with the claim: "You can kill me but you cannot judge me."

Having listened to Kurtz's razor-sharp reasoning and witnessed the result of his im/morality—a camp inhabited by crazed warriors and strewn with body parts and decapitated heads—Willard *does* eventually judge. He kills Kurtz. Coppola does not explain what criteria Willard deploys to differentiate between Kurtz, the neo-Nietzschean hero, and Kurtz, the manic monster. We are not told how Willard decides. Nor how we might judge his decision in turn. Coppola, after all, is a movie-maker, not a philosopher. It is his business to screen this age-old conundrum, not to solve it. But in dramatizing this fundamental question of discernment for a contemporary audience, Coppola has performed a critical intellectual service.

From the perspective of the scapegoating thesis, the film raises questions. Among them: How do we judge the horror? How do we distinguish between one kind of monstrosity and another? How does one differentiate between "normal" and "abnormal" actions, especially in a war like Vietnam where, in Willard's words, "charging a man with murder was like handing out speeding tickets at the Indy 500"? How is Willard to know who is on the "right" side in a war where even the Americans have changed sides, as he learns from French colonials on a lost plantation (he also learns from a French widow that "men love and kill")? And if it is true that Kurtz has welcomed his potential executioner, Willard, in an act of unconditional hospitality, has Willard been entirely just in responding to this hospitality with an act of execution? And, what is more, a summary execution without trial, in seeming defiance of Willard's own profound scruples about High Command's order to "exterminate without prejudice."

Moreover, the fact that his host, Kurtz, hangs out in a Buddhist temple and is an avid reader of Eliot's *Hollow Men*—not to mention Frazer's *The Golden Bough* and the Bible—sharpens the enigma by suggesting how deeply resolved Kurtz is to prosecute the chilling logic of war. Even if it means succumbing to its "horror." "After such knowledge what forgiveness?" as Eliot says. So, even if the demands of absolute hospitality seem impossible here, one is left wondering if the only alternative is the sacrificial killing of the monster at the heart of the labyrinth. Willard obeys his command. Theseus rules OK. But does it have to be like this?

There are two key scenes toward the close of the film which put these questions into relief. The first shows one of Willard's troops, Chef, being terrified by a tiger as they patrol the jungle. They are on the lookout for the "enemy." But what actually surprises them is an animal who is perfectly at home in his local environment. Because they are estranged from this "foreign" place the US Marines mistake one "monster" for another, confusing human and animal adversaries. At least one implication of this scene is that the "monster" Kurtz, who has gone over to the other side and assumed the mores of the natives who revere him, may also be a case of mistaken identity. A suspicion deepened by the fact that when Kurtz and Willard eventually meet at the heart of darkness, their semi-naked, sleeked figures are almost indistinguishable. The question of who is the hunter and who the hunted accentuates the problem of prejudice and judgment (Figures 10.2 and 10.3).

FIGURE 10.2 *Before the sacrifice. Final sequence of* Apocalypse Now, *directed by Francis Ford Coppola © Omni Zoetrope 1979. All rights reserved.*

FIGURE 10.3 *After the sacrifice. Final sequence of* Apocalypse Now, *directed by Francis Ford Coppola © Omni Zoetrope 1979. All rights reserved.*

The second scene, also at the film's finale, shows the statue of a Buddha in Kurtz's Cambodian hideaway just before the execution. We see the veiled statue facing Kurtz as he recites his terminal reflections on war onto a tape recorder. (He is railing against the hypocrisy of the US Army, which trains troops to drop napalm on innocents but refuses to allow the word "fuck" to be written on its planes.) In the preceding scene Kurtz is seen entering the doorway of the Buddhist temple as a caribou passes him on its way to its ritual sacrifice. Both will be offered as scapegoats to purge the community. It is significant that the twin sacrificial rites which follow—the slaughtering of the caribou juxtaposed with the killing of Kurtz in graphic montage—give rise to a scene where the "purged" Willard re-emerges through the same temple door, his bare, dark figure almost identical to Kurtz's. But with this difference: it is Willard who now wields the executioner's axe and possesses the manuscript of Kurtz's memoirs.

So here again the question is raised as to whether one is justified in executing an enemy deemed inhuman. With Kurtz's closing statement to Willard—"You have a right to kill me but not to judge me"—still ringing in our ears, the visage of the Buddha, which closes the film, gives us pause. All the more so if one is mindful of the Buddhist doctrine of non-judgment. Could Willard have executed Kurtz had he heeded such ancient Buddhist wisdom? What if Willard had forgiven Kurtz and tried to save him from this inferno, acknowledging that Kurtz was not only the ultimate symptom of US military involvement in Vietnam but also a scapegoat preserving the illusion of a clean conscience? A man who, for all his *killing*, was still capable of *loving* (his wife and son, and even, arguably, Willard, whom he refuses to slay). A man who, in his own words, hated the "stench of lies."

And yet, there is one mitigating factor in Willard's role: the confessional narrative of these events. These events are related *retrospectively*, to be sure, but they are no less cathartic for that. In acknowledging that (1) there was no way to "tell his (Kurtz's) story without telling my own" and (2) that "if his (Kurtz's) story is really a confession then so is mine," Willard admits a deep identification with the monster he has slain. He acknowledges his role as witness to Kurtz's life, before the world but most especially before Kurtz's son. "It was no accident that I got to be the caretaker of Colonel Walter E. Kurtz's memory," he concedes. Both Willard and Kurtz expose the mendacities of US military practice in Vietnam. Kurtz by his actions and Willard by telling the whole story in response to Kurtz's terminal request: "I worry that my son might not understand what I have tried to be. I want someone to tell him everything. . . . There is nothing that I hate more than lies . . . If you understand me, you'll do this for me."

These are not the words of an irredeemable monster. They are those of someone ultimately subsumed by horror. Someone for whom the truth of war won out over the truth of poetry. Someone who could not survive to tell the tale. In this Kurtz differs from Willard who, in spite of his collusion with sacrificial killing, manages to transcend the logic of scapegoating in favor of narrative testimony and wisdom: he tells the story of Kurtz, which he carries out of the temple and merges with the face of the Buddha.

Willard refuses to be divinized by Kurtz's followers after he kills the demon. As the throngs of warriors kneel before him in their bandoleers and bloodied loincloths, Willard passes through them to his waiting boat. Having defeated the Minotaur, Theseus declines the sacrificial role of replacement deity. He escapes the cycle of bloodletting. And in resisting the lure of false gods, he appears to choose the option of poetic catharsis so well described by Eliot himself when he writes:

> (The storyteller) is haunted by a demon against which he feels powerless, because in its first manifestation it has no face, no name, nothing; and the words, the poem he makes, are a kind of form of exorcism of this demon.[11]

The film *Apocalypse Now Redux* is such an exorcism as were *Heart of Darkness* and *The Hollow Men* before it. Yet the tragedy for Kurtz himself is that redemption comes, if it comes at all, *posthumously*, through the confessional voice of the film's narrator. The catharsis by pity and fear comes to Willard the narrator, and perhaps also to us viewers, but not it seems to the crazed colonial. Willard's narrative testifies to the hidden root of the alienation in Kurtz which, it transpires, is symptomatic of the war itself. When Willard finally departs from the heart of darkness, refusing the nihilism of the "Horror," he takes Kurtz's story with him. He carries the pages of testimony in his trembling hand. And in the retelling that is *Apocalypse Now Redux* the horror becomes perhaps that bit less horrible, the monster that bit less monstrous.

Conclusion

If the sleep of reason produces monsters, as Goya says, it is the perversion of reason in a certain sacrificial mood. If we are to put an end to the cycle of scapegoating, might we not begin by trying to understand our own monsters? And so doing, might we not transform some of them into creatures of passionate peace? Might we not even (who knows?) help some of those behaving monstrously "out there"—tyrants, torturers, rapists, murderers—to come to terms with their own internal monsters, and put an end to homicidal and genocidal practices of scapegoating? As Willard almost does in the final confrontation with Kurtz. Or as Ellen Ripley and the prisoners of Fiorina do at the end of *Alien 3*. Indeed, is this not the meaning of Ripley's sacrificial act as she cradles her alien offspring and holds it to her breast? But we do not have to send our Ripleys and Willards to the limits of Asia or outer space to find our monsters. Are they not lurking within us at home—in the depths of our own selves?

The notion of the stranger within is as old as civilization itself. Almost every wisdom tradition attests to it. We find it in the story of Jacob struggling with his dark double before transmuting his monster into an angel of God. We see it in the testimony of Jesus confronting demons in the desert before giving himself in an act of ultimate *caritas*. And we encounter a similar lesson being offered by the Buddha when he takes the monster of violent hatred to his heart and meditates on it until it mutates into compassionate calm. A disciple of the Tibetan Buddhist school, Milarepa, learned this truth the hard way when one day he discovered his cave taken over by a demon. After fighting with the beast for many years, he finally put himself into its jaws saying, "eat me if you want to." It was only then the demon left.[12] When violent fears go, monsters follow. Love is the casting out of fear.

The key, perhaps, is not to kill our monsters but to learn to live with them. In that way there is hope that monsters may eventually learn to live with themselves and cease to scapegoat others. Or as Nietzsche put it: "Whoever fights monsters should see to it that in the process he does not become a monster."[13] Agreed. Yet at the same time, embracing monsters doesn't mean you have to invite them to dinner—or set up house. Some monsters need to be welcomed, others struggled with. The hard thing is to tell the difference.

Notes

1 See earlier explorations of these theme in Richard Kearney, *On Stories* (London and New York: Routledge Press, 2002), especially Part Three, and *Strangers, Gods and Monsters: Interpreting Otherness* (London and New York: Routledge, 2003), chapters 1 and 2.

2 Richard Kearney, *Strangers, Gods and Monsters*, 49–53. See also Stephen Mulhall, *On Film* (London and New York: Routledge Press, 2002) and T. Beal, *Religion and Its Monsters* (London and New York: Routledge Press, 2001).

3 This is another way of describing what Heidegger and Freud identify, in their different ways, as the "uncanny" (*das Unheimlich*): that which haunts and invades our sense of social and personal security—our weird feeling of being homeless even while at home. For more on this crucial theme of the uncanny, see Richard Kearney, *Strangers, Gods, and Monsters* and *Touch: Recovering our Most Vital Sense* (New York: Columbia University Press, 2021), 52–9.

4 Richard Kearney, "Heaney, Heidegger and Freud—The Paradox of the Unhomely," in *Navigations: Collected Irish Essays 1976–2006* (Dublin: Lilliput Press/New York: Syracuse University Press, 2006), 264–6.

5 Mulhall, *On Film*, chapter 1.

6 Ibid.

7 Ibid.

8 Ibid.

9 Ibid.

10 Stanley Cavell, *The Claim of Reason: Wittgenstein, Skepticism, Morality, and Tragedy* (Oxford: Oxford University Press, 1979), 418–19. I am grateful to Stephen Mulhall for this quote.

11 T. S. Eliot, *The Three Voices of Poetry* (Cambridge: Cambridge University Press, 1943). See the fascinating discussion of this passage by Denis Donoghue in *Words Alone* (New Haven, CT: Yale University Press, 2000), 27f and Mark P. Hederman, *The Haunted Inkwell: Art and Our Future* (Dublin: Columba Press, 2001), 14.

12 See Pema Chodron, *Start Where You Are* (Boston and London: Shambhala Books, 1994).

13 F. Nietzsche, *Beyond Good and Evil* (New York: Random House, 1966), section 146.

11

A Plural Transcendence

When Film Does Phenomenology

Anna Westin

Philosophy asks us to approach the world with inquisitive wonder. We find in the ordinary stuff of life a complex and integrated majesty that allows us to see the world anew. But philosophers are not alone in this exploration. This is also the task of artists, and, particularly, filmmakers who re-imagine the world through aperture, narrative, music scores, and other cinematic processes. Film is, according to Robert Bresson, of two types: ones that *reproduce* realities, and those that use the camera and the cinematographic resources to *create* an encounter afresh.[1] This second definition is not far from the task of philosophy, and phenomenology in particular, in its definition of revelation. When examining this comparison between the task of film and philosophy, the question is whether, in its creative re-perceiving of the world, film is doing the work of philosophy.

I am aware that this is an incredibly broad question. I am also aware that my definitions of philosophy favor the phenomenological interpretation of experience, and a specific, ethically-framed representation of a particular branch of philosophy. That aside, I think that the question is still an important one. There are filmmakers who believe they are doing philosophy. There are philosophers, such as Terrence Mallick, who are filmmakers. And there are filmmakers who have no interest or experience in philosophy and just want to put a good story out into the world and evoke a response. In this chapter, I want to go back to basics. For going back to basics is just what I need to do to uncover exactly what it is that constitutes "doing philosophy," and "doing phenomenology" in particular.

In this chapter, I will first assess what we mean by the term "phenomenology," through Merleau-Ponty, who already shows a close relation between film and philosophy. I will then suggest that film requires more of Merleau-Ponty's definition concerning intersubjectivity. As opposed to someone who is "like us," the Wholly Other, as appears in the transcendental style of cinema defined by Schrader, requires that we extend the intersubjective to an experience of absolute distance. In seeking to answer this question of alterity, I will return to phenomenology via Lévinas. I will suggest that Lévinas, in turn, requires more of film in demonstrating the transcendent revelation of alterity. I will conclude by suggesting that this conversation can lead to productive encounters for both disciplines, through examining Ruben Östlund's appeal to alterity in his recent body of work. If we take the approach of phenomenology, which is particularly interested in the lived and material world, I would suggest the central question boils down to this: Does film do phenomenology—and if so, when?

Defining Phenomenology

In order to answer this question, I want to examine what phenomenology has to say about what film is doing, and contrast this to what phenomenology is. Ancient Greek philosophy focused on developing systems of thought concerning First Causes of existence. Rationalism tried to explain wisdom by appealing to reason as our source of knowledge about the world. Kant's synthetic *a priori* pushed us further to account for universal truth attached to specific, material realities. Phenomenology, introduced through Edmund Husserl and his successors, then tried to bring philosophy back to the "things themselves." The material world itself became the playground for consciousness to be explored and found.

The essence of things, then, becomes concerned with existence, in its concrete and material substance. In his exploration of phenomenology, Richard Kearney likens philosophy to tasting and knowing through the *experience* of something. He shows us that the Latin *sapiential*, wisdom, connects to the term "*sapere*," which is "to taste." *Sapere*, in turn, connects us to the French terms "*savouer*" and "*savoir*," which links the experiential tasting of wisdom to knowledge—the knowing of a thing.[2] This discussion is continued later in Kearney's book on *Touch*.[3] As such, deeply embedded in wisdom is this experiential aspect—that is, in order to be wise, we must taste and see.

This is, of course, what phenomenology wants to do—to situate the essence into the existence of the concrete world. Lévinas, Sartre, and Merleau-Ponty all reference the body as the subject of phenomenology, meaning that the wisdom that we seek as humans requires situating consciousness in concreteness, temporality, and spatiality.[4] For Merleau-Ponty, philosophy is done as phenomenology, where the "study of essences" and the definition of essences are put into existence, taking the world not as something filtered through reason but as "already there."[5] Merleau-Ponty writes that this phenomenological method of philosophy asks us to examine the world that "precedes knowledge," rather than requiring us to know in order to examine. In phenomenology, reality is a "closely woven fabric"[6] of relationships: and it is given prior to its rational understanding of the world.

I want to take time on Merleau-Ponty here because he gives us explicit connections between phenomenology and film. For him, film does the work of phenomenology[7] and is, as Vivian Sobchack writes, "perhaps the phenomenological art *par excellence*,"[8] which is why his definition of phenomenology will be particularly important to this conversation.

The relationship to the world, however, is not one of a lonely ego. Phenomenology requires relationship, and Merleau-Ponty's phenomenology of perception situates this in the lived experience of the world. This lived experience encompasses our intersubjective relation to the other than us, the *alter*. For Merleau-Ponty, the phenomenology of perception presupposes a shared experience of phenomenon. Immanence and transcendence both require one another.[9,10] The alterity of the other overlaps and "literally alters" my own reality,[11] as he explores through the description of being touched by the world, and simultaneously touching the world.

The alterity in Merleau-Ponty, however, rejects a relation to something "Wholly Other." There is some of me intertwined in the world, in the other person. This is where I will diverge from Sobchack's identification of transcendence in film, through Merleau-Ponty's phenomenology of *"transcendence in immanence."*[12] Merleau-Ponty requires reversibility, but he does not require full transcendence.[13] As such, while he rejects the idea of "fusion" with another, he also rejects a phenomenology of "infinite distance" between the self and the other.[14] If film is "doing phenomenology" for Merleau-Ponty, then film is enabling us to perceive these reversible relations between the self and the other.

Phenomenology, Film, and Problems of Transcendence

The definition of phenomenology that Merleau-Ponty offers in *Phenomenology of Perception* is an approach that aims at putting the essence back into existence. For him, according to Alberto Baracco, film acts as phenomenological art par excellence, serving as a mediated perception of the world that exists prior to rationalized thought. For Baracco, a film phenomenology is concerned with perception and understanding of the film, and how the film, in turn, interacts with the viewer and the film world that is represented.[15] Sartre, in *Apologie pour le Cinéma*,[16] equates film to the activity of consciousness. It allows viewers "an emancipation" from the "myth of interiority to things themselves." Film offers an encounter with reality that is pre-reflective. This is also what Merleau-Ponty picks up on: a perception of the world that, like phenomenology, is immediate rather than intellectual.

Consciousness is mediated through the lived body confronting the real world, and film perceives the world through encounter.[17] Baracco writes that, for Merleau-Ponty, film serves as "encounter," creating the "multiple horizons of sense and many perceptual possibilities" of reality. Thus, film can function as a mode of perceiving the world and its web of relations and possibilities, at a level that precedes thought.[18]

But film, it turns out, requires more than Merleau-Ponty's definition of experience. Our original question concerned whether film does phenomenology, and up to this point we can say that, yes, in a very broad way, one could argue that film presents a pre-rational experience of interconnected embodied beings existing in relation to their worlds. But what have we really said in this? Not much. I still have experiences of film that I cannot fit comfortably into my definitions of philosophy, and there are experiences of film that go beyond Merleau-Ponty's derivative otherness. What I feel Merleau-Ponty's definition cannot account for is the full phenomenological experience of the transcendent.

Merleau-Ponty's definition of phenomenology leads philosophers such as Baracco to suggest that film, as re-perception, is phenomenology. When examining the films of Bresson, for example, this definition of film seems to fit pretty well. In Bresson's *Notes on the Cinematograph*, he writes about the film world as a pre-rational relation to the world, mediated through the prism of relation. He writes:

> The real, when it has reached the mind, is already not real anymore. . . . Two sorts of real: (1) The crude real recorded as it is by the camera; (2) what we call real and see deformed by our memory and some wrong reckonings. Problem. To make what you see be seen, through the intermediary of a machine that does not see it as you see it.[19]

Bresson shows how the "real" that the film tries to capture is always being mediated, by, for instance, the camera. He evokes what Merleau-Ponty refers to in his description of the mediation of flesh, the experience of embodiment that both is touched by and touches the world. This relational mediation between various experiences is the phenomenon of perception, which connects the prism of experiences of being in the world.

In this instance, Bresson and Merleau-Ponty might well overlap in their definitions. However, what Merleau-Ponty's phenomenology does not adequately account for is how this pre-rational relation to the world can bring about a relation to the Wholly Other. This relation of infinite height characterizes the experience of transcendence. In Bresson, we see this grasping at the *alter*. For Bresson, the film's essence is not stringing together a coherent series of images to replicate the real, but rather "the ineffable that [the images] will disengage."[20] What Bresson wants in the encounter between the viewer and the film is an experience of transcendence.

If the series of images that portray the real are to invoke the transcendent, if this is really what Bresson wants to do when he moves the camera angle and chooses "models" to move as his characters, if his film phenomenology defines perception as pertaining to the ineffable, the Wholly Other, then we need to move beyond the vocabulary that Merleau-Ponty offers us. This requires clarifying what the transcendent means for phenomenology, and exploring how phenomenology might help us to understand film.

In Schrader's definition, the transcendental style, as expressed through Uzo and Bresson among others, defines itself by "its ability to transcend culture and personality," thereby developing into a "universal form of representation," which is "remarkably unified."[21] This "spiritual effect" is occasioned through the means of dialogue, editing process, and camera angles to produce an effect of connecting the viewer to "the ineffable and invisible" through the temporal experience.[22] This places the viewer in connection with the Wholly Other, the Ideal itself.

A Phenomenology of the Transcendent (Wholly Alter—and Yet, Human)

The transcendental style points to the "infinite distance"[23] that Merleau-Ponty fails to account for. Films that invoke transcendental style could be said to be doing philosophy in one way. But phenomenology, in its invocation of bringing "essence back into existence," needs to situate this Wholly Other in the sensible human world. This is where Lévinas becomes useful. He moves beyond Merleau-Ponty's interpretation of perception through his relation of the transcendent other, accounting for the infinite Other that the transcendental style of film requires. However, Lévinasian phenomenology, in turn, demands of film that it accounts for the height and the separation of transcendence—and brings us into a confrontation with the other that ruptures our *ipseity*, our egoic isolation, while maintaining the other's separation from us.

Lévinas agrees with Merleau-Ponty's definition of phenomenology as uncovering the "flesh of the world." Writing at the same time as Merleau-Ponty, he, too recognizes phenomenology as the pre-rational relation toward the sensible world. Responding to Merleau-Ponty, Lévinas states that this "flesh of the world" "is an excellent formula. Reality has weight when one discovers its contexts. This is the phenomenological message."[24] Both philosophers offer a cohesive definition of phenomenology. It situates consciousness in the pre-rational fabric of relationships with the world, through which we then derive knowledge. However, though they agree on the basic structure of their method, Lévinas diverges from Merleau-Ponty's definition of intersubjectivity. This Lévinasian definition of phenomenology, I will argue, helps to situate phenomenology not only as perception but as a relation of revelatory transcendence. This revelation brings about a height and separation that Merleau-Ponty's reversible relation to the world cannot account for.

The transcendent requires separation. Lévinas's transcendence is humanistic and phenomenological—it requires placing the infinite in the human face. In *Totality and Infinity*, Lévinas contrasts it with the experience of "apprehending the individual (which alone exists) not in its individuality but in its generality."[25] As such, his phenomenological transcendence is radically different to the

> transcendence of religions (in the current themataulurgic and generally lived sense of the term), from the transcendence that is already (or still) participation, submergence in the being toward which it goes, which holds the transcending being in its invisible meshes, in violence.[26]

Reducing the other to an experience of the same[27] violates the phenomenological experience of difference and otherness that is "infinitely distant from my own reality."[28] Of course, the transcendental style acknowledges the Wholly Other and this distance—but the effect is to invoke a closeness, as if able to grasp the other and become a part of it. For Lévinas, this cannot be. The other, while welcomed, remains distant. The very differentiation of ontology from phenomenology rests in resisting the urge to reduce "being" to the same. For Lévinas, this relation to the other cannot be a relation to the graspable or the same. Rather, the transcendent is exactly that "strangeness of the Other"[29] that calls into question my isolated ego and brings me into a relation of subjectivity toward the other.

A Lévinasian phenomenology of transcendence means accounting for the encounter that brings us beyond a solipsistic subjectivity of "sameness." It requires placing our relation to the world through the ethical priority of the self toward the other.[30] Simon Critchley writes that "For Lévinas, the relation to the other is asymmetrical. That is, the subject relations itself to something that exceeds its relational capacity."[31] As such, it differs from both Merleau-Ponty's relational phenomenology, and the definition of transcendence put forward by Schrader.

Exploring film through Lévinas is, of course, not something new. Film scholarship shows a distinct appreciation for what has been described as the "Lévinasian turn," despite Lévinas's own distrust in "art in general" as a way of masking what is real.[32] But Lévinas's engagement with film, and the interrogation of whether film is "doing" phenomenology, is often only interpreted through the experience of film content. For instance,

Girgus describes Lévinas's transcendent ethics applied to film as a "cinema of redemption." Film becomes the means by which the "struggle for this transformation from being" to ethical subjectivity is articulated.[33] This definition of cinema places film in the context of Lévinasian phenomenology, showing that people can be greater than they appear and that life can mean "more than can be seen, known or understood."[34] The transcendent occurs through its struggle of subordinating oneself to the prior responsibility for the other person, and the asymmetry of this relation.[35] For Girgus, this cinema of redemption seems to be played out in the content of the script, and the way it is edited, rather than the wider phenomenological experience of film that Baracco mentions earlier, and that Merleau-Ponty identifies, as a re-perception of the world.

So we return to our old question. Does film do phenomenology? Given the concerns for the lack of "height" (as in, its appeal to the infinite, Wholly Other) in previous definitions of phenomenology, which cannot do justice to films like Bresson, I have opted for Lévinas's ethical transcendence. This therefore makes the question go: "does film do phenomenology, according to Lévinas?" which, more specifically, seems to boil down to the question: What does Lévinas's kind of transcendence mean for film, and can it actually be done? Girgus proposes that this kind of Lévinasian phenomenology requires of cinema that it demonstrate a redemptive content. But this offers an examination of the story content itself, rather than the other cinematic forms—the narrative arc that is redemptive. So, in terms of it accounting for the phenomenology of film itself, that is the prismic experience that Merleau-Ponty needs us to account for, just looking at the "stuff" of the story will not be enough. In order to understand how film does phenomenology, we need to look at all the parts of its coming together—each encounter, to use the language of Lévinas, in which this revelation occurs that "is" the stuff of phenomenology.

It also requires that we get exact on our philosophy, because for scholars like Bettina Bergo, Lévinas is doing something beyond just narrative story and redemption. We really need to get precise on what is phenomenologically understood by the "transcendent." For Lévinas, the fabric of experience is one of encounter. The encounter is with someone who is like me, who is enough for me to be able to relate to them: to know that my needs are needs that they share. But it is also one that is utterly separate from me, unable to be thematized or comprehended. The description of experience is one of being affected by another, "something that disturbs it."[36] Being is disturbed because that which disturbs it is infinitely alter. The other approaches us in a "surplus of meaning" that consciousness cannot contain—the other is at once related to, and enigma.

The other evokes the transcendent.[37] This transcendence is one that cannot reduce the other to the same as us—that cannot contain and comprehend but calls us out of ourselves, revealing herself to us, expressing herself through phenomenological presence of a face that expresses a "non-physical" reality; a disturbance of myself that occurs and implicates me, prior to consciousness.[38] Here we see that the transcendent not only requires consciousness, language—but it also takes place in the phenomenological expression of the body. It is the face that speaks, revealing the other to me. In that face, we encounter the alter, the more-than, pre-conscious. Perception becomes revelation; it implicates me and involves me with the infinite, in the midst of the finite reality of death.

But Lévinas's subject needs the face. He needs corporeality of subject and a real world. It is the body that is "the mode in which a being, neither spatial nor foreign to . . . physical extension, exists separately," in which "thought" is transformed "into life." Without volition and desire, sense and sentiment, "the strictly intellectualist thesis subordinates life to representation."[39] The transcendent is played out in life. Film, in this sense, then, must reveal this phenomenological interplay between physical extension and the infinite *alter*.

This transcendent revelation is a moment of hope, because it presents the possibility of response from something outside of us. It presents us with the possibility of the separate yet infinite other. This hope of transcendence, the transcendence that Schrader points to as a "gulf of mysticism"[40] that we touch when taken up in the Wholly Other, and is brought about by the phenomenological tools of light and color, silence and "surveillance camera" non-narrative cinema,[41] at once highlights the role of the Other in film, as it diverges from the phenomenology of this relation that Lévinas requires.

For Lévinas, the problem of the "sacred otherness," which incorporates what transcendental style aims toward, is a problem of hope. This Wholly Other cannot do enough to affect the "stuff" of our existence. It does not "do" phenomenology. Bergo suggests that "the project of inscribing messianic hope [a sacred totality] into history fails for Lévinas." What Lévinas favors instead is a transcendent hope that is found in the stuff of the world, and revealed in the interhuman encounter. Lévinas "turns to sensibility . . . in the French style of a phenomenology of sensibility as desire and affectivity."[42] In *Totality and Infinity*, Lévinas claims that the other exceeds any idea that I might have of her, and the way in which this excess presents herself is through the face. So he writes: "The face of the other at each moment destroys and overflows the plastic image it leaves me, the idea of existing to my own measure and to the measure of its *ideatum*—the adequate idea."[43] The face that presents herself to me evokes the transcendent otherness that my totalizing images of that encounter cannot contain. And it is here that he situates hope. Merleau-Ponty cannot account for this hope, because the other is always mediated by my experience. There is no Wholly Other that can come from beyond to break into the immanence. For Lévinas, there is, and this revelation of hope occurs in the human face of the other. It is beyond the neo-Platonic "transcendence of the One."[44] Lévinas is caught up in a transcendent hope, as the expression of the pre-rational relation to the world—the response to the other's human face. But the transcendent hope that he qualifies as "holiness," the being-for-another, differs substantively from the "transcendence" of the sacred, where the other is enveloped in the experience of the same, that is, becoming unified with the Wholly Other. Lévinas needs to maintain plurality.

If I suggest that Lévinas's definition of phenomenology encompasses a greater recognition of embodied experience than other definitions of phenomenology, opting for a revelational understanding of transcendence, then I need to see if film actually does this work of transcendent relation. This brings us to an interesting challenge, because it means doing the Lévinasian definition of phenomenology: namely, transcendental style in cinema and ethical-revelational content of film script. Rather than understood hermeneutically with prioritization of interpreting experience through language, the "flesh becomes word."[45] Meaning is made through the confrontation with the transcendent face. Of course, a narrative can illustrate this confrontational movement toward ethical subjectivity. Grigus shows us how the cinematic retelling of transcendence is possible. But it does not address what Merleau-Ponty points to in the beginning, and what Lévinas agrees with, namely that reality takes on weight through sensibility and affectivity.

Film requires Merleau-Ponty to go further. In turn, Merleau-Ponty requires that Lévinasian philosophy accounts for experience of the sensible world. It needs to account for the actual cinematic creation itself—the use of the lens, the light, and the director's influences. Each of these permits the transcendent revelation to occur. It is all of these elements together that create both form and content of the film. Lévinas's definition of a transcendent relation to the Other actually requires addressing the relation to transcendent Otherness (differentiating it from sacred sameness) and acknowledging the sensible form of a thing, and not just its narrative content. To be truly phenomenological, we need to look at the substantive existence, that is, the form of film.

Lévinas's Transcendent in the Films of Ruben Östlund

In order to figure out if film can do phenomenology, we have now landed on a more specific subset of questions. What we are interested in here is whether film can reveal the transcendent encounter that Lévinas requires, in both narrative content and form. This section will explore whether revelational transcendence can actually happen through the medium of film. I want to say that it can. That it does. For this, I want to draw on the films by Swedish film director Ruben Östlund, who, I will argue, invokes both form and content in order to establish a cinema of transcendence that "does" the work of phenomenology.

Östlund's films are famous for their close and vibrant portrayals of modern ethical encounter. In *Play* (2011), three Swedish youths are confronted by a young gang of boys. Later *Force Majeure* (2014) documents the encounter between a husband and wife on the French ski slopes, and the effects of the husband's denial of escape in a moment of panic. More recently, *The Square* (2017) records a series of confrontations between an art curator and his colleagues, documenting a satire on freedom of expression and over-intellectualization of the arts. Narratively, each of these films creates a story where a person confronts the Other, who calls into question their "egoist spontaneity" and reveals themselves as incomprehensible, "a relation with a reality infinitely distant from my own reality,"[46] and yet central to their relational world. Lévinas's desire that "overflows the plastic image" can be seen in any number of Östlund's ethical confrontations between his dynamic characters.

But there is something else going on with Östlund's films which make me invoke him to show phenomenology's second requisite. His films document the confrontation and relation of the other narratively, as Girgus requires. However, his films also explore the transcendent through the form. Before making dramas, Östlund shot extreme skiing videos. In interviews, he has stated his main source of inspiration as YouTube, which *Film Comment* journalist Michelle Orange describes as "a vast . . . hunger . . . for something real but otherwise hidden."[47] The source of inspiration that shapes the narrative arc as well as the way in which the film is shot shows consideration for what Lévinas refers to as transcendent. Film is encounter, says Baracco. Film has a way of opening up "multiple horizons of sense and many perceptual possibilities."[48] Merleau-Ponty tells us this. Lévinas pushes us further: in order to do phenomenology, the sense and perceptual possibilities must resist generalization. The other who presents herself to me both hides and reveals herself; she is beyond my comprehension but still demands a response.[49] Östlund shows the uncomfortable closeness of the demands of the Real Other, who is not the same as us and who we cannot know.

This "real but otherwise hidden" evokes the confrontational conflict characteristic of Östlund's films. For instance, in *Play*, the unscripted segments between the children reveal a spontaneity and "liveness" to the performance. We are never sure where the confrontation will take us. Throughout the film, Östlund shoots from film angles that place us as voyeur. There are shots where the viewer is placed behind the glass of a tram door, watching pedestrians walking by, or from the height of the surveillance camera, looking down on the action. But, unlike the transcendental style, this use of shot brings us into the midst of the confrontation. The Wholly Other that we are confronting is not mystical or distant but rather revealed in the intensity of the interhuman events of the film. Östlund plays with this use of perception, creating increased discomfort as the viewers watch the other actors as voyeurs don't do anything. The viewers see the tram filling and emptying in violence, hear the parents never answer the phone, and become aware of the silence and the tangible cowardice of the crowd. Östlund plays with the response and the non-response to violence. But he also plays with the spontaneity of interhuman relationship. For me, this shows what Lévinas means by the revelatory elements that rupture any sameness of "character that is like that"—the energy.

In an interview done on the back of the release of Force Majeure, the reporter states: "The origins of Östlund's project and its animating sensibilities—a cross between extremely close observation and cool, wide-eyed style—can be seen in his earliest films, both of which are very personal documentaries."[50] Blurring between the documentary and the real, using documentaries of himself with his family as the conditions for subjectivity and relationship in his films, he reveals the other "infinitely distant" from the self. Yet it is this confrontation of the other, in content and form, that is the site of transformation, and so, in exposing the difficult and altogether too close reality, reveals the transcendent. Östlund reveals the *alter* in the intersubjective human exchange. It reveals a transcendence that echoes Lévinas's complex humanistic hope. Lévinas asks us to grow up: he presents a difficult freedom but stands firm in the understanding that it still offers a robust hope for this life. As I watch Östlund, I cannot help but wonder if film is also "growing up."

Conclusion

Does all film do phenomenology? That depends on what phenomenology is. I think that film has helped philosophers to see where their definitions of phenomenology are lacking. But in turn, phenomenology can show where film is not quite "doing" what phenomenology requires—putting transcendent essence back into the flesh of existence. Revelation par excellence. But this must mean that the film evokes the phenomenological expression in form as well as content. And it means going back to basic questions about what constitutes phenomenology in the first place, which is a good place to start.

Still, there are films that are doing this, and perhaps more so now than before, as our tools of communication and filmmaking bring us closer to what Lévinas reveals as the "face of the other" which reveals a relation that "destroys and overflows the plastic image it leaves me, the idea of existing to my own measure."[51] Using the definition of phenomenology as provided by Lévinas allows us to say, yes, sometimes film does philosophy. This does not mean that this definition can be straightforwardly applied or that it is black and white. Certainly, Bresson, in his use of models ("the thing that matters is not what they show me but what they hide from me"[52]), creates a semblance of the Lévinasian idea of the transcendent face, and Östlund uses techniques of slow cinema to develop the excruciating and drawn out conflict between the gang and the young boys in *Play*.

Personally, I am excited by what this exchange offers. I think that it shows a bi-directional conversation between phenomenology and film that is essential. As film develops and changes, so too does our understanding of what phenomenology requires of us to define and explore. As such, I think the answer to the main question remains ambiguous, but certain: film can help us to better phenomenology, and phenomenology can help us to reinvent the possibility of film. Yes, sometimes film does our work for us.

With thanks to Col Spector.

Notes

1   Robert Bresson, *Notes on the Cinematograph*, trans. Jonathan Griffin (New York: New York Review of Books, 1975/1986), 6.

2   Richard Kearney and Brian Treanor, eds., *Carnal Hermeneutics* (New York: Fordham University Press, 2015), 16.

3   Richard Kearney, *Touch: Recovering Our Most Vital Sense* (New York: Columbia University Press, 2021).

4   Kearney, *Carnal Hermeneutics*, 16.

5   Maurice Merleau-Ponty, *Phenomenology of Perception*, trans. Colin Smith (London: Routledge & Kegan Paul, 1962), vii.

6   Ibid., x.

7   Maurice Merleau-Ponty, *Sense and Nonsense*, trans. Hubert L. Dreyfus and Patricia Dreyfus (Evanston, IL: Northwestern University Press, 1964).

8   Vivian Sobchack, "'The Active Eye' (Revisited): Toward a Phenomenology of Cinematic Movement," *Studia Phaenomenologica* XVI (2016): 63. (See chapter 4 above, pp xx–xx).

9   Merleau-Ponty, *Phenomenology of Perception*, 18.

10 Jack Reynolds, "Merleau-Ponty, Lévinas, and the Alterity of the Other," *Symposium* 6, no. 1 (2002): 64.

11 Ibid., 5.

12 Sobchack, "The Active Eye," 69.

13 Reynolds, "Alterity of the Other," 69.

14 Maurice Merleau-Ponty, *The Visible and Invisible*, trans. Alphonso Lingis (Evanston, IL: Northwestern University Press, 1969), 127.

15 Albert Baracco, "Phenomenology of Film," in *Hermeneutics of the Film World* (Palgrave Macmillan, 2017), 53.

16 Jean-Paul Sartre, "Apologie pour le Cinéma. Défense et illustration d'un art international," in *Écrits de Jeunesse* (Paris: Gallimard, 1990).

17 Baracco, "Phenomenology of Film," 3.

18 Ibid., 4.

19 Bresson, *Notes on the Cinematograph*, 48.

20 Ibid., 76.

21 Paul Schrader, *Transcendental Style in Cinema* (Oakland, CA: University of California Press, 2018), 41.

22 Ibid., 36.

23 Reynolds, "Alterity of the Other," 67.

24 Emmanuel Lévinas, *Is It Righteous to Be? Interviews with Emmanuel Lévinas*, ed. Jill Robbins (Stanford, CA: Stanford University Press, 2001), 160.

25 Emmanuel Lévinas, *Totality and Infinity*, trans. Alphonso Lingis (Pittsburgh, PA: Duquesne University Press, 1969), 44.

26 Ibid., 48.

27 Ibid.

28 Ibid., 41.

29 Ibid., 43.

30 Sam B. Girgus, *Lévinas and the Cinema of Redemption: Time, Ethics and the Feminine* (New York: Columbia University Press, 2010), 3.

31 Ibid., 57.

32 Colin Davis, "Lévinas and Film," in *The Oxford Handbook of Lévinas*, ed. Michael L. Morgan (London: Oxford University Press, 2019), 515–28.

33 Girgus, *Cinema of Redemption*, 5.

34 Ibid., 4.

35 Ibid.

36 Bettina Bergo, "Thinking Hope Through a (Living) Body: Lévinas's Difficult Messianic Moment," in *Minimalist Faith, Embodied Messianism* (2009), 102. Available at: https://www.academia.edu/1662270/Minimalist_Faith_Embodied_Messianism (Accessed February 25, 2021).

37 Ibid., 103.

38 Ibid.

39 Lévinas, *Totality and Infinity*, 285.

40 Schrader, *Transcendental Style in Film*, 39.

41 Ibid., 25.

42 Bettina Bergo, "The Flesh Made Word," in *Nietzsche and Lévinas: After the Death of a Certain God*, ed. Jill Stauffer and Bettina Bergo (New York: Columbia University Press, 2009), 2.

43 Ibid., 51.

44 Emmanuel Lévinas, *Alterity and Transcendence*, trans. Michael B. Smith (New York: Columbia University Press, 1999), 11.

45 Bergo, "Thinking Hope Through a Living Body."

46 Lévinas, *Totality and Infinity*, 41.

47 Michelle Orange, "Broken Contracts," "Broken Contracts," *Film Comment*, January–February 2015. Available at: https://www.filmcomment.com/article/broken-contracts-ruben-ostlund/ (Accessed February 25, 2021).

48 Baracco, "Phenomenology in Film," 41.

49 Lévinas, *Totality and Infinity*, 44.

50 Violet Lucca, "Interview: Ruben Östlund," *Film Comment*, October 21, 2014. Available at: https://www.filmcomment.com/blog/interview-ruben-oestlund/ (Accessed February 25, 2021).

51 Lévinas, *Totality and Infinity*, 51.

52 Bresson, *Notes on the Cinematograph*, 6.

12

I Wake Up Screaming

Kansas and Beyond

Anthony J. Steinbock

Unlike westerns, detective films, or science fiction cinema, film noir is not considered to be a "genre," but rather a style or "cycle" that cuts across genres. Most interestingly, film noir emerged spontaneously as a distinctive style of film before it became conscious of itself as such. It expresses a world that has lost its hold on stable structures, a world that is trying to secure some foothold without guarantee; it evokes lives that have to navigate multiple perspectives where there are no absolutes to ground them or to give definitive answers—leaving us only with ourselves, ambiguity, contingency: "shadows." It is such a situation that is expressive of the existentialist themes of anxiety, disparity, absurdity, finitude, the rupture of linear time, the feeling of being trapped with no escape, the questioning of good and evil, and only temporary and situational triumph. In many ways, it can be seen as the harbinger of what we call today "postmodernism."

But if phenomenology, indeed, transcendental phenomenology is understood as a philosophy of transcendence; if phenomenology is the philosophical approach that lets everyday experience emerge in its fundamental strangeness and wonder, then perhaps phenomenology and film noir are more closely allied than what appears at first glance. This would mean that rather than simple entertainment, film noir in its deepest form is to be understood as taking a stand on human experience; it becomes a process of revealing as well as depicting what it means to be human; it questions and retraces the bonds that connect us to one another and to the world. As Maurice Merleau-Ponty suggests in a different context, philosophy and film—and here phenomenology and film noir—share a certain manner of being. This is certainly the case with the film by Humberstone, *I Wake Up Screaming*. In an original and novel way, human experience is portrayed through everyday trials, familiar disappointments, typical events, and restless pursuits of the real, all of which resurrect a core of human experience that has the potential not only of calling us to ourselves but of revisioning the heart of human experience.

The Maltese Falcon is often considered to be the first film noir of the classical noir period (beginning in 1941 and ending in 1958 with Orson Wells, *Touch of Evil*).[1] Released only two weeks after *The Maltese Falcon* (Houston, October 18, 1941) is another noir included in the classical catalog, namely, *I Wake Up Screaming* (October 31, 1941). Loosely based on a Steve Fisher novel of the same name, *I Wake Up Screaming* was imaginatively adapted into a screenplay by Dwight Taylor and creatively directed by H. Bruce Humberstone, with the inventive cinematographer Edward Cronjager and producer Milton Sperling.

Though shot in a more recognizable visual style, *The Maltese Falcon* has earned its titular fame not only because John Huston directed it, not only because it was based on a Dashiell Hammett novel, or because Humphrey Bogart played the starring role as Samuel Spade. Rather—and limitations of space do not allow me to elaborate here—this film called into question the familiar boundaries between appearance and reality, it exposed the lures of spiritual and economic idolatry, and, in a modest way, it advanced the arbitrariness of the "absurd man." While I do not take issue with the honorific place of *The Maltese Falcon*, the distinctive contributions of *I Wake Up Screaming* to the noir cycle are often overshadowed by this: its older fraternal twin.

Many critics have already cogently commented on the distinctive and original visual quality of *I Wake Up Screaming*. Eddie Muller, author of *Dark City*, for example, stresses in his running commentary on the film how innovative lighting, sharp shadows, and single source key lighting exhibit for us today ample and even paradigmatic examples of cinematographic techniques that have come to characterize film noir.[2] In fact, he is wont to call this film the first film noir, at least for 20th Century Fox. But even if *I Wake Up Screaming* were not the "first" film noir, there are still abundant reasons to recommend this film as an exemplary "noir," one that is both under-appreciated and/or misunderstood. Indeed, there are aspects of the film that I think if recognized would place it more securely among the canonical films of the noir cycle.

What forcefully commends its serious consideration and exemplary position in classical noir can be seen in the way in which it conveys a "new" (anti-Modern) view of the world that starkly contrasts with a former (Modern) worldview. One can argue, in fact, that its innovative visual techniques are expressive of and serve this end. The worldview portrayed in this film is at odds with an implicit optimism that things happen for a reason, that truth and universal justice can be easily discerned, that necessity will prevail over contingency, and that when all is said and done, we will be comforted by our familiar world. That is, *I Wake Up Screaming* imaginatively depicts our contemporary situation of encountering a relatively new disturbance in human existence, one in which ideals of truth, justice, trust, security—captured by the emotionally charged cipher of "home"—are radically called into question. Further, it is surprisingly anti-Modern not only in the aforementioned regard but because of the suggested way of redressing this existential trauma. It does not advocate a return to traditional Modern and classical male virtues of rationality and courage; it does not counter with Reason's naturalistic and dualistic counterpart, sheer instinct—though all of these are displayed in one way or another as alternatives; rather, it implies a way forward by retrieving what I call the order of the heart.

The anti-Modern worldview and the anti-Modern redress (i.e., the order of the heart) are two points that all the commentaries I have encountered seem to miss—despite their laudatory and critical appreciation of this film. How does this film advance its unique positions? Certainly, it presents angles askew, depth and volume through chiaroscurist lighting and shadows, upsetting frames and jarring edges, as well as inventive flashback narrative structures. Yet these originations are as much technical innovations as they are expressive elaborations of the film's thematic messages. By artistically deviating from Fisher's novel upon which the storyline is based, it originally adapts tropes, characters, and leitmotifs taken from the *then*-recent MGM box-office disappointment, *The Wizard of Oz* (Fleming, 1939), and resourcefully deploys them, evoking the dread of a new existential situation, and a possible anti-Modern challenge.[3] Thus, rather than waking up *from* a consuming nightmare to our cozy experience of being home in the world in familiar certainties and surroundings ("there's no place like home"), we instead *wake up to* a disorienting nightmare, which is the new world. This is why "I wake up screaming." The effective flashback structure; the brilliant use of shadows, angles, bars, and grills; and the character placement and displacement in the film all deliver this moral disposition.[4]

I want to illustrate this idea in five steps. After a brief summary of the basic plot, I examine the disruption, instability, and the idea of a feral humanity that is portrayed through key cinematographic and narrative devices. I then examine the main characters with an eye to their symbolic relevance with their *Wizard of Oz* parallels. This section is followed by highlighting the visual, staging, and musical clues for this interpretation of the film. I conclude with a brief summary suggesting how *I Wake Up Screaming* can be understood as one of the first original noirs presenting an anti-Modern theme and posing a possible anti-Modern challenge often ignored by Modernity.

Plot Summary

In most general outline form, here is the basic movement: on a hubristic lark, Frankie Christopher (Victor Mature), the promoter, has the idea of making the hash-slinging waitress, Vicky Lynn (Carole Landis), a glamorous model with star potential. His two friends, a passé actor, Robin Ray (Alan Mowbray), and a hack column journalist, Larry Evans (Allyn Joslyn), join him for the fun of it. The film opens, however, with the headlines that a model has been murdered, and with Frankie being interrogated for Vicky's murder. Through a series of flashbacks that then catch up with the present, the viewer learns that the lead inspector in the case, Ed Cornell (Laird Cregar), who has a perfect arrest record, is determined to find Frankie guilty of this crime and virtually harasses him at every turn. (The viewer learns later, however, that Cornell knows from very early on that Frankie did not commit the murder.) Vicky's sister, Jill (Betty Grable), and Frankie eventually fall in love and try to discern the real murderer, working through suspicions of the actor and the journalist, discovering that it is actually the creepy switchboard operator, Harry Williams (the noir staple, Elisha Cook Jr.). Sneaking into Cornell's apartment before he arrives, Frankie discovers that Cornell has an eerie obsessive fascination with Vicky: the apartment turned mausoleum/shrine is festooned with pictures of Vicki towering above tributes of flowers. After arriving on the scene, fresh bouquet in hand, Cornell explains that he blames Frankie for taking the once humble Vicky out of his reach, having given her all the ideas of fame and glamor. Having lost himself and his love, with "curtains to his brilliant career," he purposefully and fatally overdoses on his prescription tincture.

With this brief overview, let's step back now and proceed more systematically, describing the uncanny setting and atmosphere of the film, and then identifying the characters and their symbolic resonances, which lead to some of the key themes of this film that make it characteristically noir.

Disruption, Instability, and Feral Humanity

The film opens with a headline announcing the murder of a young model (Vicky Lynn) and moves immediately to a dark and boisterous interrogation room. Hemmed in by shadowy figures on all sides, Frankie Christopher is set in relief by a blinding interrogation lamp. Clearly uncomfortable, on the defensive from the very start, Frankie is accused by an impersonal accuser who remains as yet undefined behind a murky curtain of anonymity. The voice of this indicter enters the scene, but his face and identity remain veiled as a darkened silhouette.

The unsettling position of Frankie in this cave-like chamber is now mirrored by a series of temporal displacements. The beginning of the story lands the viewer clearly in the *middle* of *something*. However, rather than going forward from this ambiguous present/middle in a linear progression of time, the viewer goes backward in order to advance. The flashback—which was not part of Fisher's novel—was introduced here, a storytelling device that became solidified as a narrative technique in Wilder's *Double Indemnity* (1944), and used to great effect in Tourneur's *Out of the Past* (1947). From the onset of the film, one is oriented by disorientation, presented with a series of forced recollections that catch the viewer up to the mystery of the social dynamics and murder.

Second, there are not only temporal disturbances but also abundant forms of spatial disruption. The latter are vividly portrayed through the copious cages, grills, and bars. Not just convicts and suspects but policemen and detectives are separated and jarringly connected by see-through cages.[5] The lattice-like confines—metallic or ephemeral shadows—tend to stress our human finitude, namely, the fact that we all live under the threat of our own mortality—a pronounced theme of Maté's *D.O.A.* (1950)[6] (Figures 12.1 and 12.2).

FIGURE 12.1 *Venetian Blinds*. I Wake Up Screaming, *directed by Steve Fisher © Twentieth Century-Fox Film Corporation 1941. All rights reserved.*

FIGURE 12.2 *Cage Frankie*. I Wake Up Screaming, *directed by Steve Fisher © Twentieth Century-Fox Film Corporation 1941. All rights reserved.*

Like in the consolation bar scene, oblique lines alternate with the shift of one conversant to the next; sharp angles and tilted frames all suggest that humanity is losing its balance in a world that no longer conforms to it but to which it must adjust in order to survive.

Third, evicted from a controllable human world, the abundant images of confines and partitions suggest that the human social environment resembles a bestiary (think here of Bergman's 1953, *Sawdust and Tinsel*). It is not the Modern vision of a rupture between the human and the animal, culture and nature, but rather a vision that the "human" is all too animalistic, feral, and at root nothing more. Indeed, this film is replete with so-called reductive animalist intimations that very few characters are able to deflect. Two early comments in the film make these allusions. Looking at a photo of Vicky who Frankie just promoted, he comments: "Here. Take a look at that." Jill responds: "Hmm. Feeding time at the zoo." Or Vicky to her sister: "We've got more wolves in New York than they have in Siberia."

This is a topsy-turvy world in which human beings are in cages (police holding rooms, police offices, apartments, elevators) and feral animals are running free. I just want to highlight two occasions (though there are several more) in which human beings are purposefully evoked in terms of feral animals and where social life is reduced to manipulation by uncontrollable drives. The suggestion is that as humans we are slaves to our wild natures, our instinctual animal energies; and rather than appeal to the old concept of reason, we have to adjust to this new realization of our reality. In one scene, Frankie wakes up in his bed to a startling figure of Cornell, apparently sitting for some time in an armchair in his (Frankie's) bedroom (Figure 12.3).

FIGURE 12.3 *Panther predator.* I Wake Up Screaming, *directed by Steve Fisher ©* *Twentieth Century-Fox Film Corporation 1941. All rights reserved.*

Behind the seated wily Cornell is a painting of a black panther on a trifold room divider: the descending panther is directly over Cornell's right shoulder, and on the other panels, fleeing gazelles; outside the window is a flashing neon sign, evoking an "asphalt jungle." This feline hunter (alluding to Cornell as a predator) is featured in a couple of shots, and the light that illuminates this scene brings the panther to advantage. The juxtaposition of the two equates Cornell with the stalking instincts of the stealthy hunter, slowly but surely pursuing its prey. It is not the police chief in pursuit of truth or justice as the viewer learns, but an individual chasing his specific aims.[7]

On another noteworthy occasion following this one, Cornell wants to recapture Frankie. Jill has helped a handcuffed Frankie elude detention, but as his accomplice, she is now held in police custody with Frankie on the lam. What does Cornell do? Does he appeal to crack detective work on how to find missing criminals? Does he put out an "All Points Bulletin," like one might see happening, for example, in *The Glass Wall* (1953), trying to track down a fugitive in the streets of New York? No. Cornell appeals to the strategy of a *naturalist*. The naturalist that he alludes to here is Fabre (not "Faber"— undoubtedly, Jean-Henri Casimir Fabre, who was a French contemporary of Darwin, and for all intents and purposes, was the father of modern entomology). The book he names is the fictitiously entitled *The Sex Life of the Butterfly*.[8]

Appropriately, the district attorney asks Cornell what all this has to do with the Lynn/Christopher case. Cornell responds by recounting a story about how Fabre could not catch an exotic male specimen of an elusive butterfly from Africa. The technique was to let the female out of the glass box, and let it flit around the (Paris) apartment, and in a few hours the keeper had ten times as many rare male African butterflies filling the room. With the reduction of humans to feline predators, rodents, and insects, sexual love is reduced to chemical attraction of pheromones. The police detective is turned naturalist; criminology is turned entomology. The D.A. agreeably concedes: let Jill loose, and we will have our man in no time (and maybe more than just one!).

In sum, there is a relatively disturbing view of the human situation. Human beings are on the defensive from the very start, and in a Kafkaesque manner, facing an impersonal accuser for something they did not do. The only way forward is to go backward. To be human is to confront finitude at every turn; already imprisoned like caged animals, humans interact with one another like feral predators and prey, where social life is not governed by reason or by spiritual emotions but by sheer instinct.

The Main Characters and Their Symbolic Relevance

Let's take a look now at some of the main characters, since the main ones have an important symbolic and not merely narrative role to play in the movement of the film. Let's begin with Frankie Christopher.

Frankie Christopher is a sports promoter in New York, apparently, a well-known and successful one. There is nothing personal in what he does one way or another; it is simply his business to promote—a constant refrain—and he will promote just about anything without pangs of conscience: "from prizefighters to fan dancers," including "hockey, ice carnivals, girls. Mostly girls." Under interrogation by the still anonymous Cornell, Frankie explains why he thinks he could have made something of Vicky, replying matter-of-factly "that's my business: promotion."

In one scene, Frankie is ringside at a fight with Jill. He is standing and shouting: "Give him your left! Let 'im have your left! Give it to him again! . . . Go after his stomach, you lug! His stomach!" I cannot help but think of the 1949 film by Robert Wise starring Robert Ryan, *The Set-Up*. In this film, the audience or spectators are paradoxically the participants; their vitriolic touts, aggressive gestures, and grotesque eating habits are clearly the places of violence—not the rather regulated and controlled fighting ring. The latter at least is contained spatially by ropes and temporally by rounds and has a mediator in place if things get out of control.

Here, however, it is not so much that Frankie is invested with violence; it is more the case that he is supporting his impersonal business investment, rooting for a fighter of whom he "owns a piece." (Although, as noted later, there are hints of another side of Frankie. A personal nature slips out: "he's a great little kid," says Frankie, "I raised him from a pup." In addition, one begins to see Jill grow more enamored with his childlike spontaneous side.)

To get an even better sense of Frankie, it will be helpful to go back to the first flashback. He and his cohorts, Robin the actor and Larry the journalist, wager that they can take a rather naïve, attractive waitress and make her into a starlet. This is Frankie's idea—to spot talent and bring it into being. Frankie buys her fine clothes, takes her to a nightclub, and introduces her to high-society. Robin coaches her on acting the part; they stage an argument over her so that she gets noticed, and the journalist writes a spot in his column featuring her social debut.

Just how good of a promoter is Frankie? Apparently, he is quite good, an artistic genius, even. When Jill and Frankie are hiding from the police, Jill liberating him from handcuffs with a hacksaw, Frankie confesses to her that "Christopher" is not his real last name. Placating her worry that he changed his name because of a criminal past, he reassures her that "Christopher" was just easier to spell. His real surname? Botticelli.

The name Botticelli is chosen here, not because it is some extravagant Italian family name to emphasize Frankie's New York Italian heritage, as is often suggested. The film wanted to evoke something else. Botticelli refers to the famous fifteenth-century Italian artist Sandro Botticelli, who painted the *Birth of Venus*.[9] In apparent anticipation of this revelation, Robin alluded earlier to Frankie's artistic virtuosity: "But I doubt if even you, maestro, could make a lady out of a hash slinger."

The rise of Vicky from waitress to the alluring and promising Hollywood starlet was Frankie's creation, the birth of a "Venus." After the three men accompany Vicky back home, concluding her successful social outing as the new glamor girl, the tables have turned. She is already too good for them all. She steps into the screened elevator platform, and ascends: the goddess of love. The heads of the three men in the parquet tilt upwards as they follow her ascent. Vicky passes out of their (mortal) reach: the birth of Venus (Figure 12.4).

Although, admittedly, the following scene is directed more at the creation than the creator, Frankie nearly compares himself to a mad scientist (not a creative artist). Vicky snaps at Frankie: "Some people think I'm a very attractive girl; you didn't create that. I'm no Frankenstein, you know." Frankie: "I wonder."

Later I will return to Frankie's own transformation, which further confirms this thesis about his character and leads to another anti-Modern twist; for now it is sufficient to suggest that to the extent Frankie is the indifferent, venturing business promoter, Frankie Christopher symbolizes the Tin Man in *The Wizard of Oz*; he has no heart.

Robin Ray is the has-been, slightly portly ham actor, longing for the spotlight of younger days (he mentions his desire to have been cast recently as Romeo). Robin is also the wannabe idealistic lover wanting to run away with Vicky, to renew his acting career, as well as his hope and belief in himself. His interior persona is revealed when he is called into the police station for questioning regarding Vicky's murder. Opening with a policeman behind a grillwork cage, Robin is seated, nervously smoking a cigarette, looking at the wanted posters, then saunters to the water cooler to quench

FIGURE 12.4 *Birth of Venus*. I Wake Up Screaming, *directed by Steve Fisher* © *Twentieth Century-Fox Film Corporation 1941. All rights reserved.*

his thirst. When Frankie comes through the door and taps him on the shoulder, he startles him: "Hello, Robin." Robin jumps and spills his water.

Robin fretfully asks, "How do they go about these things? What do they do to you?" Frankie: "Oh, nothing much. It's sorta like playing handball, only you're the ball. Say, you should have worn overalls. I'm afraid you're gonna get that suit all messed up." Robin: "Are you serious?" Frankie: "What do you think?"

As they enter a special interrogation room, Robin inquires as if afraid of the dark: "No lights?" Frankie, egging him on retorts: "You're lucky. Go ahead. You're an actor. Pretend you're going to your execution." Robin sits in a dark, smoke-filled screening room, watching the screen test of Vicky (a screen test that he had originally arranged for the both of them). Wringing his gloves, eyes darting furtively from each corner, he springs for the door trying desperately to get out of the locked room, rattling the doorknob: "Let me out! Let me out of here!" He admits in the D.A.'s chambers that he had been shaken up to the point of causing an uproar when he learned that Vicky wanted to go it alone, not wanting "to hitch her wagon to a falling star." But he did not kill her. On the day of her murder, he had an alibi: he visited a sanitarium, a place he goes regularly when things get tough, "and they take care of me."[10] To console him, Frankie offers the somewhat pathetic, cowered, ashamed, defeated man a cigarette. Robin Ray owns the character of the cowardly lion.

Larry Evans, the column journalist, figures as the scarecrow. From the outset Larry is portrayed as a yellow-journalist. He seems to write as the wind blows. Perhaps one of the most convincing indications of this yellow-journalism, and in general that he lacks the smarts and an acuity of discernment, is the scene when Frankie and Jill step out to go dancing. Seeing them together, he jumps up from his table and grabs a phone calling his office: Larry tells them to scrap a story about a Japanese spy. Now, when this film was shot, the United States had not yet entered the war, and Japan had not yet bombed Pearl Harbor. But we have here a possible momentous story about Japanese espionage on US soil that could have international consequences. Instead of letting this story stand, Larry orders them to run a relatively inconsequential bit of gossip: "What sister of what recently murdered girl is stepping out with the dead girl's boyfriend? Dancing on the grave, I call it. The murderer has yet to be found."[11]

The memory of an elephant Larry has not. After returning to her apartment, chivalrously climbing in through the window to unlock the front door, Vicky announces that she is leaving for Hollywood. "You won't forget me, will you?" she asks Larry. "I won't for at least two weeks." With a little wounded pride, she probes: "Two weeks isn't very long, is it?" Larry: "It is for a columnist." The basic sense we get of Larry is that he is scattered, has a short attention span, and is not in possession of keen powers of discernment. For these reasons, he fits nicely the role of the friendly but witless scarecrow.

All three characters, Frankie, Robin, and Larry (they each discover), are given a key to Vicky's apartment—they are all travelers along the yellow brick road of Vicky's success, and each in their own way is enamored with Vicky.

From inside and outside, the inspector, Ed Cornell, is the most mysterious of figures. Notice that the heavy shadows at the very beginning of the film, the key lighting, the bright lights trained on Frankie under interrogation—all this keeps Cornell hidden from direct view while he orchestrates the events and players. He remains behind the shroud of shadows, the curtain of anonymity: the Wizard[12] (Figures 12.5 and 12.6).

FIGURE 12.5 *Cornell Wizard 1.* I Wake Up Screaming, *directed by Steve Fisher ©* *Twentieth Century-Fox Film Corporation 1941. All rights reserved.*

FIGURE 12.6 *Cornell Wizard 2.* I Wake Up Screaming, *directed by Steve Fisher ©* *Twentieth Century-Fox Film Corporation 1941. All rights reserved.*

A characteristic noir look is scripted here by the innovation of the screenplay: casting Cornell as the murky mysterious "Wizard-figure," with only his authorial voice barking accusations and orders from behind the cloak of shadows. Frankie's response to Cornell highlights the case, snapping at the shadowy figure at the left edge of the screen: "You're a pretty tough guy, aren't you, with a crowd around? Why don't you come out in the open so I can see you?" The shadowy silhouette behind the lamp [Cornell] responds curtly: "Never mind that." A little later, Frankie is staring into an interrogation lamp from whence the anonymous voice originates; Frankie can't see him and calls him only "wise guy."

The viewer does not get to meet Cornell, or at least one of Cornell's characters—matching the voice behind the drapery of shadows as the inspector—until after Jill's flashback. He is only given audibly as the interrogative and accusatory voice, and visually through Jill's flashback as the unnerving peeping tom obsessed with Vicky. It is Jill who puts them together for us after a sequence of complementing flashbacks by Frankie and Jill. No longer willing to take the insults, Jill demands to see someone in authority. Evocative of a raptor who just caught his meal, the voice [Cornell] yields: "Alright boys, keep him [Frankie] warm; I'll be right back," as he moves to the next room to hear the complaint.

On the one hand, there is a vision of a man, Cornell, who has a stellar fifteen-year career-winning streak of having never lost a conviction as police inspector. There is a vision of a man committed to the pursuit of justice: defender of the weak. He emphasizes that all of this is "simply a matter of justice" and insists on the universality and eternal nature of justice: "justice is justice."

This latter appeal to justice, however, dissonantly follows his intrusion into Jill's apartment! What is not clear yet is that justice and truth for him are not universal ideals but highly idiosyncratic manipulators. He uses the fact that he has "never been wrong yet," coupled with the definition of justice as the same justice for all and for all time, to carry out a one-time personal vendetta. He moves from an (ungrounded) assertion about reality for everyone else based on his reputation: "That man's guilty"—to the confession of intent to break the law that he pledged to uphold: "I've got a good mind to kill you myself right now"—to an implicit self-condemnation: "If that isn't the look of a guilty man, I will take the rap myself."[13]

Cornell may not have lost a conviction during his tenure as inspector, but he did lose something more important to him: his obsession, Vicky. By the end of the film, it is confirmed that Harry Williams, the switchboard operator, actually killed Vicky; Cornell discovered this, but instructed the switchboard operator to return to work and say nothing. Discovering this himself, Frankie asked for five minutes of retribution and precedes Cornell in Cornell's apartment. When he steps into the room and first turns on one set of lights, he pulls back the curtain on the Wizard.[14]

Like Frankie, the viewer is startled with a shrine of framed photographs, and below them, an altar of flower offerings to Vicky. All the lights illuminated, the second look reveals two walls fixatedly covered with a dozen model poses of Vicky, advertisements, and glamor shots. It is now Frankie hidden from Cornell. Cornell unsuspectingly walks in the room with fresh flower tributes. The surprised Cornell, desperately clinging to his former persona, utters these words to Frankie: "Have you come to give yourself up?"

Frankie had already sensed a strange compulsiveness in Cornell's action, action that had nothing to do with the pursuit of truth and the execution of justice. Portending his current discovery, Frankie charges: "You're not a cop looking for a murderer. You're crazy Cornell." With the disclosure that Frankie knows Williams is the murderer, Cornell immediately reaches for his medicine and poisons himself. Cornell confirms to his nemesis: "I'm a sick man, Frankie." Frankie: "At your soul, Cornell." Cornell: "Maybe." This points to a moral sickness, and not merely a medical condition (as in the book).

An almost tragic confession now retreats all of the dissembling curtains and shadows hiding Cornell and exposes his inner being. He describes how he had stalked Vicky for months before mustering the courage to speak to her. He felt that she took him on his own ground, and hoped that they would start to know each other better, and that he would get courage to ask her to marry him one day. So, he presumptuously took the present apartment, started to furnish it, and even stocked the perfume she liked in order to surprise her with it all.

He knew that Williams was guilty but wanted Frankie to fry. Why? For him, and him alone, Vicky was gone ("*I* lost Vicky") long before "Williams killed her." He lost her individually before she was taken universally from everyone. Therefore, universal order, right and wrong do not matter, but only *his* singular need for revenge. There are perversions and inversions of "right and wrong" on many levels here, but one of the most egregious is that Cornell uses his position as the enforcer of truth to advance his peculiar individual ends.

Cornell is no longer the hunter, the panther, the slaughter, the trapper, but is reduced in stature to a "worm looking up to a woman like that." He snaps at Frankie: "I could have killed you then, Christopher." Implicitly keeping the self-analogy of the worm, he explains why he did not kill him then: "Because I had the hook in your mouth and wanted to see you suffer."

It is not crucial at this point to try to identify all of the "Dorothy" parallels. In the first case, while there are many parallels between the Oz film and this one, there are no simple one-to-one correspondences between all the characters. That is not the point. Their functions play a much more *evocative* role. It is clear, however, that both Vicky and Jill do exhibit Dorothy-like characters (as we will see later, especially in the next two sections).[15]

Visual, Staging, and Musical Clues

Let me now call attention to a few striking clues that suggest this overall interpretation of the film, clues that help to show the novelty and significance of this original film noir.

The first clue of note is a visual clue, a rather playful one, and it greets us in the very opening of the film. It is intriguing that the opening credits to the film seem already to announce its relation to *The Wizard of Oz*. Appearing in alternating angles of the cast's names and credits, but especially in the overlapping of the producer's, and director's names, there is an outline and suggestion of a "crossroads." They are the street signs pointing us in conflicting directions (like the famous scene of *The Wizard of Oz* when Dorothy meets the scarecrow at the crossroads, pondering directions to Oz on The Yellow Brick Road: Dorothy: "Now which way do we go?" . . . Scarecrow: "Of course people do go both ways") (Figure 12.7).

It is also a rather ingenious device to place the evocation of the crossroads in these opening credits. For the opening credits do not merely forecast the film. Because of their indicative structure, they are now associated with the film. They are themselves a signpost or way to read the film, and thus are already part of the narrative (the same holds for continuing the musical theme in the ending credits as they are displayed).

The second and certainly more significant clue is musical: the refrain of "Somewhere Over the Rainbow" from *The Wizard of Oz*. For anyone who has seen this film, signaling this song will come as no surprise—the only surprise perhaps being that it has taken so long to come to something so obvious! Indeed, almost every critic who has commented on this film has

FIGURE 12.7 *Crossroads.* I Wake Up Screaming, *directed by Steve Fisher* © *Twentieth Century-Fox Film Corporation 1941. All rights reserved.*

noted the omnipresence of "Somewhere over the Rainbow." It is cited either as an unexplainable curiosity or as a distracting annoyance.[16] Others, more acutely like Muller, have recognized the patterned association of "Somewhere Over the Rainbow" with the appearance of Jill, the "good," "garden variety" sister, and the score of Alfred Newman's "Street Scene" with Vicky, the "glamour girl." Both instances tend to be associated, further, in terms of their relation with Frankie. This is especially evident when the themes oscillate from one to the other when Jill discusses Frankie's cryptic note to Vicky.

But more than this, I suggest, the *sheer repetition* of "Somewhere over the Rainbow" is just *begging* the viewer to go beyond the mere association of the song with the character, and to become one main needles of the compass to orienting us through the whole film, namely, as a distinctive elaboration of *The Wizard of Oz*, and more precisely, as anti-Oz (anti-Modern). The repetition was probably necessary to drive home the point. Let us recall that *The Wizard of Oz* appeared in 1939, only two years before this film, and had an underwhelming reception at the box office. It was re-released in its theatrical version a decade later and began to receive its widespread popularity with the television production in 1956.

The anti-Modern, anti-Oz, anti-home vision is also reflected in the staging and related visual clues. One of the most "Dorothy"-like scenes puts Jill in the kitchen of her new place, domestically bedecked at the sink with apron, dish towel in hand, drying dishes. Visually, the shot is classically edged— Jill appears through the stable, evenly proportioned and vertically balanced portico of the doorframe (Figure 12.8).

FIGURE 12.8 *Home.* I Wake Up Screaming, *directed by Steve Fisher* © *Twentieth Century-Fox Film Corporation 1941. All rights reserved.*

But for the viewer, the "home" was never really secure in the first place, because this "cozy" moment was shattered before it began when Cornell started to enter the locked door with his passkey. This stability is subsequently upset and almost violently disturbed by the re-intrusion of Cornell. Jill is doubly confronted, by Cornell's person *and* his imposing shadow (not to mention verbal assaults), and this gets represented through angular, unstable, unbalanced, skewed close-ups of unease, possibly panic, and fear (Figures 12.9–12.11).

FIGURE 12.9 *Intruder 1.* I Wake Up Screaming, *directed by Steve Fisher ©* *Twentieth Century-Fox Film Corporation 1941. All rights reserved.*

FIGURE 12.10 *Home disruption 1.* I Wake Up Screaming, *directed by Steve Fisher © Twentieth Century-Fox Film Corporation 1941. All rights reserved.*

FIGURE 12.11 *Home disruption 2.* I Wake Up Screaming, *directed by Steve Fisher © Twentieth Century-Fox Film Corporation 1941. All rights reserved.*

Conclusion: Anti-Modern Film, Anti-Modern Challenge

I Wake Up Screaming is classically noir in at least two important ways. It conveys an anti-Modern worldview, and it presents an anti-Modern challenge to this disposition that resorts neither to traditionally (masculine) Modern nor classical themes.

An Anti-Modern Noir: "Toto, I've a Feeling We're Not in Kansas Anymore"

This film, *I Wake Up Screaming*, cites and evokes *The Wizard of Oz*, not to repeat its meanings but to show that they are questioned in the new world scene. For better or ill, there is a new worldview based on a set of new experiences that have come to the fore. There is a perturbing sense of anxiety that something has changed, and there is no guarantee at all that human beings, at least in the Western world, are going to be able to get back to familiar zones of comfort after it is all over. Indeed, whatever is in store for humanity now, it will not be the same as it was; it will not be like the clever Odysseus returning full circle to his bed, or like Dorothy waking up from a dreadful nightmare to "home." Lost is the feeling of security, permanency, and familiarity.

Furthermore, the perversions of truth, justice, and social life are no longer somewhere "out there" that could be managed through rational technique or heroics. They are forces beyond our control. But worse, these forces beyond our control are within all of us, and there are no external powers that will miraculously stave the advance of corruption, unhappiness, the loss of truth, and the perversion of justice. The message is that human beings are separated from one another and juxtaposed as if in cages, alone. I do not wake up back at home in Kansas; I wake up in an uncanny new world, screaming.

These themes, devices, and motives constituted Humberstone's *I Wake Up Screaming* not only as thoroughly anti-Modern but also as a pre-eminent and exemplary film noir. But, I suggest, there is intriguingly another anti-Modern move in this film that does not reduce it to what is referred to today as the relativism of the "postmodern." It has to do with the role of the "heart."

An Anti-Modern Riposte: The Order of the Heart

Frankie Christopher is all a matter of business and promotion, personally indifferent. Like the Tin Man in *The Wizard of Oz,* the man has no heart. This is established early on and repeatedly. The mollification of this stone heart is signaled through the theme of "Somewhere Over the Rainbow." As suggested, it is not just a cipher for Jill, but for the pair of Jill and Frankie. In fact, the musical theme appears twelve main times throughout the film. Through their relationship, the viewer gains new insight into Frankie, or Frankie becomes transformed in the viewers' eyes (and in Jill's eyes). He goes from a possible killer, a heartless indifferent promoter, to a sensitive man who generously supports a slaphappy ex-fighter, a man who walks the streets of his old neighborhood, greeting friends along the way, to a man who acts like a boy going for a swim at night, a man who likes to go dancing, a man who exhibits an almost porcelain vulnerability in handcuffs, to a sensitive "artist" revealed as a passionate Italian (Botticelli). Jill to Frankie: "The trouble with you is you pretend you don't care about things, but you do." Dorothy-like or "good witch," she brings out his heart from the very first meeting.

On their date, Jill asks Frankie if he loved her sister, Vicky. Frankie responds:

> No. Do you think if I had loved her, I would have tried to exploit her the way I did. . . . that's my business. But when a man really loves a woman [and now plays 'Somewhere Over the Rainbow'] he doesn't wanna plaster her face all over the papers and magazines, he wants to keep her to himself, right in here [he gestures toward his heart].

It is only when he meets Jill, and through the repetitive softening of his calloused edges, signaled by the soundtrack of "Somewhere Over the Rainbow," that Frankie is little by little revealed to have a heart.

What is so anti-Modern about this? After all, one could exasperatingly retort: "Look, it's a romance, a melodrama; what do you expect?"

Nevertheless, I propose this idea, even if only as a very implicit motif, because of its deviation from the events in *The Wizard of Oz* and its consistent challenge to a Modern (and Classical) worldview. Let us recall that in the film *The Wizard of Oz*, the favorite character of Dorothy is the Scarecrow; but in *I Wake Up Screaming*, the only character that advances or develops is the "Tin Man" or Frankie. In the film *The Wizard of Oz*, the Scarecrow gets a brain, intelligence, reason, or rationality; the cowardly Lion gets courage. These latter two figures represent in fact traditional (Modern and Classical) male virtues, reason or rationality, and courage, respectively. But in *I Wake Up Screaming*, neither Larry (columnist/scarecrow) nor Robin (actor/lion) is changed; they remain dead ends and in fact seem to stay the same, back at the same café table where they began.

Put in the context of this film (and perhaps the larger social and political climate of portentous war in Europe and East Asia) it is not more Enlightenment rationality or more courageous warriors that will be able to redress successfully the new realities. These ideas of "home" have been and will have to be left behind. Nor is the consequence an atavistic reduction of all human emotions to mere instinct (another Modern presupposition that reduces human experience either to rationality or to instinct).

Instead, the suggestion is that if the Modern has been so disrupted by anti-Modern experiences, it cannot be a matter of ignoring the contemporary crises and anxieties by resurrecting a new Modern worldview of "home." We can't go back to 'Kansas," and it will never be the same. It is not a matter of resuscitating a predominately male Enlightenment rationality or of re-instilling the masculine virtues of war. Still less, it is a matter of reducing human coexistence to uncontrollable drives and instinct, now in order to escape the "human condition." Finally, it is not a matter of abandoning ourselves to the indifferent relativism of what is known today as the "postmodern." The suggestion is that if there is a way forward, it is by *retrieving* what was silently present in the Modern but shunned in the Modern. In this way and only in this way is it an "anti-Modern" gesture (where Modern is taken in our usual sense); if there is a way forward, it is by rehabilitating those interpersonal emotions circumscribed by the order of the heart.

As expressive both of the anti-Modern disruption of "home" and the anxiety of a new uncanny experience of the world, and an anti-Modern redress of the heart (not the virtues of rationality or courage), Huberstone's *I Wake Up Screaming* earns its place as an original and exemplary in the classical canon of film noir.

Notes

1 However, many critics consider *Stranger on the Third Floor* (Ingster, August 16, 1940) to be not just a "proto-noir"—proto, due to its "happy ending"—but

because of its visual style, the first noir of the American noir cycle. For the controversy on this issue, see, for example, Paul Schrader who holds the view I cited earlier in the text. See his "Notes on Film Noir," in *Film Noir Reader*, ed. Alain Silver and James Ursini (New York: Limelight Editions, 1999), 53–63. It is consistent, *mutatis mutandis*, with his ambiguous assessment of Carl Dreyer's *Ordet* (1955) among the "transcendental style" that we find in Bresson and Ozu. See Paul Schrader, *Transcendental Style in Film: Ozu, Bresson, Dreyer* (New York: Da Capo Press, 1972). On the other hand, Michael Stephens maintains that *Stranger on the Third Floor* was the first true film noir, and film noir has had no real ending, but only permutations. See Michael Stephens, *Film Noir: A Comprehensive Illustrated Reference to Movies, Terms, and Persons* (Jefferson, NC: McFarland & Company, Inc, Publishers, 2006).

2   Eddie Muller, *Dark City: The Lost World of Film Noir* (New York: St. Martin's Griffin, 1998). See the commentary in the "Fox Film Noir" series of this film.

3   Steve Fischer, *I Wake Up Screaming* (New York: Dodd Mead & Company, 1941). The film is *loosely* based on the novel—loosely, because of the ways in which the film makes its own points. Due to the latter there are many important deviations that have their own symbolic typologies. (Let me only cite these examples. The novel does not follow a flashback structure, there are four main characters surrounding Vicky, the protagonist is a writer, Ed Cornel is known to us in his sickness and obsessions from the outset; in this film, it is replete with flashbacks, there are three main characters, the protagonist is a businessman/promoter, and Ed Cornel remains a mystery until the end.)

A different title for this film, upon which some promotionals were based, was "Hot Spot" (in reference to an early scene in this film where it is said that Frankie is going to "fry for this"). Eventually, pressed by the cast, the title reverted to the original.

Finally, it is noteworthy, as Francis M. Nevins suggests in his biography, *Cornell Woolrich: First You Dream, Then You Die* (New York: Mysterious Press, 1988), Fischer's "Cornell" was based on the writer, Cornell Woolrich. Tony Williams further suggests that Cornell's idealization of Vicky may be based on the vulnerable man's idolatry of the female, which appears in so many of his works. See Tony Williams, "*Phantom Lady*, Cornell Woolrich, and the Masochistic Aesthetic," *Film Noir Reader*, 129–43.

4   These original dimensions peculiar to this film can be seen even more clearly when one views it alongside its 1953 remake, *Vicki*, directed by Harry Horner. In short, the "remake" is really just different film that follows a skeleton plot line.

5   We do not have the empty streets and spaces suggesting loneliness and isolation, like we see, for example, in Huston's later film, *Asphalt Jungle* (1950) or Dmytryk's 1947, *Crossfire*.

6   Venetian blinds casting bars over the characters became a common feature in classical and neo-noir films. Regarding the latter, we need only think of Hitchcock's *Psycho* (1960) in the scene with Janet Leigh and John Gavin.

7   On other occasions, Cornell tells Frankie that he will have him tied up like a pig in a slaughterhouse, and little later, Cornell equates Frankie with a "rat in a box without a hole."

8 Jean-Henri Casimir Fabre (December 22, 1823–October 11, 1915). In the
   captions of the film, it is misspelled (or mis-referenced) "Faber." Fabre was an
   astounding observer, and though a contemporary of Darwin, he was not an
   evolutionist thinker. Of the forty or so books in French, and nearly twenty in
   English I found, none appeared with such a title, although there are titles that
   suggest the social life of insects.

9 Botticelli was born in Florence, Italy, 1445–1510. This reference is also absent
   from the 1953 remake.

10 This allusion to Robin's faintheartedness is also missing from the 1953 *Vicki.*
   In the latter, he goes to a brothel to prove his manhood.

11 When Vicky is "introduced" to Larry, she remarks that she has read much
   about him. "Indeed. Flattering, I hope," he responds, "Naturally" she retorts,
   "Most of it appeared in your own column."

12 Again, in the 1953 version, *Vicki,* we know the character of Cornell right
   away.

13 But whereas Frankie went out to get drunk after he heard the news of Vicky
   leaving for Hollywood—Frankie asserting that Cornell would have done the
   same thing—Cornell has a different response. He tries to frame another person
   for murder.

14 This also unfolds differently in the 1953 version. Cornell is already in his
   apartment with lights on when "Steve" Christopher arrives on the scene to
   confront him.

15 One could even find analogies between the "wicked witch" and "good witch,"
   but I do not think that this takes us very far in terms of the main import of the
   film.

16 For example, Keaney writes that this is "an entertaining film (if you can ignore
   the constant playing of Over the Rainbow) . . ." See Michael F. Keaney, *Film
   Noir Guide* (London: McFarland & Company, Inc., 2003), 207.

13

Mediating Fairy Stories in Words and Images

Warring Magics in J. R. R. Tolkien and Peter Jackson's *Lord of the Rings*

Stephanie Rumpza

An Affair of Language?

The suggestion that it is possible to think with film is of limited use for any philosophical tradition that measures truth by logical propositions alone. Such philosophies can only shatter the integrity of the aesthetic work by trying to adapt it to their limited conceptual toolboxes; the discussion usually only stalls over dull technical details like what kind of truth claims can come out of fictional narratives. If we ask the artists, however, they would tell us that they are deeply invested in communicating something true—even in the most obviously "fictive" cases. When J. R. R. Tolkien first gave his lecture "On Fairy Stories" in 1937, he fought hard against interpretations that such tales were "irrational," "escapist," and mere "lies breathed through silver."[1] Rather than a flight from reality, Tolkien insisted, a Fairy Story is the "sub-creation" of a "secondary reality" which heals our damaged relationship to things and gives us a new glimpse of the deeper truth of our existence. An audience trained in the phenomenological hermeneutic tradition of philosophy would have granted Tolkien these points without any resistance. In *On Stories,* Richard Kearney cites Tolkien's "secondary world" as confirmation of an already well-established point.[2] Before him, Paul Ricoeur explained in *Time and Narrative* how readers enter the "world" of a text and leave with their own world transformed, while Hans-Georg Gadamer described in *Truth and Method* how the world of the artwork brings us a clearer recognition of the truth and a deeper belonging to the reality we dwell in.[3] According to phenomenology and hermeneutics, philosophers and artistic sub-creators both aim to bring things to light and communicate the truth about the world. In this, they can be said to share in a general project.

Yet even if we grant a broader definition of truth that can appreciate art's revelatory power, we must admit that this power is not always exercised in exactly the same way. In addition to the difference in artists, traditions, styles, or genres, we can also recognize a difference in media. A word does not make manifest in the same way that an image or a sound does. Perhaps this is why philosophers are often hesitant to address the medium of film, so rich with sounds and images, and why we feel more at ease with literature and poetry that share the linguistic domain which we already inhabit.

If we want to discover the way that film thinks along with philosophy, one approach would be to trace out in broad lines such differences of aesthetic media of word and image. However, if we want to think along with film, instead of from outside it, I suggest we instead explore our question in depth through one particular example of this tension of thinking in word and in image. As we have seen, Tolkien was an author who thought very deeply on the revelatory power of his art, and his widely beloved *Lord of the Rings* has had an enormous impact on literature, particularly on the genre of fantasy it inspired. By contrast, Peter Jackson's three-film cinematic adaptation (2001, 2002, 2003) was met with box office success and scholarly disdain. We do well to dismiss complaints about the film's "inaccuracy" to the book, since the very first lines of the novel narrate a fictional manuscript history for an imaginary original draft, a creative decision that places its author above any naive Middle Earth fundamentalism. Of interest to us here are the critiques that voice the prejudice philosophers are sometimes tempted by, blaming Jackson's failure on *the medium of film* itself, and particularly on its inadequacies as visual rather than verbal medium. Jane Chance suggests this in a measured way, claiming it is "in part because of the screenwriter's necessity to focus rightly on selected, representative incidents and to omit the didactic and nondramatic—nonvisual—portions" that Jackson's film sinks to the level of "an action film in which the important complex thematic meanings and characterizations are discarded or subordinated to the sentimental."[4] Verlyn Flieger, on the other hand, explicitly rejects any cinematic telling of this story, arguing the "constraining literality" of the visual medium enchanted by computer-generated techniques could never match the richness of Tolkien's prose.[5] Allison Harl argues similarly that it is not simply a problem of Jackson's flawed aesthetic vision that the priority of visual special effects "dominates the uninhibited imaginative experience of reading the written text," but a matter of "the inherent critical problems with the film medium." She concludes that "a film adaptation of the original work 'can only mock, it cannot make: not real new things of its own.'"[6] Harsh words, considering she is citing Tolkien's description of the greatest evil of his mythical universe, the corruption of Elves into Orcs. Is cinema so rotten to its core? Must a filmmaker always play the Dark Lord Morgoth of Tolkien's sub-creation?

It is tempting to dismiss these critiques as mere professional prejudice. However, spoken by a Tolkien reader, they in fact carry significant weight. It is not only a matter of contingent facts, that Tolkien was a master wordsmith by trade, with an unrivaled talent for harnessing the power of language along its poetic and historical axes to unfold an expansive imaginary world. For Tolkien himself suggests fantasy is most proper to language, even "coeval" with it. As he writes in "On Fairy-Stories," it is language that first allows us to identify and abstract from what we see, and to transpose it to new forms in the imagination: "No spell or incantation in Faërie is more potent" than an adjective, for it grants us an "enchanter's power," whereby we may "take green from grass" and put it "on man's face and produce a horror," or we may take "blue from heaven" and radiate it from a "rare and terrible" moon.[7] To tell a Fairy Story, for Tolkien, is thus most proper to words, to literature, to poetry. What would he say about cinema?

Later in his life Tolkien approved the possibility of adapting *Lord of the Rings* into film (although he rightly disparaged the one project actually pitched to him).[8] However, he does not consider the question explicitly in his 1938 essay. In fact he expresses his skepticism of visual media's ability to weave Fairy Stories as words can. From his text we can draw three reasons. First, a visual medium "imposes one visible form," whereas literature is "at once more universal and more poignantly particular," for each person embodies words in their imagination in a different way.[9] This much is true. While cinema inspires the imagination in a fashion proper to it, we are still given particular images of particular things. In this sense it lacks some of the enchanting power of the written word, whose power of abstraction calls up a meaning that must wait to be embodied according to the unique experience and imagination of each reader. On this point the power of film must cede to the power of the written word.

Tolkien further argues that literature is the only art capable of delving out the depth of world required for a secondary reality. While a talented illustrator himself, Tolkien held that visual art was "technically too easy" to be a good medium for Fairy Stories; "the hand tends to outrun the mind, or even to overthrow it."[10] In other words, visual images can suggest fantastical *things*, but lack the depth of patient craft capable of unfurling the full texture of a *world* with the "inner consistency of reality." By contrast, theatrical arts are almost incapable of the task in principle. "Drama is naturally hostile to fantasy,"[11] Tolkien declares. The illusion required to create a belief in the world of the stage does not easily extend as far as believing this stage world is also a "secondary reality." This is in part because drama is centered on characters, limited in its ability to portray settings, which are key elements of a fantasy world.[12] However, the art of the big screen suffers from none of these flaws. Already removed from the immediacy of live acting, the medium of film has an extraordinary ability to unfold a believable secondary reality. No longer limited to a stage, it has endless possibilities of portraying the wider world inhabited by the characters, and its visual capacity for effortless depth and detail in each setting can be even more vivid than a book. On this point literature may have to concede its pride of place, or at least share it. When it comes to immersing us viscerally in a secondary reality, the power of cinema is immediately evident.

But this points to a third reason which underlies both of Tolkien's prior reservations. The secondary reality of a Fairy Story has a very particular set of demands. It runs by different possibilities, a different logic than those that govern our daily life, for "Faërie itself may perhaps most nearly be translated by Magic."[13] In the world of Faërie, animals may talk, ogres may turn into mice, and in the half-light of dusk humans may stumble into the wondrous forest realms crafted by Elves. Painting has too much mechanical ease for us to feel seriously the strange new possibilities required by a magical world, while theater has too little—actors and props can only do so much. From Tolkien's perspective in 1938, we can only assume that a live-action film would share this difficulty. By the late 1990s, however, things had changed. Computer-generated special effects were sufficiently complex to resolve most problems of "mechanical success." Here again, we can no longer deny that film has the capacity to depict a secondary reality where nature believably follows different laws than our own, where frogs can turn to princes, where words can conjure fire, and where dragons hoard treasure in the mountains.

Despite Tolkien's reservations about the creative power of visual media, we have established that cinema cannot be immediately denied its power to create a coherent and tangible secondary reality. This is enough to claim it as a powerful medium of truth-telling, alongside novels and poetry, as Ricoeur, Gadamer, and Kearney would agree. However, if we want to understand whether it can actually succeed in telling a "Fairy Story" in Tolkien's sense, we must further refine our measure.

Two Warring Magics

Tolkien coins the word "fantasy" in "On Fairy Stories," but we must be cautious not to overinterpret. It takes much more than an epic with elves and dragons in a quasi-medieval setting to make a fantasy or Fairy Story in Tolkien's sense. In his days as well as in ours, many stories claiming to be a part of this genre "do not even touch upon Faërie at all."[14] As Tolkien explains, the etymology of "Faërie" is not at its core a tiny winged creature, but a place, one full of wonder and peril. If the "air that blows in that country"[15] cannot be clearly pinned down in philosophical or scientific terminology, Tolkien tries to give voice to it all the same.

"Fantasy" in Tolkien's sense must first of all serve as a recovery of our disordered relationship with the world, as well as an escape—not from reality, but from the rationalist and scientistic appropriation of it. By this sub-creative art of a Fairy Story, Tolkien explains, the world is renewed in "strangeness and wonder."[16] We do not simply see things "as they *are*," but "as we are (or were) were meant to see them"—that is "as things apart from ourselves."[17] Fairy stories clear away the banality, triteness, and possessiveness that mark our quotidian dealing with things as objects at our beck and call. When such domestication falls away, things become "free and wild" again, "dangerous and potent," wondrous and strange.[18] In the liberation of reality's primal power and resulting "repossibilization of the world"[19] we can overcome our estrangement from animals and things and recover Nature now as "a lover" and not "a slave."[20]

Once we recognize the mood of fantasy as a repossibilizing dispossession, we can appreciate what Tolkien calls the form and the "highest function" of a Fairy Story: the "Eucatastrophe."[21] In a eucatastrophe, a victory is not won or appropriated by the hard work, efforts, virtues, or cleverness of the heroes, but arrives precisely when all evidence points to defeat, in a sudden "turn" akin to "miraculous grace" given beyond all hope. The result is a piercing joy "as poignant as grief."[22] Far from mere escapism, Tolkien describes eucatastrophe to be "a glimpse of Truth" shining out behind the dark veils of history; where our nature, "chained in material cause and effect," suddenly feels as if "a major limb out of joint had suddenly snapped back."[23]

The "Magic" at the heart of a Fairy Story thus is marked by "a peculiar mood and power," which Tolkien here names "*Enchantment*." To be "enchanted" is to be as if "*inside* a song," as Jon Mentxakatorre Odriozola observes: in fact, these are the very words which Sam uses to explain his experience of the Elves.[24] This shared territory between music and "magic," between art and enchantment, is far from accidental. According to Tolkien, to create a true Fairy Story requires "a kind of elvish craft,"[25] which results in an intriguing recursion: *Art is Elvish enchantment, Elvish enchantment is essentially Art*. It takes an enchanter to voice enchantment. For Tolkien there is a small difference, in that Elvish craft is freed from "human limitations," accomplished more completely, more quickly, and with less effort than for the human sub-creator. Yet, for both, the "object is Art not Power, sub-creation not domination and tyrannous re-forming of Creation."[26]

Enchantment is fragile, always at risk of being cheated by forces of rationalization of appropriation. For "at the furthest pole" looms the corrupting influence of "the vulgar devices of the laborious, scientific, magician,"[27] a force of evil that threatens the world of Faërie at every turn.

It marks "the Enemy" almost as a logical outcome: "concerned with sheer Domination, and so the Lord of magic and machines."[28] Magic in this precise sense is thus "not an art but a technique; its desire is power in this world, domination of things and wills."[29] Tolkien's association of the "magician" with a "scientific" attitude is perhaps hasty as a generalization, but he has something specific in mind. The unrestrained advance of technology or "magic" unites both Dark Lords and the swollen scientific theory of the "Robot Age,"[30] as he called the relentless advance of industrialization which threatened his beloved English countryside.

A Fairy Story in Tolkien's sense thus involves a battle between the two "magics," enchantment and magicianship, and the risk of falling from one to the other. And as we see again and again in Tolkien's work, gravity works in one direction: the "perversion of art to power."[31] Turning to evil magic can begin as part of a good desire to "benefit the world and others,"[32] yet however good the initial impulse, the more one gives in to the use of "magic" that seeks one's ends by domination, the more one will become a servant of evil. Recalling Tolkien's identification of art and enchantment, we can conclude that the author of a Fairy Story faces the same temptation in constructing a secondary reality. "Small wonder that *spell* means both a story told, and a formula of power over living men,"[33] Tolkien observes; the real question is what *kind* of magic, what *kind* of power: that of the Elves, or that of the Magicians.

Can the visual medium of film sub-create a Fairy Story in Tolkien's own, precise sense, bringing to life this war of enchantment and magic, or is it too constrained by the "literality" and particularity of a visual medium? Does the filmmaker, like the writer, have a choice between "magics" in creating a world? The question gains a particular edge when we consider that a contemporary fantasy film trades on technologies Tolkien may well have placed in the camp of the magician-scientists. Can there be an "elvish craft of CGI" or does the advanced technical expertise required by the digital result in mere "magic"?[34] Yet this is a red herring. As Gadamer would caution us, the evaluation of a work of art does not rely on the technical process but on the event of the work itself. However different the author's craft of words may be from a green screen and an army of CGI technicians, the question concerns the dragon that appears.

Rather than press philosophically to answer for film, let us allow film to respond on its own terms. Any number of films could step forward as guide, but let us keep our focus on Peter Jackson's *Lord of the Rings*. It is clear that this trilogy falls short of Tolkien's novel in many ways. My question is why. Was it, as critics have suggested, simply because they were films? Again, my interest is not on how well they adapted this particular story, but whether this adaptation communicates the genre of Fairy Story Tolkien has laid out. In what ways do they let breathe "the air that blows in that country," and in what ways do they stifle it? Limiting our claim to one central thread: Is the visual medium of film able to illustrate the war of "magics"?

The Magician-Scientist

Let us begin with Jackson's Saruman. If this character is less subtle than in Tolkien's novel, it is not a departure from Tolkien's understanding of Fairy Stories: the Saruman of the film fully incarnates the archetype of Tolkien's magician-scientist. While Gandalf dares the dangers of travel with his companions, Saruman remains aloof, watching from his tower, influencing from afar through spies and spells and armies. To see and not to be seen: this is the pattern of magic, which seeks power and appropriation devoid of mutuality. It is no surprise that he would pursue it by any means necessary, including a Palantír, an ancient seeing-stone he proudly displays to Gandalf. And yet, just as Gandalf hastily covers it up again, the Eye of Sauron flashes across the screen, telling us that Saruman the Seer is Seen. The one who seeks to escape the Enemy by any means possible is for that very reason under the Enemy's power.

Second to the weapon of knowledge, Saruman's preferred tool is industry; as Treebeard laments, he "has a mind of metal and wheels," reflected in Orthanc's rough obsidian interiors. After an initial scene of Gandalf meeting Sauron in the verdant park surrounding the tower, the setting of Isengard is introduced by shots of trees being pulled into the red flames below, as Orcs clang at the endless fabrication of weapons. This contrast of bucolic nature and hellish industry is echoed in Frodo's vision in the Mirror of Galadriel: the Orcs' devastation of the Shire, the earth charred and the hobbit holes in ruins, their residents chained to an ugly new Orc mill on the Brandywine. If Jackson's film does not specify who is responsible for this invasion, it is all the more telling: Saruman by this point has become indistinguishable from Sauron, just as the courtyard of Isengard already visually replicates the ashen wasteland of Mordor.

If Saruman "no longer cares for growing things," as Treebeard laments, it is seen not only in destruction of nature but in his manipulation of life with a magical-scientific genetic engineering. Tolkien is cryptic on the origins of the super-Orcs, but the film imagines it for us in nightmarish detail: the Uruk-Hai rupture out of slimy, membranous pods with animal roars and a thirst for violence. The *Fellowship* film even risks over-exposition to inform us, through the tale that Saruman recounts to the Uruk's captain, that Orcs were not created but are "tortured and mutilated" remainders of Elves. In Tolkien's lore, this is the ultimate perversion of sub-creativity, the worst evil of his most evil character, Morgoth. Originally the greatest of the Valar, or demigods, Morgoth is more concerned that his voice should be the centerpiece of the creation song than that the music be beautiful. In order to seize the place of glory above all others, his song—like the creation that the Divine Ilúvatar grants to it—loses all musical quality and becomes "loud, and vain, and endlessly repeated," a "clamorous unison of many trumpets braying upon a few notes."[35] Tolkien's description of this original perversion of sub-creation is evoked for Saruman's evil through Howard Shore's score in the harsh theme of Isengard. Its rhythmic clanging and the blaring of brass is not unlike the musical leitmotif of Mordor, which also shares its jarring 5/4 time signature. The film confirms visually and musically one of the central tenets of a Tolkienian Fairy Story: that evil creates nothing of its own, but only warps the world according to its own image, which is repetitive and ugly, hellish and destructive, in one Dark Lord as in another.

Elvish Enchantment, Elvish Art

The place of enchantment is subtle in Tolkien's novel, as in Jackson's film. We usually do not see it explicitly working, and this is as it should be. Unlike the technological magic, which subjects all things to the aim of one's individual will, the aim of enchantment is to bend all of one's forces of creativity for the flourishing of the other, seeking "shared enrichment, partners in making and delight, not slaves."[36] When in the book Boromir suggests the Elvish Rings might be used to fight Sauron, Elrond responds, "They were not made as weapons of war or conquest: that is not their power. Those who made them did not desire strength or domination or hoarded wealth, but understanding, making, and healing, to preserve all things unstained."[37] Elrond is never explicitly revealed as an Elven-Ring bearer in the film, but in the prologue of the film Galadriel is. Both Elrond and Galadriel have used their power of enchantment to create refuges of peace and rest which preserve traces of the original glory of the Elves from the First Age of Middle Earth as the world around them declines and falls into danger.

It is fitting, then, that the clearest illustration of Tolkienian enchantment of this film is found in Galadriel, one of the most powerful Elves in all of Tolkien's corpus. The film evokes well the sense of danger and wonder as the Company enters the Golden Wood. The trees seem strange, as if covered by an unworldly frost. The score features singing evocative of sacred chant that is not quite like the chanting of this world, a beauty that is not quite tame. "All who look upon her are never seen again," Gimli warns, and Frodo is startled by Galadriel's whispering voice echoing his name. We see a brief extreme close-up of her star-studded eyes turning toward him, but we do not know if her glance is sly or wise, hostile or kind, and her acknowledgment of his secret is charged with tension, "You bring great evil here, *Ring-Bearer*." Galadriel's physical presence is finally revealed first by the light that falls on Frodo's face: a white glow softly washes out the lines of her figure as she descends the stair, not only evoking the watercolors of renowned Tolkien artist Alan Lee but also suggesting a presence that transcends the clarity of our comprehension. We see other hints of fragmentation: Galadriel's voice is at turns distant and warm as she speaks, and the conversation seems to be only a distraction from the real drama that is indicated only visually, with extreme close-up shots of her eyes interspersed with close-ups of the members of the Company responding to her probing gaze. Galadriel has a power we cannot pin down, while she seems able to pin us. Together these scenes confront us with what Tolkien believes is too often forgotten by our modern imagination, the age-old "the fear of the beautiful fay," the possibility that beauty and evil may be aligned. This sets us up for the tension which follows.[38]

While Saruman has a Palantír that allows him to see afar, it is alongside Galadriel's Mirror that we witness the subtlety of her enchantment give way to the possibility of becoming a magician. For as she contemplates taking the Ring which Frodo offers, she stretches out her arms to become a photographic negative of her former self, a Dark Queen with black eyes, "beautiful and terrible as the dawn," whose harsh declaration of her might is doubled over with a rumbling low voice: "All shall love me and despair!" But with a sudden cut, the cold unassailable mastery of the dream vision is gone, leaving her wide-eyed, frail, and trembling. Rejecting the temptation, she turns away and lowers her face, eyes closed, again visually performing her words, "I will diminish, and go into the West." Seeing her power allows us to appreciate all the more the significance of her restraint in bending it toward the flourishing of others. The scene ends with the powerful Lady of Lothlorien bowing to face the despairing halfling with a kind smile and a word of wisdom, which leads Frodo to close his hand around the Ring in renewed resolve.

The execution of these scenes at times falls flat under the weight of forced solemnity which verges on the melodramatic. Yet if imperfectly realized, the film at least makes the idea clear: the world that has been entered is one far beyond what we can control or comprehend, but not all power seeks domination.

Perversion of Sub-creation

Through the cases of Saruman and Galadriel, Peter Jackson has succeeded in his task in showing the two forms of Tolkienian "magic," their distinction and opposition, and the risk of falling from one to the other. Yet, Jackson as enchanter-artist faces the same temptation. Particularly in the latter two films, Jackson is not always able to resist the pull toward the devices of the scientific-magician. A Fairy Story's enchantment is meant to allow us to recover a dispossessive relationship with the world, in all its strangeness and wonder. By Jackson's hand, however, most strangeness is reduced to a plane of materialist logic easily comprehensible to his audience, who are kept in a position of control and comfort.

On the one hand, it is unquestionable that Jackson's story has succeeded in granting the films "the inner consistency of reality." The meticulous aesthetic design for each people and culture of the films is all the more remarkable as this involved not only one but two or more sets of each prop, painstakingly handcrafted to the scale requirements of humans or hobbits.

Along with the extraordinary camera tricks and size doubles, the result is a feeling of being tangibly immersed in a world inhabited by different-sized creatures like Elves and Hobbits and Dwarves. Very few viewers would notice the Rohirric rune inscription on Karl Urban's helmet, "This helmet belongs to Éomer, son of Éomund—may he ride forth with valor,"[39] and this same level of extraordinary level of care and craft saturates each frame all the same. The magnificent scale and depth of the landscape are established through extreme long shots of the characters' march across the expanse of uninhabited wilderness. Postproduction enhancement makes the marvelous and ominous of this world stand out more clearly: the fields of the Shire are made into a lush, extra-saturated green, the trees of Fangorn groan and crack with anger. The result is that the visual and sonic devices of film immerse us in wonder and makes us feel as if new detail could be discovered just around every corner.

And yet, while firmly committed to filming hobbits and elves as inhabiting the coherent world of Middle Earth, Jackson prefers to keep the environment as realistic as possible. The strange or magical is minimized: the misty dreamland of the Dead Marshes and its ghostly floating candles has become an ordinary bog inexplicably dotted with fireballs and an occasional wisp of cloud. After its first scene as an enchanted forest, Lothlorien becomes an ordinary one inhabited by a foreign civilization. And while Jackson preserves Tolkien's dialogue referencing the unnatural darkness fabricated by Mordor which turns day into night, we are shown blue skies that have been artificially desaturated to look a little overcast. While such decisions do not singularly overthrow the aim of a Fairy Story, they do indicate a trend toward the materialistic, rationalist, and technical. This is at least part of a survival strategy motivated by the concerns of New Line Cinema about Jackson's enormous budget. Tolkien observed of his own day that many people dislike the "arresting strangeness" that comes by overthrowing the domination of the "factual."[40] Perhaps this is why fantasy films had been notorious for being expensive flops. Jackson's big-budget epic was thus framed as a historical one: not "fantasy," but a "feigned history."[41] The result is that while we do find an extraordinarily believable secondary reality, which is of central importance to a Fairy Story, it comes at a heavy cost. The "secondary reality" is interpreted in a narrow and naturalistic way, as if afraid to voice the full "strangeness and wonder" essential to Tolkienian fantasy.[42]

The mysterious power of Faërie is slowly sapped by this constant reversion to "realistic" environments. But this naturalizing tendency concentrates into a real threat when it comes to the explicit conflict of magics. Rather than portray an extraordinary and unworldly struggle of good and evil through an "elvish enchantment," Jackson flattens this conflict into something concrete, graspable by a banal and materialistic imagination. Where a Fairy Story is meant to unsettle us from our seat of comfortable comprehension to a stance of humility, wonder, and vulnerability before powers beyond our control, these films simply confirm our appropriation of reality. As Jackson repeatedly crushes awe and wonder with adrenaline and brute force, his craft displays itself as "a perversion of art to power."

We see this in the degradation of all power to physical and materialistic forces. Let us pass over the most embarrassing, like the gratuitous telekinetic struggle between the wizards ("You have elected the way of *pain!*" Saruman roars while twirling Gandalf in circles, but it is the audience who winces). Consider instead the confrontation between Gandalf and the Balrog. In the *Fellowship* this battle is beautifully enchanted. We feel the heat of the demon's breath and the shadowy smoke of his evil spirit, while the sense of desperation of Gandalf's stand on the bridge is heightened by a fierce percussive chant in Tolkien's invented dwarf tongue Khuzdûl. These cinematic elements have immersed us a fairy world, with strange powers and ancient spirits lurking at the foundations of the earth. However, in *The Two Towers*, all of this is undermined in a flashback. After repeating the final moments of this confrontation, the camera tilts from Frodo's perspective of Gandalf falling to Gandalf's perspective zooming forward into the chasm like Superman. He snatches his falling sword out of the air, lands upon the back of the falling balrog, and starts hacking away, jets of fire spluttering out at each blow. Immediately, the struggling balrog ceases to be a terrifying, hellish spirit, and becomes instead a CG-painted lava-monster with a fire-whip. Are we watching a Fairy Story or a video game? What for Tolkien was a drama of incarnate Maiar, immortal angelic beings, has been reduced to a physical and materialist struggle tailored neatly to mortal comprehension. The mysterious nature of these superhuman beings has been diminished by the calculated techniques of a magician which shows us what we mere mortals were not meant to see.

Jackson admits that the monsters were "one of the real motivations for me to want to make *The Lord of the Rings*."[43] From Orcs and Trolls to the giant spider and the krakenlike "Watcher," it is hard to deny that Jackson's garden-variety monsters are quite effective. They are ugly, disgusting, and dangerous enough to keep us rooting for our heroes. Jackson even succeeds in creating monsters who terrify at a level of spiritual or cosmic significance, worthy of the enchanted air of fairy. The Ringwraiths were one of the greatest successes of the film, when given time and space to develop the effect of their terror. *The Fellowship* introduces these undead Riders with extreme close-up shots of a stamping, bloody hoof, a headless hood, a horse's crazed eye, the ominous thump of a mailed boot dismounting, which sets us up for a terrifying, unsettling enemy. In *The Two Towers* these motifs are repeated at a Ringwraith's first reappearance: an extreme close-up of a mailed glove clutching reins, a headless hood turning and sniffing, before the camera zooms out to amplify our expectations of the terrifying danger: this time the Black Rider is revealed as no longer on a horse, but a monstrous flying beast straight out of the imagination of Tolkien artist John Howe. From their unearthly, blood-curdling shrieks to the sound distortion accompanying their whispering voices, from their ragged black hoods and the distorted ghostly forms that appear when Frodo wears the Ring, they radiate a power and horror worthy of a Fairy Story evil.

Yet, when forced to choose, Jackson prioritizes his brute force empirical monsters over his subtler ones; he leaves no space for the air of Faërie to breathe, and the fear of the Ringwraith falls flat without the patient drama to set apart its horror. In the *Return of the King* we are plunged into non-stop adrenaline. All is chaos: Gondor has been breached, Orcs are running through the city, Gandalf has left his place at the front line on an urgent side-errand, when the Witch King intercepts him by landing suddenly on the wall. But it is his winged mount that dominates the scene, visually and emotionally. As the Captain of the Nine makes his threats, the close shots anchor the drama around the characters, but each wide-shot ruptures these relationships by the size of the winged monster. When Gandalf falls, we fear not the Witch King but the proximity of the gaping jaws, and when Pippin shrinks back it is not from the Witch King but from the hot breath of the roaring beast, which rears up to visually block out its rider. Tolkien's telling of this moment sets it apart as a major symbolic encounter of Light against Darkness, the two captains on horseback facing off at a moment of focused tension within the larger drama of the battle. Its sudden conclusion, a fight avoided due to Rohan's unexpected reinforcements arriving, just as dawn breaks Mordor's darkness, is a small-scale eucatastrophe and a major highlight of the book. But where Tolkien amplifies this drama by setting it apart in its significance, the film tries too hard to amplify the encounter along the calculation of a magician: manufacture more monsters, more adrenaline, more power. The result is that the scene becomes forgettable and insignificant, swallowed up as just another moment in an action-packed battle.

By far the film's worst offense against Faërie is what becomes of Sauron. Tolkien knows what any good monster movie director should: the evil that you don't see is far more terrifying than the evil that you do. For Tolkien, this is more than technique, it is of spiritual significance. In his physical absence, Sauron is felt everywhere, especially in the Ring, and thus becomes a magnetic power flushing out the evil in every heart, striving to bend all to his will. By doing this, Vincent Ferré observes, Tolkien is reconfiguring the relationship between Man and Monster, suggesting that "'evil' does not lie so much in one character than in all of them at once" as they successively struggle with their own weakness.[44] Setting aside the crudeness of interpreting Frodo's temptation as quasi-possession (complete with eye-rolling, squeaking, and fainting), some moments of the film are able to viscerally communicate the power of the Ring along the lines of Tolkien's subtle enchantment. The ominous weight of evil is tangible as the Ring slides from Bilbo's palm to the floor of Bag End without a bounce. Its warm yellow gleam brings a moment of solace from inhospitable blue nights in the wilderness, as Frodo caresses it in his palm, entranced. Shore's musical leitmotif of a boy choir envelops us within the simultaneously sweet and ominous character of the Ring's seduction, reflected in the faces of characters who hesitate before it. Such subtle reactions visualize power without materializing it.

Sauron himself is a different matter. His terrifying power of seeing from afar, of laying thoughts bare and corrupting hearts to his will has been reduced to absurd literality, which Jackson sums up in an interview: "Our main villain is an eyeball."[45] As the Eye becomes visible, the gaze does too: not only are we shown which direction the catlike eyeball is turning, but, worse, *what* he is seeing, through the beam that roves across his lands like the spotlight in a prison movie. Now that it is bound to material space and time, now that we visualize the spotlight of his gaze, we are free to escape the monster: the power of evil can be avoided simply by crouching behind a rock as it passes. The result is not only enormously silly but risks shattering the fabric of a Fairy Story at a deeper level. Applying Laura Mulvey's insights to the audiences of Jackson's films, Harl suggests that "the camera, like the Evil Eye of Sauron, puts the audience in the position of a voyeuristic, ubiquitous watcher"[46] and thus we as viewers are "cast in a role like that of Tolkien's monsters, seeking to control and dominate through the means of the visual image."[47] This means, to put it differently, that, *we* become the Eye, the magician-scientists who at least in this instance know and dominate the story, just as we know and dominate our earth. We see and appropriate all things, pierce every shadow, and no monster, no angelic spirit, or demonic force can remain obscure before our omniscient gaze.

In light of this, it is a little easier to understand Harl's accusation that Jackson can only "mock, not make"; that he has perverted the Elvish enchantment of Tolkien with the tricks of a magician. By continually reducing the story to the scope of a materialistic imagination, especially when it comes to powers that are meant to exceed what we can understand, Jackson has traded the spirit of Faërie and its Elvish enchantment for cheap magic.

Conclusion

How, in the end, must we judge Peter Jackson's cinematic rendering of Tolkien's beloved Fairy Story? Does he really stand as the Dark Lord Morgoth to Tolkien's Elvish Sub-creation? At times Jackson's film of Tolkien's Fairy Story communicates the essence of Faërie well, elaborating a beautifully crafted and credible secondary reality, which at times rises to the extraordinary possibilities within enchantment, making us feel that we are "in a song." At times the film betrays it. By prioritizing adrenaline and big action sequences, it shows too much, too objectively, tailoring a world of mysterious forces to comfortable comprehension, leaving us with appropriation instead of wonder. If Saruman has a "mind of metal and wheels" one might wonder if, at times, Peter Jackson has a "mind of monsters and special effects."

But if Tolkien is our measure, we cannot ignore Jackson's most central success: he still communicates the "truest form and highest function" of a Fairy Story, its eucatastrophe.[48] While some critics have ridiculed the "many endings" of the *Return of the King*, it is the film's way of refusing to cheapen for us the sudden turn of poignant joy with a snappy Hollywood finish. Instead, the film richly relishes every moment from Gollum's redemption of Frodo's failure to the unexpected arrival of the eagles, the joyous reunion of the Fellowship, and the inauguration of Aragorn's long-awaited reign of peace in a ceremony which ends with the mighty hosts of Middle Earth bowing to the four humble Hobbits. In all of this, the final film brings to us the wounding consolation of "a piercing glimpse of joy" that "passes outside the frame" to let a gleam of light shine through.[49] "Whatever flaws it may possess," or "confusion of purpose," Tolkien admits, "A tale that in any measure succeeds in this point has not wholly failed."[50]

There is no question about it: Jackson's talent as an enchanter does not equal Tolkien's, nor do his films achieve the possibilities Tolkien set out. Yet despite the films' failure to live up to their potential, these pioneering efforts have demonstrated that the visual medium of film *is* capable of rising to the demands of a Fairy Story, that there *is* an Elvish craft to CGI, and that despite the particularities of actors and props it *can* create a tangible secondary reality and illustrate the war of magics. In its wake, other Enchanters may in confidence employ the elven craft of cinema to liberate our thinking, and our living, "from the drab blur of triteness or familiarity"[51] and reawaken us to the truth of a world that is beautiful, marvelous, and wild, and utterly beyond our appropriation.

Notes

1   J. R. R. Tolkien, "On Fairy-Stories," in *The Tolkien Reader* (New York: Ballantine Books, 1966), 33–99.

2   Richard Kearney, *On Stories* (London: Routledge Press, 2001), 143–4; see also extended footnote 158n5.

3   Paul Ricoeur, *Time and Narrative*, vol. 2, trans. Kathleen McLaughlin and David Pellauer (Chicago, IL: University of Chicago Press, 1985); Hans-Georg Gadamer, *Truth and Method*, rev. trans. Joel Weinsheimer and Donald G. Marshall (London: Bloomsbury Press, 2014).

4   Jane Chance "Is There a Text in This Hobbit? Peter Jackson's 'Fellowship of the Ring,'" *Literature/Film Quarterly* 30, no. 2 (2002): 80.

5   Verlyn Flieger, "Sometimes One Word Is Worth a Thousand Pictures," in *Picturing Tolkien: Essays on Peter Jackson's The Lord of the Rings Film Trilogy*, ed. Janice M. Bogstad and Philip E. Kaveny (Jefferson, NC: McFarland & Company, Inc., Publishers, August 2011), 46–53.

6 Allison Harl, "The Monstrosity of the Gaze: Critical Problems with a Film Adaptation of the Lord of the Rings," *Mythlore* 25, no. 3/4 (Spring/Summer 2007): 65.

7 Tolkien, "On Fairy-Stories," 48–9.

8 Tolkien comments on film in his 1949 letter to his publisher, Allen & Unwin, n. 119 in *The Letters of J. R. R. Tolkien*, ed. Humphrey Carpenter (Boston, NY: Houghton Mifflin, 1981); see also Kristin Thompson's "Film Adaptations: Theatrical and Television Versions," for a thorough account of the Morton-Grady-Zimmerman film project of 1957–9 that roused Tolkien's ire. *A Companion to J. R. R. Tolkien*, ed. Stuart D. Lee (John Wiley & Sons, Ltd, 2014), 514–29.

9 Tolkien, "On Fairy-Stories," 95.

10 Ibid., 70; for a collection of Tolkien's art, see *J.R.R. Tolkien: Artist and Illustrator*, ed. Wayne G. Hammond and Christina Scull (Boston and New York: Houghton Mifflin Company, 2000).

11 Tolkien, "On Fairy-Stories," 70.

12 Ibid., 72.

13 Ibid, 39.

14 Ibid.

15 Ibid., 38.

16 Ibid., 68.

17 Ibid., 77, emphasis mine.

18 Ibid, 78.

19 Jean-Yves Lacoste, "Anges et hobbits: le sens des mondes possibles," *Freiburger Zeitschrift Für Philosophie und Theologie* 36 (1989): 341–73.

20 Tolkien, "On Fairy-Stories," 78.

21 Ibid., 86.

22 Ibid.

23 J. R. R. Tolkien elaborates on this idea in a 1944 letter to his son Christopher, n. 88 in *The Letters of J. R. R. Tolkien*.

24 Jon Mentxakatorre Odriozola, "J. R. R. Tolkien the Philosophical Basis of Sub-Creative Words," *Logos* 22, no. 3 (2019): 109; citing J. R. R. Tolkien, *Lord of the Rings; The Fellowship of the Ring*, II, iv (Boston, New York: Houghton Mifflin Harcourt), 351.

25 Tolkien, "On Fairy-Stories," 70, 73.

26 Tolkien expands on this idea in his 1951 Letter to Milton Waldmen, n. 131 in *Letters*.

27 Tolkien, "On Fairy-Stories," 39.

28 Tolkien, *Letters*, n. 131.

29 Tolkien, "On Fairy-Stories," 73.

30 Ibid., 80.

31 Tolkien, *Letters*, n. 131.

32 Ibid.

33 Ibid.

34 As in the title of Mark Sinker's interview, "Talking Tolkien: The Elvish Craft of CGI," *Children's Literature in Education* 36, no. 1 (March 2005): 41–54, he discusses this idea on p. 49.

35 J. R. R. Tolkien, *The Silmarillion*, ed. Christopher Tolkien (Boston: Houghton Mifflin Company, 1977), 17.

36 Tolkien, "On Fairy-Stories," 74.

37 Tolkien, *Fellowship of the Ring*, II, ii, 268.

38 Ibid., 83.

39 Kristin Thompson, *The Frodo Franchise: The Lord of the Rings and Modern Hollywood* (Berkley and Los Angeles, CA: University of California Press, 2007), 93. See Chapter 3, "Handcrafting a Blockbuster," for more examples.

40 Tolkien, "On Fairy-Stories," 69.

41 Thompson, *Frodo Franchise*, 55–6.

42 Tolkien, "On Fairy-Stories," 68.

43 Thompson, *Frodo Franchise*, 60.

44 Vincent Ferré, "Tolkien, Our Judge of Peter Jackson," in *Translating Tolkien: Text and Film*, ed. Thomas Honegger (Zollikofen: Walking Tree Publishers, 2004), 125–33.

45 Thomspon, *Frodo Franchise*, 53.

46 Harl, "The Monstrosity of the Gaze," 66; citing Laura Mulvey, "Visual Pleasure and the Narrative Cinema," in *The Norton Anthology of Theory and Criticism*, ed. Vincent B. Leitch (New York: W.W. Norton and Company, 2001), 2179–92.

47 Ibid., 61.

48 Tolkien, "On Fairy-Stories," 85.

49 Ibid., 87.

50 Ibid., 86.

51 Ibid., 77.

PART III

Thinking with Films

14

On Wim Wenders's *Paris, Texas*

Richard Kearney

Much of postmodern cinema is caught up in a "winner loses" logic. The more it strives to expose the world of pseudo-images by parodying those images, the more it seems to confirm the omnipotence of the very system it wishes to contest. The more striking the portrait of a totalizing system of false imitations, the more impotent the viewer feels. To the extent, therefore, that the filmmaker *wins* by successfully representing an omnivorous system of mass media representation, to that same extent he *loses*—"since the critical capacity of his work is thereby paralysed; and the impulses of negation and revolt, not to speak of those of social transformation, are increasingly perceived as vain and trivial in the face of the model itself."[1]

This winner loses logic is a common feature of those contemporary films which attempt to demystify the mesmeric power of mass-produced images by means of such images. Apart from Fellini's *Ginger and Fred*, one might also cite here Pakula's *Network*, Eyre's *The Ploughman's Lunch*, Truffaut's *Day for Night*, or the various film critiques of the American Dream as an alienated pseudo-image by directors such as Scorcese (*The King of Comedy*), Coppola (*One from the Heart*), Altman (*Nashville*), and Wenders (*The American Friend* and *Paris, Texas*). The problem confronting each of these directors is how to construct a parody that does not degenerate into pastiche. For with the growing threat to the individual imagination—and, by formal extension, to the very notion of a personal *style*—we find the emergence of a near global kind of media-language where the traditional ideas of a social, national, or personal identity are voided of real content and reduced to the level of empty imitations. Frederic Jameson, one of the most perceptive commentators of this postmodern trend, describes the dilemma as follows:

Parody finds itself without a vocation; it has lived and that strange new thing pastiche slowly comes to take its place. Pastiche is, like parody, the imitation of a peculiar mask, speech in a dead language; but it is a neutral practice of such mimicry, without any of parody's ulterior motives, amputated of the satiric impulse, devoid of laughter and of any conviction that alongside the abnormal tongue you have momentarily borrowed, some healthy linguistic normality exists. Pastiche is thus blank parody. . . . With the collapse of the high-modernist ideology of style—what is as unique and unmistakable as your own fingerprints— the producers of culture have nowhere to turn but to the . . . imitation of dead styles, speech through all the masks and voices stored up in the imaginary museum of a now global culture.[2]

This pervasiveness of pastiche is evidenced in the contemporary consumers' desire for a society transformed into sheer images of itself, into pure spectacle—a society where, in Guy Debord's phrase, the "image has become the final form of commodity reification."[3]

Wim Wenders's *Paris, Texas* (1984) describes the plight of imagination in the contemporary world of pastiche. The very title is a mock allusion to Paris, France: and as such it reflects the impossible quest of postmodern man for roots or origins in a society where everything has been reduced to imitation. Wenders's film explores the contemporary hankering for some authentic "memory" unadulterated by the commodification of the American Dream.

Although Wenders is himself a German director, he believes that the loss of "original memory" in today's American culture has become a generalized feature of the Western world as a whole. Through the spread of a commercial communications system, the interchangeable culture of Coca-Cola, Levi's jeans, and Burgerlands has penetrated into every corner of our globe. "The Americans have colonized our unconscious," remarks Wenders, "and recreated the so-called 'free' world according to their own image."[4] Wenders's choice of Texas as a location for his film is no doubt an allusion to the pseudo-society which has virtually become a multi-national model for our age, thanks in large part to such cult TV soap operas as *Dallas* or *Dynasty*, which had been transmitted in most countries in the world. Wenders's film, in short, is concerned with the plight of narrative imagination in a world turned Texan—a world of surfaces increasingly deprived of memory or self-reflection, where fantasy and reality have become so confused and the notion of self-identity so diluted that it no longer seems possible to tell one's story.[5]

Paris, Texas is, as Wenders informs us, constructed around the image of "a man leaving the freeway and walking straight into the desert."[6] Travis has, it would seem, abandoned the American Dream of the open highway leading to a promised land. He has also abandoned speech. Four years later, Travis returns from his desert purgatory, his dark night of the soul, mute and apparently empty. He refuses to speak his name or give his identity. And it is from this existential zero point that he will begin to retrace his narrative, to piece together the scattered fragments of his former existence. Wenders recounts Travis's quest to regain a sense of historical continuity, to become a true father to his lost son and a true son to his own dead father—by returning to a forgotten place called Paris, Texas, where he himself was first conceived.

Travis has no memory of Paris, Texas. All he possesses is a faded photograph of a derelict patch of land left to him by his parents. And, likewise, the sole record Travis has of his own wife and child is an old photomat strip. Collected from the highway motel where he has been convalescing by his brother Walt (a successful billboard advertiser), Travis is brought back to Walt's home in Los Angeles. Here Travis's son, Hunter, is being fostered. Hunter's only memory of his father and mother—Travis and Jane, who walked out on him and on each other after a traumatic split-up four years previously—is that provided by a home movie. Starting from this movie within the movie, Wenders traces the gradual attempt made by father and son to *remember* each other, to reconstruct the family scene of *le temps perdu*.

This quest for recollection takes place against a typically postmodern landscape of urban fragmentation. Their first tentative encounters are made all the more vulnerable by being graphically framed by shots of amorphous cityscapes—criss-crossing fly-overs, multi-corporation office blocks, and airport runways where screaming jets land and take off by the minute. But in spite of this incessant interference from the megapolis of noise and concrete, father and son slowly develop some kind of contact. As they come to know each other they become increasingly more aware of the missing link in their relationship. Jane, the mother, is still absent. And so leaving Los Angeles (and the foster parents) behind them, Travis and Hunter set off toward Texas in search of the *third person* of their holy trinity, the remaining member of the "original" family.

The evasive figure of the lost mother dominates the quest structure of Wenders's film. The mother is the archetypal symbol of "origin"—the very concept of which is ostensibly threatened by the postmodern culture of substitution and imitation. The mother exemplifies historical memory. She represents the possibility of returning to the source, of retelling one's personal life history. But the quest is by no means a foregone conclusion. An ominous note is struck at one point on the journey when Travis is confronted by a Crazy Man shouting (as the script tells us) "like a voice crying in the wilderness." As he wanders across an overpass spanning a gigantic sixteen-lane freeway, Travis is assailed by these words from the crazy prophet of doom:

I make you this promise on my mother's head, or right here and now, standing on the very head of my mother, our Good Green Mother Earth, which anybody who wasn't born, in a fuckin' sewer ought to know and understand to the very marrow of their bones. . . . There is nowhere, absolutely nowhere in this godforsaken valley. . . . Not one square foot of that will be a safety zone. . . . You will all be extradicted to the land of no return. You'll be flying blind to nowhere. And if you think that's going to be fun, you've got another thing coming.[7]

The location chosen for this postmodern prophecy of doom is itself highly significant. Is not the serpentine network of interlocking car lanes a typical postmodern involution of the modern American Dream of the pioneering freeway leading to a promised land? The brief description entered in Wenders's own director's script is telling: "A baffling labyrinth of intertwining highways, overpasses, entrances and exits appears." After a prolonged search—with all the trappings of a parodic "road" story à la Kerouac—Jane is finally located in the red-light underworld of Houston, Texas. The everyday reality of Jane's life is the very opposite of the "idealized" mother. She works in a peep-show club where customers pay to see her act out their sexual fantasies in a basement booth panelled with one-way mirrors, a fallen pentecostal angel hiding out in the depths of a postmodern metropolis. Moreover, there is a telling allusion to the sinister legacy of the American Dream of freedom: the outside wall of the peep-show club features a faded mural of the Statue of Liberty brandishing her flame.

Travis rents out the fantasy booth and watches Jane behind the one-way screen. But they never *see* each other face to face—only through a glass darkly. They do, however, succeed in making contact through *words*. Refusing to pursue his relationship with Jane at the level of obsessional desire—that is, the voyeuristic *imago*—Travis communicates with her by means of a telephone link. Turning aside from the see-through glass, Travis enables Jane to gradually identify him, and herself, in the story which he recounts of their past life together. And Jane eventually responds in kind by retelling and therefore remembering her own past. In this manner, they recover together the power of lost speech and lost memory. They endeavor to penetrate the false veneer of the mirror-image by narrating to each other the untold dimensions of their respective experiences for the first time. Travis and Jane are thus portrayed as latter-day versions of Orpheus and Eurydice, who seek to escape the underground maze of pseudo-images in which they have been imprisoned by renouncing the voyeuristic medium of obsessional vision. They learn the art of mutual dispossession, as it were, and reach toward a form of genuine communication, however brief, by abandoning the image in favor of the word. Their face to face is verbal, not visual. Its very condition of possibility is an unconditional postponement of vision. This renunciation of the image (as commodity possession) also entails a more general renunciation of the American Dream itself (as belief in a messianic origin and end). *Paris, Texas* refuses the traditional Hollywood tale of the family happily reunited after a long ordeal. And in a sort of parodic inversion of the Orpheus myth, it is Travis who must eventually vanish so that Jane can re-emerge into the light. Or to use the trinitarian metaphor, the father must forgo his rights of unifying possession and disappear so that the absent pentecostal mother can meet again with her son. The mirror-play of fetish images must dissolve so that language can reach through the looking glass to another kind of meaning.

But what kind of a meaning can this be? Now that Travis has told his true story, how is he to end it? Where does he go from here? Standing alone on a Houston sidewalk, surrounded on all sides by giant inter-reflecting glass high-rises, Travis would seem devoid of destination. And the concluding shot of him smiling as he drives along an Interstate highway—past a neon-lit poster for Republic Bank sporting the slogan "Together We Make It Happen"—offers no clear solution. Will he remain in some alienated no-man's-land? Will he return to the silence of the desert? Or seek solace in the aimless wandering of the highway leading nowhere? Wenders chooses to leave this question dismayingly unresolved.

Travis's narrative of origins is thus left suspended in mid-air. He still retains his tattered photograph of the patch of land in Paris, Texas. But this ancestral memory cannot be recovered as a *literal* reality. It has ceased to be a geographical place where Travis, Jane, and Hunter might recommence a life together. At best, the memory has become a kind of moral conscience, recalling a moment of past hope which must be acknowledged as *past*: a Utopian recollection which cannot be realized in the postmodern world of commodified images, but which stands nonetheless—*qua* memory—as an indictment of the existing world, a testimony to how things might have been in another kind of world. Wenders himself seems to regard this testimonial power of the photograph as a critical counterpoint to the very medium of cinema itself. He writes:

> I think that photography has remained much more intact as both form and act than has cinema. Everywhere in the world, we can still come across photographs which have a conscience and a morality of what they are about. There is a form and a style in this work whereas in cinema, style, form and the consciousness of action are vanishing more and more. Cinema has been profoundly affected and emptied by advertising and by television. But there is an ethic in the photograph in contrast to cinema which has become *catastrophic* in this regard. . . . The American dream presents itself as a nightmare through the images it produces.[8]

And we might also recall here the significance Wenders attaches to the word in *Paris, Texas*: Travis communicates with Jane through a telephone link and learns to play with Hunter through an intercom system. Indeed his parting message to Jane and Hunter is left in the form of a tape recorder. Face-to-face encounter is, curiously, made possible through the medium of the word.

So where does this leave Wenders himself as a filmmaker? If it is true that *Paris, Texas* points to the non-cinematic media of the photograph and the narrated word as possible means of contesting the postmodern cult of the pseudo-image; it is equally true that this message is conveyed through the medium of cinema itself. And so we are back once again with the paradox of cinema trying to deconstruct itself from within, trying to combat the power of the cinematic image by means of cinematic images. And even if cinema itself were to be renounced in favor of the photograph or the word, it is by no means sure that one would discover a language of reality untainted by the civilization of the commodified image. Wenders's formal quest is, in the final analysis, quite as unresolved, and perhaps unresolvable, as Travis's own narrative quest.

Notes

1 F. Jameson, "Postmodernism or the Cultural Logic of Late Capitalism," in *Postmodern Culture*, ed. H. Foster (London: Pluto Press, 1985), 111–26, at 56.

2 Ibid., 65.

3 Ibid., 66. From G. Debord, *La Société du Spectacle* (Paris: Champ Libre, 1967).

4 Quoted by D. Hounam in his review article on *Paris, Texas*, In *Dublin*, no. 214 (1984): 10–11.

5 See J. Hillman's vivid and iconoclastic account of this Texan consumerist society in *Interviews* (New York: Harper and Row, 1983), 127–8.

6 See D. Hounan, *Paris, Texas*.

7 *Paris, Texas* (Shooting Script and Stills) (Berlin: Road Movies, 1984), 45–55.

8 W. Wenders, "Arrêt sur Image," *Le Monde*, April 27–28, 1986.

15

On Larissa Shepitko's *The Ascent*

Fanny Howe

Larisa Shepitko was born in Eastern Ukraine in 1938; her mother was a schoolteacher. Her father went to the Second World War never to return to his family. Her mother raised her alone with her two siblings, and by the time Larisa graduated from school, she was on the road to Moscow to study filmmaking. She was seventeen and sure of her vocation.

She never veered from her commitment to film; she was a warrior who learned how to use large instruments to capture what she saw from close-up and far away.

Shepitko's early films were rewarded. She found her mentor in Alexander Dovzhenko, who had worked with Sergei Eisenstein, and she always kept his teachings in mind. He was a realist in the spirit of the post-war European neo-realists from Germany, Italy, and France.

She was tall, dark, and good-looking and loved her friends and her crew, and after a few years she married Elem Klimov (*Come and See*) and gave birth to a son. She went to the limits with her actors and crew into perilously cold weather, sometimes on a stretcher. Her movie *Wings* is the story of a fighter pilot who was ecstatic in the air and dulled by her return to ordinary earth as a teacher. She had a continuing fear of death that made her both superstitious and visionary. She died at age forty-one in a car crash.

Her last film, *The Ascent*, begins with an empty field of snow that slowly unfolds into a row of soldiers from the German Army. They are carrying pots, pans, and other utensils. Shots ring out like bells. Two Russians have brought on this battle, one of them shoots back, hits someone, and then they run for their lives up toward the hills and woods. All this could be seen as if through a microscope until we see one of them is wounded and we come in close enough to see them eating dried raspberries out of the cups of their hands.

The story is a simple one, a tale for every time. Two soldiers get separated from their allies. They are lashed by snow and wind. Rybak, the tougher of the two, knows where they are, and Sotnikov, the weaker (the wounded) one, follows him. They go to a house Rybak fondly remembers for the woman in it and a night he spent in bed with her. It is now ashes and ruin, and the bed broken in the rubble. Rybak is a tender man who loves life as something under his control. He can be as loving as a mother.

They walk on through the ever-deepening snow toward another wooden house; they break in and find three hungry children waiting for their mother to come home. She does. She is rough and hostile but allows the two soldiers to hide in her attic when they hear Germans coming with shouts and guns. Their brutal occupation of the house takes place swiftly, outrageously, and the mother is dragged from her children, along with the two soldiers, thrown in a truck and driven to the third place. The cries of her children are extinguished by the engines.

All this time Sotnikov is weakening from blood loss. There are glimpses of his face that begin to show him shifting between profane and sacred consciousness, one where branches are covered with glassy ice that he breaks in his hands, and another when his face looks up from the snow like a child's face buried in a sand-hole.

The third place is the room of interrogation where they will be drawn into an underground cellar after being interrogated and tortured by a German but Russian-speaking official. Two other prisoners, one a young Jewish girl, are thrown down with them, and in this grave-like hole they each acquire allegorical traits. According to the icon-maker Florensky there is no such thing as the color gold, only the mineral, and there is no way to speak of Christ unless you are a child. This film knows that and how to transcend the adult mind. "The impression of a global calamity left an indelible mark on my childhood mind," Shepitko said.

When I saw this film, in London in the 1990s, I was still very susceptible to "the Russians." Their poetry, their novels, their social reform, their composers, and drive for eternal truths. I brooded on the geographic weirdness of being at the top of the world, covering several time zones, and having so many ethnic histories. I don't know why this passion came over me so young so that I majored in European history at college and focused on revolutionary Russia. It might be because my father joined the army in 1943 and was gone two years at least and was drawn into the Red baiting days of the 1950s. He came back liking the Russians better than the British.

The Ascent shows us varieties of snow. It was shot in Belarus (White Russia), the site of a horrific genocide, switching from Soviet to Russian. Embedded in the images is more than the mortal faces we see before us, there is the glimmer-ghost of Christ, a smudge like a fingerprint.

There is a syndrome called Visual Snow Syndrome, where a person sees white dots sprinkled across their field of vision. It's compared to the "snow" we know on analog screens. Visual Snow, all you can see, the face of Christ impressed on human minds, now lives in there as the shape of a tree does; it reproduces naturally in art, though strangely not so much in life. It's like an afterimage that trails the snap glance, organizing it into the hollow face we know by now. Sometimes we see the face of Christ on the ground but rarely in a person.

Sometimes we see on a stone or glass the image of the H-bomb, smoke from napalm, and it hurts too much to face directly.

The great post-war neorealist films out of Italy, Germany, and Russia will always provide the footage to that time before we had or expected much. We still stirred the batter and shook out the broom and changed the sheets by turning them over. The child who is the only witness to all this has almost disappeared.

"Russia isn't Russia without religion," I read recently. You would not say this about many countries in the world now. Love of country—where could it ever be found? Some say God died in the Napoleonic Wars, at Jena, some say Nietzsche struck the final blow, some say God died in Auschwitz, some in the Vatican; this film could be read as the death of the *memory* of God.

God recedes but doesn't die during the feast of the Ascension of Christ which seems to me to be a celebration of liberty from earth: Jesus whirling around, even underground to check on the dead, before his astonishing hover over his friends before disappearing into the cosmos. Light in this Jesus-story is like snow (an extra apparel) and like what film can do with earth images turning them into flat radiance. Light in physics is a block of ice and we are in it. But war planes flying overhead don't dissolve but blow up or lie in old graveyards in airplane cemeteries. Larisa Shepitko's movie *Wings* shows just what I mean. A flight beyond dualism, her imagined airspace is like *The Ascension*, a continuation of consciousness in full space and of the clouds we see every day. Two minds knowing one thing. Baudelaire: "Man passes through forests of symbols which look at him with understanding eyes."

To talk about the death of God, as we knew God, in certain films especially from Russia since Russia is not Russia without religion. To talk about the effects of that death in war and in childhood.

There is no straight line of stations through which the characters mark their ways. This is partly because the snow has almost obliterated any signs of paths and stopping places. The places where action stops are either burned to the ground or about to be. There is a household where three children await their mother's return with food. There is a place of a diabolic interrogator; it is an office; outside are the gallows; down below is a basement containing prisoners.

We have come to the point where we have to assess the value of the person, a circle stretched out in the snow reduced to one face, lips, eyes, mouth, as a kind of alien thrown down from the sky. An embryo, an infinite glued to time. This film addresses such ultimacy.

Larisa Shepitko not only directed but participated physically in the iciest days on the set, got sick, and directed from a stretcher, she did not want to feel any better than her actors, most of whom were ordinary Russian citizens she found and hired. It was grueling to make but there were her crew and her husband to accompany her in her attempt to account for what she saw as a child.

It is the unyielding emptiness of the Christ-effect that fascinates me. It won't go away though the face keeps changing, the position, the landscape, the torture, the unbelief all around it. It's a remnant like a circumcision or a piece of living matter born to be infinite because it came to be in the first place. In a completely non-ironic film, a child's smile is our last hope.

The film puts artificial light on our interior unit, our senses are all we have, the awful evil in the suited man at the desk who organizes tools for torture, truly what we must remember of genocide. When the prisoner asks him what he was before he was a prosecutor, the laugh is on the prisoner when he answers, I was like you.

16

On Jim Jarmusch's *Paterson*

Brian Treanor

An Ordinary Life

In Wallace Stegner's *Crossing to Safety*, writer and teacher Larry Morgan is asked why he has not written about the life he and his wife Sally have shared with the Langs, Sid and Charity. He replies that it is not possible.

> How do you make a book that anyone will read out of lives as quiet as these? Where are the things that novelists seize upon and readers expect? Where is the high life, the conspicuous waste, the violence, the kinky sex, the death wish? Where are the suburban infidelities, the promiscuities, the convulsive divorces, the alcohol, the drugs, the lost weekends? Where are the hatreds, the political ambitions, the lust for power? Where are speed, noise, ugliness, everything that makes us who we are and makes us recognize ourselves in fiction?[1]

Of course, the irony is that *Crossing to Safety* is precisely such a novel, a tale about the intertwined lives of the Morgans and the Langs, lives that have their ups and downs but which, for all that, are indeed quiet. The crises that visit the characters—dreams deferred and eventually abandoned, professional setbacks, marital friction, the ravages of disease—are painful, but they are particular instances of the suffering we all experience. They are commonplace, mundane, prosaic—despite being depicted in a masterfully written novel.

Jim Jarmusch's *Paterson* (2016) is the story of a similarly quiet life, that of its titular character, Paterson.[2] The film is a window into one week in Paterson's life, but it is a week in which not much happens. Paterson is a man of routine. He rises early each morning, eats a solitary breakfast of Cheerios, and walks down the hill to his work as a city bus driver in Paterson, New Jersey. During the day, he drives the number 23 bus, observing the city and its people. At midday he takes his break at the nearby Great Falls of the Passaic River, where he discovers thoughtful gifts his loving wife Laura has tucked into his lunch pail alongside his food: a postcard image of Dante, an artificial flower, photos of herself. He walks home in the afternoon, always stopping to adjust the crooked mailbox outside his house. At night, he sits down to creative, if not always appetizing, meals with Laura; after this, he walks his wife's dog Marvin, stopping in at Shades, the local bar, for a single beer and a chat with the owner, Doc. During the day, he composes poetry in his head, which he jots into a journal during short breaks in his routine. This pattern repeats itself each day, with only minor variations.

Paterson is a singularly undramatic film, at least in the sense of drama as a story marked by crisis or conflict. True, there are moments of tension: on Tuesday, we sense that money is tight for Paterson and Laura; on Friday night a heartbroken man pulls a gun at Shades, and Paterson disarms him—though the gun turns out to be a fake and the man more of a dramatic type than an actual threat; and on Saturday Paterson's journal of poems is destroyed by Marvin, on the night before Paterson was to fulfill a promise to Laura to make back-up copies. And there is *dénouement*—principally Paterson's decision to take up poetry again after the destruction of his journal. But the crises of the film are not sensational or exceptional. None of these people are really threatened—physically, psychologically, or existentially. Or, better, the threats in *Paterson* (2016) are the kinds physical, psychological, and existential threats we all deal with every day.[3]

Paterson's life has problems, but no drama. When various other people speculate that his bus "could have exploded" the day it broke down, Paterson can only laugh at the hyperbole. He is an archetypal "regular guy"—outwardly unremarkable, and distinguished primarily by the internal marks of his interest in poetry and his (very private, almost solitary) intellectual and artistic life. Laura, in contrast, is a passionate woman of many eccentricities—from culinary experiments like cheddar-and-Brussel-sprout pie to continuous makeovers of both herself and the house—as well as impulsive dreams: she fantasizes, with seeming sincerity, of opening a bakery on Monday only to shift her ambition to becoming a country music star by Tuesday. Nevertheless, Paterson and Laura complement each other in many ways. They love and support each other; and together they lead an ordinary, quiet life.

Yet, despite the mundane character of Paterson's world—the commonplace routine of sleeping, eating, working, and the small, everyday interactions of an unexceptional neighborhood—the overall impression of the film is that Paterson himself is living an *extraordinary* life, one that any person with an ounce of wisdom would feel lucky to live and grateful to have lived. The film succeeds in showing us, or reminding us, that no place is unremarkable, and no life is ordinary. Or, put otherwise, that the ordinary—that which is common, local, mundane, and familiar—is, if and when we are perceptive enough, extraordinary.

The Ordinary and the Extraordinary

It is a well-worn observation that poetry represents the ordinary as extraordinary; but does poetry *make* the ordinary extraordinary, or *reveal* the ordinary to be extraordinary? The complicated truth is that it does both. Just how this is the case varies from poet to poet—for not all poets are trying to accomplish or bear witness to the same things—and would, for even a single poet, require a longer treatment that is possible here. In the present chapter, I will take up the former claim only briefly, so that I can address the latter claim in greater detail: that poetry in some way reveals or makes apparent something that is already and always present.

Although English has lost its appreciation for the etymological spirit of poetry, "poet" comes to us, via French and Latin, from the Greek ποιητής/*poētḗs*, meaning "creator" or "maker." This should give us a clue to the fact that *poiesis* is concerned with bringing something into existence.[4] In terms of the question at hand, poetry *makes* the ordinary extraordinary through its use of language. Precise diction, particular rhythm and meter, the creative use of metaphor, clever metonymy or synecdoche, and other devices are the tools the poet uses to transform, as it were, the mundane into the miraculous. It is poetry that takes up unexceptional things—things worn and rough and common—and fashions them into symbols of something shining and special. The poet takes an ordinary rose, or urban birds, or a wheelbarrow and seems to make these things say more than themselves, to imbue them with special meaning and significance.[5]

But, while there is much more to be said about the making of poetry, I want to suggest that some poets are best understood not as craftsmen but as observers, witnesses, and reporters; they discover or come to see something that is already there and, through their poetry, they can help us to do the same.

No Ideas but in Things

Paterson (2016) is obviously in dialogue with William Carlos Williams's poem of the same name: *Paterson* (1958).[6] Williams's presence is felt throughout the film, from the location of Paterson, New Jersey, to Paterson's habit of walking, to the fact that Paterson himself is committed to a "day job" rather than trying to make a living as a poet. However, perhaps the most overt nod to Williams takes place on one of Paterson's nightly walks with Marvin. Passing a neighborhood laundromat, Paterson stops to listen to a solitary rapper working on his lyrics. In between attempts to work out his own verse, the rapper repeatedly reminds himself "no ideas but in things, no ideas but in things." This is one of Williams's more famous dictums, appearing in Book I of *Paterson* (1958) itself: "—Say it, no ideas but in things—."[7] A commitment to the particularity of things is not, of course, unique to Williams's poetry; it can be found to various degrees in the poetry of Wallace Stevens, Robinson Jeffers, Saint-John Perse, Gerard Manley Hopkins, and many others, as well as in the vast phenomenological tradition of philosophy that starts with Edmund Husserl.[8] However, the commitment to things, to attending to the unique particularity of objects, people, and places, frames the vision of poetry in *Paterson* (2016).

Paterson's poems, written by poet Ron Padgett, are not epic sagas or pretentious demonstrations of esoteric form; they do not take up grand philosophical themes or weighty theological riddles. These are mostly poems about everyday things in Paterson's workaday life: the box of matches on his table, his nightly beer at Shades, the warmth of the first day of spring, and his wife. And they are often poems about things as things, not things as symbols or as representations of ideas or concepts. Occasionally, Paterson muses about something more abstruse. He observes that "there are three dimensions: / height, width, and depth," but "Then some say / there can be five, six, seven . . ." However, he never goes all the way down Alice's rabbit hole with such thoughts, and in the same poem he is soon, and happily, back to his own life: "I knock off work, / have a beer / at the bar. / I look down at the glass / and feel glad."[9] Paterson's poetry cleaves close to his experience of the particular, concrete, and local. Nevertheless, the viewer is left with the feeling that Paterson's poetry—and, more importantly, the way of being that informs his poetry—reveals his reality to be extraordinary.

The suggestion here is not that poetry makes ordinary things extraordinary by overlaying language on top of things, painting them with symbolism and metaphors, or ventriloquizing so that their mute being speaks profundities; rather, the implication is that poetry calls our attention to things that are miraculous in themselves and as they are, but which have, for us, stopped scintillating because of our familiarity and inattention.[10] To experience an extraordinary world, it is not necessary to change things, to dress them up, illuminate them with neon, and introduce them with orchestral fanfare; it is, rather, necessary to change *ourselves*, to learn to see again the plain beauty and ordinary grace that shine through things.

Returning to Things as Things

So, the question is this: What is it about a poet who works a day job and who takes the everyday as his subject matter that allows him to experience the ordinary as extraordinary? Answering this question can teach us something important, because I will maintain that we can, and ought to, experience the world poetically, whether or not we ever choose to put pen to paper.[11]

Paterson's secret is tied to his humble life; but here we must think of humility not only in the contemporary sense of modest or self-effacing but also in the etymological sense traceable to *humus*, ground, as in the soil beneath one's feet, the earth on which one is emplaced. Jarmusch's protagonist is a rara avis in the increasingly homogenized and commodified Global North: a man at home in, a man *of*, a particular place. This place-affinity is why Paterson shares a name with his home: Paterson, the bus driver, of Paterson, New Jersey. Both are characters in the film. Paterson has a relationship with Paterson, New Jersey, just as he has a relationship with Donny, or Doc, or Laura.

Silence

The first noteworthy thing about Paterson's way of being is, as I observed above, the quiet. Jarmusch emphasizes this in his depiction of Paterson, New Jersey itself. The city is muted. At most, it buzzes or hums as people go about life; but the shouts, fights, collisions, and other loud noises common in cities are absent or suppressed. The soundtrack to Paterson's daily routine is made up of the smooth, humming acceleration and deceleration of his bus, the subdued conversations of passengers, the reassuring rumbling of the Great Falls at lunch, and his quiet chats with Doc at Shades.

Paterson's own rhythms and habits are also quiet, and probably alien to many contemporary viewers. He wakes without an alarm and rises to eat breakfast alone in the morning twilight, while his wife sleeps in. There is no radio playing; and we can hear birds chirping softly outside. Although he interacts with people during his shift, much of Paterson's day passes in a kind of public solitude. After returning home, he reads or writes poetry in the late afternoon; at dinner he talks with Laura. Television is nowhere to be seen. Twenty-first-century technology, with its constant "noise"—social media updates, "doom scrolling" the news, exposure to multiple screens at once—is absent in Paterson's life; Laura has a laptop and a cell phone, but Paterson has neither. He lives in an "analog" world of physical books, pen and paper, *things*. The loudest part of his life is Laura, who is not, in fact, loud at all, but merely vibrant.

Paterson's verbal expression is subdued, reticent, laconic. He does not speak much. He does not foist his view or his opinion or his life onto others. For example, each morning he asks his supervisor Donny how things are going, and Donny responds with a litany of woe, from serious financial difficulties to minor afflictions like "a strange rash on my back." But when Donny asks after Paterson, the response is always a balanced, "I'm OK." Astonishingly, this is also Paterson's response to the destruction of his poetry by Marvin. Laura is deeply distraught, and understandably concerned about

Paterson. But Paterson reassures her, several times, "I'm OK." In fact, while Laura banishes Marvin from the house as a punishment, Paterson lets him back in the next morning. Although it seems clear that Paterson has been shaken by the destruction of his poems, we never feel he has been dismasted, or overcome with anger. He never despairs or lashes out; at most he can muster a subdued, if sincere, "I don't like you Marvin."

Why is it significant that Paterson is a quiet man? Because, if we are going to "hear" what the world has to "say," the first thing we must do is stop talking ourselves. Especially when so much contemporary talking is really just noise: speaking not for the sake of expressing something beautiful, or communicating with others, or even really to be heard by others, but merely to speak. As if to cease speaking were to cease being. But, for Paterson—and for *Paterson* (2016)—the first commandment of living poetically is to *be silent*. This requires literal silence, but it requires a broader stillness as well. We must stop imposing ourselves—our needs, our wants, our perspective, our interpretations—on to things and allow those things to "speak for themselves."

Pay Attention

Paterson's humility is self-effacing. And while some might read this as a lack of confidence (e.g., his unwillingness to call himself or even really think of himself as a poet), I don't think his self-effacement is motivated by lack of self-regard. It is, rather, an effacement of the self so that the other—in this case Paterson the city, its people, the Passaic, the light, the sky—can speak. This self-effacement is evident in things beyond Paterson's speech patterns. For example, Paterson is clearly an intelligent, disciplined, capable man. He could, one supposes, aspire to a job more financially rewarding than driving a city bus. But the *métier* of bus driver proves to be the perfect one for the poet of place. Paterson is immersed in the city and in intimate proximity with its inhabitants. He observes people on the sidewalk, going in and out of stores; he watches the play of light on the city as the day unfolds. On the bus, he overhears two children talking about Hurricane Carter, listens to construction workers falsely boasting about women and then observes the disapproving frown of a woman subjected to hearing it, hears precocious teenage "anarchists" chatting about Gaetano Bresci, and more. However, while Paterson's job puts him right in the center of the city and its people, it does so in a way in which he remains utterly overlooked, anonymous, almost invisible. The bus driver is always present, but no one interacts with him or even really notices him. Like a field biologist hidden in a blind, Paterson can observe his subjects without being observed, without disturbing the environment, allowing them to simply be themselves.[12]

I've mentioned the way Paterson's disinclination to "leash" himself to technology contributes to or facilitates his silence; he is, for example, immune to the temptation to update a social media profile, documenting, narrating, and broadcasting the minutiae of his life rather than actually living it. Who feels the need to broadcast their life in this way? And how does it change their way of being in the world? Their relationship to things? Paterson's technological ambivalence helps him to attend to the things themselves by keeping him safe from distractions. His life is spent among real things, not images, reproductions, or simulacra. And he finds that reality itself is endlessly engrossing. Like Henry David Thoreau—whose *Walden* sits on Paterson's shelf—Paterson values reality in all its wondrous diversity, including, especially, the plain, the common, the ordinary.[13] Rather than demanding that the world astonish him, or insisting on grand displays of the sublime, Paterson simply pays attention to the world around him and finds, *mirabile visu*, that the ordinary things around him *are* extraordinary. "We go about blind and deaf. . . . First we have to see, be taught to see. We have to be taught to see *here*, because here is everywhere, related to everywhere else. Of only one thing, relative to the work of art, can we be sure: it was bred of a place. It comes from an application of the senses to that place"[14]

Thus, the second fundamental law of Paterson's poetry is not "be creative"; that comes later. The fundamental law is, rather, *pay attention*. Paterson himself is a careful and committed observer of things in his life, as well as of how those things make him feel or what those things make him think; in this way, he comes to hear what things are saying to him and understand how he feels about what they are saying.

Be Patient

We all know that, even when we are quiet and open to experiences, we don't always receive what we hope for or expect. As C. S. Lewis observes, when we go to nature seeking to be overwhelmed by the experience, "nine times out of ten nothing will happen."[15] Of course, the same thing could be said for church, or the museum, or any other place people seek out extraordinary, overwhelming experiences. And that is doubly true when the place one seeks to be overwhelmed is a suburban kitchen, or the local bar, or a bus depot, places in which most people would be hard-pressed to identify anything exceptional or amazing. But the extraordinary is there, in the ordinary; we just can't expect it to show up on cue, like a nightclub act. *Pace* Protagoras, man is neither the measure nor the scheduler of all things.

> The secret of seeing is . . . the pearl of great price. If I thought he could teach me to find it and keep it forever I would stagger barefoot across a hundred deserts after any lunatic at all. But although the pearl may be found, it may not be sought. The literature of illumination reveals this above all: although it comes to those who wait for it, it is always, even to the most practiced and adept, a gift and a total surprise.[16]

Thus, the third and final commandment of Paterson's poetic way of being is this: *be patient.*

Watching *Paterson* (2016), we don't get the impression that Paterson is a demanding person; he seems unlikely to feel entitled or to insist on particular things or states of affairs, especially extraordinary things. He is dedicated to his poetry, but hardly seems to expect publication or recognition. He accepts without complaint, even with a kind of affection, things like Laura's disastrous cheddar-and-Brussel-sprout pie, Donny's daily laments, and Marvin's presence in his life. One might read Paterson's temperament as fundamentally passive and meek, but I think that would be to misread him. He is not meek; he is the only person in the bar to spring into action when Everett pulls out a gun. Nor is he passive; in fact, he is much more engaged with his world than any of the people around him, most of whom are fully occupied with themselves.

But Patterson does not expect or demand anything particular from the world.[17] And this is precisely why the world keeps revealing extraordinary things to him. When we expect or feel entitled to one thing, we often fixate on it so intently that we miss the unexpected, and equally miraculous, appearance of something else. And this is true whether or not we even get the thing which we fixated on in the first place. Like staring so intently at the sea while whale-watching—perhaps frustrated by the lack of cetaceans and feeling as if you have been "ripped off" by the tour operator—that you miss the green flash as the sun sets, or fail to appreciate the simple and familiar closeness of your partner as you stand on deck in the wind.

Paterson's patience is evident in his relationship to time. Many reviewers comment on his habit of waking early each morning without the intrusion of an alarm. The very fact that they find this so remarkable says something about both the reviewers and about Paterson. As Thoreau wrote in *Walden*, "Little is to be expected of that day, if it can be called a day, to which we are not awakened by our Genius, but by the mechanical nudgings of some servitor."[18] Other viewers might read the scenes in which we see the hands of Paterson's watch speed around the dial while he drives his bus route as a commentary on the mind-numbing, soul-crushing nature of his job. But in the context of the film there is another, more plausible, alternative. Paterson is clearly an intellectual—his bookshelf includes volumes from William Carlos Williams, Wallace Stevens, Frank O'Hara, Henry David Thoreau, and Albert Camus, among others—but he does not seem dissatisfied with his job. As I've noted, it may be that he even appreciates the way it allows him to view the world without influencing it, facilitating his observation of and attention to the things themselves. The spinning hands on Paterson's wristwatch suggest the uniformity of his routine, but not, I think, a fundamentally alienating job. He does not think the world "owes him" an impressive career or grand spectacles; he enjoys watching his city and its inhabitants. Each day brings new sights, new conversations on the bus, new revelations. Thus, we might read the incongruous speed of Paterson's watch precisely as another indication that he is not bound by "human" time, but lives in a more "natural" time.

The Extraordinary Ordinary:
Words Written on Water

If we approach the world silently and observe it carefully and patiently, what will it reveal to us? Many things, assuredly. As many combinations are there of things, and observers, and moments. An infinity of things. However, while *Paterson* (2016) reveals the importance of silence, observation, and patience, while it highlights the value of the local and particular, and while it shows us a simple life can be beautiful and profoundly rewarding, two final revelations stand out as especially significant.[19]

The first revelation is this: *be grateful for life.*

The world, Paterson observes, is a complicated place—trillions of molecules, multiple dimensions, unforeseen events—but, generally, he does not find this overwhelming. Unlike Camus, he is not compelled to revolt at his inability to comprehend the whole of reality.[20] It's not that Paterson is completely unflappable; he is clearly unsettled by the destruction of his journal and by the incident with the gun at Shades. However, despite the complexity of the world, despite his lack of full comprehension or control, despite distressing events, Paterson's general demeanor and temperament is one of gratitude: "gladness" for his simple, solitary beer at Shades; "amazement" at the love he feels for Laura and for her presence in his life; appreciation for the birds in the trees and the roar of the Great Falls and the way the light falls on the city.

> Wherever you turn your eyes the world can shine like transfiguration. You don't have to bring a thing to it except a little willingness to see.... that is, to acknowledge that there is more beauty than our eyes can bear, that precious things have been put into our hands and to do nothing to honor them is to do great harm.[21]

Paterson's principles—silence, observation, patience—rule his daily routine; and each day his patience and attention reward him by revealing beauty. Living in this way, appreciation and gratitude are natural responses; they constitute both part of the poet's work in the world—whether or not she writes and publishes—and part of a distinctly human calling.

> [Beauty] is something snatched from non-being, that shadow which creeps in on us continuously and can be held off by continuous creative act. So, simply to look on anything ... with the love that penetrates to its essence, is to widen the domain of being in the vastness of non-being. Man has no other reason for his existence.[22]

I began this chapter by observing that, despite his humble life, anyone with "an ounce of wisdom would feel lucky to live and grateful to have lived" as Paterson does. And now, we see more clearly how and why that is the case. His world is larger and more beautiful as a result of how he lives.

It would be wrong, however, to put Paterson's way of being down to naïve optimism or puerile innocence; and this leads us to a second significant revelation: *this will not last.*

When Paterson's journal is destroyed, Laura is upset, and attempts to console Paterson. However, while Paterson is clearly unsettled by the loss of the poems, he does not seem to be vengeful, or distressed, or even particularly angry. He repeatedly tells Laura, "I'm OK," but then adds, enigmatically, "They [the poems] were just words, written on water." Here again, one might be tempted to read his reaction as rooted in low self-esteem, perhaps an attempt to lessen the pain of losing the poems by pretending that they did not matter—they were no good, not worthy of saving. Some people will note that Paterson's words reflect those of John Keats, who, dying of tuberculosis, requested that his gravestone read only: "Here lies One whose Name was writ in Water." Many people speculate that Keats was distraught, in part, because he was dying young, before he had been able to fulfill his promise or establish a poetic legacy (or, on a less charitable reading, before the world had duly recognized his genius).[23] The "writ in Water" sentiment seems to prophesy that Keats will not be remembered and his work will be forgotten. Perhaps Paterson's remark gives voice to something similar: the poems were words written on water, never to find an audience. Perhaps—if one also subscribes to the view that Paterson, lacking Keats's confidence, is insecure—his appraisal of the poems goes further: the poems were not worthy of an audience. Nothing special. Just a bus driver's lark. But, as with Paterson's apparent passivity, there is another interpretation of his reaction to the loss of the poems. Perhaps Paterson recognizes the impermanence of the poems. Perhaps he recognizes, or comes to recognize after a final, influential encounter with a Japanese poet, the impermanence of everything.

The day after his journal is destroyed, Paterson goes out for a walk and finds himself back at the Great Falls of the Passaic. While there, lost in thought, he is approached by a Japanese man who, it turns out, is on holiday in Paterson, New Jersey because of his respect for William Carlos Williams. During their conversation, the tourist asks Paterson if he is a poet. To which Paterson replies, "No," and then, "I'm a bus driver myself. Just a bus driver." "Ah-ha!," replies the man (a repeated interjection in the conversation), this is "very poetic." It could be, he points out, the subject of a William Carlos Williams poem, drawing our attention to both Williams's subject matter— the local world of Paterson, New Jersey—and to the fact that Williams, like Paterson, had a day job.[24]

The two talk, and we realize that this is one of the more extended and substantive conversations in the film, and one of the few about poetry itself. Paterson remarks that the Japanese tourist must "really like poetry," to which the tourist replies with obvious sincerity: "I breathe poetry." Paterson has found a kindred spirit; he has, we sense, a dawning realization that he could, and should, say the same of himself. And he makes a crucial connection, asking the Japanese man, "so you write poetry?" It turns out that the man does write poetry, which is published. In a lesser film, this would foreshadow a shift in Paterson's ambitions, giving him the confidence to publish his work; but the point here is that someone who is a poet— someone who lives poetically, someone who *breathes* poetry—will, perforce, write poetry. As the Japanese poet departs, he gives Paterson the gift of a blank journal: "Sometimes empty page presents most possibilities."

This conversation teaches, or reminds, Paterson of a number of things: that ordinary life is poetic, that poetry is a way of being, and that for those who "breathe" poetry, it is natural to write, whether or not one publishes. But it implies, I think, something further, although without making it explicit. With the gift of the new journal, Paterson realizes that the point of his poetry is not to speak his thoughts to others or even to have them preserved in a journal, but rather to bear witness to what is revealed to his silent, observant, patient life. His poetry is an expression of his life. Thus, the first poem he pens into his new journal, "The Line," plays with lyrics of Bing Crosby's "Swinging on a Star."[25] The well-known song poses the question of whether the lives of various animals might be better than our own.

Crosby gives us the options of a mule, a pig, or a fish as the song wends on, each time reminding us of the limitations or downsides of such an incarnation. It is the final option, the life of a fish, that sticks like an earworm in Paterson's mind. Not coincidentally, Crosby's stipulation about the fish's life is that it cannot write or read, which would make the fish's life a poor one for a poet. But I'm not sure the specific limitations of any species are the point here. The point, rather, is that each of us should *be what we are*, and that one of the things about being a human is the possibility of "widening the domain of being" through bearing witness to the extraordinary shining forth in the ordinary. What matters, most fundamentally, about Paterson's poems is not whether they are ever published, or even whether they are preserved, but rather that they bear witness to the extraordinary.[26]

* * *

If this were a traditional Hollywood movie, Paterson would be "discovered" and make a name for himself with his poetry. But *Paterson* (2016) isn't that kind of story. After one week we find ourselves, by "commodious vicus of recirculation" of the Passaic rather than the Liffey, right back where we began: another Monday morning, and the same routine with which the movie opened. Paterson is a regular guy, and it seems pretty clear that he is going to live variations of the week we witness for the rest of his life. There will, we assume, be changes. Paterson and Laura may have children. Perhaps Laura will make a go of it as a baker; perhaps she will achieve some local success. But like the leaves caught in the Passaic

River, it's already clear where Paterson and Laura are going in life; they may make adjustments for good or for ill, but those choices are not going to radically alter where the story leads: the security, without luxury, of a good union job in an East Coast urban center that has seen better days, leavened by the love they have for each other and by their respective inner lives (the sober, dedicated poet and the passionate artist and free spirit). They will live, and laugh, and love; they will also struggle, decline, and, eventually, die. The things that make Paterson's life exceptional are not going to come in the form of external goods like broad recognition as a poet, professional success, or wealth, but rather in the form of internal and intrinsic goods: his relationship with Laura; his dedication to poetry; and above all his commitment to the world, his keen observation of it, and his sensitivity to and appreciation of its beauty. *That* is what makes Paterson's life extraordinary.

Notes

1   Wallace Stegner, *Crossing to Safety* (New York: The Modern Library, 2002), 230–1.

2   *Paterson* (2016). Written and directed by Jim Jarmusch. Executive Producers Oliver Simon and Daniel Baur (K5 Films). Produced by Joshua Astrachan (Animal Kingdom) and Carter Logan (Inkjet). Distributed by Amazon Studios. It has been observed that *Paterson* is one of the rare films not to use poetry merely as a backdrop (e.g., *Dead Poet's Society*), or to treat the lives of poets (e.g., *Sylvia, Kill Your Darlings*), but to be about poetry itself in some significant way.

3   One might read additional tensions or anxieties into Paterson's life. He is clearly unnerved by Everett pulling a gun at Shades, which he understandably assumes to be real. The fact that Everett is merely acting out—and that, according to Marie, "the key word is *acting*"—is not clear until after Paterson disarms him. Earlier, after Laura dreams of having twins, Paterson, ever the keen observer of his city, comes across pairs of twins everywhere: on the walk to work, on his walk home, on the bus, at Shades. However, contrary to the implication of some reviewers, this does not seem to be some manifestation of unconscious anxiety about fatherhood or the prospect of children. Likewise, Paterson and Laura clearly live frugally, if happily. The decision to purchase a guitar for Laura, which costs "a few hundred dollars," seems to be a significant one for the couple; and as far as we can see they very rarely leave their home for entertainment or socializing. When Laura makes $286.00 selling her cupcakes at the farmer's market, it is cause for celebration and a rare night out for a dinner and a movie. So, there are concerns in Paterson's life; nevertheless, the quietness and ordinariness of Paterson's life and routine seem both prominent and undeniable.

4   See Plato, *Symposium*, trans. Alexander Nehamas and Paul Woodruff (Indianapolis, IN: Hackett, 1989). For an accessible, if idiosyncratic, account

of *poiesis*, see Hubert Dreyfus and Sean Dorrance Kelly, *All Things Shining* (New York: The Free Press, 2011), 206–23.

5   See, respectively, "Every Day," "The Manoeuvre," and "The Red Wheelbarrow," in *William Carlos Williams: Selected Poems*, ed. Charles Tomlinson (New York: New Directions, 1985), 179, 167, and 56.

6   William Carlos Williams's *Paterson* (New York: New Directions, 1992) is a five-part poem written between 1946 and 1958. Williams was himself influenced by another famously place-centered narrative, Joyce's *Ulysses*; and, as with Joyce's *Finnegan's Wake*, Williams constructed his poem in conversation with a city and its river. However, Williams chose to express himself in a poetic voice that was original and self-consciously American, following the spirit of Whitman rather than of his contemporaries Pound and Eliot, who left America for Europe. Williams's vision for his *Paterson* began explicitly with the idea that "a man himself is a city, beginning, seeking, achieving and concluding his life in ways which the various aspects of a city may embody" (Williams, *Paterson*, xiv). Thus, in Jarmusch's film, Paterson the man is representative of the city, and the city of him, in fidelity to Williams's vision. To keep these references clear, I'll adopt the following convention in sentences that would otherwise be ambiguous: "*Paterson* (2016)," for Jarmusch's film; "Paterson" for the character in Jarmusch's film; "*Paterson* (1958)" for William's poem; and "Paterson, New Jersey" for the city.

7   Williams, *Paterson*, 6. And, later, "Outside / outside myself / there is a world, / he rumbled, subject to my incursions / —a world / (to me) at rest, / which I approach / concretely—" (*Paterson*, 43).

8   Wallace Stevens wrote poems including "No Ideas About the Thing but the Thing Itself" and "The Plain Sense of Things" (*The Collected Poems of Wallace Stevens* [New York: Vintage, 2015], 565 and 530). In "*Vents*," Saint-John Perse spoke of "*Non point l'écrit, mais la chose même. Prise en son vif et dans son tout*"; that is, "Not writing, but the thing itself. Taken in all its liveliness and wholeness" (Saint-John Perse, *Oeuvres completes* [Paris: Gallimard, 1972], 229). All of Robinson Jeffers's poetry was an expression of his "inhumanism," his desire to shift emphasis and significance "from man to non-man" (Robinson Jeffers, *The Double Axe & Other Poems* [New York: Random House, 1948], vii). Hopkins developed the notion of *inscape* to express the unique "selving" of particular things. See Gerard Manley Hopkins, *Poetry and Prose: Gerard Manley Hopkins* (Rutland, VT: Everyman, 1998). And, famously, Husserl sounded the call, "*Wir wollen auf die 'Sachen selbst' zurückgehen*," "we must to go back to the things themselves" (Edmund Husserl, *Logical Investigations*, vol. 1 [London: Routledge, 2001], 168). These are only a few signal instances among many possible examples.

9   "Another One" by Ron Padgett in *Paterson* (2016).

10 I cannot, in this short chapter, attend to complicated epistemological debates about the degree to and way in which human experience is, or is not, inescapably linguistic, or debates about the degree to which human imagination has a role in constituting reality, and whether and to what degree that puts "the things themselves" beyond us. These are important questions;

however, here I confine myself to focusing on a much more pressing concern for most people: how we can live lives that experience the extraordinary.

11   William Carlos Williams wrote, "It is difficult / to get the news from poems / yet men die miserably every day / for lack / of what is found there ("Asphodel, that Greeny Flower," in *Asphodel, that Greeny Flower & Other Love Poems* [New York: New Directions, 1994], 19). However, while a person may not *need* to write poetry, I will spare a word for the value of making an effort to do so: the joys and insights of production are different than those of consumption. When Thoreau decided to build his own cabin, it was, in part, so as not to "resign the pleasure of construction to the carpenter," and to taste those pleasures himself, even if the product was inferior in some ways (Henry David Thoreau, *Walden* [Princeton, NJ: Princeton University Press, 2004], 46).

12   Paterson—like William Carlos Williams, Henry David Thoreau, and others—is a devotee of walking, from his daily walk to and from work to his nightly walk with Marvin. His walking helps with his observation, and helps him to know his city more intimately. On foot, unlike in a car, we come to really know a place and the things in it. "We are here to witness," writes Annie Dillard, "that is why I take walks: to keep an eye on things," that is, to keep an eye out for the extraordinariness of the ordinary (Annie Dillard, *Teaching a Stone to Talk* [New York: HarperCollins, 1982], 90 and 91).

13   In *Walden*, Thoreau writes: "Let us settle ourselves, and work and wedge our feet downward through the mud and slush of opinion, and prejudice, and tradition, and delusion, and appearance, that alluvion which covers the globe, through Paris and London, through New York and Boston and Concord, through church and state, through poetry and philosophy and religion, till we come to a hard bottom and rocks in place, which we can call *reality*, and say, This is, and no mistake . . ." (Thoreau, *Walden*, 97–8). Elsewhere he reflects: "Think of our life in nature,—daily to be shown matter, to come into contact with it,—rocks, trees, wind on our cheeks! the *solid* earth! the *actual* world! the *common sense! Contact! Contact!*" (*The Maine Woods* [Princeton, NJ: Princeton University Press, 2004], 71). Here we read not only Thoreau's commitment to material nature, but his mentor Emerson's faith in the ordinary: "I embrace the common, I explore and sit at the feet of the familiar, the low. Give me insight into to-day, and you may have the antique and future worlds" (Ralph Waldo Emerson, "The American Scholar," in *Ralph Waldo Emerson: Lecture and Essays* [New York: The Library of America, 1983], 68–9).

14   William Carlos Williams, "Sermon with a Camera," *The New Republic*, October 10, 1938.

15   C. S. Lewis, *The Four Loves* (New York: Harvest Books, 1960), 22.

16   Annie Dillard, *Pilgrim at Tinker Creek* (New York: Harper Perennial, 2007), 35.

17   This disposition no doubt contributes to Paterson's fundamental happiness. As C. S. Lewis notes, when we expect something, we tend to move rather naturally to feeling entitled to it, even having a right to it. And, then, in cases in which we do not get what we expect from the world, we are apt to feel that some fundamental injustice has occurred. If, however, we recognize that

the world does not *owe us* anything particular, we are protected from that particular form of despair. See C. S. Lewis, *The Screwtape Letters* (New York: Harper Collins, 2001), 165–9.

18 Thoreau, *Walden*, 89.

19 This final section is more speculative than the preceding ones, and I recognize that there are legitimate reasons for interpreting Paterson, the film and the character, in a different key. Although here I downplay suggestions of Paterson's insecurity, there would be an alternative interpretation of the film that emphasized that trait and the degree to which Paterson moves beyond it in his conversation with the Japanese poet and his subsequent decision to take up poetry again.

20 See Albert Camus, *The Myth of Sisyphus*, trans. Justin O'Brien (New York: Vintage Books, 2018).

21 Marilynne Robinson, *Gilead* (New York: Farrar, Straus and Giroux, 2004), 245.

22 Nan Shepherd, *The Living Mountain* (Edinburgh: Cannongate, 2011), 102. And here we return, in a modified sense, to poetry as making. In the end the distinction between poetry making and poetry revealing is a didactic one as much as anything else. In one sense a thing is revealed to be extraordinary when I pay more attention to it; but, in another sense, it is my attention to it that makes it extraordinary. Thus, Wallace Stevens speaks of poetry as one of the "cnlargements of life," and to this I would add, with Shepherd, of being (Wallace Stevens, *The Necessary Angel* [New York: Vintage, 1951], viii).

23 That, of course, is only one interpretation. Another is that Keats recognized, as I argue further, that *everything* material and mortal is writ in water. Everything is miraculous; but nothing lasts forever.

24 The conversation obviously drives home the fact that there is no contradiction between being a bus driver and being a poet. Many excellent poets worked "day jobs": William Carlos Williams was a physician; Wallace Stevens was an insurance company executive; Dennis O'Driscoll was a civil servant in the Irish Office of the Revenue Commissioners; Dana Gioia was vice president of marketing at a major corporation; and Philip Larkin was a librarian. There are many such examples.

25 Bing Crosby sung "Swinging on a Star" in the 1944 film *Going My Way*. Directed by Leo McCarey. Lyrics by Johnny Burke, and music composed by Jimmy Van Heusen.

26 "*Verweile doch*! Last forever! Who hasn't prayed that prayer? But the *augenblick* isn't going to *verweile*. You were lucky to get it in the first place. The present is a freely given canvas. That it is constantly being ripped apart and washed downstream goes without saying; it is a canvas nonetheless" (Dillard, *Pilgrim at Tinker Creek*, 84).

17

On Sidney Lumet's *Serpico*

Sam B. Girgus

The Embattled Conscience of a Hippie Cop

Director Sidney Lumet considered Frank Serpico, the hero of his film *Serpico* (1974) as played by Al Pacino, "a native American," presumably meaning a thoroughly American character who epitomizes qualities and values inherent in American culture and consciousness.[1] As part of being such an American, Serpico, according to Lumet, "was a professional rebel." Lumet said of Serpico, "He happened to be a cop. He was a romantic, essentially."[2] Expanding on Serpico's penchant for rebellion, Lumet said, "If he hadn't been able to protest against corruption, he would have found a reason to protest about the color of his uniform. Protesting is what mattered."[3]

Serpico the New York cop in real life and in the film as portrayed by Pacino expressed his American rebellious and romantic proclivities as well as his explosive emotionality by fighting against police corruption while also adopting a so-called "hippie" style as a way of living and thinking. For Lumet he was the rebellious "Frank Serpico, the hippie dressed as a cop."[4] Similarly, Maura Spiegel in her biography of Lumet calls Serpico "an incorruptible hippie cop."[5]

Tensions and conflicts for Serpico as the hippie cop relate profoundly to his meaning for American culture. The contrast, conflict, and comparison in *Serpico* between the New York Police Department and hippie culture proffer a methodology for dramatizing and studying America during the late 1960s and 1970s. The film engages America from the two radically different perspectives of the hippie and the cop, creating a kind of interactive exchange that sometimes becomes a dialogue between them of values, beliefs, and meanings. The encounter between the two cultures of the police and the hippie becomes a crisis of divided conscience that opens a window into the America of Serpico's time and place. The influential radical philosophy at that time of Herbert Marcuse offers sharp insight into the struggle over conflicted conscience as a field for dramatizing crises of values and meaning for America.

As a policeman, Serpico represents both in his uniform and his undercover disguises the mentality and the physical power and authority of the police regime. As a hippie, he personifies an entirely different identity and consciousness of rebellion, dissidence, individual freedom, and choice. The struggle between these two parts of his identity plays out as a conflict of conscience that tears Serpico apart as he flails against police forces of conformity and corruption, on the one hand, and strives, on the other hand, for a freedom driven by an idea of culture and community infused with libidinal energy and creative imagination.

The film also proposes two different directions America could have taken in moving ahead at the time, one conservative program from the police perspective that dedicates itself to maintaining the status quo and another liberal, often radical, project for rethinking freedom and human relationships under combustible modern conditions. Lumet and Pacino pit the long-established police culture against the new consciousness of the hippies. The police as representative of the dominant culture engage Serpico's hippie identity and worldview. The NYPD's tradition of projecting images of authority, command, and regimentation even in the face of rampant corruption challenge hippie lifestyles and images.

Serpico's hippie alternative for America involves more than the pursuit of unconventional lifestyles as part of a new visual and popular culture. It was seen as the outer manifestation of the ideas and values of a so-called new counterculture, an epithet promulgated to a considerable extent by Theodore Roszak. The hippie counterculture that Serpico represents was intellectually and philosophically grounded in the work of two radical thinkers, Marcuse and Norman O. Brown. The different philosophies and approaches of Brown and Marcuse gave intellectual impetus to the counter-cultural understanding of political oppression and sexual repression. They conceptualized, theorized, and promoted fresh creative ideas and projects to achieve liberation. As Roszak writes, "The emergence of Herbert Marcuse and Norman Brown as major social theorists among the disaffiliated young of Western Europe and America must be taken as one of the defining features of the counter culture."[6]

With all of their differences as thinkers, Marcuse and Brown come together in claiming an erotic basis to culture and civilization that could be directed through a new consciousness to creating greater freedom in society. Both thinkers believed a radically revised Freudianism could provide the basis for imagining and living a new social theory and practice for liberation with the potential for rethinking classic Marx. As Roszak writes, "For it is in their work that the inevitable confrontation between Marx and Freud takes place."[7]

In spite of their common commitment to a radicalized Freudian theory, Brown and Marcuse had different world visions that diverge in regard to their relevance for understanding and appreciating Serpico's historical and cultural significance. Roszak says Brown "undertakes a revision of Freud" that relates to "the great mythical motifs of redemption and resurrection." Roszak argues, "Yet it is the Christian image of 'resurrection' that Brown finally asserts as his ideal of liberation—an image that rapidly carries him forward toward a 'body mysticism' which manages to be *both* secular *and* transcendent."[8]

It might prove difficult to find Serpico's place and purpose in hippie counterculture by looking for him through the lens of Brown's radical Freudianism that envisions a realm of mysticism and poetic sensibility and spirituality. While Brown's Christian mysticism may inform Serpico's impulse toward martyrdom, a wounded Serpico's race to the hospital in the back of a New York police car and his mental and physical condition before and after that life-saving emergency ride do not suggest a transformative resurrection and redemption of the body and the soul for him. Rather than applying Brown's theory to illuminate Serpico's role as a hippie cop, it probably would prove more helpful to use the perspective of Marcuse to provide insight into Serpico, the man of conflicted conscience.

Marcuse: A Radical Vision of a Liberated World

Marcuse built a pathway with markers of terms and ideas to lead to a philosophical theory and project for a new domain of unprecedented liberation and freedom in the modern human experience. Marcuse, as Paul Robinson says, "insisted on the real possibility of a world substantially free of guilt, misery, and injustice, a world in which the internalization and sublimation of sexuality would give way to a heightening of pleasure."[9] To reach such an extraordinary realm of such visionary hopes and possibilities would require overcoming what Marcuse dubbed "surplus repression."

Marcuse describes surplus repression as a form of "domination" that differs intrinsically from "basic" repression. He says surplus repression enforces "the restrictions necessitated by social domination" and should be "distinguished from (basic) *repression.*" Basic repression for Marcuse allows for the survival and continuity of human beings in society but without adding surplus repression for purposes of control and domination. Basic repression for Marcuse merely compels "'modifications' of the instincts necessary for the perpetuation of the human race in civilization."[10] Marcuse argues that "specific interests of domination introduce *additional* controls over and above those indispensable for civilized human association. These additional controls arising from the specific institutions of domination are what we denote as *surplus-repression.*"[11]

For Marcuse, the social effort to control sexuality employs the power of surplus repression. Surplus repression works to control the direction and organization of sexuality. As Robinson says, "The notion of surplus repression was meant to introduce a historical dimension into Freud's general equation of civilization and repression. Surplus repression denoted the *quantitative* restrictions on sexuality which resulted from economic and political domination." Developing his project to achieve a form of synthesis of Marx and Freud, Marcuse related sexual repression to historical moments and societies. As Robinson writes, "Indeed, Marcuse insisted that the *larger* portion of sexual repression in modern civilization was in fact surplus repression, repression in the service of domination."[12]

For Marcuse, "basic repression and surplus-repression have been inextricably intertwined" to control sexual organization and direction in order to secure the dominance of genitality. Marcuse maintains "the normal progress to genitality has been organized in such a way that the partial impulses and their 'zones' were all but desexualized in order to conform to the requirements of a specific social organization of the human existence."[13]

Marcuse's project argued that the creation of a new order and regime of freedom and liberation must begin by liberating sexuality from "the establishment of genital supremacy"[14] that inhibits and restrains sexuality and eroticism to the limited goal and purpose of fulfilling the demands for procreation and alienated labor. He says this repressive "process achieves the socially necessary desexualization of the body: the libido becomes concentrated in one part of the body, leaving most of the rest free for use as the instrument of labor."[15]

As opposed to such a repressive sexual regime, Marcuse presents "the notion of a non-repressive instinctual order." He writes, "Non-repressive order is possible only if the sex instincts can, by virtue of their own dynamic and under changed existential and social conditions, generate lasting erotic relations among individuals."[16] He calls for the "reactivation of polymorphous and narcissistic sexuality" that can "lead to culture-building if the organism exists not as an instrument of alienated labor but as a subject of self-realization."[17]

The hippie counterculture of Marcuse's time and place, as Christopher Hitchens and other writers and commentators state, found his critique of oppression and repression in modern technological societies refreshing and illuminating.[18] His program for freedom and liberation to counter and overcome repressive hegemonic forces inspired people with a passion for change and, for some, revolution. What was seen as the sexual and erotic basis of Marcuse's project for freedom and liberation made his project for many especially provocative and compelling.

Frank Serpico: The Divided Self

As a hippie cop, Serpico's values, beliefs, and lifestyle resonate with much of Marcuse's ambitions for a freer and liberated America, including a sexually liberated America. Marcuse's project for a counterculture to renew America puts Serpico's exploits in a broader and deeper context of psychological and social issues and challenges to America at the time of the movie.

At first, Serpico proves himself capable of making his divided self work efficiently to satisfy the conflicting demands made upon him as a young cop and a hippie. He suggests an air of almost insouciance as he adjusts to his life as a new recruit on the police force. He accommodates himself to the daily routine of policing. He learns how to work the public and official tasks and details of policing as well as the nuances of police work that occur outside public scrutiny such as being offered poor quality but free meals from restaurants as underground compensation for policing favors.

In fact, Serpico's hippie sensibility, sensitivity, and creative intelligence at times become an asset in making him a better and more effective police officer with a promising future for promotion and status in the department. He impresses an informed and intelligent commanding officer, Captain Tolkin (Gene Gross), that the police must do more to learn about and communicate with the civilian community. He says, "I think it's time we started communicating more on the street, sir." Serpico can use his background and knowledge to help the police get up to date on changes in the culture. He says, "You know the way it is, we're totally isolated, sir. We're completely out of touch with what's happening." Serpico proves so convincing that the captain urges him to continue working in his creative and unconventional disguises that the other police find grotesque and even insulting.

At times Serpico's hippie sensibility also makes him a stronger and more effective policeman fighting crime on the street. In one incident, Serpico leads in breaking up a gang rape but manages to apprehend and arrest only one of the perpetrators, a young Black man who was present at the rape but didn't participate in the actual physical assault. After a brutal beating and cruel questioning of the Black man by other policemen, Serpico approaches the young man with sensitivity and sympathy. The young offender recalls Serpico's reluctance to participate in the beating the police inflicted upon him during questioning. Serpico tells him, "That's not my kind of fun." Serpico gains the man's confidence. Serpico's modulated, refrained conversation with the young man leads to information that enables Serpico to find the rapists. In an impressive display of courage, speed, and strength, Serpico arrests the men on his own in a neighborhood park, although other police get to credit themselves for the arrest due to their seniority.

In another example where hippie experience informs Serpico's policing, both Serpico and another policeman Bob Blair, who is played by Tony Roberts, evidence clear knowledge and experience with marijuana during a police lecture designed to educate the police about the substance that was illegal at the time of the film. The other police officers in the lecture hall seem genuinely unfamiliar with marijuana while the lecturer describes it in a way that becomes laughable to Serpico and Blair. Serpico and Blair clearly exist and operate in a sphere that separates them from the other officers to such a point that in another scene a commanding officer named Barto (Ed Crowley) requires Serpico to undergo testing for drug abuse.

Serpico's hippie consciousness and being that in some ways influence the nature and success of his police work also compel him to establish a separate domain for his hippie life. He wants to keep his private life and domain separate, distinct, and distant from his police work and his Italian background and family. In a charming scene, Serpico goes to his father's shoe repair shop in an old neighborhood in Manhattan. Approaching the shop, Serpico fools with some children on the street who are enjoying some relief from the hot weather by playing in the gushing water from an open fire hydrant. In New York, police invariably show up in a patrol car to such a scene to turn off the water. In contrast to such official police activity, Serpico in this instance appreciates the opportunity to express his spontaneous joyfulness and pleasure with the children.

At the shop, his uncle Pasquale (John Medici) attends to his work while complaining to Serpico that the family has not seen much of him. Pasquale had hoped Serpico would join the family on the previous weekend to meet an Italian woman and friend of the family who might be a possible match for him. Serpico retorts that the male members of the woman's family all were policemen. He jokes that sometimes he thinks she's a policeman, clearly indicating his wish to have a life separate from the department.

The significance of Serpico's move on his own to a small apartment in Greenwich Village cannot be measured merely in terms of the few miles the change takes him from his parents, family, friends, and old Italian neighborhoods. Socially, culturally, and intellectually the move places him in a world apart from his roots and background. Although emotionally he remains the same warm, compassionate, and sympatico young man, the move to Greenwich Village confirms his identity in the hippie and counter-culture world.

With its long and important history as a bohemian and artistic center, Greenwich Village also cultivated the culture and lifestyle of the hippie counter-culture movement. Going back at least to the turn of the last century, a growing community of writers in Greenwich Village, as Christine Stansell says, "transformed an unexceptional shabby neighborhood into a place glowing with a sense of the contemporary." Over the years, assorted groups of thinkers, writers, artists, radicals, free thinkers, and non-conformists turned Greenwich Village, Stansell says, "into a beacon of American possibility in the new age."[19]

To live in Greenwich Village and to be modern and bohemian meant embracing new ways of thinking and living and to proclaim new meanings to freedom. Stansell writes of the history and people of Greenwich Village, "As they mused upon and polemicized about their favorite subjects—free speech, free love, free expression—they shaped their writings, social lives, and love affairs to conform to the new story, in which questions of sexuality and sex roles merged with those of class equality."[20]

Ironically, moving to Greenwich Village also locates Serpico and the movie closer intellectually, artistically, and culturally to Lumet's home base and the source of his being and identity on New York's Lower East Side. The vibrant atmosphere of art, culture, politics, and ethnicity of the Lower East Side that energized and cultivated Lumet throughout his life, work, and career related in many ways to the culture and life of Greenwich Village. The borders of streets and alleys and intersections between the two areas were quite porous. As Stansell notes, "In the bohemian geography of the imagination, Greenwich Village was proximate and permeable to the Jewish Lower East Side, twenty blocks to the south, crawling with its own bohemians and sizzling with its own ideas of modernity, and to the plebeian hurly-burly of Union Square to the north."[21]

For Lumet "the Village" with its history of open urban borders between communities and cultures provides the hippie environment for Serpico's journey following a Marcusian road map that takes him through a new counter-cultural geography of open social, psychological, and sexual spaces. Serpico pursues those open spaces with purpose and vigor from the moment he comes across two of the period's "flower children" on the sidewalk by his new apartment selling pet puppies they mysteriously have obtained. Greenwich Village gives him the opportunity to attend college courses on Cervantes and Don Quixote, a foreshadowing and parallel journey of his own quest and crusade. The Village and college courses also mean the opportunity for meeting another free spirit, a female free spirit named Leslie (Cornelia Sharpe).

Leslie offers access for Serpico to her friends in the arts, theater, and ballet. She takes him to wild Village parties where her friends find Serpico and his work and life as a cop intriguing. Repeating the name his friends use for him, she exclaims with glee, "Paco everybody loves you." She helps to make the two parts of his life as a hippie cop seem compatible. She becomes his instructor teaching him ballet movements and positions.

Leslie also becomes his enthusiastic and accommodating sexual partner. Everything about their relationship suggests they happily put into practice the sexual program that Marcuse and hippie sensibility preach. Their intimacy and interaction indicate a non-repressive sexual relationship that opens and appreciates the promise of polymorphous pleasure and freedom. A scene with Leslie and Serpico sharing a bathtub conveys the idea of such a relationship.

Such sexual freedom dramatically contrasts with the attitudes of some of the police about acceptable sexuality. A commanding officer named Steiger (James Tolkan) typifies a repressive, violent, homophobic view of sexuality as narrowly defined, controlled, and performed. Outraged by Serpico's unconventional hippie style and attitude, Steiger rushes after Serpico into the police station bathroom and locker room to falsely accuse him of homosexual behavior that could threaten his career under the existing rules and regulations of that time. He screams at Serpico, "In the shit house, in the dark, were you going down on him?"

Ironically, Leslie's suggestion to Serpico of marriage seems like a violation to him of the freedom and independence of their lifestyle and commitments. She leaves Serpico and her life of art and dance and returns to Amarillo, Texas, and the man named Roy who apparently had been waiting for her.

In a touching Village and New York moment, Serpico meets his second female partner in the film, a nurse named Laurie (Barbara Eda-Young) who will play an important part in his life as Serpico and the film pivot to an irreparable break and rupture between his divided hippie and cop self. Serpico and Laurie first meet each other outdoors in their adjoining apartment gardens. Serpico's recording of the amazing voice of the great Italian tenor Giuseppe di Stefano reverberates in the garden. She mistakenly thinks it's the voice of another magnificent singer and also like di Stefano a star of the Metropolitan Opera, the Swedish tenor Jussi Bjoerling. So, two New Yorkers, a nurse and a cop, evidence a sophistication about opera that would seem esoteric to many people.

The opera music and the story that Serpico listens to so carefully and that he uses to engage the attention of his attractive neighbor parallels his own story and passion. Di Stefano sings from the opera *Tosca* (1900) by Giacomo Puccini. Di Stefano sings the role of Mario Cavaradossi, a painter like so many of the artists in Greenwich Village, who is also a radical reformer. He is about to be executed at the orders of Baron Scarpia, the chief of police, who was obsessively jealous of Cavaradossi's affair with the great singer and character Tosca. Awaiting his execution on the rampart of Castel Sant'Angelo in Rome, Cavaradossi tearfully expresses his love and passion for Tosca. Serpico listens attentively to di Stefano sing, "*O dolci baci, o languide carezze*," meaning "Oh sweet kisses, oh languid caresses." A reformer and free thinker in his own right, Serpico also feels under the gun of the police, in Serpico's case fellow police officers who are threatened by his zeal for honesty, integrity, and change. Both Serpico and Cavaradossi challenge established authority and power.

Rage: Within and Without

Serpico's steady psychic deterioration under the ever-increasing pressure and hostility of fellow police officers soon becomes the center of his relationship with Laurie. The initial harmony and compatibility of their relationship leads the couple to start thinking about marriage and a family but such domestic comfort and security quickly dissipates as Serpico's tension, anxiety, and alienation worsen to a degree beyond his or Laurie's control. He turns the household into an arena for venting his rage. His outbursts become violent so that he not only disparages and chides Laurie; he also excoriates Bob Blair, his cohort on the force in the battle against corruption and crime, for not supporting him enough and for not adequately appreciating his position and situation of danger and sacrifice.

Unable to bear his tirades or the increasingly anxious atmosphere of their household, Laurie finds her growing depression and anxiety so severe as to match Serpico's distressing condition. Mostly, unable to assuage Serpico's suffering and to mitigate his self-destruction, Laurie must leave to save herself in spite of Serpico's panicky reaction to her announced departure. His passionate and earnest appeals for her to stay with him fail to convince her.

As Laurie understands, for all the vehemence of his attacks on those closest to him as well as his enmity toward corrupt and abusive officers, Serpico makes his most virulent and violent attacks against himself. He turns the direction of his sharp conscience inward. He weaponizes his conscience against himself. His redirected conscience feeds, stimulates, and directs his pervasive sense of guilt. Isolation and alienation from others exacerbate Serpico's insecurity and guilt.

Serpico succinctly summarizes the moral psychology of his dilemma. He tells Laurie, "It's amazing. I feel like a criminal because I don't take money." Serpico insinuates and lives a Freudian model of the conscience as a potentially destructive force that can operate independently of actual moral and ethical conditions and challenges. Freud propounds a theory of the conscience or super-ego as a kind of self-perpetuating power. The conscience becomes an internal policing agent that battles aggression or even the thought of aggression through the application of the power of the super-ego energized by redirected libidinal impulse. Freud in *Civilization and Its Discontents* (1930) says the individual's "aggressiveness is introjected, internalized; it is, in point of fact, sent back to where it came from—that is, it is directed toward his own ego." He says, "There it is taken over by a portion of the ego, which sets itself over against the rest of the ego as super-ego, and which now, in the form of 'conscience,' is ready to put into action against the ego the same harsh aggressiveness that the ego would have liked to satisfy upon other, extraneous individuals."[22]

As in the case of Serpico, the conscience-driven individual, according to Freud, continues to suffer from a sense of guilt that demands punishment, while the truly guilty often remain free of conscience or guilt. Freud writes, "The tension between the harsh super-ego and the ego that is subjected to it, is called by us the sense of guilt; it expresses itself as a need for punishment."[23]

While Serpico's fellow officers direct their aggression toward him and apparently feel few serious tremors of conscience or guilt, Serpico wages war against himself. As Freud says, "For the more virtuous a man is, the more severe and distrustful is its behavior, so that ultimately it is precisely those people who have carried saintliness furthest who reproach themselves with the worst sinfulness."[24]

Interestingly, Freud's notion of "saintliness" not only applies to Serpico's sense of martyrdom; it also finds confirmation in Serpico's nickname of Paco which in some translations of the Spanish form of the nickname apparently means Francis and relates to St. Francis.

Serpico's war with himself smothers and kills the hippie in him. The hippie counter-culture impulse that manifested itself for him in certain productive, promising, and pleasurable ways surrenders to what Freud theorized as the death instinct, the same drive for destruction that Marcuse hoped to engage with erotic liberation and non-repressive sexuality. Freud eclipses Marcuse. Rather than being a Thoreauvian presence of moral principle, Serpico ends up more like Mark Twain, a victim of his own brutal conscience, pervasive sense of guilt, and moral sensibility.[25]

Serpico at the end of the film sets off to sail to Europe accompanied only by Alfie, the English sheep dog he bought from street kids when he first moved into his Greenwich Village apartment. Lumet shows Serpico and Alfie headed toward the ocean liner that will take them to the old world of Europe. A broken, demoralized, and defeated Serpico leaves behind a vitiated hippie hope of achieving a new vision and world of liberation and freedom by following a path of change, love, pleasure, and play.

Notes

1   See Mort Sheinman, "Sidney Lumet: Letting It Happen," in *Sidney Lumet: Interviews*, ed. Joanna E. Rapf (Jackson, MI: University Press of Mississippi, 2006), 67.

2   Ibid., Smith, 142.

3   Ibid., Ciment, 83.

4   Ibid.

5   Maura Spiegel, *Sidney Lumet: A Life* (New York: St. Martin's Press, 2019), 255.

6   Theodore Roszak, *The Making of a Counter Culture: Reflections on the Technocratic Society and Its Youthful Opposition* (New York: Anchor Books, 1969), 84.

7   Ibid.

8   Ibid., 107, 119.

9   Paul A. Robinson, *The Freudian Left: Wilhelm Reich, Geza Roheim, Herbert Marcuse* (New York: Harper Colophon, 1969), 191.

10   Herbert Marcuse, *Eros and Civilization: A Philosophical Inquiry into Freud* (rpt; 1955. Boston: Beacon Press, 1966), 35.

11   Ibid., 37.

12   Robinson, *The Freudian Left*, 202, 203.

13   Marcus, *Eros and Civilization,* 38. As part of his theory of surplus repression and his overall philosophy of sexuality, repression, and culture, Marcuse rethinks Freud's ideas of the pleasure principle and reality principle to develop his notion of the crucial work of what he dubs the performance principle. He sees the engagement between "the unrestrained pleasure principle" and the reality principle as crucial to the development of the performance principle. He writes, "The reality

principle supersedes the pleasure principle: man learns to give up momentary, uncertain, and destructive pleasure for delayed, restrained, but 'assured' pleasure" (13). He maintains the reality principle "sustains the organism in the external world. In the case of the human organism, this is an historical world" (34).

Marcuse's performance principle advances the reality principle to what he deems a defining and salient historical context. He describes the performance principle as "the prevailing historical form of the reality principle" (35). Thinking "in terms of the specific reality principle that has governed the origins and the growth of this civilization," Marcuse says, "we designate it as performative principle" (EC: 44). The work of the performance principle relates directly to the tension between sexuality and repression. Marcuse sees the performance principle as the means for measuring and organizing the historic and social dynamics of repression and sexuality. Marcuse writes, "The organization of sexuality reflects the basic features of the performance principle and its organization of society" (48). He maintains the performance principle can help "to elucidate the scope and the limits of the prevalent repressiveness in contemporary civilization" (44).

For Marcuse, the performance principle allows for historical insight and understanding regarding repression, sexuality, and the reality principle. Working with the performative principle suggests the possibility of altering the perception and understanding of reality through a reconsideration of the relationship between sexuality and repression under historic and cultural conditions. For Marcuse, the performance principle can provide a key to rethinking sexuality and repression as the means for achieving psychological, social, and political freedom and liberation in a revolutionary transformation of society.

14   Ibid., 48.

15   Ibid.

16   Ibid., 199.

17   Ibid., 210.

18   See Christopher Hitchens, "Where Aquarius Went," *The New York Times Book Review*, Sunday, December 19, 2004, 11. See also Charles A. Reich, *The Greening of America* (New York: Random House, 1970).

19   Christine Stansell, *American Moderns: Bohemian New York and the Creation of a New Century* (New York: Metropolitan Books, 2000), 2, 3.

20   Ibid., 7.

21   Ibid., 6.

22   Sigmund Freud, *Civilization and Its Discontents*, trans. and ed. James Strachey (New York: Norton, 1972), 70.

23   Ibid.

24   Ibid., 72–3.

25   See Girgus, "Conscience and Civilization: Death and Alienation in Mark Twain," in *Desire and the Political Unconscious in American Literature* (New York: St. Martin's Press, 1990), 155–79. See also my "Conscience in Connecticut: *Civilization and Its Discontents* in Twain's *Camelot*," *The New England Quarterly* 60 (December 1978): 547–60.

18

On Antwone Fisher's *Antwone Fisher*

Alberto G. Urquidez

On the one hand, film carries the potential to disrupt thinking, challenge dominant ideologies, and open up novel perspectives. On the other hand, film carries the potential to reanimate traditional forms of thinking, reinforce dominant stereotypes, and undermine novel perspectives. In this chapter I propose that film alone is insufficient to sustain a critical philosophical perspective because what is "seen" by the viewer is largely determined by her antecedent perspective going into the film. Perhaps this thesis will seem too general. Perhaps "what is seen by the viewer" depends on genre, philosophical topic, viewer sensibilities, or other contextual matters. To avoid these objections, I will limit the scope of my thesis to films seeking to challenge racial misandric stereotypes. How might such a film undercut the invidious beliefs that (consciously or unconsciously) condition the viewer's analysis? When an antecedent ideological perspective largely conditions a viewer's interpretation, a film's prospect of undermining that perspective diminishes. Here I defend this claim in respect to the biographical drama, *Antwone Fisher*, which strikes me as one of the most powerful challenges to racial misandric stereotypes depicted in film. Evidently, this film has been unsuccessful in undermining racial misandric stereotypes among feminists who interpret it as objectionably masculinist and heteronormative. The theoretical framing feminists (or, for that matter, any other group of viewers) bring to this film is among the most powerful variables in shaping what is seen—more so than the film's intended message.

A Synopsis of *Antwone Fisher*

I begin with a synopsis of the film. Antwone Fisher, the film's main protagonist, was born in Ohio State Correctional Facility for Women, two months after the death of his father who was murdered by an ex-girlfriend for infidelity. Separated at birth and sent to a temporary orphanage, Antwone was ignorant of his mother; he had no knowledge of her name or why she was in prison. When she was released, two years later, she never claimed him. Antwone was placed in a foster home with a Black religious family, the Tates. There he faced physical abuse and torture at the hands of his foster mother. His foster father, a local preacher, was mostly absent by Antwone's account; interestingly, the film rarely depicts him in the home. Antwone was alienated. He lacked loving parents, including a positive masculine role model. Antwone was also sexually abused by his cousin, Nadine—a point I come back to, later. His foster siblings, also Black boys, were similarly abused by their foster mother—though to varying degrees, for Antwone's lighter-skinned brother was treated more favorably. All were continually reminded they had been abandoned for a reason: they were worthless, unworthy of love, and deserving of antipathy and contempt. "Nigger" was the nickname of choice, not only for Antwone, but for his siblings. Abuse went along with the daily reminder that they were bad children—hence, they could be nothing but niggers. So frequently used was the nickname that the boys could tell whom Mrs. Tate meant by how she said it.

Antwone's childhood is presented as a retrospective, which unfolds throughout the film. As a young man, Antwone recalls his painful childhood memories in reports to his Black psychiatrist, Dr. Davenport, whom he met in the navy. After being released from the Tates, and having no place to go, Antwone was homeless for a period. This experience led him to join the navy. Short-fused, Antwone was sent to Dr. Davenport for evaluation after initiating a fight with a commanding officer who teased him. This habit would prove hard for Antwone to break, each physical altercation occasioning a visit to Dr. Davenport. In this way, Dr. Davenport came to learn and empathize with Antwone's story. Evidently, two precipitating factors explain Dr. Davenport's personal investment in Antwone: an empathy established through racial solidarity and Dr. Davenport's desire to father a child (we eventually learn that his marriage was on the brink of divorce due to their inability to conceive). Taking both professional and unprofessional measures, Dr. Davenport made it a point to mentor and look after Antwone, even testifying on his behalf to ensure his good standing in the navy. He did not merely teach Antwone how to overcome fear and trauma. Additionally, he gave him lessons in manhood and self-respect. As a result, Antwone eventually overcomes his anger and the internalized racism imposed upon him as a child. This makes *Antwone Fisher* a story of hope, perseverance, self-knowledge, and triumph, but also of the possibility of cultivating a positive form of Black masculinity within a racist society.

A Feminist Critique

Antwone's story and struggle for human dignity are the stuff of captivating cinema. However, his achievement is not inexplicable in the film—it is neither miraculous nor "self-made." It depends upon the racial solidarity and community effort of Dr. Davenport, Antwone's girlfriend, and, later, his biological family. Dr. Davenport's continued insistence that the key to Antwone's psychological healing lies in "finding his real family" proves correct. As a father figure and positive role model, Dr. Davenport symbolizes the possibility of a new Black masculinity. Yet, Black masculinity is widely criticized as patriarchal.[1] Here I will consider a passage from Badia Sahar Ahad's defense of *Antwone Fisher* in her "New Normal: Black Psychic Subjectivity in Antwone Fisher."[2] On the one hand, Ahad offers an overwhelmingly sympathetic analysis and defense of the film. She argues that its appeal to three texts—John W. Blassingame's *The Slave Community*, Marcus Garvey's *Philosophy and Opinions of Marcus Garvey*, and a poem by Antwone Fisher—provides an important corrective to traditional psychoanalytic theory. On the other hand, Ahad mentions, almost in passing, that the film's heroic representation of Antwone is made possible by "displacing the contempt and disdain, typically reserved for the black masculine subject, onto the black woman." His heroic figuration apparently consists in his ability to overcome everything that is thrown his way, despite the odds heavily stacked against him. Ahad finds this objectionable because it is done at the expense of Black women: "About this, [Frank] Wilderson's analysis is astute. The film so demonizes black femaleness in general, and black motherhood in particular, that one (almost) forgets Fisher's would-be abject status—for his ability to even attempt to overcome the abuse and alienation which has come to define him creates a heroic figuration."[3] Elsewhere she claims that "*Antwone Fisher* is deeply invested in asserting the heteromasculine subjectivity of its black psychiatrist and its black analysand [i.e., Antwone Fisher]."[4]

I highlight Ahad's critique, not because it is the only feminist perspective on this film, or because this is a central theme in Ahad's paper, but because of its *prima facie* plausibility which is rooted in the devaluation of Black men. The critique is predictable and is not confined to academia— hence, its importance. Two critical issues that Ahad raises are that *Antwone Fisher* (1) depicts Black women stereotypically as abusive and unsuitable or incapable of raising children; and (2) validates a heteronormative picture of Black masculinity through its portrayal of Antwone's heroic personal achievement (his triumph over devalued Black women). Though there are other aspects to Ahad's critique, I confine my remarks to the first of these claims.

Before getting to Ahad's critique, there is a different line of critique I find illuminating in Ahad. I agree that *Antwone Fisher* fails to explicitly address white supremacy and that this would have powerfully reinforced the film's message. Unfortunately, the film settles for an implicit critique of white supremacy—conveyed only through inchoate textual references to Marcus Garvey and John W. Blassingame. One has to read Garvey, for instance, to understand the significance of Black self-reliance, militancy, and nationalism. His argument is that these values are made necessary by the fact that white people are vicious oppressors, unwilling to respond to anything other than brute force. His repeated criticisms of white people make this clear:

> For over three hundred years the white man has been our oppressor, and he naturally is not going to liberate us to the higher freedom, the truer liberty, and the truer democracy. We have to liberate ourselves.[5]

> The attitude of the white race is to subjugate, to exploit, and if necessary exterminate the weaker peoples with whom they come in contact. . . . There can be no peace among men and nations, so long as the strong continue to oppress the weak, so long as injustice is done to other people, just so long will we have cause for war, and make a lasting peace an impossibility. . . . I am not opposed to the white race as charged by my enemies. I have no time to hate anyone. All my time is devoted to the up-building and development of the Negro race. . . . Point me to a weak nation and I will show you a people oppressed, abused, taken advantage of by others. Show me a weak race and I will show you a people reduced to serfdom, peonage and slavery. Show me a well organized nation, and I will show you a people and a nation respected by the world.[6]

Because textual references of this sort are not explicitly discussed (or even mentioned) in the film, the fundamental message of the film is easy to miss. Whereas Antwone may appear to have pulled himself by his own bootstraps, it is arguable that Antwone's source of inspiration is rooted in a collective Black effort. The film channels Garvey's conception of an independent, self-sustaining Black community, which cultivates traditional virtues, as well as some insurrectionist virtues—such as tenacity and fearlessness.[7] Garvey's normative program prescribes grounding material existence in a life of education (including a strong dose of Black cultural knowledge and pride); Black entrepreneurship; and the mastery of nature, science, and medicine, among other things. A distinctive African form of life—one that is inherently cooperative, politically active, and self-reliant—is essential to his conception of Black humanization. Thus, it is arguable that the march toward human dignity in *Antwone Fisher* is symbolic of this sort of communal effort.

Disparaging Black Women?

With that, I turn to the principal feminist critique mentioned earlier. Does *Antwone Fisher* degrade or devalue Black women, as some feminists

ON ANTWONE FISHER'S *ANTWONE FISHER*   273

allege? Does the film depict Black women per se as sexual abusers of children? I argue that, while the film depicts some Black women as cruel and depraved (as a function of internalized racism), it is reasonable to extrapolate this as an essentializing depiction of Black women only by presupposing something false: that Black women are inherent victims of physical and sexual abuse and that Black men are inherent perpetrators of physical and sexual abuse. In other words, this reading depends upon the dehumanization of Black men.

The humanization of Black men, rather than the dehumanization of Black women, is clearly the intent of the film. It does, however, depict Black women as human beings that are capable of some of the worst forms of dehumanization and physical violence, including sexually violating, torturing and neglecting children. The film is a biographical drama of the abuse endured by the real person, Antwone Fisher, who is also the screenwriter of the film and co-author of the book the film is based on. However, it will be objected that the film's intent is not the central issue. For the real question is not what its creators intended but what its audience is likely to see or take away from the film. What, then, is the average viewer likely to take away about Black women? Though I do not have empirical evidence of how most people would react to the film, I would argue that the content of the film is not responsible for an essentializing racist interpretation against Black women.

First, evidence presented in the film bespeaks against the invidious depiction of Black women as abusers. Antwone's girlfriend, for example, is neither physically nor sexually abusive to Antwone, nor is she depicted as morally miscreant. On the contrary, she provides a crucial support base for Antwone that is instrumental to his healing process. Furthermore, her praiseworthy character is not bound up with her being sexually submissive or passive. Rather, Antwone and Cheryl's relationship reverses traditional masculine/feminine roles, for it is Antwone that is rendered vulnerable to Cheryl as a consequence of his physical and sexual abuse, and it is Cheryl that assumes the strong, active, and assertive role in the relationship; for example, whereas Antwone is too shy to introduce himself to Cheryl, Cheryl manifests courage in introducing herself to Antwone. Further, Cheryl manifests authority in gently initiating what is an empowering act in the film—the first sexual contact between her and Antwone, at a time when Antwone is vulnerable due to his childhood sexual trauma.

Second, the film's confrontation of Black female abuse of children, though certainly disturbing, is best understood as an honest depiction of one aspect of a wider set of complexities and sexual vulnerabilities facing certain Black households, including and especially foster homes. The film underscores the reality that Black women are not immune to being abusers of Black men and boys. Depicting some Black women as cruel and remorseless abusers would, perhaps, be gratuitous if this phenomenon were widely portrayed in popular film and media (especially without other counteracting depictions). We cannot ignore the context of white supremacy provided in *Antwone Fisher*, however. And outside the film, we cannot ignore empirical reality. The female sexual abuse of children is real, yet widely publicly unknown or at least under-discussed. Indeed, this phenomenon is largely uncharted in both academia and popular culture. The topic remains as taboo today as in 2002 when the film was released. For instance, when Derek Luke—the actor who plays Antwone Fisher in the film—was interviewed for CNN, he was asked about the sexual abuse which Antwone experiences at the hands of his cousin Nadine. "One thing that struck me about the film," says the interviewer, "was the fact that Antwone was molested by a woman. That to me is unheard of. . . . I wish I could check statistics, but it seems like it's safe to say that's pretty rare." Far from disputing the interviewer's assertion, Derek accepts the statement at face value: "It may be safe to say rare . . . it may be rare mentioning it. I don't know statistically if it's true."[8] Derek Luke could take the reporter's intuition for granted because it is culturally (ideologically) plausible, in part because sexual violence is largely depicted as perpetrated mostly by men targeting women, and in part because female sexual violence is a rarely discussed topic of conversation.[9]

During his CNN interview, Derek Luke confessed that he was personally molested as a child. This answer was in response to a question about the taboo nature of female-perpetrated child abuse. The question put to him was whether he worried about any misconceptions owing to Antwone's experience of being molested by a woman. Derek answered, "No," then went on to explain: "I think (any) molester period needs to be dealt with. I think that's the whole point of the story. If you are a molester, molestee, seeing the film . . . healing starts. You're able to relate, period. I never thought, that's a woman. I just thought, man, I know how painful that can be."[10] Derek Luke's (and his interviewer's) ignorance about the capacity of Black females to abuse children cannot be ridden off as anecdotal. Tommy Curry and Ebony Utley explain why. Here I provide a mere snippet of their argument in "She Touched Me: Five Snapshots of Adult Sexual Violations of Black Boys":

> Female perpetrators of child sexual abuse, commonly referred to as female sex offenders, remain an understudied and somewhat invisible population in the academic literature.[11] Despite the documenting of a growing demographic of female sex offenders in the child sex abuse literature,[12] cases reported to child protective services,[13] and victimization surveys,[14] there is no recognition of female sexual offenders and male victims of child sexual abuse within gender and race theory literatures regarding masculinity.[15]

Thus, while the humanization of Black males need not, and should not, require the dehumanization of Black females, it may well (and in fact seems to) require the humanization of Black females. What I mean by this is that, as human beings, Black females are as susceptible to vice and pathology as members of any other group. For example, research suggests that Black boys are vulnerable to Black women and teen girls who desire them for sexual exploits. In this context, the stereotype of male hypersexuality may be invoked to pressure and shame Black boys into their first sexual encounters.[16] Though these issues are sensitive and painful, that is no reason to ignore them. The real question is whether *Antwone Fisher* raises them responsibly, and I see no reason (or indication from Ahad) to think the film is irresponsible in this regard.

Widening the Scope of Sexualized Racism

To sum up my argument thus far, two notions must be distinguished rather. Namely, the *depiction of Black women per se as abusers of Black boys*; and the *depiction of some Black women as abusers of Black boys*. Is the latter possible without collapsing into the former? Or does any depiction of a Black woman (child) abuser automatically paint all Black women as essentially abusive? It would seem that a humanizing portrayal of Black women is and must be an honest portrayal. As no group has a monopoly on victimhood or perpetrator-hood, the acknowledgment that some Black women are abusers of children is crucial to their humanization. None of this is to deny that any such depiction must be done with care, particularly as Black women are frequently objectified and dehumanized in popular culture. The point is that depicting some Black women as abusers is distinct from depicting all Black women as such.

One way to have an honest conversation about the realities of women-perpetrated child abuse (whether committed by Black women or other ethnic/racial groups) is to develop a more nuanced understanding of racism and white supremacy. As I understand it, the premise of *Antwone Fisher* seems to be that white supremacy is the fundamental source of the Tates' internalized racism. It is internalized racism that appears to explain the cruelty and viciousness Antwone experiences in the Tates home. In the remainder of this chapter, I draw on Tommy Curry's analysis of racism as racial misandry to provide a framework for understanding female-perpetrated child abuse in *Antwone Fisher*. Thereafter, I return to the question of Black women-perpetrated child abuse.

In *The Man-Not: Race, Class, Genre, and the Dilemmas of Black Manhood*, Tommy Curry defines racism early on in the book as "a nexus of cognitive architecture . . . [that] materializ[es] the imagined inferiority and hastening the death of inferior [nonwhite] races." He quickly adds specificity to this definition by conceptualizing racism in terms of racial hatred and eroticism. To be a victim of racism, says Curry, is to be sexually targeted. A gendered analysis of racism is an old hat among feminists. Kimberlé Crenshaw's theory of intersectionality argues that Black women are victimized on the basis of their race and gender; these oppressions are not always distinct, nor are they always additive; in some cases, these categories intersect such that the resulting oppression uniquely defines the Black woman's experience.[17] Curry's argument posits that what's true for Black women and girls is true for Black men and boys. His premise is that racial dehumanization generally consists in the stripping of human categories—notably, male and female—from racialized bodies. Consequently, only white men and women are perceived as human; only white females count as *women* and only white males count as *men*. Black males and females are not-human: Black males are Not-Men or what Curry calls MAN-Nots; by implication, Black females are Not-Women or WOMAN-Nots.

The essence of MAN-Not-ness is Black male vulnerability to death and dying. Theorizing this vulnerability, however, cannot be achieved by merely extending the analytic of intersectionality. For, argues Curry, intersectionality is committed to a form of essentialism, which fails to recognize that *both* gender categories, *male* and *female*, have their roots in white patriarchy.[18] As a consequence, gender studies systematically misconstrues the sexual violence of Black men, framing their experiences of racism "as one-dimensional, narrow, and devoid of any analyses that understand the horrors of sexual violence."[19] Curry thus proposes the articulation of new categories to make sense of the sexual harms that define the Black male experience. Since the term "gendered harm" is strictly inappropriate, Curry introduces what he calls *genre* categories. Unlike gender categories (articulated by gender theorists), wherein "[g]ender becomes the symbolic representation of bodies—their intent—while race simply acts as a modifier and operates to overdetermine or lessen the power position of *maleness*," "genre expresses how the register of nonbeing distorts the categories founded upon white anthropology or that of the human."[20] A genre study is called for because Black men "are thought to be disadvantaged solely on the basis of their race. Their deaths are argued to be a consequence of racism, not of their maleness, since maleness under the present intersectional calculus supposedly gives them an advantage over women and is thought to be an entitlement of the power of patriarchy."[21] "Racism," however, is in essence "fungibility, the ease by which the Black male body is able to be disfigured and castrated without resistance—mutilated into the mold of the particular white fantasy."[22] Curry thus elaborates his theory of anti-Black male racism as a genre-d phenomenon.

In a chapter titled "Eschatological Dilemmas," Curry argues that the Black male's proximity to death (what Curry calls "Necromancy") cannot but condition the theory and conceptualization of Black men and boys. "Death conditions how Black people, and especially how Black intellectuals, approach the social reality before them."[23] Fear leads the Black scholar to examine Blackness at a distance—that is, by adopting accepted disciplinary categories that do not disturb discourses of interest to white people, that is, discourses that "preserve the illusions of freedom, democracy, citizenship, and personhood."[24] Curry calls this scholarly distance toward Blackness the "Negrophobia" of academia, a consequence of which is that Black maleness comes to be theorized as pathological. This de facto theoretical stance "imposes patriarchy on [Black men and boys] as seemingly endless and unfettered violence."[25] In reality, of course, Black male patriarchal power is nonexistent. Black male privilege is the academic counterpart to the racist trope that Black males are dangerous beasts. A consequence of necrophobia is that it becomes near impossible to theorize Black men and boys as *living* beings, as beings with the prospect of futurity. "To choose to write on Black males is to accept that you and they are in conversation with death."[26] Overcoming this theoretical limit requires nearing oneself to death—that is, fundamentally reshaping how scholars theorize topics that intersect with Black male death, such as ethics, normative values, and other "futural" notions that presuppose that the subject has a future.[27] For example, Curry argues that a "presentist" ethic that starts from Black men and boys' proximity to death is necessary. Such an ethic would surely confront the sexual victimization of Black men and boys.

Curry asks us to consider the sexual coercion of the Black male under the police state. Though widely condemned as racist, police brutality is widely unrecognized as sexualized violence. Curry describes several incidents where Black men and boys have been sexually sodomized, their testicles kicked or stomped, their anuses penetrated with fingers, plungers or other items, and their bodies raped, tortured, or mutilated by police officers or other state officials. He also describes how Black men and boys are routinely reported to be seen as larger and stronger, and sexualized as mythical beasts with grotesquely large "nigger dicks," and how this "sexual fetishization of Black male flesh" functions to rationalize beatings, convictions, rapes, mutilations, and death.[28] More generally, the American Negro is a "walking phallic symbol: which means that one pays, in one's personality, for the sexual insecurity of others."[29] Standard criticisms of such violence miss their dehumanizing nature, for rarely are they seen as genre-d:

> Our present theories used to analyze the racial oppression of Black men, the act of theoretical interpretation, leave Black men to be understood primarily by their dying and, in consequence, allow their deaths to be weighed against other political interests or more ideal subjects. . . . [I]t is not being able to think of the Black male beyond his corpse that is the real result of racism's dehumanization. Racism "thingifies" Black life, and the reduction of Black men and boys to the event of their dying leaves the aim of racism—accepting the racially oppressed as not human, nothing lost—unquestioned.[30]

Far from being anecdotes, these events are historical, hence recurring patterns. Our inability or unwillingness to conceptualize anti-Black *male* racism—the gendered vulnerability of Black males—"den[ies] the sexual motivation behind racist violence against Black males."[31] Curry locates the fundamental source of the sexual abuse of Black males in white (male and female) aggression. He underscores this emphasis in James Baldwin's disturbing story, "Going to Meet the Man" of a white heterosexual couple, both of whom are aroused by the "big black phallus."[32] Curry offers this analysis:

> Jesse's necrophilia, his sexually murderous lust, "thrives on imitating derogatory images of [B]lack men as either dangerously oversexed and/ or emasculated or dead." The white boy is made a man through the destruction of the Black male body, his conquering of the Black male beast. . . . Killing Black men is an attempt to reduce the number of black phalluses that can cause white men anxiety and worry.[33]

The complex logic of this story is incompatible with an intersectional logic. How does intersectionality explain the various levels of sexual desire and objectification of the Black male, which motivates the murdering (and pleasure obtaining from murdering) of Black men and boys? It can appeal to racism but not to sexism, for the latter is reserved for females. Curry, however, finds a way to bring sex into the picture. A plausible explanation is that, for the white sadist, Black males are not human beings; hence, they can be fucked without cheating on one's spouse, without feeling guilty or remorseful, and so on. This phenomenon goes back to rape during the period of chattel slavery: "Historically, rape during slavery was not bound by sexual designation. . . . [H]istory shows that Black 'males' were also sexually abused, and the bodies of these men and boys were sodomized throughout the diaspora."[34] Furthermore, "The rape of the Black male slave had no socially recognized justification; it was an act of white barbarism that did not pretend to maintain the moral superiority of the master. It was simply the complete brutality and the animalistic sexual domination of a Black (male) body throughout."[35]

Unlike the Black woman whose sexualized body was perceived as valuable for reproduction, the sexualized body of the Black man had no value for whites beyond their sadistic fantasies. Yet, despite their vulnerability to rape during slavery (which was no rarer an occurrence than it was for Black women[36]), enslaved Black men and boys are not widely acknowledged to be victims of rape. On the contrary, they would go on to be depicted as the rapists. This historical reality continues into the present. Black male survivors of rape often do not view themselves as victims—placing them at risk of depression and self-destructive behavior. This logic of castration and death, says Curry, surely "destabilizes the very idea of a shared maleness with white men that can be thought of as a history of patriarchy."[37] The upshot of Baldwin's story is that "all racism is erotic and sexual, which means that there is no one body or history to which gender can solely refer within an intersectional matrix."[38] All of this leads Curry to define anti-

Black male racism as *racial misandry*: "the vulnerability Black men and boys have to the obsessive hatred society directs toward them," including "the ontological program that is constantly operating to socialize the public into believing that, given the savage nature of Black men and boys, the various cruelties and stereotypes used to dehumanize them are accurate."[39]

Conclusion: Toward Depicting Black Male Vulnerability in Film

With this understanding of racism on hand I return to the feminist critique of *Antwone Fisher*. The logic of this argument parallels the logic of intersectionality Curry rejects in *The Man-Not*: "Black male vulnerability is taken to be at odds with, and thereby an erasure of, Black female suffering and, more generally, theoretically irrelevant, despite Black males' actual social condition."[40]

The notion of privileging Black men rests on a powerful intuition or gut reaction. We intuitively feel that it is absurd to depict Black men as victims of racist violence *in virtue of their maleness*. "Contending that Black men and boys are *subjects worthy of study* is such an affront under the gender morality of our day that such works demand the activism of scholars to prevent such writing from seeing the light of day."[41] While we have no problem acknowledging the putative pathological tendencies of Black men, their vulnerability to murder, rape, and violence cannot be nuanced by gender. This has dire consequences for our understanding of Black men beyond popular one-dimensional caricatures. As Curry writes:

> the most dehumanizing aspect of this paradigm is the assumption that the reporting of Black male death is no different from writing about Black male life. Saying that Black men and boys die does little to capture the causes that extinguish their lives. This reporting requires no academic engagement; it simply requires interpretation of the Black male lives lost.[42]

Recall that racial misandry is not merely the dehumanization of the Black male subject, but also the perpetual inability to *think, conceptualize* or *theorize* the Black male subject as vulnerable. This leads to the dilemma of Black manhood (echoing the subtitle of Curry's book). As I read Curry, the Black male's dilemma is that he is both alive and dead, a living corpse. "The Black male suffers an impossibility within the binary logics of theory. His existence to the world has been defined as the rapist while he has been the unseen rape victim. He is both the murderer and the corpse."[43] Curry refers to this dilemma which is a function of the Black male's phallus, "phallicism." The MAN-not is not merely not-human, his humanization is unthinkable.

The Black male can be depicted as a dead corpse in film or social media, but not as a living being, vulnerable to suffering. Ahad's critique—however well-intentioned—furthers the dehumanization of Black males. The premise that depicting Black women as abusers is harmful to Black women is motivated by an exclusive focus on the Black female subject. No similar concern is extended to the Black male subject. By accepting the proposition that Black females are never to be depicted as abusers of Black men and boys, we thereby accept the stereotype that Black men are inherently the abusers of Black women; hence, that Black male vulnerability is never to be thought, that is, acknowledged, irrespective of how pressing or urgent the need may be to attend to his trauma. If any and every portrayal of Black men as a legitimate subject of concern is tantamount to "privileging" Black men over Black women, then the only conclusion to be drawn is that Black men are not human beings worthy of concern. In this way, avoiding the erasure of Black female vulnerability demands the erasure of Black male vulnerability. Perhaps it would have us erase/cancel films like *Antwone Fisher*. The feminist critique thus seems to subscribe to a racial misandric logic.

Curry's work challenges theory to reject the *a priori* "Oppression Olympics" mindset of identity politics, which trades one devalued subject for a more desirable subject.[44] Further, it dares theory to conceptualize the Black male as *life* and not merely as death. A similar challenge exists for film: it too must dare to depict his life (and not merely his death) in film. Film can be an avenue for imagining novel life-affirming possibilities—such imaginaries, however, must be foregrounded by faithful depictions of Black male vulnerability.

I close by returning to my thesis in the opening paragraph. The challenge inherent in using film to humanize a subordinate group is that it must somehow overcome the ideological forces which shape how the film is interpreted. In the case of racialized males, I have argued that it is necessary to *bring new categories* to the interpretation of film, just as Tommy Curry's work establishes the necessity of bringing new categories to the analysis of human experience. While I do not want to deny that film has the ability to precipitate or inspire new categories or new affects that could disrupt established ideological conceptions, it is not at all clear to me that film has some intrinsic ability to overwhelm prevailing categories that have the weight of history backing them. When Black male life is rendered vulnerable in film, racial misandry is likely to double down. This, however, is no more a refutation of the medium of film than it is a refutation of the medium of philosophy. Perhaps, this is but a sobering reminder that theory, praxis, and representation must work in tandem.

Notes

1   For discussion, see Tommy J. Curry, *The Man-Not: Race, Class, Genre, and the Dilemmas of Black Manhood* (Philadelphia, PA: Temple

University Press, 2017); "Killing Boogeymen: Phallicism and the Misandric Mischaracterizations of Black Males in Theory," *Res Philosophica* 95, no. 2 (2018): 235–72. doi: 10.11612/resphil.1612.

2　Badia Sahar Ahad, "The New Normal: Black Psychic Subjectivity in Antwone Fisher," *CR: The New Centennial Review* 13, no. 3 (2013): 139–62.

3　Ibid., 144. See Frank B. Wilderson, III. *Red, White & Black: Cinema and the Structure of US Antagonisms* (Durham, NC: Duke University Press, 2010).

4　Ahad, "The New Normal," 150–1.

5　Marcus Garvey, *The Philosophy and Opinions of Marcus Garvey*, Vol. 1, ed. Amy Jacques-Garvey (Live Empowered Publishing, 2020), 17.

6　Ibid., 18–20.

7　For discussion of insurrectionist virtues, see Leonard Harris, "Insurrectionist Ethics: Advocacy, Moral Psychology, and Pragmatism," in *Ethical Issues for a New Millennium*, ed. John Howie (Carbondale, IL: Southern Illinois University Press, 2002), 192–210.

8　"Derek Luke: 'I was Molested, and I Have My Own Personal Fight,'" *CNN Interview*, December 19, 2002. http://edition.cnn.com/2002/SHOWBIZ/ Movies/12/18/sproject.ca02.luke.transcript/

9　In the case of Black males, myths of Black male hypersexuality and the disposition to rape women overdetermine the claim that Black female sexual violence is rare. For discussion, see Tommy J. Curry, "Expendables for Whom: Terry Crews and the Erasure of Black Male Victims of Sexual Assault and Rape," *Women's Studies in Communication* 42, no. 3 (2019): 287–307, https://10.1080/07491409.2019.1641874.

10　Ibid.

11　Judith V. Becker, Susan R. Hall, and Jill D. Stinson, "Female Sexual Offenders: Clinical, Legal and Policy Issues," *Journal of Forensic Psychology Practice* 1, no. 3 (2001): 31–53; Julia Hislop, *Female Sex Offenders: What Therapists, Law Enforcement and Child Protective Services Need to Know* (Ravensdale, WA: Issues Press 2001), Alana D. Grayston and Rayleen V. De Luca, "Female Perpetrators of Child Sexual Abuse: A Review of the Clinical and Empirical Literature," *Aggression and Violent Behavior* 4, no. 1 (1999): 93–106.

12　Michael Pittaro, "Demystifying Female Perpetrated Sex Crimes Against Children," *Family & Intimate Partner Violence Quarterly* 8, no. 4 (2016): 42–5.

13　David Axlyn McLeod, "Female Offenders in Child Sexual Abuse Cases: A National Picture," *Journal of Child Sexual Abuse* 24, no. 1 (2015): 97–114.

14　Franca Cortoni, Kelly M. Babchishin, and Clémence Rat, "The Proportion of Sexual Offenders Who Are Female Is Higher Than Thought: A Meta-Analysis," *Criminal Justice and Behavior* 44, no. 2 (2017): 145–62.

15　Tommy J. Curry and Ebony A. Utley, "She Touched Me: Five Snapshots of Adult Sexual Violations of Black Boys," *Kennedy Institute of Ethics Journal* 28, no. 2 (2018): 205–41, at 206–7.

16　Ibid.; Tommy J. Curry and Ebony A Utley, "She's Just a Friend (with Benefits)," *Reimagining Black Masculinities: Race, Gender, and Public Space* 33 (2020).

17 Kimberlé Crenshaw, "Demarginalizing the Intersection of Race and Sex: A Black Feminist Critique of Antidiscrimination Doctrine, Feminist Theory, and Antiracist Politics," *University of Chicago Legal Forum* 140 (1989): 139–68; "Mapping the Margins: Intersectionality, Identity Politics, and Violence Against Women of Color," *Stanford Law Review* 43, no. 6 (1991): 1241–99.

18 Tommy J. Curry, *The Man-Not*, 218–22; see also 170–6. For Curry's more recent critiques along similar lines, see Tommy J. Curry, "Reconstituting the Object: Black Male Studies and the Problem of Studying Black Men and Boys within Patriarchal Gender Theory," in *The Palgrave Handbook of Critical Race Theory and Gender*, ed. Shirley Anne Tate and Encarnación Gutiérrez Rodríguez (New York: Springer International Publishing, 2022), 525–44. Tommy J. Curry, "Decolonizing the Intersection: Black Male Studies as a Critique of Intersectionality's Indebtedness to Subculture of Violence Theory: Psychosocial Non-Alignment to Modernity/Coloniality," in *Critical Psychology Praxis* (New York: Routledge, 2021), 132–54.

19 Curry, *The Man-Not*, 4.

20 Ibid., 5, 6.

21 Ibid., 142.

22 Ibid., 143–4.

23 Ibid., 138.

24 Ibid., 137.

25 Ibid., 139.

26 Ibid., 141.

27 See Curry's discussion of anti-ethics, *The Man-Not*, 181–7. For a critical discussion of anti-ethics, see Alberto G. Urquidez, "Anti-Ethics as Insurrectionist Ethics: An Analysis of the Normative Foundations of Philosophies Born of Struggle," in *Insurrectionist Ethics: Radical Perspectives on Social Justice*, eds. Jacoby A. Carter and Darryl L. Scriven (forthcoming).

28 Curry, *The Man-Not*, 143–5.

29 Ibid., 147.

30 Ibid., 145.

31 Ibid., 146.

32 James Baldwin, *Going to Meet the Man: Stories* (New York: Vintage, 2013).

33 Curry, *The Man-Not*, 150.

34 Ibid., 156.

35 Ibid., 157.

36 Ibid., 152–63.

37 Ibid., 150.

38 Ibid., 151.

39 Ibid., 170–1.

40 Ibid., 229.

41 Ibid., 230.

42 Ibid., 231.

43 Ibid., 226.

44 For discussion, see Tommy J. Curry, "He Never Mattered: Poor Black Males and the Dark Logic of Intersectional Invisibility," in *The Movement for Black Lives: Philosophical Perspectives*, ed. Brandon Hogan, Michael Cholbi, and Alex Madva (Oxford: Oxford University Press, 2021), 59–90.

19

On Hirokazu Kore-eda's *Our Little Sister*

Paul Freaney

Our Little Sister was released in 2015, it competed for, but didn't win, the Palme D'or and might not be considered Hirokazu Kore-eda's masterwork. He won the Palme D'Or for *Shoplifters* in 2018. In many ways it is a minor film. However, it is the one that moves me.

The screenplay was an adaptation of Akimi Yoshida's manga series *Umimachi Diaries* (Seaside Diaries) which was, like the film, set in Kamakura—a heritage resort town less than an hour train ride from Tokyo central. It's a lovely town to set a film, renowned for the size and quality of its Buddhist temples and sculptures. And incidentally, the last resting place of the late great Akira Kurosawa.

The film takes place over a year—the four seasons—and follows the lives of three sisters who live in their grandparent's house. When their estranged father dies they meet their fifteen-year-old half-sister Suza at the funeral. Little Suza is now left living with her stepmother and brother—her mother is dead. It becomes clear to them that Suza had looked after their ailing father and the girls invite Suza to come and live with them in Kamakura. The three become four and Kore-eda's film intricately weaves a portrait of this family as the seasons change and the fabric of their lives grows ever more interwoven. A Japanese *Little Women*, without the melodrama, about four young women navigating their lives in a small town.

In many ways, *Our Little Sister* is not even a philosophical film. And maybe an odd choice for a reflection on cinema and philosophy. The sisters aren't artists or intellectuals, the older ones work in conventional jobs—a nurse, a bank clerk, and a shop assistant—and Suza just wants to play on the soccer team in her new school. There are few speeches with any reflective insights and generally speaking the directorial style is as modest as the women. However, I reckon this exquisite film holds some perceptive insights into how we might live.

In many ways, *Our Little Sister* is similar to Mike Leigh's 2010 film *Another Year*. It is a director at the peak of his powers relaxing into a film, not trying to prove anything, and like Leigh, Kore-eda is clearly entranced by the quality of his character's lives, unfolding together over time. These masterworks offer us perspective on how we might manage the experience of time passing and loss. Impermanence and suffering. They remind us that our time moves inexorably, that youth slips away, that sadness and loss are part of a life that we have little control over, and if we were to be attentive and kind, well . . . life might be a little more bearable, more entrancing. More like these movies.

Although *Our Little Sister* is a very Japanese film, indebted to Ozu and a national cinema, it is underpinned by a sensibility that is very worldly. Kore-eda manages to integrate the particulars of Buddhist philosophy, a Japanese aesthetic, and the detail of life and food in Kamakura, into a perspective on the character's lives that, similar to Mike Leigh, is deeply humanist and outward looking.

You can tell that Kore-eda knows the film(s) he is not making. The ones his worldly audiences have seen or might expect from his movie. His framing, camera movement and editing, his decisions on how he crafts his characters and controls his storylines are indebted to Western cinema—or more accurately, world arthouse cinema. However, he is creating his own body of work and striving for a poetic naturalism that is uncommonly hopeful and joyful.

Naturalism in European cinema tends to focus on the dispossessed and on hardship—in an attempt to make other people's suffering real—in order to encourage kindness. Kore-eda's naturalism is less concerned with the political or sociological and instead focuses on our common struggle to be kind in the battleground of family. For Kore-eda, the family offers our most profound experience of togetherness. *Our Little Sister*, like so many of his films, interrogates how we might define a family. His versions of family are always inclusive because they are never complete. His families are invariably missing someone. After all, being kind to those we call family, is no easier than being kind to strangers.

Kore-eda's films tell stories, and present characters, that might persuade us that our fortunes are not in our own hands. Not simply because fate deals cards so arbitrarily, but because life is lived together. His stories are not shaped by the individual will of single protagonists.

A few years back I visited the area around Fukushima in northern Honshū. I read testimonies and met people who were still deeply affected by the tsunami and nuclear disaster of 2011. What struck me was how they had resisted telling stories of individual loss or heroic rescue workers, of extraordinary individuals who had survived, or prevailed, despite the odds.

Stories that in America or Europe are invariably used to frame or make sense of major catastrophes. Not in Japan. It might seem like modesty or deference, but we see in Kore-eda, a Japanese philosophy of connectedness, a sense that the self is far from the measure of all things.

It may be useful to draw an imaginary line between how Eastern and Western dramatic/storytelling traditions represent agency and the individual will. It is fair to say that Western (narrative) cinema emerges out of the Western dramatic tradition, and is rooted in classical Greek thought. Western philosophy and drama attempt to distill the essence of our experiences-in-time, to abstract and articulate what can be distilled from our shared humanity. In the dramatic tradition, *plot* is a way of uncovering what is essential to our lives—the essential shapes and patterns of our shared life-stories. *Plot* dramatizes threat and requires that a protagonist, or hero, is tested in order to assert what she believes to be important; her essential values. Should *Antigone* stand so firm for the burial rites of her brother? In *Taken*, should Liam Neeson use torture and vigilante justice to save the life of his beloved daughter? They are tested by *plot*, by a change in fortune, and we—the audience—get to consider what *we* really believe, how *we* think our lives are patterned, and how we might wrestle with our fate.

Unlike many of our Western films, *Our Little Sister* is not so much about what happens, but rather how it happens—how the sisters inhabit their lives-in-the-making. The film wants us to attend to their attitude and disposition. For Kore-eda, his character's stories are also part of ancestral stories—in *Our Little Sister* each of the girls inherit their deceased father's traits, his generosity and his openness to affairs—their fortunes are inextricable from the fortunes of their families. Their actions, decisions and agency, are always played out against the responsibilities and duties they have to each other. There are no hierarchy of needs, no minor and major characters, no clear delineation between protagonist and antagonist. What a character wants or needs is always situated and defined in the complex web of other character's needs. And the individual will—the driving force of Western dramatic art—is so often thrown into relief by the passing of time, and by the seasons, wheeling back on themselves.

Our Little Sister does not set out to jeopardize and test Sachi's act of kindness in adopting her half-sister Suza. The aunt warns Sachi about how difficult it might be to raise a girl and how it might negatively affect her marriage prospects. Another filmmaker might have her suffer for her singular kindness—this is the film we are not watching. In Kore-eda's film we encounter a world where kindness is rewarded, not with wealth or personal gain, but with a quality of life—a graceful experience of interpersonal connection.

The dramatic arc of Kore-eda's film is not built on the four sisters' reckoning with fate. *Our Little Sister* is not an old-fashioned sentimental picture. We know Kore-eda has no fantasy weddings in store for us, no last-minute reversals, no tragedy or resolution in lives that will carry on. Like his master Ozu—who made over fifty films examining the minutiae of family life—it is the gesture, a revelatory incident or detail that counts the beats of this film.

The story arc of this film is not built on the cause and effect of *plot*. The sisters' lives are undoubtedly determined by the father's passing and the sister they inherit. However, the sisters seem free to smell the grass—to taste the plum wine. The *Plot* plays out to the seasons in Kamakura.

It is a remarkable feat to construct such a compelling film with so little angst or anxiety, so little struggle or heroic gesture. Kore-eda's characters are seldom at odds with themselves. Puzzled sure, and at odds with the predicaments they encounter, but Kore-eda reminds us that they are part of other schema and so, they are less the center of attention—to Kore-eda and to themselves. It might be part of Japanese temperament—however we might define that. It rains, and it snows, and houses and people get washed away, but the spring comes around again, as does the summer, and the years will pass, whether we fight them or not.

To accept and be kind to each other. It is a simple, honest, Buddhist maxim. The idea that happiness—or lightness—is independent of fate.

Of course, it is romantic, or maybe optimistic, to offer that tragedy can be overcome, or managed, with kindness. From a certain angle *Our Little Sister* can seem naïve and sentimental. It is strange to re-watch it during the pandemic. The film has so much space in it, so much innocent time. The orchestral score—although sparingly used—is, to my ear, too bathetic. It is certainly not a perfect film—a few of the key shots seem picturesque rather than crystalline. However, Kore-eda's message is crystal clear: kindness and acceptance of misfortune is ruinous to wealth and security, but it is lighter. It is more in tune with the rhythms of our passing seasons, in tune with what changes, and with what stays the same.

In Paul Schrader's recent updating of his seminal book *Transcendental Style in Cinema* he imagines cinema to be an atom, neutrons and protons bound together by the glue of narrative. He tracks how the gravitational pull of this narrative nucleus hasn't always held in the cinematic tradition, and particles have spun free, forming new taxonomies of non-narrative cinemas. In these transcendental styles, Schrader argues that the films, free from narrative hegemony, shift our experience of time to something more akin to our experience of time in the real world. Time coexists in the film and in reality. Film becomes more than just a way of abstracting or mimicking the world, it becomes a way of apprehending it. Of experiencing reality, itself.

These films conjure what Gillies Delueze called time/images. They reject the Aristotelian logic of movement/images. In classical/narrative cinema, A can never be Not-A, and time is measured spatially—an action begins and ends. In the time/image, A can be not-A, and a single moment can encapsulate change, the past present and future converging.

In his two books, *Cinema 1* and *Cinema 2*, Deleuze wanted to revitalize and develop some of Henri Bergson's ideas. Bergson had offered a critique of the notion that the actual is in the present, and instead, saw the present as a dynamic interpretation of past and future. He conceptualized the present as a multiplicity—which might unify the contradictory features of time, as heterogeneous and continuous. Deleuze wanted to work out how this idea of presence, as a multiplicity, has been captured in moving images.

For Deleuze the movement/image is useful in capturing moments of stress—or drama—when the needs and exigencies of the present require action. The time/image goes beyond the movement/image, capable of capturing the multiplicity of the present. In Kore-eda's film there are very few movement/image sequences—even when Sachi runs back to the house to fetch some plum wine for her estranged mother waiting to leave again at the train station, Kore-eda focuses on Sachi pouring the wine from the tubs. The pouring is done with such care and deliberateness that we are held back from the action, from the exigencies of the present, and reminded to interpret the moment in all its meanings and temporalities—we later learn that some of the wine was bottled by the dead grandmother.

Kore-eda frames his characters moving through the space around them, like Ozu, eschewing close-up, infusing them with a sense of otherness, of being-in-time-and-place. There is a sense of the past inhabiting each moment—most obviously in the central location of the grandparent's house with its butsudan altar—but also the sense of how the absent father, whom we never see, is present in almost every frame. If we looked closely enough we might even encounter the ghost of Kurosawa.

If we do not define the present as a singularity, then perhaps the past—our memory—might also be a multiplicity. Instead of a hierarchy of memory defined by the significance of events, defined by our individual desires or objectives, we might consider or remember the spaces, or times between. Although trauma and turmoil certainly burnish memories, it might be those summers, or years, that were not so defined by victories and defeats, so consumed with the drama of the self, that hold better clues to understanding a life. Times that resemble childhood.[1]

Our Little Sister has the quality of such a memory. Unsurprisingly, it feels like reading over the diary of a forgotten year. However, it is the little things—the whitebait on toast, the detailed observance of how a screen door was repaired, or nails were painted—that can help to illuminate the reality of our lived experience. The little things that highlight the qualities, or tonality, of that time. When we were younger. When we were young.

Although adulthood and age are beginning to impinge on the eldest Sachi, life is still full of possibility. Still full. For Kore-eda, it is not possibility and resolution, not destination, that gives life its plentitude. The film reminds us that those years, when life slips along, are surely worth remembering. Too much of cinematic storytelling relies on the extraordinary.

Our Little Sister is profound in how it questions whether drama need be so dramatic in order to dramatize life. It asks us to look at the quality of light, the hours wiled away in a local restaurant, our brief exchanges with neighbors and shopkeepers, our little kindnesses to each other, and our petty frustrations with sisters who borrow clothes or hog the bathroom.

Schrader calls for a "mature cinema" not so concerned with telling stories but with truly capturing the way we remember, or dream. Kore-eda's film offers us ways of looking at the everyday anew—the opening image of the film is middle sister Yoshino waking from sleep. It offers a viewing experience open to what Marcia Eliade called hierophanies, the experience of something sacred or something beyond ordinary time, in the ordinary.

In Mike Leigh's films one always senses a deeper political question or intent—he wants us to understand the bigger picture through the small lives he circles. With Kore-eda, I get the sense that he is attempting something similar. The lives and stories in his films are a way of directing us to the bigger picture too. Not just class inequity and how fortune is dealt, but a transcendental reality of woman in time, cyclical and ancestral, a time which reveals itself in the contemplation of everyday objects, ordinary moments, in the what is there in front of us.

It is here, in Kore-eda's cinema, that we have our hierophanies, and here that we are relieved of the weight of human time. *Our Little Sister* is light, full of light, but also light in the sense that it is joyful to watch.

The Japanese celebration of the cherry blossom—Sakura—is essentially a connection with the time/image. This moment of seasonal transition has come to represent the ephemeral and goes to the heart of Japanese aesthetics—a delicate flower that hardly lasts a week blooming with symbolism, prophecy, and tradition. Those tiny pink and white petals remind Japanese people of how brief, how precious, and how ephemeral we are. How light. When one of Sachi's patients—the restaurant owner—is dying in the terminal care ward, she remembers the cherry blossoms, and she is comforted by the fact that beauty still looks beautiful to her. Later, little sister Suza tells her sisters that their father said the same thing as he was dying. That beauty helps us accept impermanence. And maybe it does. It would be a stretch to refer to Wittgenstein as a Buddhist philosopher but he is clearly leaning Eastwards when he stated, "If we take eternity to mean not infinite temporal duration but timelessness, then eternal life belongs to those who live in the present."[2]

Re-watching the early funeral scene, I was struck by how unusual the sisters' emotional disposition is at their father's funeral. Are they more upset than they pretend? Are they hiding their true feelings? Even little step-sister Suzu, who has been nursing the dying man, seems remarkably possessed. And now, she is meeting her three siblings for the first time. And now, we find out that she is an orphan with a stepmother who cares little for her welfare. It is such an unusual scene. In fact, for most of the film the sisters seem incapable of feeling the weight of suffering and loss. Perhaps it is because they are young, and surely because they have the ballast of each other, but might it be a defense mechanism? Such a psychoanalytic read might well explain their oddly uncomplicated reaction to their father's abandonment, their apparent forgiveness of his affairs, and their reaction to his passing.

However, to read the sisters' optimism, and capacity for generosity, to be consequence of trauma, a form of sublimation, would bely what I consider the deepest intent of the film. What makes *Our Little Sister* such a remarkable and interesting film is Kore-eda's and Yoshida's very particular perspective on overcoming/managing trauma. The sisters carry the trauma of a fractured family—the father abandoned them fourteen years earlier and their mother remarried and moved up to Sendai—leaving a young Sachi to act in loco parentis. The father is now dead and yet they all seem capable of great empathy and emotional sensitivity—a reliable measure of emotional welfare. And more. This empathy and sense of responsibility to others seems not to weigh on them. At the deepest, or perhaps most straightforward level, Kore-eda might be offering us a less self-centered approach to overcoming trauma. His films advocate for the value, or buoyancy, of kindness. It is almost an ontological proposition. Kindness is the root to other people—the other people we are, now, and after we die.

It took some time to appreciate how profoundly gentle this film is with that truth. Whereas Mike Leigh lightens his films with an attitude of humor, Kore-eda lightens his with elegance, redolent images, and careful composition. His characters' humility and patience, their mutual affection and their shared pleasures, allow them the composure to negotiate and manage their travails and traumas. They manage a detachment from their unsatisfactory lives. Detachment then (from self), rather than sublimation.

And it isn't all restraint and polite bowing. As I said, these women understand and feel the sadness that imbues their lives; they drink hard and wrangle with mixed feelings. Sachi certainly carries what Lisa Tessman calls "burdened virtues," virtues that inhibit her own flourishing. Her patience with, and subservience to, the married doctor is pathetic—obviously his responsibility too. But from Yoshida and Kore-eda's perspective, her affair is a consequence of her heart, and also a direct mirror of her father's heart. Although she clearly loves the cheating MD, Sachi is no Madame Butterfly. There's no melodrama here. The affair will end and Sachi will carry on, she will remain composed, and she will find love again or she will not. Either way her broken heart will remain open. We are watching life happening, moment by moment, season by season, and whatever happens, however it turns out, Kore-eda wants us to be aware of how impermanent, how insubstantial, and of course how unsatisfactory life is. The three characteristics an enlightened Siddhartha Gautama wanted to teach.

Finally, I should say that Akimi Yoshida's original manga series can certainly be read as a feminist critique of Japanese society and the burden women are expected to carry. The four sisters are set on following their own hearts and for this they may have to pay. And pay dearly. When Sachi tells her doctor that she has decided not to take up his invitation to travel with him to Boston, he apologizes for not leaving his wife sooner. He wants to acknowledge that it is his fault their affair has foundered; he should have . . . Sachi tells him that "It's not anyone's fault." Surely, Sachi is sacrificing herself, letting him off the hook, burdening herself—he will return to his wife and she will carry the lioness' share of the emotional damage. However, she is also letting herself off the hook. It is not stoicism, not subservience, but a lightness of being. For the moment, the sisters have found a better way—a family of women. In the closing scene Suza tells the older girls that she wants it to last forever. They all do.

In this last scene on the beach the women's thoughts do turn to the philosophical as they wonder what *they* will remember when they are dying. Yoshino, sister number two, offers—"men and drinking"—the pleasures of life. Sachi, the eldest, says that she might remember—"their garden veranda"—her home in nature. However, it is very clear that Kore-eda is telling us that what they will most remember is there, now. Sadness and joy, past, present, and future, experienced together.

If you catch this film the right way, go with its drift, that moment is sublime. A simple image of four brilliant actresses strolling on a beach in winter, transformed by Kore-eda's refined craft, into a joyful and heartbreaking moment of transcendence.

Notes

1 Kore-eda has a deep fascination with the experience of childhood—In his astonishing film *Nobody Knows* 2004, he observes how four young children, again half-siblings, survive in an apartment alone. Over the course of a year— the four seasons—he presents us with a vivid and heartbreaking recreation of innocent time.

2 Wittgenstein, Ludwig, *Tractatus Logico-philosophicus* (London: Routledge & Kegan Paul, 1922).

20

On Lars von Trier's *The House That Jack Built*

John Panteleimon Manoussakis

Whose House? Which Jack?

From the beginning it was a matter of material. After all, all creation, production, and construction must begin with matter. The material Jack uses as the instrument for his first in a series of murders was a car jack. This car jack is the foundation upon which Jack's house is to be built as much as the means by which he builds it. The car jack *determines* what sort of a building Jack's house will be. In the brief diatribe on the architecture of Gothic cathedrals that Jack gives at the beginning of the film, he concludes with the following statement: "I often say that the material does the work. In other words it has a kind of will of its own and by following it, the result will be the most exquisite." It is the jack, and not Jack, that builds Jack's house—the house that Jack *is*.

Jack is an engineer and an aspiring architect. The architect is the first among the builders but he is the builder of what comes first, of the *archē*, of the beginning. Aristotle calls metaphysics an architectonic science. Verge's scornful characterization of Jack as a "theoretician" does not miss the point. After all, Jack himself signs his murder by the artistic pseudonym "Mr. Sophistication." That *sophia-* in "sophistication" is the same as our familiar sophia of the philosopher and the Sophist—two roles that Mr. Sophistication delights to play on occasion.

If, however, the tool of the Sophist's art is language and for the philosopher "language is at once the house of being,"[1] Mr. Sophistication "loath(es) a diagnosis you can just write in letters." Perhaps Jack would prefer a diagnosis incised, as Paul writes in his *Letters* (and in letters) "not with ink," "not on tablets," but "on the flesh of the human heart" (2 Cor. 3:3). The house that Jack built is not the house of language, signification, representation (*that*, as we shall see, is the house that Verge/Virgil built), but the fleshly house made by the human bodies kept in his freezer.

Isn't it the body, our body, that body we inhabit, our habitation, our house? Jack's house organizes the various bodies of his victims by replicating and reproducing, only in a "higher" level, the body's organization of its various members and, like the body, Jack's anthropomorphic house is an organism of its own, even more so since it is entirely constructed by *organic* material. The body that becomes a part or a member of Jack's house is a body that is itself a house. Like each of our bodies, borrowing again from Paul, is a member of the body of Christ (1 Cor. 12:27), namely, of the church, so each of our bodies is itself a church, a temple in which God dwells (1 Cor. 6:19). It would not be too risky, therefore, to venture the suggestion that the house that Jack builds is not *any* house but rather a *temple* (hence his opening remarks on the architecture of cathedrals) dedicated to the gods—even if these are gods who are more pleased by aesthetics than ethics. The body-temple and the temple-of-bodies as an image (*eidolon*) of the body is precisely what the Greek world knew under the name of *agalma*.

No temple, however, is consecrated without a sacrifice (literary, "to make sacred" from *sacer* and *facere*), that is, without the shedding of blood. So Jack offers his sacrificial victims at the altar of *to kalon*. If the Great Rain that washes away the traces of Jack's murders—an echo from Elijah's story in respect to both, the rain but also the slaughtering of Baal's priests—is an omen, then it is omen confirming that the gods have looked favorably upon his "sacrifices."

Yet, Jack does not see himself as a priest but as an artist. If for Foucault and Hadot philosophy is an art of living—to use the title of one of Hadot's book—Jack's art is more faithful to the Socratic definition of philosophy as "the art of dying."[2] Jack provides an explanation that is appropriately teleological and surprisingly eschatological. "The ultimate goal for the human being is not prior to death, but *after*." He goes on to explain that it is only the breakdown, the decomposition of the grape that elevates it into art—and one could add that it is only when "a corn of wheat falls into the ground and dies that brings forth much fruit" (Jn 12:24). The artwork that a human being is reaches perfection only at the end—its telos (goal) is the telos (end), when it finally becomes an exquisite corpse (*le cadavre exquis*).

There is no other material, therefore, suitable for the art that one might call *anthropotectonic* except the human body itself. If Jack fails time and again to build his house out of brick and mortar, that's because the material he needs is that which he calls "divine material," a material with its own (free) will.

Frankenstein Redux

It is more than a coincidence that *The House That Jack Built* is released exactly on the bicentennial anniversary since the publication of Mary Shelley's *Frankenstein* (1818–2018). Both, Lars von Trier's film and Mary Shelley's novel, offer a meditation on the meaning of *technē*, understood as either scientific technology or artistic creation (that Jack styles himself as an architect creates a direct relation between the *tekton* of the architect and *technē*). Both, Dr. Frankenstein and Jack, are motivated by the same desire to create—whether a living person out of a corpse or a corpse out of a living person. Even if their respective projects seem to serve opposite ends, they both share the same *material*. Creation, be it artistic or technological, is never free but always purchased at the cost of destruction, inasmuch as human creation, unlike God's creative act, is never ex nihilo, but conditioned by the givenness of a world already created which, precisely as given, human creation cannot but alter, refigure, and thus, in some sense, destroy. Both, Dr. Frankenstein and Mr. Sophistication, are not content with inert, created matter. They require a different kind of material, "divine material," that is, material proper only to divine creation. In his ambitions to architecture, Jack refers to "the Great Architect behind it all." Mary Shelley calls attention to Dr. Frankenstein's hubris by naming him "Victor," after God's name "the potent Victor" in Milton's *Paradise Lost*. Furthermore, the suggestive subtitle of *Frankenstein* "The Modern Prometheus" echoes Kant's hailing a hero of technological innovation, Benjamin Franklin, as "the Prometheus of modern times."[3]

Moreover, that the suggestion to build a house-of-bodies comes from Verge/Virgil is not accidental. Whereas the poet, such as Virgil, creates his corpus by stitching together—as the original meaning of *rhapsody* suggests—disparate limbs of various textual bodies, Jack scorns the metaphorical corpse. If he is to be an artist, he will be an artist literally (although, as we have seen, not in *litteras*). And whereas the artist commits his crimes symbolically—for the letter kills (2 Cor. 3:6), as says the old accusation that Plato brings, long before Paul, against writing[4]—Jack scorns the sublimation into art of those desires which, were they to remain in the soil from which they sprang, they would have made out of each of us a Jack (or even a Jack the Ripper). *Contra* Freud, Jack the artist rejects the deceit of an art that has formed an unholy alliance with the oppressive powers of civilization, an art that the politics of the polis instrumentalizes in order to achieve and maintain its self-preservation. "Some people claim that the atrocities we commit in our fiction are those inner desires which we cannot commit in our controlled civilization. I don't agree." Jack's anthropotectonic art demands that our aesthetic admiration be directed not to the sublimated (neutered) evil, but to evil itself. Is the sublimated atrocity any less evil than the "raw" evil of the criminal's act simply because the former is represented through the neutralizing lens of art that afford a detached ("disinterested" according to Kant's aesthetics) and thus safe place for both us, the viewers, and the artist who "commits" the atrocity with impunity? Or is the evil portrayed through art worse precisely because it is sublimated? Jack's art, on the other hand, is an art that discards the artificial; a fiction without the comfort of the fictitious; a signified naked of its signification; a presentation without representation. Such an art without mediation cannot but be an art of radical evil.[5]

The Art of the Immaterial

Even though *The House that Jack Built* seems to focus predominantly on the visual arts, as in the two-dimensional photography and the three-dimensional architecture, since these are the two fields of Jack's artistic expression, the real protagonist, however, is the non-dimensional music. Not only is the film punctuated with short videos of Glenn Gould practicing on the piano ("he represents art," as Jack explains to Verge). The juxtaposition of the artist to the criminal may suggest that Jack as a serial killer is as much of an artistic genius as Glenn Gould or, even more interestingly, that the artistic genius is as dangerous as the serial killer. The priority of music in Lars von Trier's film might become less puzzling if we were to consider that music is *the immaterial art*.[6] It is suggestive that the same preference to music, and I suspect for the same reason, is given in Plato's *Phaedo*, where the art of dying (philosophy) is taken to be identical to the dying art (music).[7]

Of all the arts, music alone retains the force and violence of its origins in murder, whether the murder of the animal (hunting), or the murder of the human (war).[8] In the story of the "Third Incident," Jack blurs the distinction between the two, thereby "hunting" a woman and her two sons. Jack's discussion of the Stuka underscores the function of the plane's sirens whose deafening sound was planned as a psychological act of war. The music of such killing machines like the Stuka (one of the many, as Jack observes, by reminding us of the trumpet of the biblical Jericho) arrests its victims well before the plane has hit its target. One may survive the bomb, but no one could escape the sound. In exposing the endemic violence of music, Jack has the support of Aeschylus, who preserves for us one of the earliest meanings of rhythm: it is by nothing else but the rhythm that Zeus restrains Prometheus on his rock.[9] Of all the arts, music alone has a place in Hell. In the film's epilogue, for which Lars von Trier chooses the term *katabasis* (which, among the many other occurrences, happens to be the very first word of Plato's *Republic* in which another famous descent is described, that of Socrates to Piraeus), Verge/Virgil explains to Jack that the buzzing sound that he hears is the sound that Hell generates. "One shouldn't focus on extracting screams and wailing, because the cries of pain of so many millions of individuals together become what you have just heard. A buzzing sound whose intensity will increase as we get ever closer to the presence of suffering." In saying this Verge/Virgil quotes himself and, more specifically, Book VI of the *Aeneid*:

> Around [the river Lethe] hovered numberless races, nations of souls, like bees in a meadowlands on a cloudless summer day.[10]

Virgil here paraphrases Sophocles—a good example of a corpus made up by textual corpses—who, in fragment from a now lost work, writes: "And the swarm of the dead buzzes as it rises up."[11] Such is the terrifying music of death.

Building Dwelling Killing

The challenge that Lars von Trier poses for the viewer of *The House That Jack Built* is the problematic relationship of ethics to aesthetics and of aesthetics to ethics. The Greek amalgamation of the Good (*Agathon*) with the Beautiful (*kalon*), according to which classical ethics were determined by aesthetics, has not been criticized enough. For the Greek culture, the ugly, the disable, and the impaired were expendable. The case of the *pharmakoi* in Athens and the Spartan *apothetai* are sufficient examples.[12] One could think of similar paradigms, closer to our times, when making personal, cultural, or natural taste the criterion of ethics have had catastrophic results. If, however, we have every good reason to liberate ethics from aesthetics, should we not, argues Lars von Trier, prevent ethical considerations from deciding the aesthetical value of a work or of an act—even if it is a crime or a house composed of decomposing corpses? Pushing von Trier's implicit logic to its provocative limit, might we not even imagine the visitor of the concentration camps of Auschwitz and Dachau taking a moment to admire the "perfection" by which an extermination of such massive scale was carried out systematically and efficiently? Isn't it the unjust suffering of the tragic hero that makes tragedy so sublime? What else is art, after all, but the process of mummifying life?[13] Art displays what is dead, or rather, art must kill that which it seeks to portray. All art is monumental, funerary, and Jack's "corporeal" house should be recognized as a true masterpiece of that function of art.

Could there be any kind of ethics for a serial killer who, following Nietzsche, declares that "only as an *aesthetic phenomenon* is existence and the world eternally *justified*"?[14] Asking about the highly improbable, on any account, possibility of the ethics of a serial killer presents us with an answer to a different question—one that we might have never considered: Why the house that Jack built is precisely a *house*? Surely, among the numerous objects and structures of the world Jack could have chosen any other. To give only one example, when Apollo kills the satyr Marsyas he builds out of the satyr's corpse a lyre or, according to other accounts, he makes a wineskin out of skin (as Jack makes a wallet out of Simple's breast).

A house is not any building. A house is a building where man dwells. According to Heidegger, "[w]e do not dwell because we have built, but we build and have built because we dwell, that is, because we are *dwellers*."[15] Indeed, "[t]o be a human being means . . . to dwell."[16] Is, therefore, the house that Jack built a profound expression, no matter how disturbing, of the human longing to make a place for oneself out of an undifferentiated space? Is Jack building a dwelling place that might rescue him from the fate of homelessness? Does the house that Jack built, insofar as he builds it as an artist and not as a builder, recover the concealment of *technē* "in the tectonics of architecture"?[17] Heidegger promises us that "[e]nough will have been gained if dwelling and building have become *worthy of questioning* and thus have remained *worthy of thought*."[18] Indeed, accepting Heidegger's invitation opens up unpredictable levels of reading Lars von Trier's film. To restrict this endeavor only to our question regarding the problematic relationship of aesthetics to ethics: the Greeks call a house, man's dwelling place: ἦθος (*ethos*).[19] We recognize the word *ethos* as the root from which we derived our term "ethics." Similarly, the Latin verb *habitare* means to dwell, to live in a place, to stay. Thus, we speak in English of inhabiting a place, a habitat. The same verb, however, gives us the term "habit" which, like the Greek *ethos*, comes to mean a characteristic trait and, therefore, one's *character*. It would seem that to build a house signifies nothing less than "to build" a character—to become oneself. If Aristotle in his *Nicomachean Ethics* describes virtue as habit, it is telling that in explaining the habituation of virtue Aristotle uses precisely the two examples we have seen in *The House That Jack Built*, namely, practicing music (Glenn Gould) and building (Jack):

> For the things we have to learn before we can do them, we learn by doing them, e.g. men become builders by building and lyre-players by playing the lyre; so too we become just by doing just acts, temperate by doing temperate acts, brave by doing brave acts. This is confirmed by what happens in states; for legislators make the citizens good by forming habits in them, and this is the wish of every legislator, and those who do not effect it miss their mark, and it is in this that a good constitution differs from a bad one. Again, it is from the same causes and by the same means that every virtue is both produced and destroyed, and similarly every art; for it is from playing the lyre that both good and bad lyre-players are produced. And the corresponding statement is true of builders and of all the rest; men will be good or bad builders as a result of building well or badly.[20]

By practice a musician becomes a *virtuoso*—that is, in the literal sense of the term, *virtuous*. Jack's series of murders is the practice of his skill. It is this "habit" that allows him to emerge at the end of the film as a true virtuoso of crime. With murder being his virtue, Jack's ethics—the true "house" that Jack built, that is, his character—could not have been anything else than an ethics of death.

Notes

1   Martin Heidegger, "Letter on 'Humanism,'" in *Pathmarks*, ed. William McNeill (Cambridge: Cambridge University Press, 1998), 274.

2   Plato, *Phaedo*, 67d.

3   Immanuel Kant, *On the Causes of Earthquakes* (1:472).

4   Plato, *Phaedrus*, 274c–277.

5   On this topic see, Manoussakis, "The Revelation according to Jacques Derrida," in *Other Testaments: Derrida & Religion*, ed. Kevin Hart and Yvonne Sherwood (London and New York: Routledge, 2005), 315.

6   On the differences between music and the rests of the arts see, Manoussakis, *God After Metaphysics* (Bloomington, IN: Indiana University Press, 2007), 109–16.

7   Plato, *Phaedo*, 61a.

8   See, Pascal Quignard, *The Hatred of Music*, trans. Matthew Amos and Fredrik Rönnbäck (New Haven, CT: Yale University Press, 2016). The ambiguous force of music was already discussed in Plato's *Republic* (see, for example, *Republic* III, 401d).

9   Aeschylus, *Prometheus Bound*, v. 242 (ὧδ' ἐρρύθμισμαι, Ζηνὶ δυσκλεὴς θέα).

10 Virgil, *The Aeneid*, VI, 705-6, trans. Robert Fagles (New York: Viking, 2006), 820.

11 Sophocles, *Fragment 879* (βομβεῖ δὲ νεκρῶν σμῆνος ἔρχεται τ'ἄνω).

12 The pharmakoi was a group of ugly people kept on public expense by the city as sacrificial victims in case that an animal sacrifice would not be enough to appease the gods or avert a natural catastrophe. When Socrates in the *Apology* proposes as his punishment to be granted free meals in the Prytaneum he might be suggesting to be used as a pharmakos. (I have written on this in more detail in my article on the *Phaedo*, "The Philosopher-Priest and the Mythology of Reason"). The apothetai was an area full of deep gorges near the Taigetos (according to Plutarch), where unwanted children were deposited. Under Spartan law the father had to have the newborn examined by the city's council of elders before starting the raising process; if the child was found to have any physical or mental defects, it was left to die in the apothetai.

13 Nietzsche made the same argument with regard to philosophy: "All that philosophers have handled for thousands of years have been concept mummies; nothing real escaped their grasp alive. When these honorable idolaters of concepts worship something, they kill it and stuff it; they threaten the life of everything they worship." *Twilight of the Idols* ("Reason" in

Philosophy, 1), in *The Portable Nietzsche*, ed. and trans. Walter Kaufmann (Penguin Books, 1982), 479.

14 Friedrich Nietzsche, *The Birth of Tragedy*, trans. Ronald Speirs (Cambridge: Cambridge University Press, 1999), 33 (emphasis in the original).

15 Martin Heidegger, "Building Dwelling Thinking," in *Poetry, Language, Thought*, trans. Albert Hofstadter (New York: Perennial Classics, 2001), 146.

16 Ibid., 145.

17 Ibid., 157.

18 Ibid., 158 (emphasis in the original).

19 See also, Martin Heidegger, "Letter on 'Humanism,'" ("ἦθος means abode, dwelling place"), 269.

20 Aristotle, *Nicomachean Ethics*, II, 1103a-b, trans. W. D. Ross.

21

On Robert Bresson's *Diary of a Country Priest*

Jake Grefenstette

Robert Bresson's Directorial Difficulty

To call a movie "inscrutable" is usually to signal disapproval. The word connotes an evening of unredemptive difficulty. We have lost our two-hour wager on arthouse pretension; nothing is to be done but forget the film and proceed to dinner. Yet there are certain films which succeed in moving us in spite of—even because of—their inscrutability. It can seem miraculous. Not professing to understand the film, we nevertheless feel we have recognized something of ourselves on the screen. Or rather, we have recognized the very part of ourselves we do not understand. At best, this latter sort of film ushers the pinnacle experience of moviegoing: post-credits, powerless to decouple from our seats, the theater staff is forced to retrieve us. We shamble home, open-mouthedly mulling this photographic diagnosis of the human condition. Plans for dinner are scrapped; life philosophies are revised.

Such is the power of the cinema of Robert Bresson. With Bresson, inscrutability is never the last word out of the critic's mouth. It is only our first point of departure. As Geoffrey Hill suggests of poetry, we recognize greatness in Bresson's films because they are as strange and difficult as we are. Gauging responses from Jean-Luc Godard to Andrei Tarkovsky, these strange and difficult masterpieces have captivated the strangest and most difficult of moviegoers. And yet Bresson's art remains open-armed, surprisingly popular among audiences otherwise allergic to arthouse. Even my dog—historically a fan of *Umberto D.* (1952) and nothing else—is taken with Balthazar. All these viewers, from Jean-Luc down to Frodo Waggins, together leave Bresson's theater frazzled—but frazzled *gainfully*.

What makes Bresson's work approachable in spite of its difficulty is the fact that our struggle to understand his films is always cognate with the struggles of his characters. We endeavor to comprehend God in tandem with Joan of Arc; we endeavor to comprehend Joan in tandem with Joan. Bresson's miserable Mouchette and pickpocketing Michel are as intractable to us as they are to themselves. Poor Balthazar's fate is no more fathomable to the audience than it is to the ass (or, indeed, to the dog). This fundamental problem of interpersonal inscrutability, of our inevitable failure to understand one another absolutely—what the director calls "the impossibility of true communication"—constitutes the common subject of Bresson's films.[1] Bresson's is an art which helps us understand the ways in which we fail to understand.

Incredibly, and as a sign of great artistic humility, Bresson makes no claim to hover above this confusion. As a cinematic translator of literary colossi—Denis Diderot, Fyodor Dostoevsky, Leo Tolstoy, Georges Bernanos, Chrétien de Troyes—Bresson himself joins us, through directorial kenosis, in the audience of interpreters. In this way, his movies comprise a communal struggle: Bresson's characters are as much a challenge to themselves as they are to each other; as they are to Bresson; as they are to us.

In this short chapter, I want to explore *Diary of a Country Priest* (*Journal d'un Curé de Campagne*; 1951) as a guide for coming to terms with this triple problem of interpretive difficulty in Bresson's films. Bresson's *Diary* stages the communicative failures which the director takes to be common to the artist, the curate, and their respective "audiences" in our world and in the world of the film. Built out from Bresson's theory of "the impossibility of true communication," *Diary* visualizes the thesis that all human discourse is doomed to some degree of cross-purpose confusion. Taking inscrutability as its subject, *Diary* demonstrates the slight and yet unbridgeable variances in perspective which haunt all efforts to communicate—the very problem echoed in Bresson's own attempts to translate novels to the screen. At the same time, *Diary* prescribes Bresson's most explicit and sanguine response to this potentially asphyxiating problem. Through his country curate, Bresson contends that artist and audience alike must cut the Gordian knot of communicative anxiety and proceed in the face of our necessary and mutual misunderstanding. The Curé de Torcy's words bear back on this common condition: although we remain mysterious to each another, one must nevertheless trudge on, must focus on "little things, from day to day, while you wait."[2] For Bresson, this humble philosophy ultimately unpetrifies the artist, audience, and priest alike. We will always fail to understand, to be understood; and yet, following the film's ecstatic coda: "What does it matter? All is grace."

Epistemological Crises: The Country Priest's Interpretation of *Diary of a Country Priest*

To illustrate Bresson's "impossibility of true communication," the plot of *Diary of a Country Priest* stages a series of breakdowns of communication. The general formula for these episodes is consistent. In each scene, we shadow the unnamed priest's efforts to decode interactions with his inscrutable parishioners. At first glance, we are lured, with the protagonist, into thinking we have interpreted a scene correctly. Invariably, however, our interpretive frameworks are undermined: by a word misheard, by a concealed double-meaning, by some evidence unknowingly withheld. Our first glance is always revealed to have been ultimately and radically insufficient. These revelations usher moments of interpretive destabilization, events the philosopher Alasdair MacIntyre dubs "epistemological crises."[3] For MacIntyre, these crises amount to experiences which jarringly illuminate previously unrecognized fissures between viewpoints. In Bresson as in the philosopher, these moments require, on threat of madness, an emergent narrative to account for our previous misinterpretations. Such is the struggle of the country priest.

In the earliest of these destabilizing episodes, we find our unnamed protagonist teaching catechism to a class of potential communicants. The priest's inaugural crisis is staged through a Kuleshov sequence, a cinematic phenomenon where a single image recurs in different contexts to different effects. In this case, the recurring image is a classroom crammed with beaming and ostensibly devoted children. After we first view this image, Bresson's camera cuts to the priest, who returns the smile. The audience is inclined to interpret the image of the schoolchildren in a positive light. These, so thinks the priest, are the children who will inherit the kingdom. This initial interpretation is reinforced by an apparently devout student who expresses special interest in the Eucharist. Yet her expression—along with the ostensible goodwill of the entire class—turns out to be only a pretext for a ruse. Summoned for an audience at the priest's desk, the young girl unexpectedly shirks the sacraments and declaims on her teacher's "beautiful eyes" as the class erupts in laughter.

Flabbergasted, the curate is flung into a state of interpretive inertia. The audience joins him in his confusion. Our initial paradigm of youthful devotion becomes suddenly and radically inadequate to explain this outburst of mockery. Turning again to the class for some interpretive clue, the camera (with the priest) sees the same set of smiling faces, but now recognizes these smiles as only ostensible. In a gestaltic moment, conspiratorial laughter renders the scene sensible by means of a new interpretation. "They had plotted it together," the curate realizes, unhappily coming to terms with his first epistemological crisis.

At this early moment, the priest's faith in his induction from behavior to intention in other minds is rudely destabilized. Following MacIntyre's model of epistemological crisis, Bresson's misinterpreting parties—here, the audience and the curate—must construct new narratives to account for our prior misinterpretations. With no motive supplied for this antagonistic behavior, the audience must shadow the priest's attempts to grapple with and schematize the children's contextless malice: "But why such hostility?" wonders the curate. "What had I done to them?" Bresson offers no reprieve for his priest or for us. We are both left to confront the inscrutable faces of his "model" actors.

The majority of Bresson's *Diary* is dedicated to compounding this problematic. In the ensuring scenes, the priest finds an anonymous note demanding his replacement. A graphological guess makes prime suspect of the sole attendee of daily Mass. This crisis likewise demands an explanatory narrative, but now with greater stakes: Does the communicant wish the young priest gone on the basis of hate? Or of admiration? Or of something unguessable from the evidence at hand?

Every conversation in *Diary*'s is in this way staged, insolvably, at cross-purposes. In the long episode of his conversation with the Countess, the priest believes he has achieved at last a mutuality of understanding. But when the Countess unexpectedly casts her medallion into the fire, he realizes the dialogue had theretofore operated on radically separate interpretations of what "giving up" her deceased son meant. "An hour ago, my life seemed to me in order," utters the Countess. "You have left nothing standing." *Diary*'s priest learns at length that while individual perspectives may overlap, an infinitude of miniscule discrepancies make complete commensurability of worldviews impossible. As he progresses through his crises, the curate thus comes to believe that the truths of his parish are not merely undisclosed, but fundamentally undisclosable; that ineradicable gulfs of understanding keep individuals at a necessary—and necessarily painful—distance.

Mutual Failures of Parishioners and Priest

Staging this series of epistemological crises, *Diary* is no facile dismantlement of a young priest's idealist illusions—as much as it may be interpreted as such. For, over the course of the priest's own crises, the townspeople struggle in parallel to pigeonhole the cleric into accustomed priestly archetypes. The Curé de Torcy, mentor to the young priest, grumbles over young ordinates who later realize the priesthood "isn't what they expected." But this oblique criticism is misdiagnostic; in *Diary*, it is rather the case that priesthood does not expect the priest.

In their efforts to understand him, parishioners invoke paradoxical archetypes of the "country priest" as "exploiter of the poor" and yet severe "ascetic"; a priest "simple" and yet "malicious." The audience is inclined to do the same. The priest's poor health, too, cycles through interpretations of saintly sickness and discrete dipsomania. The country doctor's diagnosis—

sickness from "[The wine] drunk for you, long before you came into the world"—is ostensibly scriptural, but this resonance evaporates amid later, more literal insinuations of fetal alcohol complications ("You were pickled in the stuff"). In each schema, the townspeople induce a medical or spiritual reality from mere physiognomy and glimpses of an empty bottle. The viewer easily succumbs to the same. When the doctor of Lille finally educes stomach cancer as the true cause of the priest's poor health, this wine is revealed as an interpretive red herring: the priest fits *neither* archetype of drunkard nor saint. Once again, we find we have misunderstood the priest just as radically as his parishioners.

The townspeople, like most of us, are wont to speak of "truth" as something merely "hidden." Once "the truth of the matter" is uncovered, we will understand all things absolutely. We believe, with MacIntyre's fallacious Emma, that our incorrect interpretations will be "replaced not by a more adequate interpretation, which itself in turn may one day be transcended, but simply the truth."[4] For, as we hear repeated in the priest's conversation with the Count, every soul in town is ascribed a "hand," as in a game of cards. The Count's daughter doubles this analogy: the priest and she have "cards" kept "hidden" which, were they to be laid on the table, would unravel the "malice" that cloaks the truth of things. Implicit is the notion that minds can in fact be revealed and understood on commensurate terms.

The priest initially endorses this philosophy, but it proves everywhere disastrous. On the faith of this epistemic quest, he successfully deduces the existence of a concealed letter in the pocket of Chantal, a troubled confessor. Encouraged, the priest believes his factual insight is in some way cognate with his "true knowledge" of her soul. He accordingly construes himself as a kind of saint, assuming Chantal does as well. But this is only another (and greater) moment of crisis. Over the course of her confession, Chantal instead interprets this "saintly" insight according to the opposite schema: "It must be the devil!" We finally realize—with the priest as well as MacIntyre—that our problems are more complicated than cards overturned on a table. Rather, our all-too-human condition is such that slight variances in perspective are sufficient to "yield mutually incompatible accounts of what is going on."[5]

Finally relinquishing his quest for epistemological certainty, the priest admits "no hope in breaking through the obstacle" of communication precisely because "there is no obstacle." There is, in other words, no veil which, if lifted, could reveal the "cards" concealed. For this reason, the priest concedes to a conclusion consanguine with Roman Polanski's *Chinatown*: "I know nothing of people," he decides, "and I never will." Lapsing from both his epistemological and Christian faiths, the Hamletian priest comes to inhabit an unanchored perspectivism. Abandoning prayer and homiletic duties, the priest scorns "mere human words, with no meaning except for you."

If *Diary* has in the past been read as a mere battle between a devout priest and an imprisoning parish, it has been done so in ignorance of this serious lapse of faith. As with the priest of *Sous le soleil de Satan* (both the Bernanos original [1926] and Maurice Pialat's adaptation [1987]), the claims of *Diary*'s protagonist are often discretely antithetical to Roman Catholic doctrine: "Blessed is sin if it teaches us shame," says the priest, citing damnation as spiritual "blackmail." One shrewd interlocutor voices what many critics have overlooked: "Are you just saying whatever strikes your fancy?" When the country doctor recognizes the priest as a fellow "wounded soul," it is because they have both abandoned faith in human communication. Each retains a vague resolve, but neither knows where to apply it. The doctor's mantra—"face up to it"—is always appended by an ironical condition: "But face up to what?" When the country doctor dies, the multiplicity of schemata suggested—gun malfunction, suicide—are left appropriately unresolved. Knowing the circumstances to be inscrutable, the priest makes no effort to scrutinize them. From the moment of this revelation, Bresson's priest becomes incapacitated by his epistemological anxieties. This condition persists until *Diary*'s famous coda recommends its theological solution.

Translating Bernanos: *Diary* as a Problem for Bresson

Before proceeding to the film's "solution," let us briefly consider one cinematic parallel to the priest's crisis: that is, Bresson's own task of translating the film from Bernanos's novel. Tellingly, MacIntyre suggests that both Hamlet and stage directors of *Hamlet* ask the same question: namely, "what is going on in *Hamlet*?"[6]

As director, Bresson is fully aware of the anxieties of his vocation. In the case of Bernanos's original novel, the *Diary* presents itself as a found text. Barring a brief epilogic addendum, the words published by Plon or Penguin purport to be coextensive with the narrative diary. Appropriately, Bresson's *Diary* begins by showing us this very narrative object. When Bresson's film opens on a still of this diary—its "*appartenent à*" left aptly blank—the cinematic audience is made cognizant of the camera as an additional layer of interpretation between priest and "reader."

While this distancing, movie-within-a-book mechanism is common to literary interpretations spanning *Snow White* to *The Princess Bride*, Bresson uniquely mirrors this viewership dynamic in the three shots to follow. We witness, first, a fade to an Ambricourt street sign, as if the viewer has entered the book; second, a close-up of the unnamed priest; third, a jump backward in space—the first non-fade cut of the film—to reveal a fence between camera and character. This reminder of distance visualizes Bresson's network of competing interpretations: to watch *Diary* is to negotiate between the interpretive lenses of *Diary* as film; of *Diary* as the character's diegetic diary; of the literal lens of the photographer; and of the figurative lens of the audience.

Despite the distance this dynamic implies, Bresson calls *Diary* an "interior" film: "Cinema does not describe ... You are there."[7] As Jian Yang-Yang says in *Yi Yi* (2000), photography displays the inside of the head by showing the back of the head. Accordingly, *Diary*'s initial image includes an ambiguous, Pollockian mesh (is it ink? or blood?) on the diary's blotting paper. The visuality of Bresson's medium allows for a suspension between these interior and exterior schematics. When the priest meets Chantal in the confessional, he describes a metaphoric "vision" of the truth. Bernanos is cited verbatim here, but his words play to different effect on screen: "It seemed I could read on her lips other words that went unspoken," thinks the priest. In Bresson's cinematic case, our inability to "read" her lips is a phenomenological trick intended to remind us of the competing vantages in play. Similarly, while we hear the priest's thoughts throughout the film, we see nothing of his "apparitions." The priest's pivotal "vision" of a child's face is depicted, crucially, as a black screen. The "interiority" of "being there" does not help us interpret the story: Bresson gives a face to Bernanos's name, but this only doubles our interpretive problems.

Surveying the film's directorial decisions, we find that Bresson's blocking techniques in *Diary* correspond with his characters' challenges to understand each other. In instances where the young priest attempts to align his perspective with his parishioners', they literally refuse to meet his eye. When the priest speculatively interprets the tears of Mademoiselle Louise to the Count, the ensuring scene eschews face-to-face blocking until the Count is moved to identify an interpretive fissure: "You're mad," he tells the priest. This formula is repeated in the long conversation with the Countess: when eyes finally meet, it is only to identify a cross-purpose "madness."

In his own commentaries on the film, Bresson identifies this very "madness" in himself: his effort to translate between mediums likewise constitutes an "impossible task."[8] With the priest, his communicative difficulties are stifling: "I had an infinite number of concerns of all kinds when approaching the book. Among these concerns was that I would betray the novel."[9] And yet amid this acknowledged impossibility, an artistic faith sustains his efforts: "I am quite sure that everything I took, I took from Bernanos."[10] Bresson's faith arrives, with the priest, by means of revelation. "It suddenly occurred to me," says the director, "that my faithfulness to myself would guarantee my faithfulness to Bernanos."[11] Bresson's comments summon the Bernanos source text, where the priest laments a paradoxical pastoral problem: "It's common nowadays to say that we must 'not try to understand.' But, my God, that's what we're here for!"[12] For Bresson, then, his directorial problems—and, as we shall see, solution—are cognate with the priest's.

"All Is Grace": Bresson's Solution to "the Impossibility of True Communication"

Now that we have considered the sense in which *Diary* compounds the challenges of director and priest, we can proceed to consider the film's concluding response to their joint problems. As the priest's terminal illness takes hold, he devolves into a penultimate deconstructivist streak. Recalling the words of Torcy—"Your other dream is to be loved for who you are. A true priest is never loved, remember that!"—the curate has a final lapse of faith. Through "eyes and ears," says the despairing priest, a soul is forever inscrutable; and for this reason, "A priest has no opinion." The priest's previous apprehensions over his false reputations as a drunk, a charlatan, and a heretic all dissolve: "I'd discovered, with something bordering on joy, that I had nothing to say." The priest's diary pages—the ones through which, ostensibly, we are "seeing" the story—fall into a bed of straw, literalizing the apocryphal Thomistic image of interpretive futility. Quoting the deceased doctor, the priest commits to "stand up for" nothing, to refuse to interpret the souls of his parish.

As the climax of the film arrives, however, the priest's radical perspectivism poses further problems that lead him back, in turn, to a fundamentally theistic epistemology. Through conversations with his defrocked seminarian friend, he recognizes (with MacIntyre) the impossibility of shunning interpretation altogether. His friend's Cartesian position of total schematic suspension itself implicates, as it turns out, further schemata of interpretation. And if, as he expresses to his friend, he were forced to break his vows, he would rather do it for "love" than a desiccated, so-called "intellectual life."

On his deathbed, the priest acknowledges that human challenges of communication and interpretation are agonizing. And yet he feels his moral obligation to tend to other humans *in spite of* their inscrutability is equally burdensome: "I believe if God gave us a clear idea of how closely we are bound to each other in good and evil, we truly could not live." The priest thus regains his faith and makes his conclusive resolution: that although we are doomed to mutual inscrutability, we have no option but to continue (mis) interpreting each other to the best of our abilities. Bresson's priest famously articulates this position in response to a specific doctrinal question concerning interpretation of the Viaticum. Brushing the problem aside, the curate responds that our failures do not matter: that "All is grace." The viewer's vantage in the film here ceases, so to speak, with the priest's subjectivity. This "tout est grâce" pronouncement is made beyond the bounds of the film's narrative framework: for, in the brief moments following the priest's death, his friend relates this final scene over an image of the shadow of a cross.

Bresson's great achievement in his *Diary* is to show how vocations of filmmaker, priest, and moviegoer alike require faith—artistic or theological—

in order to avoid a Hamletian abyss of interpretive doubt. Ultimately, the priest assumes the philosophy of Torcy: "Do little things, from day to day, while you wait. Little things don't seem like much, but they bring peace." As his interviews suggest, Bresson's ultimate decision to shoot an "impossible" adaptation is based on a cognate act of faith. It is fortunate for the history of cinema that Bresson was moved to take a Gordian knife to this "impossibility of true communication."[13] For the vast catalogue of *Diary*'s inheritors— *Léon Morin, prêtre* (1961); *Andrei Rublev* (1966); *Taxi Driver* (1976); *To the Wonder* (2012); *Calvary* (2014); *Fleabag* (2016, 2019); *First Reformed* (2017)—draw alike on the priest's final words. As do we. In the theater of Robert Bresson, *Diary* bares back on the moviegoing audience. It insists that our failures are not entire: that in a sea of inscrutability, we are kept afloat by the country priest's "miracle of our empty hands."

Notes

1 Robert Bresson, *Bresson on Bresson: Interviews, 1943–1983*, ed. Mylène Bresson, trans. Anna Moschovakis (New York: New York Review of Books, 2016), 210. In one of several instances, Bresson here suggests this in regard to *A Gentle Woman* (1969): "It's no exaggeration to say that the impossibility of true communication is the basis for countless dramas in every society of the world."

2 *Diary of a Country Priest*, dir. Robert Bresson (France: StudioCanal, 1951), DVD.

3 Alasdair MacIntyre, "Epistemological Crises, Dramatic Narrative and the Philosophy of Science," *The Monist* 60, no. 4 (1977): 453–72.

4 Ibid., 456.

5 Ibid., 454.

6 Ibid., 454–5.

7 Bresson, *Bresson on Bresson*, 32–3.

8 Ibid., 33.

9 Ibid., 38.

10 Ibid., 35.

11 Ibid., 38–9.

12 Georges Bernanos, *Diary of a Country Priest*, trans. Howard Curtis (London: Penguin, 1936), 5.

13 Bresson, *Bresson on Bresson*, 210.

22

On Luchino Visconti's *Death in Venice*

Joseph S. O'Leary

My three favorite films are Federico Fellini's *Satyricon* (1969), Luchino Visconti's *Death and Venice* (1971), and Ingmar Bergman's *Cries and Whispers* (1972). Sumptuously decadent last fruits of European literary tradition, they also share a groundbreaking role in bringing the portrayal of same-sex intimacy to the big screen. After fifty years, Visconti's film triumphs over Anglophone Philistines and puritans and fussy would-be defenders of Thomas Mann (1875–1955) and Gustav Mahler (1860–1911), as well as jealous champions of Benjamin Britten (1913–76), whose opera *Death in Venice* (1973) has somewhat languished in the shade cast by the film.[1] Visconti raises Mann's story to new potency, by cutting through the protagonist's wordy philosophizing, based on memories of Plato's *Phaedrus* and Nietzsche's *Birth of Tragedy*, and letting him enact his passion unencumbered. Gone too are the countless allusions to Greek mythology that saturate Mann's text, most flamboyantly in the fourth chapter, and clog the action. Mann admitted that their purpose was to keep a scabrous subject decorous. Yet the film has genuine philosophical depth, achieved with the resources proper to the seventh art, which can convey thought just as much as its haughty elder sisters, Literature and Music.

From Philosophical Lore to Cinematic Thought

Mann scholars build on his solemn musing about the tension between *Geist* and *Leben*, intellectual culture and robust life, that is explored particularly in his first two decades of writing (1893–1912), notably in *Buddenbrooks*

(1900).[2] The bearers of *Geist* in this period are inhabited by a "sympathy with death."[3] One of them finds a philosophical equivalent for his morbid instinct when he reads Part II, chapter 41, of Schopenhauer's *The World as Will and Representation*, entitled "On Death and its Relation to the Indestructibility of our Essence in Itself." "Death as dissolution, redemption, release, as transition from constraint and form into 'un-form,' as the abolition of the *principium individuationis* that governs the world of appearances and therewith the human 'life-form' is the dark happiness after which Thomas Buddenbrook unconsciously longs."[4] In Visconti, Gustav von Aschenbach's sympathy with death is shown in his smile as he listens to the clerk in Cook's relate how cholera from the Ganges is filling the morgues of Venice. The sea represents the bliss of that dissolution, notably in the final shots, the product of who knows how many "takes." Aschenbach dies smiling as the beckoning form of Tadzio moves into the alluring emptiness.[5]

For Mann, the name of Schopenhauer is inseparable from that of Wagner, who died in Venice in 1883 and whose most Schopenhauerian work, *Tristan und Isolde*, like the film, begins shipboard and ends with a *Liebestod* in the face of the sea. *Tristan* is also present in the Adagietto of Mahler's Fifth Symphony, which provides a potent love-music for the film, for its central section, when the harp falls silent, repeatedly quotes the gaze-motif of *Tristan*, a rising three notes followed by a yearning falling seventh.[6] The Adagietto's main theme orchestrates the seduction of Venice and nostalgia for its vanished past, the surge at bar 39 underlines dramatic turns, and the central section's frenetic desert of falling sevenths matches Aschenbach's desperate obsession. None of this is casual. Already in 1951 Visconti had discussed with Thomas Mann himself plans for a dramatization of "Mario and the Magician" using ballet and opera. In the four long extracts from the Adagietto in the film "the action is choreographed to the music," which functions almost as a narrative voice.[7]

Mann's other great philosophical mentor, Nietzsche, is reduced to a caricature in the sophomoric and rather comic discussions between Aschenbach and the grating "Alfred" in the Bavarian flashbacks: "The creation of beauty and purity is a spiritual act." "No, Gustav, no! Beauty belongs to the senses, only to the senses." "You cannot reach the spirit . . . you cannot reach the spirit through the senses . . . you cannot. It's only by complete domination of the senses that you can ever achieve wisdom, truth, and human dignity." This parodies the pugnacious friendship between Gustav Mahler and Arnold Schoenberg (1874–1951).[8] Such operatic simplification is preferable to the catastrophic choices of Britten's librettist to have Aschenbach deliver long philosophical lectures to himself and to represent literally the Apollo-Dionysus clash as a contest of moralizing voices—"Receive the stranger god." "No! Reject the abyss," etc.—filling in for the Dionysian phallic tumult of Aschenbach's dream (*GW* 8:515–17), which Visconti did not attempt to film.[9] Nietzsche's *Birth of Tragedy* was still fresh after forty years when Mann wrote, but a century had passed when Visconti took up the thread, by which time discussions of Apollo and Dionysus savored of obsolete cliché.[10] Britten's opera is *Hamlet* without the prince, replacing Tadzio with a pseudo-Greek high school athlete, prancing to Balinese music that destroys the work's stylistic coherence. Contrary to the idea that Tadzio had to be a non-speaking role, he chatters in French and Polish both in the novella and the film, so it would not have been impossible to supply him with a vocal part of the kind that made the "Miles" of Britten's *Turn of the Screw* so unforgettable. But Britten had no doubt exhausted the operatic possibilities of a mysterious boy soprano in that work, and since Mann specified the boy's age as about fourteen, the problem of a singer whose voice is breaking or broken would arise.[11] In Britten we do not get much outside Aschenbach's rather boring mind, and his generalized responses to Venice, whereas Visconti recreates a whole world (dismissed by critics as "opulent").

Following Nietzsche, and a Freudianism of which he already had considerable awareness, Mann sees the work of intellect as a set of screens concealing and repressing powerful unconscious or instinctual drives. Nietzsche, "incomparably the greatest and most experienced psychologist of decadence" (*GW* 12:79), is the key philosopher behind the story, who would see the Platonic allusions as Apollonian repression, though in Plato too the passion of eros can become a Dionysian mania.[12]

Nietzsche's voice is actually heard in the film, in his one great poem, the runic "Midnight Song" from *Thus Spake Zarathustra*, as set to music in Mahler's Third Symphony. Before critics had the advantage of checking their remarks by looking at a video, one critic called Aschenbach a consumptive, and another complained that the Nietzsche setting accompanies a boring scene of Aschenbach happily writing. In fact what we see as this music plays is: (1) Tadzio put in a deck chair and playing with an orange (one minute nine seconds); (2) Aschenbach writing (forty-five seconds); (3) Tadzio walking to the sea (thirty seconds); (4) seascape (ten seconds); (5) restless Aschenbach at the hotel window (twenty-four seconds); (6) twilight on the sea (ten seconds); (7) next morning, Tadzio swinging from bar to bar in Aschenbach's path (one minute eleven seconds); and (8) shattered Aschenbach almost collapsing behind the bathing huts (forty-seven seconds). There is no longueur in this packed four minutes. We do not hear the poem's last words: "Sorrow says, 'pass away,' but all joy wants eternity, wants deep, deep eternity," yet this message is intimated as part of the fabric of the film. The two seascapes during the music emblematize the poem's "*tiefe, tiefe Ewigkeit.*" As Tadzio, outgrowing juvenile games as Jaschu's horseplay turns violent, stands alone before the empty sea at the film's end, one may sense that his own youth is passing, that his life is taking an inward reflective turn. The final movement of the film is ushered in by a contextless full-screen shot of his face, which looks stern and even rather ugly, for here we take a step beyond beauty to the sublime. The funereal Mussorgsky lullaby that follows could be a lament for Tadzio: "Misfortune has come, disaster upon disaster. . . . Hush, hush, hush-a-bye!/ Your small white body lies there in the cradle,/ Your soul flies in the heavens."[13]

Love through the Eyes Alone

The sexual formula of the film, centered on a play of glances and gazes between man and boy, was provided by Mann's text:

> Nothing is stranger, more delicate (*heikler*) than the relationship between people who know each other only with their eyes—who encounter and observe each other daily, even hourly, and are forced to maintain the appearance of indifferent unacquaintedness, neither greeting nor speaking, whether from constraint of custom or from a whim of their own. Between them there is restlessness and overexcited curiosity, the hysteria of an unsatisfied, unnaturally suppressed need for knowledge and exchange and, above all, a kind of tense attentiveness. (*GW* 8:496)[14]

The filmmaker seized on this as a formula for purely visual drama and tension. Aschenbach thinks of addressing the boy and normalizing the situation, but decides not to. "The aging one did not wish for sobering" since "the excitement (*Rausch*) was too dear to him," an instinctive choice labeled "dissoluteness" (*Zügellosigkeit*) (494). The silence of both becomes an erotic pact, a rule of their game. Philip Reed writes: "In Mann, Tadzio's glances are recorded through the filter of Aschenbach's point-of-view; in Visconti, they now appear much too explicit, almost consciously seductive."[15] Visconti's Tadzio is not "almost" but obviously a conscious agent in the game of glances between adorer and adored. The film draws us into Aschenbach's point of view and we can reconstruct for every appearance of Tadzio how it is impacting on him, and can also figure out, as Aschenbach does, how the boy is reacting.

Visconti said he wanted to make a film about love without sex. In a sense Tadzio has no sex appeal, as is shown up by the contrast with Jaschu in the beach scenes. His scanty and scrawny body is underlined. The potency of his appeal is all a matter of eyes, face, hair, poise, and charm, which together compose an apparition of "Beauty." He stands alone and untouched, *eine höchst abgesonderte und verbindungslose Erscheinung* as the last page says. Aschenbach's rejection of Esmerelda in the film is not a matter of sexual impotence, repression, or even moral scruple. It is that she comes close to the Platonic ideal embodied in Tadzio, but ruins it with the prescribed postures of prostitution.

The gaze-motif, borrowed from *Tristan und Isolde*, gives erotic charge to such lines as "Their gazes crossed (*Ihre Blicken trafen sich*)" (497). The gazes in Mann are sometimes almost unnoticeable. Here is the first of them: "For some reason he turned (*wandte*) around before he crossed the threshold, and since there was no one else in the hall, his peculiar twilight-gray eyes met (*begegneten*) those of Aschenbach, who, with his newspaper on his knees, sunk in contemplation (*Anschauung*) gazed after (*nachblickte*) the group" (471). Insignificant, one might think, and vamped up by Visconti in a lewd, sensational way; but this gaze is remembered at the end of the tale: "And suddenly, as if under a memory, an impulse, he turned (*wandte*) his upper body, one hand on the hip, in a beautiful swing from his basic position and gazed (*blickte*) over his shoulder toward the strand. The gazing one (*Schauende*) sat there, as he once had sat, when first, sent back from that threshold, this twilight-gray gaze (*Blick*) had met (*begegnet*) his" (524). Philip Reed complains that "no time is allowed to insinuate Tadzio into Aschenbach's consciousness. The image of the handsome Björn Andreson [recte, Andrésen] (who plays Tadzio) is thrown at us"[16]—in fact the image is artifice as much as nature, the image not of Andrésen but of Tadzio, just the image of Aschenbach is not that of Dirk Bogarde (who in real life was the same age as Aschenbach but looked much younger). Visconti's declared ambition was to create an image to rank with the *David* or the *Mona Lisa*. The camera, in this process, does not mechanically record the model's "handsome" appearance but realizes the artist's creative thought, which generates a beautiful or even sublime image.

In the strolling players scene there is a string of very moving gazes from Tadzio to Aschenbach, all of which are the product of Visconti's coaching and selection. Note the way he shrinks back from the player and looks to Aschenbach as if for help or in solidarity of distaste,[17] then looks back and forth between the player and Aschenbach as if comparing them. The mother casts anxious glances at Tadzio even as she is being molested by the player and a little later looks really perturbed (she who is usually so imperturbable) as the long exchange of gazes between her son and the professor plays out.

The Platonic image belongs to a different world from real life, which it contradicts and is contradicted by. Recall Yeats's broodings on this: "Man is in love and loves what vanishes" ("Nineteen Hundred and Nineteen"); "Her present image floats into my mind . . . /Hollow of cheek as though it drank the wind" ("Among School Children"). The film gave Björn Andrésen (born January 26, 1955) a poisoned fame as "the most beautiful boy in the world."[18] Unlike ex-beauties such as Greta Garbo or Empress Elisabeth (Sisi), who hid their ravaged faces from the world, Andrésen reveled in the anonymity brought by the disappearance of his good looks.[19] Baron Władysław Gerard Jan Nepomuk Marya Moes (born November 17, 1900; died 1986), the original *puer mirabilis* who in May–June 1911 provided the grit around which three pearls of art were to form (Mann's, Visconti's, and Britten's), also emerged with his story.[20] But in a sense "the real Tadzio" never existed. The character is a projection of desiring imagination; and the boy actor with the nice smile provided only the raw material for Visconti's creation of an icon of Beauty (and symbolically an angel of death).

Visconti's Phenomenological Reduction

I turned against Venice in recent years, but the opening six minutes of this film restore the magic. The black ship surging out of the mist, the glimmering pink dawn;[21] then Aschenbach in his dilapidated deckchair; then radiant sandbanks with cockle pickers at their matutinal task; then, viewed from the ship's prow, the gradual emergence of Venice, majestic and mysterious; movement begins as young men on the ship view military figures jogging on land; then the ceremony of landing, with epiphanic glimpses of La Salute, S. Giorgio, and S. Marco. The whole sequence is woven hypnotically. One might say that the scene offers a phenomenological *Wesensschau* of la Serenissima, in its timeless identity, but also in its specific identity of 1911, sixty years in the past, which yet remains a "visitable past" to use Henry James's phrase about that other famous Venice novella, "The Aspern Papers."

How are such pregnant images produced? There is a documentary that shows Visconti spending an entire day on a twenty-second segment, until finally the image "clicks," in just the right nuance of hazy light. The process resembles Flaubert's fanatical perfectionism that forbade him to relax until *le mot juste* had been found. This is more than a phenomenological *Wesensschau*. It undertakes the further reduction of the world to a subjective reality: "Through the radical epoché any concern with the reality or unreality of the world is . . . put out of play. . . . The world, the objective, becomes itself a particular subjective," with the startling result that when "the I-pole and all its specific I-ness becomes a theme of inquiry into essence, they are now called in a new and still higher sense the subjective of the world."[22] Visconti imprints on every image the color of subjectivity, not Aschenbach's only, or Visconti's, but a kind of transcendental subjectivity. A world speaks to us, a past world, and with such intimacy that we experience it as a world in which we have always been at home. The camera not only sees this vanished world, but signals its own seeing, as the world it creates both resurrects a past and consigns it to the register of impossible nostalgia. The effect is realized with particular intensity in the apparitions of Silvana Mangano as the pearl-bedecked mother. Visconti wanted to film Proust, and is at his most Proustian here. The parade of gorgeous hats and dresses has the density of Renoir paintings, and is marked at every moment by a consciousness of pastness. This dimension of nostalgia is insinuated at every point, giving the objective images a subjective glow. Deleuze, in discussing the temporality of the cinematic image, classes Visconti as the cineast of "the decomposing crystal" who "could distinguish and make play according to varied relations four fundamental elements that haunted him": an aristocratic world outside of history and nature; its undermining from within; an intrusion of history that accelerates the decomposition (the pestilence in *Death in Venice*); and "the revelation that *something* has come too late," as when Aschenbach "receives from the young boy the vision of what his work has lacked: sensual beauty."[23]

Every image in the movie was filmed many times over, and this must apply especially to every image of Tadzio. The shots of him in the aristocratic black costume against a dark background in the strolling players scene where he stands still, at length, for the only time in the film are another example of the camera establishing a *Wesensschau* of his beauty. He is a creation of the camera, which may be hinted by the black camera looming in the final scene; in Mann the "photographic apparatus, seemingly masterless" that "stood on its three-legged tripod," covered with a "black cloth" (GW 8:523) is an abandoned Apollonian emblem, but in Visconti, a camera is a camera is a camera, an instrument whereby the world comes to subjective consciousness of its essence.

Demystification

Adair says: "Had he been afforded the opportunity of writing *Death in Venice* over again, Thomas insisted, he would have made it significantly less of a 'mystification.'"[24] Mann invested in mystification here more than in his other stories of sexual repression or revolt because of the dangerous nature of his pedophiliac confession. The mystification lay less in the addition of three years to Moes's age as Tadzio and twenty years to his own as Aschenbach than in strained Hellenization of every element in the story, beginning with the first appearance of Tadzio: "With astonishment Aschenbach observed that the boy was perfectly beautiful. His face, pale and gracefully compact, wreathed in honey-colored hair, with the nose falling straight, the lovely mouth, the expression of gracious and divine earnestness, recalled Greek sculptures of the noblest period" (*GW* 8:469). However, this can all be read ironically as Aschenbach's Apollonian self-mystification, as Dionysian impulses breach his defenses.

But such elaborate irony yields to high-spirited humor in Mann's *Felix Krull* (part 3, ch. 2), where the teenage waiter is pursued by fiftyish Lord Kilmarnock, who offers to employ him in Scotland, declaring, "it is the wish of a lonely heart" (*GW* 7:485). Felix tells us: "Never have I taken vain and cruel satisfaction in the sufferings of fellow-humans in whom my person aroused wishes that wisdom prevented me from fulfilling" (474). His refusal of the Lord's invitation is worthy of a diplomat: "Milord, I thank you most devotedly and implore your indulgence. I feel myself not yet mature enough for the position so generously offered me and have reached the conviction that it is better that I refrain from embarking on this path that branches away from my course" (488). As the Lord insists, offering to adopt Felix and make him his heir, he replies: "Forgive me, Milord, if I limit my answer to the repetition of my best wishes for your journey," and consoles the rejected suitor by reminding him that "there are millions of my age and natural build wandering about and aside from the little bit of uniqueness one is shaped just like the other" (490). The Lord departs graciously, giving Felix an emerald ring. "I cannot sufficiently recommend the decency of this man to the appreciation of my public" (491). Visconti projects this humor, typical of the later Mann, back into the solemn story of Aschenbach, who becomes hilariously pompous and silly, yet with no prejudice to viewers' sympathetic identification.

Mann revisited his most famous tale after forty years in another novella of the same length, "Die Betrogene" (1953), in which a German matron shocks her daughter by her unrespectable infatuation for a young G. I. The daughter relents when she learns that this passion has rejuvenated the mother to the point of restoring her menstrual flow. The lusty young man arranges to make love with the mother the following day. Alas, it is not to be, for the miraculous flow is the symptom of a fatal illness. But at the moment of death the mother declares: "Anna, speak not of Nature's betrayal and mocking cruelty. . . . Death is a great medium of life, and if it borrowed for me the shape of resurrection and pleasure of love, that was not deception but benevolence and grace. . . . Nature—I have always loved her, and Love—has shown it to her child" (*GW* 8:950). The irony in both stories is that a messy, sordid, and ultimately fatal affair, with a scandalous edge, is at the same time a triumphant love story. But the high humor of the later story dispels the portentous gloom of the earlier one. In Visconti's film the mincing campiness of the protagonist gives every opportunity to decry him with the taunt in Britten's opera: "How ridiculous you are!" But even as Aschenbach falls to bits, in novel, film, and opera alike, he acquires a heroic stature.

Visconti's film has seemed to careless viewers a crass reduction of Mann's story to a naturalistic level, making it "a queer novelette. . . . Aschenbach is far from the neurasthenic queen with a ready eye for a pretty face that was presented by Visconti."[25] But in fact Visconti conveys all the philosophic depth and mythic force of Mann's tale by sedulous pursuit of burnished images and closely observed gestures and expressions in a compositional unity pervaded by an intense elegiac sensibility nourished by Mahler, Wagner, and Proust. In his sedulous realization of a coherent cinematic vision, he works as a kind of phenomenologist, bringing out the aesthetic essence of Mann's vision in a purer reduction, centered on the labor of the image, realizing at each moment what the novelist's style conveyed in the verbal medium, and adding, thanks to the nostalgia generated by the sixty years separating the two works, an extra epiphanic glow and an extra dimension of reflective depth.

Notes

1 Colin Graham found the film "sentimental and salacious" (Donald Mitchell, ed., *Benjamin Britten: Death in Venice* [Cambridge: Cambridge University

Press, 1987], 67), but Peter Hayworth found Graham's production of the opera "disembodied" (ibid., 98). Britten's reliance on Helen T. Lowe-Porter's 1936 translation of a work so rich in nuance and tone is regrettable. Other English versions include Kenneth Burke's (1925), Martin C. Doege's (Vintage, 1989), Clayton Koelb's (Norton, 1994), Stanley Applebaum's (Dover, 1995), Joachim Neugroschel's (Penguin, 1999), Michael Henry Heim's (Ecco, 2004), and Thomas and Abby J. Hansen's (Boston: Club of Odd Volumes, 2012). Visconti presumably studied the German original.

2   See Käte Hamburger, *Thomas Manns Roman "Joseph und seine Brüder": Eine Einführung* (Stockholm: Bermann-Fischer, 1945), 13–20. For a sharp critique of the pseudo-philosophizing that this led to in much Mann criticism, see Jean Finck, *Thomas Mann und die Psychoanalyse* (Paris: Belles Lettres, 1973), 105–11.

3   Hamburger, *Thomas Manns Roman "Joseph und seine Brüder,"* 23.

4   Ibid., 20. See Arthur Schopenhauer, *Die Welt als Wille und Vorstellung,* II (Stuttgart: Cotta, 1960), 590–651; Thomas Mann, *GW* (*Gesammelte Werke* [Frankfurt: S. Fischer, 1974]), 1:654–9.

5   Some perceive Tadzio as pointing at the sun in this scene, but this is not clear; he is moving into the Adriatic, south-east from the Lido, and he points to the north-east. In the novella his gesture is less striking and enigmatic: it seems to Aschenbach "as if, releasing his hand from his hip, he were pointing forward, floating on into the promise-laden uncanny" (515).

6   In 1901, Mahler sent the Adagietto to his future wife, Alma Schindler, as a declaration of love. David Denby's snide remarks on Visconti show no awareness of the Wagnerian associations: "The *Adagietto* is used like the thick sludge of string tone composed in imitation of Mahler" by movie composers who "stole from him or watered him down to make money, but Visconti undoubtedly thinks that his corruption of the music is part of a great honor rendered to the composer" (praised as "perceptive critique" by Philip Reed, in Mitchell, ed., 181).

7   See James Larner, "Music as Narrator: Mahler, Mussorgsky, and Beethoven in Visconti's *Death in Venice," College Music Symposium* 49/50 (2009/2010): 385–91; 386. Larner points out that Visconti's aristocratic family held the controlling interest in La Scala when he was a boy, and that since 1954 he had directed operas, working with such artists as Maria Callas, Arturo Toscanini, and Leonard Bernstein. Even the *Merry Widow* waltz (1905) in the first hotel scene has significant words: "Every glance revealing/ Thoughts I may not speak/ Turn to me for I could be/ The love you seek" (quoted, 389). Thus the dismissal of the film as "operatic" contains an unwitting tribute.

8   Philip Reed, in Mitchell, ed., 180–1. When Alfred expostulates: "Evil is a necessity. It is the food of genius," Visconti may be thinking of the depiction of dodecaphony as the Devil's music in *Doktor Faustus* (1947), which greatly offended Schoenberg.

9   James Joyce was in Trieste, not very far from Venice, when the best-selling novella appeared. He drew on this dream in the third chapter of his autobiographical novel; see J. S. O'Leary, "Dionysos in *A Portrait of the Artist as a Young Man," Journal of Irish Studies* 24 (2009): 66–74.

10   Visconti's choice to make Aschenbach a musician virtually identified with
     Mahler rather than a man of letters who happens to look like Mahler and
     shares his first name, cannot be based on a belief that the events narrated
     actually happened to the composer (according to a lurid legend recounted by
     Dirk Bogarde; see Mitchell, ed., 217), since in the film a hotel porter actually
     names "Mrs Moes," showing Visconti's knowledge of the "real Tadzio."
     By linking Aschenbach with Mahler, Visconti can call up in the flashbacks
     Mahlerian associations with natural landscapes, domestic tenderness, and the
     death of children (anticipated in Mahler's own life in his *Kindertotenlieder*),
     forming a chord of beauty-love-death reinforcing that of the main narrative.

11   When rehearsing the premiere of *The Turn of the Screw* in 1954 in Venice
     Britten became so infatuated with David Hemmings (1941–2003), later the
     star of Antonioni's *Blow-Up*, that Peter Pears had to remove him from the city.

12   See Finck, *Thomas Mann und die Psychoanalyse*, 15–85; Manfred Dierks,
     "Thomas Mann und die 'jüdische' Psychoanalyse," *Thomas-Mann-Studien* 30
     (2004): 97–126; 98.

13   Quoted, Larner, "Music as Narrator," 387.

14   See Christophe Koné, "Aschenbach's Homovisual Desire: Scopophilia
     in *Der Tod in Venedig* by Thomas Mann," in *Thomas Mann: Neue
     kulturwissenschaftliche Lektüren*, ed. Georg Mein, et al. (Munich: Wilhelm
     Fink, 2012), 95–106.

15   Ibid., 182–3.

16   In Mitchell, 182.

17   Again, Visconti is following Mann's text closely (*GW* 8:506–7).

18   Germaine Greer took up this phrase of Visconti's in *The Boy* (Rizzoli, 2003).
     Andrésen was furious at her use of a photograph of him on the cover.

19   "'Adult love for adolescents is something that I am against in principle,' he
     says. 'Emotionally perhaps, and intellectually, I am disturbed by it—because
     I have some insight into what this kind of love is about.' His experience of
     'this kind of love' began at the Cannes film festival in 1970, where Visconti's
     film first became a sensation. 'I was just 16,' Andresen relates, 'and Visconti
     and the team took me to a gay nightclub. Almost all the crew were gay. The
     waiters at the club made me feel very uncomfortable. They looked at me
     uncompromisingly as if I was a nice meaty dish. I knew I couldn't react,' he
     says. 'It would have been social suicide. But it was the first of many such
     encounters'"; "When Andresen performed in Japan, he found himself mobbed
     by girls: 'You've seen the pictures of the Beatles in America? It was like that.
     There was a hysteria about it'" (Matt Seaton "I Feel Used," *The Guardian*,
     October 16, 2003). See also Ryan Gilbey, Interview: "'Death in Venice Screwed
     Up My Life.' The Tragic Story of Visconti's 'Beautiful Boy,'" *The Guardian*,
     July 15, 2021. The documentary of Andrésen's life story, *The Most Beautiful
     Boy in the World*, directed by Kristina Lindström and Kristian Petri offers a
     sad echo of Visconti's film after fifty years.

20   Gilbert Adair, *The Real Tadzio: Thomas Mann's Death in Venice and the Boy
     Who Inspired It* (Boston: Da Capo, 2003). Some say that "the real Tadzio"
     was Polish-Austrian Adam von Henzel who was fifteen in 1911 and looked

much more like the character described in the novella and in Katia Mann's *Unwritten Memories*: "the very charming, beautiful boy of about 13 was wearing a sailor suit with an open collar and very pretty lacings. He caught my husband's attention immediately. This boy was tremendously attractive, and my husband was always watching him with his companions on the beach." But Mann's correct memory of the names of Adzio and Jaschu confirms the Moes identification. Katia Mann recalls: "my uncle, Privy Counsellor Friedberg, a famous professor of canon law in Leipzig, was outraged: 'What a story! And a married man with a family!'" Edo Reents claims that the pedophile theme aroused no scandal in 1912 ("Pervers? Was für ein pfuscherisches Wort!," *Frankfurter Allemeine Zeitung*, July 23, 2012).

21 Padraig Rooney suggests that this owes something to Whistler's impressions of the Thames and Monet's "Waterloo Bridge."

22 Edmund Husserl, *Die Krisis der europäischen Wissenschaften und die transzendentale Phänomenologie* (The Hague: Nijhoff, 1954), 182–3. This is quoted by Käte Hamburger in her dense essay, "Die phänomenologische Struktur der Dichtung Rilkes," in *Rilke in neuer Sicht*, ed. K. Hamburger (Stuttgart: Kohlhammer, 1971), 83–158; 134. Her demonstration that the labor of a lyrical poet can match and confirm from afar the effort of phenomenology might be applied also to what cinema can attain.

23 Gilles Deleuze, *Cinéma 2: L'Image-temps* (Paris: Minuit, 1985), 124, 126.

24 Gilbert Adair, "In Search of the Real Tadzio," *The Independent*, December 15, 2001. Adair tells how "the six-year-old Adzio caught the eye of Henryk Sienkiewicz, . . . Nobel Prize-winning author. . . . The doting Sienkiewicz insisted that the infant come perch upon his knees, only hurriedly to offload him when he discovered that this Tiepolesque seraph had peed down the leg of his morning-suit."

25 Peter Hayworth, in Mitchell, ed., 195.

23

On Andrei Tarkovsky's
Andrei Rublev

Mark Patrick Hederman

Tarkovsky Stalking Rublev:
Cinema as Fishing by Hand

A friend of mine, Jean-Miguel Garrigues, invited me to a very rare showing of a Russian film at the Cinemathèque de Paris in 1969. There was a very long queue which extended right around the building. The film was due to start at 2:00 p.m. and we queued from early morning. We were near enough in line to view the entry door. For whatever reason, the management opened a side door and began to let people in through an alternative entrance. There was pandemonium. Everyone left the queue and began to push their way through the door that had been opened. "You are an Irishman who has played rugby," said my friend, "you barge and I'll follow." We entered the foyer in a swirling horde. A man stood up on a table in the center of the foyer and reprimanded the mob: "If you don't behave yourselves, and form an organised and orderly queue" he shouted "we won't distribute tickets to anyone!" He was swatted off the table and dumped out in the street. A woman at the guichet fled for her life. Without any tickets, we burst into the auditorium where, strangely, there seemed to be enough room for everyone. Sprawled in a sweating heap of exhaustion in a seat too near the screen, I watched mesmerized for over three hours, a film in Russian with French subtitles. I knew even then that I was present at the film of my life.

I start with this anecdote because it introduces the magic of my theme. Tarkovsky began production of *Andrei Rublev* in September 1964, two years after his first feature film, *Ivan's Childhood*, had won the Golden Lion at Venice, and one month before Nikita Khrushchev was deposed. When *Andrei Rublev* was finally completed in July 1966, the cultural thaw caused by Kruschev's departure had frozen over again in the Brezhnev regime. The state film agency demanded extensive cuts. The film was too negative, too harsh, too experimental, too frightening, too filled with nudity, and too politically complicated for release on the eve of the fiftieth anniversary of the Russian Revolution. After a single screening in Moscow, one version of the film, entitled *The Passion According to Andrei*, was shelved.

Trimmed by a quarter of an hour, a cut which Tarkovsky would later endorse, *Andrei Rublev* was scheduled for the 1967 Cannes Film Festival only to be withdrawn by the Soviet authorities at the last minute. Two years later, *Andrei Rublev* was shown at Cannes, albeit out of competition. It was screened at four o'clock in the morning on the festival's last day, but was nevertheless awarded the International Critics' Prize. Leonid Brezhnev reportedly demanded a private screening and walked out mid-film.[1]

In 1970, after five years of struggle with the authorities, Tarkovsky began writing a diary which he called "The Martyrology," recording his personal trials and, what he saw as, divine interventions on behalf of his film. Twice he recalls the miraculous recovery of the only copy of the screenplay which he had left behind in a taxi. Hours after he had left it behind, the taxi driver saw him walking along the street, in the crowd, at the same spot, stopped him, and handed back the folder.[2] Such miraculous interventions made Tarkovsky aware of some providence interested in the realization of this artistic project.

Choosing the person to play the role of Andrei Rublev was also "miraculous." Tarkovsky wanted someone who had never before been seen on screen. A little-known theater actor from Sverdlovsk, who had never played major roles in either theater or cinema, happened to read the film script, published in the journal *Iskousstvo Kino*. He left on the 2,000-kilometer journey to Moscow and presented himself at the Mosfilm studios. No one other than himself, he humbly declared, should be allowed to play the part of Andrei Rublev. He was given an audition and was proved right. Anatoly Solonitzn became a favorite actor of Tarkovsky.[3] Things must fall in place if the miracle is to happen. In something of a similar way, I turned up to see the film on the only occasion it was shown publicly in Paris and so Tarkovsky's cinematic equation was complete. Without the viewer there is no film.

Cinema Abducted

Tarkovsky saw cinema as an art form in danger of kidnap. Cinema did not exist before the twentieth century, and could not have existed before then. Cinema was also, possibly, the only art form to have arrived before its raison d'être. Or perhaps, the other way round: a shell hatched before the egg. Most other art forms were forced into existence of necessity. A receptacle had to be found which would hold the torrent of emotion pent up inside some unstoppable artist. Cinema, on the other hand, came about through curiosity and technological advance. It was the result of a number of disconnected experiments, a scientific feat which mesmerized the viewing public through its technical virtuosity. It was a container awaiting a content, a medium predating its message.

Tarkovsky describes the beginnings of cinema in terms of the Lumière brothers film *Train Arriving in the Ciotat Station*, which they made at the end of the nineteenth century and which was only half a minute long. It was so realistic and terrified the viewers that as the train approached the station on screen, the audience panicked and fled from the auditorium. That episode, according to Tarkovsky, was the moment that the art of cinematography was born. A new aesthetic principle had been realized. For the first time in the history of art, for the first time in the history of culture, we had discovered the way to pin down time, to make a print-out of the most mercurial element of existence. Cinema was the way we could stop time in its tracks. Up to that moment of this miraculous technological invention we had no control over time's illusiveness. From now on, we had been shown the way to reproduce time at will on a screen, repeat it whenever necessary, and go back over it. We were, at last, in possession of the matrix of the greatest enigma of our lives. Tarkovsky would even define the very essence of cinema as *Sculpting in Time*,[4] which was the name he gave to his important book on the subject. How to capture real time within the space of each cinematic frame became the obsessional quest for Tarkovsky; anything less was betrayal of cinema's true potential.

The Art of Cinema

The novelty of realistically moving photographs was enough to allow a motion-picture industry to mushroom at the beginning of the twentieth century. The year 1900 conveniently marks the emergence of the first motion pictures as such, where kinetic images are linked through basic editing techniques and "film narrative" takes place. The first decade of the twentieth century saw cinema moving from a prodigious novelty to a large-scale entertainment industry.

André Bazin claims that cinema's photographic basis made it very different from the more traditional arts.[5] By recording the world in all its immediacy, giving us slices of actual space and time, film puts us in a position to discover our link with more primordial sense experience. Pre-verbal, sensual, kinetic, cinema answers to the requirements of immediate physical connection with the world around us before the sophisticated gymnastics of cognitive abstraction sets in. Here is life in the raw before it is chewed into logic. We have to stop ourselves pre-empting such immediacy by translating it back into the brail to which we have become accustomed. We must refrain from writing subtitles under every image. This compulsion is the way we were educated, and the reason why we are blind to film. Experience is killed dead by recognition. This means that reality outside us is always transformed by what we supplement from the inside. We lay traps for sensation so that all we catch is the prey we are stalking. Our nets are designed to let everything else go free. We are carpetbaggers accumulating slides of life.[6]

The industry followed this proclivity: rather than delaying over the sumptuousness of each image, the emphasis was placed on speed: image after image raced past to convey a story with a beginning, a middle, and an end. We had already anticipated the ending before we had taken our seats: the guy gets the gal; and we ride off into the sunset. And if we don't get what we expect we are disappointed. Indeed, endings had to be changed when Hollywood movies failed to comply with popular demand. There are films being made which await the results of popularity polls before deciding how the ending should be.

Such determinants dictated that the story took over from the image, which became a subservient cog on the conveyor belt; each image was a vehicle for something other than itself, a carriage on the story's train of thought. The role of the image was to disintegrate as fast as the eye could see, sacrificing its own particularity to the eventual totality. Cinema became the equivalent of a "page-turner" in the world of novels; popular novels and successful plays became scripts for the first films. It was as if theater were being relayed to a wider audience. By the 1920s, the United States reached what is still its era of greatest-ever output, an average of 800 feature films annually, accounting for 82 percent of the global total.[7]

A further consideration which tipped the balance was the exorbitant cost of filmmaking. From the beginning, cinema was extravagantly expensive. A poet can write in a lonely room with a piece of paper and a pencil. Cinema involves several industries, hordes of skilled and highly paid workers, not to mention the cast and the crew, who became more and more expensive as their names grow larger on billboards. Cinema has always been dependent on financial backing from governments, businesses, or cinema-going audiences. The burgeoning industry veered between popularity and propaganda. Cinema could comply with ideological regimes or dance to the tune of popular demand. Directors, dependent on patronage, became puppets of whoever holds the purse strings.

Before the medium could assert itself and develop its own muscle and immediacy, it adapted to prevailing requirements. Tarkovsky puts it this way: "Cinema was born at the fairground with the goal of pure profit."[8]

Cinematic Forebears

Tarkovsky has acknowledged that Robert Bresson (1907–99) was his favorite director. In a small book called *Notes on Cinematography*,[9] Bresson makes a distinction between his work which he calls "cinematography" and "cinema" as most have experienced this art form to date. Cinema, according to Bresson, is no more than photographed theater, where everything is necessarily artificial. You don't expect to find real trees growing on the stage. Scenery is artificial construction. Acting, in the idiom of theater, has to participate in such artificiality. It is a calculated method. Cinema uses the camera to reproduce; cinematography uses the camera to create. Bresson hopes that cinematography can introduce us to something original, a new language of the screen, not merely photographed theater.

Bresson's film *The Diary of a Country Priest* (1950) provided one precedent for *Andrei Rublev*. It depicts the inner experience of a religious person without overstepping cinema's capabilities. Both films address a reality which cannot be captured on screen. And yet, this new language has the capacity to present the very essence of any human situation. Beyond acting and seeming there is a mysterious reality which, now and then, we catch a glimpse of, and which the camera can be ever on the alert to record. This hidden "being" of the person should be the real quarry of the cinematographer. It is there in all of us, but rarely seen, except when sometimes revealed by an involuntary gesture, a ripple from the unconscious, which the camera can capture if ready and not distracted.

The director prepares the scene for this revelation and then awaits the epiphany. All other considerations are unworthy of the art form now at our disposal. Until the twentieth century we had only produced a few cumbersome art forms to capture this mystery. Now we at last had an art form capable of tracking something of this mercurial essence, whether in a glance, a gesture, or a movement of the face.

A Film about Art and Artists

Although the protagonist of the film *Andrei Rublev* lived in the fifteenth century, Tarkovsky insists that the cine-story about him should be contemporary. The problem of talent, the question of the artist, and the relationship between art and the nation are the same in our own day. Tarkovsky wants the viewer of his film to see Rublev with today's eyes.[10]

The film comprises eight episodes during which Rublev leaves the seclusion of his monastery, is introduced to the horrors and the marvels of Russia in the fifteenth century, returns to the monastery, and creates the greatest icon ever written. Pavel Florensky, a great Russian Orthodox philosopher and theologian, holds that because Rublev's Icon of the Trinity exists, it must follow that God exists![11] The prologue and the epilogue are outside this eight-day framework and have their own particular idiom and function.

The prologue introduces a generic artistic figure who has created a contraption which will allow him to fly. He is surrounded by a hostile and jeering mob who consider his experiments blasphemous and unnatural. Efim, in the screenplay, is equipped with wings "like an angel." Tarkovsky explained after the event that they spent a long time working out how to destroy the plastic symbol on which the episode was built, and concluded that the trouble lay with the wings. To dispel the overtones of Icarus and provide a more contemporary equivalent, they decided on a hot-air balloon.[12] This "artist" as a personified emblem of all artistic endeavor climbs to the steeple of a church and launches himself over the heads of the rabble below in a stunning aerial display. He crashes to the ground in a further field out of sight. He is "anyone the artist" in any century, doomed to misunderstanding and failure.

The Buffoon, representing vulnerable art and culture, appears now and then throughout the main feature. His tongue is cut out; he is smashed against a wall and dumped in a cart by the authorities at the behest of the church (in the person of Kiril, jealous champion of Orthodoxy). The artist in any century is victim of institutional violence.

Violence throughout the century and the film stems from two sources. As well as the cruel domination of the Tartars, there is internal strife between two leading Russian princes who are brothers. The elder of these has a palace built for himself by skilled artists and artisans. These are coaxed away by his younger sibling, who intends to build a bigger and better palace for himself. One of the most violent scenes of the film is the blinding of these artists by one of their potential employers. It could mirror the unsighting of the cinema by the two major economic forces acting as patrons from the outset.

Rublev as Icon

Ostensibly *Andrei Rublev* should be the story of Russia's most renowned icon painter, who died in 1430 and is thought to have been born between 1360 and 1370. How to make a film about an artist who lived 500 years ago, about whose life next to nothing is known, and whose extant work amounts to one identifiable painting, so reworked and overladen that it hardly bears much resemblance to the original. Only this one single icon, the Old Testament Trinity, can be attributed with certainty to Rublev's hand. And yet, this artist has become a legend: canonized by the Russian Orthodox Church in 1988, at the centenary of Christianity's arrival in that country, identified as the exemplar of all authentic Russian iconography, and held up as an exemplary model for all such depiction in the future. Andrei Rublev, both the vague historical figure and the later flamboyant legend, can be seen as the pivot through which Byzantium was translated into Russian, both religiously and artistically. The traumatic century, during which Rublev lived and worked, was also the cauldron through which Russia itself became identifiable as a country in its own right. Rublev thereby becomes the hub for this politico-religious paradigm shift of the fifteenth century. In this way, he stands also as avatar for Tarkovsky and the art of cinema in the twentieth century.

The film *Andrei Rublev* is essentially about the artistic process: the transformation of horror into art. Two artists, both Russian, both living on the same landscape, enduring the same weather, surrounded by the same flora and fauna; one in the fifteenth century, one in the twentieth, viewing the world around them and translating it into a work of art. The process must be similar. Tarkovsky's filmscript at one point makes Andrei look up at thousands of crows and wonder, "are they the same ones or not?"[13] As we see the circling crows on the screen we might ask the same question. Tarkovsky helps us out. Naturalistically recorded facts, he tells us, are in themselves utterly inadequate to the creation of the cinematic image. Cinema is not a nature trail. The image in cinema is based on the ability of an artist to present "one's own perception of an object."[14] The artist must translate subjectively what the audience must receive subjectively, a translation of objectivity mediated through the image. Robert Bird[15] clarifies this further by suggesting that the screen acts as "a locus of exchange" whereupon the characters within the film, and the viewers without, create between them an "alternating current" mediated by the carefully wrought images. The screen is not a transparent window on objective reality; it is the matrix of a narrative form which requires active participation on the part of the viewer before it can fulfill its destiny. Tarkovsky insists that in creating an image, he, as artist, subordinates his own thought, which becomes insignificant in the face of that emotionally perceived image of the world that has appeared to him like a revelation.[16] For Tarkovsky the image is the instinctual go-between: the way in which the outside world is absorbed into personal subjectivity and then transmitted into cultural reality. In every case it is highly personal, and in every case it is a translation. The artist does not use "descriptions" of the world; he himself has to have a hand in its creation.[17] Film, for Tarkovsky, is the newly created artistic medium which corresponds to this immediate but illusive perception of the world outside. Expressing that amalgam of external objectivity and internal subjectivity, whether in a film or an icon, is a comparable process. It is within the experience of that process that you can correspond with artists who lived even hundreds of years before you. Andrei Rublev and Andrei Tarkovsky are artistic geminis.

Translation, at a religious and artistic level, becomes an argument in the film about painting an icon of the last judgment. The argument occurs between Rublev and the Greek master iconographer, Theophanes, who introduced the art of the icon to Russia. Traditional depiction of the Last Judgment inspires fear and trembling in the beholder, as the fierce lord of the universe metes out punishment to every sinner and wreaks vengeance on humanity for the way the second person of the Trinity was treated during his brief but violent sojourn on earth. Rublev, although living through an equivalently violent and barbaric period of history, perceives an alternative vision of the Trinity. The icon which he creates at the end of his life inspires love, harmony, and peace in the viewer. How could such a vision have come about in a country and a century torn apart by plagues, wars, violence, and treachery? Tarkovsky's film reveals that mystery in a series of poignant images. These images give birth to themselves in the artistic process. It is a mistake to talk about the artist "looking for" his subject, Tarkovsky tells us: "In fact the subject grows within him like fruit, and begins to demand expression. It is like childbirth."[18]

The birth takes place in a twofold process. You first transpose the world into "millions of metres of film." Sculpting in time then means picking out and joining together the bits of sequential fact, knowing, seeing, and hearing precisely what lies between them and what kind of chain holds them together.[19] The filmmaker assesses the blood count of the images he has shot and allows these to fuse into each other as organically linked droplets of equal blood pressure. The image is an impression of the truth, a glimpse of the truth permitted to the artist. The viewer has to be absorbed into it as into nature, "to plunge in, lose him or her self in its depth, as in the cosmos there is no bottom and no top."[20] Retaining this image of swimming in water as a way for us to approach Tarkovsky's cinema, we can learn a great deal from another source.

The Script as Novel

As well as the film itself we have an important handbook which helps to negotiate it: the so-called *Kino-roman*, which Russian directors write out in prose as a filmscript. In this case the text reads more like a novel than simply as directions for a film. There is a key moment in the filmscript which occurs as a dialogue between Andrei and Kiril, his *alter ego*: Andrei says that he can do better than Theophanes the Greek; he can represent the Trinity more accurately. And here is the exact moment in the filmscript:

> There was Andrei—a lad—jumping into a cold, clear lake; hazy pillars slanted down to touch the ghostly bed and lit up quivering, almost pulsating, algae; a startled crucian carp darted away, its gold scales dimly gleaming; a pure, sandy bank rose slowly and brightly from the depths, glistening, rippling with sunlight and water and grey shadows; the long, solitary trail of a bivalve was suddenly intersected by another, identical to it, and then stretched on into the shining warmth of the sun, to the spot where the sand bank almost touched the trembling surface of the lake (like liquid glass) towards which Andrei was swimming, eyes open under the water, arms stretched out, where he caught up with it, carefully picked it out of the sand and held it up to his eyes to watch it hide its tender, defenceless body between its ugly, convulsively clenched shutters. (32–3)

The script is telling us how the director clinches the image through the "convulsively clenched shutters" of the camera. The image is indivisible and elusive, dependent upon our consciousness and the real world that it seeks to embody. If the world is inscrutable, then the image will be so too. It is a kind of equation, signifying the correlation between truth and the human consciousness, bound as the latter is by Euclidean space. We cannot comprehend the totality of the universe, but the poetic image is able to express that totality (Filmscript, p. 106). And later, almost as if Tarkovsky, in the person of one of his young apprentices, is explaining to us, the viewers of his film, how to prepare ourselves for this experience: we have to shut our right eye so that everything we see jumps over to the right. Then we shut both eyes so that everything grows dark, and then we open our left eye to see one person standing in front of us before we open both eyes wide again. We have to scan the screen in front of us: it is all the reality that cinema can provide. And again water is used to explain the authentic experience of cinema itself: The apprentice, Foma, jumps naked into the slow, dark river; his body, heated from running, is embraced by the water, caressed, gently pushed upward from below. He swims underwater with his eyes open. A shoal of fish flash by, darting from one side to the other until eventually halting still "in the dying underwater sunlight." The genuine experience of cinema is similar to stripping ourselves of all pre-conceived ideas, diving under water and engaging in that submerged state with the images which the artist has provoked and which we try to catch in the same atmosphere in which they were originally presented. The "film" on top of the water is the go-between fleshed out in images like fish darting from one end to the other of the lighted square which stands between us. It is a question of purifying our seeing capacity, divesting ourselves of the habitual cognitive shutters which prevent all ocular innocence and preclude any possibility of adopting, even for a moment, the eyes of the artist. The images themselves are the fish we either grasp, as they are, in our hands, or let flow by in blind anonymity. Unless we see the film as it was intended to be seen it remains a wreck sunk under a sea of meaninglessness.

The Bell

The episode which would seem to represent the art of cinema as distinct from all other art forms, including the icon, is the last of the eight entitled "The Bell." Tarkovsky, if he is to be found among the characters in this film, approximates less to Andrei Rublev than to Boriska, the mere boy who is the unlikely and implausible caster of bells. Cinema is more like bell casting than icon writing. Unlike the art of the icon, "bell-casting," Tarkovsky tells us in the filmscript, "is a massive undertaking, teeming with people, involving constant din" (170). The same filmscript also provides descriptions of Boriska in words that suggest Tarkovsky's image of himself at the start of his cinema career. Boriska is at pains to conceal his own lack of confidence. He walks ahead, feeling the suspicious, searching eyes of the artisans upon him, and concentrates on an inexplicable but clear inner voice, which he himself is barely able to make out, telling him how he should behave in the face of difficulty (164). The huge assembly of workers required to produce a bell of this size (and here we can substitute the huge cost of making a film) are all thinking to themselves: "How could the Grand Prince [here read Hollywood or Moscow film] have provided this untried youngster with the finance and the wherewithal to undertake such a massive project" (77). But now the top can be seen above the pit. Slowly, as if unwillingly, swaying majestically, it starts to grow. Laboriously, with unimagined difficulty, the bell rises over the earth (178). The film eventually appears on the screen for the world to see. They wait for the sound for the sake of which they have been working for an entire year, not knowing themselves why they trusted this fanatical boy to produce it (179).

Boriska is the young son of an expert bellmaker. Men have been sent by the prince to search out his father to cast a bell for an important church. The area around his home has been ravaged by plague, the father and his family are dead. Boriska tells them that he is the only one who possesses the secret of bell casting, divulged to him by his father on his deathbed. The men are skeptical, but eventually they take him with them as a last resort and Boriska is put in charge of the project.

Finding the "right clay" is a major concern for Boriska, and his meticulous and obsessional search for such delays the project unconscionably. After seemingly endless search, Boriska trips and falls by accident into the right clay, Fat clay with no impurities, clear clay, malleable, and thick. This is what he has been longing for. He did not know that this was how it looked, he could not have described it to anyone, because he has never seen it, but he knows now for certain that this is precisely the clay that he needs (169). The search for appropriate images is the clay which makes the film. You have to wait until the exact contours take shape, sometimes quite by accident.

The process of making the bell grows into a huge, expensive endeavor with many hundreds of workers, and Boriska makes several risky decisions, guided only by his instincts. As the bell-making nears completion, Boriska's confidence slowly transforms into a stunned, detached disbelief that he has seemingly succeeded in his task. There is a quiet, agonizing tension among the crowd as the foreman slowly coaxes the bell's clapper back and forth, nudging it closer to the lip of the bell with each swing. At the critical moment the bell rings and a sigh of relief goes forth: the bell has sounded perfectly.

After the ceremony, Andrei Rublev finds Boriska in a state of nervous collapse. He confides in Rublev that his father never actually told him the bell-casting secret. It was not a craft passed on from father to son, it was a wild and crazy intuition that he had the makings of it in himself. Andrei comforts Boriska, breaking his vow of silence to do so and suggesting to the boy that they should carry on their work together: "You'll cast bells. I'll paint icons."

Beyond Iconography

The *epilogue* is the only part of the film in color. It shows vibrant details of several icons attributed to Rublev. Black and white cinema, for Tarkovsky, communicates everyday reality; color introduces an aura of fiction. Both the epilogue and the icons are placed beyond the limits of normal filmic functioning. The icon and the iconographer can only be restored to their full significance in an idiom beyond the possibilities of filmic narrative.

Tarkovsky is quite explicit about this. There will not be a single shot of Rublev painting icons in his film. He will not even be present in every scene. He will simply live and life will go on around him. The last episode will not involve the iconographer but will concentrate solely on the icons themselves. These will be shown in color and in detail with a musical background similar to that accompanying those episodes of the artist's life wherein the content and the design of the icons were conceived.[21] Music creates the link between the icons and the biographical episodes in the film.

The effect of this exotic epilogue is to distance the audience, and Tarkovsky himself, from the art of the icon. The narrative of the main film grounds the icons in a temporal reality. Cinema, as opposed to iconography, is more down-to-earth. Tarkovsky seems to distance himself from supernatural intervention in the day-to-day reality of making a film: everyone involved has a huge amount to do which cannot be outsourced to some divine hand. In fact, one gets the impression, from what Tarkovsky writes, that he is not overly impressed by the monastic vocation as such. He certainly distinguishes it from that of the artist. Rublev becomes an artist by leaving his monastery; his character is formed, his vision purified and elevated, by leaving the sheltered haven of the cloister and encountering the lived reality of the world. The art of cinema is fruit of the earth; it requires close involvement with nature and material objects as the artist works close to the bull.

In the same way that Boriska searches the earth for the "right clay," Tarkovsky has to search for the correct image. The image comes from the earth and acts as the intermediary between the director and the viewer. This requires of the image an authenticity, a transparency, a humility.

In this regard, Tarkovsky the cinematographer has been influenced by Robert Bresson. In an interview about his film *Un condamné à mort s'est échappé* [*The Escape of a Prisoner Condemned to Death*] whose subtitle was "The wind blows where it will" Bresson said that he wanted to show "the miracle of an invisible hand over the prison, directing what happens and causing such a thing to succeed for one and not for another. The film, according to Bresson, is a mystery and the Spirit breathes where it will."[22]

But the way a cinematographer "shows" this is not by giving sermons or explaining anything, nor is it by turning the story into a sensational thriller which would attract and entertain a populist audience; the way to accomplish this specific and particular miracle of the cinema is by remaining faithful to, what Eric Rohmer calls, "the miracle of objects." Everything in the film could be explained naturally. The prisoner seems to escape by his own efforts, so much so that, at one point, Bresson was tempted to call it "God helps those who help themselves." However, there is another presence felt throughout the film which never appears but which emanates from the objects, the details, the persons, and especially the images which unfold on the screen. The escape of the prisoner is, in fact, a parable about the escape of each image from its own circumscribed death-cell into another kind of movement and life. The method of such cinematography is "to translate the invisible wind by the water it sculpts in passing."[23]

This last quotation from Bresson shows where Tarkovsky derives his philosophy of "Sculpting in Time." Such cinematography makes certain demands of the audience: A highly compressed film will not yield its best at the first go. People see in it at first what seems like something they have seen before.[24] First viewing of a film could yield the bare outline of a story. The richness and the depth of each image could be reduced to mere channeling of the narrative. Bresson suggests that there should be places where in one quite small, very well-equipped cinema, only one or two films would be shown each year.[25]

Optimal appreciation of Tarkovsky's film might require such a cinema where we could stay with it long enough to no longer need voice-overs or subtitles. If we could experience the images as they unfold and allow them to hitch themselves onto the sprockets of our sensibilities, such immersion would allow us to become the final stage in Tarkovsky's vision of the making of the film: we would become "directors" who would play it in our own lives making it a reality in our own time. Has anyone said that the artist is cleverer than the people in the auditorium? Tarkovsky asks. "It is simply that the poet thinks in images, with which, unlike the audience, he can express his vision of the world."[26] However, if the genuine cinematic experience comes to pass: "The director's experience is conveyed to the audience graphically and immediately, with photographic precision, so that the audience's emotions become akin to those of a witness, if not actually of an author."[27]

In some respects, it is the resulting formation of the viewer's own vision which is the major point of the filmmaking. For Tarkovsky the film is incomplete until it is played accurately on the inner screen of the ideal viewer. Cinema is a vehicle of truth. The artist is trying to the very best of his or her ability and creativity to express such truth. The completion of this vital quest does not occur when the movie is made ready for viewing in a movie theater. The act of creation, Tarkovsky believes, takes place in the auditorium at the time of watching the film. Therefore, the viewer for me is neither my consumer nor a judge but a co-creator.

Notes

1   J. Hoberman, "Andrei Rublev: An Icon Emerges," Review originally written for the Criterion Collection in 1998.

2   Andrei Tarkovsky, *Time Within Time: The Diaries 1970–1986* (London: Faber & Faber, 1994), 122, 74.

3   "Andrei Tarkovsky parle de son film," Interview by L. & J. Schnitzer & M. Ciment conducted in Moscow in July 1969. *Andrei Roublev* (Paris: Editeurs Francais Réunis, 1970), 27.

4   Andrey Tarkovsky, *Sculpting in Time: Reflections on the Cinema*, trans. Kitty Hunter-Blair (London: The Bodley Head, 1986).

5   David Brubaker, "André Bazin on Automatically Made Images," *The Journal of Aesthetics and Art Criticism* 51, no. 1 (Winter, 1993): 59–67.

6   A contemporary artist, Bridget Reilly, paints abstract canvases of vertical stripes or interlocking diamonds. Her aim is to convey to us pure sensation. What you see in a split second out of the corner of your eye before you focus attention and label the experience. She and other contemporary artists claim that we are essentially killers of reality, that the mind destroys; that we look around us as murderers looking for booty or prey; whatever we want to see we frame freeze and gobble into our filing cabinets. We see what we already know. What we call "seeing" is, in fact, reconstruction not just from fragmentary evidence glimpsed quickly as we survey the scene, but from a whole wardrobe of accumulated past experiences which we immediately project onto the unsuspecting identity parade lined up in front of us.

7   Scott Eyman, *The Speed of Sound: Hollywood and the Talkie Revolution 1926–1930* (New York: Simon & Schuster, 1997).

8   Tarkovsky, *Sculpting in Time*, 99.

9   Robert Bresson, *Notes on Cinematography* (New York: Urizen Books, 1977).

10   Andrei Tarkovskii, Komsomolskaia Pravda, September 13, 1962, quoted in Robert Bird, *Andrei Rublev* (London: British Film Institute, 2004), 25.

11   Pavel Florensky, *Iconostasis* (Crestwood, NY: St Vladimir's Seminary Press, 1996), 68.

12   Tarkovsky, *Sculpting in Time*, 80.

13   Andrey Tarkovsky, *Andrei Rublev*, trans. Kitty Hunter-Blair (London: Faber & Faber, 1991), 181. From here onwards this filmscript will be referred to in the text by its page number surrounded by a square bracket.

14   Tarkovsky, *Sculpting in Time*, 107.

15   Bird, *Andrei Rublev*, 41.

16   Tarkovsky, *Sculpting in Time*, 37–41.

17 Ibid., 42.

18 Ibid., 43.

19 Ibid., 65.

20 Ibid., 106.

21 Cf. Bird, *Andrei Rublev*, 42.

22 *The Films of Robert Bresson* (London: Studio Vista, 1969), 68.

23 Bresson, *Notes on Cinematography*, 36.

24 Ibid.

25 Ibid., 65.

26 Tarkovsky, *Sculpting in Time*, 50.

27 Ibid., 177.

24

On Krysztof Kieślowski's
Le Double Vie de Véronique

Joseph G. Kickasola

In an interview, the Polish film director Krzysztof Kieślowski described an elusive goal for all his work:

> The realm of superstitions, fortune-telling, presentiments, intuition, dreams . . . All this is the inner life of a human being, and all this is the hardest thing to film. . . . I'm taking this direction to get as close to this as my skill allows. That's why I don't think *Véronique* betrays anything I've done before. . . . I've been trying to get there from the beginning. I'm somebody who doesn't know, somebody who's searching.[1]

The philosopher Maurice Merleau-Ponty outlined a similar objective in the work of the French painter Paul Cézanne:

> The sense of what the artist is going to say *does not exist* anywhere—not in the things, which as yet have no sense, nor in the artist himself, in his unformulated life. It calls one away from the already constituted reason in which "cultured men" are content to shut themselves, toward a reason which would embrace its origins. To Bernard's attempt to bring him back to human intelligence, Cézanne replied: "I am oriented toward the intelligence of the [79] *Pater Omnipotens*." He was, in any case, oriented toward the idea or project of an infinite Logos. . . . Cézanne's difficulties are those of the first word: He thought himself powerless because he was not omnipotent, because he was not God and wanted nevertheless to paint the world, to change it completely into a spectacle, to make *visible* how the world *touches* us.[2]

On first blush, it's difficult to find a less likely candidate for a "film as philosophy" than Krzysztof Kieślowski's *Le Double Vie de Véronique* (1991). The cinematographer for the film, Sławomir Idziak, describes it as "existing in a fairy tale," flatly stating: "we are dealing with something that is unreal."[3]

Yet, if we look past the surface trappings of the "fairy tale," we see something more philosophically interesting. In alignment with Merleau-Ponty's analysis of Paul Cézanne's work, earlier, Kieślowski uses cinematic invention to express something not so much "unreal" as "pre-realized," that primordial realm before the formulation of clear thoughts, articulations, or concretized "knowledge." Famed for his pursuit of "the truth about the world,"[4] Kieślowski remains committed to that cause, but pursues a different order of "reason which would embrace its origins."

Intuition, the Senses, and the Ground of Epistemology

This chapter explores these concerns via a set of parallels between Merleau-Ponty, a philosopher meditating on Cézanne's art, and some key aesthetic experiences Kieślowski's film engenders. Just as Cézanne's use of distortions, variations, bold colors, and non-perspectival visualizations were conceived as flights *into* "nature" rather than away from it, so, Kieślowski shapes the film as a "meditation" on knowledge at its headwaters.

Indeed, Kieślowski's agnosticism ("I'm somebody who doesn't know") generates his relentless epistemological queries and experientially delivers them: What do we know, how do we know it, and how do we know when we know it? As art, this is not philosophy as "propositions made and defended," but operational philosophy: improving our questions by placing us, the audience, in continual positions of experiential instability, uncertainty, and wonder. This productive doubt leads to an interrogation of our means of knowing anything at all, and the very nature of phenomenality itself.[5] In some ways, this work is also *proto*-philosophical, the observational and evaluative work required for philosophy to function.

Beyond "proto-philosophy," if there is one "argument" that the film puts forth it is that intuitions matter, and our multisensory experiences ground our philosophy.[6] This film puts the audience *through the paces* of encountering philosophical questions and problems as *lived* problems, returning discussion of "intuition" and "the senses" to ground zero, assuming that something critical is retrieved there. Critically, we cinematically experience things "offline," as Gregory Currie has argued.[7] That is to say, experiential truths are often subsumed amid the high stakes of living (e.g., it's difficult to philosophize about fear of nothingness, when one is perched on the edge of an abyss, but cinematic simulations can often offer less vexed, more focused analogues, with claim as experiences themselves). In this way, this film also does what good fairy tales have always done: uses exaggerated figures and narratives to reveal essential dynamics and ideas, experienced in relief.

Three Scenes

This is a modern doppelgänger story: Weronika is born in Poland on the same day that Véronique is born in France, but neither knows of the existence of the other. They look identical, possess comparable histories, suffer from similar maladies, and share a tandem existential restlessness. The first thirty minutes are given to Weronika, her young adult struggles and untimely death from a heart attack, shortly after glimpsing her double from afar. The rest of the film follows Véronique, who senses a disturbance in the universe at the moment of Weronika's death and seeks out the source of this unease. Largely through feeling and intuition, she navigates various situations and perils, including a previously unknown heart condition and a complicated, mysterious new relationship. Much of the dialogue is short and pedestrian, and many scenes move and resonate entirely at the level of the senses, offering sizable invitations to meaning without concrete resolution or conceptual articulation. Three emblematic moments reveal the power of this embodied knowledge: the opening vignettes, the mysterious phone call, and the cassette scene.

Opening Vignettes—Inversions, Distortions, and Other Productive Phenomena

We open on a wondrous image: dark on top, deep blue with red and yellow streaks on bottom, pricks of white all around, subtle movement, left to right. It is difficult to discern what we are seeing, so we must make a choice: we submit to the mystery we are beholding—to apprehend and enjoy form *as form*, sheer phenomena—or we allow ourselves to be frustrated at our lack of ability to "know" and readily "categorize" what we see.

An off-screen voice, speaking Polish, reveals a hint: that the girl has been waiting for a star, to begin Christmas Eve. The film then cuts to an upside-down child, on the lap of her mother, who intones that the haze in the image is not haze, but millions of tiny little stars.

To see more innocently and adventurously, like a child, Kieślowski revisits the site of primal perceptions and early knowledge.[8] For the viewer, having been initially forced to perceive these phenomena without categories, the mother's words carry revelation. According to the New Testament, the Magi searched for the Christ Child by following a bright star.

So, right up front, foundational themes are established and experientially delivered: cosmic phenomena, vital searching, and altered perspective become the quest for knowledge, meaning, and ultimate significance. Like so many others in Kieślowski's films, our twin protagonists will feel they lack something undefined, a spiritual vacuum they will struggle to fill.

The inverted (i.e., new, unorthodox) perspective of the first child is complemented by a different approach. Kieślowski cuts to a second child, Véronique's enormous eye (enlarged through a magnifying glass) dominating the frame. A different maternal voice speaks, this time in French, regarding the first leaf of springtime, and the delicate veins and fine down of its underside.

In the appraisal of esteemed critic Jonathan Romney, this film is "cerebral as well as sensual,"[9] which aligns with Merleau-Ponty's quote from Cézanne, regarding art and nature: "I want to unite them. Art is a personal apperception. I place this apperception in the sensations and I ask intelligence to organize them into a work."[10] Indeed, Merleau-Ponty sees a deep unity here. Dichotomies fail to describe the complete aesthetic to which Cézanne aspires:

> Cézanne did not think he had to choose between sensation and thought, as if he were deciding between chaos and order. He did not want to separate the stable things which appear before our gaze and their fleeting way of appearing. He wanted to paint matter as it takes on form, the birth of order through spontaneous organization. He makes a basic distinction not between "the senses" and "intelligence" but rather between the spontaneous order of perceived things and the human order of ideas and sciences. We perceive things; we agree about them; we are anchored in them; and it is with "nature" as our base that we construct the sciences. Cézanne wanted to paint this primordial world.[11]

These opening scenes of *Véronique* exhibit two primary modes of searching: uncategorized, intuitional, and cosmic perspective ("spontaneous order of perceived things"), complemented by a local, scientific, and microscopic view. Like Merleau-Ponty, the film portrays both approaches as complementary, but insufficient in isolation. Both children also perceive with the aid of their loving mothers (the beginnings of intersubjective, interpretive community) and through various media (through a reflective window, through a magnifying glass). The power of glass is, of course, also a reflexive gesture toward Kieślowski's own cinematic lens, which productively mediates and distorts, building yet another useful "view" that we incorporate into our own experience.

Distorted, hazy, abstract images follow as a joyful choral song emerges on the soundtrack. Amid the opening titles, we glimpse a figure in various forms of unknown activity, amid a flurry of color and movement. We do not yet know that this is a dreamy view of actions to come (a gesture toward predestination or fate). For us, these images are phenomenally present, and therefore "prescient" in us, long before their full significance becomes apparent. Just like Véronique (who witnesses similarly obscured images, later in the film) we are unclear regarding what we see or why it matters, but the experience forms a foundation for our intuitions.

The sequence ends with Weronika singing an extraordinary suspended note, the previously non-diegetic music revealing its truly diegetic nature. Or, perhaps, the music was "real" and "in the world" all along, unbeknownst to us. This elision of future and diegetic present, combined with the miraculous duration of this final pitch (testing the limits of belief), encourages us to adopt an expansive view of time (a "Pater Omnipotens" perspective, perhaps), wherein any moment may be suspended and examined. The instant plays like an aural freeze frame with abiding vitality; the clock has stopped so that time itself might breathe beyond its own typical measures. As some might recognize, this could be what Gilles Deleuze called the "crystal-image," when a bit of time "in the pure state," released from its linkage to movement, is cinematically revealed.[12] This moment marks a liminal position for Weronika, between her transcendent experience of music and all Euclidean measurement. She is challenged to consider their relation, and we must consider if aesthetic experience might reveal truths beyond our typical framing of the world.

Similarly, Cézanne's artistic quest was also philosophical: to find the truth of experience, evaluating shifts in appearances, individual perception, varied perspectives and illusions, and considering phenomena's relation to "reality" (or "nature"). The classic debates regarding ontological realism vs. idealism are hanging about here, of course. However, our focus here is on how Kieślowski and Cézanne put us through the paces of reconciling the unfamiliar and the familiar, the concrete and the fluid, the inverted and the microscopic. This is another way of saying that these artists make us see ourselves seeing and feel ourselves feeling, apart from the everyday demands of perception.

In this light, distortions may be less a deviation from "reality" and more a tool in service of it. Merleau-Ponty traces Cézanne's evolution on this point, as he moved on from Impressionistic technique (which "created a lot of atmosphere, but 'submerged the object and caused it to lose its proper weight'") and pursued "the object" again with all the lessons of Impressionism in tow. "His painting would be a paradox: investigate reality without departing from sensations, with no other guide than the immediate impression of nature, without following the contours, with no outline to enclose the color, with no perspectival or pictorial composition." Indeed, "cups and saucers" swell and expand on Cézanne's painted tables in unusual ways, eschewing perspectival rules, as if he could capture every angle at once.

The work table in his portrait of Gustave Geffroy stretches, contrary to laws of perspective, into the lower part of the picture. By departing from the outline, Cézanne would be handing himself over to the chaos of the sensations. Now, the sensations would capsize the objects and constantly suggest illusions—for example, the illusion we have when we move our heads that objects themselves are moving—if our judgment did not constantly set these appearances straight.[13]

Merleau-Ponty describes this approach (resulting in an "eternal desk," not unlike Weronika's "eternal note") as "being faithful to the phenomena."[14] In the same way Kieślowski—committed to a "deeper rather than broader" exploration of reality[15]—hopes to go deeper into the nature and *meaning* of perception.

The Phone Call—Sight and Sound before Classification

Later in the film after Véronique has quit singing, we see her sleeping; and, yet, the image is barely identifiable as such. Rather, we see patches of light in varying intensities scattered throughout a dark field and concentrated in various patterns. It might be a dark, abstract painting. Not until she moves do we understand it is a close-up of Véronique, hazily illuminated through the curtains on her window.

This initiates a critical scene bolstering the primary themes of sensory experience, intuition, and the search for understanding. The phone rings, Véronique wakes up and answers, heavy breathing is followed by the sudden entrance of music, the very piece she had been teaching her young music students earlier in the film (and, we may recall, that Weronika was performing when she died). As she struggles to understand and the music plays, the film presents a chain of warping, pulsing abstract images, which we (not Véronique) might recognize as Weronika at the moment of her death, against an infernal red background.

It seems this scene visualizes a buried intuition, not quite clear or concrete enough to be called a memory, but vivid enough to carry some weight in Véronique's consciousness. At the level of our present analysis, however, it is also a visualization of the "chaos of sensations" to which Cézanne had to surrender himself, in his quest to perceive more clearly, universally, and "naturally." ("Everything comes to us from nature; we exist through it; let us forget everything else."[16])

Likewise, as we continue to move away from "story" analysis toward phenomenological meditation, Cézanne's artistic wisdom becomes more manifestly present in Kieślowski's images:

> We forget the viscous, equivocal appearances, and by means of them we go straight to the things they present. The painter recaptures and converts into visible objects what would, without him, remain closed up in the separate life of each consciousness: the vibration of appearances which is the cradle of things. Only one emotion is possible for this painter—

the feeling of strangeness—and only one lyricism—that of the continual rebirth of existence.[17]

What Véronique perceives—at the very headwaters of perceiving itself—is another being, another herself. When we study perception, intuition, phenomenology, and epistemology, we necessarily re-engage the question of the subject, the "I" at the root of identity, a theme in the film and an experience for Véronique (and for us!) in this scene.

The Cassette Scene—A Concert of Sense amid the Chaos of Sensations

Véronique receives a mysterious audio cassette in the mail. Alexandre's sound art (present first in the phone call earlier, more explicitly here) bridges two worlds, phenomenologically (for us via cinema, for Véronique through wireless headphones). Kieślowski remains true to her experience, anchoring all the visuals in her location, but sourcing all sounds from the "elsewhere" of the recording. This scene highlights the multisensory nature of perception more than any other, a point which Merleau-Ponty would, no doubt, have appreciated. In discussing the "tactile" appeals of Cézanne's colors, he remarks:

> It is only as a result of a science of the human body that we finally learn to distinguish between our senses. The lived object is not rediscovered or constructed on the basis of the data of the senses; rather, it presents itself to us from the start as the center from which the data radiate. We *see* the depth, the smoothness, the softness, the hardness of objects; Cézanne even claimed that we see their odor.[18]

In addition to clinical synesthesia (wherein a single sensory-perceptual "input" produces a multiple sensory-perceptual output), the last few decades of neuroscience have revealed weaker but critical levels of "multisensory" experience that all human beings experience.[19] As the opening scenes of the film first suggested, and philosopher Shaun Gallagher has articulated, "perception is intermodal from the start."[20] This will prove critical in this scene, but first we should note that Véronique's engagement with the world, and Kieślowski's aesthetic approach, has been multisensory to its core throughout. Véronique generally leads with her senses, and her primary understandings of the world are sensorially directed. Kieślowski complements: the visuals are routinely sumptuous, the sounds unusual and critical, the camera often fixated on her hands, constantly lingering on her restless habits, her subtle movements. Both Weronika and Véronique are constantly touching every available surface, as if on a kind of haptic sojourn. We even have taste and smell evoked at various, unusual points of the film. The dialogue is often far less revealing than the gestures: the determined way Véronique bites the finger that bears the scar of her childhood (a wound she suspects holds more significance than she can fully grasp), or Weronika's proprioceptive confidence (her own body in space) as she skips and slides between pillars in the square amid a tense political protest in the adjoining square.

To return to our scene, as Véronique attends to various mundanities (drinking water, brushing her teeth, etc.), we hear the mysterious audiotape: equally mundane, pedestrian sounds and echoes (creaking doors, a car, things being dropped, open and shut, etc.). This bi-cameral world that is at once marvelous and disconcerting, difficult to describe, but amplifying the central feeling of the film: that two worlds might coexist, or, more tantalizingly, that the present world may be *doubly large* than previously assessed.

Sound and film theorist Michel Chion states that sounds temporalize images along several dimensions (i.e., it gives the image a sense of time). Likewise, sounds naturally tend toward "synchresis" with the image, meaning they weld a cause/effect relation between them regardless of any logical or empirical connection. In addition, the presence of sounds (their recorded "distance" and timbre) can psychologically appear to be coming from a source within the frame or, at least, the immediate diegetic region off-screen even though they clearly are not (a process he calls "spatial magnetization"). In this case, our logical understanding that the sounds are clearly *not* emanating from the frame competes with phenomena we are clearly experiencing. The fact that most ambient noises in Véronique's apartment are absent from the frame only bolsters the synthesis. The result is a "vast extension" of space in the experience (the "superfield"), to the level of the "phantom audio-vision," a term Chion reserves for the extraordinary sound design of filmmaker Andrei Tarkovsky. Chion's description of Tarkovsky's *Sacrifice* might very well apply to Kieślowski's liminal use of sound:

> [O]ne can hear sounds that already seem to come from the other side, as if they're heard by an immaterial ear, liberated from the hurly-burly of our human world. . . . it calls to another dimension, it has gone elsewhere, disengaged from the present. It can also murmur like the drone of the world, at once close and disquieting.[21]

Or, to use Cézanne's language, the sound gives us something like the "Pater Omnipotens" perspective.

So, the bicameral world we inhabit in this scene creates a fascinating aesthetic experience that points to the ways we construct our own world out of the sensory data before us. The "cognitive" question "what is it?" in hearing the sound pairs with the dominant sensory question "how can I engage it?" In developing his important concept of "motor intentionality," Merleau-Ponty argued that the fundamental mode of existing in the world is not "I think" but "I can."[22] We are oriented toward action, and our sensory perceptions are a constant call to active, bodily engagement with the sensory affordances before us. And yet, here the affordances do not cohere in a manner for which our past experience has fully prepared us. This uncanny experience creates a building multisensory perceptual puzzle we desire to solve. The film suggests this "phenomenal education" is a lifelong, never-ending process.

These building cognitive and corporeal tensions climax in a literal explosion on the soundtrack, a stand-in for the eternal "rupture" of our ordinary perceptions that will always recur with every unexplained phenomenon. There are no clues of this other presence, except the slight shake of a handheld camera, a gesture that paradoxically embodies two different cinematic codes: the authenticity of the documentary and the gliding elusive nature of the supernatural. Véronique seizes a magnifying glass, that scientific totem through which her mother first tutored her, and she holds it pensively, uncertain of its efficacy.

Of course, the suggested double-presence in the scene implies Weronika, but given the previous discussion, we see film-philosophic questions have also been raised here, yet again: To what degree is the meaning of sensory experience coextensive with an understanding of the self and others? To what degree does a phenomenon reinforce the idea of phenomenality as "given"?

Conclusion

Kieślowski states this film is "about" what is not straightforward, but critical for our existence:

> The film is about sensibility, presentiments and relationships which are difficult to name, which are irrational. Showing this on film is difficult: if I show too much the mystery disappears; I can't show too little because then nobody understands anything. My search for the right balance between the obvious and the mysterious is the reason for all the various versions made in the cutting room.[23]

Philosophers have spent considerable time thinking about what intuitions are and how they might (or might not) function in relationship to true beliefs. In this light, we might consider *The Double Life of Véronique* to be examples and/or thought experiments regarding different philosophical perspectives, such as Peter van Inwagen's suggestion that intuitions might be, "in some cases, the tendencies that make certain beliefs attractive to us, that 'move' us in the direction of accepting certain propositions without taking us all the way to acceptance."[24] In a more critical mode, we might consider the dangers of "apophenia," the human tendency to draw things into connection and relation, regardless of whether they actually are so.[25]

But applying "concepts" is to see film as primarily a mode of philosophical illustration, and this is not quite what we mean by film *doing the work* of philosophy. We have seen how film may put us through the paces of having intuitions ourselves. In that experience, we discover more about what intuition means and why it matters. It is analogous to detectives returning to the scene of the crime, with the assumption that such a localized, embodied perspective will yield something new and critical, beyond what they have pieced together back at headquarters.

The experience of the film can be an exercise in intuitional practice, embodied meaning, and an interrogation of the role of the senses in the epistemological equation. If one is willing to admit, as some have,[26] that the very experience of the cinema can be a philosophical endeavor, we have an amplified example here for all that experience might yield, and how it might complement more traditional modes of philosophy.

At the end of the film, Véronique returns to the site of her first investigation of the world, the tree outside her home that presumably bore her that first leaf below her magnifying glass. She touches it, of course, as she has relied on sensory means of understanding throughout her life. Her father intuits she is near, and he is full of affection. His love for her remains a constant in a bewildering universe. Definitive answers may not be found here, but the home he has created provides a respite from the vexing questions swirling around Véronique, and a place to renew the search for answers once again. Perhaps the relation—love—is the beginning of the answer to those questions, just as philosophy, etymologically, is "the love of wisdom."

Notes

1   Danusia Stok (ed.), *Kieślowski on Kieślowski* (London: Faber and Faber, 1993), 194.

2   Maurice Merleau-Ponty, "Cézanne's Doubt," in *The Merleau-Ponty Reader*, ed. Ted Toadvine and Leonard Lawlor (Evanston, IL: Northwestern University Press, 2007), 78–9.

3   Yonca Talu, "Interview: Sławomir Idziak," *Film Comment*, January 27, 2017. https://www.filmcomment.com/blog/interview-slawomir-idziak/ (Accessed January 26, 2021).

4   In 1981, Kieślowski wrote a manifesto in which he argued for his artistic vision, a filmmaking that goes "deeper rather than broader," built on the basic "precondition" of "the truth of the world," but reaching beyond the everyday toward "diagnoses that are wiser and more universal." He describes this vision as a necessary extension of the documentary responsibility to "describe reality." Qtd. in Paul Coates, *The Red and the White: The Cinema of the People's Poland* (London: Wallflower Press, 2005), 212.

5   On "phenomenality itself," the interested reader might consider the works of Jean-Luc Marion (e.g., *Being Given: Toward a Phenomenology of Givenness* [Stanford: Stanford University Press, 2002]).

6   See Mark Johnson, *The Body in the Mind: The Bodily Basis of Meaning, Imagination, and Reason* (Chicago, IL: University of Chicago Press, 1987),

and *The Meaning of the Body: Aesthetics of Human Understanding* (Chicago, IL: University of Chicago Press, 2012).

7   Gregory Currie, *Image and Mind. Film, Philosophy, and Cognitive Science* (New York: Cambridge University Press, 1995), 146–8, 158. Currie's Simulation hypothesis has proven influential, but has been critiqued as incomplete. One relevant supplement to Currie's ideas is the Embodied Simulation account of neuroscientist Vittorio Gallese and film scholar Michele Guerra. The discovery of "mirror neurons" (by Gallese and others) jump-started this whole approach to the arts. See "Embodying Movies: Embodied Simulation and Film Studies," *Cinema: Journal of Philosophy and Moving Images* 3 (2012): 183–210. http://cjpmi.ifilnova.pt/3-contents (Accessed February 14, 2021).

8   I argue elsewhere this strategy amounts to something like Edmund Husserl's famous phenomenological "epoché," a method for truly bracketing away the ordinary way of seeing and perceiving "the things themselves." See Joseph G. Kickasola, *The Films of Krzysztof Kieślowski: The Liminal Image* (New York: Continuum, 2004), ch. 2.

9   Jonathan Romney, "La Double Vie de Véronique," *Sight and Sound* (March 1992): 43. He refers to the adventurous French filmmaker Alain Resnais (e.g., *Hiroshima, Mon Amour,* and *Last Year at Marienbad*).

10 Ibid., 72–3.

11 Ibid.

12 Gilles Deleuze, *Cinema 2: The Time-Image* (Minneapolis, MN: University of Minnesota Press, 1985), 82, 169. This intriguing moment doesn't completely fit the "crystalline" descriptor, as cause and effect or the ordinary sense of temporal duration has not been completely renounced. However, one need not subscribe to Deleuze's ontology to see the value of his cinematic typology. After all, Deleuze's comprehensive philosophy of time is slightly at odds with (and truncated in) his writing on cinema, as James Williams has noted (*Gilles Deleuze's Philosophy of Time: A Critical Introduction and Guide* [Edinburgh: Edinburgh University Press, 2011], chapter 7).

13 Ibid., 72–3.

14 Ibid., 73–4. There is a fascinating paradox here, regarding the cinema. Merleau-Ponty says: "By remaining faithful to the phenomena in his investigations of perspective, Cézanne discovered what recent psychologists have come to formulate; the lived perspective, that of our perception, is not a geometric or photographic one. In perception, the objects that are near appear smaller, those far away larger, than they do in a photograph, as we see in the cinema when an approaching train gets bigger much faster than a real train would under the same circumstances. To say that a circle seen obliquely is seen as an ellipse is to substitute for our actual perception the schema of what we would have to see if we were cameras. In fact, we see a form which oscillates around the ellipse without *being* an ellipse." In this light, the heavily stylized cinematography here is a distinct move *away* from the "ordinary" filmic and *toward* the radically phenomenal.

15 Coates, ibid.

16 Merleau-Ponty, ibid., 72.

17 Ibid., 77.

18 Ibid., 75.

19 See Stein, Barry E., *The New Handbook of Multisensory Processing* (Cambridge, MA: MIT Press, 2012). For more on multisensory perception in media, see Joseph G. Kickasola, "Metaphor without an Answer: Cross-Modal Experience and Embodied Meaning in the Cinema," in *Embodied Metaphors in Film, Television, and Video Games: Cognitive Approaches*, ed. Kathrin Fahlenbrach (London: Routledge, 2016).

20 See *How the Body Shapes the Mind* (Oxford: Oxford University Press, 2005). Many of Gallagher's arguments regarding *prenoetic* structuring elements of perception and experience could be said to be exemplified in this film.

21 Michel Chion, *Audio-Vision: Sound on Screen* (New York: Columbia University Press, 1994), 123–4. The other ideas are found on 13, 63–70, 87, and 150.

22 Merleau-Ponty, Maurice, *Phenomenology of Perception*, trans. C. Smith (Routledge, London 2002), 158–9.

23 Stok (ed.), ibid., 173.

24 Van Inwagen, Peter, 1997, "Materialism and the Psychological-Continuity Account of Personal Identity," *Philosophical Perspectives*, 11, 309. Originally cited here: Pust, Joel, "Intuition," *The Stanford Encyclopedia of Philosophy* (Summer 2019 Edition), Edward N. Zalta (ed.). https://plato .stanford.edu/archives/sum2019/entries/intuition/ (Accessed January 28, 2021).

25 For a fascinating—and harrowing—take on apophenia and the Q-Anon phenomenon, see Reed Berkowitz, "A Game Designer's Analysis of QAnon: Playing with Reality," https://medium.com/curiouserinstitute/a-game-designers -analysis-of-qanon-580972548be5 (Accessed February 19, 2021).

26 See David Sorfa, "What is Film-Philosophy?" *Film-Philosophy* 20 (2016): 1–5. See also, Thomas E. Wartenberg, *Film as Philosophy* (London: Routledge, 2007), and Robert Sinnerbrink, *New Philosophies of Film: Thinking Images* (London: Continuum, 2011).

25

On Quentin Tarantino's
The Hateful Eight

Matthew Clemente

Not long ago, America's finest filmmaker got himself into a bit of hot water with the Twitter crowd for stating the obvious: today's superhero movies are entertaining, but they are not works of art.[1] One need not spill ink to convey such banal points (though, of course, in our age of imagined grievance and kneejerk offense, Scorsese was forced to defend this unobjectionable position with an op-ed in the *Times*). It is apparent to every thinking person that the clean, neat, Good versus Evil cosmos of the comic book has little to do with human life and thus little to do with art. Cinema, on the other hand—the real thing, the world opened up before us on the canvas of the screen—speaks by showing us ourselves. It is not, like the pellet dispenser in the gerbil's cage, a mechanism for feeding our desires, but a mirror that reveals them, a vivisection of the heart. That's not to say there is anything wrong with mere entertainment. Wish-fulfillment has its place too. Just don't call it what it's not. Old Tennessee whiskey might get you as tight as WhistlePig 15 Year Rye, but only one is worth sipping.

Now, there are filmmakers who use their art to both entertain and reveal—Scorsese happens to be a master of the genre—but few are capable of sating our lust for spectacle while also compelling us to reflect upon it. One such rare beast is Quentin Tarantino. Often chided for his overreliance on the grotesque, Tarantino stages carnivals of cruelty in which scene after bloodsoaked scene of violence, meanness, and depravity are paraded past. His films are festivals of objectification and power. In them the lust for dominance and its logical consequence—the destruction of the human form—is put on full display. Yet like children who, with puerile minds, take as literal the tale of babies arriving by stork, those who fix their gaze on whatever flashes across the screen fail to see the symbol behind the art. If Tarantino's works are brutal, they are brutally honest. The malice depicted therein is not reserved for "mean bastards," as John Ruth the Hangman is wont to say. It is the malice of our own hearts, the sadism characteristic of even the most refined among us.

Take, for instance, the unforgettable scene from *Inglourious Basterds* in which Donny Donowitz, an American soldier who has earned for himself the nickname "Bear Jew" because of the ruthlessness with which he kills Nazis, clubs a German officer to death with his Louisville Slugger. For audiences raised on *Band of Brothers* and *Saving Private Ryan*, there is something particularly satisfying about watching an American—one of Jewish descent no less—turn the tables on a medal-wearing member of Hitler's *Wehrmacht*. (Indeed, the scene is reminiscent of Upham's revenge at the end of Spielberg's great epic and it elicits a similar response.) We applaud as Donowitz makes a victim of this victimizer and turns his baseball bat—symbol of American goodness itself—into the instrument of his righteous anger. He bashes the Nazi in the head, whacking him again and again as crimson blood spatters across the screen and audiences go wild. We cheer more raucously, with more enthusiasm and more delight, than the Basterds themselves, reveling in the glory of justice attained, the beauty of evil undone, a vile wrong set right again.

But wait. What exactly are we cheering? What fills us with such mirth? Is it really the clubbing to death of an unarmed man? A man who has surrendered his weapon and is on his knees before his executioners, utterly unable to defend himself? Is that who we are? People who applaud such savagery? Who revel in the pitiless murder of a defenseless man? Do we celebrate war crimes? Do we rejoice in torture and excruciating death? Isn't that what Nazis do? Aren't they the ones who take pleasure in such barbarism, who savor the taste of their victims' blood? Something is wrong. Something is horribly wrong. Are we . . . just like the Nazis? Enemies to our fellow men? Perpetrators of the cruelest injustice? No. Shun the thought. For, if we allow ourselves some small modicum of pleasure at the bludgeoning to death of a Nazi that is only because he is a Nazi and we know he deserves it. We would never, never enjoy watching such cruelty inflicted upon an innocent victim (say, a child, the son of a wanted man—let's call him Smitty Bacall—who is forced to watch his father die at the hands of a freed slave-turned-bounty hunter. No, none of us would want to see that).

This technique of showing viewers what we are by giving us what we want is at the heart of all of Tarantino's films. But nowhere is it more evident than in his 2015 anti-Western *The Hateful Eight*. The movie opens with the image of a snow-covered cross, its frostbitten god fixed to it with nails and forgotten in the desolate Wyoming expanse. That hanged man—icon of the eternal scapegoat, stand-in for every nameless victim—will soon be replaced by a character nicknamed "the Hangman" (Kurt Russell's John Ruth), a bounty hunter whose job it is to fashion more crosses, bury more bodies in unmarked graves. But before he is supplanted, the god of the cross is, for a brief moment, joined by the man of the gallows. The two meet at a deserted crossroads, one pinned up like a signpost along the way, the other rattling past in a horse-drawn wagon. The former left out in the cold, waiting with open arms, the latter shackled to his prisoner, brandishing a pistol in each hand. John Ruth, we soon learn, is on his way to Red Rock. He is transporting a notorious criminal—Daisy Domergue (Jennifer Jason Leigh)—whom he intends to hand over to the executioner. Rambling past the frosted image of the spotless victim and yet failing to see it, Ruth descends into Tarantino's snowy wasteland never to meet the hanged man again. (That the objective correlative being employed here is reminiscent of Eliot's inferno is, I think, no accident.)[2]

John Ruth's stagecoach is being chased through the tundra by a blizzard which functions thematically as a hellhound on his trail, pushing him further into the icy depths of a Dantean hell. He is stopped along the way, however, by Major Marquis Warren (Samuel L. Jackson), a bounty hunter and Civil War veteran who fought alongside other emancipated Blacks during America's time of bitter fratricide. Ruth and Warren, we soon learn, know one another and have previously bonded over an artifact in Warren's possession, a letter written to him by the president of the United States, Abraham Lincoln. At this point, I will turn my attention away from summarizing the film—interested readers will have either seen it or ought to—and focus instead on the import of the Lincoln letter.

The letter, we come to find out, is a fraud, a deception devised by Warren in order to ingratiate himself to his white neighbors. It is, we might say, a *noble lie* (cf. Plato's *Republic*), an untruth told in the service of truth, a falsehood used to safeguard truth itself. "The only time black folks is safe," Warren explains, "is when white folks is disarmed. And this letter had the desired effect of disarming white folks." The Lincoln letter, Warren suggests, is a lie told to counteract the lie of racism, the lie of bigotry, the lie that would represent him as less human than his white interlocutors. In that sense, the audience is, I think, ready to commend it. When facing a scourge as pernicious and entrenched as racism in America—a place where human beings were literally bought and sold like cattle, where the amount of degradation suffered by human persons at the hands of human persons nauseates the stomach and boggles the mind—use whatever means necessary. Lies, deceptions, the sword. Do what works. Do what it takes.

Yet part of what is at stake in *The Hateful Eight*, it seems to me, is the question of whether or not we still see the value of such noble lies; whether, that is, we desire the (flimsy to be sure) ceasefire such lies procure or prefer to live in a world devoid of illusions—and, supposing the latter, what follows when our illusions are torn down? That the lie in question comes in the form of a letter supposedly authored by Abraham Lincoln, sent to a man whom some would prefer to see in chains, is suggestive. In the first place, it pushes us to question the integrity of other Lincoln letters, particularly those written to former slaves, the Emancipation Proclamation most of all. If one Lincoln letter could turn out to be a lie, a deception used to disarm hostile white folks, why not others—especially those as convincing to us as the film's letter is to John Ruth?

This suspicion seems to be supported by passages found in certain genuine Lincoln letters. Consider, for instance, the president's correspondence with newspaperman Horace Greeley. In one letter, written over a year after the outbreak of the Civil War, Lincoln expresses the desire to leave no doubt about the policy his administration is pursuing.

> My paramount object in this struggle is to save the Union, and is not either to save or to destroy slavery. If I could save the Union without freeing any slave I would do it, and if I could save it by freeing all the slaves I would do it; and if I could save it by freeing some and leaving others alone, I would also do that. What I do about slavery and the colored race, I do because I believe it helps to save this Union; and what I forbear, I forbear because I do not believe it would help to save the Union.

The student of history will no doubt remember that the Emancipation Proclamation was an executive order made under Lincoln's authority as "Commander-in-Chief," that is, a wartime declaration that eliminated slavery in the secessionist south but not necessarily in the Union-controlled north. (The text itself makes clear that it is merely a "war measure for suppressing . . . rebellion" and goes on to specify which states and territories must adhere to its dictates.) As such, it had as much to do with handicapping the so-called Confederacy as it did with securing the liberty of enslaved Blacks. What is more, the Proclamation includes an offer to those whom it claims to liberate: all freed slaves of "suitable condition" are encouraged to join the Union Army. (I leave it to the reader to interpret this as he will.)

Taking the obvious strategic benefits of the Proclamation along with Lincoln's own assurances to Greeley into consideration, it is fair to wonder how much truth there is in the conventional view of Lincoln as "the Great Emancipator." There is, of course, nothing particularly original in the foregoing discussion. Others have questioned the hagiography of Lincoln and have done so with greater depth and nuance than I. What I am interested in, however, is not whether the myth of Lincoln—or, for that matter, our other culture myths: the myth of the American founding, the myth of the American Dream, the myth of the Greatest Generation, and so on—is true. The question posed by Tarantino's *The Hateful Eight* is whether or not such myths are necessary. Or, said differently, what happens when we no longer hold these "truths" to be self-evident but see them for what they really are— useful lies?

We live at a time of toppling statues, when past ideals have proved to be idols and none holds up to scrutiny. For many, it is an expectant time. Revolution is in the air. The future is pregnant with possibility. ("If a temple is to be erected *a temple must be destroyed*," as the prophet of Sils Maria rightly declares.)[3] Yet Tarantino asks us to pause and consider what comes next. Sure it is fun to smash things, but where does all of that smashing get us? In answer to this question, Tarantino—in classic Tarantino fashion—gives us what we want, the destruction of the noble lie, and then shows us who we are without it.

Well. Who are we without it? It is worth noting that while the film includes depictions of extreme violence throughout, it does not present any of the near-dozen murders that take place therein until after Warren's letter is revealed to be a lie. It is as if that revelation tears down the fragile veneer of civility and allows barbarism to break through. After the lie is shown to be a lie, the "frontier justice" of which Oswaldo Mobray (Tim Roth) speaks so eloquently earlier in the film—a form of justice which is "very thirst quenching" but "apt to be wrong as it is right"—takes over. Warren provokes and murders General Sanford Smithers (Bruce Dern)—we see in horrific detail the execution of Smithers's son as well—John Ruth drowns in his own blood after being poisoned, people are indiscriminately shot, Daisy Domergue's brother surrenders his weapons only to take a bullet through the head, and the film ends with a Hamletesque bloodbath in which Domergue herself is hung by Warren and Confederate Lost Causer Chris Mannix (Walter Goggins), both of whom have been mortally wounded and are on the verge of death.

The hanging of Domergue by the neck is savage, as brutal as it is unnecessary. There is something particularly unsettling about watching two men revel in the murder of a woman. And yet, as we said before, to fixate on the spectacle is to miss the point. It is not the *presentation* of violence that matters, but the violence itself—a violence which, the film suggests, is always lurking just beneath the surface of civilized life. What constitutes the surface? What holds the violence at bay? After Domergue breathes her last breath, Mannix, the white Confederate, and Warren, the emancipated Black, share a final laugh. Mannix reads the Lincoln letter out loud and compliments the subtle touches that lend it the feel of authenticity; Warren smiles in exhaustion, no longer needing to live the lie. The truth has freed them from their hatred. It has enabled them to bridge the bitter divide. But what truth exactly? That the ceasefire won by Lincoln was unsustainable, incapable of reconciling those forced to live in the shadow of the noble lie? Perhaps. And perhaps something more too. Perhaps, with the corpse of Domergue still hanging from the ceiling, it is the realization that if we continue to mock and dismantle the lies needed to disarm hangmen like John Ruth, we will become the hangmen who replace them. Perhaps it is a warning that we are dangerously close to exchanging lies for persons, scapegoats whose deaths we use to secure the foundations of civilized life (cf. René Girard). That frostbitten god hasn't been left behind after all. He suffers and dies again and again in the dying, those whose lives we callously snuff out.

Notes

1   I am deeply indebted to my friend, colleague, and editor Jamieson de Quincey without whose works and wisdom this essay would not exist.

2   Cf. *The Waste Land*, particularly lines 54–55. Indeed, the connections to the poem are hard to miss; the name of Red Rock, for instance, is a direct reference.

3   Friedrich Nietzsche, *On the Genealogy of Morals*, trans. Walter Kaufmann (New York: Vintage, 1989), 95.

26

On Wes Anderson's
The Royal Tenenbaums

John Fardy

I have a rule that I never go to the cinema to see the same movie twice. Like most things we claim to hold dear, it's more of a habit that after years of repetition has evolved into a rule. It probably goes back to childhood and those vivid memories of going to see *The Empire Strikes Back* or the first *Superman* with Christopher Reeves and the sheer delight of imagined worlds transporting me from my dull 1980s Dublin childhood. It was such a special treat that the idea of using that treat to see something you'd already seen simply didn't compute and I guess that lingers today.

I can't actually be sure what the first film I ever saw in the cinema was but the first memory I can grab a hold of was going to see *The Spaceman and King Arthur's Court* with my father and brother. The film is actually an adaptation of Mark Twain's *A Connecticut Yankee in King Arthur's Court* and tells of an astronaut and his android double who travel back to the time of King Arthur. It's a pretty ordinary movie and hasn't aged well. But I was only five and delighted to be in the cinema and more delighted to be with my father. My parents had separated when I was a baby and my father used to "come and go" as was said in the parlance of the day. Days out with him were rare and treasured. At the time the movie was a delight. Now that might seem like a bit of an "over-share" when I'm supposed to be telling you about my favorite movie. But my first memory of going "anywhere" with my father was to the cinema.

I present the weekly film and TV show on the Irish National Radio station Newstalk and I talk to a lot of people about their favorite movies. What seems to motivate the majority of most choices is the time in a person's life when they saw a particular movie. Story, actors, themes, director are obviously always important, but they seem to be often secondary to the time or memory of seeing the film. One actress swore by *Casablanca* not simply because of its gorgeous story and its one iconic scene after another. But mostly because she first saw it when her grandmother let her stay off school to watch it and proclaimed that nothing she would learn in school that day would rival what she would see on the screen that day. There's logic to that which I find hard to argue with. Or the broadcaster who saw *Dead Poets Society* at fourteen and proceeded to record the audio of the film onto a cassette and walk around listening to the words all day. Then there was the comedian who watched *Spinal Tap* everyday for years to the point that his parents were worried about him. Movies hit us like music often does and often we can give only partial explanations for why we love them. There are often reasons that simply run so deep it's hard to articulate. They speak to us in a way that we may not even be aware of.

That's a long but necessary preamble to me declaring Wes Anderson's *The Royal Tenenbaums* as my favorite film. It is the only film that I can remember ever actively wanting to see again in the cinema and bringing my best mate with me the second time telling him that he simply had to see it. If memory serves he enjoyed it but not to the point of my subsequent obsession.

When I first saw *Tenenbaums* I was at the stage of life that you might call "transition." I had just returned from six months in Toronto. The original sojourn was meant to be longer but a love affair had turned south and I found myself back in the Old sod. I was out of work and figuring out my next move in life. I was in my mid-twenties and was by no means out of luck or on the scrap heap. Nonetheless I knew it was the time of life to start making a fist of things. But I guess I still needed a little more time to take the next step on the ladder.

It was in this mood of part hope and part melancholia that I cobbled together what little money I had to go and see *Tenenbaums* knowing only that I liked Anderson's other two movies and loved Bill Murray.

And this contradictory mood of hope and a little glumness that I found myself occupying is the mood that pervades Anderson's masterpiece. The movie centers on the multitalented three Tenenbaum children who in early life showed incredible aptitude for theater, tennis, and business, respectively. They were schooled and enabled in their endeavors by their devoted mother Etheline who is played superbly by Angelica Houston. They were a family of child geniuses who by their early middle adulthood had somewhat squandered their incredible early promise and their lives have stalled. Richie (Owen Wilson) was a tennis pro who was on the way to Wimbledon glory but "choked" at a key moment and left tennis behind. (He literally takes off his shoes and socks on Centre Court and abandons the match!) Margo, played by Gwyneth Paltrow, was writing plays since childhood but at the time of the movie hasn't written anything in seven years. Chaz played by Ben Stiller is a shrewd financier and has been running companies since he was a child. But now his life is in turmoil since the death of his wife and he is in a pressure cooker of tension as he tends to his own two young children. At the time of seeing, although I wasn't claiming to be a prodigy or genius who had come unstuck, I really fell for this idea of "stalled" lives.

Much of the Tenenbaum siblings' problems can be traced back to their mercurial yet charismatic father "Royal," played by Gene Hackman. He left the household during their early adolescence and has seen little of them since. However now falling on hard times he conducts a plan to re-enter their lives. Initially the plan seems motivated simply so he can survive, but ultimately he comes to help his children reclaim their lives. Yet this is no sentimental tale.

On some superficial level (or perhaps a little deeper) I've divided the world into the people who love *Tenenbaums* and those who simply "don't get it." If you were in my company for any length of time and the subject of film came up it wouldn't be long before conversation rolled around to your feelings for *Tenenbaums*. If you didn't like it, it's likely we'd probably not discuss cinema again should we meet. Those who don't get it are completely entitled not to, but I do see that as a failure of imagination, if I'm honest. The movie exists in a slightly different sphere to most others. (I would call it a "cult-classic" but there's always something vaguely disparaging about that term that seems to imply there's something slightly "off" with the movie. Plus the film may have been too popular to be considered such.)

I remember being in the company of a famous Irish actor who said that the director who he was working with had his own "cinematic language." I remember thinking that it was the most pretentious nonsense I'd ever heard and thinking that the Hollywood parties he had been attending for a while had gone to his head. But as, I think it was, Jacques Brel said "we're always in danger of becoming the thing we claim to hate" and I find myself now telling you that Wes Anderson has his own Cinematic Language and nowhere is he more fluent in that language than in *The Royal Tenenbaums*.

What first strikes you when you watch *Tenenbaums* is its vaguely magic-realist quality. Are they the streets of New York or some imagined New York? The film was shot in New York but it's more some imagined New York–like place. The only traffic we ever really see are these strange gypsy cabs that pass up and down the street and are always available for pick-ups. The house the *Tenenbaums* call home seems like a raucous art-deco pile on some upper eastside Corner but looks just slightly too odd for even New York.

The movie also purposefully feels like a book; along with prologues and chapter headings, it actually begins with someone in a library borrowing a book called *The Royal Tenenbaums*, complete with a dust jacket for the movie you are about to watch. This clever act of self-reference doesn't seem to be some kind of postmodern statement about not knowing the book from the movie but rather just a way for Anderson to create his own world with its own internal logic.

Anderson has now become so stylized a filmmaker that there is a recent book that details pictures of houses and buildings around the world that look like they belong in Anderson movies!

The music is also other worldly with a harpsichord version of The Beatles' "Hey Jude." The clothes are also of a type. Chaz, despite being wildly wealthy, spends much of the movie dressed in a tracksuit as do his two children, while Royal holds cigarette holders. Margot wears a fur coat for most of the movie and has eyes made up that look like nothing you've ever seen. Richie's tan suit and headband evoke a tennis player having some kind of crisis of confidence. Such was the fondness for the fashion in the movie that the styles could be seen being aped on Fall Runways in the following year.

It also seems somewhat "out of time"; it's hard to tell when it's set and may not actually be set at any particular time. Sometime in the mid- to late twentieth century seems about as close as we can posit. Every stylistic choice combines to give this slightly ethereal quality; it's real but only just.

Nothing is wasted in the movie; not one camera angle or one choice of music or one word of dialogue. There's no wasted meat on the bones of the movie anywhere and this is where it's magic lies. So complete is it's style and the fact that it's such a fully realized movie means that it "feels" like nothing else I've ever seen.

A recurrent motive in Wes Anderson movies is the absent or missing or downright shoddy father and Tenenbaums dials that up to the max. Anderson said that Bill Murray is so regularly cast in his movies because he seems like a cool dad or a Dad his generation would love to have as their own father. Anderson wrote the character of Royal specifically for Hackman despite Hackman pleading with him not to do that. But the strength of the material won out and Hackman had his head turned. And as a wayward father Hackman is brilliant. Having found his way back into the family home he takes his grandsons to a dog fight. He constantly introduces his daughter Margo who is adopted as his "adopted" daughter. He fibs his way back into the house by claiming he has cancer. But he is also world-weary and almost unbeknownst to himself is seeking redemption in the family he abandoned.

If Tolstoy is right and every family is indeed tragic in its own unique way, then the Tenenbaums are getting their fair share of burdens. Richie's tennis career and his life has become so dysfunctional because he's in love with his sister, albeit his adopted sister, Margo. Margo in turn is also lost; possibly for the same reason and also due to her strained relationship with her father. She is currently married to a brilliant but dull neurologist played by Anderson regular Bill Murray. Chaz is a widower who's struggling to come to terms with the death of his wife. To add further fuel to the filial fire there is Eli Cash who is a neighbor of the Tenenbaums since childhood who has in essence lived at their house most of his life. Now grown up to be a successful novelist he longs to be a Tenenbaum and has begun an affair with Margo. He also has a drug problem to boot.

But all this tragedy is firmly wound in comedy and to my mind no movie has ever quite rode the line between comedy and tragedy so coherently and entertainingly. "Dramedy" is what I've heard many writers and directors claim for their work in twenty-first-century TV and movies but none do it as well as *Tenenbaums*. Much of the humor in the movie comes from Royal's observing his now adult children and how they are making their way in the world and his poor sensitivity to their problems and pains. While taking the children to visit his mother's grave he's reminded of Chaz's deceased wife being in the same cemetery and he merrily says, "well, we better swing by her grave too" much to Chaz's disdain.

But there's also tremendous warmth to the movie as the three Tenenbaum siblings all decide that they will return to the family home. With Royal now also back in the bosom of the family nest there's a glorious feeling of safety as the children and Dad attempt to heal their wings back in the house that spawned them.

Favorite movies tend to occupy a space in your brain where they somehow allow scenes to randomly pop into your mind unbidden at the most unexpected of times, and *Tenenbaums* is laced with those; Margo getting off the Greenline bus in slow motion while "These Days" by Nico plays mournfully, as Richie stares at his sister desperately in love and desperately terrified. Or the sight of Royal taking his grandkids on a larceny-ridden tour of the city which involves them stealing milk from a convenience store or riding on the back of Trash Lorries. And, as grim as a list it is to top, the movie contains perhaps the most effecting suicide scene ever committed to celluloid when Richie, unable to manage his troubling feelings for his sister and spurred on by details of her previous lovers, courtesy of a private investigator, attempts an act of serious self-harm that you're not quite sure is happening at first and all against the doleful tune of Elliot Smith's "Needle in the Hay"—who himself died in an apparent suicide three years after the film.

As the movie moves toward its end with the Tenenbaums trying to repair their brokenness, the film comes to a head on Etheline's wedding day to her new husband. But as it's a Tenenbaum event there's trouble. There's a car crash and the death of a treasured pet. Characters like Eli and Chaz openly break down and admit that they need help.

But the true climax of the movie comes just after these events on the wedding day in the form of a wish-fulfillment for Anderson and perhaps lots of young men who see it today. Royal manages to replace the dead dog for Chaz's sad sons. Chaz tells his somewhat reformed father that "we've had a rough year" and Royal puts a hand on his shoulder and says, "I know you have, Chazy." Those simple words represent the rapprochement between father and son that all Anderson fans secretly long for. Chief among them is me. For a young man in his mid-twenties trying to figure out life, the movie spoke to me in a way none ever has and continues to do so. Perhaps I haven't fully explained why but maybe that's the point of a favorite movie.

My own stalled life that I mentioned when I first saw *Tenenbaums* didn't take long to find a path again. Way lead onto way and I grew up. But despite some level of maturity and responsibility *Tenenbaums* still casts a spell.

With that responsibility has come the arrival of my own little "royal" family. One of the delights of being a father to three small kids is bringing them to the cinema and also showing them my own favorite movies. The oldest is only eight so I haven't shown him *Raging Bull* or anything like that. But I have loved him watching *Star Wars*, and indeed *Superman* with him, as well as his own contemporary blockbusters like *Avengers Endgame*. Some day way down the line I'll show him *Tenenbaums*. Hopefully he'll like its rye style and charm but maybe not to the same extent as me. All going to plan he won't have as much need for the figure of the missing and returning father who makes amends.

27

On Persichetti, Ramsey, and Rothman's
Spider-man

Anne M. Carpenter

Spider-man: Into the Spider-verse is a confrontation with self, with being a self in the world: that is, with what it means to arrive at an autonomy that realizes that "autonomy decides what autonomy is to be."[1] The film brings its audience to an alternate New York, one of many in a multi-verse, and it poses as its problem what it means to "wear the mask" of the superhero Spider-man. Through narrative action, through visual vocabulary rooted in comic books, and through physical action, *Into the Spider-verse* articulates Miles Morales's confrontation with himself, and his decision of what he is to be. This chapter focuses on the nature of Miles's confrontation, on the vision of the self that is presented through the various media of the film. And in that technique is a curious and illuminating complexity, which is that Miles is a multiracial character in a city of dense diversity; this is significant for the film's intended audience, but not—in terms of the action—for Miles himself. In other words, Miles himself is not asked to articulate himself *for* himself despite his race, and in this sense the film poses in its fiction a world without the barrier of race. But such a world is not so for the film's real-world audience, in which race is engrained. Miles *to the audience* is a racialized figure, and that he is not so to himself renders the film a kind of revelation: of the autonomous self concealed in the real world by race, especially the autonomous self of the person of color, and of the concealing of self in the first place that race effects. Thus for *Into the Spider-verse* becoming oneself is, at its outermost limit, the eruption of race and the emergence of free responsibility.

The Art of Being a Self

The creative team behind *Into the Spider-verse* deliberately mimicked comic book layouts in their CG animation. One of their major decisions involved recreating the look of (Ben-Day) dot-printed pages, which would have been the coloring method deployed in the decade of Spider-man's first appearance in *Amazing Fantasy* no.15 in 1961. Dot-printing uses closely placed dots to effect various shades, allowing for primary and, through overlapping, some secondary colors. The animation team imitated the way color offsets in the old dot-printing method sometimes become misaligned, resulting in shades and shadows in the wrong places in a kind of halo-effect. Danny Dimian, the film's visual effects supervisor, explains: "we splintered and offset the image in a way that is similar to a misprint. [. . .] it creates this illusion that something is printed on the screen."[2] Similarly, the team emulated the stark contrasts of vibrant colors and deep darks common to comic books from the 1960s and today. This vibrancy comes from a tradition of hand-drawing in comics, with two different artists performing the tasks of drawing lines and of coloring, respectively. Imitating hand-drawn effects in the film involved fighting the way computer animation is designed to work, which is smoothly, accurately, and realistically, through complex simulation software. Dean Gordon, the film's art director, describes their decisions in terms of shapes and colors: "We worked on painting textures that are less naturalistic, definitely more abstract. [. . .] We worked to get away from soft transitions between colors and values, which is what computers naturally do. In our artwork we broke down colors and values into defined shapes with short or no transitions to give them a more illustrative feel."[3] Thus, rather than effecting realism, the film's artists worked to effect the "feel" or experience of drawing, and not just any drawing, but the drawing techniques common to comic books, with their vividly contrasting colors and stylized shapes.

Emphasizing the work as "drawn" instead of as what it was, which was computer-generated, extended to the action and motion of the film. As a first layer, working in an animated environment allowed the artists to "break" physics in ways impossible to a live-action film but far closer to the universe of drawn comic books.[4] They extended this notion into the way the animation articulated the motions of the characters, so that any pause of the screen would reveal an image that looked drawn.[5] Their most notable effort here was the elimination of motion blurs, which is normally how CG animation transitions between quick character positions. Instead, they animated multiple images to serve as in-between positions, and rendered the backgrounds more abstractly, the latter of which is a commonly drawn technique to evoke movement on a static page.[6]

For the makers of *Into the Spider-verse*, the decision to imitate hand-drawn comic books is more than an effort at homage. Justin K. Thompson, the film's production designer, indicates the way that the plot of the film pulls together the basic connection between the everyday struggles of comic book readers and the "heightened" stakes of comic book heroes, which are world-altering.[7] In Miles Morales's case, the mundane or everyday question of who he wants to be runs directly into the problem of superpowers and a particle collider that will destroy Brooklyn. "Who am I?" blooms, backdropped by extreme risk and, since Miles's decisions doubly determine who he is and the fate of his neighborhood, the question of selfhood also becomes decisively one of risk.

The color palettes of Miles's environments situate the basic tensions of Miles's life. Cool blues dominate the dizzying high towers of Manhattan, Miles's new and high-pressure academic setting, and the scientific lab spaces of one of the plot's major action sequences, emphasizing unwelcoming worlds in which Miles's decisions are both important and potentially devastating. The harsh and calculating gaze of this outer world is in direct contrast with Miles's home with his family in Brooklyn, which is saturated in warm tones and which underlines Miles's supportive family and neighborhood.[8] Finally, green appears in characters and backgrounds—most notably in the film's version of Spider-man's nemesis "Doc Oc"—in order to stress anxiety and duress.[9] Thus by way of color the film establishes the situation of its thirteen-year-old main character, who comes from a supportive home, faces a harsh new world of decisions, and endures the anxiety of coming to be "Spider-man."

At more than one point, the animation imitates the paneling that in comic books serves as the central method of sequencing narration and action. Dialogue boxes for inner monologues appear, staggered moments of developing action are stacked together in a single frame, and so forth. Two such moments put forward a particularly important transformation that Miles undergoes. Each of these moments imitates one another, and the visual set-up is simple: two panels sit side by side on a single screen, cutting the image in half. In the first, the door and wall of Miles's school dorm split apart Miles on one side and his father, Jefferson, a police officer, on the other. Miles here is at his lowest point, wrapped in webs to his chair, unable to use his new powers at will and unable to help his fellow Spider heroes return to their own universes.–And what is more, Miles's Uncle Aaron, Jefferson's brother, has been revealed as the Prowler, an assassin, and has died, shot by his employer Kingpin for refusing to murder his nephew. Father and son stand apart, split visually like comic book panels, and across the distance Jefferson offers his support to Miles. This bridge is mirrored later in the story, after the climax and its victory, where the two are again split across the screen. Here, though, the moment is not one of separation but of intimacy, as Miles calls his father on the phone to check in with him, and in the next moment hugs him.

Miles's relationship with his father, which is loving, thus forms one of the central hinges on which the plot turns. In the beginning of the story,

Miles struggles with his police officer father's high expectations for him. This is represented visually and scholastically: Miles is assigned an essay on who he wants to be (with the novel *Great Expectations* backgrounded here), and Miles spray paints himself breaking through a wall of brightly colored expectations. Uncle Aaron at this point serves as another model for who Miles might be, this one much more free and easy, released, as it were, of expectations—though Miles does not know Aaron's dark secret. Both of these adults encourage Miles to express his emotions and both articulate a desire that Miles lay hold of his own freedom, though in different ways. Even when Aaron is revealed as the Prowler and is shot for refusing to kill Miles, Aaron's dying words emphasize his love for Miles and Miles's own goodness. In this way, the contrastive "split" that Miles endures does not reveal a choice between good and evil as such, nor between mere law and non-law. Miles's environment is fundamentally one of nurturing love. The question for him really is whether he will allow that support to serve as a bridge into greater responsibility for himself and his world. To return to a theme: when Miles speaks to his father in the split screen after the climax, he is dressed as Spider-man, that is, as the responsibility he has freely laid hold of, and his father's love has made possible this transition, even as Miles's new responsibility is what enables him to return his father's love more freely. Indeed, Miles finishes his essay and his father helps him spray paint a new mural, one dedicated to Aaron.

The aesthetics of *Into the Spider-verse* combined with its narrative puts forward a theory of becoming oneself, and there is one moment in particular that becomes essential. During the low point of the film, split across the screen, Jefferson tells his son that his "spark" is his own, and "whatever you do with it, you'll be great." Miles's father then reminds Miles that he loves him, and walks away. This loving affirmation of Miles's autonomy, that it is up to him to decide who he is to be, provides the literal spark that activates Miles's control over his own powers. The film stresses Miles's new arrival to his autonomy in several ways: through a voice-over that repeats his family's support, through the appearance of a Spider-man costume that fits Miles and that he customizes, through an underlying soundtrack with a song that literally greets danger, and finally through Miles's leap from the top of a Manhattan tower and in the act of swinging through the city on his spiderweb. It is important to note the following characteristics of this sequence: Miles does not arrive at self-as-autonomous by himself; his autonomy expresses itself as rising to responsibility for the world; this shared self is a becoming of himself as himself; and it is this becoming that is marked most of all with risk, rather than the "mere" risk of Brooklyn destroyed in a black hole through the particle collider.

In terms of its emotional catharsis, the film is basically complete once Miles is able to take his leap and navigate the heart of New York as his own version of Spider-man. The rest of the film resolves its plot, but this resolution is at its heart the playing-out of this prior moment. And the moment itself is visually remarkable: the animation warps the buildings to emphasize Miles's extreme height as he leaps, and when he plunges downward, the movement is inverted visually so that his descent into the city becomes a literal ascent. Miles struggles for a moment before taking control of his fall and managing his webbed swing, again a literal seizing of his own direction, one underlined with the reappearance of comic book paneling to frame his expression of focus and determination.

That Miles lays hold of his own becoming for the sake of others but also through the support of others is highly suggestive of the notion that becoming oneself is not the product of pure individuality. Thus the film presses against an atomized or secluded notion of selfhood. But becoming a self is also a product of becoming a personality, inasmuch as Miles places his own mark on being Spider-man, one with unique powers and a unique look. In other words, he is being himself. Being himself involves rising to a sense of responsibility, but this responsibility is not "outside" of the hero; it instead emerges from out of his being himself in the world. And the most significant comment on this "being oneself" that the film makes is that being oneself is the being that is most fraught with risk, rather than the risk of rescuing New York. After all, it is this first leap into being himself responsibly that allows Miles to leap into battle with Kingpin and his catalogue of goons. The film in this way subverts not only absolutized individuality but also the superhero archetype. Rather than stressing a hero in their immensity or the uniqueness of their responsibility or their vast power, the film stresses a person becoming more himself as *the* essential drama at hand, rather than these other notions. In one sense, this subversion is directly from the Spider-man tradition: he is the hero who is just a regular person. But the film's unflinching center of focus on Miles *as* Miles breaks open this tradition in a new way with a new effectiveness. One aspect of that newness is simply the new alchemy of selfhood in the art, the animation, and its narrative. But another has to do with Miles himself.

It is difficult here to properly place Miles in his racial, multiethnic significance, and this difficulty is in a way *Into the Spider-verse*'s genius, and it is deserving of attention as a final manner of understanding the film. The difficulty at hand has to do with how Miles, who is both Black and Puerto-Rican, is at once a racialized character—he "has" race—and a character for whom race is never problematized. Within the logic of the narrative, Miles does not experience his racial identity as an obstacle to his arrival at identity and responsibility. In this sense, the film is post-racial, since, in the traditions of thinkers like Frantz Fanon and James Baldwin, race is a fiction and a lie that serves as a barrier to the self. "In America," explains Baldwin, "the color of my skin had stood between myself and me."[10] But even if Miles's race is not problematized for him, it is unavoidably so for his audience, and in two ways. One reveals the autonomous self in the midst of becoming, which is concealed underneath the person of color by their color in the (Western) society that they live in, emphasizing therefore the selfhood of people of color. The second way reveals how race conceals this autonomous subjectivity, since after all it should not be a revelation that these human beings are autonomous, are selves.

In its complex portrait of a young person of color being himself, *Into the Spider-verse* speaks to its own concrete context in the Western world, which is a world that knows the concealing fiction of race. At the same time, the revelation of Miles being himself sunders the effects or illusions of race, exploiting the mechanism to see its demise, and in doing so it supposes that being a self transcends the constraints of a racialized context. And perhaps most significantly, the film emphasizes that this arrival at autonomous self, though ever-precarious an achievement, is the most important one.[11]

Conclusion

In this chapter, I have emphasized the ways that, aesthetically and narratively, the film *Into the Spider-verse* is a confrontation with becoming oneself. That confrontation is achieved through the artistic decision to imitate the hand-drawn work of "classic" or "Golden Age" comics, borrowing their heightened stakes to tell a new story around a multiethnic young Miles Morales, the Spider-man of the film's particular version of the universe in a multi-verse. This new story thinks beyond race by emphasizing Miles's own becoming of himself, and by—in its art and in its plot—emphasizing that it is this becoming that is the real drama of being alive. Being a superhero is sublated to this other, more central drama. And so the becoming of self that *Into the Spider-verse* articulates is a self for its time, but also a self whose responsible becoming is available beyond the pure context of its time. The "being oneself" at the heart of the film is an ascent to responsibility, an ascent accomplished not alone, but together.

Notes

1 Bernard Lonergan, "Existenz and Aggiornomento," in *Collected Works of Bernard Lonergan: Collection*, ed. Frederick E. Crowe and Robert M. Doran (Toronto: University of Toronto Press, 1993), 224.

2 Ramin Zahed, *Spider-man: Into the Spider-verse: The Art of the Movie* (London: Titan Books, 2018), 13.

3 Ibid., 12.

4 Ibid., 13.

5 Ibid., 183–5.

6 Ibid., 184.

7 Ibid., 11.

8   Ibid., 14, 34, 59.
9   Ibid., 102–3.
10 James Baldwin, "Introduction," in *Collected Essays*, ed. Toni Morrison (New York: Penguin Random House, 1998), 135.
11 Cf. Lonergan, "Existenz and Aggiornomento," 229.

28

On the Dardenne Brothers' *Young Ahmed*

Joel Mayward

In May 2019, I had the opportunity to attend the Festival de Cannes in France, where I saw the premiere of *Le Jeune Ahmed* (*Young Ahmed*), a powerful and provocative film from Belgian filmmakers Jean-Pierre and Luc Dardenne. Internationally acclaimed, the Dardenne Brothers are part of an elite group of directors who have twice won the Palme d'Or at Cannes. *Young Ahmed* won them "Best Director" at Cannes 2019, and in 2020 they were awarded the Lumière Award in Lyon, the cinematic equivalent of the Nobel Prize for Literature.[1] They have also been recognized for creating post-secular cinema imbued with philosophical and theological significance. "Post-secular" as I am using it here suggests a dynamic porous relationship between the religious and the secular spheres in the wake of Max Weber's so-called "disenchantment" of modern Western society. In their collection, *Immanent Frames*, film-philosophers John Caruana and Mark Cauchi describe post-secular cinema as "the work of those filmmakers whose films explicitly hover over that grey zone that dissolves the strict boundaries that are often established between belief and unbelief," thereby challenging many simplistic dichotomies which prevail in the popular imagination.[2] Following Caruana and Cauchi, as well as film scholars Sarah Cooper and Catherine Wheatley,[3] I contend that the Dardenne Brothers are indeed post-secular filmmakers who employ religious allusions within their ostensibly non-religious social realist films about individuals facing moral dilemmas within the urban margins of post-industrial Europe. I want to suggest that *Young Ahmed* may be considered a post-secular cinematic parable which subversively provokes philosophical thought via the brothers' distinctive audiovisual style and approach to narrative structure. In order to demonstrate this claim, I draw upon the work of Paul Ricoeur, specifically his view of "parable" as a "narrative-metaphor" which provokes a "re-orientation by disorientation" in an audience's imagination.

Ricoeurian Parables

Paul Ricoeur's remarkable capacity to reconcile seemingly disparate views and disciplines makes him an ideal mediator between cinema, philosophy, and religion, particularly via his appreciation of parables. As I have explored this idea extensively elsewhere,[4] I will aim to be brief: in his 1975 article "Biblical Hermeneutics," Ricoeur describes "parable" as the conjunction of a *narrative form* and a *metaphorical process*.[5] This narrative-metaphor points to a third element, an external referent beyond the parable which Ricoeur calls "limit-experiences." Limit-experiences are human encounters with the horizon of knowledge and material reality, or immanence colliding with transcendence. In this way, a parable indirectly redescribes the religious dimension of human existence without resorting to overtly religious discourse, thus provoking a variety of valid interpretations. Through what Ricoeur calls "signs of metaphoricity,"[6] a parable refers to something *beyond* what was literally told in the narrative, even as the story remains coherent in itself. John Dominic Crossan summarizes Ricoeur's threefold description of parable as *narrativity*, *metaphoricity*, and *paradoxicality*.[7]

Realism, in both its aesthetic and cinematic sense, is an essential trait for Ricoeurian cinematic parables. Parables are "narratives of normalcy" which could have actually occurred to typical people in everyday life, yet contain a peculiarity or eccentricity, only not through supernatural or magical elements. As Ricoeur puts it, parables depict "the extraordinary within the ordinary"[8] through the "fantastic of the everyday."[9] Ricoeur describes the structure underlying this peculiarity: "parables are ordinary stories whose entire metaphorical power is concentrated in a moment of crisis and in a denouement that is either tragic or comic."[10] This crisis elicits a response as the parable is received and appropriated by the audience—parables produce a "re-orientation by disorientation" in our imagination, opening us up to new possible ways of knowing.[11] Thus, true Ricoeurian parables may generate a diversity of interpretations and applications out of a single narrative-metaphor, reorienting our philosophical, religious, and moral imaginations. To rephrase a classic Ricoeurian proverb, *the parable gives rise to thought*. With Ricoeur's understanding of a parable in view, we can turn our attention to *Young Ahmed*.

Young Ahmed

At eighty-four suspenseful minutes, *Young Ahmed* is the Dardennes' shortest feature-length film. It is also the first of the brothers' nine films without their regular cinematographer, Alain Marcoen; cameraman Benoît Dervaux stepped into the role, as Marcoen was ill at the time of filming and requested that Dervaux take his place.[12] *Young Ahmed* nevertheless remains strongly anchored within the Dardennes' sui generis visual style and thematic interests, namely the moral formation of young people and the ethical question of taking a human life. In its consideration of religious fundamentalism, *Young Ahmed* is a post-secular parable: through its formal subversion of conventions, it interrogates both religion and Western secularism as it prompts queries about our contemporary social imagination. Its premise is perhaps the most controversial and certainly the most divisive of the brothers' films: a young Belgian teenager hatches a plot to kill his teacher after embracing an extremist interpretation of the Qur'an, leading to his imprisonment and attempted rehabilitation (Figure 28.1).

Having observed the increase in religious fanaticism and violence around the world—especially in Belgium with various terrorist attacks, but also the rise of nationalist, racist, and anti-immigrant sentiments throughout Europe and America—the Dardennes hoped to make a film not about a person becoming radicalized, but rather what it might take to *de-radicalize* someone, especially within the present globalized context. Ahmed's very biological makeup—he has an absentee North African father and a white Belgian mother—symbolize an in-between status as he strives to be both a faithful Muslim and a faithful Belgian. Without ever using the term "post-secular," the Dardennes' stated motivations for making *Young Ahmed* are

FIGURE 28.1 *Inès and Ahmed.* Young Ahmed, *directed by Jean-Pierre and Luc Dardenne. Film still. ©Christine Plenus.*

precisely the same phenomena observed by Jürgen Habermas in "Notes on Post-Secular Society": the mutual rise of pluralism and fundamentalism within globalization, prompting a "return to religion" in the public sphere.[13] That is, *Young Ahmed* is addressing post-secularism through a post-secular cinematic aesthetic—it *is* post-secular and it is *about* our post-secular world.

In his published journal, *On the Back of Our Images*, Luc Dardenne states that Italian filmmaker Roberto Rossellini's neorealist masterpiece *Germany Year Zero* is the "model" for all of the brothers' films.[14] *Young Ahmed* is arguably the Dardennes' own *Germany Year Zero*: it is the thematic culmination of all their previous works, a concentrated narrative-metaphor about an adolescent boy's moral corruption by a violent ideology, which culminates in a heartbreaking open-ended conclusion precipitated by the boy's literal and metaphorical fall. The eponymous Ahmed, a thirteen-year-old multiethnic Belgian teen, is portrayed with quiet sincerity by newcomer Idir Ben Addi, one of the Dardennes' non-professional discoveries. Ahmed attends afterschool classes taught by Inès (Myriem Akheddiou), a kind and confident teacher who previously helped Ahmed overcome dyslexia when he was younger. Akin to the characters of Assita in *The Promise* (1996) and Samantha in *The Kid with a Bike* (2011), Inès is a Dardennean maternal figure who takes a troubled boy under her care out of sheer decency. But Ahmed has recently become antagonistic toward her; he's captivated by his local imam (Othmane Moumen) and extremist teachings (Figure 28.2), as well as the memory of his deceased cousin, a jihadist terrorist. The parallels

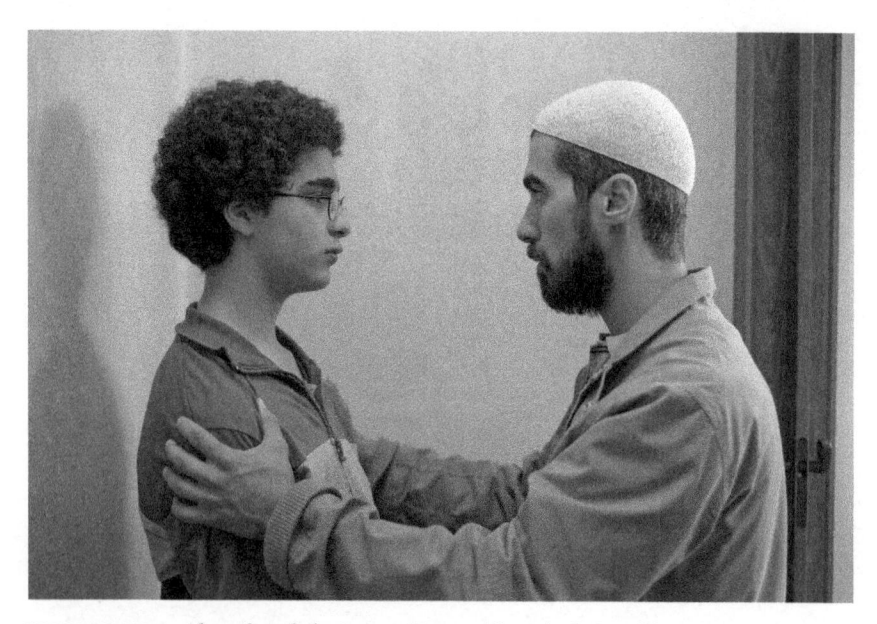

FIGURE 28.2 *Ahmed and the imam.* Young Ahmed, *directed by Jean-Pierre and Luc Dardenne. Film still. ©Christine Plenus.*

between the imam in *Young Ahmed* and the Nazi schoolteacher in *Germany Year Zero* are noteworthy—both men take the adolescent protagonist under their wing and inspire the youth to kill another human being, yet ultimately disown the boy when their preached violent beliefs are put into practice. Though the imam declares Inès an apostate "bitch," we can see how Inès is a faithful Muslim who embodies the Islamic pillar of charity via her generous actions toward educating young people in her community in urban Seraing. When Inès invites Ahmed to have a conversation about their differing interpretations of the Qur'an, he rejects her harshly, saying he can't discuss sacred texts with a woman. Where Inès appears to emphasize the spirit of the text through acts of generosity and mercy, Ahmed's view is a rigidly literalist hermeneutic. Their scripture-informed worldviews are at odds, creating a conflict of interpretations which ultimately leads Ahmed to unsuccessfully attack Inès with a knife.

Ahmed is depicted as being an ordinary person who suddenly becomes a hostile and violent outsider due to his extraordinary religious convictions. We're provoked to wonder: *Why* do people adopt such extreme beliefs, religious or otherwise? Even if we are inclined to view Ahmed's actions as immoral or detrimental, the film formally presents him as a subjective mystery, never giving satisfying reasons for his newfound views. To borrow language from Ricoeur's *Lectures on Ideology and Utopia*,[15] we could interpret Ahmed as representing a quasi-utopian vision which confronts modern secular liberal ideologies, or we could interpret him as being entrenched within a rigid religious ideology which requires a utopian alternative in order to be freed. In this resistance to offering clear or simple explanations for such beliefs and behaviors, the parable makes us aware of our own interpretive process, as well as the implicit cultural values which form our social imagination. Thus, even as *Young Ahmed* is *about* characters' interpretations, it also prompts the audience to *make* interpretations.

One way *Young Ahmed* elicits such interpretations is in how the Dardennes deliberately disallow us from knowing what Ahmed is thinking and feeling. There is no explanatory voice-over narration, and Ahmed's face generally exhibits a Bressonian blankness. Ahmed himself often seems unsure as to his intentions and reasoning, often acting impulsively out of his fervent devotion. As we are thrown in medias res with Ahmed already radicalized, we are not made privy to what motivated his conversion to a fundamentalist ideology; in an interview, Jean-Pierre calls this a "fascinating opacity."[16] Some critics have expressed frustration at this opacity, viewing it as a poor lead performance or even an Islamophobic screenplay, but Addi portrays Ahmed as a typical early adolescent boy—inarticulate, awkward, sometimes harsh while at other times kindhearted—while the positive role of Inès complicates claims of Islamophobia. Ahmed wears wiry glasses with thick lenses, a key metaphorical motif as the story progresses—this is how he sees the world, and the lenses we look through affect our interpretations of reality. In the scene of the attack on Inès, he uses rubber bands to secure his glasses around his ears, as if to keep his ideology fixed in place. As the film generates inquiries about ideological entrenchment and religious beliefs, the audience is also invited to evaluate their own lenses of interpretation. Through Ahmed, it presents a philosophical anthropology not unlike Ricoeur's, but that of a finite subject which is fallible-yet-capable and requires interpretation for self-understanding. In this way, *Young Ahmed* parabolically makes us aware of the ethical significance of hermeneutics, of being able to see *how* we are seeing and how our interpretations—of texts, of others, of ourselves—affect our moral actions.

Though Ahmed shows small signs of progress, the numerous individuals representing state systems and institutions—lawyers, judges, therapists, teachers, and even Ahmed's own mother—all ultimately fall short in converting Ahmed away from his fundamentalist devotion. The only person who seems to reach him is Louise (Victoria Bluck), a confident and affable teen girl Ahmed meets on a local farm as part of the rehabilitation process. She befriends and flirts with Ahmed, even asking to wear his glasses, to which he surprisingly agrees. With his glasses—his interpretative lenses—on her face, she asks if she looks hazy or clear to him before announcing that she would like to kiss him. The spontaneous smile which erupts on Ahmed's face at her request is a standout moment as we see a tiny breakthrough in Ahmed's rigid defenses. The teens later kiss in a field, an idyllic scene in the greenery of nature far from the post-industrial urban complex of Seraing (Figure 28.3). Where much of *Young Ahmed* is located in confined

FIGURE 28.3 *Ahmed and Louise.* Young Ahmed, *directed by Jean-Pierre and Luc Dardenne. Film still. ©Christine Plenus.*

interior spaces, these farm scenes connote openness and growth, what the Dardennes describe as "the fragility of life" and "an element of hope."[17] When Louise attempts a French kiss, the intimacy startles Ahmed, and he backs away, troubled. Later, after Louise understandably refuses Ahmed's insistence that she convert to Islam in order to legitimize their romance—a non-believer, she responds "I won't be forced"—he pushes her away in anger. Metaphorically, a marriage between religion (Ahmed) and secularism (Louise) cannot be consummated by coercion or duress.

Fueled by this rejection, Ahmed dramatically escapes from his caseworker (Olivier Bonnaud), traveling across town until he reaches Inès's school office, apparently still on his jihadist mission. In a long-take, Ahmed scales the school's exterior in order to break inside the locked building from an open window and attack Inès with a metal piton. As he nears the second-floor window, his handhold gives way and Ahmed falls backward off the roof to the garden below. This shocking moment strongly parallels the climactic falls in both *Germany Year Zero* and *The Kid with a Bike*. Where Edmund's suicide in *Germany Year Zero* is intentional, Ahmed's fall is both accidental and more redemptive. With the camera positioned above him in a quasi-God's eye view shot, he lies on his back semi-paralyzed, blood trickling from his ear. His glasses—his ideology—lie broken and out of reach. Ahmed pitifully calls out, "Mama! Mama!" but no one is there to listen. He slowly drags his body to a nearby fence and strikes the piton on the metal—his weapon now becomes his signal for help. Responding to the sound, Inès comes into the garden courtyard, approaching the injured boy with mild hesitation. In an earlier scene with a judge as mediator, she couldn't even look at Ahmed without bursting into tears and leaving the room. Here, seeing the injured boy prone on the ground, she maintains her composure. Reaching toward her, Ahmed cries, "I'm sorry, Madame Inès!" as she compassionately takes his hand in hers. She then rises and goes to call for an ambulance. Ahmed's eyes flutter as the film abruptly cuts to black (Figure 28.4).

Some film critics have argued that *Young Ahmed*'s ending is too rushed and offers simplistic resolutions; as the critic for *Cahiers du Cinéma* put it, "Everything is predictable, and as soon as Ahmed climbs a wall, we know how it will end: by this same fall and that same Christian redemption that the filmmakers have filmed a hundred times before."[18] Yet despite the poignant denouement, it remains unclear if and how Ahmed has been transformed by his physical fall. Has he given up his murderous ideology in the face of his own mortality, or is his cry of forgiveness an act meant only for survival? Even if it is initially sincere, will this conversion last? And what does it imply that only suffering or imminent death can engender such repentance? The Dardennes admit that Ahmed did die in early versions of the script; alternatively, they ended the film on the silent shot of his hand reaching for Inès, with any reconciliation remaining unclear. The willingness of Inès in the final version to grab hold of Ahmed's hand as he asks for forgiveness is one of hopeful possibility—this affecting touch echoes a stated

FIGURE 28.4 *Cannes Press Conference for* Young Ahmed. *Photo by Joel Mayward, 2019.*

desire in Luc's journals to "make a film that would be a handshake."[19] As Luc puts it in an interview, "Finally, he had to speak, in that he apologizes to Madame Inès for being alive. This is not a confession. It is a child who asks for forgiveness. Ahmed wants to return to life. Though earlier he did not want to touch Madame Inès anymore, now he touches her."[20] However, even as the final shot carries traces of Emmanuel Levinas and "the face of the Other"—with the exception of *Lorna's Silence* (2008), every one of the Dardennes' cinematic parables concludes with an affecting Levinasian face-to-face encounter—the sudden cut to black refuses us definitive conclusions. We are not even sure as to whether Ahmed will survive his injuries or what physical state the fall has left him in—it is entirely possible that his cries for forgiveness are his final words. Thus, it remains open (yet hopeful) as to whether or not Ahmed has been truly redeemed.

To shift from film-text to action, we could ask: How might contemporary societies respond to a repentant radicalized person? Is it possible to sympathize with or even forgive individuals who have become entrenched in dangerous ideologies? What can or should be done to help de-radicalize people caught in such paradigms (e.g., the recent QAnon conspiracy phenomenon)? These are the kinds of questions raised by such cinematic parables, not merely through religious or philosophical content, but through affective visual styles and provocative structures as narrative-metaphors. *Young Ahmed* challenges our capacity for empathy as it interrogates the limits of modern liberalism and Western secular institutions for effectively addressing religious fundamentalism. The parable also challenges the progressive-conservative dichotomy, having been criticized as both "the folly of liberal sentimentality"[21] and a "highly conservative work."[22] Interpreted one way, *Young Ahmed* can be viewed as a critical indictment of secular state-run systems; seen another way, the film is an affirmation of how such systems may play a role in rehabilitation and healing. If secular approaches alone cannot wholly redeem an individual from out of religious fundamentalism, the film seems to suggest a partnership of secular *and* sacred—in other words, post-secular—in order to bring about full restoration. As both a good teacher and a good Muslim, Inès overcomes the sacred-secular divide in a receptive post-secular posture—her actions offer a possible way forward, an openly religious paradigm operating successfully within the secular public sphere.

One interpretive clue lies in the film's title: Ahmed is *young*, still malleable and maturing, his values not yet cemented into static systems or rigid ideologies. Jean-Pierre states, "We chose a character of 13-years-old because it is an age where we can still be molded and shaped. It's still the age of a child."[23] For the Dardennes, moral transformation is possible, but it requires patience and hope. As Bonnaud's caseworker says to Ahmed (and to us), "understanding takes time." Indeed, one of the brothers' primary influences is philosopher Ernst Bloch. In his magnum opus, *The Principle of Hope*, Bloch describes "guiding images," or cultural works which carry within them the possibility of utopian virtue. He calls these guiding images "wishful portraits of being truly human."[24] This phrase perfectly describes the Dardennes' post-secular cinema; their humanistic guiding images invite us to interpret (and re-interpret) our world through a lens of hope.[25]

Notes

1 Frédéric Ponsard, "The Dardenne Brothers are Honoured at Forward-Looking Lumière Festival," *Euronews*, October 20, 2020. https://www.euronews.com /2020/10/20/the-dardenne-brothers-are-honoured-at-forward-looking-lumiere -festival.

2 John Caruana and Mark Cauchi, eds., *Immanent Frames: Postsecular Cinema between Malick and von Trier* (Albany, NY: SUNY Press, 2018), 1–5.

3 Sarah Cooper, "Mortal Ethics: Reading Levinas with the Dardenne Brothers," *Film-Philosophy* 11, no. 2 (2007): 66–87; Sarah Cooper, "'Put Yourself in My Place': *Two Days, One Night* and the Journal Back to Life," in Caruana and Cauchi, 229–244; Catherine Wheatley, "The Third City: The Post Secular Space of the Dardennes' Seraing," *Film-Philosophy* 23, no. 3 (2019): 264–81.

4 See Joel Mayward, "The Fantastic of the Everyday: Re-Forming Definitions of Cinematic Parables with Paul Ricoeur," *Horizons* 47, no. 2 (December 2020): 283–314.

5   Paul Ricoeur, "Biblical Hermeneutics," *Semeia* 4 (1975): 29–148.

6   Ibid., 96–7.

7   John Dominic Crossan, *Cliffs of Fall: Paradox and Polyvalence in the Parables of Jesus* (New York: Seabury Press, 1980), 2.

8   Paul Ricoeur, *Figuring the Sacred: Religion, Narrative, and Imagination*, trans. David Pellauer, ed. Mark I. Wallace (Minneapolis, MM: Fortress Press, 1995), 60.

9   Paul Ricoeur, "The 'Kingdom' in the Parables of Jesus," *Anglican Theological Review* 63, no. 2 (April 1981): 167.

10 Ibid.

11 Ricoeur, "Biblical Hermeneutics," 108–14.

12 Nick Newman, "Jean-Pierre and Luc Dardenne on *Young Ahmed*, Arabic Teachings, and Taking Religion Seriously," *The Film Stage*, February 21, 2020. https://thefilmstage.com/jean-pierre-and-luc-dardenne-on-young-ahmed-arabic-teachings-and-taking-religion-seriously/.

13 Jürgen Habermas, "Notes on Post-Secular Society," *NPQ: New Perspectives Quarterly* 25, no. 4 (2008): 19–21.

14 Luc Dardenne, *On the Back of Our Images, Volume One: 1991–2005*, trans. Jeffrey Zuckerman and Sammi Skolmoski (Chicago, IL: Featherproof Books, 2019), 27.

15 Paul Ricoeur, *Lectures on Ideology and Utopia*, ed. George H. Taylor (New York: Columbia University Press, 1986).

16 Yves Alion, "Le Jeune Ahmed Dossier," *L'Avant Scène Cinéma* no. 666 (October 2019): 7.

17 Eileen G'Sell, "Innocence to the Extreme: An Interview with Cannes Best Director Winners Luc and Jean-Pierre Dardenne," *Los Angeles Review of Books*, April 13, 2020. https://lareviewofbooks.org/article/innocence-extreme-interview-cannes-best-director-winners-luc-jean-pierre-dardenne/.

18 Alion, "Le Jeune Ahmed Dossier," 62.

19 Dardenne, *On the Back of Our Images*, 11.

20 Alion, "Le Jeune Ahmed Dossier," 17.

21 Armond White, "*Young Ahmed* Shows Terrorism as Youthful Indiscretion," *National Review*, May 27, 2020. https://www.nationalreview.com/2020/05/movie-review-young-ahmed-shows-terrorism-as-youthful-indiscretion/.

22 David Walsh, "*Young Ahmed*: A Portrait of a Youthful Religious Zealot—From the Dardenne Brothers," *World Socialist Web Site*, December 17, 2020. https://www.wsws.org/en/articles/2020/12/18/ahme-d18.html.

23 Alion, "Le Jeune Ahmed Dossier," 9.

24 Ernst Bloch, *The Principle of Hope, Volumes 1–3*, trans. Neville Plaice, Stephen Plaice, and Paul Knight (Cambridge, MA: MIT Press), 931–2.

25 For more philosophical reflections on *Young Ahmed*, see Joel Mayward, *The Dardenne Brothers' Cinematic Parables: Integrating Theology, Philosophy, and Film* (London: Routledge, 2022), 178–86.

29

On John Huston's *The Dead*

Magnus Ferguson

John Huston's 1987 adaptation of James Joyce's *The Dead* is a film about memory, loss, and the lasting power of the dead over the living. Over the course of a festive dinner party, guests find themselves haunted by spectral figures of an older, near-forgotten Dublin. For Gretta Conroy, the music and storytelling of the evening awaken memories of an intense and tragic childhood romance. The cathartic final scenes of the film, in which Gretta tells her husband about young Michael Furey, leave audiences to ponder the strange hold of the past over the present, as well as the impenetrable alterity of those who are closest to us.

The original *New York Times* review of Huston's *The Dead* describes the film as an "immensely faithful adaptation,"[1] and similar praise has been repeated by film critics and scholars alike. But what does it mean for a film to be faithful to its source material? One lesson we might draw from Huston's film is that faithful adaptation does not consist in merely replicating an original text. After all, in rewriting the script Tony Huston (the director's son) reassigned numerous lines to different characters, expanded Freddy Malins's role to add an element of slapstick comedy, and wholly invented the character of Mr. Grace and his dramatic recitation of the eighth-century-poem "Donal Og." Beyond these narrative interventions, the transition to film had profound effects on the pacing of the story.[2] Joyce's writing famously grants the reader privileged access to Gabriel's internal stream of consciousness, meaning that the slow pace of the Morkans' dinner party is quickened by Gabriel's rapidly shifting observations, memories, and emotional responses. This complicated vantage point is practically impossible to replicate on the screen. Instead, audiences watch the action from behind the camera, only once accessing the protagonist's internal monologue as a voice-over at the end of the film.

Huston's challenge, then, was not only to transpose *The Dead* into a visual medium but also (and almost paradoxically) to alter the story in a faithful way. Answering to this double-task—to preserve and to transform—is more the work of translation than replication. By translation, I do not only mean the passage between two languages or between words in the same language. The medieval *translatio* referred to the practice of moving holy relics, which often took the form of the corpses of saints.[3] To translate in this sense is to ferry the dead from one consecrated space to another. Many such translations were covert in nature, and were sometimes called *furta sacra*—that is, "holy theft." By way of what Patrick Geary describes as "a ritual kidnapping by which the saints passed from one community to another,"[4] a saint's influence was preserved and renewed.

In a way, "holy theft" is an appropriate description for Joyce's "original" short story, which is itself a literary adaptation of a story related to Joyce by his wife, Nora Barnacle. The character of Gretta in *The Dead* appears to be modeled directly after Barnacle, as Joyce makes explicit in a 1909 letter: "Do you remember the three adjectives I had used in *The Dead* in speaking of your body. They are these: 'musical and strange and perfumed.'"[5] Moreover, there is ample evidence that Barnacle (like Gretta) had a powerful romance in her youth with a man named Michael Bodkin (in the story, Michael Furey). Barnacle's childhood friend Mary O'Hollderan confirms that "Nora knew another boy whom she was very fond of his name was Michael (Sonny) Bodkin . . . Sonny Bodkin died very young."[6] Barnacle would go to "Mr. Bodkin's sweetshop at No. 2 Prospect Hill"[7] with the express purpose of seeing Michael, and the two quickly struck up a flirtatious courtship. Sadly, just like Furey, Bodkin contracted tuberculosis quite suddenly and was consigned to the county infirmary. In his final days, he snuck out of his bed and walked through the rain to Barnacles' house to sing her a ballad, *The Lass of Aughrim*, before passing away on February 11, 1900.[8]

The young man's death left an enormous impression on Barnacle, and in the first year of her relationship with Joyce she told him about Bodkin's romantic gesture. Joyce judged it to be so important to her formation that he mentioned Bodkin in a letter to his brother Stanislaus in December of 1904: "She has told me something of her youth. . . . She has had many love-affairs, one when quite young with a boy who died. She was laid up at news of his death."[9] Eight years later, Joyce even paid a visit to Bodkin's grave and wrote to Stanislaus that "the graveyard of *The Dead*" was "exactly as I imagined it."[10] Given his general obsession with (and jealousy about) Nora's past romances, it is perhaps unsurprising that Joyce would write a short story inspired by the shadow of Bodkin's memory over his own relationship with Barnacle.

What makes Joyce's short story a holy theft of sorts is the fact that he not only alters Bodkin's name to Furey but also literally relocates Bodkin's corpse by moving his place of rest to Oughterard. (In actuality, Bodkin was almost certainly buried in Rahoon.[11]) Still, this substitution is not necessarily a betrayal. Translated memories, like translated relics, can change over the course of their journeys. *The Dead* is not only about the lingering power that the dead hold over the living but also the practices by which the living preserve memories of the dead through revisionist storytelling. Conversation at the party is full of nostalgic impressions of an older, almost mythical Dublin, evident in Ms. Ivor's confrontation with Gabriel over his modern, continental tendencies, as well as the numerous remembrances over dinner of opera singers from the past. ("Those were the days, [Mr. Browne] said, when there was something like singing to be heard in Dublin."[12])

Tellingly, when Gabriel shares the story of his grandfather's old horse, "[t]he never-to-be-forgotten Johnny,"[13] his aunts point out a number of embellishments in his tale. For example, the late Patrick Morkan was a starch miller, not a "glue-boiler," and he didn't live in an "ancestral mansion somewhere near Back Lane."[14] Still, the liberties that Gabriel takes in his retelling revitalize his grandfather's memory, as if altering it in order to summon it to the present.

Barnacle, Joyce, and Huston's translations—an intimate confession, a short story, and a film—of Bodkin's memory also accomplish this curious mixture of preservation and embellishment. They remind me of the complicated ways in which traditional ballads (which feature prominently across Joyce's writing and Huston's film) develop over time, often trading melodies, themes, metaphors, and characters. The oldest records of English-language ballads were printed broadsheets that included only lyrics, likely because musical notation was not widely accessible. This apparent archival limitation has given rise to a diversity of melodies, meaning that any given performance evokes only a partial thread of a ballad's regional and historical variations. The exchange of words, melodies, and even dramatis personae between variants over time has allowed these stories to survive across centuries.

Joyce was intimately familiar with traditional ballads, and he frequently wove them into his fiction. Huston's adaptation has the natural advantage of allowing audiences to listen to and be directly affected by musical performance. In the film, Bartell D'Arcy's haunting rendition of *The Lass of Aughrim* (an Irish variant of a Scottish ballad) is especially poignant because Huston commits the audience to three full verses, as opposed to the single verse that Joyce includes in his story. Here, the notably slower pace of the film actually serves to deepen the audience's connection to the ballad, lending the scene a solemn weight that is only described second-hand through Gabriel's eyes and ears on the page. The film's orchestral accompaniment, which enters with the final reprise, marks Gretta's rekindled memories of her past romance with Michael Furey in a uniquely musical way that the written word simply cannot imitate.

Joyce scholar Donagh MacDonagh stumbled upon the connection between the Irish and Scottish variants entirely by chance. His daughter knew a version of the ballad called *Lord Gregory* from a 1965 Judy Collins recording. According to MacDonagh, he was reading some of Joyce's letters in his office when his daughter "by coincidence came by strumming her guitar and singing an unfamiliar air to faintly familiar words."[15] In a way, MacDonagh's experience resembles Gretta's hesitant recognition of the ballad, which she also only hears in passing through the walls of the Morkans' house. (In the film, Huston lightly muffles the vocal performance to give it a sense of distance, reinforcing that the audience is eavesdropping on D'Arcy's rendition.) Given that only three lines of *The Lass of Aughrim* are actually printed in Joyce's story ("O, the rain falls on my heavy locks / And the dew wets my skin / My babe lies cold,"[16] this is almost certainly the verse that MacDonagh recognized in Collins's rendition.

Most versions of *The Lass of Aughrim* and its associated variants (including *Lord Gregory*, *The Lass of Ocram*, *The Lass of Lochryan*, and *The Lass of Roch Royal*) tell the story of a young mother and her infant seeking shelter from the rain at Lord Gregory's home.[17] Gregory's mother impersonates her son's voice from behind the door and demands that the young woman produce evidence to prove her identity. After much pleading and cruel interrogation, the young woman is turned away and dies in the night. Some versions go on to describe Gregory's discovery of his mother's treachery, and his tragic search for his lover's body. Beyond serving as a transition point between the bustling, social atmosphere of the Morkans' party and the quiet intimacy of the story's final pages, several scholars have identified thematic connections between the ballad and the story. The image of a lover standing outside in the rain at risk of her life, for example, foreshadows Gretta's tale of Michael Furey's romantic gesture,[18] and Gregory's mother's cruelty parallels Gabriel's mother's dismissal of Gretta as "country cute."[19] Moreover, *The Lass of Aughrim* also held great personal significance for Joyce. In a letter to Barnacle, he writes:

> My dear little runaway Nora I am writing this to you sitting at the kitchen table in your mother's house!! I have been here all day talking with her and I see that she is my darling's mother and I like her very much. She sang for me *The Lass of Aughrim* but she does not like to sing me the last verses in which the lovers exchange their tokens.[20]

Ellmann claims that on this particular visit to see Annie Healy (Barnacle's mother), Joyce was "[n]ot sure of his welcome, [so] he sent [his son] Giorgio into the house ahead of him."[21] Unlike Gregory's mother in the ballad, however, Healy met Joyce with warm hospitality: she welcomed them both into her home, sat them down in her kitchen, and sang them a ballad about a mother who fails to welcome her child's lover into her home. Her rendition was so moving that Joyce mentions it again in a separate letter to Barnacle less than a week later: "I was singing an hour ago your song *The Lass of Aughrim*. The tears come into my eyes and my voice trembles with emotion when I sing that lovely air. It was worth coming to Ireland to have got it from your poor kind mother."[22]

We can only speculate as to the specific variant of *The Lass of Aughrim* that Healy sang that day in August 1909, but what we do know is that it was radically different from the version that appears in Huston's film. A number of scholars have pointed out that the melody sung by Frank Patterson in the film is likely Scottish in origin, not Irish.[23] This substitution of a more operatic, Ionian melody for what was likely a brooding, Mixolydian lament is no accident. Alex North, a composer and longtime collaborator of Huston's who developed the score for the film, was certainly aware of traditional Irish melodies, and he even penciled down a transcription of a Mixolydian variant that perfectly taps into what Gabriel describes in the story as "the old Irish tonality."[24] Nevertheless, Huston and North chose to substitute a "less authentic" version of the ballad with which the classically trained opera singer D'Arcy would be familiar, even knowing that it differed greatly from the version that Joyce likely had in mind (and the variant that Michael Bodkin sang to Barnacle.) The substitution of a sweeter, more accessible melody also allowed Huston to slyly insert the ballad into a number of scenes throughout the film, a move that both foreshadows Gretta's eventual confession and also renders the melody faintly familiar to the audience by the time they hear the ballad performed in the pivotal staircase scene.

If the Italian saying "*Traduttore, traditore,*"[25] or "translator, traitor," suggests that in translation, fidelity and betrayal go hand in hand, then perhaps Huston's *The Dead* can be considered something like a "faithful betrayal." As the melody of *The Lass of Aughrim* sounds for the last time in the background of the closing scene, it is as if it marks the persistent memory of a young Michael with a new surname, a different resting place, and an unfamiliar song. When asked in an interview about his interventions on the original story, Huston remarked: "What we wanted to do was not so much to adhere paragraph for paragraph to Joyce's prose, but to capture a certain mood, an exuberance for life that exists in the story."[26] For me, his film drives home the suggestion (already present in Joyce's story) that a love for life can also express itself as a complicated love for the dead. The film is as much an ode to Joyce as it is to a near-forgotten generation—that of Aunt Julia, Mr. Browne, Patrick Morkan, and Parkinson, who Aunt Kate remembers as "the purest tenor voice that was ever put into a man's throat."[27] In what he knew to be his final film, Huston reminds us of the strange double-duty required of us if we are to make space for the dead.

Notes

1   Vincent Canby, "Film: *The Dead*, by Huston," *The New York Times*, Thursday, December 17, 1987.

2   Anelise R. Corseuil, "John Huston's Adaptation of James Joyce's *The Dead*: The Interrelationship between Description and Focalization," *Cadernos de Tradução* 1 (2001): 67–79.

3   Anastasia Ulanowicz, "Reassembling Sacred Relics: Translation, Disapora, and Andriy Chaikovsky's *Za Sestroyu*," *Children's Literature Association Quarterly* 43, no. 4 (2018): 412–33, at 412.

4   Patrick Geary, *Furta Sacra: Thefts of Relics in the Central Middle Ages* (Princeton, NJ: Princeton University Press 1990), xiii.

5   James Joyce, *Letters of James Joyce*, Vol. II–III, ed. Richard Ellmann (New York: The Viking Press, 1966), 239.

6   Donagh MacDonagh, "The Lass of Aughrim or the Betrayal of James Joyce," in *The Celtic Master: Contributions to the First James Joyce Symposium Held in Dublin, 1967*, ed. Maurice Harmon (Dublin: Dolmen, 1969), 17–25, 18.

7   Padraic Ó Laoi, *Nora Barnacle Joyce: A Portrait* (Galway: Kenny Bookshop and Art Galleries, 1982), 23.

8   Ibid., 29–30.

9   Joyce, *Letters*, 72.

10 Joyce, *Letters*, 300.

11 Nathan Halper, "The Grave of Michael Bodkin," *James Joyce Quarterly* 12, no. 3 (1975): 273–80, at 276.

12 James Joyce, "The Dead," in *Dubliners*, ed. Shane Weller (New York: Dover Publications, 1991), 119–52, 135.

13 Ibid., 141.

14 Ibid.

15 MacDonagh, "The Lass of Aughrim," 21.

16 Joyce, "The Dead," 143.

17 Francis James Child, *English and Scottish Popular Ballads*, ed. Helen Child Sargent and George Lyman Kittredge (Boston: Houghton Mifflin Company, 1904), 161–4.

18 Richard Ellmann, *James Joyce* (Oxford: Oxford University Press, 1982), 248.

19 George Geckle, "The Dead Lass of Aughrim," *Éire-Ireland* 9, no. 3 (1974): 86–96, at 88.

20 Joyce, *Letters*, 240.

21 Ellmann, *James Joyce*, 286.

22 Joyce, *Letters*, 241.

23 Hugh Shields, "The History of 'The Lass of Aughrim,'" in *Irish Musical Studies*, ed. Gerard Gillen and Harry White (Dublin: Irish Academic Press, 1990), 58–73; Martin Dowling, "'Thought-Tormented Music': Joyce and the Music of the Irish Revival," *James Joyce Quarterly* 45, no. 1 (2008): 437–58; Gerry Smyth, *Music in Irish Cultural History* (Dublin: Irish Academic Press, 2009).

24 Joyce, "The Dead," 143.

25 Richard Kearney, "Linguistic Hospitality—The Risk of Translation," *Research in Phenomenology* 49 (2019): 1–8.

26 English, "Huston Meets Joyce."

27 Joyce, "The Dead," 136.

30

On Terrence Malick's *The Tree of Life*

Jason M. Wirth

I Will Be True to You, Whatever Comes

In the soundscape at the beginning of Terrence Malick's groundbreaking film, *A Tree of Life* (2011), Mrs. O'Brien's voice invokes the mystery of grace by recollecting a distinction found in Thomas à Kempis's *De Imitatione Christi* that she had learned from the nuns. "They taught us that no one who loves the way of grace . . . ever comes to a bad end. I will be true to you. Whatever comes." Does this not seem pollyannish, flying in the face of the ineluctable suffering and pain of human living, the relentless ways in which the lives and aspirations of the living come to a bad end? Moreover, does not such "positive thinking" render us complicitous with our suffering as we set ourselves up to fail? Is this not the miserable Sisyphean life in which, after coming to a bad end, we start again, only to come once again to a bad end, until finally, the last bad end, death itself, relieves us from this injurious cycle? Is this not the folly of "positive thinking" and "healthy-mindedness" that William James denigrated "as a philosophical doctrine, because the evil facts which it refuses positively to account for are a genuine portion of reality"?[1]

Yet Malick's film opens with an epigram from Yahweh's response to Job in the unimaginably bad end of his pit: "Where were you when I laid the foundation of the earth. . . . When the morning stars sang together, and all the sons of God shouted for joy?" (Job 38:4, 7). Grace does not come into relief in the happiness of our good fortunes, but rather in their absence and loss. "One sees the moon after one's house burns down" as

Bashō's student Mizuta Masahide (1657–1723) memorably put it. Grace is found in mourning and convalescence, in the *felix culpa*, and before the event of such experiences, it is merely the stuff of wishful belief and magical thinking.

As difficult as such a thought may be philosophically, how does one think it cinematically without sacrificing the unique powers of cinema as a medium by confusing it with discursive pedantry? How can film, true to its possibilities as a medium, do what only film can do, and imagine the presence of the tree of life in the valley of darkness?

I pursue these questions by way of a philosophical consideration of what I consider to be the central cinematic problem at the core of Malick's *The Tree of Life*: *How to create a cinematic image of the divine, in itself unimaginable, that simultaneously reveals the grace and healing power of the cinematic image?*

The Funereal Image
(Seeing the Divine in Loss)

Most films that have resorted to anything religious—think of the idolatrous exercises in religious ideology like *The Ten Commandments* or *Jesus of Nazareth* or *The Passion of the Christ* or *The Greatest Story Ever Told*—were content to represent or illustrate with overweening piety the well-worn ideas about what matters in religion. And to be fair: religion itself is increasingly a contested and opaque concept as we grapple with the history of the violence that its institutions have wrought. Malick's film has also flabbergasted (and divided) critics as they struggle to say anything halfway intelligent about it. It deftly avoids the *idolatry* of religious cinematic thinking, that is, it refuses the task of *representing* God and the realm of religious experience, while also avoiding a partisan reading of doctrinal issues.

Nonetheless, Malick's oeuvre is religious, albeit in a philosophically and artistically subtle and profound manner. Malick's films, like his religiosity, are not conspicuously philosophical because he is *cinematically* presenting, not philosophically representing, religious experience. Malick's films are conspicuously thoughtful by exploring the nether limits of cinema's singular powers. Malick's cinema is consequently not philosophy by other means. It does not present discursive arguments and it does not illustrate philosophical themes. It thinks in a manner exclusive to film as a medium. As Malick said in 1975, "I don't feel one can film philosophy."[2] Philosophical thought about the religious dimensions of human experience is translated and transformed into a uniquely cinematic manner of thinking. It is his cinematic solutions to such problems that produce what Robert Sinnerbrink felicitously called Malick's "*cinematic thinking*"[3] or what Stuart Kendall and Thomas Deane Tucker have called "a certain kind of filmmaking relevant to philosophy."[4] It is the character of this relevance that here concerns me.

The great Andrei Tarkovsky, to whose cinema Malick's *The Tree of Life* has clear resonances and affinities—think of the central motif of Alexander and Little Man planting a tree in *The Sacrifice* (1986)—claimed that in "creating an image" an artist "subordinates his own thought, which becomes insignificant in the face of that emotionally perceived image of the world that has appeared to him like a revelation. For thought is brief, whereas the image is absolute."[5] This led Tarkovsky to draw an analogy between the potency of an artistic image and a "purely religious experience" (ST, 41). The image as such, whether or not it presents anything explicitly religious, is, when successful, already analogous to religious experience. Images, Tarkovsky writes, are "governed by the dynamic of revelation. It's a question of sudden flashes of illumination—like scales falling from the eyes; not in relation to the parts, however, but to the whole, to the infinite, to what does not fit into any conscious thought" (ST, 41). The image is not concerned with "illustrating some idea" (ST, 25), but is rather a "hieroglyphic of absolute truth" such that "through the image is sustained an awareness of the infinite: the eternal within the finite, the spiritual within matter, the limitless given form" (ST, 37). Images do not somehow *represent* the absolute. They are monads that in their own singular manner *express* the absolute. What makes an image an image does not reduce to what it is literally an image *of*, and the art of this kind of cinema is to produce an anti-ideological cinema grounded in the epiphany of the revelatory power of the image, in its power to show what cannot be seen in what can be seen. It is the art of constructing images that reveal the revelatory character of image.

Hence for Tarkovsky the image is like a "monad" (ST, 47), saying in its singular and irreducible way the inexhaustible unimaginability of that which it paradoxically reveals. For Malick this is the "grace" of the image that asks, as does the adult Jack O'Brien in *The Tree of Life*: "How did you come to me? In what shape? What disguise?" Like the early Augustine, "I didn't know how to name you then." At the end of his life, after a deep religious awakening, Tolstoy spoke of art's power of "infection" such that "the evolution of feelings takes place by means of art, replacing lower feelings, less kind and less needed for the good of humanity, by kinder feelings, more needed for that good. This is the purpose of art."[6] Tarkovsky and Malick are less convinced that art has quite this kind of power and it is not the task of art to preach about how we should live. For Tarkovsky art nonetheless has the power of "shock and catharsis." In themselves artistic images and other works cannot make us good but they can awaken us from the profanity of our lives of quiet desperation and make us "receptive to good" (ST, 50). Indeed for Tarkovsky art in its own way does what Plato in the *Phaedo* claims for philosophy in its own way: "The aim of art is to prepare a person for death, to plough and harrow his soul, rendering it capable of turning to good" (ST, 43).[7] Malick, before abandoning public interviews over four decades ago, made the same kind of point: "For an hour, or for two days, or longer, these films can enable small changes of heart, changes that mean the same thing: to live better and to love more."[8]

Despite the abundant promise evident in his translation of and introduction to Heidegger's *Vom Wesen des Grundes*,[9] Malick wrote nothing like Tarkovsky's remarkable book and has conscientiously (and contractually) avoided public discourse. Malick's silence speaks volumes and his careful constellations of cinematic images and soundscapes speak more eloquently than their reduction to any set of philosophical theses. They form the cinematic enactment of a new restoration of Eden—a healing of our relationship to the earth and our way of being upon it. As Michel Chion has astutely remarked, Malick's films "all seem to speak of an 'earthly paradise' that is at once lost and ever-present."[10] It is not that the earth has fallen. The problem is rather our eyes, which can no longer see the Eden now repressed within the human world. Malick's cinema is teaching us how better to see and hear, leading the senses back through the gate of their banishment as they are encouraged to see as the cinematic eye sees and to hear as the cinematic ear hears.

In part, our relationship to nature is broken because we suffer, sometimes horribly, and all that lives is born to die. The earth that grants life displays no allegiance to anything living. Religion that reacts to the brokenness of our relationship to nature (that we have fallen from Eden, forgotten the Buddha lands) imagines that it can solve this problem by denying the ultimate existence of pain, suffering, evil, and death. In heaven we find only the part of the earth that we like, and in infinite and imperishable supply. Just suffer through this thing with a pure heart, and get to the real life, which is always elsewhere, provoking Nietzsche to quip in *Beyond Good and Evil* that "a will has dominated Europe for 1800 years that wants to make a *sublime miscarriage* out of humans."[11] Wittgenstein, another of Malick's early philosophical inspirations, demoted the doctrine of predestination to the status of "pain language," more akin to screaming ouch when you step on a nail than to metaphysics. This kind of religion is the desperate magical thinking that attempts to solve the problem of pain in the terms set by pain, that is, it responds to the problem of pain by acting in ways that preserve and even enhance pain. The pain of our inability to affirm life on its own terms drives us to the kind of religion that institutionalizes, reinforces, and preys upon this refusal.

Martin Sheen, star of Malick's first film, *Badlands* and a radical Catholic activist whose work includes years of protest against the School of the Americas in Georgia, spoke of Malick as his "spiritual mentor," recalling that Malick had given him a copy of *The Brothers Karamazov*, which "had a very profound effect on my spiritual life, and that was like the final door that I had to go through."[12] *The Tree of Life* is filled with images of doors and passageways. Malick's production designer Jack Fisk recalls that

Malick "has always loved gates. . . . I believe gates and doors are passage into another world, another part of our lives."[13] (Think of the forlorn gate standing in the wheatfields in Malick's second film, *Days of Heaven*.) One of Malick's principal camera operators, Jörg Widmer (who eventually became Malick's DP for *A Hidden Life*), reflects that "during the shooting we are always, literally, crossing borders. *The Tree of Life* is about crossing borders and crossing spaces. Getting out of something into the light. Stairs, ladders, going up to heaven, or going into something—these are always the philosophical elements of his movies" (TMRU, 297). The film opens with Jack confessing, "Brother. Mother. It was they who led me to your door."

The Brothers Karamazov itself is hardly a defense of religious practice as usual. It powerfully contrasts the grace of Alyosha with the Job-like recriminations of Ivan, who rebels against creation and advocates for the Grand Inquisitor who, upon learning of the return of Jesus, condemns him to death so that the institutional religious control over the scandal of creation, including the barbarism of the human, can continue. Ivan's anguish is mirrored in the Inquisitor's willful deployment of Satan's three temptations that Jesus resisted in the desert: miracles (religion provides magical solutions so that we do not have to accept things the way they are), mystery (the mystification of the intellect so that it is uncritical of magical church teachings), and might (the church exerts its control over the scandal of life by the sword). The Inquisitor "corrected" Jesus's deed and marshalled institutional violence to prevent us from acting in accord with our worst instincts.

And the power of Jesus and Alyosha? The vulnerable, wholly exposed, wholly unprotected kiss, the embrace that endures all because it loves all. This tension, between Jesus and the Grand Inquisitor, Alyosha and the broken-hearted and betrayed Ivan, repeatedly plays itself out in Malick's work. In *The Thin Red Line*, it is the relationship between First Sergeant Welsh (Sean Penn), who thinks that one should become an island and leave no flank of one's life exposed, and Witt (Jim Caviezel), who saw a "spark" in Welsh, and who died so that his men could live. In *The Tree of Life* it is the tension between Mrs. O'Brien (Jessica Chastain), "the way of grace," and her husband (Brad Pitt), "the way of nature." Mrs. O'Brien sounds like Zosima when she counsels, "unless you love, your life will flash by" and "love everything. Love every leaf, every drop of rain." In the beginning of the film, against the forebodingly plaintive soundscape of John Tavener's *Funeral Canticle*, Mrs. O'Brien, as a young girl admiring cows in a pasture, tells us:

> The nuns taught us there are two ways through life . . . *the way of nature* and *the way of grace*. You have to choose which one you'll follow. Grace doesn't try to please itself. Accepts being slighted, forgotten, disliked. Accepts insults and injuries. Nature only wants to please itself. Get others to please it too. Likes to lord it over them. To have its own way. It finds

reasons to be unhappy . . . when all the world is shining around it . . . when love is smiling through all things. They taught us that no one who loves the way of grace . . . ever comes to a bad end. I will be true to you. Whatever comes.

Mrs. O'Brien's description of Grace and Nature is lifted almost word for word from *De Imitatione Christi* where the fifteenth-century-German-Dutch Canon Regular Thomas à Kempis wrote that "Grace doesn't try to please itself. Accepts being slighted, forgotten, disliked. Accepts insults and injuries. . . . Nature only wants to please itself. Get others to please it over them. To have its own way" (Book 3, Chapter 54).[14] Jessica Chastain recalls her process working on this character. Malick was "looking for something universal from my character, something out of time . . . a kind of love that didn't serve her, a kind of love that was only for others" (TMRU, 341). To prepare, Chastain did a lot of calming gratitude meditation and "would try and envision opening my heart to the world" (TMRU, 341).

Mourning as the Struggle between Nature and Grace

Yet the flower is crushed by the wind and kindness is destroyed by the bullet. Like her son R. L. who commits suicide at an early age, Mrs. O'Brien has all of the power and fragility of a kiss, a kind word, a sunflower blowing in the wind. She will be crushed. To be crushed by death is the way of all things, tyrants and flowers alike, but the latter is almost wholly without defenses. The shock upon receiving the telegram of her son's suicide overwhelms her openness to the world and, as she howls and weeps, she only wants "to die and be with" her son.

Mr. O'Brien is the power of nature, which wants to "have its own way." He tells his boys that it "takes a fierce will to get ahead." Indeed, a propos of the American Dream and the devastation of the earth, "You make yourself what you are. You have control of your own destiny." You have to take charge of life and make it bend to your will, "Get them by the nuts if you pardon my French." Like Ahab amid the infinite and placeless sea, Mr. O'Brien experienced life as an immense desert, an endless lack and cheat, and you have to rebel against it and make up for its mistakes. "Your mother's naive. It takes fierce will to get ahead in this world. If you're good, people take advantage of you." One refuses to be cheated any longer. "Nature has regard for temporal wealth and rejoices in earthly gains. It is sad over a loss and irritated by a slight, injurious word," Thomas à Kempis counsels us. Driving ruefully past the mansions of the wealthy, endlessly patenting his ideas, always waiting and hoping for the big break that would confirm that he was not nothing, losing again in court, callously being fired from his job—"I never missed a day of work"—and being offered a new job that nobody wants, fighting violently with his wife and his children, he is a kind of Texas Willie Loman, allegedly in control of his destiny, but a complete worldly failure, a nobody in a nowheresville Texas town (Waco, but filmed in Smithville). He is invisible to the grand march of history and winners.

In the extended version of the film,[15] we encounter Mr. O'Brien's father. His son ruefully reflects, "I took my father for granted. I thought he was weak." He worked tirelessly without success until he was finally destroyed. Nature seems as if it has no predilection for justice and fairness. His father did not get what he deserved. He was used by the system and then spit out as garbage. Later his son concludes that "the world lives by trickery. If you want to succeed, you can't be too good." After seeing a boy drown, his oldest son, speaking to the skies, spitefully concludes, "Why should I be good if You aren't?" To be clear: those who embrace nature's self-insistence, only to feel betrayed, like Ivan Karamazov's assessment that life is not worth the price of admission, are not unreasonable. They are outraged by the presence of injustice as if the way of all things is scandalous. Human self-insistence is to stand up for oneself in the face of the indifference of nature's self-insistence and then to gnash one's teeth at the subsequent futility of doing so.

The origins of the vice grip of nature begin early, as they did with Augustine confessing his sins, even as a baby: Mrs. O'Brien firmly telling her son, "No!" The young child grabbing a piece of cake, imperiously declaring, "It's mine!" Mrs. O'Brien shielding her child's eyes from a scene of violence. Mr. O'Brien drawing an invisible line in the grass over which one should not cross. A beautiful butterfly lying on the grass, and a hungry cat eyeing it. Suddenly seeing a three-legged dog. Seeing your mother bleed after cutting her hand badly in a kitchen accident and then the sudden epiphany: "Will you die, too?" Playing on the graves in the cemetery. Sickness, old age, suffering, death: "Can it happen to anyone? No one talks about it."

No one is wholly marked by either grace or nature. Mrs. O'Brien howls in grief upon receiving the news of her son's suicide and would rather die than be among the cows and sunflowers. Mr. O'Brien is not without self-knowledge and regret. He momentarily realizes that his sons not only were the only good he had ever done, but that they were enough. "I wanted to be loved because I was a great man. . . . Now I'm nothing. Look at the world around us. The trees and birds. I lived in shame. I dishonored it all and didn't notice the glory. A foolish man." (We might here remember in *The Brothers Karamazov* that, as Zosima's brother was dying, he apologized to the birds.)

Their eldest son, Jack O'Brien (Hunter McCracken and Sean Penn), feels the two possibilities warring within himself. "Mother, father, always you wrestle inside me, always you will." This is the battle within between water and the desert, affirmation and lamentation. As a child he recognizes that he is more like his father—"I'm more like you than like her"—and this begins with what he regards as the injustice in having such a hypocritical and controlling father. "What I want to do, I can't do. I do what I hate."

Like nature's self-insistence, he demands, "I want to do what I want" and then prays, "Please God, kill him." Asked to come here by his mother, he defiantly refuses, "No! I'm gonna do what I want to do, and you let him walk all over you." The film abounds with images of youthful willfulness, and these scenes are multiplied in the extended cut: blowing up birds' eggs with firecrackers, tying a frog to a skyrocket and igniting it, throwing rocks through an abandoned window, fighting and taunting each other, coaxing R. L. to put his finger at the end of the barrel of a BB gun so that Jack can fire it, even sneaking away to steal his comely neighbor's underwear.

Jack has succeeded where his hapless father had not. He is a successful architect who works in a shiny yet antiseptic Texas urban office building, lives in a stylish and expensive house, and wears Armani suits, but he has not forgotten his childhood, his mother, his anguished father, and the fragile, powerful innocence of his brother R. L. whose suicide is announced at the beginning of the film. A tree grows forlornly and pitifully in the arid office courtyard, much like Jack's own languishing life in the spiritual desert. He is still mourning them, and he lights a ritual candle as unreconciled memories of his childhood and the death of his brother involuntarily return. Mourning is the war between grace and nature, infinity and the diminution of form, within us all. Nature refuses the diminishment of loss while grace releases the past in affirmation. If we were pure grace, we would love everything but be attached to nothing. Time would flow like a river, unobstructed by memory and aspiration. If we were pure nature, we would not let go of anything and eventually be crushed by the weight of memory and its catalogue of scandals, injustices, disappointments, and failures. We mourn at funerals as grace gives nature its due, but endeavors to have the final word.

This is the struggle within memory between nature and grace, traumatic, involuntary recollection and the acceptance and release of loss, as Jack O'Brien struggles to come to terms with the suicide of his brother. Is not the wound of memory—the recurrence of a past event that one cannot accept and release—the lingering presence of Job's lament? That life itself comes to be seen as not acceptable, that, given what it has revealed itself to be, it should not have been? Since it is not what it should have been, it should not have been at all? Ivan Karamazov, as well as Alyosha, as he struggled with his teacher's putrefaction, are rebels, but they do not rebel against the creator. It is creation itself that is found wanting; it is the world that they refuse. It is creation that Yahweh redeems for Job, not the divine.

The Tree of Life

The tree of life itself, which resonates in the sacred writings of all of the peoples of the Book and in many other traditions, was planted in the Garden of Eden along with the tree of the knowledge of good and evil (Gen. 2:9). The fruit of the latter tree led to the fall from nature and the diremption of life into the good and acceptable on the one hand, and the evil, deplorable, abject, and detestable on the other hand. In the 22nd chapter of the book of Revelation, this curse—that our lives and life itself are more than we can fully bear—is lifted. Eden, that is, *the unconditional affirmation of all of nature*, is restored:

> Then the angel showed me the river of the water of life, as clear as crystal, flowing from the throne of God and of the Lamb down the middle of the great street of the city. On each side of the river stood the tree of life, bearing twelve crops of fruit, yielding its fruit every month. And the leaves of the tree are for the healing of the nations. No longer will there be any curse. (NIV Rev. 22:1-4)

The tree of life and the water that makes it possible—no water, no life in any real sense of the word—is not the fantasy that there is only life. Driven from the affirmation of nature by death, pain, and suffering, there is now a healing of this wound. Malick is in no way a Gnostic, denigrating the shining of the earth as somehow fallen and calling for escape. It is humans who are fallen, not the earth. Although we blame the earth for the poverty of our vision, we do so easily because our eyes are so poor that they do not easily recognize their poverty. *Malick's cinema is an exercise in seeing more fully*.

Malick is not a dualist. The latter is precisely the problem of the tree of the knowledge of good and evil which "knowingly" severs the earth into an ontologically distinct duality. That being said, this is precisely where we always begin: the division of the earth into the bearable and unbearable, the graceful flowing of affirmation and the traumatic wounds that congeal memory, turning it against affirmation and its ready yielding to the movement of time as well as its forgiveness of wounds. The radical *anamnesis* of nature, the remembering and healing of its fall and internal conflict, is a prominent motif in all of Malick's films. As Private Train (John Dee Smith) mused at the beginning of *The Thin Red Line*, "What is this war in the heart of nature? Why does nature vie with itself . . . the land contest with the sea? Is there an avenging power in nature? Not one power, but two?"

Light and darkness contest each other yet are inseparably intertwined with each other. Malick uses little artificial light in his films, although the scenes in *The Tree of Life* when the adult Jack O'Brien mourns his past while sitting in his office in a Texas urban high rise or in his fancy house, make the light itself appear fallen, as if Jack O'Brien were in a pit, detached from the light.

In addition to the glimmering of light against the darkness (flames burning against the absence of light, the crepuscular sun filtering through trees, the bright and seemingly unyielding sun illuminating our memories of youth), Malick deploys frequent images of the "the river of the water of life, as clear as crystal, flowing from the throne of God and of the Lamb." There are ferocious waterfalls as well as water flowing into the sink from the faucet. The first forms of life emerge from the water; children play in the water; lava flows into the ocean and cools, making new land. The sea teems with creatures (sea snakes, hammerhead sharks, etc.), the local river flows, and the family has goldfish in a bowl. In a striking image of amniotic fluid, a young Jack swims out of the door of his room and into the light of the day and then Malick cuts to him as a baby being pulled from the womb. *Grace is the flowing of life in the purity of its affirmation.* Malick asked the composer Alexander Desplat to write music that is "flowing like a body of water."[16]

Yet water is also interfused with ruin and death. A young boy drowns while swimming in Barton Springs, a plesiosaur bleeds on the beach while another dinosaur lies dying in a stream. The hammerheads and sea snakes are not vegans any more than the raptor who deigns to let an injured dinosaur die in peace. In the most quietly sublime image in the film, the immense super fauna and biotic extravagance of the Age of the Great Reptiles come to an end in a hush as a giant asteroid is seen falling into the earth from space. *Gate, gate, para gate, parasam gate*—gone, gone, really gone, utterly and consummately gone.[17]

The struggle between the twin calls of emptiness and form, grace and nature, is also imagined as the strife between fluidity and aridity, plenty and paucity, *water and desert*. In the final series of images, the adult Jack O'Brien, led by a ghostly memory of himself as a child, walks upon the desert with all of the ghosts that haunt his memory. Some hasty critics have confused this sequence with a fantasy about heaven and the afterlife, as if, at the last minute, Malick lost his Dostoevskyian nerve, and posited a mystifying deus ex machina about the purity of life without death. The sequence is shot in locations like Death Valley and the desiccated floor of Mono Lake—hardly images of Paradise! Heaven was the fantasy about an enduring place of plenty, not the barrenness of the desert. As he walks among the ghosts of the dead whose memory and being are kept alive by mourning, it is to the soundtrack of the *Agnus Dei* of Berlioz's *Requiem*, the point in the funeral where we attempt to make our peace with nature and yield to the grace of acceptance and affirm loss. Yes, this is a scene of expiation, but it is the expiation in which the funereal weeping that begins the film comes to accept death itself and release it. As the desert meets the water, Mrs. O'Brien is heard saying, "I give him to You. I give You my son." This is no less than Job retracting his rebellion and, like Alyosha, watering the earth with his tears of gratitude in the wake of Zosima's death and putrefaction. "I knew You, but only by rumor; my eye has beheld You today. I retract. I even take comfort for dust and ashes" (Job 42:5).[18] Mourning is the journey through the desert in search of lost water. It seeks to soothe the agony of division.

Job and the Rebellion against Being

Just as the film begins and ends with the image of a flame, the adult Jack O'Brien, which as an acronym reads JOB, lights a ritual candle, which frames the involuntary flood of memory that is mourning. This framing of our mourning, this concentration and expiation of its forces, is the ritual of the funeral, and the whole film follows the mournful, expiatory logic of this ritual. The film, with its remarkable soundscape, begins with both funeral music and the call of the graceful sea, including the sounds of seabirds. The power of "nature" (form, meaning, justice) cannot solve the problem of pain by putting it into intellectual perspective and explaining it away. The book of Job, after all, was not a theodicy and it did not seek to justify and legitimate the Ways of God in a world of traumatizing pain. It redeems nature itself as the grace of being. "Where were you when I laid the foundation of the earth. . . . When the morning stars sang together, and all the sons of God shouted for joy?" (Job 38:4, 7). The problem of nature is not that it is nature but rather that it is seen and felt as the trauma of nature.

The trauma of nature brings nature to the edge of its powers and to the precipice of both despair and grace. As Father Haynes (Kelly Koonee), giving a Kierkegaardian sermon on Job, asks: "Or does not also the one see God's hand, who sees that he takes away? Or does he alone see God, who sees God turn his face towards him? Does not also he see God, who sees God turn his back?" The back of God is not other than God, although in trauma we see it as the traumatic fallenness of nature. The back of God is nature absconding, receding from our hopes and plans, its crushing flow away from our attachments and our settling into time by trying to hold it in place. The death of a loved one is the river of time carrying them away from us, leaving us bereft and alone. The good lord gives (the front of God) and the good lord takes away (the back of God). It is easy to affirm the grace of the front, but we are crushed by the back and feel betrayed by it and respond to it with the self-insistence of nature. "Job imagined he might build his nest on high. That the integrity of his behavior would protect him against misfortune" (Father Haynes). There is no protection from the back of God. Malick, like all of us, knew the back of God and knew the crippling difficulty of affirming it as God. He had his own R. L. to mourn:

> Larry, the youngest, went to Spain to study with the guitar virtuoso Segovia. Terry discovered in the summer of 1968 that Larry had broken his own hands, seemingly despondent over his lack of progress. Emil [Malick's father], concerned, went to Spain and returned with Larry's body; it appeared the young man had committed suicide. (quoted in SG, 3)

After R. L.'s death is communicated at the beginning of the film, one sees an abandoned guitar sitting on its stand in his room. Memories of the young and graceful R. L., trusting the world and often thereby being left open to hurt and abuse, include images of him playing his guitar. How can one explain away the suffering and death of the innocent? One cannot. This was what obsessed Ivan Karamazov as he collected horrible story after horrible story of the cruelty unleashed upon innocent children and animals.

Ivan's "view" of the scandal of life enervates any justification of life and threatens thereby to make life look worthless, a trick or a fraud, something that rightly and justly should never have been. Schopenhauer, inadvertently the nineteenth century's clearest and most rigorous enactment of Job's lamentations in the pit, held "the conviction that the world, and therefore also humans, are something that really should not have been";[19] we are but a "needlessly disturbing episode in the blessed stillness of the nothing" and life "as a whole" is, and here Schopenhauer uses English, a "disappointment, nay a cheat," or, "to speak German," it is *eine Prellerei*, a swindle or fraud. All in all, there is "utter disappointment with all of life" (VLW, 321; ES, 10). Job curses the fact that he is alive as a swindle: he should have died in the womb or, barring that, died during birth, or, barring that, died early. He should never have been! "For my sighs are brought to me for bread, and my cries poured out for water" (Job 3: 24). As Father Haynes asks, "Is there some fraud in the scheme of the universe?" Indeed, "there is no hiding place in the world where trouble may not find you. No one knows when sorrow might visit his house any more than Job did."

The grandmother (Fiona Shaw), much like Job's putative friends (Bildad, Zophar, and Eliphaz) who visited him in his pit, encapsulates all those who want to neutralize the pain of Job's loss by putting it into some kind of tidy perspective. Each of her platitudes is galling. (1) *You still have your memories*. Curse memories, they are the haunting presence of the crushed precisely as crushed. They mock us. (2) *The pain will pass*. All things pass. That is precisely the problem. (3) *Life goes on*. Again, that is the nub of the problem. It goes on but in reckless and absolute abandon for the living. (4) *Nothing stays the same*. Unfortunately that is true. That is why I am weeping. As Father Haynes in his sermon reflects, "We vanish as a cloud. We wither as the autumn grass and like a tree we are rooted up." (5) *You still have the other two*. At most funerals this feeble attempt at consolation gets you slapped. No life is substitutable. In the reigning great extinction event, shall we take comfort in the fact that at least we still have our zoos? (6) *The Lord gives and the Lord takes away*. This was the very platitude that Job offered to himself and his wife after the death of their children, the destruction of their estate, and his contraction of boils (Job 2:10). That is just words. Within a few sentences, Job declares to Bildad, Zophar, and Eliphaz: "Blot out the day that I was born" (Job 3:1). (7) *God sends flies to wounds so that they may heal*. That the suicide of the innocent would be part of our healing process wounds us further.

The power of pain to undo meaning and tear the measure asunder is the thrust of Antonio Negri's remarkable essay, *The Labor of Job*.[20] Enduring the pain of the ongoing humiliation of labor, the collapse of the Left, and the lack of a viable alternative to the worldwide suffering of the proletariat, Negri discovered an unexpected opening in Job. As Job's friends try to console him, it is clear that it is first and foremost they who are unsettled. Unnerved by the enormity of the injustice of Job's suffering, they are trying to console and reassure themselves. The absurdity that Job could have done something that justifies his condition as a fitting punishment or a helpful moral lesson or the silver lining of an unexpected spiritual exercise, or that Mrs. O'Brien could reconcile and put in proper perspective the suicide of her son as her mother urges, obliterates the expectation that we can make a contract with life and negotiate fair terms. As they desperately attempt to console Job as he mourns the loss of everything that he held dear and now sits on a dung hill in his pit with his shard to scratch his boils, they are unable to confront what Negri calls the immeasurable (*smisurato*) reality of his pain and their counsel, and solace, amounts to little more than vainly grasping at some conventions and deals that would allow life to be measured and justice to be apportioned.

But Job is like the young Jack's memory of the drowned boy in Barton Springs. "Where were you? You let a boy drown. You'll do anything." Or upon seeing the sullen and anguished prisoners, he asks, "Can it happen to anyone? No one talks about it." Pain silences the measure. This is the lie of theodicies that attempt, like Zophar, Eliphaz, and Bildad, to spin pain into something reasonable, manageable, and just. Grace exceeds justice. It is not regulated by justice. "It is necessary," Negri argues, "*to go beyond the justification of pain and comprehend the practical transfiguration of pain*" (LJ, 68). This transfiguration included the failed theodicy of the Left as it tried to solve the scandal of Capital and its devastation of the earth by bringing it under some measure and opposing it with the administration of a more just counter-measure. Pain exposes the immeasurability of the ground: "for this reason the remaining credibility that any theodicy of capital would need to be based upon falls away to nothing—whereas the destructive character of its grasp of the world is accentuated. Capital is truly Behemoth and Leviathan, Hiroshima and Auschwitz" (LJ, 75).[21]

On the one hand, Job awakens to the de-authorizing power of unjustifiable pain as even Yahweh castigates Job's friends for bearing false witness to Job (Job 42:6-9). One does not cut a deal with life anymore than one bargains or makes a contract with the Leviathan. It was the folly of Melville's Ahab that he thought he could bring the Leviathan under his control and exact vengeance upon it for its injustices. The value and power of Yahweh's immeasurability exposes the measure's ultimate lack of value. On the other hand, what Yahweh's speech exposes is the immeasurable power of vulnerability and love. Turning to Aquinas, Negri remarks that the "virtue of charity represents our extraordinary capacity to love God as he loves himself," which is "beyond measure, not because its immeasurableness is chaotic but simply because it cannot be measured; it cannot be measured because love, charity, creativity are not measured but are measuring, and are, therefore, superior to all other virtues whose mode of existence is to be measured" (LJ, 74–5). Or in the *eye* of Malick's cinema, the retrieval of once lost grace enables one to *see* the world the way God *sees* the world, and to love it as God loves it—"all things shining" (*The Thin Red Line*). "I want to know what You are. I want to see what You see," prays the young Jack.

Mrs. O'Brien experienced "love . . . smiling through all things," but does it smile even through the suffering and death of the innocent or through the incomprehensibly ruinous scale of the Sixth Great Extinction event? Mrs. O'Brien recalls that the nuns "told us that those who live in the way of grace never come to a bad end." Yet R. L., child of grace, is crushed. "Where were you? Did you know what happened? Do you care?" she asks, right before the onset of Malick's extraordinary cinematic evocation of Yahweh's answer to Job, "a story from before we can remember" (R. L.). Yahweh's response as the unfolding of the genesis of being and eventually life on earth—"why is there something rather than nothing" as Malick explicitly reposes Leibniz's question in *The Voyage of Time: Life's Journey* (2016)—is accompanied by Zbigniew Preisner's tremulous *Lacrimosa* from his *Requiem for My Friend*. Preisner wrote this achingly beautiful and doleful music on the occasion of the death of his friend and longtime artistic partner, the great director Krzysztof Kieślowski, who died during open-heart surgery at the age of fifty-four. The universe's natality is punctuated by *lacrimosa*—weeping—for its simultaneous fatality. The *lacrimosa* is neither an avoidable nor a final word. As the film opens with a demonstration of the back of God (the suicide of R. L), it is preceded by an announcement of the front of God in the form of an epigram taken from the beginning of the first of Yahweh's two replies to Job: "Where were you when I laid the foundation of the earth. . . . When the morning stars sang together, and all the sons of God shouted for joy?" (Job 38:4, 7)

The desert finds its way to the water and mourning finds its way to acceptance—"I give him to You. I give you my son"—just as Job comes to accept all things, even death. "I even take comfort for dust and ashes" (Job 42:5). Death itself is not an argument against the glory of the tree of life, whose shining is like what Paul said of the messianic: "For he himself is our peace, who has made the two one and has destroyed the barrier, the dividing wall of hostility" (NIV Eph. 2:14). The film reveals as belonging together, without dialectical resolution but with "the healing of the nations," water and desert, the front and back of life, because it is also a tree of life, namely, the hidden power of the cinematic image as it *sees the grace of nature shining through the agony of nature*.[22] The front and the back, water and desert, was this not what Private Train discovered in *The Thin Red Line*? The thin red line itself holds together opposites and serves as the gateway or passage from one to the other: "One man looks at a dying bird and thinks there's nothing but unanswered pain. That death's got the final word, it's laughing at him. Another man sees that same bird, feels the glory, feels something smiling through it."

Notes

1   William James, *The Varieties of Religious Experience* (New York: Modern Library, 2002), 182.

2   See James Morrison and Thomas Schur, *The Films of Terence Malick* (Westport, CT: Praeger, 2003), 97. See also Jonathan Beever and Vernon W. Cisney, "Introduction: In the Midst of the Garden," in *The Way of Nature and the Way of Grace: Philosophical Footholds on Terrence Malick's The Tree of Life* (Evanston, IL: Northwestern University Press, 2016), 5–6. Henceforth WNWG.

3   Robert Sinnerbrink, "Belief in the World: Aesthetic Mythology in Terrence Malick's *The Tree of Life*," WNWG, 99.

4   *Terrence Malick: Film and Philosophy*, ed. Thomas Deane Tucker and Stuart Kendall (New York and London, 2011), 1.

5   Andrey Tarkovsky, *Sculpting in Time: Reflections on the Cinema*, trans. Kitty Hunter-Blair (Austin, TX: University of Texas Press, 1987), 41. Henceforth ST.

6   Leo Tolstoy, *What is Art?* (1897), trans. Richard Pevear and Larissa Volokhonsky (London: Penguin, 1995), 123–4.

7   "I am afraid that other people do not realize that the one aim of those who practice philosophy in the proper manner is to practice for dying and death" (64a). Note that Socrates insisted that philosophy was not first and foremost epistemology or ethics but rather a particular practice, namely the practice of our mortality. I have here used Grube's translation, revised by John M. Cooper, in *Five Dialogues*, 2nd ed. (Indianapolis/Cambridge: Hackett, 2002), 101.

8   See: http://terrencemalick.me/category/terrence-malick-interviews/.

9   Martin Heidegger, *The Essence of Reasons*, trans. Terrence Malick (Evanston, IL: Northwestern University Press, 1969).

10 Michel Chion, *The Thin Red Line* (BFI Film Classics), trans. Trista Selous (London: BFI, 2004), 8. As Chion remarked already a propos of *The Thin Red Line*, "Why are we born into the world and part of the world, while at the same time feeling that we have been exiled from it? Why doesn't the world's haunting beauty prevent us from being alone and suffering?" (7).

11 Friedrich Nietzsche, *Kritische Studienausgabe*, ed. Giorgio Colli and Mazzino Montinari (Munich and Berlin: Deutscher Taschenbuch Verlag and Walter de Gruyter, 1980), volume 5, 83.

12 Quoted in Peter J. Leithart, *Shining Glory: Theological Reflections on Terrence Malick's Tree of Life* (Eugene, OR: Cascade Books, 2013), 15n7. Henceforth SG.

13 *Terrence Malick: Rehearsing the Unexpected*, ed. Carlo Hintermann and Daniele Villa in collaboration with Luciano Barcaroli and Gerardo Panichi (London: Faber and Faber, 2015), 296. Henceforth TMRU.

14 The relationship between nature and grace is also a central theme for Thomas Aquinas. See the first part of the second part of the *Summa Theologiae*, question 109.

15 This is the extended version of the film, fifty minutes longer than the theatrical version, released by the Criterion Collection in 2018 (release no. 942).

16 James Wierzbicki, *Terrence Malick: Sonic Style* (New York: Routledge, 2019), 93–4.

17 This is the concluding mantra of the *Heart Sutra*.

18 Quotations from the book of Job are from the translation of Raymond P. Scheindlin (New York and London: Norton, 1998). The exception is Job 38:4, 7, the epigram to *The Tree of Life,* which seems to have been taken from *The New American Standard Bible* (an appropriate choice for a director whose work also meditated so assiduously on the space and time of *The New World*).

19 "*Nachträge zur Lehre vom Leiden der Welt*" is the twelfth chapter of the second volume of *Parerga und Paralipomena*. It can be found in Frauenstädt's *Arthur Schopenhauers Sämmtliche Werke*, second edition (Leipzig: Brockhaus, 1891), volume 6, 312–27. This citation is at 312–13. Henceforth VLW, followed by the English translation found in *The Essential Schopenhauer*, ed. Wolfgang Schirmacher (New York: Harper, 2010), 2, henceforth ES.

20 Antonio Negri, *The Labor of Job: The Biblical Text as a Parable of Human Labor*, trans. Matteo Mandarini (Durham and London: Duke University Press, 2009). Henceforth LJ. "The reality of our wretchedness is that of Job, the questions and the answers that we pose to the world are the same as Job's" (LJ, 15).

21 "Job is not patient, he is powerful" (LJ, 81).

22 As Robert Sinnerbrink aptly argues, "nature and grace are not opposed but co-exist in a dynamic unity of opposites." *Terrence Malick: Filmmaker and Philosopher* (London and New York: Bloomsbury, 2019), 146.

CONTRIBUTORS

Anne M. Carpenter is an associate professor of theology at Saint Mary's College of California. She has written and published essays on the Trinity, Maurice Blondel, Charles Péguy, Thomistic metaphysics, and Benedictine monasticism. Her publications include *Theo-Poetics: Hans Urs von Balthasar and the Risk of Art and Being* (2015), which discusses the theologian Hans Urs von Balthasar's use of poetic and metaphysical modes of argumentation together, and its implications for his theology; and *Nothing Gained is Eternal: A Theology of Tradition (2022)* which focuses on theologies of tradition, especially in Blondel and Péguy; the retrieval of Thomas Aquinas in both Balthasar and Bernard Lonergan; and the interaction or collision between theological aesthetics and decolonial thought.

Stanley Cavell (1926–2018) was the Walter M. Cabot Professor of Aesthetics and the General Theory of Value at Harvard University. His work bridged many fields, bringing together Anglo-American tradition (especially Austin and Wittgenstein) with moments of the Continental tradition (e.g., Heidegger and Nietzsche); with American philosophy (especially Emerson and Thoreau); with the arts (e.g., Shakespeare, film, and opera); and with psychoanalysis. He was the recipient of numerous awards, including a MacArthur Fellowship, and was author of eighteen books, including *The World Viewed: Reflections on the Ontology of Film* (1971); *The Claim of Reason* (1979); *Pursuits of Happiness: The Hollywood Comedy of Remarriage* (1981); *Contesting Tears: The Hollywood Melodrama of the Unknown Woman* (1996); and *Cities of Words* (2004).

Matthew Clemente is a husband and father of four. He is a Research Fellow in the *Center for Psychological Humanities and Ethics* at Boston College and the Coeditor in Chief of the *Journal of Continental Philosophy and Religion*. His books include *Eros Crucified* (2019), *Posttraumatic Joy* (2023), and *Technology and Its Discontents* (with David Goodman, 2024).

David Deamer is a writer and free scholar whose research explores cinema, culture, and the philosophy of Gilles Deleuze, Henri Bergson, and Friedrich Nietzsche. He is the author of *Deleuze's* Cinema *Books: Three Introductions* *to the Taxonomy of Images* (2016) and *Deleuze, Japanese Cinema and the Atom Bomb: The Spectre of Impossibility* (2014). He publishes here and there in edited collections and journals; speaks at academic conferences and seminars; and blogs and podcasts online. Deamer was a lecturer in film theory at Manchester Metropolitan University (1999–2017) and has been working on a book on Nietzsche and cinema for some time. See www .daviddeamer.com.

Gilles Deleuze (1925–95) was a French philosopher who wrote on philosophy, literature, painting, music, and cinema and who taught at the University of Paris VIII. His first major philosophical work, *Difference and Repetition* (1968), confronted the concept of identity through explorations of time, space, and consciousness. In the early 1970s, Deleuze forged a collaborative writing partnership with French psychotherapist Félix Guattari, together producing the books *Anti-Oedipus* (1972), *Kafka* (1975), *A Thousand Plateaus* (1980), and *What Is Philosophy?* (1991). During this second period Deleuze also continued to publish on his own, including *The Logic of Sense* (1969), *Francis Bacon: The Logic of Sensation* (1981), the *Cinema* books (1983; 1985), *Foucault* (1986), and *The Fold: Leibniz and the Baroque* (1988).

John Fardy presents the weekly film and TV show "Screentime" on the Irish National Radio Station Newstalk. Previous guests have included people as diverse as Will Ferrell, Glenn Close, Neil Jordan, and Ricky Gervais. John holds a master's degree in philosophy from the University College Dublin. He is married with three children and lives in Dundalk in Co. Louth in Ireland.

Magnus Ferguson received his doctorate from the Philosophy Department at Boston College. His work draws from a wide range of philosophical traditions, including social epistemology, philosophical hermeneutics, feminist philosophy, and moral psychology. His dissertation was on the role that emotion can play in prompting us to take on expanded political responsibilities. He is currently the Robert Merrihew Adams—Charlotte W. Necombe Fellow in Philosophy at the Institute for Citizens & Scholars, and a visiting lecturer at Tufts University in Medford, Massachusetts.

Paul Freaney teaches cinema history and screenwriting at the National Film School, at IADT, in Dublin. For more than twenty years he has been chair of the prestigious *Masters in Screenwriting for Film and Television*. He has a master's degree in philosophy from the University College Dublin. He has written a number of screenplays, made documentaries, and works as a script-editor.

Sam B. Girgus is a retired professor of English and American Studies who has taught at Vanderbilt University and the Universities of New Mexico,

Alabama, and Oregon. A recipient of a Rockefeller Humanities Fellowship, he has written and published more than ten books on film, modernism, and American literature, thought, and culture.

Jake E. Grefenstette is a PhD candidate in the Faculty of Divinity studies at King's College, University of Cambridge. His research examines the relationship between theology and the arts in the 19th and 20th centuries, particularly with respect to the Romantic legacy.

Mark Patrick Hederman is a monk of the Irish Benedictine monastery at Glenstal Abbey in Limerick. He has been abbot of the community and headmaster of the school in his turn. His academic specialisms are meant to be philosophy and theology but his secret passion is for cinema. As monastery librarian for the last fifteen years he has amassed for the community a DVD collection of over a thousand Art House Movies among which Tarkovsky takes pride of place.

Fanny Howe is the author of more than twenty books of poetry and prose, most recently the novel *The Lives of a Spirit/Glasstown: Where Something Got Broken*, the book of poetry *On the Ground,* and a book of essays, *The Wedding Dress: Meditations on Word and Life*. She has received numerous awards and fellowships, including the Ruth Lilly Poetry Prize and the Lenore Marshall Poetry Prize, and she was twice shortlisted for the Griffin Poetry Prize. Professor Emerita of Writing and Literature at the University of California, San Diego, she now lives in Massachusetts.

Richard Kearney holds the Charles Seelig chair of philosophy at Boston College. He is Director of the Guestbook Project for creative peace pedagogy and he has written many books that have been translated into over a dozen languages. Notable titles include *Wake of the Imagination* (1988), *The God Who May Be* (2001), *On Stories* (2002), *Strangers Gods and Monsters* (2003), *Anatheism: Returning to God after God* (2009) and *Touch: Our Most Vital Sense* (2021). In addition to his many books in philosophy, he has also written several novels, including the forthcoming *Salvage* (2023).

Joseph G. Kickasola is Professor of Film and Digital Media, Baylor University in Waco, Texas. He specializes in embodied film theory, aesthetics, and religion and film, and is the author of *The Films of Krzysztof Kieślowski: The Liminal Image*. He has published widely in numerous academic and popular venues, including *Cinema: Journal of Philosophy and the Moving Image* and *The Routledge Companion to Philosophy and Film*. He lives in New York City, where he directs the Baylor in New York Program.

Sandra Laugier has studied at the Ecole normale supérieure and Harvard University and is currently Professor of Philosophy at Université Paris

1 Panthéon Sorbonne, Paris, France, and a senior fellow of Institut Universitaire de France. She has extensively published on ordinary language philosophy (Wittgenstein, Austin, Cavell), moral and political philosophy, gender studies and the ethics of care, and popular culture. She has translated most of Stanley Cavell's work and is an editor of his *Nachlass*. Her recent publications include *Why We Need Ordinary Language Philosophy* (2013), *Recommencer la philosophie. Stanley Cavell et la philosophie en Amérique* (2014), *Etica e politica dell'ordinario* (Milano, 2015), *Politics of the Ordinary. Care, Ethics, and Forms of life* (Leuven 2020), and *Cavell's* Must We Mean What We Say? *at Fifty* (ed. with Greg Chase and Juliet Floyd) (2021). She is also a columnist at the French Journal *Libération* (www .liberation.fr/auteur/6377-sandra-laugier).

M. E. Littlejohn is a professor of philosophy at University of New Brunswick in Canada. He is also a visiting researcher at Sorbonne Université where he is working on recent developments in French philosophy. His research and teaching works along the tear of the continental and analytic traditions.

John Panteleimon Manoussakis is Associate Professor of philosophy at the College of the Holy Cross (Worcester, MA) and editor-in-chief (with Brian Becker) of the *Journal for Continental Philosophy of Religion*. His publications focus on philosophy of religion, phenomenology, Plato and the Neo-Platonic tradition, Patristics, and psychoanalysis. He is the author of *God after Metaphysics: A Theological Aesthetic* (Indiana, 2007, translated into Russian and Romanian), *For the Unity of All* (2015, translated into Italian), and more recently of *The Ethics of Time: Phenomenology and Hermeneutics of Change* (2017).

Joel Mayward (PhD, University of St Andrews, Scotland) is Assistant Professor of Christian Ministries, Theology and the Arts at George Fox University, where he also serves as a Faculty Fellow in the Honors Program. A professional freelance film critic, Joel is the author of *The Dardenne Brothers' Cinematic Parables: Integrating Theology, Philosophy, and Film* (Routledge, 2022) His interdisciplinary research weaves together theology, philosophy, and film theory to understand how audiovisual art and media affect our religious and moral imaginations.

Stephen Mulhall is the Russell H. Carpenter fellow in philosophy at New College, Oxford. His research interests include Wittgenstein, Heidegger, and Nietzsche; ethics, religion and theology; and the relation between philosophy and the arts (especially literature and film). His recent books include *On Film: 3rd Edition*, *The Great Riddle*, and *The Ascetic Ideal: Genealogies of Life-Denial in Religion, Morality, Art, Science and Philosophy*; *In Other Words: Transpositions of Philosophy in J. M. Coetzee's "Jesus" Trilogy* appeared in 2022.

Joseph S. O'Leary, born in Cork in 1949, studied literature, theology, and philosophy in Maynooth, Rome, and Paris, and taught English Literature at Sophia University, Tokyo, from 1988 to 2015. He was the Roche Professor for Interreligious Research at Nanzan University, Nagoya, 2015–16. Recent publications include *Conventional and Ultimate Truth* (2015) and *Joysis Crisis: Rereading James Joyce Theomasochistically* (2021).

Stephanie Rumpza is a researcher in philosophy at Sorbonne Université in Paris and author of *Phenomenology of the Icon: Mediating God through the Image* (2023). Her current work explores the concept of mediation in the philosophy of language, aesthetics, and religion across the continental and analytic traditions.

Naomi Scheman is Professor Emerita of philosophy and gender, women, and sexuality studies at the University of Minnesota. She was one of the first philosophers to read Wittgenstein in a feminist light and to bring his ideas to feminism, and she co-edited *Feminist Interpretations of Wittgenstein* (2002). Her essays in feminist epistemology and metaphysics have been collected in two volumes: *Engenderings: Constructions of Knowledge, Authority, and Privilege* (1993) and *Shifting Ground: Knowledge and Reality, Transgression and Trustworthiness* (2011).

Robert Sinnerbrink is Associate Professor of philosophy at Macquarie University, Sydney. He is the author of *New Philosophies of Film: An Introduction to Cinema as a Way of Thinking*, 2nd edition (2022), *Terrence Malick: Filmmaker and Philosopher* (2019), *Cinematic Ethics: Exploring Ethical Experience through Film* (2016), *New Philosophies of Film: Thinking Images* (2011), and *Understanding Hegelianism* (2007/2014). He is also a member of the editorial boards of the journals *Film-Philosophy*, *Film and Philosophy*, and *Projections: The Journal of Movies and Mind*.

Vivian Sobchack is Professor Emerita of critical media studies in the Department of Film, Television, and Digital Media and former associate dean of the School of Theater, Film, and Television at the University of California, Los Angeles. She was the first woman elected president of the society for cinema and media studies and, in 2012, was the recipient of its distinguished career achievement award. Her research interests are eclectic: American film genres, philosophy and film theory, history and phenomenology of perception, historiography and cultural studies. Her essays have appeared in journals such as *Quarterly Review of Film and Video*, *Film Comment*, *camera obscura*, *Film Quarterly*, and *Representations*. Her books include *Screening Space: The American Science Fiction Film*; *The Address of the Eye: A Phenomenology of Film Experience*; and *Carnal Thoughts: Embodiment and Moving Image Culture*, and she has edited two anthologies: *Meta-Morphing: Visual Transformation and the Culture* of *Quick-Change* and *The Persistence of History: Cinema, Television, and the Modern Event*.

Anthony J. Steinbock is Professor of philosophy at Stony Brook University, and Director of Phenomenology Research Center. He works in the areas of phenomenology, social ontology, aesthetics, and religious philosophy. His publications include works on generative phenomenology, religious experience, and the emotions. His most recent works include *It's Not about the Gift: From Givenness to Loving* (2018) and *Knowing by Heart: Loving as Participation and Critique* (2021). He is also the translator of Edmund Husserl's *Analyses Concerning Passive and Active Synthesis* (2021). He is editor-in-chief of *Continental Philosophy Review* and General Editor of "SPEP" Series.

Brian Treanor is Professor of Philosophy and Charles S. Casassa, SJ Chair at Loyola Marymount University in Los Angeles. His teaching and writing engage a wide range of issues and themes, with particular attention to environmental philosophy, philosophy of religion, and ethics. He is the author or editor of ten books, including *Emplotting Virtue* (2014), *Carnal Hermeneutics* (2015), and, most recently, *Melancholic Joy* (2021).

Alberto G. Urquidez is a visiting assistant professor of philosophy at St. Olaf College, St. Olaf, Minnesota. He is the author of *(Re-)Defining Racism: A Philosophical Analysis*.

Anna Westin is a lecturer in philosophy and ethics. She has published on the intersection between philosophy, health ethics and the arts. Her most recent book is *Embodied Trauma and Healing: Critical Conversations on the Concept of Health*. Anna is currently a Lecturer and Tutor at St. Mellitus College, East Midlands, and a Visiting Lecturer and Research Fellow at The Bakhita Centre for the Study of Modern Slavery, Exploitation and Abuse at St. Mary's University, Twickenham. She is Director of The Willow Institute, an academic collective of artists engaged in trauma and care work, and The JAM Network UK, a creative anti-trafficking community based in London. Anna is also a songwriter and poet.

Jason M. Wirth is Professor of philosophy at Seattle University and works and teaches in the areas of Continental Philosophy, Buddhist Philosophy, Aesthetics, and Environmental Philosophy. His recent books include *Nietzsche and Other Buddhas: Philosophy after Comparative Philosophy* (2019), *Mountains, Rivers, and the Great Earth: Reading Gary Snyder and Dōgen in an Age of Ecological Crisis* (2017), a monograph on Milan Kundera (*Commiserating with Devastated Things*, Fordham 2015), *Schelling's Practice of the Wild* (2015), and the co-edited volume (with Bret Davis and Brian Schroeder), *Japanese and Continental Philosophy:*

Conversations with the Kyoto School (2011). He is the associate editor and book review editor of the journal *Comparative and Continental Philosophy*. He is currently completing a manuscript on the cinema of Terrence Malick as well as a work of ecological philosophy called *Turtle Island Anarchy*.

INDEX